Arthur Cox Employment Law Yearbook 2024

Disclaimer

This publication is a summary of selected developments in the area of employment law in 2024. Case reports and summaries of decisions are based solely on the publicly available copies of the relevant judgments, recommendations and determinations. There may be cases reported in this publication which, unknown to the authors and the publishers, have been appealed and/or overturned, or subsequently settled.

Whilst every care has been taken to ensure the accuracy of this work, this publication is not a definitive statement of the law and is not intended to constitute legal advice. The authors, editors and publishers do not accept any liability or responsibility for errors or omission. No responsibility for loss occasioned by any person acting or refraining from action as a result of any statement in the publication can be accepted by any of the authors, editors or the publishers.

Arthur Cox Employment Law Yearbook 2024

Bloomsbury Professional
DUBLIN · LONDON · EDINBURGH · NEW DELHI · NEW YORK · SYDNEY

BLOOMSBURY PROFESSIONAL

An imprint of Bloomsbury Publishing plc

Bloomsbury Professional Plc

50 Bedford Square, London, WC1B 3DP, UK

1385 Broadway, New York, NY 10018, USA

Bloomsbury Publishing Ireland Limited, 29 Earlsfort Terrace, Dublin 2, D02 AY28, Ireland

BLOOMSBURY and the Diana logo are trademarks of Bloomsbury Publishing Plc

© Arthur Cox 2025

The authors have asserted their right under the Copyright, Designs and Patents Act 1988 to be identified as Authors of this work.

All rights reserved. No part of this publication may be: i) reproduced or transmitted in any form, electronic or mechanical, including photocopying, recording or by means of any information storage or retrieval system without prior permission in writing from the publishers; or ii) used or reproduced in any way for the training, development or operation of artificial intelligence (AI) technologies, including generative AI technologies. The rights holders expressly reserve this publication from the text and data mining exception as per Article 4(3) of the Digital Single Market Directive (EU) 2019/790.

While every care has been taken to ensure the accuracy of this work, no responsibility for loss or damage occasioned to any person acting or refraining from action as a result of any statement in it can be accepted by the authors, editors or publishers.

British Library Cataloguing-in-Publication Data

A catalogue record for this book is available from the British Library.

ISBN: PB: 978 1 52653 116 2
ePDF: 978 1 52653 118 6
ePub: 978 1 52653 117 9

Typeset by Compuscript Ltd, Shannon
Printed and bound in Great Britain by CPI Group (UK) Ltd, Croydon, CR0 4YY

For product safety related questions contact productsafety@bloomsbury.com

To find out more about our authors and books visit www.bloomsburyprofessional.com. Here you will find extracts, author information, details of forthcoming events and the option to sign up for our newsletters

Practice Areas Involved in the *Arthur Cox Employment Law Yearbook 2024*

Employment and Industrial Relations
Kevin Langford
Cian Beecher
Louise O'Byrne
Séamus Given
Niamh Fennelly
Ailbhe Moloney
Ciara McDermott
Declan MacQuillan
Grace-Ann Meghen
Hannah O'Farrell
Sally Doyle
Sarah Falkner
Sarah Lawn
Aedín McHugh, Arthur Cox Editor
Aisling Kerins
Gavan Mc Laughlin
Katie Rooney
Melissa O'Sullivan
Rosanna McAleese
Róisín O'Donoghue
Sonam Gaitonde

Tax
David Kilty
Ailish Finnerty
Fintan Clancy
Orlaith Kane
Elaine Mooney
Mary Dineen
Michael Tansley
Ciara Fagan
Cristina Susanu
Dearbhla Ní Fhloinn
Lebo Motsumi Nkoloti
Nicola Cavey

Paulina Serafieva
Ciara Murphy
Edwina Hilton
Fiona Hughes
Isobel D'Arcy
Jessica Lewis
Mari Woulfe
Rachel Coyle
Ruth O'Sullivan

Pensions
Philip Smith
Sarah McCague
Daniel Watters
Deirdre Cummins
Michael Shovlin
Anne Corrigan
Katie Lawless
Ross Neill
Alan Harney
Martha McGarry

Technology and Innovation
Colin Rooney
Rob Corbet
Olivia Mullooly
Ian Duffy
Aoife Mac Ardle
Rachel Benson
Aoife Coll
Ciara Anderson
Rosemarie Blake
David O'Connor
Dr Robert Clark
Fionn Henderson
Kerry Burns

Practice Areas

Laura Dunne
Laura McFadden
Lorraine Sheridan
Lucy Robinson
Lukas Mitterlechner
Rory Curtis
Sarah Courtney

Shay Buckley
Vivian Spies

Arthur Cox Belfast
Rosemarie Lundy
Chris Fullerton
Ruth McIlwaine

Introduction

This is the fourteenth volume of the *Arthur Cox Employment Law Yearbook*, which is designed to set out the latest developments and information on employment law and related areas of law in Ireland in 2024. The *Arthur Cox Employment Law Yearbooks* are a unique resource for lawyers, human resource professionals, public and private sector employers, employees and trade unions, for whom keeping up to date with employment law is an ever-present challenge.

There continues to be a high volume of employment litigation in the Workplace Relations Commission and the Labour Court. There have also been many employment cases of note in the civil courts in Ireland, including applications for judicial review and interlocutory injunctions. Key decisions of the Court of Justice of the European Union and of the Employment Appeal Tribunal, the High Court, the Court of Appeal and the Supreme Court in the neighbouring jurisdiction are also noted.

The material for the *2024 Yearbook* have been carefully selected by experienced Arthur Cox lawyers in the fields of employment law, data protection, pensions and taxation. The line for inclusion in the *2024 Yearbook* was drawn as of 1 December 2024. Work on the *Arthur Cox Employment Law Yearbook 2025* is already in progress.

A particular word of thanks must go to David Hand BL who worked with Arthur Cox to put together the internal monthly employment law update briefings on which the *2024 Yearbook* is based, and to Siobhán Mulholland for her unfailing expertise, guidance and support to the Arthur Cox team.

Others deserving of special thanks are the team at Bloomsbury Professional, in particular Amy Hayes for her continued guidance and assistance, Andrew Turner for indexing, Caroline Ion for tabling, Compuscript for typesetting and Abby Somers for co-ordinating the cover design process.

Sincere thanks also to all those in Arthur Cox who contributed to the *2024 Yearbook*, in particular our subject matter experts, Aisling Kerins (the *2023 Yearbook* Editor) and our then Trainees (Niamh McCarthy, Róisín O'Donoghue and Patrick McWalter) and for their hard work and outstanding efforts in collating the cases for inclusion in the text.

Aedín McHugh, Arthur Cox Editor

January 2025

Contents

Practice Areas Involved in the Arthur Cox Employment Law Yearbook 2024 .... *v*
Introduction .... *vii*
Table of Cases .... *xix*
Table of Statutes .... *xxxiii*
Table of Statutory Instruments .... *xxxix*
Table of EU and other Legislation .... *xlv*

Chapter 1 Contract of Employment 1
Introduction 1
    Agency Employees 1
    Bonus 1
    Breach of Confidence 1
    Entitlement to Employee Benefits Post Termination of Employment 1
    Fiduciary Duty 1
    Right to Silence and the Contract of Employment 2
    Terms of Employment 2
Agency Employees 2
Bonus 3
Breach of Confidence 5
Entitlement to Employee Benefits Post Termination of Employment 6
Fiduciary Duty 7
Right to Silence and the Contract of Employment 9
Terms of Employment 10

Chapter 2 Data Protection/Privacy 13
Introduction 13
European Data Protection Supervisory Authorities' Sanctions 14
Data Protection Commission—Guidance 18
    Guidance on the Use of CCTV—for Data Controllers 18
Data Protection Commission—2023 Annual Report 21
Data Protection Commission—Investigations, Decisions and Fines 22
European Data Protection Board—Guidance 29
    EDPB's Report on Coordinated Enforcement Action, Designation
        and Position of DPOs —Important Considerations for Organisations
        and DPOs 30
EDPB Opinions 31
EDPB Strategy 2024–2027 33
Artificial Intelligence 34
    DPC Statement: AI, Large Language Models and Data Protection 34

Contents

EDPB Report on the ChatGPT Taskforce 36
EDPB Statement 3/2024 on data protection authorities' role in the Artificial Intelligence Act framework (adopted on 16 July 2024) 36
Trans-Atlantic Transfers 37
    EU-US Data Privacy Framework 37
    EDPB Information Note on the redress mechanism for EU/EEA individuals 38
    EU-US Data Privacy Framework FAQ for European individuals, (adopted on 16 July 2024) 38
Data Protection Caselaw 39
EU Caselaw 39
    Right to Compensation: Article 82 GDPR 45
    European Court of Human Rights 55
Irish and UK Caselaw 57

Chapter 3 Employment Equality 63
Introduction 63
    Age—Occupational Qualification 63
    Age—Mandatory Retirement 63
    Age—Eligibility for Post-Retirement Employee Benefits 63
    Age—Harassment 63
    Age—Occupational Benefit Scheme 64
    Associative Discrimination 64
    Burden of Proof 64
    Compensation 64
    Disability 64
    Gender 65
    Gender—Affirmative Action 65
    Gender—Equal Pay 65
    Gender—Harassment 65
    Gender Recognition 65
    Pregnancy and Maternity Leave 65
    Inducing a Discriminatory Act 66
    Race 66
    Race—Harassment 66
    Religion 66
Age—Occupational Qualification 67
Age—Mandatory Retirement 68
Age—Eligibility for Post-Retirement Employee Benefits 71
Age—Harassment 73
Age—Occupational Benefit Scheme 73
Associative Discrimination 74
Burden of Proof 75
Compensation 76
Disability 78
Gender 97
Gender—Affirmative Action 100

Gender—Equal Pay 101
Gender—Harassment 104
Gender Recognition 107
Pregnancy and Maternity Leave 109
Inducing a Discriminatory Act 112
Race 114
Race—Harassment 122
Religion 123

Chapter 4 Employment Litigation 129
Introduction 129
    Abuse of Process 129
    Anonymity Order 129
    Application for Adjournment 129
    Costs 129
    Diplomatic Immunity 130
    Disclosure Orders 130
    Employment Status 130
    Frivolous and Vexatious Appeals 130
    Identification of Employer 130
    Press Freedom 130
    Res Judicata 131
    Settlement Agreements 131
    Strike Out 131
    Territorial Jurisdiction 131
    Time Limits—Claims 131
    Time Limits—Appeals 132
    Without Prejudice Privilege 132
Abuse of Process 132
Anonymity Order 133
Application for Adjournment 134
Costs 136
Diplomatic Immunity 136
Disclosure Orders 137
Employment Status 139
Frivolous and Vexatious Appeals 145
Identification of Employer 146
Press Freedom 147
Res Judicata 147
Settlement Agreements 149
Strike Out 153
Territorial Jurisdiction 154
Time Limits—Claims 156
Time Limits—Appeals 168
Without Prejudice Privilege 170

Chapter 5 Employment-Related Torts 173
Introduction 173
    Defamation and Injurious Falsehood 173
    Personal Injury 173
    Vicarious Liability 173
Defamation and Injurious Falsehood 174
Personal Injury 175
Vicarious Liability 176

Chapter 6 European Law 179
Introduction 179
    European Company—Employee Involvement 179
    Free Movement of Workers 179
    Posting of Workers 179
    Recognition of Professional Qualifications 179
    Social Security 180
    Sports/Competition Law 180
    VAT Liability—Employee Fraud 180
European Company—Employee Involvement 180
Free Movement of Workers 182
Posting of Workers 184
Recognition of Professional Qualifications 188
Social Security 191
Sports/Competition Law 193
VAT Liability—Employee Fraud 195

Chapter 7 Fixed-Term Work 197
Introduction 197
    Contract of Indefinite Duration 197
    Less Favourable Treatment 197
Contract of Indefinite Duration 198
Less Favourable Treatment 203

Chapter 8 Health and Safety 207
Introduction 207
    Penalisation 207
Penalisation 207

Chapter 9 Immigration 213
Introduction 213
    Employment Permit 213
    Penalisation 213
Employment Permit 213
Penalisation 215

Chapter 10 Industrial Relations and Trade Unions 217
Introduction 217
    Defamation of a Trade Union 217
    European Works Council 217
    Industrial Relations Act 1969 217
    Penalisation for Taking Part in Industrial Action 218
    Rectification of Collective Agreements 218
    Sectoral Employment Orders 218
    Trade Union Recognition 218
    Trade Unions—Interference with the Right to Organise 218
Defamation of a Trade Union 219
European Works Council 219
Industrial Relations Act 1969 222
Penalisation for Taking Part in Industrial Action 224
Rectification of Collective Agreements 226
Sectoral Employment Orders 227
Trade Union Recognition 228
Trade Unions—Interference with the Right to Organise 229

Chapter 11 Injunctions 233
Introduction 233
    Disciplinary Process 233
    Dismissal 233
    Non-compete 233
    Picket Injunctions 233
    Stalking 234
    Unknown Defendant Injunctions 234
Disciplinary Process 234
Dismissal 238
Non-compete 244
Picket Injunctions 250
Stalking 255
Unknown Defendant Injunctions 256

Chapter 12 Judicial Review 259
Introduction 259
    Conduct of Hearing 259
    Discharge from Defence Forces 259
    Employment Equality 259
    Garda Disciplinary Process 259
Conduct of Hearing 260
Discharge from Defence Forces 261
Employment Equality 262
Garda Disciplinary Process 263

Contents

Chapter 13 Legislation 2024 265
Introduction 265
   Acts 265
   Code of Practice on Determining Employment Status (October 2024) 266
Acts 266
Code of Practice on Determining Employment Status (October 2024) 274
   The Questions to be Considered 275
   Exchange of Wage or Other Remuneration for Work 276
   Personal Service 276
   Control 277
   All of the Circumstances of the Engagement 277
   The Legislative Context 277
   Typical Characteristics of an Employee 278
   Typical Characteristics of Self-Employment 279
   Special Circumstances and Developments in the Labour Market 280
   False/Bogus Self-Employment and PRSI Arrears 280
   Health and Safety Matters 280
Statutory Instruments 281

Chapter 14 Part-Time Work 299
Introduction 299
Less Favourable Treatment 299

Chapter 15 Pensions 303
Budget 2025 303
Irish Updates 303
   Automatic Enrolment Retirement Savings System Act 2024 303
   State Pension 304
   Financial Services and Pensions Ombudsman (Amendment) Bill 2023 305
   Occupational Pension Schemes (Fees) (Amendment) Regulations 2023 305
European Legislation 306
   Digital Operational Resilience Act ('DORA') 306
Regulatory Updates 307
   Authority Publishes Investment Strategy (Liquidity Risk) Guidance
      for Trustees 307
   FSPO Publishes Overview of 2023 Complaints 308
   EIOPA Quarterly Updates of Occupational Pensions Risk Dashboard 308
   Authority Launches Consultation on Revised Code of Conduct
      for PRSA Providers 308
Revenue Update—No More Retirement Annuity Contracts 309
Case Law 309
   Ireland 309
   Interpretation of Trust Deed and Rules 309
   UK 312

Chapter 16 Redundancy **317**
Introduction 317
    Collective Redundancy 317
    Redundancy Payments—Layoff 317
    Statutory Redundancy 317
Collective Redundancy 317
Redundancy Payments—Layoff 321
Statutory Redundancy 323

Chapter 17 Taxation **325**
Introduction 325
    Karshan 325
    Enhanced Reporting for Employee Benefits 325
    Tax Costs 325
Revenue eBrief Updates 326
    Relief for Key Employees Engaged in Research and Development
        Activities 326
    Employer-Provided Vehicles 327
    Guidelines on PAYE Assessments 327
    The Employers' Guide to PAYE from 1 January 2019 327
    Revenue Guidelines for Determining Employment Status 328
    Special Assignee Relief Programme 328
    Schedule E Basis of Charge 328
    PAYE Reviews Where Week 53 Applies 329
    Tax Treatment of the Reimbursement of Expenses of Travel and
        Subsistence to Office Holders and Employees 329
    Returns by Employers in Relation to Reportable Benefits—Enhanced
        Reporting Requirements 329
    Determining Employment Status for Taxation Purposes 331
    Decision Tree from Revenue Guidelines for Determining Employment
        Status for Taxation Purposes 333
    Provision of Miscellaneous Benefits 334
    Returns by Employers in Relation to Reportable Benefits—Enhanced
        Reporting Requirements 334
    Pension Manual Chapter 14 Amended 335
    Employee (PAYE) Tax Credit 335
    Income Tax Credits and Reliefs for Individuals Over 65 and Individuals
        Caring for Those Over 65 335
    Remote Working Relief 335
    Revenue Documentation to Verify Personal Addresses for Non-Revenue
        Purposes 335
    Loss Relief for Self-Employed Individuals Adversely Impacted
        by Covid-19 Restrictions 336

Contents

    Income Tax Return 2023—ROS Form 11 337
    Income Tax (Employments) Regulations 2024 337
    Salary Sacrifice Arrangements 338
    Arrears of Pay Being Paid to an Employee Who Has Left an Employment 338
    Road Haulier Drivers Employees—Subsistence Rates 339
    Taxation of Couriers 339
    Code of Practice on Determining Employment Status (Employed or
        Self-Employed) 340
Employment Tax Cases 340
Irish Tax Appeals Commission 340
Irish High Court 351
UK Case Law 356
    Determination of Employment Status 356

Chapter 18 Transfer of Undertakings **373**
Introduction 373
    Dismissal 373
    Post-Transfer Changes 373
    Transfer? 373
Dismissal 374
Post-Transfer Changes 375
Transfer? 376

Chapter 19 Unfair Dismissal **381**
Introduction 381
    Agency Workers 381
    Capability 381
    Choice of Employer 381
    Compensation 381
    Conduct 382
    Conduct—Freedom of Expression 382
    Constructive Dismissal 382
    Dismissal or Resignation? 382
    Notice 382
    Other Substantial Grounds—Refusal to be Vaccinated 382
    Redundancy 382
    Re-engagement 383
    Retirement 383
    Trade Union Activities 383
Agency Workers 383
Capability 385
Choice of Employer 387
Compensation 388
Conduct 390

Conduct—Freedom of Expression 392
Constructive Dismissal 393
Dismissal or Resignation? 397
Notice 398
Other Substantial Grounds—Refusal to be Vaccinated 399
Redundancy 400
Re-engagement 403
Retirement 407
Trade Union Activities 408

Chapter 20 Wages **409**
Introduction 409
    Covid-19—Pay Cuts 409
    National Minimum Wage 409
    Payment of Wages 409
    Payment of Wages Act—Bonus 409
    Payment of Wages Act—Deductions 409
Covid-19—Pay Cuts 410
National Minimum Wage 410
Payment of Wages 411
Payment of Wages Act—Bonus 412
Payment of Wages Act—Deductions 414

Chapter 21 Whistleblowing **421**
Introduction 421
    Compensation 421
    Criminal Justice Act 2011 421
    Detriment—Penalisation 421
    Dismissal 421
    Employer's Knowledge 422
    Protected Disclosure? 422
    Relevant Wrongdoing/Reasonable Belief 422
    Vicarious Liability 422
    Worker 422
Compensation 422
Criminal Justice Act 2011 423
Detriment—Penalisation 424
Dismissal 429
Employer's Knowledge 431
Protected Disclosure? 433
Relevant Wrongdoing/Reasonable Belief 436
Vicarious Liability 437
Worker 437

Contents

Chapter 22 Working Time **439**
Introduction 439
    Annual Leave 439
    Holiday Pay 439
    Maternity Leave 439
    Night Workers 439
    Parent's Leave 440
    Public Holiday Pay 440
    Remote Working 440
    Standby 440
Annual Leave 440
Holiday Pay 443
Maternity Leave 445
Night Workers 446
Parent's Leave 447
Public Holiday Pay 448
Remote Working 448
Standby 449

Chapter 23 Northern Ireland—2024 in Outline **451**
Introduction 451
Legislative Developments 451
    The 'Good Jobs' Employment Rights Bill Consultation 451
    Domestic Abuse—Safe Leave Consultation 453
    The Fair Employment (School Teachers) Act (Northern Ireland) 2022 453
    Unfair Dismissal 453
Caselaw Highlights 454
    Unfair Dismissal 454
    Equal Pay 455

Index **457**

Table of Cases

A

A Multi Academy Trust v RR [2024] UKUT 9 (AAC) 3.01, **3.16**
A v Patērētāju tiesību aizsardzības centrs (Case C-507/23)................................**2.56**
AB v University of East London; Shina v Rendall and Rittner Ltd;
  Rehman v Healthbridge Direct; Adams v Power X Equipment Ltd;
  Samuels v Searcy Tansley and Co Ltd [2024] EAT 157 ....4.01, **4.45**
abrdn (SLSPS) Pension Trustee Co Ltd, Petitioner, Re [2023]
  CSIH 31..**15.15**
Abtran Unlimited v Sumaili, EDA2452...4.01, **4.21**
Adekoya v Heathrow Express Operating Co Ltd [2024] EAT 72..................1.01, **1.05**
AEPD: Inadequate notification of biometric data to employees
  (No: EXP202202960 12 February 2024) **2.07**
AEPD: Unauthorised sharing of employee data (No: EXP202310230
  24 January 2024) **2.06**
AEPD: Unlawful distribution of employee video surveillance
  (No: EXP202300692 20 June 2024) **2.08**
Aer Lingus v Fennell, PWD2426..20.01, **20.02**
Aer Lingus v Linehan, UDD2418..19.01, **19.08**
Agentsia po vpisvaniyata v OL (Case C-200/23) **2.57**
Aghajanyan v Armenia, App No 41675/12 ....19.01, **19.11**
Al Sadeq v Dechert LLP [2024] EWCA Civ 28 ....4.01, **4.08**
An Bord Banistíochta Gaelscoil Moshíológ v Ó Súird, UD/18/102.................19.20
An Bord Banistíochta, Gaelscoil Moshíológ v Labour Court (No 1)
  [2023] IEHC 484 ....19.20
An Bord Banistíochta, Gaelscoil Moshíológ v Labour Court (No 2)
  [2023] IEHC 497..19.20
An Bord Banistíochta, Gaelscoil Moshíológ v Labour Court [2023]
  IESCDET 128 ....19.20
An Bord Banistíochta, Gaelscoil Moshíológ v Labour Court [2024]
  IESC 38 ....19.01, **19.20**
An Post v Dowling, EDA2451..3.01, **3.07**
An Post v Dowling, HSD2410..3.07, 8.01, **8.02**
Analog Devices BV v Zurich Insurance Co [2005] 1 IR 274 ....17.35
Anderson v CAE Crewing Services Ltd [2024] EAT 78 ....3.01, **3.18**
Aramark Ltd v HMRC [2024] UKFTT 832 (TC)...**17.42**
Aronmar Plant Ltd v Brzezinski, DWT2422 ....4.01, **4.37**
Astha Ltd and Chakraborty v Grewal [2023] EAT 170 ....19.1, **19.06**

Table of Cases

ASTI v Ireland, 180/2019 .... 10.01, **10.13**
Atholl House Productions v HMRC [2024] UKFTT 37 .... **17.41**
Atif v Dolce & Gabbana UK Ltd [2024] EAT 47 .... 3.01, **3.40**
Atlantic Troy Ltd v Conroy, EDA2426 .... 3.01, **3.12**
Augustine v Data Cars Ltd [2024] EAT 117 .... 14.01, **14.02**
AV, BT, CV and DW v Ministero della Giustizia (Case C-41/23) 7.01, **7.02**
Avon Cosmetics Ltd v Dalriada Trustees Ltd [2024] EWHC 317 (Ch) **15.17**
Avon Cosmetics Ltd v Dalriada Trustees Ltd [2024] EWHC 34 .... 15.17

B

Bailey v Stonewall Equality Ltd, Garden Court Chambers Ltd,
  Menon KC and Harrison KC [2024] EAT 19 .... 3.01, **3.36**
Baldwin v Cleves School, Hodges and Miller [2024] EAT 66 .... 3.01, **3.19**
Ballerino v The Racecourse Association Ltd [2024] EAT 98 .... 3.01, **3.35**
Ballymun Regional Youth Resource v Davis, RPD249 .... 18.01, **18.04**
Barnard v Hampshire and Isle of Wight Fire and Rescue [2024]
  EAT 12 .... 3.01, **3.35**
Bathgate v Technip Singapore Pte Ltd [2023] CSIH 48, [2024]
  IRLR 326 .... 4.01, **4.22**, 4.23
BBC v BBC Pension Trust Ltd [2024] EWCA Civ 767 .... **15.14**
Beaumont Hospital v Thomas, EDA2431 .... 3.01, **3.42**
Belfry Hospitality Services Ltd v McCaul, DWT2413 .... 4.1, **4.42**
Bellinger v Bellinger [2003] UKHL 21 .... 3.33
Bennett v London Borough of Islington [2024] EAT 118 .... 4.01, **4.04**
Bicknell and The British Medical Association v NHS Nottingham
  and Nottinghamshire Integrated Commissioning Board [2024]
  EAT 103 .... 18.01, **18.07**
Bilfinger Salmis UK Ltd v HMRC [2024] UKFTT 736 (TC) 17.42
Bird v IRC [1989] AC 300 .... 17.31
BL v MediaMarktSaturn Hagen-Iserlohn GmbH (Case C-687/21) **2.58**
Blanc de Provence Ltd v Thu Lieu Ha [2023] EAT 160 .... 3.01, **3.31**
Bodis v Lindfield Christian Care Home Ltd [2024] EAT 65 .... 3.01, **3.17**
Bonnington Castings Ltd v Wardlaw [1956] AC 613, [1956] 3 WLUK 6 .... 5.04
Boohene v The Royal Parks Ltd [2024] EWCA Civ 583 .... 3.01, **3.39**
Boyle v Caterpillar (NI) Ltd [2024] NIIT 9826/18 .... **23.08**
British Airways plc v Mello and Ors [2024] EAT 53 .... 22.01, **22.04**
British Airways plc v Rollett [2024] EAT 131 .... 3.01, **3.44**
British Bung Manufacturing Co Ltd v King and Finn [2023] EAT 165 .... 3.01, **3.32**
British Council v Beldica [2024] EAT 92 .... 4.01, **4.25**
BU v Commune di Copertino (Case C-218/22) 22.01, **22.03**
Bugden v The Royal Mail Group Ltd [2024] EAT 80 .... 3.01, **3.21**
Buildmaster Construction Services Ltd v Al-Naimi [2024] EAT 101 .... 20.01, **20.13**

Bwg Foods Unlimited Co v Eldic, UDD2433 .... 4.01, **4.37**
Bwg Foods Unlimited Co, Unit D and E v Eldic PWD2451 .... 4.37
Bwg Foods Unlimited Co, Unit D and E v Eldic UDD2434 .... 4.37
Bye (Inspector of Taxes) v Coren [1986] STC 393 .... 17.31

C

C & S v Shaw and Live Active Leisure [2023] CSIH 36 .... 5.01, **5.05**
Cairns v The Royal Mail Group Ltd [2024] EAT 129 .... 3.01, **3.20**
Campbell v Irish Prison Service [2023] IEHC 706 .... 11.01, **11.05**
Campbell v NHS Business Services Authority [2023] EWCA
  Civ 1377 .... **15.16**
Care Choice v McCarthy, UDD2411 .... 4.01, **4.33**
Carey Glass UC v Unite the Union [2023] IEHC 705 .... 11.01, **11.15**
Carozzi v University of Hertfordshire and Anor [2024] EAT 169 .... 3.01, **3.43**
CCC v Tesorería General de la Seguridad Social & Instituto
  Nacional de la Seguridad Social (Case C-673/22) 22.01, **22.05**
Charpentier v Verizon Ireland Ltd, ADJ-00034402 .... 10.04
CHEZ Razpredelenie Bulgaria AD v Komisia za zashita ot
  discriminatsia (Case C-83/14) 3.44
Chief Constable of the Police Service of Northern Ireland and
  Northern Ireland Policing Board v Agnew [2019] NICA 32 .... 23.06
Chief Constable of the Police Service of Northern Ireland and
  Northern Ireland Policing Board v Agnew [2023] UKSC 33 .... 22.04, 23.06
CJ v PC [2024] EAT 182 .... 3.01, **3.10**
CL, GO, GN, VO, TI, HZ, DN and DL v DB and Fondo de Garantía
  Salarial (Fogasa) (Case C-196/23) 16.01, **16.02**
Clayson v Ministry of Justice, Lord Chancellor and Secretary of
  State for Justice [2024] EAT 99 .... 14.01, **14.03**
Clifford v IBM United Kingdom Ltd [2024] EAT 90 .... 4.01, **4.23**
CM v TimePartner Personalmanagement GmbH (C-311/21) 1.1, 1.2
CNIL: Excessive employee data collection and surveillance
  (Decision SAN-2023-021 of 27 December 2023) **2.05**
CNIL: Unjustified collection of job applicant data of (simplified
  decision procedure of 22 December 2023) **2.04**
Colhoun v Royal Mail Group Ltd [2023] NICA 88 .... **23.07**
Collins v FBD Insurance plc [2013] IEHC 137 .... 2.62
Commissioners for Revenue and Customs v Lees of Scotland Ltd
  [2024] EAT 120 .... 20.01, **20.03**
Creganna Ltd v Cullen and Lake Region Medical Ltd [2024]
  IEHC 231 .... 11.01, **11.10**
Crystal Valet Centre Ltd v Serao, PWD2455 .... 20.01, **20.08**
Cunningham v Irish Prison Service [2020] IEHC 282 .... 3.14

D

De Bank Haycocks v ADP RPO UK Ltd [2024] EWCA Civ 1291 .... 19.01, **19.19**
Debenhams Retail (Ireland) Ltd v Crowe, PED241 .... 16.01, **16.03**
Decotek Automotive v 60 Siptu Members, LCR23011 .... 10.01, **10.12**
Department of Justice & An Garda Síochána v Doherty, CJD231 .... 21.01, **21.03**
Department of Justice & An Garda Síochána v Doherty, TED2317................ 1.01, **1.08**
Department of Justice and An Garda Síochána v Doherty, PWD2454........ 20.01, **20.07**
Derma Med Ltd and Peal Athena Ltd v Ally, Zackally Ltd and
    Qasemzahi [2024] EWCA Civ 175 .... 11.01, **11.11**
Determination 60TACD2024..**17.32**
Determination 63TACD2024..**17.31**
Determination 85TACD2024..**17.30**
Determination 148TACD2024..**17.33**
Deutsche Wohnen SE v Staatsanwaltschaft Berlin (Case C-807/21).........................**2.51**
DHL Supply Chain (Ireland) Ltd v McAndrew, EDA2341 .... 3.01, **3.11**,
    19.01, **19.12**
Donegal Investment Group Plc v Danbywiske and Others [2017]
    IESC 14 ....**17.31**
Donoher v Minister for Defence, Ireland and the Attorney General
    [2024] IEHC 370.. 12.01, **12.03**
Doolin v Eir Business Eircom Ltd, ADJ-00045261... 3.01, **3.05**
Dowding v The Character Group plc [2024] EAT 153 ....21.01, **21.07**
Doyle Shipping Group v Troy, UDD2342 .... 19.01, **19.22**
Dundalk Institute of Technology v Honari, TED2424..................................... 1.01, **1.10**
Durnin v Horse's Mouth Ltd trading as Sportcaller [2024] IEHC 532........ 11.01, **11.07**

E

EA v Artemis Security SAS (Case C-367/23)...22.01, **22.06**
Edwards v Bairstow [1956] AC 14 ....**17.40**
Element Pictures v Arkins, UDD2414... 19.01, **19.04**
Emagine v Teke, PLBD241 ....22.01, **22.07**
Erhard-Jensen Ontological/Phenomenological Initiative Ltd v
    Rogerson [2024] EAT 135...21.01, **21.06**
ESB v Sharkey [2024] IEHC 65 .... 1.01, **1.07**
European Commission v Czech Republic (Case C-75/22)............................. 6.01, **6.07**
Excel Roofing Systems Ltd v Porter, PWD2444 .... 20.01, **20.10**

F

Farley v Sunderland City Council [2024] EAT 115... 3.01, **3.25**
Fasano v Reckitt Benckiser Group plc [2024] EAT 7..................................... 3.01, **3.06**
Federal Republic of Nigeria v Ogbonna [2012] I WLR 139 ....**4.07**

Fédération Internationale de Football Association v BZ
 (Case C-650/22) 6.01, **6.06**
First Greater Western Ltd v Moussa [2024] EAT 82 ....21.01, **21.05**
Flutter Entertainment Plc v Long, UDD2442 ....4.01, **4.40**
Forstater v Centre for Global Development [2021] EAT 87............................**4.40**
Forstater v CGD Europe [2022] ET/2200909/2019..**4.40**
Forte Healthcare Ltd v Duffy, UDD2440 ....19.01, **19.13**
Frank McHale t/a Stacks Bar v Joyce, RPD2416 ....16.01, **16.06**

G

Gallagher v McKinnon's Auto and Tyres Ltd [2024] EAT 174 ....4.01, **4.46**
Galway and Roscommon Education Board v Moran, PAT241 ....4.01, **4.29**
George v Cannell [2024] UKSC 19 ....5.01, **5.02**
Glasson v The Insolvency Service [2024] EAT 5 ....3.01, **3.23**
Godfrey v Natwest Market plc [2024] EAT 81 ....3.01, **3.24**
Goodwin v UK, App No 28957/95 ....**3.33**
GP v Juris GmbH (Case C-741/21)..**2.54**
Grainger plc v Nicholson [2010] ICR 360...**3.47**
Greater Glasgow Health Board v Mullen [2023] EAT 122 ....19.01, **19.10**
Groom v Maritime and Coastguard Agency [2024] EAT 71 ....4.01, **4.12**
Gupta v DB Group Services Ltd [2024] EWHC 2297 (KB) 1.01, **1.03**

H

HA O'Neil Ltd v Unite the Union [2024] IESC 8 .... 11.01, **11.14**
Hanley v PBR Restaurants Ltd t/a Fish Shack Café [2024]
 IEHC 662..4.01, **4.10**
Harrison v Cameron [2024] EWHC 1377 (KB) **2.65**
Hastings-Bass, Re [1975] Ch 25 ....**15.17**
Henderson v Henderson [1843–60] All ER 378, [1843] 7 WLUK 87...........4.06, 12.05
HM v Departamento de Justicia de la Generalitat de Catalunya
 (Case C-332/22) 7.01, **7.03**
HMRC v Atholl House Productions Ltd (Kaye Adams) [2022]
 EWCA Civ 501, [2022] BTC 12 ....17.37, 17.39, 17.41
HMRC v Atholl House Productions Ltd [2021] UKUT 37 ....17.39
HMRC v Basic Broadcasting [2024] UKUT 165 ....**17.39**
HMRC v Marlborough DP Ltd [2024] UKUT 98 ....**17.40**
HMRC v Professional Game Match Officials Ltd [2020] UKUT
 147 (TCC) 4.13
HMRC v Professional Game Match Officials Ltd [2021] EWCA
 Civ 1370, [2021] BTC 27 ....17.37
HMRC v Professional Game Match Officials Ltd [2024]
 UKSC 29 ....4.13, 17.01, **17.36**

Table of Cases

HMRC v RALC Consulting Ltd [2024] UKUT 99 .... **17.37**
HMRC v Ritchie [2019] UKUT 71 .... 17.39
HMRC v S&L Barnes [2024] UKUT 262 .... **17.38**
HMRC v Vermilion Holdings Ltd [2023] UKSC 37 .... **17.30**
Holbrook v Cosgrove KC, Coppel KC, Findlay KC, Bhose KC,
 Townsend, Kohli, Green, Beglan, Williams and Bowes [2023]
 EAT 168 ....4.01, **4.40**
Holland v HSE and Midland Louth Meath Mental Health Services
 [2024] IEHC 533 .... 12.01, **12.04**
Holmes v Poeton Holdings Ltd [2023] EWCA Civ 1377 .... 5.01, **5.04**
HSBC European Works Council and HSBC Continental Europe,
 Central Arbitration Committee, Case No EWC/38/2021 .... 10.03
HSBC European Works Council v HSBC Continental Europe
 [2024] EAT 104 .... 10.01, **10.03**
HSE v McMahon, PWD2460 .... 20.01, **20.09**
HSE v Okafor, EDA2415 .... 3.01, **3.38**

I

IBM Ireland v Keane, RPD244 .... 4.01, **4.34**
IK and CM v KfH Kuratorium für Dialyse und Nierentransplantation
 e.V (Case C-184/22) 3.01, **3.26**
Inland Revenue Commissioners v Muller & Co's Margarine Ltd
 [1901] AC 217 .... 17.31
Inspire Wellbeing Ltd v Conlon DWT2412 .... 4.01, **4.38**
Irish Prison Service v Cunningham, EDA2434 .... 3.01, **3.14**
Irish Prison Service v Cunningham [2020] IEHC 282 .... **3.14**
Irish Prison Service v Cunningham [2021] IECA 19 .... 3.14
Ivers v Commissioner of An Garda Síochána [2024] IEHC 626 .... 12.01, **12.05**

J

JMP v AP Assistenzprofis GmbH (Case C 518/22) 3.01, **3.02**
Jones v Aer Lingus, PWD2248 .... 20.02
Jones v Secretary of State for Health and Social Care [2024] EAT 2 .... 4.01, **4.41**

K

Karabko v Tiktok Technology Ltd, ADJ-00051600 .... 22.01, **22.09**
Karpicz v Graham O'Sullivan Restaurants Ltd [2024] IEHC 432 .... 3.01, **3.34**
Karshan v HMRC [2022] IECA 124 .... 4.10
Keane v Central Statistics Office [2024] IEHC 20 .... **2.62**
Kerry County Council v McGaley, EDA2427 .... 3.01, **3.13**

Kickabout Productions Ltd v HMRC [2022] EWCA Civ 502 .... 17.39
Kikwera-Akaka v Salvation Army Trading Co Ltd [2024] EAT 49 .... 19.01, **19.03**
KL v X sp z oo (Case C-715/20) 7.01, **7.05**
Koninklijke Nederlandse Lawn Tennisbond v Autoriteit
    Persoonsgegevens (Case C-621/22) 2.31
Konzernbetriebsrat der O SE & Co KG v Vorstand der O Holding
    SE (Case C-706/22) 6.01, **6.04**
Kostal Ireland Gmbh v Cannon, PWD2452 .... 20.01, **20.11**
KT v Dirección General de la Función Pública Catalunya
    (Case C-331/22) 7.01, **7.03**
KV v Consiglio Nazionale delle Ricerche (Case C-439/23) 7.01, **7.06**

L

Law Society of Ireland v Ellis [2023] IEHC 728 .... 4.01, **4.17**
Law Society of Ireland v MIBI [2017] IESC 31 .... 15.12, 17.35
Leaney v Loughborough University [2023] EAT 155 .... 19.01, **19.14**
Lee v Revenue Commissioners [2021] IECA 18 .... 17.31
Leeks v University College London Hospitals NHS Foundation
    Trust [2024] EAT 134 .... 4.01, **4.24**
Leicester City Council v Parmar [2024] EAT 85 .... 3.01, **3.09**
Leslie Easton & Co Ltd and Easton v Donlon [2024] EAT 126 .... 4.01, **4.05**
Lewis v Dow Silicones UK Ltd, UKEAT/0155/20/LA 18.02
Lewis v Dow Silicones UK Ltd [2024] EAT 51 .... 18.01, **18.02**
Literacy Capital plc v Webb [2024] EWHC 2026 (KB) 11.01, **11.13**
LM v Omnitel Comunicaciones SL and Ors (Case C-441/23) 19.01, **19.02**
Lobo v University College London Hospital NHS Foundation
    Trust [2024] EAT 91 .... 7.01, **7.04**
LVX Remedies Holdings Ltd v Kelleher, HSD239 .... 8.01, **8.03**

M

MacLennan v The British Psychological Society [2024] EAT 166 .... 21.01, **21.15**
Madigan's Pharmacy Kilkenny Ltd v Murphy, UDD2424 .... 21.01, **21.08**
Mallon v Minister for Justice, Ireland and the Attorney General
    [2022] IEHC 546 .... 3.03
Mallon v Minister for Justice, Ireland and the Attorney General
    [2024] IESC 20 .... 3.01, **3.03**
Mansfield Care Ltd v Newman and Ors and Rollandene Ltd
    [2024] EAT 128 .... 18.01, **18.06**
Martompol v Tomiak, LCR22943 .... 10.01, **10.11**
Masiero, Hussain, Chadwick and Dimitrova v Barchester
    Healthcare Ltd [2024] EAT 112 .... 19.01, **19.18**
Masterson and Others v Córas Iompair Éireann [2024] IEHC 222 .... **15.13**

Table of Cases

Mater Misericordiae University Hospital v Stefan, DWT2415 .... 22.01, **22.08**
McCabe v AA Ireland Ltd [2024] IECC 6 .... **2.63**
McKeown (Inspector of Taxes) v Roe, ITR 214 .... 17.30
Mendy v Manchester City Football Club Ltd, 2411709/2023 .... 20.10, **20.12**
Menolly Homes Ltd v Appeal Commissioners [2010] IEHC 49 .... 17.33, 17.35
Mercer v Alternative Future Group Ltd and Pritchard [2022]
  EWCA Civ 379 .... 10.09
Mercer v Alternative Future Group Ltd and Pritchard, UKEAT/
  0196/20/JOJ 10.09
Merck Sharp & Dohme Corporation v Clonmel Healthcare Ltd
  [2019] IESC 65, [2020] 2 IR 1 .... 11.14
Meta Platforms Inc v Bundeskartellamt (Case C-252/21) 2.25, 2.44, 2.48
Metropolitan Films International Ltd v Lyons, FTD247 .... 4.01, **4.16**
Metropolitan Films International Ltd v McCarthy, TED2411 .... 4.01, **4.15**
Microsoft v A Job Offeree, LCR23018 .... 10.01, **10.07**
Minis Childcare Ltd v Hilton-Webb [2024] EAT 108 .... 3.01, **3.22**
Moloney v Dunne [2024] IEHC 84 .... 5.01, **5.03**
Moon v Slater & Gordon UK Ltd [2024] EAT 144 .... 20.01, **20.06**
Moorehall Disability Services t/a Moorehall Living v Novak,
  PDD242 .... 21.01, 21.11, **21.13**
Moorehall Disability Services t/a Moorehall Living v Novak,
  UDD2419 .... 21.01, **21.11**
Moorilla Estate Pty Ltd v Lau [2024] TASSC 49 .... 3.01, **3.28**
Munnelly v Hassett, Cremin and Anor [2023] IESC 29 .... 4.06
Munnelly v Hassett, Cremin and City Learning Ltd [2024] IESC 41 .... 4.01, **4.06**
Munster Technological University Kerry v O'Sullivan, EDA2438 .... 3.01, **3.27**

N

N Notaro Homes Ltd v Keirle, Nash, Owens and Mead [2024]
  EAT 122 .... 19.01, **19.07**
Nacionalinis visuomenės sveikatos centras prie Sveikatos apsaugos
  ministerijos v Valstybinė duomenų apsaugos inspekcija
  (Case C-683/21) **2.50**
National Union of Rail, Maritime and Transport Workers and Anor v
  Tyne and Wear Passenger Transport Executive t/a Nexus [2024]
  UKSC 37 .... 10.01, **10.10**
Natus Manufacturing Ltd v Callanan, PWD2447 .... 20.01, **20.05**
Nelson v Renfrewshire Council [2024] EAT 132 .... 19.01, **19.15**
Nicholls v London Borough of Croydon [2019] ICR 542 .... 18.07
Nicol v World Travel and Tourism Council, Guevara and Gracia
  [2024] EAT 42 .... 21.01, **21.10**
Nolan v Science Foundation Ireland [2024] IEHC 368 .... 11.01, **11.06**

Nord Vest Pro Sani Pro SRL v Administrația Județeană a Finanțelor
    Publice Satu Mare and Direcția Generală Regională a Finanțelor
    Publice Cluj-Napoca (Case C-387/22) 6.01, **6.03**
North Leinster Citizens Information Centre v Gerety, HSD248 .... 4.01, **4.20**
Northway Personnel Ltd v Nacu, RPD2418 .... 16.01, **16.04**
Novak v Intesa Sanpaolo Life DAC [2024] IEHC 262 .... 4.01, **4.14**
NSL Ltd v Zaluski [2024] EAT 86 .... 3.01, **3.41**
NWL Ltd v Woods (The Nawala) (No 2) [1979] 3 All E.R. 614 .... 11.14

O

O'Brien (Case C-432/17) 7.06
O'Reilly and O'Neill v Atlantic Troy Ltd [2024] IEHC 541 .... 12.01, **12.02**
Onyemekeihia v Minister for Justice and Equality [2023] IEHC 697 .... 3.01, **3.37**

P

P sp. z o.o. v Dyrektor Izby Administracji Skarbowej w Lublinie
    (Case C-442/22) 6.01, **6.09**
Pady v HMRC [2024] EAT 73 .... 4.01, **4.02**
Pamukkale Trading Co Ltd Anatolia Café and Restaurant v Turkay,
    DWT2426 .... 4.01, **4.39**
Parnell v Royal Mail Group Ltd [2024] EAT 130 .... 4.01, **4.19**
Parnells GAA Club v Fogarty RPD2419 .... 16.01, **16.05**
Parnells GAA Club v Fogarty RPD2420 .... 16.01, **16.05**
Parry v Cleaver [1970] UKHL 4 .... 3.10
Presentation Secondary School Board of Management v Murphy,
    UDD2437 .... 19.01, **19.21**
Prospect v Evans [2024] EWHC 1533 (KB) 10.01, **10.02**
PSN Recruitments Ltd v Ludley [2023] EWHC 3153 .... 1.01, **1.04**

Q

Quashie v Stringfellows Restaurant Ltd [2012] EWCA Civ 1735 .... 17.37

R

R (on the application of Castellucci) v Gender Recognition Panel
    [2024] EWHC 54 (Admin) 3.01, **3.33**
R (on the application of Karmakar and The British Medical Council) v
    The Royal College of General Practitioners [2024] EWHC 2211
    (Admin) 3.01, **3.15**

Table of Cases

R (on the application of the3million and Open Rights Group) v Secretary of State for the Home Department [2023] EWCA Civ 1474 .... **2.64**
R (on the application of the3million and Open Rights Group) v Secretary of State for the Home Department [2021] EWCA Civ 800 ....2.64
R (on the application of TTT) v Michaela Community Schools Trust and London Borough of Brent [2024] EWHC 843 (Admin).............................3.01, **3.46**
Railways Pension Trustee Co Ltd v Atos IT Services UK Ltd [2022] EWHC 3236 (Ch) (16 December 2022)..**15.30**
Rajpal v HSE [2024] IECA 194...11.01, 11.02, **11.03**, 11.04
Rajpal v HSE [2024] IEHC 70..11.01, **11.02**, 11.03, 11.04
Rajpal v HSE [2024] IESCDET 121...11.01, 11.02, 11.03, **11.04**
Ralph v Salvation Army, ADJ-00046755...8.01, **8.06**
RBT v YLA [2024] EWHC 1855 (KB) 11.01, **11.16**
Ready Mixed Concrete (South East) Ltd v Minister of Pensions and National Insurance [1968] 2 QB 497 ....17.37, 17.38, 17.39, 17.41
Revenue Commissioners v Aidan Hennessy and Gerard Hennessy [2024] IEHC 245.. 17.01, **17.34**
Revenue Commissioners v Karshan (Midlands) Ltd t/a Domino's Pizza [2023] IESC 24..4.1, 4.10, 13.06, 17.01, 17.13, 17.14, 17.28, 17.29, 17.33
Ridley v HB Kirtley t/a Queen's Court Business Centre; Kostrova v McDermott International; Taylor v Lloyds Pharmacy Ltd (In Liquidation) [2024] EWCA Civ 884 ....4.01, **4.44**
Ringsend Community Services Forum Clg v Moore, MND249 .... 19.01, **19.17**
Ringsend Community Services Forum Clg v Moore, PWD2450.................20.01, **20.04**
Ringsend Community Services Forum Clg v Moore, TED2416......................1.01, **1.09**
Ringsend Community Services Forum Clg v Moore, UDD2432 .... 19.01, **19.09**, 19.17, 20.01, 20.04
Ritson v Milan Babic Architects Ltd [2024] EAT 95....................................21.01, **21.09**
Rose Hospitality Ltd v Scanlon, UDD2429...4.01, **4.30**
Rotunda Hospital v McNally, EDA2416 ....4.01, **4.32**
Royal Embassy of Saudi Arabia v Alhayali [2023] EAT 149 ....4.01, **4.07**
Royal Parks Ltd v Boohene & Ors [2023] EAT 69...3.39
Ryanair DAC & Storm Global Ltd v Lutz [2023] EAT 146 ....1.01, **1.02**
Ryanair Holdings plc v A Worker, LCR23002... 10.01, **10.05**

S

SA Royal Antwerp Football Club (Case C-680/21)..6.01, **6.05**
Saint John of God Community Services v Oyegoke, UDD2415................. 19.01, **19.16**
Scalable Capital GmbH (Joined Cases C-182/22 and C-189/22) **2.55**

Schrems v Meta Platforms Ireland Ltd (Case C-446/21) 2.01, **2.48**
Sean Pong Tyres Ltd v Moore [2024] EAT 1 .... 18.01, **18.05**
Secretary of State for Trade and Business v Mercer [2024] UKSC 12 .... 10.01, **10.09**
Siddiqi v Revenue Commissioners [2024] IEHC 195 .... 17.01, **17.35**
SN v Staatssecretaris van Justitie en Veiligheid (Case C-540/22) 6.01, **6.02**
South Dublin County Council v A Worker, LCR22963 .... 10.01, **10.08**
Sparta Global Ltd v Hayes [2024] EWHC 100 .... 11.01, **11.12**
SPI Spirits (UK) Ltd & Shefler v Zabelin [2023] EAT 147 .... 21.01, **21.02**
Spijkers v Gebroeders Benedik Abbatoir CV (Case C-24/85)
  [1986] ECR 119 .... 17.32
St Vincent's Private Hospital v Pickford, EDA2448 .... 4.01, **4.43**
St Vincent's Private Hospital v Pickford, TED2420 .... 4.01, **4.43**
Stena Drilling Pte Ltd v Smith [2024] EAT 57 .... 4.01, **4.26**
Sullivan v Isle of Wight Council [2024] EAT 3 .... 21.01, **21.04**
Sutcliffe v Secretary of State for Education [2024] EWHC 1878
  (Admin) 3.01, **3.45**

T

TC v Firma Haus Jacobus Alten und Altenpflegeheim GmbH
  (Case C-284/23) 4.01, **4.27**
Teagasc v Reid, EDA2437 .... 3.01, **3.29**
Templederry Renewable Energy Supply Ltd Community Power v
  Kelly, UDD2425 .... 4.01, **4.11**
Tennant v Smith (Surveyor of Taxes) [1892] AC 150 .... 17.33
Tesco Stores Ltd v USDAW, Webb, Singh and Kumar [2022]
  EWCA Civ 978 .... 11.08
TF v Sparkasse Südpfalz (Case C-206/22) 22.01, **22.02**
The Square Dental Services Ltd v Ling, EPD241 .... 9.01, **9.03**
Thomas v Surrey and Borders Partnership NHS Foundation Trust
  and Brett [2024] EAT 141 .... 3.01, **3.47**
Three Ireland Ltd v A Worker, LCR22926 .... 10.01, **10.06**
Timis and Sage v Osipov [2018] EWCA Civ 2321 .... 21.14
Tonchev v Bulgaria (Application No 40519/15) 2.61
TR v Land Hessen (Case C-768/21) 2.49
Transdev Dublin Light Rail Ltd v Doody, EDA243 .... 3.01, **3.04**
Transdev Light Rail Ltd v Chrzanowski, ADE/16/52 .... 3.04
Treadwell v Barton Turns Development Ltd [2024] EAT 137 .... 21.01, **21.14**
Trinity College Dublin v Malone, EDA2435 .... 3.01, **3.08**
Trinity Motors Ltd v Breslin, TUD2410 .... 18.01, **18.04**
Trinity Motors Ltd v Breslin, TUD249 .... 18.01, **18.04**
Tyne and Wear Passenger Transport Executive t/a Nexus v National
  Union of Rail, Maritime and Transport Workers [2022] EWCA Civ 1408 ...... 10.10

U

Uber BV v Aslam [2021] UKSC 5..17.36
Union of Shop, Distributive and Allied Workers and Ors v Tesco
  Stores Ltd [2022] EWHC 201 (QB)..11.08
Union of Shop, Distributive and Allied Workers and Ors v Tesco
  Stores Ltd [2024] UKSC 28.. 11.01, **11.08**
University College Cork v Cooper, HSD246......................................8.01, **8.04**

V

VB v Natsionalna Agentsia za Prihodite (Case C-340/21).........................**2.60**
Verizon Ireland Ltd v Charpentier, TID241.....................................10.01, **10.04**
Verizon Ireland Ltd v Charpentier, TID242.....................................10.01, **10.04**
Victoria Hall Management Ltd v Cox [2024] IEHC 674..................1.01, **1.06**
Virgin Atlantic Airways Ltd v Loverseed, Fenton and O'Connor
  [2024] EAT 79...4.01, **4.09**
Vodafone Ireland Ltd v Farrell [2024] IEHC 280.....................................**15.12**
VX, AT v Gemeinde Ummendorf (Case C-456/22)...................................**2.59**

W

Walsh v Kerry County Council [2023] IEHC 719...........................22.01, **22.10**
Waterford Health Park Pharmacy Ltd v Foley, UDD2412..............19.01, **19.05**
Watson v Wallwork Nelson Johnson and Johnson [2024] EAT 105.......4.01, **4.13**
Wexford County Council v O'Connor, HSD243................................8.01, **8.05**
Whelton t/a Whelton Dental v Corkery, TUD247................................4.01, **4.31**
William v Lewisham and Greenwich NHS Trust [2024] EAT 58..........21.01, **21.12**
Wolverhampton City Council v London Gypsies and Travellers
  [2023] UKSC 47.. 11.01, **11.09**

X

Xerox (Ireland) Pension Scheme v Gavagan, PAT231 ....4.01, **4.18**, **4.28**
Xerox (Ireland) Pension Scheme v Gavagan, PAT242 ....4.01, **4.28**
X-FAB Dresden GmbH & Co KG v FC (Case C-453/21)........................**2.32**
XXXX v Sozialministeriumservice (Case C-116/23).........................6.01, **6.08**

Y

Yoon v The Minister for Enterprise, Trade and Employment
  [2024] IEHC 548..9.01, **9.02**

Z

Z v Commerzbank AG [2023] UKET 2203396/2020.......................................4.01, **4.03**
Zalewski v Adjudication Officer, the WRC, Ireland and the Attorney
  General [2021] IESC 24,..15.04
ZQ v Medizinischer Dienst der Krankenversicherung Nordrhein,
  Körperschaft des öffentlichen Rechts (Case C-667/21)......................................**2.53**

DPC DECISIONS

Airbnb Ireland UC ('Airbnb') – DPC decision 31 January 2024 ....**2.27**
Apple Distribution International Ltd ('Apple') – DPC decision 7 March 2024.......**2.28**
Mediahuis Ireland Group Ltd – DPC decision 7 June 2024 ....**2.29**
Meta Platforms Ireland Ltd ('Meta') – DPC decision 27 September 2024 ....**2.30**
Meta Platforms Ireland Ltd ('Meta') – DPC enforcement notice,
  10 November 2023 ....**2.25**
Microsoft Ireland Operations Ltd ('Microsoft') – DPC decision
  15 November 2023 ....**2.26**

Table of Statutes

IRELAND

A

Automatic Enrolment Retirement
   Savings System Act 2024 .... 13.01, **13.02**, 15.02

C

Companies Act 2014 .... 13.03, 13.49
   s 1590 .... 13.49
      (1), (2) 13.49
   1596 .... 13.49
      (1), (2) 13.49
   1616 .... 13.49
Companies (Rescue Process for
   Small and Micro Companies)
   Act 2021 .... 13.03
Court Officers Act 1945 .... 3.03
   s 12(6)(b) 3.03
Criminal Justice Act 2011 .... 21.01, 21.03
   s 20(2) 21.03

E

Education Act 1998 .... 19.20
Employment (Collective Redundancies
   and Miscellaneous Provisions)
   and Companies (Amendment)
   Act 2024 .... 13.01, **13.03**
Employment Equality
   Act 1998 .... 3.13, 3.33
Employment Equality
   Acts 1998–2015 .... 4.21
   s 83(1) 4.21
      (2) 3.04

Employment Equality
   Acts 1998–2021 .... 3.05, 3.07, 3.08, 3.11, 3.14, 3.34, 3.37, 4.01, 4.21, 4.32, 4.43, 13.05
   s 14A 3.37
    14B 13.05
    77 .... 3.05
      (3) 3.34
      (5)(a) 3.42
      (6A) 3.42
      (6) 4.32
    83(1) 3.08, 3.11, 3.12, 3.13, 3.14, 3.27, 3.29, 3.38, 3.42, 4.21, 4.32, 4.43
Employment Permits Act 2006 .... 9.03
   s 12(3) 9.02
   Sch 2 .... 9.03
Employment Permits Act 2024 ...... 13.01, **13.04**
Equal Status Acts 2000 .... 12.02

F

Finance Act 2022 .... 17.03
Finance Act 2023 .... 17.18
Finance Act (No 2) 2023 .... 17.03, 17.04, 17.05
   s 17 .... 15.11
Financial Emergencies Measures
   in the Public Interest
   Act 2013 .... 10.13
Financial Services and Pensions
   Ombudsman (Amendment)
   Bill 2023 .... 15.04

H

Health Act 1970 .... 11.04

Table of Statutes

I

Industrial Relations
  Acts 1946–2015 .... 10.06
Industrial Relations
  Acts 1946–2019 .... 4.29
Industrial Relations Act 1969 .... 10.01,
                                  10.05, 10.06
  s 13 .... 10.07
  20(1) 10.01, 10.05,
                                  10.08, 10.12
Industrial Relations Act 1990 .... 11.15
  s 10–14 .... 11.14
  19(2) 11.14
Industrial Relations (Amendment)
  Act 2015
  s 8(3)(d) 10.14
  23 .... 10.11
Industrial Training Act 1967 .... 13.28,
                                              13.36

M

Maternity Protection Act 1994
  s 14C 13.60
Maternity Protection, Employment
  Equality and Preservation of
  Certain Records Act 2024 .... 13.01,
                                              13.05
  s 6 .... 13.60
  14B 13.05
Minimum Notice and Terms of
  Employment Acts 1973–2005 ... 19.17

N

National Minimum Wage
  Acts 2000–2015 .... 20.04

O

Organisation of Working Time
  Act 1997 .... 4.35, 4.38,
                                          4.39, 4.42
  s 11 .... 4.35
  15(1)(a) 4.35
  17(1) 4.35
  28(1) 4.38, 22.08

P

Parent's Leave and Benefit
  Act 2019 .... 13.15
  s 5(1) 13.44
  16(1) 13.44
  19 .... 22.07
Payment of Wages Act 1991 .... 4.42,
                                  20.05, 20.07,
                                  20.08, 20.11
  s 7(1) 20.02, 20.04,
                                  20.07, 20.09,
                                  20.10, 20.11
Pensions Act 1990 .... 3.08, 4.01,
                                  4.18, 4.29, 15.07,
                                  15.10, 15.13
  s 33 .... 13.35
  81E 4.28, 4.29
Pensions Acts 1990–2014
  s 81(1) 4.18
Personal Injuries Assessment
  Board Act 2003 ...... 2.62, 13.09, 13.10
  s 11 .... 13.09
Postal and Telecommunications
  Service Act 1983 .... 15.12
Protected Disclosures Act 2014 .... 4.10,
                                              21.11
  s 12(2) 21.13
Protection of Employees
  (Fixed-Term Work)
  Act 2003 .... 4.16, 12.04
  s 8 .... 4.16
Protection of Employment
  Act 1977 .... 16.03
  s 12 .... 13.46
Protection of Employment
  Acts 1977–2014 .... 13.03
Public Service Pay and Pensions
  Act 2017 .... 10.13
  s 13 .... 10.13
Public Service Superannuation
  (Age of Retirement) Act 2018 ..... 3.03
Public Service Superannuation
  (Miscellaneous Provisions)
  Act 2004
  s 3A 12.04

R

Redundancy Payments
  Act 1967 .... 4.34, 17.32,
                                        18.04, 19.05
Redundancy Payments
  Acts 1967–2014 .... 16.05, 16.06,
                                        18.04
    s 12 .... 16.04
    19 .... 16.06
    24 .... 4.34

S

Safety, Health and Welfare at Work
  Act 2005 .... 8.02, 8.03,
                                         8.04, 13.06
    s 28 .... 8.06
Safety, Health and Welfare at
  Work Acts 2005–2014 .... 4.20
    s 27 .... 8.02, 8.04,
                                                    8.05
    29(1) 4.20, 8.02, 8.03, 8.05
Sick Leave Act 2022 .... 13.21
Social Welfare and Civil Law
  (Miscellaneous Provisions)
  Act 2024 .... 13.39
    Pt 2 (s 3) 13.40
Social Welfare Consolidation
  Act 2005 .... 13.01, 13.06,
                                 13.15, 13.16, 13.26
    s 47 .... 13.60
    69(2) 13.27
Social Welfare (Miscellaneous
  Provisions) Act 2023 .... 13.14,
                                         13.16, 15.03
    Pt 4 (ss 29–53)................. 13.15, 13.26
Social Welfare (Miscellaneous
  Provisions) Act 2024 ..... 13.01, **13.06**

T

Taxes Consolidation Act 1997
  s 12 .... 17.31
    Sch E....................... 17.30, 17.31,
                                         17.32, 17.33
    Sch F....................... 17.31, 17.31

Taxes Consolidation Act 1997 – *contd*
  s 19 .... 17.31
    81 .... 17.30
    97(2)(k)..................................... 17.23
    112 .... 17.30, 17.31,
                                         17.32, 17.33
    112B... 17.12
    123 .... 17.32,
                                                    17.35
      (1).. 17.35
    192A 17.01, 17.35
      (2)–(4) 17.35
    200A... 17.23
    201 .... 17.32
      (2)(a) 17.35
    203 .... 17.32
    304(3A) 17.22
    395A 17.22
    436A... 17.30
    472 .... 17.34
      (1)(a) 17.01,
                                                    17.34
    766C... 17.03
    784 .... 15.11
    825 .... 17.34
    825A... 17.34
      (2)(c) 17.34
    897C... 13.19,
                                                    17.12
    1077F 17.22
    Sch 3.. 17.32
Terms of Employment
  (Information) Act 1994................. 1.10
Terms of Employment
  (Information) Acts 1994–2014 .... 1.09
    s 5(1)... 1.08
    8(1).................................... 1.08, 1.09
Transnational Information and
  Consultation of Employees
  Act 1996
    s 17B... 10.04

U

Unfair Dismissals Act 1977 .... 4.14
  s 6 .... 19.20

Unfair Dismissals
 Acts 1977–2015................. 4.10, 4.11,
  4.14, 4.36, 4.37, 19.05,
  19.12, 19.13, 20.04, 22.07
  s 1 .... 19.13
  6 ....4.10
   (2)(a) 19.22
  7 .... 19.05
  8(2).. 4.33
  8A................. 4.11, 4.30, 4.33, 4.36,
   19.04, 19.08, 19.09,
   19.13, 19.16, 19.22,
   21.08, 21.11
  10A... 4.10

W

Work Life Balance and
 Miscellaneous Provisions
 Act 2023 .... 13.30, 13.31,
  13.32, 22.01, 22.09
 Pt 2 (ss 2–15).................. 13.31, 13.32
 s 8 .... 13.31
  12(a)..................................... 13.31
  13, 14 .... 13.31
 Pt 3 (ss 16–29)............................ 13.32
Workplace Relations
 Act 2015 .... 4.10, 4.14
 s 40 .... 13.30
  41 .... 4.42
  44 .... 4.42
   (1)... 4.10
  46 .... 19.20

BUNREACHT NA hÉIREANN

Constitution of Ireland 1937
 art 34.5.3.................................... 11.04

UNITED KINGDOM

C

Civil Jurisdiction and Judgments Act
 1982.. 4.26

D

Data Protection Act 1988 .... 2.62
 s 7 .... 2.62
Data Protection Act 2018.................. 2.65
 s 43(1).. 2.29
  71 .... 2.63
  110 .... 2.24
  117 .... 2.63
   (4)(b) 2.63
  133(9), (10)............................... 2.25
Defamation Act 1952
 s 3(1).. 5.02
Domestic Abuse (Safe Leave)
 Act (Northern Ireland) 2022...... 23.03

E

Education Act 2002
 s 141B... 3.45
Employment Act 2002 .... 19.06
Employment Act (Northern
 Ireland) 2016 .... 23.01
 s 19 .... 23.01
Employment Relations Act 1999
 s 13(1)(a) 4.12
Employment Rights
 Act 1996 .... 3.35, 4.25, 4.26,
  4.46, 10.10,
  19.06, 20.06,
  20.12, 20.13
 s 13 .... 10.10, 20.12
  24 .... 10.10
  47B........................... 21.09, 21.10,
   21.12, 21.15
 Pt 10 (ss 94–134A)....................... 3.21
 s 94 .... 3.32
  95(1)(c) 18.02, 19.15
  98 .... 3.32
  103A............................. 21.09, 21.10, 21.14
  105 .... 21.09
  111A.. 4.46
  123 .... 19.07
  230 .... 4.12, 4.13
   (1)...................................... 18.06

Equality Act 2010 .... 3.01, 3.06,
                                    3.10, 3.15,
                                    3.16, 3.23,
                                    3.31, 3.46,
                                    4.22, 4.25,
                                    4.26, 4.40
  s 10 .... 3.47
    13 .... 3.24, 3.35, 4.23
    15 .... 3.17, 3.18, 3.19,
                                    3.20, 3.24,
                                    4.19, 4.23
    18 .... 3.35
    19 .... 3.44, 4.23
    20 .... 3.20, 3.21, 4.19
    21 .... 4.19
    26 .... 3.32, 3.43
    27 .... 3.19, 3.43,
                                    21.05
    30 .... 3.32
    109 .... 3.18
    111 .... 3.36
    123(3) 3.18
    136 .... 3.40

F

Fair Employment (School Teachers)
  Act (Northern Ireland) 2022 ...... 23.04

G

Gender Recognition Act 2004 .... 3.01,
                                    3.33, 3.36

H

Health and Social Care Act 2012 .... 18.07
Human Rights Act 1998 .... 3.33, 4.25,
                                    10.09

I

Income Tax (Earnings and Pensions)
  Act 2003 .... 17.37, 17.41
    s 48–61 .... 17.41
      49(1)(c)(i) 17.37
    Pt 7 (ss 417–554) 17.40
    Pt 7A (ss 554A–554Z21) 17.40
    s 554A 17.40
      (1)(c) 17.40

J

Judicial Pensions and Retirement Act
  1993 .... 14.03

S

State Immunity Act 1978 .... 4.07

T

Trade Union and Labour Relations
  (Consolidation) Act 1992 .... 10.02,
                                    10.10,
                                    11.08, 18.06
    s 146 .... 10.09
      179(1) 10.10

Table of Statutory Instruments

IRELAND

A

Agricultural Workers Joint
  Labour Committee 1976
  (SI 198/1976).............................. 13.25

C

Catering Joint Labour Committee
  2018 (SI 591/2018)..................... 13.25
Civil Aviation (Working Time)
  Regulations 2004 (SI 756/
  2004)... 22.04
Contract Cleaning Joint Labour
  Committee 2007 (SI 626/
  2007)... 13.25
Córas Iompair Éireann Superannuation
  Scheme 1951 (SI 353/1951)...... 15.13
  r 20 .... 15.13

E

Early Years' Service Joint Labour
  Committee 2021
  (SI 292/2021)............................. 13.25
Employment (Collective Redundancies
  and Miscellaneous Provisions)
  and Companies (Amendment)
  Act 2024 (Commencement)
  Order 2024 (SI 303/2024) 13.03
Employment Equality Act 1998
  (Section 20A) (Gender Pay Gap
  Information) (Amendment)
  Regulations 2024 (SI 259/
  2024)... **13.38**
Employment Equality Act 1998
  (Section 20A) (Gender Pay Gap
  Information) Regulations 2022
  (SI 264/2022).............................. 13.38

Employment Permits Act 2024
  (Commencement) Order 2024
  (SI 443/2024).............................. 13.04
Employment Permits (Amendment)
  (No 2) Regulations 2024
  (SI 12/2024)................................ **13.22**
Employment Permits (Amendment)
  (No 3) Regulations 2024
  (SI 328/2024).............................. **13.47**
Employment Permits (Amendment)
  (No 4) Regulations 2024
  (SI 598/2024).............................. **13.54**
Employment Permits (Amendment)
  Regulations 2024 (SI 8/2024) ... **13.20**
Employment Permits Regulations
  2017 (SI 95/2017).......... 13.04, 13.20,
                                              13.22, 13.47
  Sch 4 .... 9.02
Employment Regulation (Amendment)
  Order (Contract Cleaning Industry
  Joint Labour Committee) 2024
  (SI 255/2024).............................. **13.37**
Employment Regulation
  (Amendment) Order (Early
  Years' Service Joint
  Labour Committee) Order
  No 1 2024 (SI 296/2024)............ **13.42**
Employment Regulation
  (Amendment) Order (Early Years'
  Service Joint
  Labour Committee) Order
  No 2 2024 (SI 297/2024)............ **13.43**
Employment Regulation Order
  (Early Years' Service Joint
  Labour Committee) No 1 2022
  (SI 457/2022).............................. 13.42
Employment Regulation Order
  (Early Years' Service Joint
  Labour Committee) No 2 2022
  (SI 458/2022).............................. 13.43

Employment Regulation Order
(Security Industry Joint Labour
Committee) 2023
(SI 424/2023).............................. 13.45
Employment Regulation Order
(Security Industry Joint
Labour Committee) 2024
(SI 319/2024).............................. **13.45**
English Language Schools Joint
Labour Committee 2020
(SI 24/2020)................................ 13.25
European Communities (Protection
of Employees on Transfer of
Undertakings) Regulations
2003 (SI 131/2003).......... 4.01, 18.03,
18.04
reg 8 .... 18.03
11(1) 4.31, 18.03
European Union (Adequate Minimum
Wages) Regulations 2024
(SI 633/2024).............................. **13.57**
European Union (Corporate
Sustainability Reporting)
Regulations 2024
(SI 336/2024).............................. **13.49**
European Union (Disclosure of
Non-Financial and Diversity
Information by certain large
undertakings and groups)
Regulations 2017
(SI 360/2017).............................. 13.49
European Union (International Labour
Organisation Work in Fishing
Convention) (Working Hours)
(Amendment) Regulations 2024
(SI 25/2024)................................ **13.24**
European Union (Workers on Board
Seagoing Fishing Vessels)
(Organisation of Working Time)
(Share Fishermen) (Amendment)
Regulations 2024 (SI 24/2024) **13.23**
European Union (Workers on Board
Seagoing Fishing Vessels)
(Organisation of Working Time)
(Share Fishermen) Regulations
2020 (SI 585/2020).......... 13.23, 13.24

G

Garda Síochána Act 2005
(Retirement) (Amendment)
Regulations 2024
(SI 438/2024).............................. 13.52
Garda Síochána Act 2005
(Retirement) Regulations
2018 (SI 28/2018) 13.52
reg 2(b) 13.52
Garda Síochána (Admissions
and Appointments)
(Amendment)
Regulations 2023
(SI 611/2023).............................. **13.08**
Garda Síochána (Discipline)
Regulations 2007
(SI 214/2007).............................. 12.05
Garda Síochána (Reserve
Members) Regulations
2024 (SI 64/2024)....................... **13.29**
Garda Síochána (Retirement)
(Amendment) (No 2)
Regulations 2024
(SI 440/2024) 13.52
Garda Síochána (Retirement)
(Amendment) Regulations
2024 (SI 439/2024) 13.52
Garda Síochána (Retirement)
(No 2) Regulations 1951
(SI 335/1951) 13.52
reg 6 .... 13.52
Garda Síochána (Retirement)
Regulations 1996
(SI 16/1996) 13.52
reg 3 .... 13.52
Garda Síochána (Retirement)
Regulations 2024
(SI 437/2024).............................. **13.52**

H

Hairdressing Joint Labour
Committee 1964
(SI 212/1964).............................. 13.25
Hotels Joint Labour Committee
1965 (SI 81/1965)....................... 13.25

I

Immigration Act 2004 (Visas) (Amendment) (No 2) Order 2024 (SI 335/2024) **13.48**

Immigration Act 2004 (Visas) Order 2014 (SI 473/2014) 13.48

Income Tax (Employments) Regulations 2018 (SI 345/2018) 13.19, 17.24
    reg 2(1) 17.24
        10(1) 17.24
        10A 17.24
        23 .... 17.24

Income Tax (Employments) Regulations 2024 (SI 1/2024) **13.19**, 17.24
    reg 2 .... 17.26

Industrial Training (Beauty Therapy Industry) Order 2024 (SI 56/2024) **13.28**

Industrial Training (Social Work Industry) Order 2024 (SI 177/2024) **13.36**

J

Joint Labour Committees (Statutory Review) Order 2024 (SI 29/2024) **13.25**

L

Local Government Act 2001 (Retirement of Firefighters) Regulations 2024 (SI 420/2024) **13.50**

Local Government (Superannuation) (Consolidation) (Amendment) Scheme 2024 (SI 421/2024) **13.51**

M

Maternity Protection, Employment Equality and Preservation of Certain Records Act 2024 (Section 6) (Commencement) Order 2024 (SI 640/2024) **13.60**

N

National Minimum Wage Order 2024 (SI 563/2024) **13.53**

O

Occupational Pension Schemes (Revaluation) Regulations 2024 (SI 124/2024) **13.35**

P

Parent's Leave and Benefit Act 2019 (Extension of Periods of Leave) Order 2024 (SI 300/2024) **13.44**

Personal Injuries Assessment Board Rules 2023 (No 2) (SI 617/2023) **13.09**

Personal Injuries Resolution Board Act 2022 (Change of Name of Board) Order 2023 (SI 627/2023) **13.12**

Personal Injuries Resolution Board Act 2022 (Commencement of Certain Provisions) (No 3) Order 2023 (SI 626/2023) **13.10**

Protection of Employment Act 1977 (Notification of Proposed Collective Redundancies) Regulations 2024 (SI 324/2024) **13.46**

Public Service Pay and Pensions Act 2017 (Section 42) Payments to General Practitioners) (Amendment) Regulations 2024 (SI 120/2024) **13.33**

Public Service Pay and Pensions Act 2017 (Section 42) (Payments to General Practitioners) Regulations 2019 (SI 692/2019) 13.33

R

Registered Employment Agreement (Overhead Powerline Contractors Group) Order 2024 (SI 267/2024) **13.41**

Table of Statutory Instruments

Retail, Grocery and Allied Trades
Joint Labour Committee 1991
(SI 58/1991).................................. 13.25

S

Safety, Health and Welfare at Work
(Carcinogens, Mutagens and
Reprotoxic Substances)
Regulations 2024
(SI 122/2024).............................. **13.34**
Sectoral Employment Order
(Construction Sector) 2019
(SI 234/2019).............................. 10.11
Sectoral Employment Order
(Construction Sector) 2024
(SI 620/2024).............................. **13.55**
Security Industry Joint Labour
Committee 1998
(SI 377/1998).............................. 13.25
Sick Leave Act 2022 (Increase of
Statutory Sick Leave Days)
Order 2024 (SI 10/2024) **13.21**
Social Welfare and Civil Law
(Miscellaneous Provisions)
Act 2024 (Part 2)
(Commencement) Order 2024
(SI 263/2024).............................. **13.40**
Social Welfare (Consolidated
Claims, Payments and Control)
(Amendment) (No 2) (Days
not to be treated as days of
unemployment) Regulations
2024 (SI 35/2024)....................... **13.27**
Social Welfare (Consolidated
Claims, Payments and Control)
(Amendment) (No 2) (State
Pension (Contributory))
Regulations 2019
(SI 40/2019)................................ 13.17
Social Welfare (Consolidated
Claims, Payments and Control)
(Amendment) (No 8) (Child
Maintenance and Liable
Relatives) Regulations 2024
(SI 262/2024).............................. **13.39**

Social Welfare (Consolidated
Claims, Payments and Control)
(Amendment) (No 8) (Days
not to be treated as days of
unemployment) Regulations
2023 (SI 362/2023)..................... 13.27
Social Welfare (Consolidated
Claims, Payments and Control)
(Amendment) (No 10) (Days
Not to Be Treated as Days of
Unemployment) Regulations
2023 (SI 512/2023)..................... 13.27
Social Welfare (Consolidated
Claims, Payments and Control)
(Amendment) (No 12)
(State Pension (Contributory) –
Long Term Carer's Qualifying
Contribution) Regulations 2023
(SI 690/2023).............................. **13.17**
Social Welfare (Consolidated Claims,
Payments and Control)
(Amendment) (No 13)
(Notifications Where Claimant
Wishes For Certain Payments to
Continue After Attaining
Pensionable Age) Regulations
2023(SI 689/2023)...................... **13.16**
Social Welfare (Consolidated Claims,
Payments and Control)
(Amendment) (No 15) (Jobseeker's
Pay-Related Benefit)
Regulations 2024
(SI 635/2024).............................. **13.58**
Social Welfare (Consolidated
Claims, Payments and Control)
(Amendment) (No 16)
(Jobseeker's Pay-Related
Benefit) Regulations 2024
(SI 636/2024).............................. **13.59**
Social Welfare (Consolidated
Claims, Payment and Control)
Regulations 2007
(SI 142/2007)...... 13.16, 13.17, 13.27,
13.39, 13.58, 13.59
Pt 2 (reg 20–115)........................ 13.59
reg 44(1)(b) 13.27

Social Welfare (Consolidated
 Contributions and Insurability)
 (Amendment) (No 1) (Credited
 Contributions) Regulations 2023
 (SI 688/2023)............................. **13.15**
Social Welfare (Consolidated
 Contributions and Insurability)
 (Amendment) (No 1)
 (Employment Contributions –
 Miscellaneous Amendments)
 Regulations 2024
 (SI 34/2024).............................. **13.26**
Social Welfare (Consolidated
 Contributions and Insurability)
 Regulations 1996
 (SI 312/1996)................. 13.15, **13.26**
 reg 31... 13.26
 88... 13.26
Social Welfare (Consolidated
 Occupational Injuries)
 Regulations 2023
 (SI 687/2023)............................. **13.14**
Social Welfare (Consolidated
 Occupational Injuries)
 Regulations 2024
 (SI 632/2024)............................. **13.56**
Social Welfare (Temporary
 Provisions – Increase for
 Qualified Child) Regulations
 2023 (SI 633/2023).................... **13.12**
Social Welfare (Temporary
 Provisions) (No 3)
 Regulations 2023
 (SI 634/2023)............................. **13.13**
Solicitors Acts 1954 to 1994
 (Apprenticeship and
 Education) Regulations 2001
 (SI 546/2001)............................. 13.07
Solicitors Acts 1954 to 2011
 (Apprenticeship and
 Education) (Amendment)
 Regulations 2019
 (SI 503/2019)............................. 13.07
Solicitors Acts 1954 to 2015
 (Apprentices' Fees) Regulations
 2023 (SI 602/2023).................... **13.07**

W

Work Life Balance and
 Miscellaneous Provisions
 Act 2023 (Commencement)
 (No 2) Order 2024
 (SI 91/2024)............................... **13.31**
Work Life Balance and
 Miscellaneous Provisions
 Act 2023 (Commencement)
 Order 2024 (SI 90/2024)........... **13.30**
Work Life Balance and
 Miscellaneous Provisions
 Act 2023 (Workplace Relations
 Commission Code of Practice
 on the Right to Request
 Flexible Working and the
 Right to Request Remote
 Working) Order 2024
 (SI 92/2024)............................... **13.32**
Workplace Relations Act 2015
 (Fixed Payment Notice)
 Regulations 2023
 (SI 705/2023)............................. **13.18**

UNITED KINGDOM

A

Agency Workers Regulations 2010
 (SI 2010/93)................................ 1.02

E

Employment Appeal Tribunal
 Rules 1993 (SI 1993/2854) 4.44
Employment Rights (Northern
 Ireland) Order 1996
 (SI 1996/1919 (NI 16))............... 23.07
 Pt XI (art 126–169A)................. 23.07

F

Fair Employment and Treatment
 (NI) Order 1998 (SI 1998/3162
 (NI 21))
 art 71.. 23.04

N

National Health Service Pension Scheme Regulations 1995 (SI 1995/300) 15.16

O

Occupational Pension Schemes (Administration, Investment, Charges and Governance) (Amendment) Regulations 2021 (Draft) 15.07

Occupational Pension Schemes (Fees) (Amendment) Regulations 2023 (Draft) 15.05

P

Part-Time Workers (Prevention of Less Favourable Treatment) Regulations 2000 (SI 2000/1551) 14.02

S

Sex Discrimination (Northern Ireland) Order 1976 (SI 1976/1042 (NI 15)) 23.08

Social Security (Categorisation of Earners) Regulations 1978 (SI 1978/1689)
   reg 5A 17.42
      para 9 .... 17.42

Social Security Contributions (Intermediaries) Regulations 2000 (SI 2000/727)
   reg 5, 6 .... 17.41

T

Transfer of Undertakings (Protection of Employment) Regulations 2006 (SI 2006/246) 18.02, 18.06, 18.07
   reg 3 .... 18.06
      4(9) 18.02

W

Working Time Regulations (Northern Ireland) 1998 (SI 1998/386) 23.06

Table of EU and other Legislation

DIRECTIVES

Directive 92/85/EEC (on the introduction of measures to encourage improvements in the safety and health at work of pregnant workers and workers who have recently given birth or are breastfeeding) 4.27
    art 10 .... 4.27
        (2) 3.34
    12 .... 4.27
Directive 95/46/EC (general data protection) 2.01, 2.62
    art 23(1) 2.62
Directive 97/81/EC (concerning the Framework Agreement on part-time work) 3.26, 7.06
Directive 98/24/EC (on the protection of the health and safety of workers from the risks related to chemical agents at work) 13.34
Directive 98/59/EC (on collective redundancies) 16.01
    art 1(1) 16.02
        (a) 16.01, 16.02
    2 .... 16.01, 16.02
Directive 99/70/EC (framework agreement) 7.01, 7.03, 7.05, 7.06
    cl 2 .... 7.02
        (1) 7.02
    4 .... 7.02, 7.05, 7.06
        (1) 3.26, 7.06
        (2) 3.26
    5 .... 7.02, 7.03
        (1) 7.03
            (a) 7.02

Directive 2000/78/EC (establishing a general framework for equal treatment in employment and occupation) 3.02
    art 2(2) 3.02
        (5) 3.02
    3(1) 3.02
    4(1) 3.02
    6(1) 3.02
    7 .... 3.02
Directive 2000/79/EC (concerning the European Agreement on the Organisation of Working Time of Mobile Workers in Civil Aviation) 22.04
Directive 2001/86/EC (supplementing the Statute for a European company with regard to the involvement of employees) 6.01
    art 3–7 .... 6.04
    11 .... 6.04
Directive 2003/88/EC (on certain aspects of the organisation of working time) 22.02
    art 7 .... 7.02, 22.02, 22.03
        (1) 22.02, 22.03
        (2) 22.03
    9(1)(a) 22.06
Directive 2004/37/EC (on the protection of workers from the risks related to exposure to carcinogens or mutagens at work) 13.34
Directive 2005/36/EC (on the recognition of professional qualifications) 6.01, 6.07
    art 3 .... 6.07
        (1)(g), (h) 6.07
    6 .... 6.07

Directive 2005/36/EC (on the recognition of professional qualifications) – *contd*
   art 6(1)(b) 6.07
      7(3) 6.07
      21(6) 6.07
      31(3) 6.07
      45(2) 6.07
          (c), (e)–(j) 6.07
          (3) 6.07
      50(1) 6.07
      51(1) 6.07
   Annex VII 6.07

Directive 2005/71/EC (on a specific procedure for admitting third-country nationals for the purposes of scientific research) 13.04

Directive 2006/54/EC (recast equal treatment) 19.02
   art 2(1)(b) 3.26
      (2) 19.02
      4 .... 3.26
         (1) 3.26
      15 .... 19.02

Directive 2006/112/EC (on the common system of value added tax)
   art 9 .... 6.09
      203 .... 6.09

Directive 2006/123/EC (on services in the internal market)
   art 20 .... 6.03

Directive 2008/104/EC (temporary agency work) 19.02
   art 3(1) 19.02
      5(1) 19.02

Directive 2009/38/EC (on the establishment of a European Works Council or a procedure in Community-scale undertakings and Community-scale groups of undertakings for the purposes of informing and consulting employees) 10.03, 10.04

Directive 2013/55/EU (on administrative cooperation through the Internal Market Information System) 6.01, 6.07

Directive 2017/1132/EU (relating to certain aspects of company law) 2.57

Directive 2019/1158/EU (on work-life balance for parents and carers) 22.05
   art 5 .... 22.05

Directive 2022/431/EU (amending Directive 2004/37/EC on the protection of workers from the risks related to exposure to carcinogens or mutagens at work) 13.34

Directive 2022/2041/EU (on adequate minimum wages in the European Union) 13.57

Directive 2022/2464/EU (amending Regulation (EU) No 537/2014, Directive 2004/109/EC, Directive 2006/43/EC and Directive 2013/34/EU, as regards corporate sustainability reporting) 13.49

REGULATIONS

Regulation 2157/2001/EC (on the Statute for a European company) 6.01
   art 12(2) 6.04

Regulation 883/2004/EC (on the coordination of social security systems) 6.01, 6.08
   art 3 .... 6.08
        (1)(a), (b) 6.08
      4 .... 6.08
      5 .... 6.08
      7 .... 6.08
      11(3)(a) 6.08
      14 .... 6.08
      21 .... 6.08
         (1) 6.08

Regulation 492/2011/EC (on freedom of movement for workers within the Union)
art 7(2) 6.08
Regulation 679/2016/EU (European Court of Justice, Rules of General Data Protection) 2.01, 2.48
Recital 36 .... 2.39
       75 .... 2.55
       85 .... 2.55
art 3(2) 2.03
    4(2) 2.50
      (7) 2.50, 2.51, 2.65
      (8) 2.50
      (11) 2.25
      (16)(a) 2.39
    5 .... 2.01, 2.48, 2.50, 2.58, 2.60
      (1) 2.30, 2.63, 2.64
        (a) 2.10, 2.25, 2.48, 2.51
        (b) 2.04, 2.48, 2.48
        (c) 2.05, 2.10, 2.27, 2.48, 2.51
        (e) 2.10, 2.48, 2.51
        (f) 2.08
      (2) 2.32, 2.48
    6 .... 2.05, 2.56, 2.63
      (1) 2.06
        (b) 2.25
        (f) 2.25, 2.27, 2.31
    9(1) 2.10, 2.48
      (2) 2.48
        (e) 2.48
    12 .... 2.05, 2.25, 2.26, 2.28
      (4) 2.26
    13 .... 2.05, 2.07, 2.10, 2.25, 2.28, 2.50
      (1)(c) 2.48
    15 .... 2.64
      (1)(c) 2.65
    17 .... 2.26, 2.28, 2.32
      (1) 2.28
    23 .... 2.64
      (2) 2.64
    24 .... 2.32, 2.58, 2.60
      (1) 2.60

Regulation 679/2016/EU (European Court of Justice, Rules of General Data Protection) – *contd*
art 25(1) 2.51
      (2) 2.48
    26 .... 2.50
      (1) 2.50
    28 .... 2.34, 2.36, 2.38
    29 .... 2.54
    30 .... 2.13
    32 .... 2.05, 2.28, 2.50, 2.58, 2.60
      (1) 2.30, 2.60
      (2) 2.60
    33(1), (5) 2.30
    35 .... 2.07, 2.50
    44 .... 2.03
    57(1)(a) 2.49
        (f) 2.49
    58(2) 2.49, 2.51
        (b) 2.26, 2.27, 2.30
        (i) 2.30, 2.51
    60 .... 2.22, 2.25
    64(2) 2.33
    65 .... 2.25
    66 .... 2.25
      (2) 2.25
    70 .... 2.33
      (1) 2.33
    77(1) 2.49
    81(1) 2.59
    82 .... 2.52, 2.53, 2.54, 2.55, 2.56, 2.58, 2.59, 2.60, 2.63
      (1) 2.53, 2.55, 2.56, 2.57, 2.58, 2.59, 2.60
      (2) 2.60
      (3) 2.54, 2.60
    83 .... 2.30, 2.49, 2.50, 2.51, 2.54
      (1) 2.50, 2.51
      (2), (3) 2.51
      (4)–(6) 2.50, 2.51
    85 .... 2.29
Regulation 2554/2022/EU (EU Digital Operational Resilience Act) 15.06
art 30 .... 15.06

Regulation 1689/2024/EU
    (laying down harmonised
    rules on artificial intelligence,
    EU Artificial Intelligence Act).....2.01
    art 2(7)..2.44
        70..2.44
            (3), (9)..................................2.44

TABLE OF AGREEMENTS, CHARTERS, CONVENTIONS, PROCEDURES AND TREATIES

Charter of Fundamental Rights
    of the European Union.....1.02, 22.02
    art 7......................................2.48, 6.08
        8..2.48
            (1)..2.38
        21..7.05
        26..3.02
        27..16.02
        30.................................7.05, 16.02
        31..1.02
            (2)..........................22.02, 22.03
        32(2)..22.03
        47..........................1.02, 7.03, 7.05
        52(1)..22.03
Data Protection Working Party
    art 29..2.31
European Convention on
    Human Rights and
    Fundamental Freedoms.................2.64
    art 2..19.18
        5..19.18
        6..4.25
        8......................................2.61, 3.33,
                                            4.03, 19.18
        9..........................3.01, 3.45, 3.46
        10...........................3.45, 19.11,
                                            21.04, 21.15
        11.......................3.47, 10.01, 10.09
        14.........................3.33, 21.04,
                                            21.15
        17..3.47
Revised European Social Charter
    art 5..10.13

Treaty on the Functioning of the
    European Union..........................2.38
    art 6..................................6.05, 21.06
        art 18..6.08
        21(1)...6.02
        26..6.03
        45..........................6.05, 6.06, 6.08
            (2)..6.08
        56......................................6.02, 6.03
        57...6.02
        101...................................6.05, 6.06
            (1), (3)..................................6.05
        157..3.26
        165..6.05
        288..2.33
UN Convention on the Rights
    of Persons with Disabilities
    art 19..3.02

EDPB GUIDELINES AND RECOMMENDATIONS ETC

EDPB 2023: 'Coordinated
    Enforcement Action Designation
    and Position of Data Protection
    Officers', (adopted
    16 January 2024)..........................2.32
EDPB Opinion 22/2024 on certain
    obligations following from the
    reliance on processor(s) and
    sub-processor(s)...........................**2.34**
EDPB Opinion 04/2024 on the
    notion of main establishment
    of a controller in the Union
    under article 4(16)(a) GDPR
    (adopted on 13 February
    2024)...**2.39**
EDPB Report of the work
    undertaken by the ChatGPT
    Taskforce. 23 May 2024...............**2.43**
EDPB Statement 3/2024 on data
    protection authorities' role
    in the Artificial Intelligence
    Act framework (adopted on
    16 July 2024).......................2.01, **2.44**

EDPB Guidelines 1/2024 on Processing
of Personal Data Based on
Article 6(1)(f) GDPR **2.31**

TABLE OF INTERNATIONAL LEGISLATION

Australia

Anti-Discrimination Act 1998
(Tasmania)
   s 16(e) 3.28
   26 .... 3.28

Italy

Use of facial recognition to monitor
employee attendance (Order
of 6 June 2024 [10029500]) 2.09

USA

Executive Order 14086 on
'Enhancing Safeguards for
United States Signals
Intelligence Activities' adopted
in October 2022 .... 2.45
Executive Order 14086 on
Regulation on the Data
Protection Review Court
issued by the US Attorney
General 2.45
Foreign Intelligence Surveillance
Act
   s 702 .... 2.45
Freedom of Information
Act 2.46

Chapter 1

Contract of Employment

INTRODUCTION

[1.01]

Agency Employees

The UK EAT considered the status of contracted pilots in *Ryanair DAC & Storm Global Ltd v Lutz*.

Bonus

The High Court of England and Wales considered whether a decision not to award a discretionary bonus could amount to breach of contract in *Gupta v DB Group Services Ltd*.

Breach of Confidence

In *PSN Recruitments Ltd v Ludley*, the High Court of England and Wales considered whether loss and damage is required in a breach of confidence claim.

Entitlement to Employee Benefits Post Termination of Employment

In upholding one ground of appeal, the UK EAT in *Adekoya* dealt with whether the employment tribunal had properly determined that the claimants were contractually entitled to a lifelong rail travel discount in a redundancy situation.

Fiduciary Duty

In *Victoria Hall Management Ltd v Cox*, the High Court delivered a notable decision on the fiduciary duties owed by a senior executive to their employer group in relation to commercial opportunities.

Right to Silence and the Contract of Employment

In another key judgment, *ESB v Sharkey*, the High Court considered the limits on the right to silence that may be enjoyed by employees in disciplinary proceedings where there is a contemporaneous criminal investigation.

Terms of Employment

There are three Labour Court cases in relation to terms of employment. In *Department of Justice & An Garda Síochána v Doherty*, the Court considered an appeal against a decision of the WRC in relation to whether pay increases arising from collective agreements must be notified to employees. In *Ringsend Community Services Forum Clg v Moore*, the Court considered defects in a written contract of employment which did not set out the basic terms. In *Dundalk Institute of Technology v Honari*, the Court considered the five-day statutory timeframe for employers to provide employees with a written statement of employment terms.

AGENCY EMPLOYEES

[1.02] ***Ryanair DAC & Storm Global Ltd v Lutz***[1]—***UK Employment Appeal Tribunal—appeal from employment tribunal—Charter of Fundamental Rights of the European Union—status of claimant—agency work—purpose and nature of work—whether the employment tribunal erred in concluding that the claimant was a temporary worker***

The respondent companies appealed from a preliminary decision of an employment tribunal which related to the status of the claimant pilot.

The claimant was one of a pool of 'contracted pilots' who flew Ryanair's aircraft. He was supplied to Ryanair by Storm Global, with which he had a contract, and from which he claimed accrued annual leave on the basis that he was a 'crew member' within the meaning of the relevant domestic and European working time legislation, and that he was a 'worker' under arts 31 and 47 of the Charter of Fundamental Rights of the European Union (the 'Charter'). The claimant sought the same conditions as would apply had he been directly employed by Ryanair, in particular in relation to pay and annual leave, on the basis that he was an 'agency worker' under UK Agency Worker Regulations.

The employment tribunal accepted the claimant's arguments. It was common ground that the claimant had a five-year, fixed-term contract with Storm Global and that he was 'supplied' to Ryanair to work as a pilot under its direction. The employment tribunal's unchallenged findings were that the claimant was not in business on his own account and the respondents were not his clients; there was a complete imbalance of power, and

---

1 *Ryanair DAC & Storm Global Ltd v Lutz* [2023] EAT 146.

the claimant was not able to alter anything about the arrangements; a service company which the claimant was required to use was a fiction; the claimant had no right of substitution and the substitution clause in the written agreement was a sham; and the dominant purpose of the arrangement was for the claimant to provide personal service to Ryanair.

On appeal, Ryanair argued that the employment tribunal wrongly treated the five-year, fixed-term contract as determinative of the temporary nature of the claimant's work and had not focused on the purpose and nature of the work. It was emphasised that, at the expiry of five years 'any contracted pilot who remained was, without exception, issued with a new five-year contract'. Storm Global, emphasised that contracted pilots were not used to provide cover and were integrated into Ryanair's pool of pilots and rostered in the same way. It also stressed the length of the arrangement between itself and Ryanair for the supply of pilots, dating back to 2011.

The UK EAT held that the employment tribunal's findings were sufficient to support a conclusion that the claimant was employed by Storm Global. The tribunal had been entitled to conclude that the claimant's contract was to perform work or services personally and its reasoning disclosed no material error of law. It had been correct to take into account fetters to the right to substitution arising from airline safety regulatory requirements. It had not erred in concluding that the supply of the claimant on a five-year, fixed term was 'temporary' work within the meaning of the Regulations. It had correctly decided that the supply was terminable on a condition being satisfied, rather than an open-ended indefinite arrangement. Its findings of fact indicated that the agreed five-year term represented the basis of the supply.

The appeal was, accordingly, dismissed.

BONUS

[1.03]   *Gupta v DB Group Services Ltd*[2]—*High Court of England and Wales— Howells J—breach of contract—unreasonable or irrational exercise of discretionary power—discretionary bonus scheme—assurance of discretionary bonus— affordability considerations—unique and exceptional circumstances of the employee*

The claimant alleged breach of contract arising from the respondent's decision not to award her a bonus under a discretionary bonus scheme.

The claimant was employed by the respondent in its 'non-core operations unit' ('NCOU'), the purpose of which was to dispose of the respondent's high-risk assets. The NCOU had a temporary mandate and the claimant knew that there was a risk that she would be made redundant in late 2016 or early 2017, when the unit came to a close. She was well remunerated and, in addition to her salary, had always received a bonus. The claimant had no contractual entitlement to a bonus, merely an entitlement to be considered for one. However, she alleged that in 2016 she was given oral 'assurances'

---

[2]   *Gupta v DB Group Services Ltd* [2024] EWHC 2297 (KB).

by the respondent that if she performed well and achieved her targets, she would be paid multiples of previous years' bonuses. Her case was that she relied upon those assurances and remained in the respondent's employ as she expected to be rewarded once the NCOU's work was complete.

The claimant was made redundant from 31 March 2017. For the year ending 2016, neither she nor any employee of her seniority and above received individual bonuses. The claimant did receive a group bonus, though this was lower than she expected. She argued that the respondent failed to pay her the appropriate bonus and that it failed to take into account assurances that it would do so. She claimed that the decision not to award her an individual bonus was unlawful. Alternatively, the decision was irrational, not supported by reasons, and inconsistent with the contractual purpose.

For its part, the respondent contended that the claimant was never given assurances upon which she could rely. Any decision as to the payment of bonuses was entirely within the respondent's discretion, as set out in its compensation policy documents. It was decided that, in the wake of a penalty imposed by the US Department of Justice, further individual bonus payments were not affordable. The respondent admitted to telling the claimant in or about April 2016 to 'focus on her job', not to 'worry', and that she would 'be treated fairly'.

The Court found the evidence in support of the claimant's case to be 'unclear, nebulous and ... inconsistent'. It accepted the respondent's case that, 'although certain aspirations and hopes may have been expressed, there was nothing said or done which could amount to an assurance'. In any event, assurances of future remuneration would need to have been given 'in such a way that it could be expected that someone would place a degree of reliance upon them'. The claimant's evidence lacked clarity as to what she was told and by whom, and the Court did not accept that she was given any direct assurances by the respondent; rather a 'general expectation based on past history'.

It was clear from publicly available documents that the respondent's bonus pool had significantly reduced, there was a limit to what bonuses could be paid, compared to salary. The claimant was not unique in her position and any remuneration assurances must equally have applied to others in the NCOU. This context made it unlikely that the respondent would have given the alleged assurances. It was also notable that in 2015, the respondent, in order to ensure retention of NCOU employees, who were effectively 'working themselves out of a job', offered the claimant and others significant increases in salary and significant off-cycle payments. In that context, the likelihood of the alleged assurances having been provided was 'extremely weak'. Finally, there was an absence of any documentation that the respondent made the assurances as alleged or at all.

Even had reliable assurances been given, the respondent was entitled to determine that affordability was the paramount consideration in deciding whether to award individual bonuses that year. As a commercial organisation operating in a tightly regulated environment, the payment of bonuses threatened the respondent's financial viability, and so the decision was 'entirely rational'. The claimant did not establish that her particular circumstances were unique and exceptional, so that the decision was not illogical. It followed that the decision was not unreasonable in the *Wednesbury* sense.

The respondent had also given its reasoning on various company-wide communications and the claimant had sufficient information as to its decision-making process.

In conclusion, the claimant had not proven her case. The respondent was not in breach of its contract, nor was its exercise of its discretionary decision-making power unreasonable or irrational.

See also decision of Labour Court in *Natus Manufacturing Ltd v Callanan*,[3] at **[20.05]**; and decision of UK EAT in *Moon v Slater & Gordon UK Ltd*,[4] at **[20.06]**, both relating to bonuses in the context of payment of wages claims.

BREACH OF CONFIDENCE

[1.04] *PSN Recruitments Ltd v Ludley*[5]—*High Court of England and Wales—Clarke J—passing off—breach of confidence—whether the claimant suffered loss and damage—quantity of loss and damage—confidential information—liability for breach of confidence*

The claimant, a specialist recruitment agency in the landscape, horticulture and gardening sector, brought an action in passing off and breach of confidence against the respondent, who was employed as a recruitment agent by the claimant. Several months into his employment, the respondent began forwarding documents and data belonging to the claimant to his own accounts. These included spreadsheets and folders with titles such as 'live jobs', 'financials' and 'campaigns'. The respondent notified the claimant of his resignation, stating (falsely, he accepted in evidence) that he had obtained alternative employment. He subsequently incorporated a company, trading as Greenscape, for the purpose of working as a recruitment agent on his own account. He then sent an email ('the email') to over 500 of the claimant's clients and the claimant's HR administrator, misrepresenting that Greenscape was the claimant's new trading name.

The respondent denied that any loss or damage was caused by the email and argued that none of its recipients were misled to the extent that 'when they did business with Greenscape, they thought they were dealing with the claimant', and that he 'suspected' they probably ignored the email. The respondent denied that the claimant's client list was confidential and asserted that it was no more than a collection of well-known contact details.

The Court found both witnesses for the claimant to be credible and reliable. The respondent in his evidence made a number of concessions and admissions of wrongdoing (including destroying evidence of information taken from the claimant) and denied having seen the confidentiality obligations set out in the claimant's employees handbook, which he had signed and, the Court was satisfied, had indeed probably seen.

---

[3] *Natus Manufacturing Ltd v Callanan* PWD2447.
[4] *Moon v Slater & Gordon UK Ltd* [2024] EAT 144.
[5] *PSN Recruitments Ltd v Ludley* [2023] EWHC 3153.

The Court found the respondent untruthful in his evidence about why he sent the email, stating that it was 'a mistake', and was satisfied that he did so with the intention of directing the claimant's business to his new venture. The Court accepted the claimant's evidence about the time and effort it had expended in assembling its customer relationship management database, and the confusion that the email caused among its client base. It was clear that the respondent began working with clients of the claimant 'almost immediately' following the sending of the email, without correcting the misrepresentation. The Court was sympathetic to the claimant's difficulties in quantifying its losses, given the respondent's approach to the evidence overall. It was satisfied that the claimant suffered loss and damage by the respondent's passing off and proceeded to quantify same.

The Court found that the claimant's client list was confidential information, and that the claimant was liable for breach of confidence.

ENTITLEMENT TO EMPLOYEE BENEFITS POST TERMINATION OF EMPLOYMENT

[1.05] *Adekoya v Heathrow Express Operating Company Ltd[6]—UK Employment Appeal Tribunal—appeal from employment tribunal—breach of contract—withdrawal of contractual benefit under reciprocal agreement with a third party—jurisdiction—incorporation of terms of reciprocal agreement into claimants' contracts of employment*

The claimants appealed against an employment tribunal's dismissal of their claim for want of jurisdiction.

The claimants were all employed by the respondent, which runs the Heathrow Express train service. Following a consultation process, they were made voluntarily redundant. The claimants alleged breach of contract. They contended that, because they all had five years or more of service and had been made redundant, they were entitled to discounted rail travel for life.

The respondent denied that the claimants were entitled to benefit from the rail discount scheme, and, even if they were, they had been bought out of that entitlement as part of a settlement agreement. The scheme was administered by a third party, the Rail Delivery Group, which had determined that the scheme would no longer apply to former employees of UK rail companies, including the respondent. More importantly, the respondent argued successfully that the employment tribunal did not have statutory jurisdiction to hear the claims, as no breach of contract had arisen from the dismissals.

The claimants submitted that the employment tribunal erred in its finding that this 'reciprocal agreement' between the third party and the respondent was incorporated into the claimants' contracts of employment.

---

[6] *Adekoya v Heathrow Express Operating Company Ltd* [2024] EAT 72.

The UK EAT was satisfied that, at least initially, the claimants were contractually entitled to the rail travel discount. It seemed that the tribunal's implicit reasoning was that, under a reciprocal agreement between the third party and the respondent, the third party was entitled to withdraw the benefit of the scheme, and the respondent would not be contractually liable if it did so. The tribunal's reasons did not explain why it considered that these withdrawal provisions were incorporated into the terms of the claimants' contracts of employment. Although the claimants would have been aware that the benefit was being operated by a third party, it was agreed that the claimants were never given a copy of the reciprocal agreement and, indeed, did not know about it until litigation had commenced. Hence, the tribunal could not properly have found that the terms of the reciprocal agreement were incorporated into the claimants' contracts of employment. That ground of appeal was, accordingly, upheld.

The EAT did not accept an argument from the respondent that it was able to unilaterally vary the provision of the benefit without placing itself in breach of contract with the claimants. This argument did not appear to have been advanced at the tribunal hearing and had not informed the tribunal's reasoning nor its decision, which wholly turned on a finding that the withdrawal provisions were incorporated into the contracts of employment.

The matter was remitted to the employment tribunal for a fresh consideration of the issues of jurisdiction and whether the claimant's right to continued enjoyment of the benefit was compromised by a settlement agreement.

FIDUCIARY DUTY

[1.06] *Victoria Hall Management Ltd v Cox*[7]*—High Court—Quinn J—fiduciary duties—corporate governance—senior executive liability—conflict of interest—misuse of corporate opportunities—equitable remedies—constructive trust—duty of loyalty—breach of fiduciary duty—defences in equity*

The plaintiff brought a claim in damages against the defendant for breaches of fiduciary duty arising from his alleged diversion of a lucrative commercial opportunity for his personal benefit. The plaintiff sought declarations, an account of profits, and other remedies to address the defendant's conduct, which was said to have contravened the high standards of loyalty, good faith, and integrity expected of someone in his position.

The defendant was a senior executive within the O'Flynn Group, of which the plaintiff was part. The O'Flynn Group operated a corporate structure that included the plaintiff and other entities engaged in property development and management. The defendant's formal role was as an employee of Tiger Developments, a central company within the group, which carried out significant property investment and development activities. In this capacity, the defendant had a strategic leadership role, which included sourcing and managing investment opportunities and participating in high-level decisions that affected the group's commercial ventures.

---

[7] *Victoria Hall Management Ltd and Ors v Cox and Ors* [2024] IEHC 674.

Although the defendant was not directly employed by the plaintiff, his role extended across the O'Flynn Group, encompassing responsibilities that impacted the plaintiff's operations. The High Court held that the defendant owed fiduciary duties to the plaintiff because of his position of trust, authority, and influence within the group. His access to sensitive commercial information and the scope of his decision-making authority made him accountable to the plaintiff as a fiduciary, particularly in relation to opportunities and transactions relevant to the group's business. Thus, his relationship to the plaintiff was one of trust and confidence, with a corresponding duty to act in the plaintiff's best interests.

The primary breach of duty concerned the Gardiner Street student accommodation project, a highly valuable development opportunity. The Court found that the defendant had diverted this project for his personal benefit and that of his co-defendants. He failed to disclose the opportunity to the plaintiff, as required by his fiduciary obligations, and actively concealed his actions. The plaintiff emphasised the defendant's use of confidential documents and proprietary information belonging to the plaintiff to further his own interests. These materials, which he misappropriated, included commercially sensitive data that provided him with a significant advantage in acquiring the Gardiner Street project. By engaging in these acts, the defendant not only breached his duty to avoid conflicts of interest but also his fundamental duty of loyalty to the plaintiff.

The defendant argued that he had been given oral consent by the plaintiff to pursue personal projects outside his work with the group. The Court found no credible evidence to support this assertion, noting inconsistencies in the defendant's testimony and the lack of corroboration. Written consent was also invoked by the defendant, but the Court held that any such consent did not extend to the Gardiner Street project or the actions he had taken in relation to it. Further, the defendant contended that the documents and information he used were not confidential or commercially sensitive. The Court rejected this, finding that the materials were integral to the plaintiff's business operations and had been clearly marked as proprietary. The defendant also sought to argue that his relationship with the plaintiff was limited to a consultancy arrangement and that no fiduciary obligations applied. The Court disagreed, emphasising that his fiduciary duties arose from the trust, reliance, and authority placed in him by virtue of his senior role in the organisation.

In addressing remedies, the Court held that the defendant was accountable to the plaintiff for all profits derived from the Gardiner Street project. The Court declared that the profits were held on constructive trust for the plaintiff, reflecting the principle that a fiduciary must not profit from their position without proper authorisation. The defendant was ordered to account for and pay the full profits of the project to the plaintiff, with interest. In instances where profits could not be recovered, the defendant was required to pay damages equivalent to the value of the lost profits. The Court declined to award aggravated damages, concluding that, while the defendant's conduct amounted to a serious breach of fiduciary duty, it did not meet the threshold of egregiousness required for such a remedy.

The Court reiterated that fiduciaries must act in the best interests of their beneficiaries and must avoid conflicts of interest or personal exploitation of their roles. The defendant's actions in this case—concealing an opportunity, misappropriating proprietary information, and failing to disclose material facts—constituted a stark departure from these principles. He was not entitled to profit from his breaches of fiduciary duty and the beneficiaries were entitled to full redress for the harm caused.

RIGHT TO SILENCE AND THE CONTRACT OF EMPLOYMENT

[1.07]   *ESB v Sharkey*[8]*—High Court—Mulcahy J—repudiatory breach—refusal to comply with instruction to answer questions—right to silence—contemporaneous criminal investigation—whether right to silence may only be invoked in relation to parties acting on behalf of the State*

This case raised the question of whether an employee could rely on his right to silence when directed by his employer to respond to its request for information.

The defendant was a network technician who commenced employment with the plaintiff in 2017. In May 2022, the plaintiff was made aware of allegations from two developers that certain ESB employees were demanding cash payments to expedite works on a development site. It was also alleged that the defendant had approached a site foreman to arrange for a tiler on site to carry out work at the defendant's home for 'probably well below cost'. The plaintiff notified An Garda Síochána of the allegations and an investigation followed.

The plaintiff wrote to the defendant requesting answers to questions regarding this incident, alleged to have occurred during the course of his employment, in respect of which the defendant was the subject of the criminal investigation. The defendant, acting on legal advice, denied wrongdoing but otherwise refused to answer any questions, invoking his right to silence. The plaintiff sought a declaration that the defendant had, thereby, repudiated his contract of employment.

In its request for information from the defendant in February 2023, the plaintiff advised the defendant that it was involved in High Court proceedings with the two developers in which it sought documentation relevant to the allegations (this would ultimately be granted). Since these were public proceedings, details about the allegations—including the fact that the defendant was one of the persons against whom they were made—were in the public domain. In light of this, the defendant was asked to confirm whether he had ever asked for or received any payment or other emolument from a third party in connection with his duties with the ESB, and to provide full details of same. The letter advised that this was a 'formal instruction' in connection with the defendant's employment with the plaintiff.

The Court observed that no disciplinary proceedings had commenced against the defendant in relation to the allegations. The defendant remained in his employment

---

[8]   *ESB v Sharkey* [2024] IEHC 65.

and had not been suspended. The plaintiff had not raised any queries with the defendant until some nine months after it first became aware of the allegations. It did not seek to commence disciplinary proceedings in relation to the defendant's refusal to answer the questions; rather, it sought to summarily dismiss him. Given that the defendant was clearly acting on legal advice in refusing to answer the questions, the Court accepted that he would be entitled to be given a further opportunity to reconsider his position if the case were decided against him.

The plaintiff's contention, broadly, was that the defendant's reliance on the right to silence was misconceived and that privilege against self-incrimination is concerned with protecting individuals against compulsion by those acting on behalf of the State. Accordingly, the right did not have horizontal effect and the consequence of the defendant's refusal to answer the questions was a matter of private law. The defendant, for his part, argued that his privilege against self-incrimination, for the duration of the criminal investigation at least, entitled him to refuse to answer the questions. The Court noted that both sides approached the question from extreme positions, with neither adopting a balancing exercise.

The Court concluded that, although the right or privilege against self-incrimination is not absolute, no authority suggests that a person may only invoke it to guard against State abuse. The Irish Courts 'have long recognised that the constitutional rights to fair procedure ... are also guaranteed in any proceedings, such as a disciplinary proceeding'. Demanding answers to a question on the basis of a threat of dismissal could be regarded as 'impermissible compulsion'. While the Court considered that it would be wholly premature for the plaintiff to regard the defendant's contract as repudiated, it would not be appropriate in the absence of a balancing exercise to simply injunct that the plaintiff could never discipline the defendant for failing to answer the questions. It was therefore incumbent on the plaintiff to carry out its own assessment of the competing interests involved, including the urgency in commencing disciplinary proceedings in advance of the criminal investigation's conclusion. Such an assessment would be reviewed by the Court if necessary.

Thus, the defendant was entitled to refuse to comply with the directions issued by the plaintiff for the time being; however, that entitlement would cease once the criminal investigation ended, or if the plaintiff could show that 'its interest in insisting on the performance by the defendant of his contractual obligations outweighs the risk of infringement of the defendant's constitutionally protected right to silence'.

TERMS OF EMPLOYMENT

[1.08] *Department of Justice & An Garda Síochána v Doherty*[9]—*Labour Court—appeal from Workplace Relations Commission—Terms of Employment (Information) Acts 1994 to 2014, s 8(1)—pay increases arising from collective agreements excluded from the Acts*

---

[9] *Department of Justice & An Garda Síochána v Doherty* TED2317.

The claimant appealed against a decision of the WRC dismissing her complaint under the Terms of Employment (Information) Acts 1994 to 2014 (the 'Acts'). She complained that the respondent did not provide her with information in respect of changes to her terms and conditions of employment.

The claimant was a member of An Garda Síochána. During the relevant period, she was on unpaid suspension as she was serving a 20-month prison sentence. The claimant submitted that during the cognisable period, changes occurred to her terms and conditions of employment of which she was not notified, including, *inter alia*, changes to her rates of pay, circulars in respect of acceptance of gifts, hospitality, sponsorship, and notification of a course in fraud and e-crime. The respondent submitted that only two relevant circulars issued during that period, both of which concerned pay increases arising from a collective bargaining agreement, and from which the claimant had not benefited in any event, as she had been suspended without pay.

The Court held that it was clear from the legislation that payments under collective agreements are excluded from s 5(1) of the Acts. The claimant did not dispute the respondent's submission that the only relevant circulars related to collective agreements, from which she could not benefit.

Accordingly, the appeal failed and the decision of the Adjudication Officer was upheld.

[1.09] ***Ringsend Community Services Forum Clg v Moore*[10]—*Labour Court—appeal from Workplace Relations Commission—Terms of Employment (Information) Acts 1994 to 2014, s 8(1)—written statement of terms of employment—employer's failure to provide basic terms of employment in writing***

The claimant appealed against a WRC decision that dismissed her complaint under the Terms of Employment (Information) Acts 1994 to 2014. The respondent did not attend the hearing at first instance.

The claimant submitted that her contract of employment was in breach of the Terms of Employment (Information) Acts 1994 to 2014 in that it did not set out the basic terms of employment in writing.

The respondent accepted the defects in the written statement of terms and conditions of employment.

The Labour Court found that the complaint was well founded. The respondent was ordered to pay €1,150 in compensation.

[1.10] ***Dundalk Institute of Technology v Honari*[11]—*Labour Court—appeal from Workplace Relations Commission—Terms of Employment (Information) Acts 1994 to 2014—terms of employment—written statement—'day 5 statement'—compensation award***

---

[10] *Ringsend Community Services Forum Clg v Moore* TED2416.
[11] *Dundalk Institute of Technology v Honari* TED2424.

The claimant appealed against a decision of the WRC upholding his complaint under the Terms of Employment (Information) Act 1994 (the '1994 Act') and awarding him €2,000 in compensation. The case arose from the respondent failing to provide the claimant with a written statement of employment terms within the statutory timeframe. The claimant challenged the level of the award.

The claimant began working with the respondent as an hourly-paid assistant lecturer in computing science and mathematics on 3 October 2022, a fixed-term role set to end on 16 December 2022. Under the 1994 Act, the respondent was obliged to issue a 'day 5 statement' detailing the essential terms of employment within five days of commencement. However, the respondent only issued the required statement on 22 November 2022, significantly after the statutory deadline.

The claimant argued that this failure to provide timely employment terms prevented him from making an informed decision about whether to accept the contract. He also contended that the respondent's failure to include a public sector pay adjustment in the issued contract exacerbated the breach. He sought the maximum compensation of four weeks' remuneration and additional remedies for the alleged underpayment during his employment.

The respondent admitted to breaching the 1994 Act by failing to issue the day 5 statement in the required timeframe. However, it attributed the delay to uncertainty regarding the maximum hours for the claimant's role. It maintained that once this detail was resolved, the contract was promptly issued. The respondent also argued that the dispute over the claimant's rate of pay was outside the scope of the 1994 Act and not part of the Labour Court's jurisdiction. It requested a lower award than the maximum permissible under the 1994 Act, citing its efforts to rectify the omission.

The Labour Court confirmed that its role was limited to determining whether the respondent had breached its obligations under the 1994 Act and did not extend to adjudicating disputes over pay or other contractual terms. It found that the respondent's failure to issue the written terms of employment within the statutory timeframe constituted a clear breach of the 1994 Act.

In considering the appropriate compensation, the Court took into account the claimant's weekly hours and rate of pay, as well as the circumstances of the delay. It determined that an award of €2,000 was just and equitable, reflecting the respondent's admitted breach.

Consequently, the Labour Court upheld the WRC's decision affirming the award of €2,000 to the claimant.

Chapter 2

Data Protection/Privacy

INTRODUCTION

[2.01] Artificial intelligence ('AI'), and more specifically the interaction between the General Data Protection Regulation[1] ('GDPR') and AI, continued to occupy the resources of the DPC and we can expect this to continue in 2025. The authority became the lead supervisory authority for cross-border processing carried out by OpenAI in February 2024. It issued a statement identifying data protection risks associated with AI systems in April.[2] August saw the DPC engage with X in relation to its processing of certain personal data used for training its AI 'Grok',[3] and, in September, the Data Protection Commission ('DPC') announced a cross-border statutory inquiry into Google Ireland Limited concerning the use of personal data in the development of its foundational AI model.[4]

Similarly, the European Data Protection Board ('EDPB') has continued its focus on AI. In anticipation of the entry into force of the EU Artificial Intelligence Act,[5] the EDPB adopted a Statement on 16 July 2024 highlighting supervision and coordination issues that could result from the designation of competent authorities by the Member States in areas linked to personal data protection matters.[6] AI, and its deployment by and within an organisation, is discussed in more detail below.[7]

---

[1] Regulation (EU) 2016/679 on the protection of natural persons with regard to the processing of personal data and on the free movement of such data, and repealing Directive 95/46/EC ('General Data Protection Regulation'/'GDPR').

[2] 'AI, Large Language Models and Data Protection', Data Protection Commission, 18 July 2024, available at: *https://www.dataprotection.ie/en/dpc-guidance/blogs/AI-LLMs-and-Data-Protection*.

[3] 'Data Protection Commission welcomes conclusion of proceedings relating to X's AI tool "Grok"', Data Protection Commission, 4 September 2024, available at: *https://www.dataprotection.ie/en/news-media/press-releases/data-protection-commission-welcomes-conclusion-proceedings-relating-xs-ai-tool-grok#Grok*. Addressed in more detail below.

[4] 'Data Protection Commission launches inquiry into Google AI model', Data Protection Commission, 12 September 2024, available at: *https://www.dataprotection.ie/en/news-media/press-releases/data-protection-commission-launches-inquiry-google-ai-model*. Addressed in more detail below.

[5] Regulation (EU) 2024/1689 laying down harmonised rules on artificial intelligence ('Artificial Intelligence Act').

[6] EDPB Statement 3/2024 on data protection authorities' role in the Artificial Intelligence Act framework, (adopted 16 July 2024), available at: *https://www.edpb.europa.eu/system/files/2024-07/edpb_statement_202403_dpasroleaiact_en.pdf*.

[7] See [2.41–2.42] below.

How to lawfully process personal data for the purpose of behavioural and targeted advertising was another area of focus for courts and regulators in 2024, and illustrates the efforts, ongoing since 2018, to comprehensively interpret and apply art 5 GDPR. The ECJ delivered its judgment in *Schrems v Meta Platforms Ireland Limited*,[8] finding that the fact that a person has made a statement about his or her sexual orientation in public does not authorise the operator of an online social network platform to process other data relating to that person's sexual orientation for the purpose of personalised advertising. The Court also held that personal data obtained by a controller from the data subject or third parties may not be processed for the purposes of targeted advertising without restriction as to time and without distinction as to type of data.

Behavioural advertising by large online platforms implemented using 'consent or pay' models was the subject of an opinion from the EDPB examining how this can be done in a way that constitutes valid and freely given consent. The opinion gave rise to much commentary, as well as an action by Meta before the European Court of Justice ('ECJ') seeking to annul the opinion. The EDPB organised a remote stakeholder event in November 2024 to collect stakeholders' input concerning future guidelines on the application of data protection legislation in the context of 'consent or pay' models.[9]

EUROPEAN DATA PROTECTION SUPERVISORY AUTHORITIES' SANCTIONS

[2.02] European data protection supervisory authorities ('supervisory authorities') have continued to exercise vigilance in investigating employee complaints as to data breaches by employers in processing the personal data of employees. The following represents a sample of fines imposed by various supervisory authorities in 2024.

AP: Transfer of personal data to the US without appropriate safeguards[10]

[2.03] On 22 July 2024, the Dutch Data Protection Authority, the *Autoriteit Persoonsgegevens* ('AP'), imposed a fine of EUR €290 million on Uber for failing to appropriately safeguard its drivers' personal data transferred to its parent company in the US for processing on centralised IT infrastructure and servers. Uber has appealed this finding of an infringement of art 44 GDPR.

The European Commission plans to open a public consultation on new Standard Contractual Clauses ('SCCs') in the fourth quarter of 2024.[11] These new SCCs will

---

[8] *Schrems v Meta Platforms Ireland Limited* (Case C-446/21), see **[2.48]** below.
[9] In July, the European Commission informed Meta of its preliminary findings that its 'pay or consent' advertising model failed to comply with the EU Digital Markets Act ('DMA'), which seeks to regulate the behaviour of certain large online platforms.
[10] 'AP fines Uber 290 million euros for transferring data from drivers to the US', Dutch Data Protection Authority, available on the Dutch DPA website: *https://autoriteitpersoonsgegevens.nl*.
[11] 'Standard contractual clauses for the transfer of data to third country controllers and processors subject to the GDPR', available at: *https://ec.europa.eu/info/law/better-regulation/have-your-say/initiatives/14404-Standard-contractual-clauses-for-the-transfer-of-data-to-third-country-controllers-and-processors-subject-to-the-GDPR_en*.

address the situation, which applied in the Uber case, where the data importer is based outside of the European Economic Area ('EEA') but is directly subject to the GDPR due to art 3(2) GDPR, ie, its processing activities are related to the offering of goods and services to data subjects in the EU, or the monitoring of data subjects' behaviour within the EU.

CNIL: Unjustified collection of job applicant data[12]

[2.04] On 22 December 2023, the French Data Protection Authority, *Commission Nationale de l'Informatique et des Libertés* (the 'CNIL'), issued a fine under its new simplified procedure against an unnamed company for unjustified collection of job applicant data. The fine was one of five issued by the CNIL with an aggregate total of EUR €44,000. The CNIL's simplified procedure is available for matters which it determines to be of limited complexity or seriousness, with most of the details of the sanctions remaining non-public. In this case, the company collected the locations, countries of birth and social security numbers of applicants for jobs to act as extras or hosts for televised events. As the collection of this data did not have a direct and necessary link with the job offered and with the assessment of professional skills, the CNIL found it to be a breach of art 5(1)(b) GDPR under the principle of data collection for specified, explicit and legitimate purposes. The CNIL clarified that the company's decision to modify its application form in the period prior to the issuance of the fine by the CNIL did not absolve the company from its responsibility for past actions.

CNIL: Excessive employee data collection and surveillance[13]

[2.05] The recent decision of the French supervisory authority, CNIL, to fine Amazon for 'an excessively intrusive system for monitoring the activity and performance of employees' provides a timely reminder of the need for careful analysis if monitoring employees in the workplace, whether conducted remotely or on an in-office basis.

In the case of Amazon's monitoring practices, scanners were put in place for its warehouse workers to document how long it took them to carry out certain tasks, and to quality check articles within a certain minimum time frame. This information was stored and used to calculate indicators providing information on the quality, productivity, and periods of inactivity of each employee, and was further utilised as part of employee coaching and performance reviews.

The CNIL found that Amazon's practices failed to comply with the data minimisation principle under art 5(1)(c) GDPR, and a failure to ensure lawful processing under art 6 GDPR.

---

[12] CNIL: Unjustified collection of job applicant data of (simplified decision procedure of 22 December 2023).
[13] CNIL: Excessive employee data collection and surveillance (Decision SAN-2023-021 of 27 December 2023).

Regarding the type of personal data processed, three indicators processed by the company were found to be non-compliant:

— the 'Stow Machine Gun' indicator, which provided an error message when an employee scanned an item 'too quickly' (ie, in less than 1.25 seconds after scanning a previous item);

— the 'idle time' indicator, which signaled periods of scanner downtime of 10 minutes or more;

— the 'latency under 10 minutes' indicator, which signaled periods of scanner interruption between 1 and 10 minutes.

The CNIL found that the processing of all three indicators could not be based on legitimate interest, as it led to excessive monitoring of the employee, when balanced against the commercial objectives pursued by Amazon.

The CNIL noted that Amazon already had access to numerous indicators in real time, both individual and aggregated, to achieve its objective of quality and safety in its warehouses. It also noted that, as implemented, the processing required employees to justify every break or interruption to their work. Accordingly, the processing was found to be excessively intrusive. The decision also found that the company had failed to properly inform employees that their personal data would be processed by the scanners in advance of their data being collected, leading to a breach of its obligation to provide information and transparency under arts 12 and 13 GDPR, and a failure to comply with the obligation to ensure the security of personal data captured under art 32 GDPR. On 27 December 2023, Amazon France Logistique was fined EUR €32 million by the CNIL. The CNIL's decision is currently under appeal so employers should watch out for further guidance.

The DPC has noted in previous guidance on data protection in the workplace that employers have a legitimate interest in protecting their business, reputation, resources and equipment. The DPC cautioned within this guidance that any limitation of employees' right to privacy in the workplace, particularly with regard to monitoring software, should be proportionate to the likely impact on the employer's legitimate interests. The DPC further notes that in the ordinary course of business, employers should consider implementing other less intrusive means of monitoring employees.

AEPD: Unauthorised sharing of employee data[14]

[2.06] On 24 January 2024, the Spanish Data Protection Authority, *Agencia Espanola Proteccion Datos* (the 'AEPD') imposed a fine of EUR €2,000 on Vukmal Trade SL, reduced to EUR €1,200 for early payment and acknowledgement of the violation, for requiring employees to use their personal mobile phones for work and sharing employees' personal numbers without consent. This use involved requiring employees to install an application on their personal mobile phones. In filing a complaint with the

---

14 AEPD: Unauthorised sharing of employee data (No: EXP202310230 24 January 2024).

AEPD, an ex-employee outlined that after leaving the company, their phone number remained part of two work WhatsApp groups. As a result, they continued to receive messages from former colleagues, with their name and phone number still visible. The AEPD ruled that the processing activities by Vukmal Trade SL violated art 6(1) GDPR, and accordingly imposed an administrative fine.

AEPD: Inadequate notification of biometric data to employees[15]

[2.07] On 12 February 2024, the AEPD imposed a fine of EUR €365,000 on CTC Externalización for breach of GDPR, as a result of failing to provide any information to employees regarding the collection, processing or storage of fingerprint data which was to be taken for the implementation of a fingerprint sign-in system. The company did not communicate to employees that fingerprint data would be stored in the employee portal. The AEPD found that this failure to inform employees about such storage was a breach of art 13 GDPR. Additionally, as the company had failed to verify the security measures implemented to access the data or to prove how the erasure of the data after capture was guaranteed, the company also violated art 35 GDPR. Further, the failure of the company to consider the processing of such biometric data as processing special categories of data and as such failing to carry out a data protection impact assessment ('DPIA') was a breach of art 35 GDPR. In addition to the fine imposed, the AEPD required the company to limit the processing of the data until it had carried out and passed a valid DPIA. They also requested the company to prove within six months that they had informed all employees of the processing, established the necessary security measures and were in compliance with GDPR.

AEPD: Unlawful distribution of employee video surveillance[16]

[2.08] On 20 June 2024, the AEPD imposed an administrative fine of EUR €42,000 on CUI ZSQ FOOD S.L for unlawful distribution of video surveillance footage of employees in the workplace. The AEPD investigated a complaint that the company used video surveillance to observe an employee's absence from his post for a bathroom break for 18 minutes and then sent the footage into a WECHAT group chat, asking other employees if the employee in question should have the money subtracted from his pay. The company argued that no employee was identified in the message and that all employees were given a privacy policy, which mentioned the use of video surveillance for monitoring the work of employees. The AEPD found that the distribution of the video surveillance footage in the WECHAT group chat lacked legal basis and violated the confidentiality of the complainant's personal data, along with other employees visible in the video. This constituted a violation of art 5(f) GDPR. The AEPD imposed a fine of EUR €70,000, which was subsequently reduced by 40% by the company acknowledging its responsibility for the violations and paying the reduced sanction of EUR €42,000.

---

[15] AEPD: Inadequate notification of biometric data to employees (No: EXP202202960 12 February 2024).
[16] AEPD: Unlawful distribution of employee video surveillance (No: EXP202300692 20 June 2024).

Persónuvernd: Monitoring of an employee's work returns

[2.09] On 20 March 2024, *Persónuvernd*, the Icelandic Data Protection Authority, imposed an administrative fine of ISK 1,500,000 on *Stärnan ehf.*, the operator of Subway in Iceland, due to its unlawful electronic monitoring of employees. Documents submitted with the complaint showed that the store's manager had taken a number of screenshots of the complainant from the restaurant's surveillance cameras to record what the complainant was doing at a given time. *Persónuvernd* concluded that this monitoring had not been in accordance with the stated purpose in the context of employment. This, and the fact that the company failed to inform its employees that monitoring was taking place, in addition to failing to keeping a register of processing activities, resulted in the administrative fine imposed.

Garante: Use of facial recognition to monitor employee attendance[17]

[2.10] On 6 June 2024, the Italian Data Protection Authority, *Garante*, imposed an administrative fine of EUR €120,000 on car dealership *Capello Giovanni & Figli srl* for the use of facial recognition systems to monitor employee attendance. A complaint was made by an employee who challenged the processing of personal data through a biometric system installed at the workplace. *Garante* found that this processing of biometric data was without proper legal basis. It explained that this is special category data, and due to the imbalanced nature of the employment relationship, the consent given by employees cannot be considered a valid basis for such processing. *Garante* found there to be a violation of art 9(1) GDPR by the company. Further, *Garante* found that this processing violated the principle of data minimisation under art 5(1)(c) GDPR as it found that the controller was unable to prove that the processing was necessary and proportionate, particularly as there are less intrusive ways of registering employee attendance. *Garante* additionally found that the company violated art 5(1)(e) GDPR for storage of data for excessive periods, art 13 GDPR for an incomplete privacy policy, and art 5(1)(a) GDPR for violating principles of transparency and fairness. On these grounds, *Garante* issued a fine of EUR €120,000.

DATA PROTECTION COMMISSION—GUIDANCE

Guidance on the Use of CCTV—for Data Controllers[18]

[2.11] In November 2023, the DPC updated its Guidance Note: Guidance on the Use of CCTV—for Data Controllers. This Guidance aims to help owners and occupiers of premises (including employers) to understand their data protection obligations when using CCTV on their premises. Where employers operate CCTV, they are acting as data controllers with respect to personal data collected by the CCTV, to include the personal data of their employees and of other individuals on the premises.

---

[17] Garante: Use of facial recognition to monitor employee attendance (Order of 6 June 2024 [10029500]).
[18] *Guidance on the Use of CCTV—For Data Controllers* (November 2023).

The detailed Guidance is helpful for employers in exploring how they can operate CCTV in compliance with data protection law.

(i) Considerations prior to installing a CCTV system

[2.12] Before installing a CCTV system, the Guidance advises that best practice is to create a CCTV Data Protection Policy ('Policy'). The Policy should set out: the purpose and legality of installing CCTV (including why it is necessary and proportionate to do so); the security measures that will be put in place to safeguard the personal data collected through the use of CCTV; the retention periods for the CCTV recordings; and how to make the whole system transparent for data subjects. Where an employer develops such a policy, employees should be made aware of it so that they are fully informed of the fact that, and way in which, the CCTV system processes their personal data.

Employers should clearly identify the purpose of using CCTV. They must have a lawful basis for processing personal data through CCTV, in addition to identifying the purpose for the processing. When assessing necessity, employers should consider whether other actions that do not involve the processing of personal data could effectively achieve the same purpose. To assess proportionality employers must consider whether the manner in which the CCTV system will operate is reasonable, by examining factors such as the size of areas covered by CCTV, the number of CCTV cameras employed, the number of employees affected, the nature of the workplace areas involved, and the extent to which the CCTV will monitor employees while working. How the CCTV footage will be stored must be considered by the employer, and appropriate technical and organisation security measures and robust policies and procedures should be put in place to assure its security. The CCTV footage should not be kept for longer than needed to achieve the purpose for which it was processed. Data subjects must be adequately informed that their personal data is processed through the use of CCTV.

(ii) Accountability for the use of CCTV

[2.13] Records of data processing activities that employers are legally required to maintain under art 30 GDPR must include the use of CCTV and set out any risks involved. The assessment that is done as part of the development of the CCTV Data Protection Policy should be recorded in such a way that clearly shows how the CCTV system was determined to be necessary and proportionate and how this decision was reached.

(iii) Data protection by design and default

[2.14] Data protection by default will impact the manner in which the CCTV system is designed and set up. Employers should ensure only personal data that is necessary to be collected for the identified purpose(s) is collected by the CCTV. This may involve consideration of, for example, the area where cameras are placed, how they are focused, whether they can pan, tilt or zoom, and whether there are privacy-masking features.

(iv) Third-party data processors

[2.15] Where the CCTV systems in place at a workplace are managed or maintained by a third-party security company, employers should have a contract with the security company that specifies what the security company can do with the data, what level of security is required in relation to the system and how long the security company can retain the data.

(v) Disclosing CCTV footage to third parties

[2.16] The Guidance acknowledges that there may be times where data controllers are asked to disclose CCTV footage to third parties for a purpose that is different to the purpose for which the footage was obtained and discusses how to assess compliance in different circumstances.

(vi) Access to CCTV by data subjects

[2.17] The Guidance provides that generally, a data controller must respond to a request from a data subject to access personal data obtained through CCTV within one month and discusses clarifications that might be sought and other factors to consider in fulfilling the request.

(vii) Covert surveillance

[2.18] Generally, using CCTV to obtain data without a person's knowledge is unlawful. Only in exceptional cases is this permitted, ie, where the data is required for the purpose of preventing, detecting or investigating offences, or apprehending or prosecuting criminal offenders. There must be a written policy in place dealing with this kind of processing. A DPIA should also be carried out before covert CCTV systems are implemented.

(viii) Facial recognition and biometric data

[2.19] Employers should be aware that where CCTV systems use facial recognition software, special category personal data is being processed as this software is considered biometric processing. Employers must comply with the obligations relating to special category data in GDPR in relation to this processing. This processing is considered as separate processing to the general use of the CCTV system.

(ix) Use of CCTV in areas of an increased expectation of privacy

[2.20] The Guidance expands upon what is expected of data controllers in relation to the use of CCTV in areas where data subjects have an increased expectation of privacy. Using CCTV in such areas, for example in bathrooms, will likely always be in breach of GDPR, unless the controller can show that the use of the CCTV meets the principles of data protection and pursues a legitimate aim, is necessary and proportionate and the risks associated with the processing have been identified, assessed and mitigated to an acceptable level.

(x) Mitigating risks and engaging with the DPC

[2.21] The Guidance strongly recommends that employers conduct a DPIA and a legitimate interests assessment when planning to install CCTV. The Guidance also states that a data controller should be able to produce retention, risk management and CCTV policies, processing agreements with any third-party CCTV providers, procedures for managing data subject rights requests, and documented assessments of the data processing that have had the full involvement of the DPO or other expert. If the DPC is inspecting the premises or investigating a complaint, they are likely to seek access to these documents.

DATA PROTECTION COMMISSION—2023 ANNUAL REPORT

[2.22] On 29 May 2024, the Data Protection Commission released its 2023 Annual Report revealing that the year was another busy one for the authority. In addition to receiving 11,200 new cases, the DPC concluded 11,147 cases in 2023, of which 3,218 were resolved through the formal complaint-handling process.

Moreover, following several cross-border and national inquiries, the Commission issued a number of record fines and corrective orders and by the end of 2023, it had imposed fines totaling €1.55 billion. Of note was the conclusion of the DPC's investigation into Meta Platforms Ireland Limited (Facebook) in relation to transatlantic data flows.[19] The DPC adopted its final decision on 12 May 2023, imposing an administrative fine on the organisation in the amount of €1.2 billion, among other measures. In September 2023, the DPC issued its final decision to Tiktok Technology Limited following an own-volition inquiry into the processing of children's personal data by the organisation, resulting in a fine of €345 million.[20]

Once again, the Annual Report contains many case studies detailing how complaints made to the authority were resolved and providing valuable guidance for employers. In 2023, the most frequent GDPR topics for queries and complaints continued to be: access requests; fair-processing; disclosure; direct marketing; and right to erasure.

In 2023, the DPC received 6,991 valid GDPR data breach notifications, an increase on the GDPR data breach numbers reported in 2022. In keeping with the trends over previous years, public sector bodies and banks accounted for the 'top ten' organisations with the highest number of breach notifications recorded against them, with insurance and telecom companies featuring prominently in the top 20. Notably, the DPC has continued to see situations where correspondence was issued to incorrect recipients because

---

[19] See *Arthur Cox Employment Law Yearbook 2023* at [2.45].
[20] See *Arthur Cox Employment Law Yearbook 2023* at [2.20].

of poor operational practices and human error, eg, inserting the wrong document into an envelope addressed to an unrelated third party.

In November 2023, the DPC's decisions to impose administrative fines on five different organisations were confirmed in the Dublin Circuit Court. These comprised:

- VIEC t/a Virtue Eldercare; a fine of €100,000;
- A&G Couriers t/a Fastway Couriers; a fine of €15,000;
- Kildare County Council; a fine of €50,000;
- Centric Health; a fine of €460,000;
- Bank of Ireland; a fine of €750,000.

As of 31 December 2023, the DPC was conducting 89 statutory inquiries, including 51 cross-border inquiries. Four DPC draft decisions in large-scale inquiries had been referred to the EU co-decision making process (art 60 GDPR).

The DPC continues to work towards the 2022–2027 regulatory strategy to prioritise the protection of children and vulnerable adults. As part of this strategic goal, throughout 2023, the DPC engaged with several financial institutions and representative bodies regarding concerns that GDPR and data protection law are being used as a barrier to access services. It will continue to prioritise this work throughout 2024. The DPC also participated in the 2023 Coordinated Enforcement Framework ('CEF') on the designation and position of Data Protection Officers.[21] In 2024, the DPC is participating in the CEF action on the implementation of the right of access by controllers. The DPC's staff numbers and budgetary allocation grew in 2023, with 44 new members brought on board and a budgetary allocation of €26.364 million.

DATA PROTECTION COMMISSION—INVESTIGATIONS, DECISIONS AND FINES

[2.23]   Some notable inquiries and decisions made by the DPC in the past 12 months, including the cases noted below.

Data Protection Commission: inquiry into Ryanair's customer verification process[22]

[2.24]   On 4 October 2024, the DPC announced that it had launched an inquiry into Ryanair's customer verification processes under s 110 of the Data Protection Act 2018. These processes require additional verification of identity from customers who purchase flights on third-party websites that have not been authorised by Ryanair rather than buying directly from Ryanair itself. Additional verification measures include facial recognition technology based on biometric data. The cross-border inquiry will

---

21 See [2.32] below.
22 'Data Protection Commission launches inquiry into Ryanair's Customer Verification Process', Data Protection Commission, 4 October 2024, available at: https://www.dataprotection.ie/en/news-media/press-releases/data-protection-commission-launches-inquiry-ryanairs-customer-verification-process.

investigate whether Ryanair has infringed GDPR, in particular, the principles relating to the lawfulness and transparency of data processing.

Meta Platforms Ireland Limited ('Meta')—DPC enforcement notice, 10 November 2023[23]—behavioural advertising—consent or pay model

[2.25] This DPC enforcement notice addressed to Meta and dated 10 November 2023 imposed (and required Meta to implement and give effect to) a ban on processing by Meta of personal data collected on Meta's products for behavioural advertising purposes on the basis of arts 6(1)(b) and 6(1)(f) GDPR. The ban was effective one week after the notification of the decision to Meta.

Events were first set in motion on 25 May 2018, the day GDPR entered into force, when complaints were made about the Facebook and Instagram services. In anticipation of GDPR, Meta changed its terms of service for Facebook and Instagram. It would no longer be relying on consent as the legal basis for processing users' data for the delivery of Facebook and Instagram's services, which included behavioural advertising. Instead, Meta informed users that it would now rely on contractual necessity under art 6(1)(b) GDPR. The complainants challenged the reliance on contractual necessity for behavioural advertising on Facebook and Instagram.

In its preliminary decision on this complaint, the DPC found that GDPR, the jurisprudence and EDPB guidance did not preclude Meta from relying on art 6(1)(b) GDPR as a legal basis to carry out the personal data processing activities involved in the provision of its service to users, including behavioural advertising, insofar as that process forms a core part of the service, which it found that it did for Facebook and Instagram. The DPC found that Meta breached the principle of transparency in failing to clearly outline to users what processing was being conducted on their personal data and the legal basis on which it was relying, thereby infringing arts 5(1)(a), 12 and 13(1)(c) GDPR.

A consensus could not be reached on this preliminary decision between the concerned supervisory authorities ('CSAs'), and the points in dispute were referred to the EDPB under the art 65 GDPR dispute resolution procedure.

The EDPB upheld the DPC's finding on transparency and inserted an additional breach of the fairness principle. However, the EDPB found that use of user data for behavioural advertising purposes by Meta in the context of Facebook and Instagram was objectively not necessary for the performance of Meta's contract with users, was not an essential or core element of these services and therefore Meta was not entitled to rely on contractual necessity for behavioural advertising.[24] The DPC's final decision included these findings, increased fines of €210 million (in the case of Facebook) and

---

[23] Enforcement notice in the matter of Meta Platforms Ireland Limited made pursuant to Sections 133(9) and 133(10) of the Data Protection Act, 2018 and Articles 60 and 66 of the General Data Protection Regulation, available on the website of the EDPB at: *https://www.edpb.europa.eu/our-work-tools/consistency-findings/register-decisions/2023/enforcement-notice-matter-meta_en*.

[24] EDPB Instagram decision: 'Binding Decision 4/2022 on the dispute submitted by the Irish SA on Meta Platforms Ireland Limited and its Instagram service (Art. 65 GDPR)', (adopted on 5 December 2022), available at: *https://www.edpb.europa.eu/our-work-tools/our-documents/binding-decision-board-art-65/binding-decision-42022-dispute-submitted_en*.

€180 million (in the case of Instagram), and imposed a three-month deadline to bring processing operations into compliance with the GDPR.

In response to this decision, on 5 April 2023, Meta changed the lawful basis for use of on-Facebook/Instagram data for behavioural advertising purposes from contractual necessity to legitimate interest under art 6(1)(f) GDPR. Consent continued to be the lawful basis for the collection of off-Facebook/Instagram data for behavioural advertising.

However, on 14 July 2023, the Norway SA issued a temporary ban under the art 66 GDPR urgency procedure (bypassing the one-stop-shop mechanism) and issued a three-month ban on Meta using Norwegian user data to personalise ads on Facebook and Instagram, grounded on the basis of contractual necessity and legitimate interests. This resulted in an urgent decision adopted on 27 October 2023 by the EDPB confirming and extending the ban across the EEA, on the basis that Meta could not rely on contractual necessity or legitimate interests for the processing of on-Facebook/Instagram data for behavioural advertising.[25] In light of the risk of harm to data subjects in the absence of final measures, the EDPB ordered the DPC to adopt the ban on the processing of personal data collected on Meta's platforms for the purpose of behavioural advertising on the basis of contractual necessity or legitimate interest.

In response, from November 2023, Meta offered Instagram and Facebook users the option to either: (a) pay for a service that does not show advertising and does not use on-Facebook/Instagram data for behavioural advertising; or (b) consent to the use of on-Facebook/Instagram data for behavioural advertising. The EDPB subsequently issued an Opinion in relation to 'consent or pay' models which refers to the *Bundeskartellamt* judgment[26] in examining the question of whether consent given by the user of an online social network may be regarded as satisfying the conditions of validity laid down in art 4(11) GDPR. The main criteria to be taken into account in assessing whether consent is 'freely given' and valid relates to: the possibility of detriment being suffered by not consenting; the imbalance of power between controller and user; the request to consent to processing activities not objectively necessary for the contract to gain access (conditionality); and the ability to consent to different processing operations (granularity). Any fee imposed in a 'consent or pay' model cannot be such as to effectively inhibit users from making a free choice, with the EDPB finding that offering a paid alternative only to a service which includes processing for behavioural advertising purposes should not be the default way forward for large online platforms. The recommendation of introducing an 'equivalent alternative' option for users will, it says, operate toward ensuring consent is freely given and valid.

EDPB Facebook decision: 'Binding Decision 3/2022 on the dispute submitted by the Irish SA on Meta Platforms Ireland Limited and its Facebook service (Art. 65 GDPR)', (adopted on 5 December 2022), available at: *https://www.edpb.europa.eu/our-work-tools/our-documents/binding-decision-board-art-65/binding-decision-32022-dispute-submitted_en*.

[25] EDPB: 'Urgent Binding Decision 01/2023 requested by the Norwegian SA for the ordering of final measures regarding Meta Platforms Ireland Ltd (Art. 66(2) GDPR)', (adopted on 27 October 2023), available at: *https://www.edpb.europa.eu/our-work-tools/our-documents/urgent-binding-decision-board-art-66/urgent-binding-decision-012023_en*.

[26] *Meta Platforms Inc v Bundeskartellamt* (Case C-252/21), EU:C:2023:537, judgment of the Court of Justice of the European Union, 4 July 2023.

Microsoft Ireland Operations Limited ('Microsoft')—DPC decision 15 November 2023[27]—erasure request—public interest—failure to inform complainant of ability to see judicial review of decision to refuse

[2.26] The complainant submitted a 'right to be forgotten form' to Microsoft on 22 March 2021 requesting the removal of four URLs from the Bing search engine. Microsoft responded to the complainant on 27 March 2021, informing him that two URLs would be removed, but that no action would be taken in relation to the two other URLs on the basis that the public interest 'outweighs [his] interest in privacy'. On 9 October 2021, the complainant submitted another right to be forgotten form to Microsoft requesting the removal of three URLs. Microsoft responded to the complainant on 17 October 2021, informing him that, as it had determined that there was a significant public interest in accessing the information as it pertained to the complainant's work life, it had decided to take no action to remove the three URLs.

On 12 November 2021, the DPC commenced the process of complaint-handling, as lead supervisory authority. After back-and-forth correspondence, Microsoft confirmed on 14 March 2022 that the complainant's personal data had been removed. The DPC informed the complainant of this. The complainant rejected an amicable resolution, citing reasons such as the length of time it took for Microsoft to complete his erasure request and his concerns over the possible disclosure of his personal data to third parties.

The DPC commenced its inquiry into the matter, the scope of which involved an examination into whether Microsoft's handling of the complainant's erasure requests infringed arts 12 and 17 GDPR. The DPC found that Microsoft breached art 12(4) GDPR in relation to the March 2021 and October 2021 requests, as it failed on both occasions to inform the complainant of the ability to seek a judicial remedy when Microsoft informed him of its decision to take no action. The DPC also found that Microsoft infringed art 17 GDPR as it failed to erase the personal data pertaining to the October 2021 erasure request without undue delay. The DPC issued a reprimand to Microsoft under art 58(2)(b) GDPR requiring it to bring its procedures into compliance with the GDPR to prevent similar infringements occurring in the future. However, no administrative fine was imposed.

Airbnb Ireland UC ('Airbnb')—DPC decision 31 January 2024[28]—request for a copy of identification (ID) to verify identity and erase data—date minimisation—alternative means of verification

[2.27] As part of its registration process, Airbnb required the complainant to verify his identity through providing a copy of his ID. Upon receiving this request, the complainant decided to withdraw from the registration process. He then accessed an internal area of the platform through providing his email address and creating a

---

[27] Inquiry into Microsoft Ireland Operations Limited—November 2023, available at: *https://www.dataprotection.ie/sites/default/files/uploads/2023-12/13.12.2023%20Microsoft%20Ireland%20Operations%20Limited%20Decision.pdf*.

[28] Inquiry into Airbnb Ireland UC—January 2024, available at: *https://www.dataprotection.ie/sites/default/files/uploads/2024-04/Inquiry-into-Airbnb-Ireland-UC-31-January-2024-EN_0.pdf*.

password in order to ask Airbnb to delete all of his personal data to prevent it being transferred to third parties. The complainant stated that he was informed by the platform that it would not be possible to erase his data without a copy of his ID. The complainant alleged that this practice does not have any legal basis and that it infringed his right to erasure of personal data.

The DPC considered whether:

1. Airbnb had a lawful basis for requesting a copy of the complainant's ID both at the time of registration and at the point when he requested the erasure of his data;
2. Airbnb complied with the principle of data minimisation in requesting the complainant's ID; and
3. Airbnb complied with the principle of transparency and provision of information at the time when the complainant's personal data was provided by him.

The DPC noted that no evidence was provided by the complainant in relation to his allegation that Airbnb required a copy of his ID during the registration process and consequently found no infringement on this point. However, evidence was produced showing that Airbnb had asked for the complainant's ID in order to process his request for erasure of his personal data. Airbnb argued that this request was made on the basis of legitimate interest in protecting users' accounts from being deleted in illegitimate or otherwise inappropriate circumstances. The DPC noted that Airbnb was capable of verifying the complainant's identity through other means, namely through his account login, and accordingly found that Airbnb did not have a valid legal basis under art 6(1)(f) GDPR. Similarly, as the DPC was of the view that Airbnb had alternative means of verifying the complainant's identity, it concluded that Airbnb had not complied with the principle of data minimisation when requesting a copy of his ID and had thus infringed art 5(1)(c) GDPR. The DPC found no infringement on the third point as Airbnb's terms of service explained the platform's reasons for collecting identity verification information, thus the complainant was on notice that he may be required to verify his identity.

The DPC noted that Airbnb discontinued the practice of requesting a copy of ID in order to verify identity in order to process erasure requests and that on foot of a previous DPC decision, Airbnb had already revised its policies to prevent infringements of art 5(1)(c) GDPR. The DPC concluded that an administrative fine would not be necessary, proportionate nor dissuasive and instead issued a reprimand to Airbnb under art 58(2)(b) GDPR.

Apple Distribution International Limited ('Apple')—DPC decision 7 March 2024[29]—erasure request—retention of personal data in hashed form—legitimate interests—financial reporting

[2.28] On foot of receiving an erasure request from the data subject, Apple confirmed that it would delete the complainant's Apple ID and all data associated with it. Two years

---

[29] Inquiry into Apple Distribution International Limited, 7 March 2024, available at: *https://www.dataprotection.ie/en/dpc-guidance/law/decisions-made-under-data-protection-act-2018/Apple-Distribution-International-Limited-March-2024*.

later, the complainant attempted to create a new Apple account and received a notification that the email address he had inputted could not be used because it was already associated with another Apple account. The complainant then submitted a complaint to the DPC that Apple had breached his right to erasure and right to be forgotten under art 17 GDPR. Apple responded that it had retained a hashed value of the complainant's email address and that it had carried out such processing for the purposes of legitimate interests including to:

(a) demonstrate compliance with the complainant's erasure request made under art 17(1) GDPR;
(b) demonstrate compliance with security of processing obligations under art 32 GDPR; and
(c) protect its users against fraud.

Apple also informed the DPC that it retains data associated with purchases for 10 years in order to comply with the retention periods specified by various applicable laws governing financial reporting, and that these retention practices are subject to periodic reviews.

The DPC assessed Apple's arguments as outlined above and came to the conclusion that Apple validly relied on the legitimate interests basis, that it had given due consideration to the principle of data minimisation because the retention practices are reviewed, and that it had complied with the requirements under arts 12 and 17 GDPR in relation to the processing of the erasure request. However, the DPC found that Apple had infringed its transparency obligations under art 13 GDPR by failing to inform the complainant that a hashed value of his email would be retained and the reasons for this processing. Apple was issued with a reprimand requiring it to update its terms to address this lack of transparency.

Mediahuis Ireland Group Limited—DPC decision 7 June 2024[30]—Data Protection Act 2018, s 43(1)—balancing fundamental rights—freedom of expression and information

[2.29] The data subject submitted a complaint regarding news reports published in Mediahuis' newspapers in which they claimed their medical data was processed. Mediahuis Ireland Group Limited ('MIG') claimed that the processing was exempt under s 43(1) of the Data Protection Act 2018 as it was for the purpose of exercising the right to freedom of expression and information, including processing for journalistic purposes.

The DPC examined its jurisdiction to conduct an inquiry into the news outlet in light of the exemption provided for in s 43(1) and the balance required to be struck between the right to freedom of expression and information and the right to protection of personal data.

---

[30] Inquiry concerning Mediahuis Ireland Group Limited (MIG), 7 June 2024, available at: *https://www.dataprotection.ie/en/dpc-guidance/law/decisions-made-under-data-protection-act-2018/inquiry-concerning-mediahuis-ireland-group-limited-june-2024.*

First, the DPC found that it has the power to conduct inquiries relating to data subjects' data protection rights which also engage data controllers' rights to freedom of expression and information. The explicit acknowledgment in art 85 GDPR of the potential incompatibility between data protection rights and the right to freedom of expression highlights the importance of the DPC's involvement in assessing the very applicability of the exemption under s 43(1) of the Data Protection Act 2018.

Second, the DPC determined whether or not the s 43(1) exemption applied to MIG's publication. The DPC deployed a two-part test in this regard:

1. The processing in question must be for the purpose of exercising the right to freedom of expression and information, including processing for journalistic purposes or for the purposes of academic, artistic or literary expression.
2. Compliance with the relevant provisions of GDPR must be incompatible with those purposes, having regard to the importance of the freedom of expression right in a democratic society.

The DPC noted that the balance between data protection rights and the right to freedom of expression and information will favour the latter where information is published in the public interest so long as the information contributes to a debate of general interest. The DPC further stated that the balance may tip in favour of the data subject's rights (which is likely to include their right to privacy) where the person is not a public figure and the information relates to their private life. The DPC acknowledged that while medical information does require a very high level of protection, it did not result in an automatic determination of the balance weighing in favour of the data subject's rights. The DPC concluded that the exemption under s 43(1) of the Data Protection Act 2018 applies. In this case, there was a connection between the personal data published and the debate in the general interest and accordingly dismissed the complaint.

Meta Platforms Ireland Limited ('Meta')—DPC decision 27 September 2024[31]—personal data breach—passwords visible to Facebook employees

[2.30] As part of its routine security checks, Meta noticed that it had inadvertently stored some Facebook users' passwords in a readable format (ie in plain text without encryption). In January 2019, Meta issued an announcement online upon discovering the issue, in which it stated that the passwords were never visible to anyone outside of Facebook, nor did it find any evidence that the passwords had been improperly used. Meta also announced that it would be informing the affected users. Meta notified the DPC in March 2019 and the DPC commenced an inquiry in April 2019 to investigate whether Meta had infringed the GDPR, and specifically whether Meta had in place security measures appropriate to the level of risk regarding the processing of passwords, and whether it complied with the requirements to document and notify the DPC of personal data breaches.

In its decision, issued on 27 September 2024, the DPC found: that Meta had infringed art 33(1) GDPR for failing to notify the DPC of the personal data breach; that Meta had

---

[31] Inquiry into Meta Platforms Ireland Limited, 27 September 2024, available at: *https://www.dataprotection.ie/en/news-media/press-releases/DPC-announces-91-million-fine-of-Meta*.

infringed art 33(5) GDPR for failing to document the personal data breach; and that Meta had infringed arts 5(1) and 32(1) GDPR for its failure to implement technical and organisational measures to ensure the security of the passwords appropriate to the level of risk associated with storing such passwords. The DPC issued a reprimand under art 58(2)(b) GDPR and fined Meta €91 million under arts 58(2)(i) and 83 GDPR.

EUROPEAN DATA PROTECTION BOARD—GUIDANCE

Guidelines 1/2024 on Processing of Personal Data Based on Article 6(1)(f) GDPR[32]

[2.31] On 8 October 2024, the EDPB published Guidelines for public consultation analysing the criteria that controllers must meet, set down in art 6(1)(f) GDPR, to lawfully engage in the processing of personal data that is 'necessary for the purposes of the legitimate interests pursued by the controller or by a third party'. The Guidelines build upon and update the previous 2014 opinion from the Article 29 Data Protection Working Party on the notion of legitimate interests of the data controller and take into account the decision of the ECJ in *Koninklijke Nederlandse Lawn Tennisbond*.[33] The Guidelines were open for public consultation until 20 November 2024.

The Guidelines will be useful to employers in interpreting art 6(1)(f) GDPR and applying that article in the context of their data processing activities and strategy. They also advise as to how an art 6(1)(f) GDPR assessment should be carried out in practice, including in a number of specific contexts where this legal basis may be considered, eg, fraud prevention, direct marketing, information security, etc. For processing to be based on art 6(1)(f) GDPR, three cumulative conditions must be fulfilled:

— First, the pursuit of a legitimate interest by the controller or by a third party. In this regard, not all interests of the controller or a third party may be deemed legitimate; only those interests that are lawful, precisely articulated and present, may be validly invoked to rely on art 6(1)(f) GDPR as a legal basis.

---

[32] Guidelines 1/2024 on Processing of Personal Data Based on Article 6(1)(f) GDPR: Version 1.0, 8 October 2024.

[33] In its judgment delivered on 4 October 2024, in *Koninklijke Nederlandse Lawn Tennisbond v Autoriteit Persoonsgegevens* (Case C-621/22), the Court was asked, in the context of art 6(1)(f) GDPR, to interpret the term 'legitimate interest', and in particular, to consider should a purely commercial interest, such as the provision of personal data in return for payment without the consent of the data subject concerned, be regarded as a legitimate interest under certain circumstances? It held that the disclosure, for consideration, of personal data of the members of a sports federation, in order to satisfy a commercial interest of the controller, may be regarded as necessary for the purposes of the legitimate interests pursued by that controller, within the meaning of art 6(1)(f), only on condition that that processing is strictly necessary for the purposes of the legitimate interest in question and that, in the light of all the relevant circumstances, the interests or fundamental rights and freedoms of those members do not override that legitimate interest. While a legitimate interest under art 6(1)(f) GDPR must be lawful, it does not require that such an interest be determined by law, available at: *https://curia.europa.eu/ juris/document/document.jsf?mode=DOC&pageIndex=0&docid=290688&part=1&doclang=EN& text=&dir=&occ=first&cid=366396#:~:text=2%20The%20request%20has%20been,on%20the%20 KNLTB%20for%20infringement.*

— Second, the need to process personal data for the purposes of the legitimate interest(s) pursued. Controllers should ask if these interests can be achieved just as effectively by other means, less restrictive of the fundamental rights and freedoms of data subjects?
— Third, the interests or fundamental freedoms and rights of the concerned data subjects do not take precedence over the legitimate interest(s) of the controller or of a third party. The outcome of this balancing exercise must be that the legitimate interests being pursued are not overridden by the data subjects' interests, rights and freedoms.

EDPB's Report on Coordinated Enforcement Action, Designation and Position of DPOs —Important Considerations for Organisations and DPOs

[2.32] On 17 January 2024, the European Data Protection Board adopted the second report of the Coordinated Enforcement Framework ('CEF') on the designation and position of data protection officers ('DPOs') across the EEA (the 'Report').[34] The Report provides guidance for organisations and DPOs on how to enhance the role of the DPO within an organisation and identifies issues for potential regulatory focus and scrutiny. Some of the key points raised in the Report are set out below:

1. **Organisations should ensure that sufficient resources are allocated to the DPO:** The Report makes a number of recommendations as to adequately resourcing the DPO. For example, it recommends ensuring that the DPO is full time and adequately supported by a team and deputy DPO. The Report also recommends that the DPO is given control over their own budget as this would enable the DPO to manage their resources in an appropriately responsive and independent manner. Controllers and processors should be performing an appropriate, case-by-case analysis of what resources a DPO needs.
2. **Organisations should ensure that their DPO has sufficient expertise and training:** The Report recommends that controllers and processors provide DPOs with sufficient opportunities, time and resources to allow them to keep up to date with developments in data protection and privacy, including if relevant, new EU digital- and AI-related legislation. Controllers and processors should also ensure they are documenting their organisation's knowledge and training needs and progress (to ensure compliance with arts 24 and 5(2) GDPR).
3. **Organisations should ensure that DPOs are entrusted with all tasks required under GDPR:** The Report recommends organisations adequately set out the job description for DPOs, promote the (independent) role of the DPO internally, and work with the DPO to build up the roles in an appropriately comprehensive

---

[34] EDPB 2023: 'Coordinated Enforcement Action Designation and Position of Data Protection Officers', (adopted 16 January 2024).

and independent way. The Report also recommends that organisations actively review and improve the DPO's involvement in matters relating to the protection of personal data.

4. **Organisations should prevent conflict of interests and ensure the independence of the DPO:** The Report highlights that certain situations could potentially give rise to a conflict of interest (subject to an evaluation on a case-by-case basis, as is required by *X-Fab Dresden*[35]). Examples of these conflicts of interest include: the DPO holding position (or having duties) related to the (highest) management level of their organisations; or the DPO being required to act simultaneously in two roles (such as DPO for both the controller and the processor). Recommendations include formalising the duties and terms and conditions via an 'engagement letter' and enabling the DPO to collect evidence of interferences with their independence.

The Report notes many areas where the EDPB and supervisory authorities could provide further guidance, developed on the basis on the survey results. Controllers and processors should consult any new guidance developed by the EDPB and DPC to guide the role, resources and activities of their DPO.

The Coordinated Enforcement Action for 2024 focused on the right of access to personal data and the report on the outcome is due to be adopted at the beginning of 2025. For 2025, the EDPB has selected the implementation of the right to erasure ('right to be forgotten') by controllers (art 17 GDPR).

EDPB OPINIONS

[2.33] Article 70 GDPR empowers the EDPB to issue guidelines, recommendations, best practices and opinions in the manner described in art 70(1) GDPR. Article 64(2) GDPR provides that any supervisory authority may request that any matter of general application or producing effects in more than one Member State be examined by the EDPB with a view to obtaining an opinion. In 2024, the EDPB issued a number of art 64(2) GDPR opinions on matters of general application on request from supervisory authorities. We expect this to continue in 2025, and indeed, note from the EDPB's October plenary that the Board intends to issue an art 64(2) GDPR opinion on AI following a request by the DPC. However, an opinion is not a legally binding instrument.[36] The concern for stakeholders when supervisory authorities seek an opinion to contribute to a harmonised interpretation of GDPR, is the potential for an EDPB opinion to create new quasi-legal standards reflecting regulatory expectations across the EEA, without undergoing the usual checks and balances incorporated into mechanisms for the making of binding Union law.

---

[35] *X-Fab Dresden GmbH & Co. KG* (Case C-453/21), ECLI:EU:C:2023:79, judgment of 9 February 2023.
[36] See Treaty on the Functioning of the European Union, art 288—'Recommendations and opinions shall have no binding force', available at: *https://eur-lex.europa.eu/legal-content/EN/TXT/PDF/?uri=OJ:C:2012:326:FULL*.

EDPB Opinion 22/2024 on certain obligations following from the reliance on processor(s) and sub-processor(s)

[2.34] The EDPB issued this opinion in October 2024 on foot of a request from the Danish SA. The opinion addresses questions on the interpretation of certain duties of controllers relying on processors and sub-processors, arising in particular from art 28 GDPR, as well as the wording of controller-processor contracts. The questions address processing of personal data in the EEA as well processing following a transfer to a third country. The opinion will be of interest to employers who outsource payroll, or other HR functions, to third-party providers, as well as to those controllers who engage processors as part of their business processes.

(i) Identification of sub-processors

[2.35] Controllers must be able to identify all processors and sub-processors in the processing chain. Processors should provide all relevant information about how the processing activity will be carried out, including lists of all sub-processors and descriptions of their involvement. Processors should be under a proactive obligation to provide this information.

(ii) Verification of guarantees of sub-processors

[2.36] Article 28 GDPR requires controllers only to engage processors who can provide sufficient guarantees to implement appropriate technical and organisational measures to meet the requirements of GDPR. The EDPB states that this obligation falls on the controller with respect to all links in the processing chain, no matter how complex or long. The Opinion discusses the controller's obligation to verify that the (sub-) processors present sufficient guarantees to implement the measures that the controller requires to protect the personal data, and provides guidance as to the limits of that obligation and how to demonstrate compliance.

(iii) Processor to sub-processor international transfers

[2.37] The EDPB stresses that the decision to send personal data outside the EEA falls with the controller. Where a processor engages a sub-processor based outside the EEA, the controller is still ultimately responsible for, and liable for, the transfer and should engage in diligence to ensure the transfer is in compliance with GDPR before such transfer occurs. The controller should ensure this involves receiving the transfer impact assessment carried out by the sub-processor.

(iv) Can a processor process personal data to comply with third-country law?

[2.38] Article 28 GDPR provides that processors may not process personal data, other than on the instructions of the controller, unless required to do so by EU or Member State law. The Opinion accepts that GDPR does not prevent, in principle, the inclusion of wording in a contract that addresses third-country law requirements (given that processors are required to comply with their own local laws). However, the contract should include provisions ensuring that the third-country law respects the essence of GDPR, the Treaty on the Functioning of the European Union and art 8(1) of the Charter of Fundamental Rights of the European Union.

EDPB Opinion 04/2024 on the notion of main establishment of a controller in the Union under article 4(16)(a) GDPR[37]

[2.39] This opinion will be of interest to employers with a multi-national presence that are engaged in cross-border processing of personal data and wish to avail of the one-stop-shop mechanism. In this Opinion, the EDPB considers that art 4(16)(a) GDPR, as informed by Recital 36, together with the context in which art 4(16)(a) GDPR appears and the general objective of the one-stop-shop mechanism, support its position that to be considered as a main establishment under art 4(16)(a) GDPR, a controller's 'place of central administration' in the Union must be the place where it takes the decisions on the purposes and means of the processing of personal data and where it has power to have these decisions implemented.

As a first step in assessing main establishment, the Board advises that it is necessary to identify the processing at issue, as well as the (joint-) controller(s) for the processing. The burden of proof as to the location of the main establishment falls on controllers and the EDPB reiterates that controllers have a duty to co-operate with supervisory authorities in this regard. If the decisions on the purposes and means and the power to have such decisions implemented are exercised outside of the Union, the Opinion confirms that there should be no main establishment under art 4(16)(a) GDPR, and the one-stop-shop mechanism should not apply. Supervisory authorities also have a duty to co-operate with each other in order to identify the main establishment of the controller and they may challenge the controller's claim, based on an objective assessment of the facts. The Opinion addresses how the supervisory authorities should apply art 4(16)(a) GDPR to ensure its consistent application.

EDPB STRATEGY 2024–2027

[2.40] In April 2024, the EDPB published its strategy for 2024–2027, setting out its priorities for the coming years. The priorities are grouped around four pillars: enhancing harmonisation and promoting compliance; reinforcing a common enforcement culture and effective co-operation; safeguarding data protection in the developing digital and cross-regulatory landscape; and contributing to the global dialogue on data protection. It notes that a new aspect of the strategy is the focus on the interplay of data protection law with the new regulatory digital framework.

The EDPB strategy confirms that the EDPB will continue to provide guidance on key issues, to include, for example, guidance on the application of GDPR to particularly

---

[37] EDPB Opinion 04/2024 on the notion of main establishment of a controller in the Union under article 4(16)(a) GDPR, (adopted on 13 February 2024).

vulnerable data subjects, such as children, and on the application of particularly notable provisions. It also intends to create information streams tailored for non-experts, including SMEs. Employers can benefit from these resources to better understand and comply with data protection laws.

On 8 October 2024, the EDPB published its 2024–2025 Work Programme based on the priorities set out in the EDPB Strategy and grouped under the same pillars.[38] For employers, some of the key actions of interest include:

— Further improvements and promotion of the EDPB Data Protection Guide for Small Businesses.[39]
— Opinions on transfer tools, ie, Binding Corporate Rules, certification as a tool for transfers and standard contractual clauses and *ad-hoc* contractual clauses.
— Update of Referential for BCR Processor.

ARTIFICIAL INTELLIGENCE

[2.41] The necessity for AI systems to absorb large volumes of data for training purposes, and the resulting incorporation of that data into AI systems, has meant the application of GDPR is an important consideration in evaluating the provision, deployment and use of AI systems. Helpfully for employers engaging in AI, whether as deployer, provider or otherwise, in July 2024, the Data Protection Commission issued a statement on AI, Large Language Models and Data Protection and the EDPB has announced plans to develop guidelines on the interplay between EU data protection law, the AI Act, as well as on generative AI—data scraping.[40]

DPC Statement: AI, Large Language Models and Data Protection[41]

[2.42] The DPC published a statement on the interaction between AI and data protection on 18 July 2024. This statement discusses the potential for data processing activity to take place during the initial training and re-training/fine-tuning of AI models. It notes that the training of large language models ('LLMs') often involves the use of large datasets to teach the model how to answer questions or perform tasks based on the input/instructions they are given.

The statement identifies risks to data subjects, which may arise when an AI model is being trained or retrained. For example, using personal data during the training phase of an AI model, where it is not necessary to do so and without the data subjects' knowledge

---

[38] Available at: *https://www.edpb.europa.eu/system/files/2024-10/edpb_work_programme_2024-2025_en.pdf*.
[39] EDPB: 'EDPB Data Protection Guide for Small Business', available at: *https://www.edpb.europa.eu/sme-data-protection-guide/home_en*.
[40] EDPB 2024–2025 Work Programme.
[41] EDPB: 'AI, Large Language Models and Data Protection' (July 2024).

or permission and the risk that an AI model might retain or generate inaccurate personal data. This may be of particular concern where AI outputs are used in decision-making processes.

Organisations need to be aware of the risks of using various AI systems so that they choose a model that will comply with GDPR in how it processes personal data. Some of the risks identified by the DPC are as follows:

(i) Risks arising from processing personal data without a data subject's permission or knowledge, or unnecessarily processing personal data to train or re-train an AI model. Organisations need to ensure that they would be able to comply with a data subject request to exercise any of their rights in relation to their personal data.
(ii) Organisations need to ensure that there is human intervention in processes involving AI systems being used to make decisions about people to ensure that harmful automated decision making does not occur due to AI models that are biased or inaccurate.
(iii) Organisations need to ensure they comply with the principle of storage limitation when retaining personal data used in AI models.

The statement identifies data protection points to be considered by AI product designers, developers and providers. For example, when considering the use of publicly available personal data, they should consider the purposes for which those people have made that data available and what their reasonable expectations are about the way in which it can be used. The DPC reminds those involved in AI that a data protection impact assessment may be required to assess the risks of the AI model at all stages of its development and use, particularly where the risks involved in the processing are higher due to, for example, novel processing activities or use of personal data of more vulnerable members of society. Processing must be transparent. Data subjects should be informed as to what processing is being carried out, how it is being carried out and how their rights can be exercised. Further data protection considerations are set out in the statement.

Employers would be well advised to consider the following in managing AI within their organisation:

— understand where and how AI systems are being used within the organisation and keep an inventory;
— understand the role of the organisation and related regulatory obligations for each AI system;
— review procurement, outsourcing and contracting processes and structures to ensure they are fit for purpose;
— educate employees on AI usage and governance considerations;
— develop AI and data ethics policy that aligns with the principles of the AI Act, regulatory guidance and good industry practice;
— adapt existing governance structures to ensure robust supplier reporting, clear allocation of responsibility, effective internal lines of reporting and appropriate oversight;

- consider where AI usage impacts on other governance and compliance matters; and
- integrate AI considerations into broader risk management activities.

EDPB Report on the ChatGPT Taskforce

[2.43] The EDPB set up the ChatGPT Taskforce in April 2023 to ensure co-operation in investigating ChatGPT among the EU Member State supervisory authorities ('SAs'). The coordinated EU approach followed a decision by the Italian data protection authority, Garante, temporarily banning ChatGPT in March 2023.[42] At that time, the One-Stop Shop mechanism was not applicable to OpenAI. However, since February 2024, OpenAI is deemed to have single establishment in the EU in Ireland. Therefore the cross-border processing carried out by OpenAI falls within the remit of the One-Stop Shop, specifically the corrective powers are to be exercised by the DPC as the lead supervisory authority.

The views set out in the report issued in May 2024 are of a preliminary nature as investigations instigated by SAs prior to February 2024 had not concluded at that point. The report focuses on interpreting key provisions of GDPR that are relevant to ongoing ChatGPT investigations.[43] These include lawfulness, fairness, transparency and information obligations, data accuracy and rights of the data subject. The report contains a set of questions developed within the context of the ChatGPT Taskforce and these may be helpful for controllers considering the provision of generative AI.

EDPB Statement 3/2024 on data protection authorities' role in the Artificial Intelligence Act framework (adopted on 16 July 2024)[44]

[2.44] On 16 July 2024, the EDPB released a statement on DPAs' role in the AI Act framework. The statement notes the complementary and mutually reinforcing nature of the AI Act and EU data protection legislation, emphasising that EU data protection laws apply fully to the processing of personal data by AI systems, as stated in art 2(7) of the AI Act. The EDPB also stresses that the processing of personal data is a core element in the development of AI systems, particularly those which present a high risk to fundamental rights, therefore DPAs will play a prominent role in ensuring safe and rights-oriented AI deployment.

Article 70 of the AI Act requires Member States to appoint market surveillance authorities ('MSAs') before 2 August 2025, to supervise and enforce the AI Act.

---

[42] See *Arthur Cox Employment Law Yearbook 2023* at [2.38].
[43] EDPB Report of the work undertaken by the ChatGPT Taskforce. 23 May 2024.
[44] EDPB Statement 3/2024 on data protection authorities' role in the Artificial Intelligence Act framework, (adopted 16 July 2024), available at: https://www.edpb.europa.eu/system/files/2024-07/edpb_statement_202403_dpasroleaiact_en.pdf.

The EDPB recommends that DPAs be designated as MSAs for high-risk AI systems, referencing:

— the benefits for entities of having a single point of contact for AI and data protection;
— the existing technical and legal expertise within DPAs, including in areas referred to in art 70(3) of the AI Act, such as data computing and data security;
— the common independence requirements for DPAs and MSAs under EU law; and
— the dual role of the EDPS as the supervisory authority under data protection law and art 70(9) of the AI Act.

The EDPB further emphasises the importance of 'sincere co-operation' between MSAs and other entities tasked with supervising AI systems, as highlighted by the ECJ in *Bundeskartellamt*.[45]

TRANS-ATLANTIC TRANSFERS

EU-US Data Privacy Framework

[2.45] The EU-US Data Privacy Framework ('DPF') is a self-certification mechanism for US-certified companies to transfer personal data from the EEA to the United States of America (the 'US'), without the need to put in place further safeguards or obtain an authorisation. The DPF includes Executive Order 14086 ('E.O. 14086') which seeks to enhance safeguards around US intelligence activities and establishes a new redress mechanism to resolve complaints from data subjects in the EU and EEA. This redress mechanism applies regardless of the transfer tool used to transfer the complainants' personal data to the US. The DPF is of relevance to those US multinational employers in Ireland who have certified to the DPF to support the centralised processing of HR data by their US headquarters.

On 9 October 2024, the European Commission published a report following the first review of its decision of 10 July 2023, finding that the DPF provides an adequate level of protection for personal data transferred from the EU to organisations in the US.[46] Based on the information gathered during the review, the Commission has concluded that the US authorities have the necessary structures and procedures to ensure that the DPF functions effectively.

The Commission will closely monitor relevant developments, paying particular attention to:

(1) the upcoming reports of the Privacy and Civil Liberties Oversight Board ('PCLOB') on the implementation of EO 14086 and the functioning of the signals' intelligence redress mechanism, in particular the Data Protection Review Court ('DPRC');

---

[45] *Meta v Bundeskartellamt* (Case C-252/21).
[46] Report on the first periodic review of the functioning of the adequacy decision on the EU-US Data Privacy Framework, 9 October 2024, available at: *https://commission.europa.eu/document/ 25695177-8073-4ce3-bf81-eb816dc6b468_en*.

(2) possible further amendments of s 702 FISA; and
(3) the nomination and appointment of members to the PCLOB to fill upcoming vacancies.

The Report also contains a number of recommendations to ensure that the DPF continues to function effectively, such as developing common guidance between US authorities and EU data protection authorities on key DPF requirements.

EDPB Information Note on the redress mechanism for EU/EEA individuals[47]

[2.46] The EDPB released an Information Note on the Redress Mechanism for National Security Purposes which outlines the process for EU/EEA individuals to address alleged violations of US law regarding their data collected by US authorities for national security purposes. The process includes a mechanism for review conducted by the DPRC, which can obtain relevant information from elements of the US Intelligence Community and take binding remedial decisions. The decision of the DPRC is binding and final.

The note also outlines the role of the US Department of Commerce ('DOC') in relation to declassified information concerning complaints reviewed by the PCLOB or DPRC. The DOC will periodically contact the US Intelligence Community requesting declassified information that was subject to a review by the PCLOB or DPRC. If such information is declassified, the DOC, *via* the EDPB and the relevant DPA, will inform the complainant. The complainant may then request access to said information via applicable US law, such as the US Freedom of Information Act.

EU-US Data Privacy Framework FAQ for European individuals, (adopted on 16 July 2024)[48]

[2.47] The EDPB released a FAQ document for individuals to better understand the DPF. The FAQ document sets out what the DPF covers, and outlines the benefits for individuals where a company has self-certified, including the right to be informed about data transfers, access their data, and correct or delete any incorrect or unlawfully handled data. It explains how individuals can verify if a US company is certified under the DPF by checking the online EU-US Data Privacy Framework List.

The FAQ document sets out that, as a first step, any questions or concerns about the processing of personal data by a company certified under the DPF, should be directed to

---

[47] EDPB Information Note on the redress mechanism for EU/EEA individuals in relation to alleged violations of US law with respect to their data collected by US authorities competent for national security, available at: *https://www.edpb.europa.eu/system/files/2024-04/edpb_information-note_dpf-redress-mechanism-national-security-purposes_en.pdf*.

[48] EU-US Data Privacy Framework F.A.Q. for European individuals, (adopted on 16 July 2024), available at: *https://www.edpb.europa.eu/system/files/2024-07/edpb_dpf_faq-for-individuals_en_0.pdf*.

the company. It sets out a number of redress avenues available where a person believes a US company has violated their rights.

When a complaint is lodged with a national Data Protection Authority, two scenarios may occur:

1. **Informal panel of EU DPAs**: If the complaint involves HR data transferred to a US company or if the US company has chosen the EU DPAs as its recourse mechanism, an informal panel of EU DPAs will investigate. Both parties can present their views, and the panel can issue binding advice to the US company.
2. **Referral to US authorities**: If the complaint does not involve HR data or the US company has not agreed to co-operate with the EU DPAs, the national DPA may refer the complaint to US authorities. The national DPA may also directly exercise its powers, such as prohibiting or suspending data transfers.

DATA PROTECTION CASELAW

EU CASELAW

[2.48] *Schrems v Meta Platforms Ireland Ltd, formerly Facebook Ireland Ltd*[49]—*European Court of Justice—reference for a preliminary ruling from Germany—Regulation (EU) 2016/679 ('GDPR')*[50]—*protection of natural persons with regard to the processing of personal data—online social networks—general terms of use relating to contracts concluded between a digital platform and a user—personalised advertising—art 5(1)(b) GDPR—principle of purpose limitation—art 5(1)(c) GDPR—principle of data minimisation—art 9(1) and (2) GDPR—processing of special categories of personal data—data concerning sexual orientation—data made public by the data subject*

Meta collects user- and device-related data about user activities on and off the social network and links that data with the Facebook accounts of the users concerned. It uses 'cookies', 'social plug-ins' and 'pixels', as indicated by its terms of use and policies. Facebook's social plug-ins are 'embedded' by third-party website operators into their pages and this means that the URL of the page visited and various log data are transmitted to Meta each time the website is visited. With the data available to it, Meta is able to identify the data subject's interest in sensitive topics, such as health, sexual orientation, ethnic groups and political parties.

The applicant received advertising concerning an Austrian politician, which Meta provided to him as its analysis indicated that he had points in common with other users who had 'liked' that politician. The applicant also regularly received advertising targeting homosexual persons and invitations to related events, although he had

---

[49] *Schrems v Meta Platforms Ireland Ltd, formerly Facebook Ireland Ltd* (Case C-446/21).
[50] Regulation (EU) 2016/679 on the protection of natural persons with regard to the processing of personal data and on the free movement of such data ('GDPR').

never previously shown any interest in those events and did not know where they were to be held. The list of his activities outside Facebook, held by Meta included, 'inter alia, dating apps and dating websites for homosexuals, as well as the website of an Austrian political party' and also included an email address which was not provided on his Facebook profile, but which he had used to send requests to Meta. Further, during a panel discussion organised by the Representation of the European Commission in Vienna (Austria) and held on 12 February 2019, the applicant publicly disclosed his homosexuality, but this had not been published on his Facebook profile.

The applicant brought an action before the Landesgericht für Zivilrechtssachen Wien (Regional Court for Civil Matters, Vienna, Austria), on the basis that the processing of his personal data by Meta infringed a number of provisions of GDPR. Four questions as regards the application of GDPR were addressed to the ECJ, two of which have been addressed in an earlier decision in *Meta Platforms and Others (General terms of use of a social network)* (Case C-252/21).[51] The remaining questions addressed by the ECJ in this judgment, in essence, are as follows:

1. Is art 5 (1)(c) GDPR to be interpreted as meaning that all personal data held by a platform may be aggregated, analysed and processed for the purposes of targeted advertising without restriction as to time or type of data?
2. Is art 5(1)(b) GDPR, read in conjunction with art 9(2)(e) GDPR, to be interpreted as meaning that a statement made by a person about his or her own sexual orientation for the purposes of a panel discussion permits the processing of other data concerning sexual orientation with a view of aggregating and analysing the data for the purposes of personalised advertising?

In assessing the first question, the ECJ confirmed that the principles relating to the processing of personal data set out in art 5 GDPR apply cumulatively. It considered art 5(1)(a), (b), (c) and (e), the principle of accountability laid down in art 5(2) GDPR and transparency in art 13(1)(c) GDPR, as well as the requirement under art 25(2) GDPR to implement appropriate measures for ensuring that, by default, only personal data which is necessary for each specific purpose of processing is processed. The Court remarked that, as previously held in an earlier judgment concerning *Meta Platforms and Others (General terms of use of a social network)* (Case C-252/21),[52] the processing by Meta is particularly extensive since it relates to potentially unlimited data and has a significant impact on the user. It noted that the processing of data at issue is characterised by a serious interference with the fundamental rights of the data subjects, in particular their right to respect for their private life and the protection of personal data guaranteed by arts 7 and 8 of the Charter of Fundamental Rights of the European Union, and subject to verification by the national Court, this does not appear to be reasonably justified in the light of the objective of the dissemination of targeted advertising.

The Court went on to find that art 5(1)(c) GDPR must be interpreted as meaning that the principle of data minimisation precludes all of the personal data obtained by a

---

51 *Schrems v Meta Platforms Ireland Ltd, formerly Facebook Ireland Ltd* (Case C 446/21) at [37].
52 *Schrems v Meta Platforms Ireland Ltd, formerly Facebook Ireland Ltd.* (Case C-446/21) at [62].

controller, such as the operator of an online social network platform, from the data subject or third parties and collected either on or outside that platform, from being aggregated, analysed and processed for the purposes of targeted advertising without restriction as to time and without distinction as to type of data.

In addressing the second question above, the Court clarified as a preliminary point, that the panel discussion in the context of which the applicant made a statement concerning his sexual orientation, was held on 12 February 2019 and Meta was already processing personal data concerning his sexual orientation on that date. For this reason, it examined the second question in the context of potential processing of data relating to the applicant's sexual orientation carried out by Meta after 12 February 2019. Although the ECJ held that it is for the national Court to confirm, the Court concluded that the possibility cannot be ruled out that that statement at the panel discussion, constituted an act by which the applicant manifestly made his sexual orientation public within the meaning of art 9(2)(e) GDPR, with the effect that the derogation from the prohibition laid down in art 9(1) GDPR would apply.

However, the ECJ found that making this statement by itself, would not authorise the processing of other personal data relating to a data subject's sexual orientation. Accordingly, the Court held that art 9(2)(e) GDPR must be interpreted as meaning that the fact that a person has made a statement about his or her sexual orientation, on the occasion of a panel discussion open to the public, does not authorise the operator of an online social network platform to process other data relating to that person's sexual orientation, obtained, as the case may be, outside that platform using partner third-party websites and apps, with a view to aggregating and analysing those data, in order to offer that person personalised advertising.

[2.49] *TR v Land Hessen*[53]—*European Court of Justice—reference for a preliminary ruling from Germany—Regulation (EU) 2016/679 ('GDPR')*[54]—*protection of natural persons with regard to the processing of personal data—art 57(1)(a) and (f) GDPR—tasks of the supervisory authority—art 58(2) GDPR—corrective powers—administrative fine—discretion of the supervisory authority—limits*

This preliminary reference to the ECJ for an interpretation of art 57(1)(a) and (f), art 58(2) and art 77(1) GDPR was made in the context of an action before a German Court, asking it to order the Hessen Commissioner for Data Protection and Freedom of Information, Germany (the 'Commissioner for Data Protection') to take action against *Sparkasse* (the 'savings bank') and, in particular, to impose on it a fine.

One of the employees of the savings bank had, on several occasions, unlawfully accessed personal data of TR, one of its customers. While the bank notified the Commissioner for Data Protection, it did not notify TR of the breach of his personal data on the basis that the bank's DPO made the assessment that there was not a high risk to TR's rights and

---

[53] *TR v Land Hessen* (Case C-768/21).
[54] Regulation (EU) 2016/679 on the protection of natural persons with regard to the processing of personal data and on the free movement of such data ('GDPR').

freedoms. Disciplinary measures had been taken against the employee concerned and she had confirmed in writing that she had neither copied nor retained the personal data, that she had not transferred it to third parties and that she would not do so in the future.

TR lodged a complaint with the Commissioner for Data Protection after he became aware that his personal data had been improperly consulted. Upon investigation, the Commissioner for Data Protection informed TR of its finding that the savings bank had not infringed art 34 GDPR.

The ECJ noted that the system of sanctions provided for by the EU legislature allows supervisory authorities to impose the most appropriate and justified penalties depending on the circumstances of each individual case, taking into consideration the need to ensure that GDPR is fully enforced and to ensure a consistent and high level of protection of personal data through strong enforcement of the rules. It follows that it cannot be inferred either from art 58(2) GDPR or from art 83 GDPR that the supervisory authority is under an obligation to exercise, in all cases where it finds a breach of personal data, a corrective power. They must react appropriately to remedy the shortcoming found. Accordingly, when a breach of personal data has been established, the supervisory authority is not required to exercise a corrective power, in particular the power to impose an administrative fine, under art 58(2) GDPR where such action is not appropriate, necessary or proportionate to remedy the shortcoming found and to ensure that the GDPR is fully enforced.

This case reflects the practical experience of controllers in Ireland. In the vast majority of cases where a personal data breach is reported to the Data Protection Commission, the DPC will not exercise any corrective powers, particularly where the reporting controller can demonstrate that it has taken measures to mitigate the risks to data subjects and to avoid a recurrence.

[2.50] *Nacionalinis visuomenės sveikatos centras prie Sveikatos apsaugos ministerijos v Valstybinė duomenų apsaugos inspekcija[55]—European Court of Justice—reference for a preliminary ruling from Lithuania—Regulation (EU) 2016/679 ('GDPR')[56]—protection of natural persons with regard to the processing of personal data—art 4(2) and (7) GDPR—concepts of 'processing' and 'controller'—development of a mobile IT application—art 26 GDPR—joint control—art 83 GDPR —imposition of administrative fines—conditions—requirement that the infringement be intentional or negligent—responsibility and liability of the controller for the processing of personal data carried out by a processor.*

In March 2020, Nacionalinis visuomenės sveikatos centras prie Sveikatos apsaugos ministerijos (the Lithuanian National Public Health Centre under the Ministry of Health, 'NVSC') selected an IT company, IT sprendimai sėkmei ('ITSS'), to develop an app capable of recording and monitoring exposure of members of the public to

---

[55] *Nacionalinis visuomenės sveikatos centras prie Sveikatos apsaugos ministerijos v Valstybinė duomenų apsaugos inspekcija* (Case C-683/21).
[56] Regulation (EU) 2016/679 on the protection of natural persons with regard to the processing of personal data and on the free movement of such data ('GDPR').

Covid-19. The app collected information on users' name, phone number, national identification number, location and address. The privacy policy of the app described NVSC and ITSS as controllers of the personal data.

In April 2020, the Minister for Health instructed the Director of the NVSC to organise the acquisition of the app from ITSS. However, no public contract for the official acquisition of the app by the NVSC was ever concluded between NVSC and ITSS.

In May 2020, the Lithuanian data protection authority ('DPA') opened an investigation into the app and in February 2021 it concluded that the app violated arts 5, 13, 32 and 35 GDPR and issued administrative fines to NVSC and ITSS as joint controllers. NVSC challenged this decision arguing that ITSS should be considered the sole controller within the meaning of art 4(7) GDPR, while ITSS contended that it acted as a processor, within the meaning of art 4(8) GDPR, on the instruction of the NVSC who, in ITSS' view, was the sole controller. The Lithuanian national Court referred the following questions in essence to the European Court of Justice ('ECJ') for a preliminary ruling:

1. Can a 'controller', as set out in art 4(7) GDPR, consist of an entity intending to acquire the data collection app despite no formal contract being concluded?
2. Can a 'controller', as set out in art 4(7) GDPR, consist of an entity which has not acquired ownership nor taken possession of the data collection app but where the app provides links to that entity and the privacy policy specifies that entity itself as a controller?
3. Can a 'controller', as set out in art 4(7) GDPR, consist of an entity which has not performed any actual data processing operations as defined in art 4(2) GDPR and has not provided clear consent to the performance of such operations?
4. Can the definition of 'processing' of personal data, as set out in art 4(2) GDPR, include situations in which copies of personal data have been used for the testing of IT systems in the process for the acquisition of an app?
5. Can joint control of data under art 4(7) and art 26(1) GDPR be interpreted exclusively as involving deliberately coordinated actions in respect of the determination of the purpose and means of data processing, or can that concept also cover situations in which there is no clear 'arrangement' in respect of the purpose and means of data processing and/or actions are not coordinated between the entities?
6. Do improper personal data processing actions carried out by the processor give rise to strict liability on the part of a controller for the purpose of art 83(1) GDPR?

On the first three questions, the ECJ held that an entity which has entrusted a company with the development of a mobile application and which has, in that context, participated in the determination of the purposes and means of the processing of personal data carried out through that application may be regarded as a controller for the purposes of art 4(7) GDPR. This is the case even where that entity has not acquired the application and has not itself performed any processing, unless, prior to the app being made available to the public, that entity expressly objected to making said app available and to the subsequent processing of personal data.

On the fourth question, the ECJ found that 'processing' of personal data as set out in art 4(2) GDPR can include situations in which copies of personal data have been used for the testing of IT systems unless the personal data has been anonymised such that the data subjects are no longer identifiable.

On the fifth question, the ECJ noted that art 4(7) and art 26(1) GDPR do not require a specific arrangement between two entities regarding the determination of the purposes and means of the processing of personal data in order for them to be considered joint controllers.

On the sixth question, the ECJ first stated that an administrative fine may only be imposed where the controller or processor has intentionally or negligently committed an infringement referred to in art 83(4) to art 83(6) GDPR. The Court further held that a controller can be held liable for such infringement by a processor if the processor performed processing operations on the controller's behalf, unless the processor carried out the processing for its own purposes or in a manner incompatible with the framework for the processing in place between the controller and processor.

For employers, this case illustrates the importance of correctly defining and recording the data protection roles they and other parties play in respect of various processing operations. All processing operations carried out on their behalf by processors should be accurately and consistently recorded.

[2.51] *Deutsche Wohnen SE v Staatsanwaltschaft Berlin*[57]—*European Court of Justice—reference for a preliminary ruling from Germany—Regulation (EU) 2016/679 ('GDPR')*[58]—*protection of natural persons with regard to the processing of personal data—art 4(7) GDPR—concept of 'controller'—art 58(2) GDPR—powers of supervisory authorities to apply corrective measures—art 83 GDPR—imposition of administrative fines on a legal person—discretion of the Member States—requirement that the infringement be intentional or negligent.*

Deutsche Wohnen SE ('DW') is a real estate company responsible for the central management of a group of companies of which it is part, while its subsidiaries carry on the operational side of the business. DW and its group companies process personal data of tenants of the units it owns, including proof of identity, tax, social security and health data.

On foot of an investigation, the German DPA imposed an administrative fine on DW on the basis that it infringed art 5(1)(a), (c) and (e) and art 25(1) GDPR for intentionally failing to implement measures for data erasure where the data was no longer necessary and for erroneously storing data. DW challenged the decision arguing that domestic legislation only permits the imposition of an administrative fine against a legal person where the infringement is attributable to a natural person, including representatives of the legal person or of members of bodies thereof.

The national German Court viewed the limited liability regime of legal persons under national law as a conflict with the regime of direct liability of undertakings laid down

---

[57] *Deutsche Wohnen SE v Staatsanwaltschaft Berlin* (Case C-807/21).
[58] Regulation (EU) 2016/679 on the protection of natural persons with regard to the processing of personal data and on the free movement of such data ('GDPR').

in art 83 GDPR and sought a preliminary ruling from the ECJ. The national German Court sought clarification firstly on whether art 58(2) and art 83(1) to (6) GDPR must be interpreted as precluding national legislation which requires an infringement to be attributed to an identified natural person in order to impose an administrative fine on a legal person, and secondly on whether a fine can only be imposed where the controller intentionally or negligently committed an infringement of the GDPR.

In relation to the first question, the ECJ held that art 58(2)(i) and art 83(1) to (6) GDPR must be interpreted as precluding domestic legislation which provides that an administrative fine can only be imposed on a legal person in its capacity as controller in respect of an infringement referred to in art 83(4) to (6) GDPR if that infringement has previously been attributed to an identified natural person. As the first question was answered in the affirmative, the ECJ then considered the second question and concluded that a supervisory authority may only impose an administrative fine where it is established that the controller, which can be a natural or legal person, intentionally or negligently committed an infringement referred to in art 83(4) to 83(6) GDPR.

Right to Compensation: Article 82 GDPR

[2.52] Over the course of several preliminary references during 2023 and 2024, the European Court of Justice ('ECJ') has clarified the circumstances in which data subjects will be entitled to compensation under art 82 GDPR. The following decisions will be of interest to controllers who are concerned about litigation by data subjects claiming compensation for an infringement of GDPR, particularly in cases where the controller claims that they are not responsible for the breach and where the claimant suffers non-material damage. A typical scenario is where an aggrieved employee or former employee asserts that there has been an infringement of their GDPR rights in the context of a broader employment grievance and where a compensation claim is asserted under art 82 GDPR, typically coupled with an employment law claim. As can be seen below, the ECJ has considered a variety of fact patterns in respect of which compensation was claimed under art 82 GDPR during the course of 2024 and this caselaw will help employers identify the potential scale of damages (if any) that may arise, which in turn will inform their defence strategy.

[2.53] *ZQ v Medizinischer Dienst der Krankenversicherung Nordrhein*[59]*— European Court of Justice—request for a preliminary ruling from Germany— Regulation (EU) 2016/679 ('GDPR')*[60]*—data subject's capacity to work*

This case is of particular interest to employers and it concerned the processing of personal data relating to the data subject's capacity to work. In answering the German Court's questions relating to art 82 GDPR, the ECJ held that the establishment of

---

[59] *ZQ v Medizinischer Dienst der Krankenversicherung Nordrhein* (Case C-667/21), judgment delivered in December 2023, see *Arthur Cox Employment Law Yearbook 2023* at [2.53] for Opinion of Advocate General Campos Sánchez-Bordona, delivered on 25 May 2023.
[60] Regulation (EU) 2016/679 on the protection of natural persons with regard to the processing of personal data and on the free movement of such data ('GDPR').

liability on the part of the controller is subject to the existence of a fault committed by the controller. The ECJ explained that this fault is presumed unless the controller proves that it is in no way responsible for the event giving rise to the damage. This reversal of the burden of proof somewhat lowers the bar for data subject litigants and heightens the potential exposure for controllers, thus showing the importance of having secure data processing practices in place should a controller wish to rebut the presumption of fault.

In relation to art 82(1) GDPR, the referring Court enquired whether the degree of fault on the part of the controller or processor is a factor to consider when assessing the amount of non-material damage to be compensated. It specifically asked whether 'non-existent or minor fault on the part of the controller or processor can be taken into account in their favour'. The ECJ held that, as the right to compensation under art 82 GDPR does not fulfil a punitive function, the degree of seriousness of the controller or processor's fault in causing the damage is not relevant when determining the amount of damages to be awarded.

[2.54] ***GP v Juris GmbH*[61]—*European Court of Justice—request for a preliminary ruling from Germany—Regulation (EU) 2016/679 ('GDPR')*[62]—*protection of natural persons with regard to the processing of personal data—art 82 GDPR—right to compensation for damage caused by data processing—concept of 'non-material damage'—impact of the seriousness of the damage suffered—liability of the controller***

The case concerned a customer of a business who realised his personal data was being used for the purposes of direct marketing and subsequently revoked all consents to receive information from that company and objected to this processing of his data. He later received two advertising leaflets for which he claimed compensation under art 82 GDPR for alleged unlawful processing.

The ECJ clarified that it is not sufficient for a controller to claim that the damage was caused by the failure or negligence of a person acting under the controller's authority, within the meaning of art 29 GDPR in order to avail of the exemption from liability under art 82(3) GDPR. The ECJ also held that, as art 82 GDPR is compensatory in nature, in contrast to art 83 GDPR which is punitive, the criteria used for determining the amounts of administrative fines under art 83 GDPR cannot be used to determine the amount of damages under art 82 GDPR. The Court followed on from the reasoning that, as art 82 GDPR is compensatory rather than punitive, the fact that several infringements have been committed by the controller in relation to the same data subject cannot constitute a relevant criterion for the purposes of assessing the compensation to be awarded to that data subject under art 82 GDPR. It further held that only the damage actually suffered by that person must be taken into consideration in order to determine the amount of monetary compensation.

---

[61] *GP v Juris GmbH* (Case C-741/21), judgment delivered April 2024.
[62] Regulation (EU) 2016/679 on the protection of natural persons with regard to the processing of personal data and on the free movement of such data ('GDPR').

[2.55] *Scalable Capital GmbH[63]—European Court of Justice—request for a preliminary ruling from Germany—Regulation (EU) 2016/679 ('GDPR')[64]—protection of natural persons with regard to the processing of personal data—art 82 GDPR—right to compensation for damage caused by data processing—concept of non-material damage—compensation of a punitive nature or purely in respect of damages and satisfaction—minimal or symbolic compensation—theft of personal data stored on a trading application—identity theft or fraud*

The ECJ considered the interpretation of art 82 GDPR in the context of two sets of joined proceedings concerning compensation for non-material damage. The applicants in the main proceedings opened an account with Scalable Capital. Personal data and data relating to a deposit made by those applicants were seized by third parties whose identity was unknown. The applicants sought compensation for the non-material damage that they alleged to have suffered as a result of the theft. According to Scalable Capital, the personal data had not been used fraudulently.

GDPR does not establish a hierarchy between physical, material or non-material damage and to assume that physical injury is more serious than non-material damage would risk being contrary to the principle of full and effective compensation for the damage suffered.

Where damage is established but where that damage is not serious, the national Court can compensate the data subject by awarding minimal compensation, provided it compensates the data subject in full for the damage suffered.

The theft of personal data alone cannot give rise to a claim of identity theft or fraud.

Article 82(1) GDPR, in light of Recitals 75 and 85, must be interpreted as meaning that, in order for identity theft to be classified as such and to give rise to a right to compensation for non-material damage, the identity of a person affected by a theft of personal data must actually be misused by a third party. However, compensation for non-material damage caused by the theft of personal data, under art 82(1) GDPR, cannot be limited to cases where it is shown that that data theft subsequently gave rise to identity theft or fraud.

[2.56] *A v Patērētāju tiesību aizsardzības centrs[65]—European Court of Justice—request for a preliminary ruling from Latvia—Regulation (EU) 2016/679 ('GDPR')[66]—protection of personal data—art 82(1) GDPR—right to compensation and liability—unlawful processing of data—concept of damage—compensation for non-material damage in the form of apologies—principle of effectiveness—assessment of the form and level of compensation—attitude and motivation of the controller*

The European Court of Justice considered the interpretation of art 82 GDPR in the context of proceedings between a well-known journalist in Latvia and the Patērētāju

---

[63] *Scalable Capital GmbH* (Joined Cases C-182/22 and C-189/22), judgment delivered June 2024.
[64] Regulation (EU) 2016/679 on the protection of natural persons with regard to the processing of personal data and on the free movement of such data ('GDPR').
[65] *A v Patērētāju tiesību aizsardzības centrs* (Case C-507/23), judgment delivered October 2024.
[66] Regulation (EU) 2016/679 on the protection of natural persons with regard to the processing of personal data and on the free movement of such data ('GDPR').

tiesību aizsardzības centrs (Latvian Consumer Rights Protection Centre, the 'Centre'). As part of a campaign to make consumers aware of the risks involved in purchasing a second-hand vehicle, the Centre had distributed a video on several internet sites featuring a character imitating the journalist, without his consent. The Regional Administrative Court in Latvia confirmed that the processing of personal data by the Centre was unlawful on the basis of art 6 GDPR, and ordered that conduct to cease, as well as the publication of an apology on the relevant websites.

The issue of compensation for non-material damage subsequently came before the ECJ in questions referred for a preliminary ruling. The ECJ considered previous caselaw on art 82(1) GDPR and held that:

(i) an infringement of the GDPR is not sufficient, in itself, to constitute 'damage' within the meaning of art 82(1) GDPR;
(ii) the making of an apology may constitute sufficient compensation for non-material damage, *inter alia* where it is impossible to restore the situation that existed prior to the occurrence of that damage, provided that that form of redress is such as to compensate in full the damage suffered by the data subject; and
(iii) art 82(1) GDPR precludes taking into account the attitude and motivation of the controller in order to award compensation to the data subject that is lower than the damage he or she has actually suffered.

[2.57] *Agentsia po vpisvaniyata v OL*[67]—*European Court of Justice—request for a preliminary ruling from Bulgaria—Regulation (EU) 2016/679 ('GDPR')*[68]—*publication in the commercial register of a company's constitutive instrument containing personal data—Directive (EU) 2017/1132*[69]—*non-compulsory personal data—lack of consent of the data subject—right to erasure—non-material damage*

Personal data of the applicant, including the surname, first name, identification number, identity card number, date and place of issue of that card, as well as her address and signature, was made available to the public in the commercial register by the Registration Agency in Bulgaria (the 'Agency'). The data was contained in a company's constitution instrument, of which the applicant was a member, that was submitted to the Agency. The applicant sought the erasure of her personal data in the constitution instrument. In response to the request, the Agency sought an authenticated copy of the constitution instrument concerned, in which the personal data of the company members, other than the personal data required by law, were redacted, to be sent to it in order to grant the erasure request.

The referring Court in Bulgaria referred a number of questions on the interpretation of the relevant EU laws to the European Court of Justice. As regards art 82(1) GDPR, the ECJ held that a loss of control, for a limited period, by the data subject over his or her personal data, on account of that data being made available online to the public, in the

---

[67] Agentsia po vpisvaniyata v OL (Case C-200/23), judgment delivered October 2024.
[68] Regulation (EU) 2016/679 on the protection of natural persons with regard to the processing of personal data and on the free movement of such data ('GDPR').
[69] Directive (EU) 2017/1132 relating to certain aspects of company law.

commercial register of a Member State, may suffice to cause 'non-material damage', provided that that data subject demonstrates that he or she has actually suffered such damage, however minimal, without that concept of 'non-material damage' requiring that the existence of additional tangible adverse consequences be demonstrated.

[2.58] *BL v MediaMarktSaturn Hagen-Iserlohn GmbH*[70]—*European Court of Justice—reference for a preliminary ruling from Germany—protection of natural persons with regard to the processing of personal data—Regulation (EU) 2016/679 ('GDPR'),*[71] *arts 5, 24, 32 & 82—assessment of validity of art 82—admissibility of request—right to compensation for infringement—transmission of data to unauthorised third parties in error—protective measures taken by controller*

This request for a preliminary ruling concerned the interpretation of various provisions of the GDPR. There was also a request for an assessment of the validity of art 82 GDPR. These requests were made in proceedings between the applicant, BL, and the respondent company, Saturn. The main dispute concerned a claim in non-material damage caused by accidental transmission of the applicant's personal data to a third party.

The applicant visited the respondent's outlet, where he purchased an electrical household appliance. A sales contract and credit agreement were drawn up by an employee of the respondent. In the process, the applicant's name, address, name of employer, income and bank details were entered in the respondent's information system. Contracts containing that personal data were printed and signed. These documents were brought by the applicant to employees at the collection counter, who inadvertently gave both the appliance and the documents to an individual who had surreptitiously jumped the queue, and who then left with everything. The error was quickly discovered, and the items were returned within half an hour. The appliance was offered free of charge to the applicant, who did not consider this adequate compensation.

The applicant brought proceedings in the Local Court in Hagen, Germany (the 'referring Court'), where the respondent argued that the severity threshold for a GDPR infringement had not been reached, and that the applicant had not suffered any damage. The referring Court decided to stay the proceedings and refer several questions to the ECJ for preliminary ruling.

By its first question, the referring Court asked in essence whether art 82 GDPR is invalid in so far as it lacks detail on compensation for non-material damage. This question was declared inadmissible as it was not accompanied by the requisite statement of reasons, *per* the Court's rules.

Next, the referring Court asked whether arts 5, 24, 32 and 82 GDPR, read together, must be interpreted so that, in an action for compensation, circumstances such as those

---

[70] *BL v MediaMarktSaturn Hagen-Iserlohn GmbH* (Case C-687/21).
[71] Regulation (EU) 2016/679 on the protection of natural persons with regard to the processing of personal data and on the free movement of such data ('GDPR').

pertaining to the applicant's claim are sufficient, in themselves, to consider the protective measures implemented by the data controller 'not appropriate', within the meaning of arts 24 and 32 GDPR. The ECJ held that, it is apparent from the wording of those articles, that the controller is responsible for assessing the appropriateness of protective measures implemented by it. The controller is obliged to mitigate the risk of personal data breaches; though not to prevent all such breaches. Existing caselaw from the ECJ holds that unauthorised disclosure of personal data, or access to that data by a third party, are not sufficient, in themselves, to conclude that the protective measures implemented by the controller are not appropriate; the measures taken must be assessed 'in a concrete manner'.

In the present case, the fact that employees of the controller provided, in error, a document containing personal data to a third party was 'capable of indicating' that the protective measures implemented by the controller were not appropriate. Such circumstances may have arisen as a result of negligence, or a failure in the controller's organisation, for instance. In an action for compensation under art 82 GDPR, the burden of proof is on the controller to show that the personal data was processed securely. Accordingly, the controller bears that burden in relation to the appropriateness of the protective measures implemented by it. The ECJ found that the circumstances of the present case were not, in themselves, determinative of the issue and the referring Court would have to take into account all of the evidence provided by the controller in that respect.

Next, the referring Court asked whether art 82 GDPR must be interpreted as meaning that the right to compensation in the case of non-material damage fulfils a 'punitive' function, and whether the severity of the infringement must be taken into consideration for the purposes of compensation. ECJ caselaw has made it clear that art 82 GDPR fulfils a compensatory function, as opposed to being a deterrent. It does not require the severity of the fault to be taken into consideration when setting the amount of compensation allocated for non-material damage. It is for the national Court to apply its internal rules when assessing compensation payable, provided that amount is set in a way that the damage 'actually suffered' as a result of the infringement is compensated in full.

The existence of 'damage' or 'harm' which has been 'suffered' is one of the conditions for the right to compensation, as is the existence of a causal link between that damage and the infringement. Article 82(1) GDPR has been interpreted as precluding a national rule or practice which makes compensation for non-material damage subject to that damage reaching a certain degree of seriousness. The fear experienced by a data subject with regard to a possible misuse of his or her personal data by third parties as a result of an infringement of art 82 GDPR 'is capable, in itself, of constituting non-material damage'. Loss of control of the personal data, even for a short period of time, may cause the data subject non-material damage giving rise to a right to compensation, 'subject to that person demonstrating having actually suffered such damage, however minimal, bearing in mind that the mere infringement … is not sufficient to confer a right to compensation on that basis'. Were it established, however, that the unauthorised third party did not become aware of the personal data at issue, non-material damage would not arise merely because the data subject was put in fear.

[2.59] **VX, AT v Gemeinde Ummendorf**[72]—*European Court of Justice—reference for a preliminary ruling from Germany—Regulation (EU) 2016/679 ('GDPR'),*[73] *art 82—protection of personal data—right to compensation—liability—non-material damage—publication without consent of data subject*

This request for a preliminary ruling from Germany concerned the interpretation of art 82(1) GDPR. The request was made in proceedings between the applicants, VX and AT, and the respondent, the Municipality of Ummendorf, Germany. The applicants sought compensation for alleged suffering arising from the disclosure of the applicants' personal data without their consent on the respondent's website.

The respondent published the agenda of a meeting of the municipal council on its website. The agenda mentioned the applicants' names on several occasions, as well as a Court judgment referencing their names and addresses (the identities of other parties had been deleted). These documents were accessible on the homepage of the respondent's website for a period of three days. The applicants contended that the unlawful disclosure of personal data of an individual constituted 'damage' within the meaning of art 82, and that a '*de minimis* threshold' would run contrary to the scheme of the GDPR and to the deterrent effect of art 82 GDPR. The respondent argued that compensation for non-material damage requires 'proof of a noticeable disadvantage and an objectively comprehensible impairment of personal interests'.

The Regional Court in Ravensburg, Germany (the 'referring Court') decided to stay the proceedings and to refer a question to the European Court of Justice for preliminary ruling. In essence, it asked whether art 82(1) GDPR must be interpreted as precluding national legislation or a national practice which sets a *de minimis* threshold for establishing non-material damage.

According to the ECJ's caselaw, the existence of 'damage' or 'harm' which has been 'suffered' is one of the conditions for the right to compensation under art 82(1) GDPR, as is the existence of a causal link between that damage and the infringement. These conditions are 'necessary and sufficient' for a right to compensation. In the absence of any reference in art 82(1) GDPR to the national law of Member States, the concept of 'non-material damage' must be given an autonomous and uniform definition specific to EU law. Article 82(1) GDPR has been interpreted as precluding a national rule or practice which makes compensation for non-material damage subject to that damage reaching a certain degree of seriousness. Thus, it follows that art 82(1) GDPR does not require a *de minimis* threshold for establishing non-material damage caused by a proven infringement.

A person affected by an infringement of the GDPR is required to show that the consequences of that infringement constitute non-material damage within art 82 GDPR. In the present case, although there was nothing to preclude the respondent's actions from causing the applicants non-material damage, it would be for the applicants to demonstrate that they had 'actually suffered such damage, however minimal'.

---

[72] *VX, AT v Gemeinde Ummendorf* (Case C-456/22).
[73] Regulation (EU) 2016/679 on the protection of natural persons with regard to the processing of personal data and on the free movement of such data ('GDPR').

[2.60] *VB v Natsionalna Agentsia za Prihodite*[74]—*European Court of Justice—reference for a preliminary ruling from Bulgaria—Regulation (EU) 2016/679 ('GDPR'),*[75] *art 5—principles relating to processing of personal data—art 24, accountability of the controller—art 32, measures implemented to ensure security of processing—assessment of appropriateness of such measures—scope of judicial review—taking of evidence—art 82, compensation and liability—possible exemption from liability—claim in non-material damages for fear of potential misuse of personal data*

This request for a preliminary ruling from Bulgaria concerned the interpretation of various provisions of the GDPR. The request was made in proceedings between the applicant, VB, and the respondent, Bulgaria's national revenue agency. The applicant sought compensation for non-material damage as a result of a personal data breach.

The respondent was a data controller within the meaning of the GDPR. In July 2019, the media reported a cyberattack on the respondent's IT system, resulting in the publication of personal data from that system on the internet. More than six million natural persons were affected. Several hundred of them, including the applicant, brought actions against the respondent.

In the applicant's case, the non-material damage consisted of 'fear that her personal data, having been published without her consent, might be misused in the future, or that she herself might be blackmailed, assaulted or even kidnapped'. The respondent contended that the applicant had not sought information concerning the precise data disclosed from it. It also gave evidence to the effect that it had taken all necessary measures in advance to prevent the data breach, and subsequently to limit the effects of that breach and to reassure citizens. It disputed the causal link between the breach and the non-material damage and argued that it could not be held liable in any event, since it had suffered a malicious attack by third parties who were not employees. The action was dismissed.

On appeal, the Supreme Administrative Court (the 'referring Court') considered that the fact that a personal data breach had occurred might, on its own, lead to the conclusion that the measures implemented by the data controller were not 'appropriate' within arts 24 and 32 GDPR. However, in the event that this was not dispositive, the referring Court queried the scope of the review to be carried out by a court in its assessment of the appropriateness of those measures. Second, it queried the rules on the taking of evidence in that context. Third, the referring Court asked whether a data controller is systematically exempt from liability for damage caused to data subjects as a result of the actions of third parties. Finally, it asked whether fear of potential misuse of the data subject's personal data is capable in itself of constituting 'non-material damage'. The referring Court decided to stay the proceedings and to refer a number of questions to the ECJ for preliminary ruling.

---

[74] *VB v Natsionalna Agentsia za Prihodite* (Case C-340/21).
[75] Regulation (EU) 2016/679 on the protection of natural persons with regard to the processing of personal data and on the free movement of such data ('GDPR').

First, the referring Court asked in essence whether arts 24 and 32 GDPR must be interpreted as meaning that unauthorised disclosure of personal data, or access to that data by third parties, are sufficient, in themselves, to conclude that the protective measures implemented by the controller were not 'appropriate'. As is apparent from the wording of those articles, the controller is required to adopt 'technical and organisational measures' intended to avoid, 'in so far as it is at all possible', any personal data breach. The appropriateness of such measures is to be assessed 'in a concrete manner', with reference to the type of processing in question, in particular data protection needs and associated risks. Hence, the unauthorised disclosure of personal data, or access to that data by a third party, are not sufficient to conclude that the protective measures implemented by the controller were not appropriate. A finding to the contrary would deprive the data controller of a rebuttable presumption, allowing it to demonstrate that it had implemented appropriate measures.

Second, the referring Court asked in essence whether art 32 GDPR must be interpreted as meaning that the appropriateness of protective measures implemented by the controller must be assessed by the national Courts 'in a concrete manner', having particular regard for risk associated with the processing concerned. Here, it was apparent from art 32(1) and (2) GDPR that 'appropriateness' must be assessed in two stages: first, by identifying the associated risks, including their likelihood and severity, and possible consequences for the rights of natural persons; and second, by ascertaining whether the protective measures implemented are appropriate to those risks. While it is true that the controller has 'some discretion' in determining the appropriate technical and organisational measures to ensure a level of security commensurate with the risk, it remains that a national Court must be able 'to evaluate the complex assessment carried out by the controller', and in doing so make sure those measures are appropriate. Such an examination requires a 'concrete analysis' of the nature and content of the measures implemented by the controller, the manner in which they were applied and their practical effects, having regard to the risks inherent in that processing.

Third, the referring Court asked in essence whether the 'principle of accountability' must be interpreted as meaning that, in an action for damages, the controller bears the burden of proving the appropriateness of security measures implemented by it. It was noted that both arts 24(1) and 32(1) GDPR require the controller 'to implement appropriate technical and organisational measures to ensure and be able to demonstrate that [processing of personal data] is carried out in accordance with that regulation'. Hence, it is clear from the wording of those provisions that the controller carries the burden of proving that personal data is processed securely. Accordingly, the controller bears that burden in relation to the appropriateness of the protective measures implemented by it. It is for Member States to establish procedural rules for actions intended to safeguard art 82 GDPR rights, in particular rules of evidence. It may not be 'systematically necessary' to rely on experts' reports in the light of other evidence before the Court, provided that evidence is recent.

Next, the referring Court asked in essence whether art 82(3) GDPR must be interpreted as meaning that the controller is exempt from liability solely because the damage arises from the actions of third parties. As was clear from art 82(2) GDPR, a controller can be exempt from liability 'only if it proves that it is in no way responsible for the event giving rise to that damage'. The circumstances in which a controller may claim to be exempt from liability 'must be strictly limited to those in which the controller is able to demonstrate that the damage is not attributable to it'. In the present case, the infringement could not be attributable to the controller, unless the controller made that infringement possible by failing to comply with a GDPR obligation. Thus, the controller may repel liability by proving that there is no causal link between the alleged breach of a data protection obligation and the damage suffered by the natural person. It may not, however, do so solely because the damage arises from the actions of third parties.

Finally, the referring Court asked in essence whether art 82(1) GDPR must be interpreted as meaning that the fear experienced by a data subject of potential misuse of his or her personal data by third parties as a result if an infringement is capable in itself of constituting 'non-material damage'. Previous ECJ caselaw holds that the existence of 'damage' or 'harm' which has been 'suffered' is one of the conditions for the right to compensation under art 82(1) GDPR, as is the existence of a causal link between that damage and the infringement. Article 82(1) GDPR has been interpreted as precluding a national rule or practice which makes compensation for non-material damage subject to that damage reaching a certain degree of seriousness. Thus, such fear is capable of constituting non-material damage, subject to the national Court verifying that the fear can be regarded as well founded in all of the circumstances.

Key principles include

— A mere infringement of GDPR by a controller is not sufficient to be entitled to compensation. The claimant must also establish that the infringement caused them damage (material or non-material).
— There is no seriousness threshold of damage which must be met to be entitled to compensation.
— Non-material damage may include a loss of control over personal data or fear about potential future misuse, but the claimant must prove a well-founded fear that the data will be misused and that the risk is not hypothetical.
— Damages under art 82 GDPR are compensatory and not punitive in nature.
— The concept of damage must be interpreted autonomously across all Member States, but national legal systems can prescribe procedural rules to determine the amount of compensation.
— Where the damage established is not serious, a national Court can award minimal compensation, provided it compensates the data subject in full for the damage suffered.
— Theft of personal data alone cannot give rise to a claim for compensation based on alleged identity theft, rather the data subject must prove that their stolen data has been misused by a third party.

— An apology may sufficiently compensate the non-material damage suffered by a data subject, if it compensates the damage in full.
— Loss of control of personal data for a limited period may constitute 'non-material damage', provided that that data subject demonstrates that he or she has actually suffered such damage, however minimal.

European Court of Human Rights

[2.61] *Tonchev v Bulgaria*[76]—*European Court of Human Rights—European Convention on Human Rights, art 8—private life—ongoing retention of data about a penalty incurred by the applicant—relevant regulations vague enough to cause confusion—not sufficiently foreseeable—interference not in accordance with law*

The applicant complained under art 8 ECHR about the retention and disclosure of his criminal records by the respondent, the Bulgarian Government. The key issue was whether the allegedly indefinite retention of data about a criminal matter, that was disposed of without marking a conviction against the applicant, was 'in accordance with the law' and whether it was consistent with data protection law.

In March 2004, the applicant applied for a prison guard position. In support of his application he submitted certification to show that he had no criminal convictions. He was appointed to the role in June 2004. Meanwhile, in May 2004, the applicant had been caught drink driving, and in September 2004 he was convicted of the offence, though criminal liability was waived and, instead, an administrative fine was imposed. As required by national regulations, a record card for the penalty was produced and stored in the Troyan District Court's criminal records bureau. The fine was paid.

In July 2012, the Ministry of Justice opened a competition for posts in the directorate for the security to the judiciary. The applicant applied for a post and, on 14 August 2012, the directorate sought and obtained a criminal record mentioning his 'substitute administrative penalty' from 2004. This report came from data obtained electronically from the record card stored in the Troyan District Court's criminal records bureau. On 23 August 2012, the directorate again sought and obtained a criminal record report which also mentioned the penalty, but added that, on 20 August 2012, the physical record card had been earmarked for destruction as it was expired. On the basis of the electronically-obtained data, the applicant was disqualified from participating in the competition.

The criminal record report of 14 August 2012 also issued to the applicant's employer, the Chief Directorate for the Execution of Punishments. The employer made its own

---

[76] *Tonchev v Bulgaria* (Application No. 40519/15).

enquiries and, on 28 November 2012, obtained a electronic criminal record report on him. The applicant was dismissed in March 2013 on the basis of the criminal record report disclosing the substitute administrative penalty.

The applicant sought judicial review of his dismissal and argued that the data about his penalty was obtained unlawfully. His case was that criminal record reports could only be used for law enforcement purposes; the only way an employer could access criminal record data was by way of a conviction certificate. The claim was dismissed by the Sofia City Administrative Court, which held that the lawfulness of the dismissal was unaffected. The applicant appealed; he argued that, after the lawful destruction of his record card, it became impermissible to obtain that data by other means. That appeal was rejected by the Supreme Administrative Court, which held that, by law, prison officers with substitute administrative penalties had to be dismissed. It went on to find that the law did not require that data about those penalties be obtained by the employer in any particular way. The existence of the criminal record report mentioning the penalty was sufficient.

The applicant complained to the Commission for the Protection of Personal Data that the Ministry had processed his personal data unlawfully, since the Troyan bureau had retained the record card beyond its five-year lifespan (the penalty having expired in October 2009). In June 2013, the Commission unanimously upheld the complaint. It found that the retention of the data after the five-year period had been devoid of any legal basis and breached national data protection law.

The Troyan District Court sought judicial review of the Commission's decision. The Sofia City Administrative Court declared the Commission's decision null and void as the applicant had since withdrawn his complaint. The Commission appealed and the Supreme Administrative Court upheld the lower Court's judgment. It found that, while the record card was to be destroyed after five years under national regulations, there was no provision for the electronic data to be deleted as well. On the contrary, the data was to be retained and archived in accordance with another regulation.

The European Court of Human Rights ('ECtHR') stated that, to be 'in accordance with law', an interference with an art 8 ECHR right must not only have a basis in law, but that law must be accessible and sufficiently foreseeable. With regard to the processing of criminal record data, 'clear and detailed rules governing the scope and application of such measures, and minimum safeguards' are essential. The regulations governing the ongoing retention of the applicant's data, while clear regarding the time limit for keeping record cards, were ambiguous on whether electronic data derived from the cards was to be deleted alongside them or retained for longer, or indefinitely. The Ministry of Justice, which drafted the regulations, argued for the indefinite retention of that electronic data. By contrast, the Commission argued for its deletion, along with the record cards. The ECtHR found that regulations which were vague enough to cause confusion 'even among the national authorities in charge of their interpretation and application' were not sufficiently foreseeable. Thus, the ongoing retention of the data concerning the applicant's penalty was not in accordance with law and there had been a violation of art 8 ECHR.

IRISH AND UK CASELAW

[2.62] *Keane v Central Statistics Office[77]—High Court—O'Donnell J—Data Protection Act 1988—Directive 95/46/EEC[78]—breach of data privacy—Personal Injuries Assessment Board Act 2003—definition of a 'wrong'—definition of 'personal injury'—requirement to make an application to PIAB for assessment of claims*

The plaintiff was an employee of the defendant, who processed sensitive personal data about her, such as information on her pay and tax information. A data breach occurred in which the defendant accidentally disclosed the plaintiff's P45 to third parties. The plaintiff alleged that she suffered distress, anxiety and a worsening of a condition she suffered from, psoriatic arthritis, because of this breach. The plaintiff claimed her data protection rights had been breached and sought an order that the defendant disclose the identity of the third parties who received her information; she also sought damages for that breach, among other causes of action. The defendant raised a preliminary issue that, as the plaintiff was only claiming damages for personal injuries, she should have made an application to PIAB prior to bringing this action, as required under the Personal Injuries Assessment Board Act 2003 (the '2003 Act'). The Circuit Court agreed, and found that while the plaintiff's proceedings remained extant, the principal remedy sought by the plaintiff was damages for personal injury, and that aspect of the claim was bound to fail because of her failure to obtain prior authorisation under the 2003 Act.

On appeal to the High Court, O'Donnell J considered whether the plaintiff should have brought an application to PIAB before instituting the proceedings.

In relation to the plaintiff's claim regarding breach of data protection legislation, as the proceedings pre-dated GDPR, the elements of the processing regarding breach of data protection rights fell to be determined under the Data Protection Act 1988 and Directive 95/46/EEC. The Court referred to art 23(1) of Directive 95/46/EEC which provides that:

> 'Member States shall provide that any person who suffered damage as a result of an unlawful processing operation or of any act incompatible with the national provisions adopted pursuant to this Directive is entitled to receive compensation from the controller for the damage suffered'.

Section 7 of the Data Protection Act 1988 Act provides that, for the purposes of the law of tort, a data controller or processor shall owe a duty of care to data subjects about whom they collect personal data. The Court referred to the decision of the High Court in *Collins v FBD Insurance plc*,[79] which held that s 7 of the Data Protection Act 1988 does not provide for the automatic payment of compensation, or for strict liability. Therefore, a plaintiff had to show proof of damage in order to recover compensation.

---

[77] *Keane v Central Statistics Office* [2024] IEHC 20.
[78] Directive 95/46/EC on the protection of individuals with regard to the processing of personal data and on the free movement of such data.
[79] *Collins v FBD Insurance plc* [2013] IEHC 137.

The only damage alleged by the plaintiff was personal injuries (anxiety, distress and an aggravation of her psoriatic arthritis). Because of this, the Court held that the plaintiff should have applied to PIAB before bringing these proceedings, in accordance with the 2003 Act and the plaintiff's claims as regards damages for personal injuries could not proceed.

[2.63] *McCabe v AA Ireland Ltd*[80]—*Circuit Court—O'Brien J—Regulation (EU) 2016/679 ('GDPR')*[81]—*arts 5(1), 6 & 82 GDPR—Data Protection Act 2018—ss 71 & 117—video recording of employee by employer while employee off premises—failure to account for erasure or destruction—compensation*

The plaintiff was an employee of the defendant company and was absent from work on sick leave. On the last day of his leave, he was assisting a family member with work in the garden when senior managers of the defendant company drove up in a vehicle. The operations manager, who was present in the vehicle, took a mobile phone video recording of the plaintiff engaging in the work. The plaintiff was angry that this had occurred and claimed that he had been unlawfully recorded without his consent. The following day, a meeting was scheduled with the operations manager at which the plaintiff was suspended from his employment without pay, pending an investigation. He was told at this meeting that the video evidence would not be used as there were credible witnesses.

The plaintiff subsequently attended a disciplinary hearing, following which he was dismissed. The decision to suspend the plaintiff was a result of his ability to engage in physical work while on sick leave and the aggressive manner in which the plaintiff responded to the video being taken. No investigation was taken against the defendant's operations manager for possibly breaching the defendant company's data protection policy, as set out the employee guide. It was claimed that the plaintiff's personal data was recorded, used and processed in breach of data protection laws as this took place without the plaintiff's permission and for an unlawful purpose. The plaintiff sought access to the video. The defendant claimed that the video had been deleted. The defendant claimed that no processing of personal data took place as the video was not handed over to anyone else in the company and wasn't used in the disciplinary process.

The Court examined whether the actions of the defendant in recording, using and processing the data took place in breach of data protection laws, and, whether the defendants had an obligation to provide the plaintiff with a copy of the recording and account to the plaintiff for its potential destruction or loss, in accordance with the principle of accountability under GDPR.

The Court held that while the video wasn't directly relied on as part of the disciplinary process, there was clearly a connection between the recording and the plaintiff's dismissal as the grounds for his dismissal cited by the defendant included the plaintiff's reaction to the video being taken. It was therefore necessary for the defendant to

---

[80] *McCabe v AA Ireland Ltd* [2024] IECC 6.
[81] Regulation (EU) 2016/679 on the protection of natural persons with regard to the processing of personal data and on the free movement of such data ('GDPR').

account to the plaintiff for the deletion of the recording. While the defendant claimed that the video had been deleted, they did not produce any sworn testimony that this had been done and therefore the current status of the video was not certain.

Further, due to the seriousness of the consequences for the plaintiff and the reasons the defendant gave for these consequences (ie, the plaintiff's reaction to being recorded), the plaintiff should have received a copy of the video or been given reliable information about whether it had been destroyed. The plaintiff should have received such information under the principles of fairness and transparency. Such information would have assisted the plaintiff in his defence or in other litigation. As an employee, the plaintiff also had a right to data collected by his employer where this data was closely connected to his role as an employee.

The question of whether processing was within the legitimate interests of the defendant was not of relevance here given that the defendant claimed they did not rely on the video in making the decisions regarding the plaintiff's dismissal. This defence could only be considered if the use of the video was proved, or admitted by the defendant.

The Court held that the defendant, its servant and or agents breached the personal data rights of the plaintiff. The Court directed the defendant to account to the plaintiff for the deletion or loss of the recording and to provide sworn testimony regarding the current status of the recording. The defendant was also directed to pay compensation of €5,500 to the plaintiff for damage suffered, under s 117(4)(b) of the Data Protection Act 2018.

[2.64] *R (the3million and Open Rights Group) v Secretary of State for the Home Department*[82]—*Court of Appeal of England and Wales*—*Lewison, Singh & Laing LJJ*—*appeal from High Court of England and Wales*—*data protection and privacy*—*derogating Regulations*—*UK GDPR*[83]—*immigration exemption*

These proceedings concerned the lawfulness of the UK Government's second attempt at creating an 'immigration exemption' from key data subject rights under the UK GDPR. The original exempting Regulations had been held to be unlawful by the Court of Appeal of England and Wales.[84] In this instance, the Government appealed against a High Court finding of unlawfulness following a judicial review challenge to the amended version of the Regulations.

The amended Regulations introduced a number of qualifications to the immigration exemption, notably limiting the scope of the exemption to personal data processed 'by the Secretary of State', and only if he or she has an 'immigration exemption policy document' ('IEPD') in place. Such an IEPD would be required to be published, kept

---

[82] *R (the3million and Open Rights Group) v Secretary of State for the Home Department* [2023] EWCA Civ 1474.
[83] UK GDPR is a part of 'retained' law, ie, it derives from EU law but, since the UK's departure from the EU, is now part of domestic law. The UK GDPR originated from Regulation (EU) 2016/679 on the protection of natural persons with regard to the processing of personal data and on the free movement of such data.
[84] *R (the3million and Open Rights Group) v Secretary of State for the Home Department* [2021] EWCA Civ 800.

under review and updated as appropriate. The Regulations would require the Secretary of State to 'have regard' to the relevant IEPD and to make a case-by-case assessment of the extent to which application of the relevant GDPR provision 'would be likely to prejudice' the immigration process. Having made an assessment of likely prejudice to the immigration process, the Secretary of State would then be required to record and inform the data subject of that determination, provided it would not be prejudicial to the immigration process to do so.

Article 23(2) GDPR sets what is required of derogations from fundamental rights, including that they be made by way of legislation, be clear and precise, legally binding, accessible and foreseeable, and that they set out safeguards. The trial Judge had observed that an IEPD was 'not a legislative measure', but a 'readily changeable government policy' not subject to Parliamentary oversight. The trial Judge upheld complaints that the Regulations did not comply with art 23(2) GDPR, in that they did not make specific provisions for 'safeguards to prevent abuse or unlawful access or transfer', or for 'risks to the rights and freedoms of the data subject'. The trial Judge also accepted that the requirement of a balancing exercise 'needs to be made clear on the face of the legislation and cannot be regarded simply as implicit', as in the case of the 'likely to prejudice' test.

The Court of Appeal saw 'no dispute' that the immigration exemption had a legitimate aim, and indeed sought to advance 'important public interests'. Furthermore, the trial Judge had rightly identified that the case was fundamentally about the rule of law, a constitutional principle. The rule of law calls for 'specific' provisions, rather than general principles of human rights or administrative law 'to reduce the risk of abuse of broad powers'. A non-statutory policy document could in principle meet that purpose, if worded with sufficient precision. In the case of the immigration exemption, 'binding rules rather than simply policies', and, crucially, Parliamentary scrutiny, were required. Therefore the trial Judge had properly concluded that the immigration exemption was not compliant with art 23(2) GDPR.

The Court of Appeal expressed agreement with the trial Judge that the Regulations themselves did not specify what safeguards were to be set out in the IEPD, and that this was 'fundamentally deficient'. Further, the trial Judge was correct that a bare requirement to 'have regard' to the IEPD (as opposed to a duty of 'due regard') encouraged a 'generalised, non-prescriptive document, rather than one of detail and specificity'. The only document in which any assessment of risk to GDPR rights appeared was in an unpublished 'rationale and reasoning' note, and the trial Judge had correctly identified this too as a fundamental defect. Even if this document were made available to Parliament, it would be defective in that it only referred to GDPR rights, making no reference to other rights such as those in the European Convention on Human Rights.

In relation to cross-appeals brought by the respondents, the Court of Appeal held that the trial Judge had been correct to reject a complaint that the term 'effective immigration control' was so vague as to amount to an open-ended exemption. The trial Judge had correctly concluded that 'effective immigration control' is a clear concept 'used without difficulty in other statutes'. The Court of Appeal held that the trial Judge had also correctly rejected a complaint of insufficient safeguards relating to the 'storage' of the data concerned, observing that the immigration exemption applied only when, and for as long as, the 'likely to prejudice' test was satisfied. In any event, art 5(1) GDPR makes provision for the keeping of personal data 'for longer than is necessary for the purposes which the personal data are processed'. Further, it is open to the data subject to make another request under art 15 GDPR which is to be treated on its own merits. Thus, an express 'review period' in the Regulations was unnecessary.

The Court of Appeal, accordingly, upheld the trial Judge's declaration of incompatibility of the immigration exemption with art 23 GDPR, suspending the declaration for a period of three months. The appeal was, accordingly, dismissed.

[2.65] *Harrison v Cameron & Others*[85]—*High Court of England and Wales— Steyn J—UK GDPR*[86]—*Data Protection Act 2018—voice recordings—purely personal/household exemption—art 4(7)—whether directors considered data controllers where they determine means and purpose of processing data by company—art 15(1)(c)—subject access rights—disclosure of recipients of personal data—'rights of others' exemption*

The claimant, on two phone calls with the first-named defendant (who was the owner and director of the second-named defendant company), made various threats to the first-named defendant. The first-named defendant recorded these calls and shared the recordings with various people, including employees, friends and family. Some of these recipients further shared the recordings with other people. The claimant made a data access request seeking information regarding the identity of the recipients to whom the recordings had been disclosed.

The issues for the Court to consider were: whether the director's processing of the claimants' personal data occurred as part of a solely personal activity and was therefore outside the scope of the relevant data protection legislation; whether the director was a data controller when acting in his personal capacity; and, if the claim did fall within the scope of UK GDPR, whether the defendants were entitled not to disclose the identities of the recipients on the basis that the request was manifestly unfounded or excessive, or on the basis that the defendant was protecting the rights and freedoms of others, as set out in UK law.

The Court held that the processing of the claimant's personal data did not fall outside the scope of UK GDPR. When the calls were recorded by the first-named defendant, he did this in his capacity as a director of the defendant company. The conversation that took place on the phone calls related to the termination of a business contract between the claimant and the defendant company. Therefore, the calls were business calls and were, at least partially, recorded for business purposes. When the recordings were sent by the first-named defendant to his friends and family, he was not acting in the course of a purely personal activity. He was sharing personal data held by the defendant company

---

[85] *Harrison v Cameron & Others* [2024] EWHC 1377 (KB).
[86] UK GDPR is a part of 'retained' law, ie, it derives from EU law but, since the UK's departure from the EU, is now part of domestic law. The UK GDPR originated from Regulation (EU) 2016/679 on the protection of natural persons with regard to the processing of personal data and on the free movement of such data.

that related to its business and was seeking advice from those with whom it was shared on the termination of the contract, as well as in relation to threats the claimant made. Therefore, the processing did not fall outside the scope of UK GDPR.

The first-named defendant was not considered to be a data controller under the relevant data protection legislation. When he recorded and shared the calls, he was deciding the means and purposes of processing while acing in his capacity as a director of the defendant company. His role as a director of the company, whereby he processed data as an agent for the company, did not make him a controller himself. The defendant company was a data controller, but he was not. If an employee or director was to process data in an unauthorised manner, then that might result in them being a data controller. However, that did not occur in this case.

The Court outlined that the right of access to personal data that has been disclosed to others imposes on data controllers an obligation to disclose the identity of such recipients to data subjects, unless it is not possible to identify them or unless the request is manifestly unfounded or excessive. The defendants tried to draw a distinction between employee recipients and external recipients of the recordings, but the Court held that this could not be done—both of these categories were 'recipients' under UK GDPR of whom the data subject had a right to know the identity. It was held not to be manifestly unfounded or excessive in this case for the defendant company to disclose the identities of the recipients of the recordings. This exception could not be relied upon to refuse disclosure.

However, the Court held that the defendant company did not have to comply with the claimant's access request, as the rights and freedoms of others exemption applied to the information in these circumstances. In deciding this, the Court considered the fact that none of the recipients of the recordings gave their consent to their identity being disclosed to the claimant, and therefore the question was whether it was reasonable for the company, as controller, to disclose their identities without their consent. The Court referred to the wide margin of discretion controllers have under law in balancing the various considerations that must be taken into account when assessing reasonableness, such as the type of information that would be disclosed, the duty of confidentiality owed to other individuals, and the circumstances in which consent has not been given. The company decided it would be unreasonable to disclose the identity of recipients where this would give rise to a significant risk of them being harassed, intimidated or made subject to hostile litigation by the claimant. This view was formed due to, among other things, the behaviour of the claimant towards the first-named defendant, the fact that intimidating legal correspondence had been sent by the claimant to many employees of the defendant company, and the fact that the employees who had previous contact with the claimant feared him. Further, the recipients of the data had said they would give their consent if the claimant gave undertakings not to threaten or harass them, but the claimant did not give such undertakings. Based on these facts, the company was acting well within its discretion in deciding that it was not reasonable to disclose the identity of the recipients to the claimant and it was not unreasonable for them to give more weight to 'such sustained and menacing behaviour' demonstrated by the claimant.

The claim against both defendants was dismissed.

Chapter 3

Employment Equality

INTRODUCTION

[3.01]

Age—Occupational Qualification

The European Court of Justice considered the legality of a job offer stating ideal minimum and maximum ages for applicants in *JMP*.

Age—Mandatory Retirement

Mandatory retirement age for revenue sheriffs was considered by the Supreme Court in *Mallon v Minister for Justice*.

In *Transdev*, the Labour Court determined that the issue of the compulsory retirement ages for tram drivers was *res judicata*, by reference to a previous Labour Court determination.

The WRC considered the compatibility of the stated legitimate aim of a retirement policy with an employee's individual characteristics in *Doolin*.

Age—Eligibility for Post-Retirement Employee Benefits

In *Fasano*, the UK EAT considered the eligibility for post-retirement employee benefits.

Age—Harassment

An Post v Dowling concerned a Labour Court decision in relation to harassment on the grounds of age.

Age—Occupational Benefit Scheme

In *Trinity College Dublin v Malone*, the Labour Court considered a claim of age discrimination in the context of an occupational benefit scheme which prohibited those aged 66 and above from joining, in circumstances where the employer was neither a party nor a contributor to the scheme.

Associative Discrimination

In *Rollett*, the UK EAT considered associative discrimination and whether a claimant who does not have the same protected characteristic as a relevant disadvantaged group but who suffers the same disadvantage can bring a claim for indirect discrimination.

Burden of Proof

In *Leicester City Council v Parmar*, the UK EAT considered the burden of proof in a claim for less favourable treatment on the grounds of race.

Compensation

In *CJ*, the UK EAT considered the method for calculating compensation, including the interaction between ill-health retirement pensions and mitigation of loss requirements.

Disability

The Labour Court dealt with reasonable accommodation and disability discrimination in *DHL, Atlantic Troy, Kerry County Council v McGaley* and *Irish Prison Service v Cunningham*.

In *Karmakar*, the High Court of England and Wales considered whether a blanket college policy of refusing to void previous unsuccessful exam attempts contradicted the duty to make reasonable adjustments.

The UK Upper Tribunal, in *A Multi Academy Trust v RR* examined the statutory test for 'substantial disadvantage' in relation to the duty to make reasonable adjustments.

The UK EAT delivered a number of decisions concerning disability discrimination, including *Bodis, Anderson, Baldwin, Cairns and Bugden*. In *Minis*, the UK EAT considered indirect disability discrimination.

Finally, knowledge in the context of disability claims was considered by the UK EAT in *Glasson, Godfrey* and *Farley*.

Gender

The European Court of Justice considered the treatment of part-time workers in relation to indirect discrimination on the grounds of gender in *IK*.

In *O'Sullivan*, the Labour Court considered a claim of discrimination on the grounds of age and gender in relation to an interview and selection process.

Gender—Affirmative Action

Affirmative action in relation to gender was considered by the Supreme Court of Tasmania in *Moorilla Estate Pty v Lau*.

Gender—Equal Pay

Equal pay and the burden of proof required to establish 'like work' in the chosen comparator were considered by the Labour Court in *Teagasc v Reid*.

In *Barnard*, the UK EAT adjudicated on equal pay for firefighters.

Gender—Harassment

The UK EAT decision in *Blanc de Provence Ltd* concerned harassment on the basis of gender.

In the decision of the UK EAT in *King*, harassment for reasons related to sex was considered.

Gender Recognition

Gender recognition and the omission of a definition of the word 'gender' in the Gender Recognition Act 2004 was the subject of the *Castellucci* judgment of the High Court of England and Wales, which determined that public interest for legislative and administrative coherence and the administrative costs of amending a statute were relevant factors to be balanced against the claimant's interest in having their gender recognised in the UK.

Pregnancy and Maternity Leave

The High Court in *Karpicz* determined that the issuing of a P45 in error to a woman on maternity leave constituted a dismissal.

In *Ballerino*, the UK EAT considered discrimination while on maternity leave.

Inducing a Discriminatory Act

The issue before the UK EAT in *Bailey* was the inducement of a discriminatory act, where the claimant, a tenant barrister in chambers, alleged that a complaint received from a charity regarding tweets published by him influenced a chambers investigation into acts of the claimant.

Race

In *Onyemekeihia*, the High Court considered a claim of racial abuse of a prison officer by prisoners.

In *Okafor*, the issue before the Labour Court was whether race discrimination had occurred in the appointment of a chief medical scientist.

Boohene, a judgment of the Court of Appeal of England and Wales, concerned a claim of indirect race discrimination arising from the failure to pay the appellants the London living wage.

The UK EAT considered the burden of proof in a claim for race discrimination in *Atif*. In *Zaluski*, the EAT considered whether the employment tribunal had erred in awarding aggravated damages in a case of indirect discrimination and harassment related to race.

In *Beaumont Hospital v Thomas*, the Labour Court determined that, as the claimant had failed to establish a *prima facie* case within the cognisable period, the Court could not address the contention that events occurring within that period were part of a continuum of discrimination.

Race—Harassment

In *Carozzi*, the UK EAT considered whether an accent amounted to a protected characteristic under the race ground of the Equality Act 2010.

Religion

In *Sutcliffe*, the High Court of England and Wales considered whether an order prohibiting a teacher from teaching by reason of professional misconduct amounted to discrimination on the basis of religious belief.

In *TTT*, the High Court considered whether a policy prohibiting pupils' prayer rituals on school premises interfered with the freedom to manifest one's religion or belief under art 9 of the European Convention on Human Rights or subjected the claimant pupil to detriment under the Equality Act 2010.

In *Thomas*, the issue before the UK EAT was whether the claimant's anti-Islamic views were a protected characteristic under the Equality Act 2010 or the European Convention on Human Rights.

AGE—OCCUPATIONAL QUALIFICATION

[3.02] *JMP v AP Assistenzprofis GmbH[1]—European Court of Justice—reference for a preliminary ruling from Germany—Directive 2000/78/EC,[2] art 2(5)—equal treatment in employment and occupation—prohibition of discrimination on grounds of age—UN Convention on the Rights of Persons with Disabilities, art 19—Charter of Fundamental Rights of the European Union, art 26—social and occupational integration of persons with disabilities—job offer stating minimum and maximum age requirements—justification*

This request for a preliminary ruling concerned the interpretation of arts 2(5), 4(1), 6(1) and 7 of Directive 2000/78/EC establishing a general framework for equal treatment in occupation, read in the light of the Charter of Fundamental Rights of the European Union (the 'Charter') and the UN Convention on the Rights of Persons with Disabilities (the 'UN Convention'). The request was made in proceedings between the applicant and the respondent, a company offering assistance and advisory services to persons with disabilities. The proceedings related to an action for discrimination on the grounds of age occurring in the context of a recruitment process.

In July 2018, the respondent advertised a job, stating that a 26-year-old female student was looking for a female personal assistant, 'preferably between 18 and 30 years old'. The applicant, who was born in 1968, applied for the position and was rejected by the respondent. The applicant brought the discrimination action against the respondent before the Labour Court in Cologne, Germany. The respondent pointed to the importance, enshrined in national legislation, of taking into account the 'legitimate wishes' and 'subjective needs' of each person in receipt of personal assistance. In this instance, the respondent argued that the legitimate wish that the personal assistant be of a certain age should be regarded as being a 'genuine and determining occupational requirement' within the meaning of the national legislation, in order to protect the right of personality.

Both the Labour Court and, on appeal, the Higher Labour Court upheld the applicant's complaint, and the respondent appealed on a point of law to the Federal Labour Court, the referring Court, which decided to stay the proceedings and to refer a question to the European Court of Justice (the 'ECJ') for a preliminary ruling. It asked, in essence, whether arts 2(5), 4(1), 6(1) and/or 7 of Directive 2000/78/EC, read in the light of the Charter and art 19 of the UN Convention:

> 'must be interpreted as precluding the recruitment of a person providing personal assistance from being subject to an age requirement pursuant to national legislation under which account is to be taken of the individual wishes of the persons who are entitled to personal assistance services as a result of disability'.

The ECJ noted that the situation fell within the scope of Directive 2000/78/EC, concerning as it did 'conditions for access to employment ... including selection criteria and

---

[1] *JMP v AP Assistenzprofis GmbH* (Case C-518/22).
[2] Directive 2000/78/EC on establishing a general framework for equal treatment in employment and occupation.

recruitment conditions' within the meaning of art 3(1). It appeared that the applicant was rejected on account of her age, and this constituted 'direct discrimination on grounds of age' within the meaning of art 2(2). It therefore fell to be determined whether the difference in treatment on grounds of age could be justified under the Directive, and any exception to the prohibition of discrimination under art 2(5) would fall to be interpreted strictly.

The national legislation at issue required providers of personal assistance to respect:

> 'the legitimate wishes of the [disabled] persons entitled to receive those services ... in so far as those wishes are reasonable and by taking account of those persons' personal circumstances, age, sex, family and religious and philosophical needs'.

It was apparent to the Court that the legislation giving rise to that measure pursued an objective of protecting the self-determination of persons with disabilities. Such an objective, it was noted, comes within the scope of art 2(5), inasmuch as it is intended to protect this right to self-determination. In particular, the right 'to express wishes and to choose freely' gives 'specific expression' to the integration of persons with disabilities under art 26 of the Charter, and the right to self-determination endorsed by art 19 of the UN Convention.

Here, the stated preference in the job offer for a certain age range was explained by the fact that the desired candidate 'had to be able to fit easily in [the service user's] personal, social and university circle'. It thus appeared that the difference of treatment on grounds of age at issue in the main proceedings was the result of a measure that was necessary for the protection of the rights and freedoms of others within art 2(5), and therefore, the question of the referring Court was answered in the negative.

AGE—MANDATORY RETIREMENT

[3.03] *Mallon v Minister for Justice[3]—Supreme Court—Collins J—appeal from High Court—Court Officers Act 1945, s 12(6)(b)—discrimination on age grounds—mandatory retirement age for revenue sheriffs—justified under Directive 2000/78/EC[4]—legitimate aims—appropriate and necessary*

The appellant was appointed revenue sheriff for Cavan and Monaghan in 1987. He was responsible for the execution of certificates of tax liability under what would become the Taxes Consolidation Act 1997.

The Court Officers Act 1945 provides that the office of revenue sheriff is non-pensionable and that the age of retirement is 70. There is no provision for the extension or variation of that statutory retirement age. Revenue sheriffs are not paid a salary, but

---

[3] Mallon v Minister for Justice, Ireland and the Attorney General [2024] IESC 20. See *Arthur Cox Employment Law Yearbook 2022* at **[3.09]** for the decision of the High Court in *Mallon v Minister for Justice, Ireland and the Attorney General* [2022] IEHC 546.

[4] Directive 2000/78/EC on establishing a general framework for equal treatment in employment and occupation.

instead receive annual retainers plus recovery fees from which they must provide the necessary staff and discharge all relevant expenses. On his appointment, the appellant was entitled to remain in private practice as a solicitor and did so throughout his appointment and to his retirement at age 70.

In July 2020, the Sheriff's Association, the representative body of which the appellant was a member, made submissions to the Minister for Justice arguing for the increase of the statutory retirement age to 72. The Minister's response, in a communication dated 20 April 2021, indicated that approval to remain beyond the age of 70 would not be forthcoming. It explained that the standard compulsory retirement age in the public service had been consolidated 'to the greatest extent possible, at the age of 70', following the enactment of the Public Service Superannuation (Age of Retirement) Act 2018.

The appellant brought judicial review proceedings challenging the lawfulness of the mandatory retirement age, which he contended was objectively discriminatory on the grounds of age, and was not justifiable. He also asserted that the mandatory retirement age for revenue sheriffs was unlawfully discriminatory when compared with the recently increased (from 70 to 72) mandatory retirement age for coroners.

The High Court held that the mandatory retirement age was 'no doubt' discriminatory on age grounds but that the aims identified by the Minister fell within the broad discretion of the State and were legitimate policy aims within the Employment Equality Directive, ie:

> 'to allow for planning at the level of the individual and at the level of the organisation, the creation of an age balance in the workforce, personal and professional dignity, intergenerational fairness, and standardising the retirement age in the public service'.

The fact that those aims did not apply with equal force across the public service did not undermine their legitimacy. Importantly, revenue sheriffs were distinguishable from public service workers generally, being the subject of specific legislation and provision. This being so, the application of a mandatory retirement age, even without a ministerial power to vary it, could still be considered proportionate. Revenue sheriffs were entitled to access State pension schemes and were not precluded from engaging in other professional activities. The High Court was therefore satisfied that the mandatory retirement age was proportionate and necessary, and the reliefs were refused.

On appeal to the Supreme Court, the appellant argued that a blanket mandatory retirement age is not justifiable where individual assessment is possible. The Supreme Court expressed agreement with the High Court that the absence of flexibility on a 'case by case or role by role basis' does not, on its own, render a measure disproportionate. Indeed, European Court of Justice jurisprudence recognises that Member States may reasonably adopt 'generally applicable mandatory retirement rules', without any requirement for individual capacity assessment. The Supreme Court accepted the State's argument that, provided the aims are legitimate, and the measure proportionate, a mandatory retirement rule does not offend the Employment Equality Directive's prohibition on age discrimination. The High Court was satisfied that the State had identified legitimate aims for the mandatory retirement policy. The appellant had not demonstrated any error in that conclusion. Indeed, the Supreme Court could not 'in truth … see how any other conclusion would have been open to the [trial judge] on the basis of the material before her'.

Similarly, the issue of whether the State was reasonably entitled to the view that the mandatory retirement age for sheriffs was 'necessary and appropriate' to achieve those aims 'would appear to admit of only one answer'. It was difficult to identify any circumstances in which a retirement age of 70 might be said to be disproportionate. Indeed, it was higher than many mandatory retirement thresholds considered 'without criticism or condemnation' by the European Court of Justice; and higher than mandatory retirement ages in other areas of public service, including An Garda Síochána, the Permanent Defence Forces and the fire services. As a matter of principle, the State may provide for different retirement ages applicable to specific categories of public servants where there is a rational and objective basis for doing so, including the effective delivery of public services in that area. Hence, the decision to increase the retirement age for coroners from 70 to 72 was, on the evidence, one which the Government and the Oireachtas were entitled to take.

In the circumstances, the trial Judge was entitled to conclude that the mandatory retirement age was justified under the Employment Equality Directive and the appeal failed.

[3.04] *Transdev Dublin Light Rail Ltd v Doody*[5]—*Labour Court—appeal from Workplace Relations Commission—Employment Equality Acts 1998 to 2015, s 83(2)—res judicata*

The claimant appealed against the WRC's determination that the claimant was estopped from proceeding with his claim of discriminatory dismissal against the respondent on the age ground as it was *res judicata*. The Labour Court had previously determined that the respondent's policy of compulsory retirement for tram drivers at age 65 is objectively justified.[6]

Referring to its earlier determination, the Labour Court concluded that the claimant was so estopped.

[3.05] *Doolin v Eir Business Eircom Ltd*[7]—*Workplace Relations Commission—Employment Equality Acts 1998 to 2021, s 77—discrimination on grounds of age—mandatory retirement—objective justification—compatibility of stated legitimate aim of retirement policy with employee's individual characteristics*

The claimant, who was employed as a desktop support agent, alleged discrimination on the grounds of age. In January 2023, the respondent issued the claimant with a notice of an intention to retire him from employment on 1 July 2023, the date of his 65th birthday. Having requested an extension of his retirement date, the claimant was told on

---

5   *Transdev Dublin Light Rail Ltd v Doody* EDA243.
6   *Transdev Light Rail Ltd v Chrzanowski* ADE/16/52, see *Arthur Cox Employment Law Yearbook 2016* at **[4.08]**.
7   *Doolin v Eir Business Eircom Ltd* ADJ-00045261.

14 March 2023 that he would not be allowed to work beyond his 65th birthday and he was served with a notice of termination accordingly.

The respondent's case was that, following a review its pension schemes, it had made the decision to align the retirement age of the Defined Contribution Pension Scheme with the Defined Benefit Pension Scheme, which was age 65. Staff were notified of the change to the mandatory retirement age in April 2020, and the change came into effect on 1 July 2020.

The WRC noted that the revised retirement policy was not applied universally and that three employees were retained by the respondent after turning 65. It was satisfied from the respondent's evidence, however, that these had been exceptional cases and that they did not undermine the respondent's policy.

Nevertheless, the WRC was not persuaded that the respondent's mandatory retirement age policy was objectively justified by a legitimate aim, which was, on the respondent's evidence, to 'promote intergenerational fairness' and ensure smooth 'succession planning'. In particular, the WRC was unconvinced that retaining the claimant in his (non-critical, relatively junior) role as a desktop support agent would have impeded the career progression of any other employee. Health and safety concerns cited by the respondent were also deemed irrelevant, given the desk-based nature of the claimant's role. The respondent's decision of 14 March 2023 'clearly lacked an element of individual assessment' and there was 'no evidence of a test of compatibility of the purported legitimate aims, directed specifically at the individual characteristics of the [claimant]'.

Finally, the WRC noted the claimant's limited skillset, that he was still seeking work and that his only income since turning 65 was just over €200 per week in social welfare payments. There was no evidence to suggest that the respondent considered the claimant's future job prospects and reduction in his income when it decided to terminate his employment.

Thus, the claimant had established a *prima facie* case of discrimination, which the respondent had failed to successfully rebut. Accordingly, the complaint was upheld, and the respondent was directed to reinstate or re-engage the claimant.

AGE—ELIGIBILITY FOR POST-RETIREMENT EMPLOYEE BENEFITS

[3.06] *Fasano v RB Group plc*[8]—*UK Employment Appeal Tribunal—appeal from employment tribunal—indirect age discrimination—provision, criterion or policy—justification—agency*

The claimant appealed against the dismissal of his claim of indirect age discrimination by an employment tribunal.

---

[8] *Fasano v Reckitt Benckiser Group plc* [2024] EAT 7.

The claimant was employed by RB Health, a wholly-owned subsidiary of RB Group (the respondents), from 1997 until his retirement in June 2019, latterly in the senior role as chief supply officer. As an employee, the claimant was eligible to participate in the RB Group's 'long term incentive plan'. That scheme provided for the award of shares and share options to employees, subject to conditions which included the group's performance over a certain period. Those conditions could be waived or changed by the group in certain circumstances. On those terms, the claimant was awarded 32,000 shares and 64,000 share options.

The claimant was informed, prior to retiring, that his shares and share options under the scheme for 2017 may vest in May 2020, subject to the group's performance at the end of 2019, and that they would be 'pro-rated for service up to retirement'. In actuality, the performance of the group's shares was such that it became clear that no 2017 award was going to vest for anyone. These awards, historically, had comprised a large part of the remuneration for senior staff and were an important incentive to remain in the respondents' employ. The group therefore resolved on 18 September 2019 to change the performance criteria for the 2017 award in order to retain existing staff in senior management roles. The claimant, having retired before that date, did not benefit from the changes. Six participants in the scheme, who were still employed by the respondent in September 2019, but who had agreed to leave their employment in the near future, did benefit from the changes.

The claimant alleged that being deprived of the award (which would have been substantial) under the amended terms, by virtue of not being employed on 18 September 2019 amounted to indirect discrimination based on age under the Equality Act 2010. The tribunal concluded that RB Group was acting as an agent of RB Health when providing the long-term incentive plan, including the amending of its terms. While the amended terms did put people over the age of 57 at a particular advantage compared with those under the age of 57, 'it was a proportionate means of achieving the legitimate aim of retaining staff and was therefore justified'.

The UK EAT found the tribunal's reasoning on justification deficient: it was the provision, criterion or policy ('PCP') of requiring that participants be employed on 18 September 2019 in order to benefit from the amended terms that needed to be justified, not the changes to the scheme as a whole. Even if there was a need for a qualifying cut-off date, the PCP in question could not contribute to the retention of staff and its only real justification was to avoid unnecessary payments to those who could not be retained, ie to save money. The respondents had never made this case, nor had they argued that they could not afford to pay participants in the 2017 award, who had left their employment before 18 September 2019. The appeal was therefore allowed on that point.

On the agency point, the EAT agreed with the respondents that it was perverse to categorise RB Group as an agent of RB Health in relation to the long-term incentive plan. It was plain that the subsidiary had no control over the group's actions or decisions in relation to the scheme. There was no basis for saying that the subsidiary authorised the group to act in relation to the scheme, or that the group was acting on behalf of the subsidiary when it was making the changes to the long-term incentive plan and imposing the PCP. The cross-appeal on that point was therefore allowed.

The EAT concluded that while the PCP was not justified, RB Group was not acting as agent for RB Health in imposing the PCP, with the result that neither respondent was liable to the claimant. It followed that the appeal was dismissed.

AGE—HARASSMENT

[3.07] *An Post v Dowling*[9]—*Labour Court—appeal from Workplace Relations Commission—Employment Equality Acts 1998 to 2021, s 83(1)—harassment on the grounds of age—discrimination on the grounds of disability—prima facie case*

The claimant appealed against the WRC's dismissal of her complaint under the Employment Equality Acts 1998 to 2021. The Adjudication Officer found there was no *prima facie* case of discrimination on the grounds of disability, victimisation or failure to provide reasonable accommodation. The claimant was, however, found to have been discriminated against and harassed on the grounds of age and was awarded €1,000 in compensation.

The claimant's case on appeal was that she was ridiculed and was made the target of jokes about her age by her supervisor and two junior members of staff. The employees in question laughed at her and remarked that a song on the radio by Gilbert O'Sullivan was 'her vintage'. Her supervisor set a tone in the workplace which was discriminatory and did not respect the claimant's right to dignity at work.

For its part, the respondent, An Post, was unclear if the appeal related to the level of compensation awarded, or the finding that the claimant was not discriminated against on the grounds of age and disability. There was no evidence that the claimant was subject to unfavourable treatment on the grounds of disability. Otherwise, the WRC's findings of age-related harassment and the level of compensation were not being cross-appealed.

The Labour Court, like the WRC, found that no *prima facie* case of disability discrimination had been made out, no such evidence having been presented by the claimant. The Court was satisfied that the respondent was liable for the harassment suffered by the claimant and the award of compensation was left untouched. Thus, the WRC's decision was upheld.

AGE—OCCUPATIONAL BENEFIT SCHEME

[3.08] *Trinity College Dublin v Malone*[10]—*Labour Court—appeal from Workplace Relations Commission—Employment Equality Acts 1998 to 2021, s 83(1)—occupational benefit scheme—statutory basis of complaint—employer contributions to scheme*

---

[9] *An Post v Dowling* EDA2451, see also related case *An Post v Dowling* HSD2410 at **[8.02]**.
[10] *Trinity College Dublin v Malone* EDA2435.

The claimant appealed against the WRC's dismissal of her complaint of discrimination on the ground of age.

The claimant submitted that she was prevented from opting in to a voluntary income protection and life assurance scheme because she was aged 66 or over. The scheme was facilitated by the respondent but, crucially, it did not make any contributions to it.

The respondent submitted that the scheme to which the claimant referred was an occupational benefit scheme, and so the complaint ought properly have been pursued under the Pensions Act 1990. However, that Act excluded schemes to which the employer is not a party or to which contributions are voluntary.

The Labour Court concluded that the claimant had failed to identify an act of discrimination under the Employment Equality Acts 1998–2021, and so the appeal failed.

ASSOCIATIVE DISCRIMINATION

[3.09] *British Airways plc v Rollett*[11]—*UK Employment Appeal Tribunal—appeal from employment tribunal—Equality Act 2010, s 19—indirect discrimination—whether a claimant not having the same protected characteristic as a relevant disadvantaged group but who suffers the same disadvantage as a result of a PCP can bring a claim in indirect discrimination*

The respondent appealed against an employment tribunal's decision that it had jurisdiction to hear the 49 claimants' indirect discrimination claims.

The claimants were cabin crew based at Heathrow Airport. Their claims arose from a restructuring exercise, including scheduling changes, undertaken by the respondent during the COVID-19 pandemic. The claimants argued that the scheduling changes particularly disadvantaged those (predominantly non-British nationals) who lived abroad and commuted to Heathrow from abroad, when compared to those commuting from within the UK, as well as disadvantaging those (predominantly women) with caring responsibilities, when compared to those without such responsibilities. Claims of 'ordinary' indirect discrimination were brought by those with the relevant protected characteristics (for example, non-British nationals and women). Importantly, those claimants who did not have the relevant protected characteristics brought claims of 'associative' indirect discrimination, in that they allegedly suffered the 'same disadvantage'.

The employment tribunal concluded, in light of ECJ authority,[12] that the UK equality legislation must be read without the requirement for the claimant to share the protected characteristic of the protected group. Accordingly, the tribunal had jurisdiction to hear

---

[11] *British Airways plc v Rollett* [2024] EAT 131.
[12] *CHEZ Razpredelenie Bulgaria AD v Komisia za zashtita ot discriminatsia* (Case C-83/14).

the indirect discrimination claims. In an appeal on a point of law, the respondent challenged that finding.

Dismissing the appeal, the EAT did not see that the employment tribunal's construction of the legislation could be said to 'go against the grain'. On the contrary, it seemed entirely consistent with a statute 'that seeks to harmonise discrimination law and to strengthen the law to support progress on equality'. It was certainly consistent with the legislative purpose of applying the EU definition of indirect discrimination in domestic law. The decision was in no way 'repugnant' to the legislative purpose and the tribunal had made no error of law.

Accordingly, the appeal was dismissed.

BURDEN OF PROOF

[3.10] *Leicester City Council v Parmar*[13]—*UK Employment Appeal Tribunal— appeal from employment tribunal—race discrimination—less favourable treatment—prima facie case of discrimination—burden of proof*

The respondent appealed against an employment tribunal's decision upholding a complaint of race discrimination.

The claimant, a British national of Indian origin, was a long-serving employee of the respondent. She had an extensive career in social work dating back to 1989, and was promoted in 2005 to the position of head of service within the respondent's adult social care and safeguarding division. Before the events in question, she had an unblemished record, with no history of disciplinary action.

The claimant alleged that she was subjected to less favourable treatment than her white colleagues, specifically by her line manager. Relations between the service area headed by the claimant, and another area—contact and response—led by a white British colleague, HM, were often strained. These conflicts and complaints about staff conduct eventually culminated in disciplinary proceedings against the claimant. HM swore inappropriately during a phone call that was overheard in the office and later sent a divisive email to staff. Despite staff objections and grievances against HM, the line manager opted to address these matters informally, rather than initiating disciplinary action. Conversely, allegations of workplace issues involving the claimant's service area led to the claimant facing a formal investigation.

In January 2021, the claimant's line manager decided to temporarily transfer the claimant from her role pending a disciplinary investigation. Allegations against her were vaguely worded and included accusations of failing to uphold management standards and creating a detrimental work environment. As the investigation dragged on,

---

[13] *Leicester City Council v Parmar* [2024] EAT 85.

the claimant repeatedly sought clarification as to the misconduct of which she was accused. Ultimately, the investigation concluded in May 2021 with a finding of no case to answer. The prolonged process caused significant stress for the claimant.

The employment tribunal noted stark contrasts in how disciplinary issues were handled. For instance, HM's conduct of swearing and sending inflammatory emails was dealt with informally, as was the conduct of another, JR, who allegedly denigrated a colleague. By contrast, the claimant faced a formal investigation for comparatively minor or unsubstantiated allegations. The tribunal also criticised the respondent for its failure to disclose key evidence, such as notes and recordings of investigation meetings, which undermined its credibility. It found that the respondent treated the claimant less favourably than white colleagues in similar circumstances. The tribunal concluded that race played a part in the decision to instigate disciplinary proceedings against the claimant, noting that her line manager had never initiated formal investigations against white employees of comparable seniority. The burden of proof having shifted, the respondent failed to provide a credible, non-discriminatory explanation for its actions. The tribunal criticised the disciplinary process as unnecessary and lacking substantive justification. It noted that mediation or informal measures, used for white employees, were not considered for the claimant. The respondent's failure to disclose relevant evidence further supported the inference of discrimination.

On appeal, the respondent argued that the employment tribunal had misapplied the law and failed to consider each allegation separately. It contended that the tribunal relied too heavily on disparities in treatment without sufficient evidence, that unfair treatment alone was insufficient to establish discrimination, and that the tribunal erred in shifting the burden of proof without clear evidence of discriminatory intent.

Dismissing the appeal, the EAT held that the employment tribunal appropriately considered evidence of disparate treatment and the wider context, which supported an inference of discrimination. While not every disparity alone proved discrimination, taken collectively, the evidence was compelling. The tribunal correctly shifted the burden of proof after establishing a *prima facie* case of discrimination. The respondent's explanations were deemed insufficient to rebut the presumption of discrimination. Finally, the EAT rejected the respondent's argument that the tribunal failed to analyse each allegation separately, noting that the tribunal's conclusions were consistent with the evidence as a whole.

COMPENSATION

[3.11] *CJ v PC*[14]—UK Employment Appeal Tribunal—appeal from employment tribunal—Equality Act 2010—discrimination and victimisation—ill-health retirement—mitigation of loss—pension and compensation offset—freelance

---

[14] *CJ v PC* [2024] EAT 182.

earnings—deduction—future loss compensation—professional negligence—injury to feelings—finality in litigation

The claimant appealed the employment tribunal's remedy judgment in her claims of discrimination arising from disability and victimisation. The case concerned the appropriate method for calculating compensation, including the interaction between ill-health retirement pensions and mitigation of loss under the Equality Act 2010.

The claimant was employed as a HR adviser by the respondent local authority. She suffered from multiple disabilities, including epilepsy, a benign brain tumour, anxiety, and functional neurological disorder. These conditions caused her to take extensive periods of sick leave and, ultimately, to retire on ill-health grounds at the age of 42. The claimant succeeded in her discrimination claims at the employment tribunal, which found that the respondent discriminated against her by reducing her pay to half-pay during two periods in 2019, and that the respondent victimised her by subjecting her to a 'trust and confidence' meeting in January 2020, leading to her ill-health retirement in November 2020.

The employment tribunal awarded compensation, including £20,793.81 for lost earnings, but offset her ill-health retirement pension and other earnings against her financial losses. It declined to award future loss compensation, finding that her pension and additional income exceeded her former salary.

Compensation was calculated by deducting the claimant's ill-health pension (£33,000 annually) and earnings from freelance work (such as TV and events work) from her lost salary. This approach was agreed upon during the remedy hearing, based on the claimant's schedule of loss. The tribunal applied a general duty to mitigate loss, setting off the claimant's additional earnings from freelance work against her lost earnings. It found no future financial loss, reasoning that the claimant's pension and other income would exceed her pre-retirement salary. Awards included £35,000 for injury to feelings, £15,256 for psychiatric injury, and £13,834.85 in interest.

On appeal, the claimant argued that the employment tribunal erred by offsetting her pension against her lost earnings. She pointed to the principle in *Parry v Cleaver*,[15] under which pensions should not reduce damages for loss of earnings as they constitute insurance-type payments. The claimant also contended that the tribunal wrongly required her to mitigate losses by engaging in freelance work during ill-health retirement. She argued that deductions of freelance earnings and pay in *lieu* of notice were improperly applied, as these were not causally linked to the victimisation.

While the EAT acknowledged that the employment tribunal erred in not applying the *Parry v Cleaver* principle, it refused to allow this argument to be raised on appeal. The claimant's schedule of loss had explicitly deducted the pension from her lost earnings, and introducing this new argument would necessitate a rehearing. The EAT emphasised the importance of finality in litigation and noted that the claimant could pursue her

---

[15] *Parry v Cleaver* [1970] UKHL 4.

representatives for professional negligence if she believed their failure to raise this point caused her loss.

The EAT rejected the claimant's argument that retirees are exempt from the duty to mitigate loss. Compensation for discrimination is based on tortious principles, which impose a general duty to mitigate losses. The employment tribunal reasonably found that the claimant had mitigated her losses by engaging in freelance work and was likely to continue doing so. It also upheld the tribunal's deductions of additional earnings, finding they were appropriately set off against her financial losses. The tribunal had correctly assessed causation, ensuring only those losses attributable to the unlawful conduct were compensated.

The EAT dismissed the appeal, affirming the employment tribunal's judgment. The claimant was awarded approximately £32,000 in financial compensation, alongside non-pecuniary awards totaling £64,090.85.

DISABILITY

[3.12] *DHL Supply Chain (Ireland) Ltd v McAndrew*[16]—*Labour Court—appeal from Workplace Relations Commission—Employment Equality Acts 1998 to 2021, s 83(1)—reasonable accommodation for disability—complaint of victimisation on the disability and race grounds*

The claimant appealed against the WRC's dismissal of his complaint under the Employment Equality Acts 1998 to 2021. He did not appear at the first-instance hearing, which he attributed to a miscommunication.

The claimant, who was Scottish, suffered from hypertension and depression. He was employed by the respondent as a HGV driver, working a pattern of day and night shifts. He submitted that the respondent failed to make reasonable accommodation for his hypertension by not removing him from night duties, contrary to medical advice from his GP. He also complained of harassment from a colleague, including racist remarks and comments about his mental health condition, which he alleged the respondent failed to investigate. He further alleged victimisation on the disability and race grounds, arising from the shift pattern he was required to work when the respondent became aware of his inability to work nights. The claimant submitted that his pay was reduced by 20% from the end of July 2021 as a consequence of his inability to work night shifts.

In July 2020, following a period of absence from work with severely swollen lymph nodes, the claimant informed the respondent that he had been advised by his GP to take time off from night duties for health reasons. He was, thereafter, rostered on day shifts only. In November 2020, the claimant presented a medical certificate to the respondent in which he was declared unfit to perform night duties from 15 November 2020

---

[16] *DHL Supply Chain (Ireland) Ltd v McAndrew* EDA2341.

until 15 January 2021 'due to cardiac investigations'. The claimant was examined by the respondent's occupational health advisor on 8 December 2020, and the report that issued afterwards informed the respondent, for the first time, that the claimant had been suffering from high blood pressure for two months by that time, but that no medication had been necessary to date. The report opined that the claimant remained fit to work, in a full-time capacity, but that he would be unfit for night work until the end of January 2021. Subsequently, the claimant remained rostered on day shifts only and, in a letter dated 28 June 2021, the respondent confirmed that it intended to remove the claimant's night shift premium. Separately, the claimant described certain encounters over several months with a named colleague, who, the claimant asserted, appeared to know about the outcome of a grievance complaint made by the claimant to management.

The Court found it 'abundantly clear' that the respondent was first informed of the claimant's hypertension in the report from its own occupational health advisor, dated 8 December 2020. The claimant had accepted in evidence that he did not work any night shifts between July 2020 and his resignation from his employment in October 2021. It followed that his complaint of failure to make reasonable accommodation for his disability 'simply did not stand up'.

The Court also found no evidence that the respondent was ever notified of the claimant's depression. The complaint of harassment by a colleague amounted to a 'mere series of assertions' and 'conjecture' about breaches of confidentiality by management to staff. These fell well short of the requirement of the claimant to establish facts from which an inference of discrimination could be made (thus shifting the burden of proof to the respondent). That aspect of the claim was therefore not well founded.

Finally, in relation to the victimisation complaint, the Court noted that the claimant's own evidence had been that, prior to the onset of his hypertension, he was regularly working a combination of day and night shifts, which included working unsociable hours. The respondent's decision to cease paying him the night shift premium (thereby reducing his pay by 20% from July 2021 onwards) was commensurate with the reduction in the claimant's contractual duties, in circumstances where there was 'no reasonable prospect of him resuming his full contractual duties in the foreseeable future'. Accordingly, the complaint of penalisation was not well founded.

It followed that the claimant's appeal failed in all respects.

[3.13] *Atlantic Troy Ltd v Conroy*[17]—*Labour Court—appeal from Workplace Relations Commission—Employment Equality Acts 1998 to 2021, s 83(1)—disability discrimination— failure to prove any actual or constructive knowledge of the disability*

The claimant appealed against the WRC's dismissal of his complaints of disability discrimination, failure to make reasonable accommodation, and discriminatory dismissal under the Employment Equality Acts 1998 to 2021.

---

[17] *Atlantic Troy Ltd v Conroy* EDA2426.

The claimant was employed by the respondent, working as a porter between March and May 2022, when his employment was terminated. The claimant stated that he had a registered disability but declined to share the nature of that disability with the Court.

The respondent denied any actual or constructive knowledge of the disability. The claimant accepted that at no point during his employment had he told the respondent that he had a disability, nor had he sought reasonable accommodation for that disability.

The Court was therefore not satisfied that the claimant had established facts to indicate that he had a disability at any material time. Nor did it accept that the respondent could have had direct or constructive knowledge indicating such a disability. The onus of proving the absence of discrimination had not shifted to the respondent, and so the appeal failed. The decision of the Adjudication Officer was upheld accordingly.

[3.14] *Kerry County Council v McGaley*[18]*—Labour Court—appeal from Workplace Relations Commission—Employment Equality Acts 1998 to 2021, s 83(1)—reasonable accommodation—facts from which the occurrence of an act of discrimination could be inferred*

The respondent appealed against a WRC decision, which upheld a complaint under the Employment Equality Act 1998.

The claimant contended that she suffered a disability from 2016 onwards and that the respondent failed to provide her with reasonable accommodation. The respondent disputed this and submitted that her complaint was out of time.

The claimant's case was that she was unable to work full days and that the respondent's solution—that she be afforded four half-days while being required to work one full day—was inadequate and discriminatory. She submitted that she had been the subject of a 'continuum' of discrimination on grounds of disability since 2016, and that the latest act of discrimination occurred on or after 14 December 2022, when she wrote to the chief executive of the respondent to set out a range of issues, including what she alleged was a continuing failure to afford her the working pattern she had suggested to her GP (and with which her GP had agreed). The latest act of discrimination was the respondent's failure to reply to that letter, which, the claimant argued, occurred within the cognisable period of the complaint.

The Labour Court found that the letter of 14 December 2022, in substance, amounted to a 'recounting' of a 'narrative' alleging failings of the respondent over a period of some six years. The content of the letter did not amount to any 'new event' occurring in the cognisable period for the complaint. It was common case that the letter was in fact responded to on 18 January 2023, and so the contention that the respondent had committed a discriminatory act was not a reasonable assertion. It followed that the claimant had not established facts from which a further act of discrimination could be inferred and the appeal therefore succeeded.

---

[18] *Kerry County Council v McGaley* EDA2427.

[3.15] *Irish Prison Service v Cunningham*[19]—*Labour Court—appeal from Workplace Relations Commission—Employment Equality Acts 1998 to 2021, s 83(1)—reasonable accommodation—whether the worker had a disability at the relevant time—difference in medical opinion—burden of proof*

The respondent appealed against a WRC decision which upheld a complaint under the Employment Equality Acts 1998 to 2021. The WRC found that the claimant was not afforded reasonable accommodation to enable his return to work post-surgery. He was awarded €40,000 in compensation.

The claimant was employed as a prison officer by the respondent from 2005. He was assigned to Cloverhill Prison, where he served as a prison officer for over six years. In 2011, he was transferred to the Midlands Prison. The claimant underwent back surgery in 2015 and sought to return to work, albeit on restricted duties. The respondent's CMO deemed him medically fit to return to 'non-prisoner contact duties' (ie, no control and restraint of prisoners).

The claimant submitted that, on a number of occasions, he sought to engage with the respondent about his return to work, but was advised that his return could not be facilitated and that the only options open to him were ill-health retirement or a transfer to administration support work. Otherwise, the claimant was advised that he was welcome to return to work for three months under the respondent's accommodation policy, after which, without improvement, he would have to go back on sick leave. The claimant submitted that he was treated differently on the basis of a disability or an imputed disability, in that he was denied a return to work, both at the relevant time and on a 'continuous basis'.

The respondent referred to a contemporaneous report from the claimant's treating neurosurgeon which sanctioned the claimant's 'unrestricted' return to work, albeit with 'common-sense advice' regarding heavy-lifting activities. The respondent submitted that had this information been available to it at the relevant time, the claimant could have been facilitated with a full return to work. It was submitted that the claimant, while initially reliant on that medical opinion in order to assert that he was fit to return to work, later resiled from it in order to rely on the CMO's report.

The Court noted that the medical professionals were in disagreement as to whether the claimant had a disability at the relevant time. Both doctors were called as witnesses by the respondent and the claimant did not give evidence in respect of his disability. Indeed, his own treating surgeon gave evidence that he did not have a disability. Given that the burden of proof lay with the claimant, the Court found on the balance of probabilities that the claimant had failed to establish that he had a disability at the relevant time.

The appeal was therefore upheld.

---

[19] *Irish Prison Service v Cunningham* EDA2434. For related cases see also: *Cunningham v Irish Prison Service* [2020] IEHC 282 in *Arthur Cox Employment Law Yearbook 2020* at [4.10] and *Irish Prison Service v Cunningham* [2021] IECA 19 in *Arthur Cox Employment Law Yearbook 2021* at [5.18].

[3.16]   R (Karmakar) v The Royal College of General Practitioners[20]—High Court of England and Wales—Garnham J—Equality Act 2010—judicial review—certiorari—blanket college policy of refusing to void previous unsuccessful exam attempts—rationality of policy—duty to make reasonable adjustments—indirect discrimination

The applicant applied to the High Court of England and Wales for an order of certiorari quashing a decision of the respondent refusing to grant her a further attempt at the respondent's written exams.

In order to qualify for membership of the respondent college, and thus practise as a GP, candidates were required to sit and pass three assessment exams. This case specifically challenged a policy adopted by the respondent that permitted only four attempts at each of those exams, with a fifth attempt permitted 'exceptionally and solely' on the basis of additional educational attainment. The respondent's policy was that candidates who, subsequent to an unsuccessful attempt, received a late diagnosis of a disability that would have entitled them to reasonable adjustments, could not have an additional attempt and could not have previous unsuccessful attempts voided.

The applicant was a trainee GP in Northampton. She attempted the written exams on three occasions prior to November 2020, failing on each attempt. In November 2020, the applicant's educational supervisor told her he felt that she was 'struggling organisationally on busy clinic days' and that he suspected she may have a neurodiverse condition, something the applicant had not previously considered. She was referred for a neurodiversity assessment, which concluded that the applicant did indeed have a 'neurodiverse cognitive profile, characterised by … relative weaknesses in working memory and processing speed'.

In light of that diagnosis, the applicant, with the support of her educational supervisor, applied for reasonable adjustments for her fourth attempt. She was granted 25% extra time. On this occasion, the applicant scored 66%, failing by 4.5%. The respondent's exam department refused the applicant's request to void her previous attempts, but she was granted an exceptional fifth attempt. On that occasion, she failed by 6.5%. Citing its policy, the respondent again refused to void her first three attempts. The applicant challenged that decision.

The Court was satisfied in the first instance that the matter was justiciable. The respondent's 'bald assertion' that it would 'take a view' on the issue 'in light of its understanding of its candidates, their training, the assessment and the requirements of the profession' amounted to nothing more than the college being guided by its 'instinctive feel', which was clearly not an academic judgement.

The Court was further satisfied that judicial review was an appropriate remedy. It did not agree with the respondent's submission that the more appropriate remedy lay with

---

[20]   *R (Karmakar and The British Medical Council) v The Royal College of General Practitioners* [2024] EWHC 2211 (Admin).

an employment tribunal. Here, there were no significant factual issues. The extent and nature of the applicant's disability were not in dispute and the timeline of events was readily ascertainable. The Court considered itself 'as well placed as the tribunal' to decide upon the issue of reasonable adjustments and indirect discrimination. More importantly, the remedy ultimately sought by the applicant—a quashing order—could not be obtained from an employment tribunal. The Court held that judicial review provided the most 'convenient, expeditious and effective means of fairly disposing of the issues raised'.

The Court rejected the applicant's submission that, in reaching its decision, the respondent had 'fettered its discretion' by refusing to consider allowing someone in the applicant's position a further attempt at the examination. The respondent's powers were not statutory in nature but derived from a Royal Charter, an act of royal prerogative. It was clear from the face of the relevant documents that the respondent was not limited by internal legal constraints from determining its own rules of membership. Its power was therefore not akin to a statutorily-derived power, nor could it be said to be a 'residual' common law power. Subject to equality legislation, the respondent had a wide discretion for deciding upon its criteria for admission to the college, provided those criteria were rational.

There was, however, nothing in the Royal Charter limiting the respondent's ability to void any previous attempts for a candidate retrospectively applying for reasonable adjustments, either for a 'progressive disability' or a 'new disability'. On the contrary, the instrument gave the respondent 'a wide power to determine the length and content of the training required and a power to deal exceptionally with exceptional cases'. In this instance, the respondent had simply chosen to frame its policy on refusing to offer an additional attempt as 'absolute' and had 'failed entirely to provide a coherent justification' for that policy. Nor could the Court see any justification that could be advanced for a policy allowing disabled candidates, who knew of their disability, to benefit from reasonable adjustments, while refusing to make equivalent allowance for disabled candidates who discovered their disability after failed attempts at the test. That difference in treatment was held to be irrational.

In the circumstances, the appropriate remedy was an order quashing the respondent's decision and quashing the rule as it related to the written exams. The applicant therefore succeeded.

The Court went on to find that the respondent had 'in general a consistent and committed approach to equality'. Since the provision, criterion or policy ('PCP') advanced, ie, that the respondent 'will never make a reasonable adjustment for a disabled trainee who received a late diagnosis' could not be applied to both disabled and non-disabled candidates, the reasonable adjustments and indirect discrimination challenges failed. The respondent, moreover, did not know and could not have known that the applicant was disabled when she initially sat the exams and suffered the detriment of which she complained. The respondent was therefore not in breach of its duty to make reasonable adjustments and was not guilty of indirect discrimination.

[3.17] A Multi Academy Trust v RR[21]—UK Upper Tribunal—appeal from First-Tier Tribunal (Health, Education and Social Care Chamber)—Equality Act 2010—discrimination arising from disability—failure to make a reasonable adjustment—statutory test for 'substantial disadvantage'—hypothetical comparator

The claimant brought claims under the Equality Act 2010 against the respondent proprietor of a special school (the 'school'). The First-Tier Tribunal dismissed all but one of the claims, upholding a complaint that the respondent had discriminated against the claimant's child (the 'pupil'), who was a year-10 pupil at the school, by failing to make a reasonable adjustment in its approach to the school year transition. The respondent appealed this finding.

The First-Tier Tribunal found that, while there had been 'some planning' during the summer term of 2021 for the pupil's transition to year 10 that September, there was no 'documented transition plan' for the pupil, and so there was 'a lack of certainty and clarity as to the support which [would] be in place during transition and how that support [would] be organised'. It considered that the lack of a documented transition plan placed 'disabled pupils generally' at a substantial disadvantage compared with 'non-disabled pupils'.

On appeal, the respondent submitted that the First-Tier Tribunal misapplied the statutory test for 'substantial disadvantage', in particular the requirement for the substantial disadvantage to be experienced by 'disabled pupils generally'. The respondent also submitted that the First-Tier Tribunal had not identified the comparator group by reference to which the pupil had experienced substantial disadvantage. On both points, it was argued, the decision had been inadequate in its reasoning.

The Upper Tribunal found it clear from the words 'disabled persons generally', contained in the legislation and read in the context of a school, that it is the impact of the provision, criterion or practice ('PCP') 'on a group of pupils rather than a particular pupil, which falls to be examined'. It found that the authorities state that the legislation is not referring to all disabled pupils but a category or sub-category of disabled pupils. The Upper Tribunal also held that the comparator group should be 'persons who are not disabled', as opposed to persons who are not 'disabled in the same way' (as was submitted by the claimant). It did not accept the respondent's submission that the comparator *must* be someone to whom the school could apply the PCP, and it was satisfied that a hypothetical comparator is permitted by the legislation. The appropriate comparator in this case was a non-disabled child about to move to a new school year with new demands.

The Upper Tribunal held that the First-Tier Tribunal fell into error by not clarifying in its reference to 'disabled pupils generally' whether it meant 'any and all disabled pupils or some sub-set of them and if so, what'. It also erred in making a comparison with 'non-disabled pupils' without explanation. The fact that the school may have had few or no non-disabled pupils permitted comparison with a hypothetical non-disabled

---

[21] *A Multi Academy Trust v RR* [2024] UKUT 9 (AAC).

pupil, though it was not clear that this was what the First-Tier Tribunal meant. Further, there was no evidence about the effect of a lack of a documented transition plan on a hypothetical non-disabled pupil.

The decision of the First-Tier Tribunal was, accordingly, set aside.

[3.18] *Bodis v Lindfield Christian Care Home Ltd*[22]—*UK Employment Appeal Tribunal—appeal from employment tribunal—Equality Act 2010, s 15—discrimination arising from disability—treatment because of something arising in consequence of a disability—employee's demeanour in an investigative meeting—failure to appeal against a finding that the treatment was justified—unfair dismissal*

The claimant appealed against an employment tribunal's dismissal of her complaints of disability discrimination and unfair dismissal. It found that the respondent reasonably concluded, after an investigation, that the claimant was guilty of gross misconduct and that dismissal fell within the band of reasonable responses.

The respondent company operated Compton House care home. The claimant started working for the respondent as a domestic assistant in 2008 and was appointed as an activities coordinator the following year. The respondent employed 60 to 70 members of staff, mostly part time.

From October 2018, a series of unusual incidents started to occur at Compton House with such frequency that they were logged by the respondent. These included acts of vandalism and involved, among other things, paper towels being stuck down the staff lavatories, oil from a reed diffuser being spilled over the manager's workstation, and photographs of the manager and deputy manager being repeatedly defaced. The employment tribunal held that the respondent was entitled to conclude that one such incident was an implied criticism of the manager. In January 2019, a maintenance technician discovered that the boiler had been turned off. The tribunal held that this could not have been accidental.

The respondent commenced an investigation and, in February 2019, held a meeting with staff to discuss the incidents. A few days later the claimant's photograph was found to have been defaced with a drawing of a cat. The employment tribunal found that the respondent concluded, on reasonable grounds, that it was likely that a staff member was involved because of the restricted locations, the defacing of staff photographs and the apparent criticism of management. The claimant conceded during the hearing that it was not unreasonable for the respondent to confine its enquiries to staff. Records showed that the claimant was the only member of staff on duty when all of the incidents occurred. The respondent concluded that the claimant's signature on time sheets was similar to handwriting on a defaced poster and a paper towel. The respondent decided that the claimant had a case to answer, though no motive could be identified.

---

[22] *Bodis v Lindfield Christian Care Home Ltd* [2024] EAT 65.

The claimant was disabled with anxiety and depression at all material times, though the investigating officer did not know this. The claimant was invited to an investigative meeting. Under the respondent's disciplinary procedure, she did not have the right to be accompanied or represented and she was not given advance notice of the matters to be discussed (the tribunal upheld complaints of failure to make reasonable adjustments in that regard). The claimant did not say during the interview that she was suffering from a mental health condition and the investigating officer's evidence was that, had he been so informed, he would not have used the fact that her answers 'were sometimes brief and not to the point' as a basis for proceeding to a disciplinary process. The respondent concluded that the claimant was the likely perpetrator of 'several, if not all, of the incidents'.

In March 2019, the claimant was suspended pending a disciplinary hearing. At the start of the disciplinary hearing, she was asked if she was fit to continue and she stated that she was. She was found guilty of gross misconduct and was summarily dismissed. The employment tribunal noted that no further similar incidents occurred following the claimant's dismissal.

On appeal, the claimant argued that the employment tribunal erred in law in failing to consider whether the dismissal was rendered unfair by the respondent's taking account of the manner in which the claimant responded to questions put to her in the investigative meeting. For its part, the tribunal did not accept that the investigating officer could reasonably rely on the claimant's demeanour in the interview in support of his recommendation for disciplinary proceedings. However, it held that 'that error did not infect the disciplinary hearing', as the claimant's demeanour was a 'trivial' factor and not 'the' effective cause of the decision to refer the claimant to a disciplinary hearing. The UK EAT was not in agreement. The claimant's demeanour was, on the tribunal's own findings of fact, 'a contributing factor in the decision, albeit a minor one', and therefore, her treatment was something arising in consequence of her disability.

Critically, the employment tribunal reasoned, in the alternative, that the treatment was a proportionate means of achieving a legitimate aim and was therefore 'justified'. There was no appeal against this finding; this was fatal to the complaint, and so that aspect of the appeal failed.

The claimant also argued that the employment tribunal erred in law in rejecting the complaint of unfair dismissal because it had not expressly taken account of the respondent's failure to notify the claimant of the matters to be discussed at the investigatory meeting and its refusal to allow the claimant to be accompanied. The EAT pointed out that these were never asserted as being the reasons why the dismissal was unfair, and so the employment tribunal could not properly be criticised for not referring to them specifically. In any event, the test for unfair dismissal is different to that of failure to make reasonable adjustments. There was no proper basis to conclude that the tribunal did not take account of all the relevant factors in concluding that the dismissal was fair.

The appeal was therefore dismissed.

[3.19] *Anderson v CAE Crewing Services Ltd*[23]—*UK Employment Appeal Tribunal—appeal from employment tribunal—Equality Act 2010, s 109—agency—vicarious liability—s 15—disability discrimination—time limits—s 123(3)—conduct extending over a period of time*

The claimant appealed against an employment tribunal's dismissal of her complaints of direct disability discrimination, discrimination because of something arising in consequence of disability, and harassment. She also challenged the finding of a separate tribunal that a number of alleged acts of disability discrimination were out of time.

The respondent supplied cabin crew to airlines. The claimant entered into a fixed-term contract with the respondent in January 2019. Members of cabin crew were required to hold 'fit to fly' certificates ('FTFCs') issued by aviation medical examiners ('AMEs') following a medical assessment. These AMEs were approved by the UK's Civil Aviation Authority. The employment tribunal held that AMEs were independent of the respondent and the authority.

The claimant described herself as having bipolar disorder and a heart condition. She notified the respondent of a recent cardiac episode and was referred to an AME. The claimant disclosed that she had bipolar disorder in a form she was required to complete as part of the assessment process. The AME, Dr Watts, did not consider that he was qualified to assess the claimant in relation to her bipolar condition and he advised her to attend an appointment with a psychiatrist for the purpose of obtaining a report. Dr Watts would not accept a report from the claimant's GP and the claimant asserted that he incorrectly categorised bipolar as a 'delusional' disorder.

The claimant arranged a consultation with an alternative AME, Dr Rowley, who issued her with an FTFC.

In view of the conflicting medical opinions, the respondent decided that the claimant should be referred to a third AME, Dr King. He too concluded that the claimant should be examined by a psychiatrist. The claimant asserted that Dr King made inappropriate comments about her bipolar condition.

The claimant accepted that Dr Watts and Dr King were not employees of the respondent. She argued that Dr Watts was an agent of the respondent 'given the extent to which the respondent was keen to justify and uphold his opinion'. Rather than being a 'one-off action' on Dr Watts' part, the claimant argued that the respondent 'constantly sought to uphold [Dr Watts'] opinion and failed to investigate his harassing and discriminatory acts', while refusing to allow the claimant to rely on Dr Rowley's certificate. Nothing was specifically said about Dr King.

The employment tribunal found that Dr Watts and Dr King were both independent contractors engaged to provide a specific service, namely assessments for FTFCs. Hence, there was no relationship akin to employment which would render the respondent vicariously liable for discriminatory acts on their part, and so there was no agency involved.

---

[23] *Anderson v CAE Crewing Services Ltd* [2024] EAT 78.

The UK EAT concluded that the employment tribunal adopted an incorrect analysis. Rather, the question was whether the AMEs 'were acting as agents of the respondent and, if so, whether they did so with the authority of the respondent, whether or not the acts complained of were done with the respondent's knowledge or approval'. The question of agency was not necessarily answered by determining whether the AMEs were independent contractors (though factors in support of that conclusion could be highly relevant to agency). While some of the features identified by the tribunal pointed against agency, it could not be said that there was only one possible answer in that regard. The tribunal had made 'only limited findings' about the contractual arrangements between the respondent and Dr Watts and Dr King; and there had been 'little consideration' of the statutory and regulatory context. This issue was therefore remitted for re-determination.

The employment tribunal went on to consider (should it be wrong about the agency issue) whether Dr Watts and Dr King were guilty of any disability discrimination for which the respondent could be liable. In doing so, it gave its reasoning in what appeared to be draft form without reaching a conclusion. The claimant argued that this was a serious procedural irregularity in that the tribunal's findings were incomplete. The EAT considered that aspect of the judgment unsafe and allowed the appeal, remitting the issue for re-determination to a new employment tribunal.

The time appeal related to a number of alleged acts of disability discrimination on the respondent's part, including: questioning the claimant's request for reasonable adjustments during an interview for promotion; a requirement to wear high heels; telling the claimant that she was incapable of doing her job for not being able to wear high heels and a blazer in a hot working environment; mocking and humiliating the claimant for weight gain; and the claimant's being subjected to online abuse by colleagues.

The claimant submitted that the tribunal erred in failing to consider whether there was merit in the claimant's argument that the respondent's attitude towards her had changed following its knowledge of her bipolar condition. This, she argued, could have resulted in a conclusion that there was 'conduct extending over a period'.

The EAT observed that the vast majority of the conduct was said to relate to the claimant's heart condition, and that the complaints were of different types of disability discrimination involving different people. There was nothing to suggest that they knew of the claimant's bipolar condition, and so the EAT did not consider that there was any error of law in the tribunal's analysis.

As regards the complaint of unfavourable treatment because of something arising in consequence of a disability, which was in time, the claimant submitted that the tribunal did not properly consider whether the acts of initiating disciplinary proceedings and issuing a final written warning amounted to detriments.

Although the tribunal properly concluded that the claimant was not forced to resign—on her own evidence that she considered resignation financially preferable to dismissal or redundancy—the EAT considered the tribunal's reasoning 'a little opaque' as far as the other complaints of detriment were concerned. Accordingly, those issues were remitted for re-determination by the same employment tribunal.

[3.20] Baldwin v Cleves School[24]—UK Employment Appeal Tribunal—appeal from employment tribunal—Equality Act 2010, ss 15 & 27—direct disability discrimination—discrimination arising from disability—victimisation—harassment—individual liability—employees and agents—perversity challenge

The claimant appealed against an employment tribunal's dismissal of all, bar one, of her complaints of discrimination arising from disability, as well as complaints of victimisation and harassment. The tribunal also upheld one complaint of direct disability discrimination.

The claimant was employed by the respondent school as a newly qualified teacher from September 2014 until her resignation in March 2015. At the time of accepting the role, she had not completed her postgraduate certificate in education ('PGCE'). The claimant was disabled at the relevant time and during the first term of her formal induction year she was absent on a number of occasions.

The proven act of direct disability discrimination arose from an email exchange in October 2014 between a teacher at the school, who was the claimant's designated 'mentor', and the claimant's PGCE tutor, in which the former enquired about the claimant's ill-health and asked that the conversation be kept between the two of them. The employment tribunal considered this exchange indicative of the respondent's suspicion that the claimant had significant health issues, which had not been disclosed to the school. One such email was seen by the claimant, who challenged her mentor for discussing her health 'behind her back', which she viewed as unprofessional conduct.

The proven act of discrimination arising from disability concerned an evaluation report completed by the school principal at the end of the claimant's first term. In the report, the claimant was commented upon as having 'not acted with integrity at all times'. The employment tribunal found no sufficient evidence to support this view and found that the matter had not been raised with the claimant beforehand. The claimant objected to the report at the time and eventually resigned.

In the first instance, the claimant challenged the employment tribunal's finding that her designated mentor and the school principal were not individually liable as employees or agents of the respondent for the proven acts of discrimination, and the consequent dismissal of those claims against them. The UK EAT's analysis concluded that the tribunal had no discretion to refuse to make such a finding of a contravention just because the employer was found liable, provided the conditions for liability of employees and agents under the relevant legislation were met.

Next, the claimant submitted that the employment tribunal failed to address an alleged protected act raised by the claimant, namely the conversation between the claimant and her mentor concerning the latter's handling of the email in October 2014. The EAT accepted that the tribunal had decided at the relevant time that the discussion did not amount to a protected act but had omitted to mention it in its written reasons.

---

[24] *Baldwin v Cleves School, Hodges and Miller* [2024] EAT 66.

Finally, the claimant challenged as perverse the dismissal of her complaint of harassment arising from an email from the school principal in November 2014. She argued that the only rational conclusion open to the employment tribunal in light of the email's contents was that it amounted to harassment. Having considered the email, the tribunal found that the school principal was expressing concern about the claimant's absences and the impact of the claimant's health on her induction year. The EAT rejected this ground of appeal. In the first instance, it was not persuaded that this matter was ever alleged as an act of harassment. The tribunal was therefore correct to state, to the extent it was considering the email at all, that it was not one of the allegations of harassment in the claim. In any event, the EAT did not consider this ground as coming close to meeting the threshold for a perversity challenge.

The first ground of appeal was therefore allowed and the remainder of the grounds were dismissed.

[3.21] *Cairns v The Royal Mail Group Ltd[25]—UK Employment Appeal Tribunal—appeal from employment tribunal—Equality Act 2010, ss 15 & 20—disability discrimination—failure to make reasonable adjustments—failure to engage with the claimant's substantive case*

The claimant appealed against an employment tribunal's dismissal of his complaints of discrimination arising from disability and failure to make reasonable adjustment.

The claimant was employed as a postman for the respondent, working in the Hendon office in London. He had worked in his role since 1990. In 2016, he twisted his knee in an accident and an operation the following year revealed osteoarthritis. The claimant was confined to working restricted indoor duties. There was no dispute that he was a disabled person and that he could no longer perform outdoor deliveries. At the relevant time he was carrying out duties in a supernumerary role.

In January 2018, an occupational health report advised that the claimant met the criteria for ill-health retirement. The matter was discussed in a meeting between the claimant's manager and union representative. They also discussed a planned merger between the Hendon office and the Mill Hill office, though it was not known at the time when the merger would in fact take place. The respondent enquired of delivery managers in the area whether they had suitable vacancies for someone with the claimant's restrictions, albeit without success. The respondent was also given to understand that the merger would reduce the number of indoor jobs.

In February 2018, the claimant was retired on ill-health grounds. He appealed. At the appeal hearing, which took place in May 2018, it was suggested by the claimant's union representative that the merger was only four weeks away and that it would be wrong not to keep the claimant's current job open until an indoor role could be found for him at the merged depot. The claimant's manager countered that no date was set for the merger at that stage and that there was no indoor role for the claimant until the merger went ahead.

---

[25] *Cairns v The Royal Mail Group Ltd* [2024] EAT 129.

The employment tribunal was satisfied that the dismissal was a proportionate means of achieving a legitimate aim, namely ensuring the efficient and economic operation of the delivery office. The claimant was in a role that had been created temporarily for him, preparing work for delivery postmen and other *ad hoc* duties, including some outdoor deliveries to cover sick leave. It concluded that there was no relevant alternative employment to offer the claimant as a reasonable adjustment, either before or after the merger.

The EAT found that the employment tribunal failed to engage with the substance of the claimant's case, ie: that the merger was expected, at the time of the appeal hearing, to take place in June 2018; that the claimant could have been given an indoor role at the merged depot; that it would have been reasonable not to require him to carry on performing *ad hoc* duties, such as covering the outdoor deliveries; and that it would have been reasonable to keep him in his supernumerary role until he could take up that alternative employment. The claimant's case was that this would have been a reasonable adjustment. Dismissal would have been neither proportionate nor justified had the claimant been redeployed into an actual role.

The employment tribunal also failed to address whether it would have been reasonable to keep the claimant on for a few weeks until the merger, then assign him an indoor role at the merged depot.

For those reasons, the appeal was upheld.

[3.22] *Bugden v The Royal Mail Group Ltd*[26]—*UK Employment Appeal Tribunal—appeal from employment tribunal—Equality Act 2010, s 20—Employment Rights Act 1996, Pt 10—reasonable adjustments—unfair dismissal—whether the employment tribunal ought to have considered redeployment as a reasonable adjustment*

The claimant appealed against an employment tribunal's dismissal of his complaints of unfair dismissal and breach of duty to make reasonable adjustments.

The claimant was employed as a postal worker by the respondent, Royal Mail, from 1994 to 2019. He was dismissed with notice as a result of regular and substantial periods of absence, totaling 297 days between 2015 and 2019. Some of these absences were related to long-term medical conditions, though there was no suggestion that any of the absences were for other than genuine reasons. The respondent conceded that the claimant was disabled by reason of anxiety and depression, visual migraines, musculoskeletal disorders and bladder issues. He was offered a reduction in his working hours, as recommended by an occupational therapist's report, but he refused it on financial grounds.

On appeal, the claimant submitted that the employment tribunal erred by failing to consider redeployment as a reasonable adjustment, and by failing to take into account the potential for redeployment as an alternative to dismissal when determining whether the dismissal was fair. The question of redeployment had not been raised by the claimant, who

---

[26] *Bugden v The Royal Mail Group Ltd* [2024] EAT 80.

was self-represented at the tribunal hearing. It was argued, however, that redeployment was an 'obvious' and indeed 'fundamental' point which the tribunal itself ought to have raised when addressing the reasonable adjustments claim and the unfair dismissal claim.

The EAT did not accept on the facts that redeployment was an immediately obvious reasonable adjustment to alleviate the alleged substantial disadvantage (the taking into account of disability-related absences) caused by application of the provision, criterion or practice ('PCP') of requiring the claimant to attend for work. From the material before the tribunal, absences resulting from the claimant's mental health condition—purportedly linked to a difficult relationship with a certain manager—were only 'one part of the overall picture', given the claimant's other disabilities and resulting absences. Moreover, it was 'far from clear' on the evidence what effect, if any, being managed by that individual had on the claimant's mental health, and the absences resulting therefrom, such that it was not incumbent on the tribunal to canvass, of its own accord, a potential adjustment only subsequently contended for on appeal. Redeployment was not suggested by the occupational health reports, nor was it raised by the claimant during the dismissal process. That ground therefore failed.

In relation to the unfair dismissal claim, however, the EAT accepted that, since the issue for determination by the employment tribunal was whether dismissal was within the range of reasonable responses, the question of redeployment should have been addressed by the tribunal, even if it had not been raised by the parties. The appeal was allowed on that ground and the matter was remitted to the same tribunal for further consideration.

[3.23] *Minis Childcare Ltd v Hilton-Webb*[27]—*UK Employment Appeal Tribunal—appeal from employment tribunal—indirect disability discrimination—provision, criterion or practice—justification—legitimate aim*

The respondent appealed against an employment tribunal's decision upholding a complaint of indirect disability discrimination. The tribunal also dismissed a complaint of failure to make reasonable adjustments, having found that the respondent lacked the requisite knowledge.

The claimant was a disabled person with Apert Syndrome, a condition resulting in impaired vision. At the relevant time, the claimant had not told the respondent that she had difficulty reading standard documents. Nevertheless, the employment tribunal held that she was the subject of indirect disability discrimination by the respondent providing documentation in 'small' font sizes. The respondent accepted that it applied the 'provision, criterion or practice' ('PCP') of providing documents with a 'small' font size (between 10 and 12 point), and that this placed the claimant at a substantial disadvantage in comparison with people who did not have Apert Syndrome.

The respondent relied on the legitimate aim of 'efficient management'. Nevertheless, the employment tribunal was categorical that there was 'simply no objective justification' and 'no legitimate aim' for the PCP.

---

[27] *Minis Childcare Ltd v Hilton-Webb* [2024] EAT 108.

The EAT was unclear what the employment tribunal meant when it said that there was 'no legitimate aim' for the PCP, in circumstances where the respondent had asserted its aim. The complaint was therefore remitted to the same employment tribunal for redetermination, and so the appeal succeeded.

[3.24]   Glasson v The Insolvency Service[28]—UK Employment Appeal Tribunal— appeal from employment tribunal—Equality Act 2010—discrimination arising from disability—failure to make reasonable adjustments—substantial disadvantage— actual or constructive knowledge of the disadvantage

The claimant worked for the respondent from 2005. It was known to the respondent that the claimant spoke with a stammer. In 2020, the claimant applied for a promotion to a position for which there were two vacancies. Prior to a remote interview, the claimant indicated on a pre-interview form that, due to his stammer, he may require more time to respond to questions put to him. The claimant performed well in the interview but scored one point below the second most successful candidate who, along with the highest scorer, was awarded the position.

The claimant brought claims under the Equality Act 2010 for failure to make reasonable adjustments and discrimination arising from disability. He relied on the fact that, during the interview, he went into what he described as 'restrictive mode', giving shorter answers in order to avoid stammering, but he did not mention this effect of his stammer on his pre-interview form. The employment tribunal accepted that the 'restrictive mode' was something that arose from the claimant's stammer, which had in fact impacted his performance in the interview. However, the reasonable adjustment complaints failed on a finding that the respondent did not have actual or constructive knowledge of the disadvantage relied upon, as he had not included it on his form.

The tribunal also dismissed his complaint of discrimination arising from disability, observing that the claimant was working to a high standard in his role; that he had participated in a remote interview previously without issue; and that he had raised no concerns in advance of this particular interview, in which he provided answers which were 'reasonably competent, albeit not as detailed as the panel expected'.

On appeal, the claimant argued that the tribunal failed to take a structured approach to the reasonable adjustment complaints. He submitted that it should have first identified the substantial disadvantage before making a finding on knowledge. By failing to do so, the tribunal had not made clear of what it considered the respondent did not have knowledge. Further, it was perverse to conclude that the respondent had no knowledge of the disadvantage, or that he had raised no concerns in advance of the interview, having found that the claimant referred to his stammer in the interview form and did not communicate some of his answers fully. In addition to knowledge, the tribunal failed to consider whether the respondent could not have reasonably been expected to know that the claimant was likely to be placed at the substantial disadvantage. To that end, it should have asked itself whether the respondent should have made further enquiries about how the claimant's

---

[28]   *Glasson v The Insolvency Service* [2024] EAT 5.

stammer affected him in interviews and, indeed, should have been prompted to do so by some of his answers. The tribunal should have considered the claimant's performance in the interview relative to the candidates with whom he was competing.

In relation to the complaint of discrimination arising from disability, the claimant argued that the tribunal erred by considering whether the use of remote interviewing was justified, whereas it should have considered whether the unfavourable treatment, ie, the lower scoring in the interview, was justified.

The UK EAT was satisfied that the tribunal had not erred in concluding that the respondent had neither actual nor constructive knowledge of the disadvantage relied upon. It had understood and correctly set out the provisions, criteria or practices ('PCPs') relied upon, and had identified the relevant substantial disadvantage before considering knowledge of the disadvantage. Nor had the tribunal erred by failing to consider whether the less detailed nature of the claimant's answers should have put the respondent on enquiry. It was undisputed that the claimant did not at the time specifically refer to the possibility that he might go into 'restrictive mode', or seek any adjustment in that regard when completing the pre-interview form. In reaching its conclusion on constructive knowledge, the tribunal had properly regarded the factual background, the claimant's general high performance at work, a previous remote interview, and his good performance overall in this particular interview.

Further, the tribunal had not erred in dismissing the complaint of discrimination arising from disability. It had been entitled to conclude that the defence of justification was made out and had rightly considered what needed to be justified.

The appeal was dismissed.

[3.25] *Godfrey v Natwest Market plc*[29]—*UK Employment Appeal Tribunal—appeal from employment tribunal—Equality Act 2010, ss 13 & 15—disability discrimination—knowledge of disability—whether the employment tribunal properly considered the question of knowledge by reference to relevant factual features of the disability, rather than its diagnosis*

The claimant appealed against an employment tribunal's dismissal of his complaints of disability discrimination, including direct discrimination and unfavourable treatment because of something arising in consequence of his disability. The tribunal found (unanimously) that the respondent did not have actual knowledge of the claimant's autism spectrum condition and (by a majority) that it did not have constructive knowledge of the disability.

The claimant had previously been employed by the respondent from September 2006 until his resignation in January 2011. He alleged that the respondent subsequently refused to appoint him, or consider him for appointment, to various vacancies arising between March 2017 and January 2019. The claimant was diagnosed with Asperger's

---

[29] *Godfrey v Natwest Market plc* [2024] EAT 81.

syndrome in 2018. That condition is lifelong, however, and the claimant would not have engaged in conversation and social interactions in the same way as others.

While only learning of the impact of his condition since his diagnosis, the claimant's case was that those who sat around him at work would nevertheless have been fully aware of his communication and social interaction difficulties on a daily basis. Indeed, he referred to repeated experiences of cruel language and comments from co-workers, though he did not elaborate upon them in evidence. For its part, the tribunal found no evidence that 'the claimant's behaviour in the workplace itself was such as to give rise to comment', apart from contributing to the perception that he was 'sensitive', 'irritating' and 'slightly arrogant'. The majority did not consider this sufficient to put the respondent on notice that the claimant had a disability. It found that there was no factor which would have caused the respondent, absent in-depth training, to conclude that the claimant's differences might be the result of mental impairment or an autistic spectrum disorder.

The UK EAT considered the employment tribunal to have correctly directed itself to the relevant legal test, thereafter carrying out a 'wide-ranging assessment' of the evidence as to how the claimant would have presented during his earlier period of employment with the respondent. However, the tribunal's reasoning did not expressly answer the question required of it, ie, whether the respondent had demonstrated that it was not put on notice that the claimant suffered a mental impairment. Rather, the majority's reasoning suggested that it reached its decision by imposing a requirement that the respondent had been put on notice that the claimant 'might have suffered from an autistic spectrum disorder'. Its reasoning was, thus, focused on the respondent having notice of a particular medical diagnosis, rather than the possible effects of a mental impairment generally.

To the extent that this decision was unsafe, however, it was not fatal. The majority of the employment tribunal was satisfied on the evidence that, had the respondent sought to make further enquiry, the claimant would have resisted any suggestion that he should undergo psychiatric assessment. This was a finding of fact which was open to the majority. The appeal was therefore dismissed.

[3.26] *Farley v Sunderland City Council*[30]*—UK Employment Appeal Tribunal—appeal from employment tribunal—disability discrimination—requisite knowledge—reasonable adjustment—whether the employee was disabled*

The claimant appealed against an employment tribunal's dismissal of his complaint of indirect disability discrimination.

The claimant was employed by the respondent as a technical officer. His duties included dealing with service requests from members of the public living in rented accommodation. The claimant had various periods of sickness absence, first in November 2019 for a back-related problem, then in January 2020 for a chest infection. Thereafter,

---

[30] *Farley v Sunderland City Council* [2024] EAT 115.

the claimant was on continuous sick leave up to the date of the employment tribunal hearing.

In March 2020, the claimant's team was informed that all staff were to avoid face-to-face contact, unless absolutely necessary. The claimant agreed to volunteer to work at the crematorium on assurances that his existing contractual terms would be met and his existing role would remain open for him. He did not raise any issues about his health or PPE at the time. The claimant worked at the crematorium for one day only. He advised the respondent that he would not be returning to the crematorium and agreed to return to the office.

In April 2020, the UK Government issued a 'stay at home' direction. The claimant informed the respondent that he was unwilling to come back to the office. He continued to work from home. The claimant declined a request to carry out lockdown-compliance inspections of businesses in the city, citing concerns for his own health and safety. A fitness note from his GP stated that the claimant was 'under investigation for respiratory symptoms' and that he was to avoid client visits and observe social distancing rules.

In June 2020, the claimant brought a formal grievance. This referred to 'work-related stress' but made no mention of the claimant working in the crematorium or in the office. In November 2020 (after the alleged discrimination), the claimant was suspected of having asthma. At the employment tribunal hearing, the claimant relied on the disability of 'physical impairment of the lungs'. The 'provision, criterion or practice' ('PCP') was instructing him to work at the office in April 2020. In a reasonable adjustment claim, he complained that he was put at a substantial disadvantage in comparison with a non-disabled person when he agreed to work at the crematorium.

The employment tribunal found that the claimant was not a disabled person for the purposes of equality legislation, and that the respondent did not have the requisite knowledge of the alleged disability in any event. There was no requirement that the claimant work in the crematorium or the office, and no substantial disadvantage when he was working there. The alleged PCPs were not applied.

On appeal, the claimant submitted that the employment tribunal erred in failing to consider the significance of an inhaler which the claimant had been prescribed and which he was using. This was not accepted by the EAT. Although the tribunal's judgment mentioned an occupational health report, referring to his being given an inhaler 'which he continued to use on an as-needed basis', there was no evidence that the claimant had in fact used an inhaler in April 2020. The tribunal also made clear findings that the claimant's 'flu-like symptoms' had been treated with antibiotics, and that he had made a full recovery. The claimant's witness statement made no reference to his using an inhaler at the material time.

The claimant's description of his disabilities as being asthma/bronchitis were not supported by contemporaneous medical evidence. There was no formal diagnosis, other than a note—post-dating the alleged discrimination—to say that he was suspected of having asthma. Medical records supported the employment tribunal's findings that the claimant's 'chest infection', 'flu-like illness' and 'chronic cough' were treated with antibiotics and that he had made a full recovery. The tribunal was therefore correct to find that the claimant was not disabled.

The EAT also rejected a perversity challenge. The employment tribunal was entitled to its factual finding that the respondent did not have the necessary knowledge of the claimant's disability.

Finally, the employment tribunal permissibly concluded that there was no PCP applied to the claimant requiring that he work in the crematorium or the office. The claimant's case was simply not made out on the facts. It followed that the remaining reasonable adjustment ground also failed.

The appeal was, accordingly, dismissed.

GENDER

[3.27] *IK v KfH Kuratorium für Dialyse und Nierentransplantation e.V*[31]*— European Court of Justice—reference for a preliminary ruling from Germany— social policy—Treaty on the Functioning of the European Union, art 157—equal treatment between men and women in matters of employment and occupation— Directive 2006/54/EC,*[32] *art 2(1)(b) & art 4—prohibition of indirect discrimination on grounds of sex—Directive 97/81/EC,*[33] *Framework Agreement on part-time work, clause 4—prohibition on treating part-time workers less favourably than comparable full-time workers—payment of additional pay only for overtime worked by full-time workers*

This reference for a preliminary ruling concerned the interpretation of art 157 TFEU, art 2(1)(b) and art 4(1) of Directive 2006/54/EC on the implementation of the principle of equal opportunities and equal treatment of men and women in matters of employment and occupation, and clause 4(1) and (2) of the Framework Agreement on part-time work (the 'Framework Agreement'). The requests were made in German proceedings between the applicants, two part-time care assistants, and the respondent employer. The dispute related to overtime pay.

The respondent provided out-patient dialysis services throughout Germany; of its 5,000 employees, more than half worked part time. The majority of those part-time workers were women. The two applicants, who were female part-time workers, were separately required to perform 40% and 80% of the normal working hours of full-time employees. Under German law, part-time workers were only entitled to overtime pay for hours worked in excess of 'normal' working hours, ie, those of full-time employees.

---

[31] *IK and CM v KfH Kuratorium für Dialyse und Nierentransplantation e.V* (Case C-184/22). See also **Ch 14**, Part-Time Work.
[32] Directive 2006/54/EC on the implementation of the principle of equal opportunities and equal treatment of men and women in matters of employment and occupation.
[33] Directive 97/81/EC concerning the Framework Agreement on part-time work concluded by UNICE, CEEP and the ETUC, aka Framework agreement on part-time work.

The applicants brought an action before the Labour Court in which they asserted they were entitled to additional pay for overtime worked in excess of their agreed working hours. They argued that the respondent was treating them less fairly than full-time workers on the ground that they worked part time. They also claimed indirect discrimination on grounds of sex insofar as the respondent employed mostly women part time. The action was dismissed.

The applicants appealed to the Higher Labour Court, which ordered the respondent to credit the additional overtime pay which was due to them, but refused their claim for damages in German equality legislation. The applicants appealed against that aspect of the decision to the Federal Labour Court (the referring Court), asserting entitlement to damages. The respondent also cross-appealed.

In order to decide on the issues, the referring Court needed to ascertain whether the applicants were discriminated against on grounds of sex or their status as part-time workers. In the circumstances, the referring Court decided to stay the proceedings and to refer a number of questions to the European Court of Justice ('ECJ') for a preliminary ruling.

The referring Court asked, in essence, whether clauses 4(1) and (2) of the Framework Agreement were to be interpreted as meaning that the national law at issue in the main proceedings brought about 'less favourable' treatment for part-time workers, and whether such treatment could be justified on 'objective grounds'; in this instance, the objective of deterring employers from requiring employees to work overtime in excess of their agreed working hours, and the objective of ensuring full-time workers were not treated less favourably than part-time workers.

The ECJ was first satisfied that overtime pay falls within the concept of 'employment conditions' referred to in clause 4(1). The referring Court alone would have jurisdiction to determine whether the services performed by the applicants were comparable to those performed by full-time employees of the respondent. The ECJ referred to settled caselaw, under which the remuneration of part-time workers must be equivalent to that of full-time workers, subject to the principle of *pro rata temporis*. On this basis, it appeared that part-time care assistants were treated 'less favourably' than full-time care assistants, though the referring Court would have to verify this. Such treatment would be prohibited by clause 4(1) of the Framework Agreement unless justified by objective grounds, again this was for the referring Court to determine. However, the ECJ found it was clear that, for part-time workers, the national provision did not achieve the objectives mentioned by the referring Court. The referring Court pointed out that the law in practice encouraged employers to impose overtime on part-time workers, since this incurred no extra expense and was cheaper than supplementing overtime for full-time workers. Parity of overtime pay between part-time and full-time workers would not give rise to less favourable treatment of the latter, since they would be equal under the principle of *pro rata temporis*.

It followed that the national law did cause less favourable treatment for part-time workers within the meaning of the Framework Agreement, and that this could not be justified on the grounds relied upon.

Next, the referring Court asked, in essence, whether art 157 TFEU and arts 2(1)(b) and 4(1) of Directive 2005/54 were to be interpreted as meaning that the national provision at issue was indirectly discriminatory on grounds of sex, and whether that too could be justified by the objective of deterring employers from requiring employees to work overtime in excess of their agreed working hours, and the objective of ensuring full-time workers were not treated less favourably than part-time workers.

The ECJ found that it would be a matter for the referring Court to appraise the facts giving rise to the complaint of indirect discrimination, including with reference to statistical evidence. The referring Court would be required to compare the respective proportions of men versus women in the workplace who were and were not affected by the legislation. It was not necessary that there be considerably more male than female full-time employees in order to establish indirect discrimination on grounds of sex—the referring Court would have to examine 'all relevant factors of a qualitative nature' in order to determine whether a disadvantage existed. If the referring Court concluded from the statistical data that the legislation disadvantaged a significantly higher proportion of women than men, such legislation would be contrary to art 2(1)(b) unless objectively justified by a legitimate aim.

The ECJ observed that the objectives mentioned by the referring Court did not provide such justification.

[3.28] *Munster Technological University Kerry v O'Sullivan*[34]—*Labour Court—appeal from Workplace Relations Commission—Employment Equality Acts 1998 to 2021, s 83(1)—discrimination on the ground of age or gender—recruitment—selection process—interview process—gender of applicants—relevance of comparators—prima facie case*

The claimant appealed against the WRC's dismissal of his complaint of discrimination on the ground of age or gender.

In May 2022, the claimant, at the time a 51-year-old male, was interviewed for the position of assistant lecturer in pharmacy at the respondent. He claimed that the respondent had a 'preferred type of employee', all female and predominantly under 30 years of age. He submitted that the respondent 'bypassed' its own recruitment process and gave the job to a female candidate who did not have the necessary qualifications or experience for the role but was of a similar age to the other assistant lecturers in pharmacy employed by the respondent.

The claimant submitted that the interview process itself was flawed and that he noticed an additional person on the four-person interview panel at the interview, which was conducted remotely. This person, whom the claimant claimed to be the owner of a local pharmacy, moved out of sight, without any explanation given for her presence. The claimant believed that she had an undue influence on the selection process.

---

[34] *Munster Technological University Kerry v O'Sullivan* EDA2438.

The claimant submitted that he would have been the only candidate for the role if the respondent's screening process was applied correctly.

The respondent rejected any suggestion of discrimination in its selection process and contended that the successful candidate had the requisite three years' post-graduate experience. She had scored higher than the claimant in all bar two of the respondent's selection criteria. While the claimant had experience as a retail pharmacist, he did not have any disclosed experience in lecturing or academia. Neither gender nor age were relevant factors for the selection of candidates. Rather, the candidate pool for pharmacy was predominantly female (83% of qualified applicants) and this had a bearing on the gender makeup of appointees. The application form used in the recruitment of staff did not request a candidate's age, meaning it was not possible to confirm the age of candidates. The respondent categorically rejected the claimant's assertion that there was an undeclared fifth person present at the interview.

The claimant cited as comparators the successful candidate in the May 2022 competition as well as the three other assistant lecturers in pharmacy employed by the respondent, all of whom were female and younger than the claimant. The Court noted that no evidence was offered by the claimant to show how the three assistant lecturers, employed prior to the May 2022 competition, were relevant to his complaint of direct discrimination. Nor was there any basis to the claimant's assertion that the respondent bypassed its selection policy when it screened the successful candidates for interview—the respondent was entitled to take account of the candidate's work experience gained 'during and in conjunction with' her post-graduate studies.

In all of the circumstances, the claimant had not established sufficient facts from which discrimination might be inferred. The Court was satisfied that the respondent had applied its selection criteria and that the claimant was outscored by the successful candidate at interview.

Having failed the establish a *prima facie* case, the claimant's appeal failed.

GENDER—AFFIRMATIVE ACTION

[3.29] *Moorilla Estate Pty v Lau*[35]—*Supreme Court of Tasmania—Marshall AJ—appeal from decision of Tasmanian Civil and Administrative Tribunal—Anti-Discrimination Act 1998 (Tas), s 16(e)—direct discrimination on the basis of gender—equal opportunity measure—s 26*

The appellant company was the owner of The Museum of Old and New Art ('MONA'), a significant tourist attraction in the state of Tasmania, Australia. In 2020, MONA opened an exhibition of artwork titled the 'Ladies Lounge', a private lounge enclosed by a curtain. Entry to the lounge was prohibited to anyone not identifying as female.

---

[35] *Moorilla Estate Pty Ltd v Lau* [2024] TASSC 49.

As a 'participatory installation', the process of being admitted or refused entry to the lounge was part of the concept.

In April 2023, the respondent having paid for admission to MONA was refused entry to the Ladies Lounge because he was male.

The respondent complained to Tasmania's Anti-Discrimination Commissioner, who referred the complaint to the Tasmanian Civil and Administrative Tribunal. The tribunal made a finding of direct discrimination contrary to State legislation. It ordered the appellant to 'cease refusing entry to the Ladies Lounge to persons who did not identify as ladies'. The appellant challenged that decision before the Supreme Court of Tasmania.

The issue before that Court was whether the Ladies Lounge was permitted under anti-discrimination law as an 'arrangement designed to promote equal opportunity to a group of people who are disadvantaged or have a special need because of their gender', in this instance women.

The appellant submitted that the Ladies Lounge provided an environment where female disadvantage is not present but male disadvantage is, thereby enabling female participation 'in a concept which is ordinarily foreign to them', ie, experiencing 'female advantage' and witnessing 'male disadvantage'. The concept was a response to the historical exclusion of women from spaces, designed to highlight past and current societal discrimination against women and provide a 'flipped universe' where the 'commonly prevailing power imbalance between the sexes in Australia' was reversed.

The Supreme Court found the tribunal to have erred in its characterisation of the appellant's evidence. In doing so, the tribunal asked itself the wrong question by considering whether the 'relevant disadvantage' for the purposes of statute was the disadvantage experienced by female artists in the context of having their work displayed. This was a mischaracterisation of the Ladies Lounge which, on the evidence, was never intended to display the work of female artists exclusively. Rather, the exhibition addressed 'current and ongoing gender disadvantage'. Equal opportunity was thus promoted by highlighting that disadvantage, ie, the lack of opportunity for women generally prevalent in society.

The appeal was therefore allowed. The tribunal's decision was quashed and the matter was remitted for fresh consideration.

GENDER—EQUAL PAY

[3.30]   *Teagasc v Reid*[36]—*Labour Court—appeal from Workplace Relations Commission—Employment Equality Acts 1998 to 2021, s 83(1)—complaint of gender discrimination—equal pay—comparator—whether claimant and comparator engaged in 'like work'—burden of proof*

---

[36]   *Teagasc v Reid* EDA2437.

The respondent appealed against a WRC decision upholding a complaint of gender discrimination. The Adjudication Officer ordered that the claimant be placed on the appropriate pay scale from 1 May 2017 with arrears. The claimant was also awarded compensation of €40,000 and the respondent ordered to apologise to her for its handling of the matter.

The claimant's case was that she had 45 years of experience with the respondent and was the only woman to have worked as a statistician in the organisation. She was appointed to that role in 2001, working in the food programme. The comparator, a man, was appointed to the role of senior research officer in the production programme in 2005, but took up the role in 2006 as he was required to complete a MSc in Statistics at UCD (he already had a PhD at the time). While the comparator was undertaking further education, the claimant took on both roles. For 15 years, the claimant and the comparator were the respondent's only statisticians. At the time the claimant lodged her complaint, she earned approximately €20,000 per annum less than the comparator. She contended that her role had evolved over the years, so that, in practice, she operated at senior research level. As such, she and the comparator were engaged in 'like work', as they had the same or similar duties; provided identical supporting roles; and had the same qualification.

There was a long-running industrial relations dispute between the parties, centred around the fact that the claimant was never placed on the higher research salary scale, despite her 20 years of experience as a statistician. This also meant she was often not credited as an author in peer-reviewed publications. As a 'last resort', in 2009, the claimant contended that she accepted an offer to be re-classified as a technological grade 2, but that offer was reneged upon by the respondent. The claimant was prevented from competing in promotion competitions in research grades because she was not designated a research officer. Meanwhile, there was no objective basis for the comparator to be 'promoted' into the role of senior research officer.

The respondent submitted that the claimant failed to identify an appropriate comparator: the claimant was a technician statistician on an experimental officer grade salary (a legacy grade), whereas the comparator was a senior research officer with a different level of responsibility and broader range of duties. The two were not engaged in 'like' work. The claimant had never applied for any research officer roles. Had she done so, and been successful, she would have been eligible to compete for the senior research officer role. In 2009, following agreement with her union, the claimant was to be assimilated into a new grade, technologist grade 2, which was the appropriate grade based on her competency skill set. That agreement stalled due to the government's moratorium on recruitment pay and promotion in the public sector. When the moratorium ended in 2015, the claimant did not agree to the implementation date proposed. That dispute was never resolved and explained why the claimant remained on a legacy pay grade.

In its findings, the Labour Court noted that the claimant had no direct knowledge of the comparator's 'day-to-day' role. Instead, she relied on other facts to assert that they engaged in 'like work' as statisticians, such as responding to the same job advert, having the same job title, the same qualifications, the same reporting line, and similar intranet profiles. While supportive, these were not sufficient to meet the burden of proof for 'like work' (though the Court noted 'a clear lack of transparency' around the comparator's appointment in 2006).

On the extensive evidence, the Court found that the comparator's role in research design and analysis was broader in remit than that of the claimant. The comparator also delivered more training and at a more advanced level, had more peer-reviewed publications to his name, and provided 'intellectual input' on large-scale research projects. The claimant and her comparator were not engaged in like work, and so the respondent was entitled to pay the claimant a different rate of pay. The respondent did not discriminate against the claimant in paying her less than her comparator. Accordingly, the appeal succeeded.

[3.31] *Barnard v Hampshire and Isle of Wight Fire and Rescue Authority*[37]—*UK Employment Appeal Tribunal—appeal from employment tribunal—equal pay—indirect discrimination—constructive dismissal—differential—justification*

The claimant was employed by the respondent authority for an initial spell in 2005, re-entering the respondent's employment in 2009 and resigning in June 2017. She brought claims for equal pay and constructive dismissal. The equal pay claim covered the period from the end of 2011 until her resignation. At issue were two sets of nationally-agreed terms: 'grey book terms', which applied to staff trained as operational firefighters; and 'green book terms', which applied to local government employees. The claimant, who was on green book terms throughout her employment, sought parity of terms with two comparators who were on grey book terms.

In the case of the first comparator, both he and the claimant were seconded into a new business support officer role from December 2011 to October 2012; the comparator was on grey book terms while the claimant remained on green book terms.

In October 2012, the claimant was promoted to the role of fire safety officer. From June 2014 until her resignation, she was an office manager. The second comparator for the 2012 to 2017 period had, himself, been a fire safety officer on grey book terms before being promoted to office manager at the same time as the claimant; again, he was on grey book terms while the claimant continued on green book terms.

The roles carried out by each comparator during the periods of comparison were not, themselves, firefighting roles; however, the tribunal accepted the respondent's evidence that all grey book firefighters were expected to maintain operational effectiveness, regardless of role. While pay and annual leave entitlements were more generous for grey book staff, they were required to remain physically fit and available for any operational role consistent with their ranking. Conversely, green book employees were not subject to such requirements, and, while in one sense the claimant was a 'trailblazer'—occupying roles of greater responsibility than would usually be the case of green book employees—she was aware of the very different terms and conditions pertaining to operational firefighters and made it clear that she had no wish to train in firefighting.

---

[37] *Barnard v Hampshire and Isle of Wight Fire and Rescue* [2024] EAT 12.

The tribunal found that there was indirect sex discrimination. However, it accepted that the respondent had the legitimate aims of providing an effective and efficient service, ensuring the safety of the public, and rewarding firefighters for being on-call and competent for operational deployment. It also accepted that keeping employees at the claimant's level on separate terms and conditions of service was a proportionate means of achieving those legitimate aims.

As regards the complaint of constructive dismissal, the tribunal found that the respondent was not in fundamental breach of the contract of employment—the equal pay claim having failed—nor was there a breach of implied duty of trust and confidence. Hence the complaints were dismissed.

On appeal, the UK EAT rejected the claimant's contention that the tribunal had erred by not making a finding as to whether the comparators in fact fully complied with their requirement to maintain operational competence during their secondments. One strand of the respondent's defence was that the comparators were required to maintain operational competence during their secondments, since they could be called upon to engage in some operational duties during that time, and it was important to maintain competencies associated with the roles to which they would eventually return. The tribunal had found this requirement to be genuine and it was entitled to find that the requirement was a contributory cause of the difference in pay.

The EAT also considered that the tribunal was fully entitled 'to accept as a common sense starting point ... that employees who had the particular more onerous responsibilities ... would expect that to be reflected in their level of remuneration'. Failure to maintain that differential risked damaging morale and undermining the aims that the tribunal had already found to be legitimate. The fact that the respondent had previously 'experimented' with moving a group of green book employees onto the same terms as grey book employees did not undermine the respondent's case. Hence, the claimant's challenge on justification failed.

As these issues disposed of the matter, the appeal was dismissed.

GENDER—HARASSMENT

[3.32] *Blanc de Provence Ltd v Ha[38]—UK Employment Appeal Tribunal—appeal from employment tribunal—Equality Act 2010—sex-related harassment—identifiable evidence linking the behaviour to the protected characteristic—procedural fairness—feature of the behaviour inherently linked to sexism or gender bias*

The respondent appealed against the decision of an employment tribunal which upholding a complaint of sex-related harassment.

The claimant was employed as a tailor by the respondent in January 2019. At the relevant time, she worked in the respondent's Marylebone store. Disciplinary proceedings

---

[38] *Blanc de Provence Ltd v Thu Lieu Ha* [2023] EAT 160.

were brought against the claimant for her 'abrupt attitude' towards her manager and for her having posted an inappropriate message on the respondent's internal messaging system. The claimant refused to participate in the process and, in March 2020, a hearing took place in her absence, resulting in the issue of a first written warning.

At the same time, the respondent was considering making redundancies amid Covid-19-related business disruptions. The claimant was visited at the store by the respondent's director and its head of operations (both males) for the purpose of informing her that she was being made redundant. The claimant's two female colleagues were instructed to leave the vicinity and the store was locked. The claimant objected to being left alone with the two male managers and requested a female companion, but her request was denied. The meeting took place in the store's basement, with the managers standing over her as she sat at her workstation.

These events formed the basis of the claimant's complaint of sex-related harassment. She alleged that the environment was intimidating and hostile. The employment tribunal upheld the complaint, primarily due to the power imbalance and gender dynamics involved. It noted, in particular, that the claimant was left alone as the only female in the store, despite her expressed discomfort; that the store was locked, and the meeting occurred in a confined setting; and that the respondent's approach created an intimidating and hostile environment, exacerbated by the denial of her request for a female companion. The tribunal concluded that the respondent's conduct was related to the claimant's sex, in that it was not likely to have treated a male employee in the same manner. It emphasised the need for professional and considerate handling of such meetings, suggesting alternative venues or the presence of a female witness as best practice.

On appeal, the respondent asserted that the employment tribunal's conclusion that the treatment was related to sex was not adequately supported by its factual findings. In addition, the managers were not given a fair opportunity to respond to the allegation that their actions were influenced by the claimant's sex. Finally, the tribunal was overly reliant on the claimant's perception of events without robust analysis of whether the conduct objectively related to her sex.

The EAT identified errors in the employment tribunal's reasoning. It clarified that conduct 'related to' sex must be supported by identifiable evidence linking the behaviour to the protected characteristic. The tribunal's reasoning that the respondent 'might not have treated a man the same way' lacked sufficient factual basis. As regards procedural fairness, the two managers were not explicitly questioned about whether their conduct was influenced by the claimant's sex. This was a critical procedural omission. The EAT emphasised that, while the respondent's actions were inappropriate, the managers' gender alone did not render the conduct sex-related harassment. It was for the tribunal to assess whether any feature of the behaviour was inherently linked to sexism or gender bias.

The appeal therefore succeeded and the matter was remitted to a differently constituted tribunal.

[3.33] British Bung Manufacturing Co Ltd v King[39]—UK Employment Appeal Tribunal—appeal from employment tribunal—Equality Act 2010, ss 26 & 30—harassment for reasons related to sex—ambit of protected characteristic of sex—Employment Rights Act 1996, ss 94 & 98—unfair dismissal—wrongful dismissal—perversity challenge

The respondent appealed against an employment tribunal's decision upholding complaints of harassment related to sex, and unfair and wrongful dismissal.

The claimant was employed by the respondent as an electrician from September 1997 to May 2021, when he was summarily dismissed for gross misconduct. The respondent was a small family business with around 30 employees, most (if not all) of whom were male. 'Industrial language' was found to have been commonplace on the shop floor. In July 2019, an altercation took place between the claimant and a co-worker, who called the claimant a 'bald c**t' and threatened him with physical violence. The claimant's evidence was that he decided to draw a line under the matter and move on, having been told that his aggressor was a single parent who risked losing his job. A second altercation took place in March 2021, in which the same co-worker was found to have threatened the claimant. In a distressed state, the claimant told the respondent that he had had enough of his co-worker's behaviour and that, if they did not fire him, 'that would be it'. The claimant walked out of the workplace and a period of furlough followed, during which time he received statutory sick pay from the respondent.

In April 2021, the respondent invited the claimant to attend an investigation meeting. With the help of his son, a police officer, the claimant prepared a written statement of events in advance of the meeting. This statement was written on a template 'witness statement' which was headed 'West Yorkshire Police' and endorsed with a statement of truth signed by the claimant. The employment tribunal found that this document induced the respondent to believe that the March incident had been reported to the police. The claimant was suspended on full pay. The respondent alerted West Yorkshire Police to the existence of the document, and the involvement of the claimant's son in preparing it, and sought assurances that the incident was not within their purview. The respondent also demanded a written explanation from the claimant as to how the statement came to be made. The claimant was invited to attend the disciplinary hearing that would lead to his summary dismissal.

The disciplinary hearing concluded that the witness statement was presented 'as a form of threat or harassment' designed to 'purposely mislead' the respondent that an employment issue had been reported to police as a crime. The respondent did not believe this to have been an honest mistake. In light of the claimant's 'failure to apologise' and 'insistence that [he had] done nothing wrong', the respondent informed him that it was now impossible to have trust and confidence in him as an employee.

---

[39] *British Bung Manufacturing Co Ltd v King and Finn* [2023] EAT 165.

Although the claimant was summarily dismissed two working days later, the employment tribunal found that he was led to believe that no decision would be taken by the respondent pending the outcome of their enquiries with the police. This, it concluded, was an act of bad faith and breached the requirements of natural justice. The complaint of unfair dismissal succeeded on that basis, although compensation was reduced to take account of the claimant's 'foolish' and 'bloody-minded' conduct. As blameworthy as that conduct was, however, it was not intended to undermine the relationship between the claimant and the respondent, but rather to preserve it. The claimant was not therefore in repudiatory breach of contract, and so the wrongful dismissal complaint also succeeded.

The employment tribunal took the view that the 'bald c**t' remark amounted to unwanted conduct, which was uttered with the purpose of violating the claimant's dignity and creating an intimidating, hostile environment. In its judgment, there was a connection between 'bald' and the protected characteristic of sex ('as all three members of the tribunal will vouchsafe, baldness is much more prevalent in men than women'). Thus, the complaint of harassment related to sex was upheld.

On appeal, the EAT rejected the argument that the tribunal erred in law or reached a perverse conclusion in finding that use of the term 'bald c**t' had been related to the protected characteristic of sex. The respondent's submission that, in order for unwanted conduct to relate to sex, it must relate to a matter 'which is *both* inherent in the gender in question *and* in no-one of the opposite gender' (emphasis added) was not rooted in authority and ran contrary to the purpose of the equality legislation. It was open to the tribunal to find that it was 'much more likely that a person on the receiving end of a remark such as that ... would be male'. The tribunal's findings of unfair and wrongful dismissal showed no error of law or perversity.

The appeal was, accordingly, dismissed.

GENDER RECOGNITION

[3.34]   *R (Castellucci) v Gender Recognition Panel*[40]—*High Court of England and Wales—Laing LJ & Williams J—Gender Recognition Act 2004—European Convention on Human Rights, art 14—recognition of a person's gender as non-binary in the UK where that person has been recognised as such under the law of another State or territory—statutory interpretation*

The claimant was born male and was recognised in the State of California as non-binary. They applied to the respondent panel for similar recognition in the UK in the form of a Gender Recognition Certificate ('GRC'). It was not the respondent's practice to issue such a GRC and, as such, the claimant was not issued one. The claimant brought the following three sets of proceedings challenging the respondent's position: by way of a statutory appeal, the claimant sought an order granting them a GRC recording their gender as non-binary; by way of judicial review they sought an order quashing

---

[40]   *R (Castellucci) v Gender Recognition Panel* [2024] EWHC 54 (Admin).

the respondent's decision and/or an order granting them their preferred GRC; and they also sought declaratory relief and damages under the Human Rights Act 1998.

The claimant argued, first, that the respondent had misinterpreted the Gender Recognition Act 2004 (the '2004 Act'), which, properly understood, obliged the respondent to issue the claimant a GRC describing their gender as non-binary because their change of gender from male to non-binary was recognised in the State of California. They argued in the alternative that the 2004 Act was discriminatory contrary to art 14 of the European Convention on Human Rights ('ECHR') (read with art 8) on the ground of their status as a non-binary person, and that the 2004 Act must be read in accordance with the Human Rights Act 1998 so as to oblige the respondent to issue the GRC. Alternatively, they sought a declaration of incompatibility of the 2004 Act with art 14.

This matter concerned the appeal and the application for leave to apply for judicial review, which were heard together. Ultimately, the two issues pursued by the claimant were whether 'on an ordinary construction' the 2004 Act permits 'the recognition of a foreign-acquired gender that could not otherwise be obtained under English law', and an allegation of a breach of the claimant's art 14 rights.

The claimant conceded that, for the purposes of a domestic application under the 2004 Act, 'gender' is binary, so that an application can only be made by a person of the female or male gender, and neither could apply to be registered as non-binary. They also accepted that the UK is not subject to a positive obligation under art 8 ECHR to permit such a change to the statutory scheme. It was argued that the position is different in the case of an applicant who has 'changed gender' under the law of a country or territory outside the UK. Here, the claimant submitted, the reference to 'either gender' in the 2004 Act is not restrictive, but must refer to the applicant's gender before the change under foreign law, and so 'gender' need not be either male or female but the 'gender' as changed under the law of the approved country or territory, whatever that may be. Were the claimant's submissions in that regard to be rejected, the result would be discrimination contrary to art 14 between an individual who has changed to the 'opposite' gender (ie, male or female) under Californian law, and one in the claimant's position who has changed their gender to non-binary.

The High Court of England and Wales did not consider that the construction of the 2004 Act, as advanced by the claimant, was one for which Parliament had made 'express and advertent provision'. Rather, it was doubtful that Parliament had this case in mind when the 2004 Act was enacted, and the claimant's submission, if correct, had latent consequences flowing from the statutory language. The 2004 Act was enacted to correct breaches of the ECHR concerning the non-recognition of a change of gender by a post-operative transsexual,[41] and the inability of a post-operative transsexual to marry a person of the same sex as the applicant's natal sex.[42] The purpose of the 2004 Act was 'plainly to right those wrongs', which arose against the background of a 'binary

---

[41] *Goodwin v UK* App No 28957/95.
[42] *Bellinger v Bellinger* [2003] UKHL 21.

concept of biological sex'. With this in mind, the Court did not consider it likely that, when Parliament enacted the 2004 Act, it did so intending to do anything 'other than to deal with the legal status of people who had gender dysphoria', by creating a procedure by which they could change their legal status.

The Court rejected the claimant's submission that 'gender' could mean different things in the domestic and foreign provisions of the 2004 Act. The fact that 'gender' is not defined in the 2004 Act was not of assistance to the claimant because 'it went without saying' that, when the 2004 Act was enacted, 'gender' referred to a binary concept and this was supported by the various provisions of the 2004 Act. Contextual and linguistic factors pointed to 'gender' having the same meaning throughout the 2004 Act and, as such, the claimant's argument was rejected. The Court nevertheless accepted that the ground was arguable and permitted the claimant to apply for judicial review of the respondent's decision not to issue the claimant with their preferred GRC.

Turning to the art 14 ground, although the Court considered the complaint to fall within the ambit of art 8—and accepted that there was a difference in treatment which could only be justified by 'very weighty reasons'—it did not accept that it was possible to separate a foreign case from the wider issues: 'A system which held that it is justified not to recognise non-binary gender in a domestic case, but that it is not justified to fail to recognise a non-binary gender under foreign law would be incoherent'. Thus, the public interest for legislative and administrative coherence, and the administrative costs of change, were relevant factors to be balanced against the claimant's interest in having their gender recognised in the UK, as well as the psychological effect of non-recognition. Also of relevance was the wide margin of appreciation enjoyed by Member States owing to the sensitivity of the issue and a lack of international consensus. This was 'pre-eminently' a question for Parliament to consider and the difference in treatment was held to be justified. The art 14 ground was therefore dismissed.

PREGNANCY AND MATERNITY LEAVE

[3.35]   *Karpicz v Graham O'Sullivan Restaurants Ltd*[43]—*High Court—Gearty J—appeal from Circuit Court—Employment Equality Acts 1998 to 2021, s 77(3)—Directive 92/85/EEC,*[44] *art 10(2)—discrimination—worker dismissed during pregnancy—substantial grounds for dismissal*

The defendant appealed against an award made by the Circuit Court under the Employment Equality Acts 1998–2021. The plaintiff was found to have been dismissed while pregnant. The fact of dismissal was in dispute.

The plaintiff received her P45. This, she argued, was sufficient indication that she had been dismissed. The defendant submitted that the P45 was issued in error and that the

---

[43] *Karpicz v Graham O'Sullivan Restaurants Ltd* [2024] IEHC 432.
[44] Directive 92/85/EEC on the introduction of measures to encourage improvements in the safety and health at work of pregnant workers and workers who have recently given birth or are breastfeeding.

plaintiff should have queried the matter, either with her manager or with the owner of the business.

The plaintiff was hired as a barista in one of the defendant's four restaurants in November 2017, and was subsequently promoted to general assistant. Of the 45 employees in the defendant's restaurants, between 38 and 40 were women. In July 2018, the plaintiff notified the defendant that she was six weeks pregnant. At the same time, five other employees of the defendant were either pregnant or on maternity leave. The general manager of the defendant's branch, on learning of the plaintiff's pregnancy, congratulated her and commented, 'there must be something in the water', in reference to the other pregnant employees. The plaintiff did not perceive the comment to be friendly and the Court observed that the defendant 'did not welcome the news generally'.

In November 2018, the plaintiff received her P45 at her workplace. She had returned to work following a period of sick leave due to the effects of her pregnancy. The dismissal followed a meeting between the plaintiff and the general manager. The defendant maintained that, in the meeting, he reassured the plaintiff that her job was safe. The plaintiff claimed that she was encouraged to apply for social welfare benefits. The Court was not convinced by the defendant's explanation—that the general manager believed that the plaintiff requested her P45, and, thinking that she resigned, he did not attempt to correct the misunderstanding.

Having argued that the P45 issued in error, the defendant did not explain how it came to be filed with the Revenue. After her dismissal, the plaintiff noticed her own job being advertised, full time. The Court found that the defendant could not satisfactorily explain this.

In all of the circumstances, the sending of the P45 constituted a dismissal. In the Court's view, to expect a woman, 'who is aware that five members of an overwhelmingly female staff are pregnant or on maternity leave, and is herself physically ill due to her pregnancy, to negotiate with the owner of the business when she unceremoniously receives a P45' was 'unrealistic'. If the P45 did issue in error, it was difficult to understand how the error was not immediately corrected. In context, the effect of delivering the P45 to the plaintiff was to dismiss her.

The plaintiff was entitled to damages for discrimination, as well as her costs. The appeal failed.

[3.36] *Ballerino v The Racecourse Association Ltd*[45]*—UK Employment Appeal Tribunal—appeal from employment tribunal—Equality Act 2010, ss 13 and 18—Employment Rights Act 1996—discrimination—direct discrimination because of sex, maternity and pregnancy—unfair dismissal—automatic unfair dismissal—maternity and parental leave*

The claimant appealed against an employment tribunal's dismissal of her complaints of direct sex discrimination, pregnancy and maternity discrimination, and in the

---

[45] *Ballerino v The Racecourse Association Ltd* [2024] EAT 98.

alternative, of automatic unfair dismissal in the context of what she claimed was a sham redundancy.

In August 2018, the claimant commenced part-time employment as a financial accountant with the respondent. This was a relatively new role and there was a degree of uncertainty as to how many hours it actually required. The claimant was pregnant at the time and she started maternity leave in December 2018.

During the claimant's maternity leave, the respondent created the full-time role of 'business and financial analyst'. That position was advertised externally and five candidates were shortlisted. While initially it was not suggested that the new role would include the claimant's workload, between the first and second rounds of interviews it was expanded to do just that. Two candidates were invited to second-round interviews for the expanded position. Meanwhile, the claimant was told that her role was at risk of redundancy as a result of the decision to incorporate her role into the new role. The claimant was invited to apply for the new role, but at the same time she was given a draft settlement agreement and instructed that if she wished to accept it, she should do so within five days. The claimant was highly critical of the respondent's approach and, following extended communication between the parties, she was notified in July 2019 that she was being dismissed with immediate effect.

The employment tribunal found that, although the new role encompassed the claimant's previous role, it was 'almost completely different' in every other respect, being mainly concerned with business analysis and being full time and office based (the claimant worked mainly from home). Hence, the respondent was under no obligation to offer it as a 'suitable alternative vacancy'; it was an entirely different role on terms that were less favourable to the claimant. As regards the discrimination complaints, the tribunal found that while the burden of proof had shifted to the respondent, it did not accept that the redundancy had been devised to terminate the claimant's employment while she was on maternity leave. It therefore accepted that the respondent's business reorganisation was genuine.

As regards the unfair dismissal complaint, it was common case in the appeal that the employment tribunal was statutorily required to determine whether or not there was a redundancy. While in some cases, it might be permissible to go straight to the question of whether there was a suitable alternative vacancy, the EAT took the view that the facts of this case did not lead inexorably to a conclusion that there was a redundancy at first glance; the claimant's role was itself relatively new, and there was uncertainty as to the number of hours it required. The fact that there had been a reorganisation, with the addition of a new role, did not necessarily mean there was a redundancy. Even a finding that there was a redundancy might have had a bearing on the question of the suitability of the role for the claimant. Either way, the tribunal erred in failing to address the question.

As to the discrimination complaints, both parties accepted that once the burden of proof had shifted to the respondent, the employment tribunal was then bound to consider whether it should accept the respondent's explanation for the claimant's dismissal as being by reason of redundancy. A striking feature of the case had been the respondent's reliance on there having been a genuine redundancy situation, and the claimant's contention that it was a sham. In light of the tribunal's failure to engage with that issue in the first place, its decision in relation to the discrimination complaints was rendered unsafe.

Therefore, the appeal was allowed.

INDUCING A DISCRIMINATORY ACT

[3.37] *Bailey v Stonewall Equality Ltd*[46]—*UK Employment Appeal Tribunal—appeal from employment tribunal—Equality Act 2010, s 111—inducing a discriminatory act—protected belief—detriment—liability of agent*

The claimant appealed against an employment tribunal's dismissal of her claim of inducing a discriminatory act. The claimant was a barrister and a tenant of Garden Court Chambers. Her claim of direct discrimination against the chambers succeeded. An aspect of her case, however, was that an employee of the respondent charity, Stonewall, induced one of the chambers' discriminatory acts against the claimant.

The claimant became a tenant of Garden Court Chambers (the 'chambers') in November 2004. The chambers had a particular focus on fighting inequality and protecting human rights. The claimant, who was a lesbian, believed that a woman is defined by her biological sex, and not her gender identity. The belief that women are defined by sex, and the belief that gender is a matter of self-identity are both protected under UK equality legislation.

In November 2018, the chambers signed up to the respondent's Diversity Champions scheme, whereby in exchange for an annual fee, they would receive: a dedicated account manager to advise on best practice and to meet with stakeholders; free places at seminars; use of the Diversity Champions logo; access to research publications; and discounted rates for conferences. The barrister tenants were notified of this development by email. In a 'reply all', the claimant objected to the chambers' collaboration with the respondent. She took issue with the respondent's stance on amending the Gender Recognition Act 2004 to include a self-identification process. A number of tenants made adverse comments about the claimant's email.

In late 2019, one tenant made a complaint to the heads of chambers about tweets posted by the claimant that were critical of the chambers' trans-rights events. The tweets drew negative comments to the chambers' website. In October 2019, the claimant posted a tweet announcing the launch of the LGB Alliance (a breakaway association from the respondent founded on gender critical principles). The employment tribunal found that that tweet 'generated a strong reaction on Twitter, some of which was specifically directed at [the chambers]'.

Subsequently, the chambers hosted a meeting of the Trans Organisational Network, which was attended by representatives of various groups, including the respondent.

---

[46] *Bailey v Stonewall Equality Ltd, Garden Court Chambers Ltd, Menon KC and Harrison KC* [2024] EAT 19.

Those in attendance were encouraged to write to the chambers to express their concern about the claimant's tweets.

In light of complaints from inside and outside chambers, the claimant was informed that there would be an investigation in accordance with the chambers' complaints procedure. In a tweet (the 'response tweet'), the chambers announced that they would be investigating concerns raised about the claimant's comments, which, they stated, were expressed in a 'personal capacity' and did not represent their adopted position. The employment tribunal identified the response tweet as a detriment inflicted on the claimant due to her holding protected beliefs.

A draft report found that the claimant's comments were 'deliberately provocative' but not transphobic. It concluded that there was 'nothing to investigate'. Importantly, while this report was being drafted, an employee of the respondent sent his own complaint to the chambers (the 'Stonewall complaint'). That complaint had links to tweets posted by the claimant. It stated that the claimant's actions 'put us in a difficult position with yourselves'. The chambers, while initially minded to investigate the Stonewall complaint separately, decided to deal with all the complaints in a single report, so as to avoid more than one 'media storm'. This report, in draft form, stated that there was a 'risk' of a breach of Bar Standards Board ('BSB') guidelines. The final report, however, stated that the tweets were 'likely' to breach BSB guidelines. In December 2019, the claimant was informed that the heads of chambers accepted the report. The claimant was asked to delete certain tweets. The employment tribunal found that the outcome of the Stonewall complaint was the other detriment inflicted on the claimant; both of which amounted to discrimination against the claimant.

Crucially, the employment tribunal found that the Stonewall complaint did not influence the chambers' investigation process in any way, absolving the respondent. The Stonewall complaint was just that—a form of protest by someone in an advocacy role—and the respondent could not be blamed for deficiencies in the chambers' investigation. The complaint 'contained nothing in the nature of an instruction to ... discriminate against [the claimant] because of her protected views, and nothing in the nature of an inducement, actual or attempted'. The EAT was in agreement.

The EAT did not accept that the employment tribunal erred by wrongly focusing on the Stonewall employee's subjective intentions. While it was clear that the employee was significantly influenced by the claimant's protected beliefs, it was not wrong of the tribunal to ask what that employee intended to achieve, since his subjective intentions were relevant to the fairness or reasonableness of finding the respondent liable. In any event, it was unlikely that the chambers' response to the complaint was influenced by the mere fact that the claimant held protected beliefs; the investigators were barristers specialising in equality law and could be expected to weigh the complaint impartially. The tribunal was entitled to find the respondent was not reasonably liable for causing the basic contraventions. Nor had it induced the chambers, or attempted to do so. The chambers alone were responsible for determining the complaint in a discriminatory way.

The appeal was, accordingly, dismissed.

RACE

[3.38]   Onyemekeihia v Minister for Justice and Equality[47]**—High Court—O'Regan J—appeal from Labour Court—Employment Equality Acts 1998 to 2021, s 14A—rationality of decision—contradictory findings—failure to give reasons**

The appellant sought to set aside a decision of the Labour Court dismissing his appeal.

While working as a prison officer in Mountjoy Prison, the appellant alleged that he was subjected to constant racial abuse by some prisoners over the years. He argued that the racial abuse was within the meaning of the Employment Equality Acts 1998 to 2021 (the 'Acts') and that the Irish Prison Service had not taken sufficient steps to discourage the behaviour. The respondent Minister argued that the prison environment is unique, but that its rules incorporate sanctions for prisoners who misconduct themselves and that this was sufficient to satisfy the reasonably practicable defence requirements in the Acts.

The appellant challenged as irrational the Labour Court's finding that the respondent 'has consistently taken a robust approach in dealing with racist behaviour' and that its sanctions regime was 'meaningful and proportionate', while nevertheless finding 'merit' in the argument that the Prison Service had not given racism and racial harassment the level of attention they require and directing the Prison Service to conduct a 'thorough review' of its anti-racism strategy and policies.

The High Court remarked that it was difficult to reconcile these apparent contradictions, all the more so given that the Labour Court had not explained why it considered them to be harmonious. The Court did not accept the respondent's argument that the reference to racism not being given the level of attention required was *obiter*, and it supported the appellant's submission that the decision was irrational and that the Labour Court had not fulfilled its obligation to provide reasons. The High Court found that the Labour Court had, moreover, 'ignored completely' submissions relating to indirect discrimination, which, while not a 'key issue' should have been referenced in its decision.

Thus, the High Court found, the appellant was entitled to the reliefs sought.

[3.39]   HSE v Okafor[48]**—Labour Court—appeal from Workplace Relations Commission—Employment Equality Acts 1998 to 2021, s 83(1)—race discrimination—burden of proof**

The claimant appealed against a WRC decision that his complaints of gender and race discrimination were not well founded; only the complaint of race discrimination proceeded on appeal.

The claimant, who was of Nigerian origin, was employed as a medical scientist at Our Lady of Lourdes Hospital in Navan from 2004. In 2014, he was promoted to the role of

---

[47] *Onyemekeihia v Minister for Justice and Equality* [2023] IEHC 697.
[48] *HSE v Okafor* EDA2415.

senior medical scientist in the blood transfusion department, initially on a part-time and temporary basis but became regularised on a full-time basis in 2018. The department also employed another senior medical scientist, KC, who had been *in situ* since 2005, converting from part time to full time in 2020.

In 2021, posts were being filled at chief medical scientist level in a number of departments, including blood transfusion, in accordance with the terms of a 2003 agreement between the Health Services Employers Agency and the Medical Laboratory Scientists Association ('the 2003 agreement'). Having been 'in overall charge' of the blood transfusion department, KC was considered appropriate for promotion, though she did not hold a master's degree as required by the Department of Health and Children for appointment at that level.

The laboratory manager, then unaware of the claimant's past appointment as senior medical scientist, proposed that the post in the blood transfusion department be filled by way of 'confined competition' in line with the 2003 agreement. He identified the claimant as one of two eligible participants. The claimant was unhappy with that proposal as he believed he was entitled to be appointed on the basis that he was the more appropriate candidate. The claimant held the necessary master's qualification and had been deputy lead in his department. Separately, KC sought the appointment, requesting that she be permitted to complete a master's degree within a specified timeframe post-appointment.

Following a full review of the claimant's personnel records, the laboratory manager deemed the claimant eligible for appointment as chief medical scientist in the blood transfusion department. In August 2022, the claimant was retrospectively offered, and accepted, the position.

The Labour Court considered the delay in filling the post to be attributable to a 'genuine confusion' that arose in relation to the interpretation of the 2003 agreement and its application to the circumstances 'not only of the [claimant] himself but also to those of his colleague, KC'. It appeared that each candidate had a stateable case which was supported by their trade union. Having given due consideration to all the relevant facts, management eventually resolved the matter in the claimant's favour. The claimant's appointment and salary were backdated, meaning that he suffered no detriment as a result of the delay.

It followed that the claimant had not established any facts from which an inference that he was treated less favourably by the respondent because of his race could be drawn. Therefore, the appeal was dismissed.

[3.40] ***Boohene v The Royal Parks Ltd[49]—Court of Appeal of England and Wales—Underhill, Jackson & Lewis LJJ—appeal from UK Employment Appeal Tribunal—indirect racial discrimination—remuneration of outsourced workers—disparate impact on BME workers—correct comparison pool—existence of a claim against the principal—failure to prove case as pleaded***

---

[49] *Boohene v The Royal Parks Ltd* [2024] EWCA Civ 583, see *Arthur Cox Employment Law Yearbook 2023* at [3.30] for the decision of the UK EAT in *The Royal Parks Ltd v Boohene* [2023] EAT 69.

An employment tribunal upheld a complaint of indirect race discrimination by 16 contract workers. That decision was overturned by the UK EAT and the workers appealed to the Court of Appeal of England and Wales.

The alleged discrimination concerned the failure to pay the appellants the London living wage ('LLW'), an hourly rate of pay in excess of the UK's national minimum wage. It is recommended by the Living Wage Foundation and has no statutory status.

The respondent is a charity, managing eight of London's Royal parks and other open spaces. It took over responsibility from the Royal Parks Agency, an agency of the UK's Department of Culture, Media and Sport. The appellants were employees of Vinci Construction UK Ltd ('Vinci'), which had a toilet maintenance and cleaning services contract with the respondent, having successfully tendered in 2014, at an hourly rate of pay of £7. At the time, the respondent's predecessor was given the option of accepting a bid whereby staff would be paid the LLW rate (then £9.15) but it decided not to take that up. The evidence had been that it was not affordable to do so. Indeed, at all material times, it was the respondent's policy not to require its contractors to pay the LLW. Meanwhile, the 160 predominantly white 'direct employees' of the respondent were paid the LLW.

In June 2017, trade unions representing the outsourced workers submitted a request that the respondent consider extending the LLW to all employees of contractors. In June 2019, the appellants' trade union wrote to Vinci, pointing out that the vast majority of their cohort was paid below the LLW and asking that Vinci respond with a proposal for wholesale implementation of the LLW. In their annual pay claim that year, the trade unions submitted that the respondent should 'extend payment of the living wage to the employees of all its contractors, by incorporating a clause to this effect as part of the procurement process'.

The respondent's position remained unchanged until a board meeting in September 2019, when it was agreed that the respondent and all of its contractors should pay the LLW to all staff as soon as possible after the contracts came up for renewal, and by April 2023 at the very latest. Vinci's contract was renewed and it was agreed that the respondent would meet the costs of the LLW.

In their complaint of indirect race discrimination, the appellants—all but one of whom were from a black or minority ethnic ('BME') background—argued that the contractual arrangements put in place by the respondent for determining the pay of outsourced workers treated them less favourably than the respondent's direct employees. The effect was a 'disparate impact' on BME workers, who are more likely to find themselves in outsourced roles.

Importantly, no evidence was adduced about the details of the respondent's outsourcing contracts with any other contractor—or about the workers employed under them—except for Vinci. Evidence adduced on the disparate impact issue related only to a pool consisting of the respondent's direct employees and the Vinci workers, to the exclusion of the 'indirectly-employed' workforce generally—something the EAT concluded was a fundamental error on the employment tribunal's part. The appellants challenged that finding. In the alternative, they contended that if the EAT was correct, the claim should have been remitted to the tribunal, and not dismissed.

For its part, the respondent took issue with a number of matters rejected by the EAT. In the first instance it contended that its conduct as principal in not requiring Vinci to pay the LLW, or funding its payment, did not discriminate as to the terms on which it allowed the appellants to work or subject them to any other detriment. Next, it argued that there were material differences between its employees and the Vinci workers, such that they could not be treated as comparable. Finally, it contended that it did not 'apply' any provision, criterion or practice ('PCP') to the appellants.

Addressing the issues raised by the respondent first, the Court of Appeal concluded that the appellants had no claim against the respondent for discrimination as contract workers, since the allegation related to the remuneration payable under their contracts with Vinci. The claim concerned rights arising from the employer-worker relationship and had nothing directly to do with the principal-worker relationship, irrespective of any influence the respondent may have had over the content of those rights. The Court pointed out that the worker would always have the right to claim against its own employer for any discriminatory terms of his or her contract with it. Hence, the respondent did not subject the appellants to any detriment as regards the terms of their contracts with Vinci. It followed that the respondent could not be regarded as having applied a PCP to them.

Although strictly unnecessary to consider the appeal, the Court did so. It agreed with the EAT's conclusion that the pool as pleaded by the appellants consisted of the respondent's direct employees plus the *entirety* of the indirectly-employed workforce. It was 'impossible on an objective construction' to read the appellants' pleading in the way the employment tribunal did—a reading which led it to wrongly choose a 'Vinci-only pool'. Though the appellants' pleaded case was analytically the correct one, it was not proved because they did not adduce any evidence about the indirectly-employed workforce, and in particular its ethnic composition. This was essential in order to prove the PCP had a disparate impact on BME members of the pool. The EAT's decision not to remit was found to be correct, as the appellants had not adduced the evidence necessary to prove their case. It was their responsibility to prove their case as pleaded, and so 'there could be no question of their being given a second chance'.

Thus, irrespective of the Court's conclusions on the respondent's points, the appeal would have been dismissed.

[3.41] *Atif v Dolce & Gabbana UK Ltd*[50]—*UK Employment Appeal Tribunal—appeal from employment tribunal—Equality Act 2010, s 136—race discrimination—burden of proof*

The claimant appealed against an employment tribunal's dismissal of her complaints of unfair dismissal and race discrimination. This appeal concerned the race discrimination complaint.

---

[50] *Atif v Dolce & Gabbana UK Ltd* [2024] EAT 47.

The claimant worked for the respondent, Dolce & Gabbana's UK subsidiary, as a client advisor at their Harrod's concession from 2013 until she was dismissed in 2020 for 'systematically abusing' the respondent's sick absence policy. The claimant was Algerian and Arabic speaking. She had a difficult relationship with her immediate manager, who was Italian, as was the respondent company.

In October 2019, the claimant complained about her manager's treatment of her, in particular in relation to the allocation of late shifts. She complained that no Arabic speakers had lasted in the team. In November 2019, she requested 2 days' leave on 30 and 31 December. When this was refused, she told colleagues that she would take them anyway, as sick leave. She complained of discrimination to the European HR manager as a result of being rostered for both Christmas and the New Year. Following a roster adjustment, the claimant was permitted leave on 31 December only. In December 2019, the deputy store director and the claimant's manager shared concerns over the claimant's repeated requests about the number of sick days she 'had left'; the claimant called in sick on 30 December. The claimant returned to work on 4 January 2020. Two days later she complained about her treatment by her manager since returning to work. The claimant's sicknesses were investigated, leading in due course to her dismissal for gross misconduct in March 2020. An internal appeal was unsuccessful.

The claimant submitted that her race discrimination complaint should have been upheld by the tribunal; that she had been investigated, disciplined and dismissed because of her race. The UK EAT noted the tribunal's finding that it had not received evidence giving rise to that inference, and so had decided that the burden of proof did not shift to the respondent. The EAT reached the view that the tribunal ought to have concluded that the burden did indeed shift, looking at the facts in combination. Nevertheless, the finding of no discrimination was not perverse and it was clear that the tribunal had engaged with the evidence in detail and formed its conclusions. Notwithstanding the route it took, the tribunal had been entitled to its decision, which, it seemed, would have been no different had the respondent been put on proof.

Therefore, the appeal was dismissed.

[3.42] ***NSL Ltd v Zaluski*[51]—UK Employment Appeal Tribunal—appeal from employment tribunal—indirect discrimination—impact—justification—harassment related to race—aggravated damages***

The respondent appealed against an employment tribunal's decision upholding complaints of indirect discrimination and harassment related to race, and awarded aggravated damages to the claimant, who was a Polish national.

The claimant had been employed by the respondent since 2013 and was responsible for enforcing parking regulations in the London Borough of Wandsworth. He had a period of unauthorised leave in January 2020, when he travelled to Poland following the death of his mother-in-law. The respondent took no action at the time and it was recorded that the claimant had a good excuse 'this time'. Subsequently, the claimant asked for three

---

[51] *NSL Ltd v Zaluski* [2024] EAT 86.

weeks' leave to go to Poland in August 2020, but was only granted the first and third weeks of that month. On account of sickness, he did not in fact return to the UK until November 2020, when, due to the Covid-19 pandemic, he was required to quarantine for 14 days. The respondent, suspecting the claimant to have pre-planned this, referred the matter to a disciplinary process, though no sanction was imposed on that occasion as the absence was considered unplanned. Still, the employment tribunal found that the respondent held the claimant's 'history of not returning on the due date' against him.

The claimant's father died in December 2020. In February 2021, he requested three weeks' leave, from 21 February to 14 March 2021, in order to return to Poland to organise a funeral and attend to his father's affairs. The respondent refused the request, citing operational reasons and the mandatory quarantine period, which would apply on the claimant's return to the UK. The respondent instead authorised leave from 22 February to 3 March 2021. In an email, the claimant was warned that he was to return to work on 3 March and that any unauthorised absence would be treated as a disciplinary matter. In light of the respondent's awareness of the mandatory 14-day quarantine period, the employment tribunal found these instructions 'unclear', 'ambiguous', and 'clearly not practical'.

The claimant's leave was then extended to 15 March, though the respondent continued to express concern that the claimant had not yet booked a return flight. He was again warned in an email that failure to return to work on the due date would be considered misconduct. The employment tribunal observed that 'again this still did not allow the claimant the full time in Poland he had requested'. In the event, the claimant was required to quarantine for 10 days upon his arrival in Poland. The tribunal was satisfied that this was genuinely unexpected by him.

The claimant contacted the respondent, explaining that the earliest return flight he could book was 24 March. He was warned that any absence beyond 15 March would be unauthorised and he was urged to take all possible steps to return on the agreed date. The tribunal observed that the implication of this was that the claimant would have had to return in order to quarantine in the UK without attending his father's funeral.

The claimant returned to work on 6 April 2021, where he received a final written warning. He was criticised for failing to keep the respondent sufficiently informed of events as they unfolded. On appeal, the warning was upheld.

The employment tribunal concluded that the provision, criterion or practice ('PCP') of requiring that staff return promptly from authorised leave during the COVID-19 pandemic, regardless of changing events due to the pandemic—and that quarantine be factored into authorised leave—put the claimant at a substantial disadvantage, 'particularly as the respondent did not approve sufficient leave in the first place'. The PCPs were not considered an appropriate means of achieving the aim of ensuring there were sufficient enforcement officers on the streets and, indeed, there was a 'good chance' they would have pushed the claimant and his colleagues to leave, with the attendant risk of unfair dismissal claims. The PCPs would not have impacted the claimant had he not been an overseas national. The respondent, furthermore, 'had a prejudicial view of the claimant having a tendency to take unauthorised leave based on two previous examples, despite the findings in favour of the claimant in both cases'—this contributed to an intimidating and hostile environment.

Aggravated damages were awarded on the basis that the 'perpetrator' of the discrimination was paid to attend the hearing, whereas the claimant had taken unpaid leave to do so.

As regards the indirect discrimination complaint, the EAT's analysis concluded that the employment tribunal, when weighing the disadvantageous impact of the PCPs, erred by focusing 'exclusively, or at least predominantly' on the particular circumstances of the claimant's case, giving insufficient consideration to the more general 'group impact'.

The tribunal, moreover, did not rely upon any specific evidence in support of there being a 'good chance' that application of the PCPs would 'push' the claimant and his colleagues to leave. This assertion formed a significant part of the tribunal's reasoning, informing its conclusions as to whether the PCPs were justified. It was not a factual matter to which the tribunal was entitled to take judicial notice, and so its reliance upon it was misplaced.

As regards the harassment complaint, the employment tribunal was entitled to its finding that the respondent's emails made repeated 'threats' of disciplinary action, informed by its negative view of the claimant's prior history. The tribunal was, similarly, entitled to its finding that the threats, which amounted to harassment, were influenced by the claimant's nationality. Hence, it did not err in upholding that complaint.

Finally, the award of aggravated damages was not reflective of conduct that was of such an egregious character as to exacerbate the distress caused by the original wrong. The presence of the perpetrator at the hearing, or the fact that he was paid, did not meet the high bar for triggering such an award, and so the employment tribunal erred in making it.

The issue of justification for indirect discrimination was remitted to a different tribunal for consideration.

[3.43] *Beaumont Hospital v Thomas[52]—Labour Court—appeal from Workplace Relations Commission—Employment Equality Acts 1998 to 2021, s 83(1)—discrimination on the grounds of race—adverse treatment—continuing discrimination, s 77(5)(a) & (6A)—cognisable period*

The claimant appealed against the WRC's dismissal of her complaint of discrimination.

The claimant was originally from Kerala, India. She commenced employment as a staff nurse with the respondent hospital in June 2004. She submitted that, in the period from August 2007 to January 2018, she was consistently passed over for promotion in favour of less experienced or less qualified candidates. Citing 14 such instances in total, with the most recent occurring in late 2017 and early 2018, the claimant alleged that she was discriminated against on the grounds of race and that no adequate explanation was provided by the respondent for not appointing her to any of the positions. In support

---

[52] *Beaumont Hospital v Thomas* EDA2431.

of her claim, she submitted that overseas nurses were under-represented in managerial positions at the respondent generally.

The respondent denied the allegations. Further, it contended that any incidents alleged over six months prior to the lodging of the complaint were time barred. The competitions referred to by the claimant were 'standalone events' and did not form a continuum.

The Labour Court pointed out that it had no authority in a situation such as this 'to conduct a wide ranging inquiry into discrimination generally' at the hospital and that it could only inquire into referred incidents of discrimination. It first considered the claims of alleged discrimination falling within the six-month cognisable period.

The claimant contended that she was subject to adverse treatment, when competing for the post of respiratory candidate advanced nurse practitioner in October 2017, because she had lodged a complaint of discrimination against the respondent to the WRC in December 2016. She complained that the respondent refused to extend her interview date when she was unable to attend due to a medical appointment. This was categorically denied by the respondent and, indeed, on the facts; the Court was satisfied that the claimant was facilitated with an extension but denied a further extension for the clear reason that the HSE required a successful recruit by a specified date. This had been set out in a letter to the claimant explaining the position. The claimant contended that because she was already on a panel for the same post since 2016, the post should automatically have been offered to her. The Court was satisfied from the correspondence before it that the claimant was advised in October 2017 that this panel had expired and that she had been notified of the panel's expiry date in advance. The claimant proffered no evidence in support of her assertion that she was advised that the 2016 panel was to be extended.

The claimant also asserted that she was discriminated against on the race ground when a white Irish national with less experience and qualifications was appointed to a clinical nurse manager/specialist post following interviews held in December 2017 and January 2018. She asserted that she was also subject to adverse treatment when she was not paneled for the clinical nurse manager post, despite her obvious experience and qualifications, and that the respondent failed to implement an open and transparent selection process. The respondent rejected this, stating that the claimant was not the most suitable candidate for either post, as reflected in her lower interview scores. The claimant took issue with the composition of the interview board, which she asserted included individuals who were the subject of her pending action against the hospital. The respondent denied any procedural or substantive unfairness. Here, the Court found that the claimant provided no evidence to support her assertion that she had made a formal complaint or grievance against the individuals in question. Nor were any facts presented to infer that the marks awarded in the interview, as between the claimant and the successful candidate, were 'illogical' or 'unfair', or that the interview process was carried out 'in an unprofessional manner'.

In relation to the interviews for the post of clinical nurse specialist in January 2018, the respondent agreed, at the request of the claimant's union, to include one external member on the panel. The claimant objected to the external member that was appointed as she came from another hospital within the respondent 'group' and, in the claimant's view, could not be independent. In the Court's view, however, this appointment was a reasonable approach to the request. As was the case with the December 2017 interview, no facts were presented by the claimant to infer that the marks awarded were illogical or unfair or that the process was unprofessional. The Court further noted that the successful white Irish candidate was promoted out of the post and that the next candidate on the panel, who was of Indian origin, was appointed instead. It was satisfied that the claimant's failure to be paneled for the post was because of her lower marks at interview.

In all of the circumstances, the Court did not accept that sufficient facts were established by the claimant to infer discrimination or victimisation on the race ground. As the claimant had failed to establish a *prima facie* case within the cognisable period, the Court could not address the contention that events occurring within that period were part of a continuum of discrimination. It therefore lacked jurisdiction to consider the complaints outside that period and the appeal, accordingly, failed.

RACE—HARASSMENT

[3.44] *Carozzi v University of Hertfordshire*[53]—**UK Employment Appeal Tribunal**—*appeal from employment tribunal*—*Equality Act 2010, s 26*—*harassment related to protected characteristic*—*accent and race/nationality*—*victimisation, s 27*—*protected acts*—*constructive dismissal*—*mental element*—*procedural bias*—*burden of proof*

The claimant appealed against an employment tribunal's dismissal of her complaints of harassment, victimisation, and procedural bias.

The claimant, a Brazilian national of Jewish heritage, was employed by the respondent under a probationary contract. Her probation period, initially six months, was extended twice but remained incomplete when she resigned. She brought claims alleging constructive dismissal; harassment related to her race, nationality and accent; victimisation for having raised complaints; and direct discrimination based on religion and race. Among these were complaints about remarks made by her line manager about her accent and the refusal of another colleague to disclose meeting notes that, she argued, contained vital information.

The claimant's case was complex, involving 36 allegations of detrimental treatment. The employment tribunal dismissed most of the claims, finding that the line manager's comments about the claimant's accent related solely to legitimate concerns about her intelligibility rather than her race or nationality. As such, the comments were not 'related to' her race or nationality. It also rejected the victimisation complaint on the basis that the refusal to disclose notes did not amount to detrimental treatment under the Equality Act 2010, as the respondent would have acted similarly with other

---

[53] *Carozzi v University of Hertfordshire and Anor* [2024] EAT 169.

employees who had not engaged in protected acts. Allegations that the employment Judge made prejudicial comments during the hearing were dismissed as unsupported by evidence.

On appeal, the claimant argued that the employment tribunal incorrectly required a 'mental element', akin to direct discrimination, to establish a link between the comments about her accent and her race or nationality. She contended that the tribunal failed to properly assess whether the refusal to disclose notes was materially influenced by her protected acts. Finally, the claimant alleged that the employment Judge's remarks and interruptions during the hearing created an appearance of bias.

The EAT concluded that the employment tribunal misapplied the law by conflating 'harassment' with 'direct discrimination'. It clarified that comments about a person's accent can relate to race or nationality if the conduct violates dignity or creates an offensive environment, irrespective of intent. The harassment complaint was remitted for reconsideration. The tribunal also erred in its comparator analysis. The proper question was whether the refusal to disclose notes was materially influenced by the claimant's protected acts, not whether others in similar circumstances were treated alike. That complaint was also remitted. The EAT rejected the claimant's allegations of bias, finding no evidence of improper conduct or unfair treatment by the employment Judge.

The EAT remitted the harassment and victimisation complaints to a differently constituted employment tribunal, noting that the original tribunal's flawed approach to harassment necessitated fresh consideration. The EAT emphasised that the rehearing should be proportionate and focused only on the remitted issues.

Therefore, the appeal was allowed in part.

RELIGION

[3.45] *Sutcliffe v Secretary of State for Education*[54]*—High Court of England and Wales—Pepperall J—Education Act 2002, s 141B—teachers' standards—claimant prohibited from teaching for professional misconduct—religious beliefs and professional duties, conflict—European Convention on Human Rights and Fundamental Freedoms, art 9*

The claimant challenged the respondent's decision to make an order prohibiting him from teaching.

The claimant was a maths teacher at The Cherwell School in Oxfordshire. He was also an Evangelical Christian who preached on the streets and online. He had strong and sincerely held views about gender identity, homosexuality, the sanctity of marriage, the role of men and women in society, and Islam. The claimant deliberately used female pronouns to refer to a transgender male pupil, both in the classroom and in an interview

---

[54] *Sutcliffe v Secretary of State for Education* [2024] EWHC 1878 (Admin).

on ITV's *This Morning*, in which he described the pupil, effectively 'outing' him. He told his class that homosexuality is a sin and implied that homosexuals might be 'cured' by God.

The claimant's religious convictions conflicted with his professional duties as a teacher. This led to a complaint about his conduct, and ultimately his dismissal in February 2018. Further complaints led to his resignation from subsequent employment at St Aloysius College in Islington, where he showed pupils a video entitled 'Make Men Masculine Again'.

The respondent appointed a professional conduct panel in accordance with legislation. The panel found the claimant guilty of 'unacceptable professional conduct' and 'conduct that may bring the teaching profession into disrepute'. Specifically, it found that the claimant 'failed to treat his pupils with dignity, or build relationships rooted in mutual respect'. The panel concluded that it would be a proportionate and appropriate response to recommend a prohibition order. The respondent accepted the panel's recommendation and made the order which prohibited the claimant from teaching, with a two-year review period. The decision was confirmed in May 2023.

In a wide-ranging appeal, the claimant submitted, broadly, that the panel's decision infringed his rights under arts 9 and 10 ECHR, and that his conduct was not actionable under equality legislation.

The respondent stressed that the panel was correct to focus on the issue of whether the claimant was guilty of misconduct as a teacher.

The Court rejected the claimant's challenge on human rights and equality grounds, pointing out that arts 9 and 10 ECHR are qualified rights. It is fundamental that teachers not only educate, but at all times treat the children in their care with dignity and respect and safeguard their wellbeing. The restrictions were no doubt proportionate. It was not the function of the panel to determine the veracity, reasonableness or otherwise of the claimant's beliefs. Similarly, the case did not concern whether the school was right or wrong to accept the pupil's request to use his preferred pronouns.

While the prohibition order was a severe sanction, the claimant had not demonstrated any error in the approach taken by the respondent. Therefore, the appeal was dismissed.

[3.46] ***R (TTT) v Michaela Community Schools Trust*[55]—*High Court of England and Wales—Linden J—European Convention on Human Rights, art 9—secular state school—religious discrimination—policy prohibiting pupils' prayer rituals on premises***

The claimant pupil challenged the decision of her school's governing body to prohibit its pupils from performing prayer rituals on its premises (the 'prayer rituals policy').

---

[55] *R (TTT) v Michaela Community Schools Trust and London Borough of Brent* [2024] EWHC 843 (Admin).

The school, a state secondary school, was strictly secular and prided itself on its exceptionally good academic results.

While the policy applied to all prayer rituals, regardless of religion, there was no evidence that pupils of any religion other than Islam wished to pray during the school day. In the autumn and winter months, the window for performing *Duhr* prayers overlapped with the school lunch break. The claimant wished to have 25 minutes during the lunch break in which to perform *Duhr*. She argued that the school's refusal to permit her to do so was in breach of art 9 ECHR and that the policy indirectly discriminated against Muslim pupils contrary to the Equality Act 2010. In introducing the prayer rituals policy, she argued, the respondent failed to have 'due regard' to the need to eliminate discrimination, and advance equality of opportunity.

In March 2023, the claimant was excluded for two days. She, along with other pupils, had prayed in the schoolyard using prayer mats. When reprimanded, she had displayed rudeness towards a teacher. In April 2023, she was excluded for five days when certain threats were made to another pupil. The claimant contended that the exclusions were procedurally unfair in that she was not given an opportunity to respond to what was alleged against her before the decisions to exclude her were made by the headteacher.

The respondent submitted that the prayer rituals policy did not 'interfere' with the claimant's freedom to manifest her religion or belief under art 9 ECHR, nor did it subject her to a detriment under the Equality Act 2010. It argued that Islam would permit the claimant to make up for missing *Duhr* by performing *Qada* prayers later in the day. Even if this were not so, the claimant had chosen a secular school with a strict behavioural regime and she was free to transfer to a non-secular school if she wished. Any interference with the claimant's religious freedom was in any event justified, as was any indirect discriminatory effect of the prayer rituals policy since the performance of ritual prayers conflicted with the school's ethos and rules. The respondent asserted that it did have 'due regard' to the Equality Act 2010 when the policy was introduced.

Rejecting all except the final ground of the claim, the High Court of England and Wales did not accept that there had been any interference with the claimant's art 9 rights. It did so on the strength of ECHR caselaw, reflecting the fact that art 9 protects 'freedom' to manifest belief, rather than conferring an 'absolute right' to do so. The claimant had 'at the very least impliedly accepted', when she enrolled, that she would be subject to restrictions on her ability to manifest her religion. She knew that the school was secular and her evidence had been that her mother wished for her to attend there 'because it was known to be strict'. It was not until 'the best part of the way through year 9' that the claimant indicated any objection to the policy, which had been introduced during her third year. The claimant had not satisfied the burden of proof of showing undue hardship or inconvenience if she were to move to a different school within travelling distance, that would permit prayer during the school day; or that it would be impossible to enrol in such a school; or that no such school existed. While less satisfactory, under the teachings of Islam, the claimant was nevertheless able to manifest her belief through *Qada*, for which purpose the prayer rituals policy constituted a 'good reason' not to perform *Duhr*.

The Court accepted that the aims relied on by the respondent to justify not permitting or facilitating indoor prayer rituals were legitimate (it being readily accepted that outdoor prayer would be inappropriate). It could not be discounted that allowing indoor prayer would lead to logistical difficulties and behavioural issues, including peer pressure and bullying of Muslim pupils who might otherwise not wish to participate in prayer (as had happened in March 2023). The Court accepted the headteacher's predictive judgement in that regard. There was a rational connection between the aim of promoting the school's ethos and the prayer rituals policy.

It was true that the claimant was subject to a 'detriment' within the meaning of the Equality Act 2010, in that the prayer rituals policy prevented her from praying when she could and should otherwise do so. Nevertheless, the policy was a proportionate means of achieving a legitimate aim. The Court concluded that the respondent had due regard to the Equality Act 2010. The respondent governing body was likely to have had a degree of familiarity with the workings of the school, was entitled to rely on the headteacher's inquiries and judgement, and could be taken to have carefully considered information provided in a briefing note on the events of March and April 2023, of which it was likely already aware.

While no procedural unfairness tainted the two-day exclusion, in the case of the investigation leading to the five-day exclusion, the decision to interview pupils who were not party to the conversation in which the threats were uttered, and not to ask the claimant for her account, were neither fair nor appropriate, and school had not acted in a manner consistent with its policies. The claim succeeded on this final point alone and was otherwise dismissed.

[3.47] *Thomas v Surrey and Borders Partnership NHS Foundation Trust*[56]—*UK Employment Appeal Tribunal—Sheldon J—appeal from employment tribunal—Equality Act 2010, s 10—protected belief—anti-Muslim views—whether employee's beliefs were a protected characteristic—European Convention on Human Rights, art 17*

The claimant appealed against an employment tribunal's dismissal of his complaint of belief discrimination. He challenged the tribunal's finding that his belief in English nationalism, which included anti-Islamic views, was not a protected belief under equality legislation.

The claimant had been engaged through an agency to provide consultancy services to the respondent NHS Trust for just under three months. He was then notified by the agency that his employment was being terminated because it had come to light that he had failed to declare an unspent criminal conviction. The claimant believed the true rationale for his dismissal to be his 'philosophical belief' and political affiliation with English nationalism—he had stood for political office between 2004 and 2016 for the English Democrats. He alleged discrimination.

---

[56] *Thomas v Surrey and Borders Partnership NHS Foundation Trust and Brett* [2024] EAT 141.

The respondent contended that the claimant's dismissal was due to his providing misleading information on his CV and candidate application form. In any event, it denied that the claimant's belief was protected by equality legislation. In a preliminary hearing, the employment tribunal addressed the latter issue.

The employment tribunal was satisfied that the evidence (including, *inter alia*, past use of the hashtag *RemoveAllMuslims*) provided 'more than an adequate basis for finding that the claimant held anti-Muslim views', including a belief in the 'coercive removal' of Muslims from the UK, and that these formed part of his belief in English nationalism. Other online posts, advocating the use of armed violence against migrants, demonstrated the claimant's intolerance of illegal migration 'as an extension of his nationalist views'. In the tribunal's opinion, such posts represented a 'snapshot' of the views the claimant had publicly posted and demonstrated what English nationalism meant to him.

The tribunal's analysis concluded that, although English nationalism is capable of constituting a philosophical belief for the purposes of equality legislation, the claimant held anti-Islamic views as part of that philosophical belief at the relevant time. Those anti-Islamic views did not satisfy the '*Grainger* criteria' (formulated by the leading EAT decision, *Grainger plc v Nicholson*),[57] in that they were not worthy of respect in a democratic society, were incompatible with human dignity, and conflicted with the fundamental rights of others. The claimant's views thus prevented his belief in English nationalism from being a protected characteristic.

On appeal, the EAT was clear that the *Grainger* criteria in question were intended to be consistent with art 17 ECHR. The employment tribunal's findings demonstrated that the claimant's beliefs, characterised as they were by a 'disdainful and prejudiced focus on Islam', were 'more than offensive, shocking or disturbing', thus setting them apart from views which would otherwise be protected by art 11 ECHR. While recognising some 'dissonance' in the ECtHR jurisprudence, the EAT considered the tribunal was entitled to its conclusion that the claimant's beliefs were not protected by the ECHR. Although these beliefs 'would not have the effect of inciting violence towards Muslims, they [did] espouse and would necessarily stir up disdain, and therefore, hatred of Islam and Muslims'. As such, the language used by the claimant fell within the 'grave forms' of hate speech identified by the ECtHR and was inconsistent with art 17 ECHR.

Accordingly, the appeal was dismissed.

---

[57] *Grainger plc v Nicholson* [2010] ICR 360.

Chapter 4

Employment Litigation

INTRODUCTION

[4.01]

Abuse of Process

In *Pady*, the UK EAT considered whether the employment tribunal had erred in dismissing claims of direct discrimination in relation to redundancy payments when there were ongoing claims relating to that redundancy scheme, including an appeal.

Anonymity Order

In *Z*, the UK EAT heard an appeal from the employment tribunal's dismissal of a claim for discrimination where there was alleged untruthful evidence provided and the lifting of 'privacy orders' that had been granted in respect of the claimant.

Application for Adjournment

In *Bennett*, the UK EAT considered whether the employment tribunal had erred in refusing an adjournment application in circumstances where the claimant's representative ceased to represent the claimant. In *Leslie Easton & Co Ltd*, the UK EAT considered whether the refusal to grant an adjournment in a case of sexual harassment and victimisation was lawful.

Costs

In *Munnelly*, the Supreme Court considered whether a costs order was merited where the unsuccessful party was unrepresented.

Diplomatic Immunity

In *Alhayali*, the UK EAT considered whether a statutory 'tort exception' to state immunity applied to psychiatric injury.

Disclosure Orders

In *Al Sadeq*, the Court of Appeal of England and Wales considered litigation privilege and legal advice privilege in relation to disclosure orders, and the exception of iniquity. In *Loverseed*, the UK EAT considered the relevance of material ordered to be disclosed in a disclosure order relating to internal management documents, including financial information in unredacted form.

Employment Status

In a notable judgment of the High Court, *Hanley v PBR Restaurants Ltd t/a Fish Shack Café*, the Court looked at whether the Labour Court had erred in not applying the test laid out in *Karshan* in relation to employment status, and in determining that it could not hear claims based on protected disclosures that were not properly raised at first instance.

In *Kelly*, the Labour Court considered whether a worker was engaged under a contract of service or a contract for services.

In *Groom*, the UK EAT considered whether a volunteer was a worker, and in *Watson*, the UK EAT considered the intention of the parties in relation to the worker status of the claimant.

Frivolous and Vexatious Appeals

Novak saw the High Court determine whether an appeal should be struck out as being frivolous and vexatious.

Identification of Employer

In the two *Metropolitan Films International Ltd* cases, the Labour Court considered the identification of the correct employer for the claimant.

Press Freedom

In *Law Society of Ireland v Ellis*, the High Court heard an application to take up a transcript of a digital audio recording made by the respondent in underlying proceedings.

Res Judicata

The principle of *res judicata* was considered in the Labour Court decision in *Xerox* and the UK EAT decision in *Parnell*.

Settlement Agreements

The Labour Court in *Gerety* and *Sumaili* considered whether it had jurisdiction to hear complaints in circumstances where settlement agreements had been entered into.

In *Bathgate*, the Court of Session of Scotland determined whether a waiver in respect of future claims, that was included in a settlement agreement, was valid in the context of post-employment discrimination claims.

In *Clifford*, the UK EAT considered an appeal from the employment tribunal's decision to strike out a disability claim as having no reasonable prospect of success where a settlement agreement had been entered into.

Strike Out

In *Leeks*, the UK EAT considered whether the employment tribunal's decision to strike out a claim was proportionate in a case where the claimant had unreasonably delayed proceedings.

Territorial Jurisdiction

In *Beldica*, the UK EAT considered whether the employment tribunal had jurisdiction to hear an extra-territorial employment claim where the claimant worked in Dubai but was employed by the British Council. In *Stena Drilling Pte Ltd*, the UK EAT considered whether the employment tribunal had jurisdiction to hear the claim in circumstances where the claimant was non-resident for the purpose of UK tax and spent no more than 90 days per year in the UK.

Time Limits—Claims

In *TC*, the European Court of Justice considered circumstances where a worker became aware of her pregnancy after the expiry of the time limit for bringing an action challenging her dismissal. In *Xerox* and *Moran*, the Labour Court looked at whether claims under the Pensions Act 1990 were out of time. The Labour Court decision in *Rose Hospitality Ltd v Scanlon* concerned the issue where the incorrect respondent had been named on the appeal form. In *Whelton* and *McNally*, the Labour Court considered whether claims under the European Communities (Protection of Employees on the

Transfer of Undertakings) Regulations 2003 and the Employment Equality Acts 1998 to 2021, respectively, were out of time. Note also the decisions in *McCarthy*, *Keane* and *McCaul*. The UK EAT considered the same issue in *Holbrook*.

Time Limits—Appeals

The Labour Court delivered a number of decisions on the time limits for appeals. Note the decisions in *Brzezinski*, the two *Pickford* cases, *Long*, the two *Eldic* cases, *Conlon* and *Turkay*. The Court of Appeal in England and Wales also considered the time limit for appeals in *Ridley*, and the UK EAT considered it in *AB* and *Jones*.

Without Prejudice Privilege

In *Gallagher*, the UK EAT heard an appeal from a ruling by the employment tribunal that evidence of pre-termination negotiations was inadmissible in a complaint of unfair dismissal.

ABUSE OF PROCESS

[4.02] *Pady v HMRC*[1]—*UK Employment Appeal Tribunal—appeal from employment tribunal—direct age discrimination—multiple ongoing claims concerning the same issue—res judicata—claimants seeking to re-litigate an issue already decided upon—abuse of process*

The claimants, members of a civil and public service trade union, appealed against an employment tribunal's dismissal of their claims of direct age discrimination in relation to redundancy payments under a civil service compensation scheme.

At the time the complaints were lodged, the claimants were aware that there were already ongoing claims relating to that redundancy scheme, including an appeal. Those claims were the subject of a case management order which was extended to apply to this matter. A preliminary hearing of sample cases upheld the respondent's defence of justification and the sample claims were dismissed. The claimants nevertheless sought to pursue their claims. The employment tribunal took the view that to permit them to do so would be an abuse of process, and so the claims were struck out in accordance with its rules.

Although there is no presumption that re-litigation in civil proceedings is an abuse, the UK EAT held that, in this instance, the employment tribunal was entitled to so conclude. The tribunal's powers to strike out a claim as an abuse of process is an 'exceptional jurisdiction'; in this case underpinned by the need for 'finality in litigation' and the principle that a party 'should not be vexed twice in the same matter'.

---

[1] *Pady v HMRC* [2024] EAT 73.

The claimants were parties to proceedings that had been case managed. Had the claimants sought to participate in the preliminary hearing on justification, it was inconceivable that their involvement would not be accommodated. To re-litigate a point that had been determined would undermine the case management of the proceedings, putting the respondents at risk of repeat litigation.

The employment tribunal had therefore correctly concluded that allowing the issue of justification to be re-litigated would be manifestly unfair to the respondents and would bring the administration of justice into disrepute. The appeal was, accordingly, dismissed.

ANONYMITY ORDER

[4.03]   *Z v Commerzbank AG[2]—UK Employment Appeal Tribunal—appeal from employment tribunal—anonymity order—holiday pay—costs order—dishonest and untruthful evidence*

The claimant started working for the respondent bank as an analyst in May 2019. His employment did not go smoothly, and the claimant made a number of allegations against the respondent, including discrimination, sexual harassment and sexual assault. Various meetings took place between the parties to discuss matters. The claimant was dismissed with pay in lieu of notice in November 2019. He exited the respondent's premises assisted by security personnel.

The employment tribunal dismissed the claimant's claim; his complaints related mainly to discrimination and the tribunal did not believe his evidence. The claimant appealed to the UK EAT, where he challenged the tribunal's decision to revoke anonymity orders protecting his identity. He also appealed against the dismissal of his claim for outstanding holiday pay and challenged an order that he pay a contribution of £20,000 towards the respondents' costs.

In the course of the tribunal proceedings, the respondent applied for an anonymity order and a restricted reporting order in respect of the individual against whom the claimant was alleging sexual assault and sexual harassment. The next day, the claimant applied for similar orders in respect of himself. All of these 'privacy orders' were granted by the tribunal.

The tribunal went on to dismiss all of the claimant's claims, describing the claimant as 'a witness contemptuous of his duty to tell the truth and unworthy of belief'. The tribunal acceded to the respondent's request to lift the privacy orders in respect of the claimant and made the impugned costs order.

The EAT concluded that the tribunal had been right to decide that there was a material change in circumstances once it concluded that the complaints of sexual harassment and sexual assault were fabricated. Indeed, it found that it was 'difficult to think of a more striking change of circumstances'. It held that the tribunal was therefore 'amply justified' in revoking the privacy orders in respect of the claimant. It had also been correct in its reasoning that the claimant no longer had 'a sustainable right to litigate

---

[2]   *Z v Commerzbank AG* [2023] UKET 2203396/2020.

anonymously' and could not therefore invoke his art 8 ECHR rights in that respect. The revocation orders would therefore stand.

As regards loss of holiday pay, the claimant had given oral evidence of having agreed with the respondent that three days of annual leave which he had taken would be treated as sick days. The tribunal had found this evidence to be false. The claimant argued that the issue was not whether this agreement was reached, but whether the claimant was 'off sick' and therefore unable to take his annual leave. This ground was rejected; the claimant could not go behind the tribunal's finding as to his dishonesty and untruthfulness.

Finally, the EAT found no error in the tribunal's decision on costs, which was upheld. Accordingly, the appeal failed and was dismissed.

APPLICATION FOR ADJOURNMENT

[4.04] *Bennett v London Borough of Islington[3]—UK Employment Appeal Tribunal—appeal from employment tribunal—application for adjournment—whether the tribunal erred in refusing the adjournment application*

The claimant appealed against an employment tribunal's refusal to grant an adjournment of her hearing.

The claimant was employed by the respondent from 2005. By the time of her dismissal in June 2019, she was a senior business support officer. She was dismissed on the ground of capability and brought claims of unfair dismissal and disability discrimination. The claimant was a disabled person with PTSD.

On the first day of what was to be a 10-day hearing, the employment tribunal refused an application made by the claimant's representative to adjourn the hearing on grounds of the representative's ill-health. The application was renewed the following day and was again refused on the basis that there had been no material change of circumstances since the previous day. Neither the claimant nor her representative were in attendance when the hearing got underway. It proceeded in any event and the tribunal went on to dismiss the claim.

On appeal, the EAT considered that the employment tribunal erred in refusing the second adjournment. Whereas on the previous day, the tribunal had concluded that the claimant could continue to be represented by her representative with adjustments, by the following day it was evident that the representative would not be representing the claimant. This required the tribunal to consider whether the claimant could fairly be expected represent herself. The fact that the tribunal was not persuaded that the claimant's representative was not well enough to attend 'did not absolve it from considering the implications of his departure for the claimant'.

The appeal therefore succeeded and a fresh trial before a differently constituted tribunal was directed.

---

[3] *Bennett v London Borough of Islington* [2024] EAT 118.

[4.05] *Leslie Easton & Co Ltd v Donlon*[4]—*UK Employment Appeal Tribunal—appeal from employment tribunal—sexual harassment—legitimate doubt as to witness capacity to give evidence—whether the tribunal erred in refusing an adjournment*

The respondents, Leslie Easton & Co Ltd and one of its directors, appealed against the employment tribunal's refusal to grant an adjournment. The tribunal would go on to uphold complaints of sexual harassment and victimisation. The claimant was awarded £19,000 compensation.

The claimant worked as an administrative assistant for the respondent, a glass business, from April 2014 until May 2020. The claimant brought proceedings alleging unfair dismissal, wrongful dismissal, sexual harassment and victimisation. The latter allegations were against a co-owner of the respondent, who was one of its directors.

In a preliminary hearing, it was noted that the director in question was elderly and in poor health. He had suffered a stroke and was awaiting 'another heart operation'. No medical evidence was provided. At the outset of the hearing, it was indicated that the director's evidence would be confined to a letter, unsigned and undated, and apparently written by him. On the third day, when called to give evidence, the director disavowed the letter, denied its contents and said that anyone claiming otherwise was lying. He was questioned by the tribunal and denied, contrary to the submission of his representative, that he suffered any memory problems. He denied instructing his representative that he would be relying on the letter in evidence.

Following a brief recess, the respondents applied for an adjournment to obtain a medical report on the issue of whether the director was fit to give evidence. It was indicated that the director would not be called as a witness without such a report. The employment tribunal refused the adjournment, criticising the respondents for not raising the issue earlier, or providing any evidence of capacity. The tribunal said that it could not be sure whether the problem arose because of a failure to take proper instructions, or that the concerns were genuine.

The respondents submitted that the employment tribunal erred in law in not granting an adjournment so that up-to-date medical evidence could be obtained as to the director's fitness to give evidence. By the appeal stage, the director was deceased.

It appeared to the EAT that there was good reason for concern and legitimate doubt as to the director's capacity. The employment tribunal should have followed set guidance and allowed time for a report to be obtained. The fact that the issue had not been raised earlier was 'really beside the point' if a legitimate doubt had arisen at that stage. It was not good enough for the tribunal to ask the director himself about his cognitive skills. The EAT found that the tribunal's suggestions that there was a failure to take proper instructions, or that the concerns were not genuine, were unfair.

The appeal was therefore allowed and the case was remitted to a new employment tribunal.

---

[4] *Leslie Easton & Co Ltd and Easton v Donlon* [2024] EAT 126.

COSTS

[4.06] *Munnelly v Hassett, Cremin and City Learning Ltd*[5]—*Supreme Court— O'Donnell CJ, Dunne, Hogan, Murray, Collins JJ—costs—successful party seeking costs of appeal—unsuccessful party unrepresented—whether a costs order against the unsuccessful party merited*

In a judgment delivered in November 2023, the Supreme Court allowed the respondents' appeal in its entirely and dismissed the appellant's claim as to costs.[6]

The background concerned a dispute that followed the appellant's departure from City Learning Ltd ('the company'), one of three respondents. The appellant represented herself at all stages. The respondents argued that the action was barred by the rule in *Henderson v Henderson*, the appellant having previously brought proceedings against the company which were dismissed in the Circuit Court. It would ultimately fall to the Supreme Court to decide on the true interpretation of the rule in *Henderson v Henderson* and, in particular, whether the rule could be invoked by parties who had not been party to the earlier proceedings. It did so in the respondents' favour. This ruling dealt with the respondents' application for costs, having been wholly successful in the appeal.

Noting that the appeal involved an issue of general public importance which extended 'beyond the facts of the case'; that the appellant would otherwise have been entitled to her costs in the High Court; that the award would further aggravate ill-feeling between the parties; and the fact that the respondents' legal teams were assigned under the *ad hoc* scheme, and therefore did not incur costs in defending the appeal, the Supreme Court decided that the merits of the case were best met by making 'no order' as to costs.

DIPLOMATIC IMMUNITY

[4.07] *The Royal Embassy of Saudi Arabia v Alhayali*[7]—*UK Employment Appeal Tribunal—appeal from employment tribunal—psychiatric injury—state immunity— application of correct legal test—whether claimant's employment was sufficiently close to employer's exercise of sovereign authority—whether employer had waived state immunity—whether a statutory 'tort exception' to state immunity applied to psychiatric injury*

The respondent embassy appealed against a preliminary decision of an employment tribunal, which held that the respondent had validly submitted to its jurisdiction, and that the claimant's employment was not an exercise of sovereign authority.

The claimant had been employed in the respondent's academic and cultural affairs departments between 2013 and 2018. In January 2018, she brought a number of complaints

---

[5] *Munnelly v Hassett, Cremin and City Learning Ltd* [2024] IESC 41.
[6] See *Arthur Cox Employment Law Yearbook 2023* at [4.29] for decision of Supreme Court in *Munnelly v Hassett, Cremin and Anor* [2023] IESC 29.
[7] *The Royal Embassy of Saudi Arabia v Alhayali* [2023] EAT 149.

before the employment tribunal, including a personal injury claim for psychiatric injury. The respondent initially asserted state immunity under the State Immunity Act 1978. On foot of a direction from the employment judge, however, by email dated 9 April 2019 the respondent's then solicitors accepted that the employment tribunal had jurisdiction over 'such claims as were derived from EU law'; these included discrimination on grounds of religion and belief, discrimination on grounds of disability, harassment related to sex and religion, victimisation and unpaid holiday leave. On 4 August 2021, the substantive hearing having been listed, the respondent 'reasserted' state immunity, claiming that no authority had been given to its former solicitors to waive immunity.

The EAT was in no doubt that the work of the respondent's academic and cultural affairs department—which included looking after the interests of Saudi students in the UK and promoting Saudi academic and artistic endeavour—involved the exercise of sovereign authority. Such functions are indeed contemplated by the Vienna Convention. On this basis, the EAT found that the employment tribunal had 'elided' the correct legal test, which was whether the claimant's work—which was 'ancillary and supportive' to the exercise of the respondent's sovereign authority—was *sufficiently close* to that exercise. Applying the correct test of 'sufficiently close', rather than 'ancillary and supportive', the EAT held that certain aspects of the claimant's employment (disregarding those of a purely clerical nature) played a part, 'even if only a small one, in protecting the interests of the Saudi state and its nationals in the UK and in promoting Saudi culture in the UK'. The EAT nevertheless conceded that the case was 'borderline' and 'difficult'.

The EAT rejected the respondent's argument that a statutory exception to state immunity in claims of personal injury did not extend to pure psychiatric injury. It observed that the leading authority in that regard, *Federal Republic of Nigeria v Ogbonna*,[8] held that the relevant international conventions do not support a restrictive reading of the phrase 'personal injuries', which should, accordingly, be given its normal meaning in domestic law, 'covering psychiatric as well as physical injury'. The EAT expressed agreement with that construction and saw no reason to depart from *Ogbonna*.

The EAT invited further submissions from the parties as to whether there was any need for the issue of waiver to be remitted to a differently constituted tribunal.

DISCLOSURE ORDERS

[4.08] *Al Sadeq v Dechert LLP*[9]—*Court of Appeal of England and Wales—appeal from High Court of England and Wales—Underhill, Males & Popplewell LJJ—disclosure—litigation privilege—legal advice privilege—iniquity exceptions*

The appellant appealed against a decision of the High Court of England and Wales dismissing his challenge to assertions of legal professional privilege made by the respondents, a law firm based in London.

---

[8] *Federal Republic of Nigeria v Ogbonna* [2012] I WLR 139.
[9] *Al Sadeq v Dechert LLP* [2024] EWCA Civ 28.

The appellant was a qualified lawyer in his native Jordan. In November 2008, he started working as a legal advisor for the Ras Al Khaimah Investment Authority ('RAKIA'), the sovereign wealth fund for Ras Al Khaimah ('RAK') in the United Arab Emirates. He was promoted to group legal director of RAKIA in 2010, becoming deputy CEO in June 2011. In 2012, he resigned and moved to Dubai, where he established an investment business.

RAKIA contended that, around this time, it discovered that its CEO, Dr Masaad, and associates had been involved in systematic and wide-ranging fraud against RAKIA and its various arms and entities, including the misappropriation of some hundreds of millions of dollars. In 2014, the appellant was arrested at his home in Dubai and brought to RAK where he was tried, convicted and imprisoned for fraud. He maintained his innocence and contended that the trials were politically motivated.

The respondents in these proceedings were, respectively, an international law firm and three named individuals who, at the material times, were its partners. The respondent law firm was engaged by the RAK Government in connection with an investigation into the activities and transactions of subsidiary companies controlled by RAKIA under the instruction of Dr Masaad.

The appellant's case was that the respondent law firm and three of its partners used threats and/or mistreatment and/or other unlawful methods to force the appellant to give evidence, including false evidence, in an effort to build a case against Dr Masaad and his alleged co-conspirators at the behest of the ruler of RAK. The appellant sought compensation in the High Court of England and Wales for physical, emotional, psychological, moral and financial harm, loss and damage he sustained on his rendition to RAK.

There followed a two-day disclosure hearing in the High Court, dealing with issues of litigation privilege, legal advice privilege and iniquity exceptions pertaining thereto. In a reserved judgment, the trial Judge refused the appellant's application in its entirety, on the grounds that the iniquity exception does not apply if the document is generated by, or reports on, the iniquitous conduct.

The Court of Appeal overturned the High Court. The Court of Appeal held that iniquity need only be established on the balance of probabilities and that the material provided by the appellant clearly established a prima *facie case* of iniquity. This included: the appellant's detention and rendition to RAK, and subsequent detention there; the conditions in which he was held in detention; and lack of access to legal representation during his detention. Its analysis concluded that the iniquity exception is not limited to documents created in furtherance of, or as part of the iniquity. The exception includes documents which report on or reveal the iniquitous conduct in question. It followed that the disclosure exercise would have to be re-undertaken to address documentation withheld by the respondents as a result of the misapplication of the iniquity exception.

The Court went on to confirm that litigation privilege is not confined to parties to litigation but can apply in respect of non-parties, such as victims of alleged crimes, provided that the relevant document was prepared for the dominant purpose of seeking or obtaining legal advice, information or evidence in connection with litigation in reasonable contemplation.

[4.09] *Virgin Atlantic Airways Ltd v Loverseed[10]—UK Employment Appeal Tribunal—appeal from employment tribunal—redundancy—indirect discrimination—disclosure—relevance of material disclosed*

The respondent appealed against an employment tribunal's order that it make disclosure of internal management documents, including financial information in unredacted form, to the claimant pilots. The documents were produced by the respondent for the purposes of decision making which led to the claimants' dismissal by reason of redundancy.

The various complaints related to alleged unfair dismissal and indirect discrimination on grounds of age and sex. The claimants contended that the financial information, which related to pilot costs and potential savings, was relevant to their pleaded cases which, among other things, challenged the selection criteria adopted by the respondent as part of the redundancy exercise. The claimants' case in that respect was that the redundancy was 'opportunistic' and disguised an attempt to maximise savings by removing the most 'expensive' pilots.

In dismissing the appeal, the EAT held that the employment Judge had directed herself correctly. It was apparent that she was conscious of the scope of the pleadings and properly concluded that the unredacted material was relevant to the disputed issues, namely what selection criteria had been used by the respondent and whether it was fair. As regards the complaints of indirect discrimination, the material had a bearing on the question of whether the selection criteria could be justified as a proportionate means of achieving a legitimate business aim.

EMPLOYMENT STATUS[11]

[4.10] *Hanley v PBR Restaurants Ltd t/a Fish Shack Café[12]—High Court—Bolger J—application to set aside decision of Labour Court—Unfair Dismissals Acts 1977 to 2015, ss 6 & 10A—Protected Disclosures Act 2014—protected disclosures—unfair dismissal—employment status—mutuality of obligation—de novo appeal—Labour Court jurisdiction—Workplace Relations Commission Act 2015, s 44(1)—Karshan (Midlands) test*

The claimant alleged that he was unfairly dismissed under the guise of redundancy. His claim was first lodged with the WRC, which determined that he lacked the requisite 12 months of continuous service as an employee. The WRC applied a mutuality of obligation test and concluded that, prior to December 2019, the appellant was self-employed, thus disqualifying him from pursuing an unfair dismissal claim. He appealed to the Labour Court.

---

[10] *Virgin Atlantic Airways Ltd v Loverseed, Fenton and O'Connor* [2024] EAT 79.
[11] On Employment Status, see also Chapter 17, Taxation.
[12] *Hanley v PBR Restaurants Ltd t/a Fish Shack Café* [2024] IEHC 662.

The Labour Court proceedings took an unexpected turn when, for the first time, the claimant explicitly argued that his dismissal was connected to protected disclosures, thereby negating the statutory service requirement under the Unfair Dismissals Acts 1977 to 2015. The claimant contended that this argument was implicit in his earlier filings. The respondent argued that raising the protected disclosures issue constituted an entirely new claim and that the Labour Court lacked jurisdiction to consider it on appeal. The Labour Court agreed, ruling that it could not hear the claims based on protected disclosures as they were not properly raised at first instance. It further concluded that the claimant's employment status prior to December 2019 precluded him from qualifying as an employee, reaffirming the WRC's earlier finding.

The claimant subsequently appealed to the High Court on two grounds. First, he argued that the Labour Court erred in refusing to hear evidence regarding protected disclosures, contrary to its *de novo* appellate jurisdiction. Second, the Labour Court misapplied the mutuality of obligation test in determining his employment status, especially in light of recent Supreme Court jurisprudence.[13]

Addressing the first ground of appeal, the High Court emphasised that the Labour Court, as an appellate body, is mandated by the Workplace Relations Act 2015 to conduct full rehearings. This includes hearing new evidence relevant to appeals. A *de novo* appeal requires the appellate body to exercise its own judgment independently of the first instance decision. The Labour Court's refusal to hear evidence on protected disclosures therefore amounted to a serious legal error. The High Court noted that raising new factual grounds under the Unfair Dismissals Acts 1977 to 2015—such as protected disclosures—does not transform an unfair dismissal claim into a separate claim under the Protected Disclosures Act 2014. Rather, protected disclosures represent one of many possible grounds for an unfair dismissal claim. The Labour Court's jurisdictional ruling thus failed to appreciate the statutory framework underpinning the claim.

Turning to the second ground, the High Court evaluated the Labour Court's reliance on mutuality of obligation as a decisive factor in determining the claimant's employment status. While the Labour Court had considered other tests, such as control and carrying on business on one's own account, it ultimately relied on the absence of mutuality to disqualify the claimant as an employee. The High Court observed that this approach was inconsistent with the Supreme Court's recent decision in *Karshan*, which rejected mutuality of obligation as a standalone or decisive test, favouring a more holistic approach that includes the contractual and factual realities of the working relationship. By applying outdated legal principles, the Labour Court had committed a fundamental error of law. The High Court noted that any rehearing of the case must be guided by the updated principles established in *Karshan*.

Accordingly, the High Court set aside the Labour Court's determination and remitted the matter for a full rehearing.

---

13   *Revenue Commissioners v Karshan (Midlands) Ltd t/a Domino's Pizza* [2023] IESC 24, see *Arthur Cox Employment Law Yearbook 2023* at [4.14].

[4.11] ***Templederry Renewable Energy Supply Ltd Community Power v Kelly***[14]*—Labour Court—appeal from Workplace Relations Commission—Unfair Dismissals Acts 1977 to 2015, s 8A—employee status—whether the worker was engaged under a contract of service or a contract for services*

The claimant appealed against the WRC's dismissal of his complaint under the Unfair Dismissals Acts 1977 to 2015. It found that the claimant 'was not at any time an employee of the respondent engaged on a contract of service'.

The respondent submitted that the claimant was a self-employed contractor on a contract for services. The claimant's evidence was that he agreed to undergo a three-month 'trial period' with the respondent, working three days a week and supplying invoices for payment, on the understanding that his contractual situation would be 'regularised' after that period. He claimed that he was 'strung along' for two years without his contract being 'regularised'.

The Labour Court found that the claimant's evidence did not establish that he was 'in reality' engaged on a contract of service with the respondent. Even if he had a genuine expectation that there was an offer of engagement, the claimant had 'nevertheless readily agreed to a most unusual "trial period" during which he was content to be paid on an invoice basis without the deduction of tax, PRSI or USC'. The claimant had allowed that arrangement to continue for over two years. Even when the claimant did formulate a proposal in writing to 'regularise' his situation, he expressed a preference to continue invoicing through a limited company.

The appeal therefore failed and the decision of the WRC was upheld.

[4.12] ***Groom v Maritime and Coastguard Agency***[15]*—UK Employment Appeal Tribunal—appeal from employment tribunal—Employment Relations Act 1999, s 13(1)(a)—Employment Rights Act 1996, s 230—whether a volunteer was a 'worker'—status of a voluntary relationship—whether there was a contract—entitlement to remuneration—provision of services*

The claimant appealed against an employment tribunal's finding that he was not a 'worker' for the purposes of UK employment legislation.

The claimant was a volunteer in the Coastal Rescue Service ('CRS') from 1985. In May 2020, the claimant was invited to a disciplinary hearing. He was refused permission to be accompanied by a trade union representative—the basis of his claim. The employment tribunal decided that, on a proper construction of the documents governing their relationship, there was no contract at all between the claimant and the respondent.

A 'volunteer handbook' stated that 'no contract of employment exists' between a volunteer and the respondent. The handbook provided that volunteers should abide by a code of conduct. This code of conduct stated that volunteers were 'expected to agree to keep

---

[14] *Templederry Renewable Energy Supply Ltd Community Power v Kelly* UDD2425.
[15] *Groom v Maritime and Coastguard Agency* [2024] EAT 71.

up certain standards', follow coastguard rules, and 'maintain the professional image of the CRS'. It cautioned that failure to abide by the code of conduct could result in cancellation of membership. Under the heading 'payment', the handbook stated that volunteers were permitted to submit monthly claims to cover minor costs and any disruption incidental to authorised activities 'if they wished', but that some volunteers chose not to. Payment was calculated at an hourly rate, with P60 forms issuing at the end of the year and P45s issuing on termination of membership.

Volunteers were required to attend training regularly. They were not subject to a 'minimum response commitment' but were required to 'maintain a reasonable level of incident attendance'. They were required to 'act in line with CRS policies, procedures and processes' and to 'carry out all reasonable requests' by coastguard management when responding to callouts or undertaking training.

In deciding that there was no contractual relationship between the parties, the employment tribunal was persuaded by the facts that the purported agreement was described as a 'voluntary' agreement; that there was no 'automatic' remuneration for any activity and, in any event, many volunteers did not claim; that the 'degree of control' did not appear to be 'particularly significant'; and that a HMRC investigation had concluded the volunteers were not workers, and this was 'clearly significant'. While none of these factors were individually decisive, the tribunal considered that, together, they pointed to a 'genuine voluntary relationship'.

The claimant argued that there was an overarching contract between the parties or, in the alternative, there was a contract in respect of each individual activity undertaken. The UK EAT held that the claimant had not advanced the case of there being an overarching contract before the tribunal, and so he was not permitted to proceed with that line of argument.

The EAT rejected the respondent's argument that volunteering, as a category of relationship, is *sui generis*. This was not supported by any authority, nor, it stated, did the law provide that a volunteer provides service on a non-contractual basis. Describing a relationship as 'voluntary' is not determinative of absence of a contract. The EAT also rejected an argument that money payable for attendance was not in the nature of an entitlement to an hourly rate of remuneration, but analogous to the recovery of expenses. The remuneration document drew a clear distinction between 'remuneration claims' (calculated at an hourly rate) and 'expense claims'. Payments in this case were correctly described as remuneration, rather than arising in the context of a collateral agreement. It was immaterial whether the contract could be described as unilateral or otherwise.

The EAT found that the tribunal erred in holding that there was no contract at all between the parties. It was wrong to regard the question of automatic right to payment as a relevant factor. In doing so, it lost sight of the fact that the claimant had the right to be remunerated for many activities; something which pointed in favour of the existence of a contract. The tribunal also erred in its consideration of whether a contract arose when a volunteer undertook an activity. It reasoned that a volunteer could cease to assist part-way through the activity. There was no factual basis for that notion, which did not sit well with the code of conduct. In any event, such a finding was not inconsistent with a volunteer being a worker when they did attend.

The EAT concluded that the only proper construction of the documents was that a contract came into existence when a volunteer attended an activity in respect of which there was an entitlement to remuneration. That contract was for the provision of services, and not a collateral contract for the reimbursement of expenses. Activities took place in the context of a code of conduct, setting minimum levels of attendance. The use of the term 'volunteer' was not determinative.

The EAT therefore substituted a finding that the claimant was a 'worker'.

[4.13] *Watson v Wallwork Nelson Johnson*[16]*—UK Employment Appeal Tribunal—appeal from employment tribunal—Employment Rights Act 1996, s 230—status of claimant—whether worker, employee, or self-employed—intention of parties*

The claimant appealed against an employment tribunal's finding that he was not an employee, and was therefore not entitled to pursue claims of unfair dismissal or breach of contract.

The claimant was an experienced tax accountant and started employment with the respondent, an accountancy practice, in 2010. He qualified as a tax adviser in 2013 and was promoted, along with two others, to the role of associate in 2018. It was not in dispute that the claimant was an employee of the respondent up to 31 March 2019; he was paid a monthly salary, was auto-enrolled in a pension scheme, was paid overtime, and was treated as an employee for tax and national insurance purposes.

In April 2019, having obtained the requisite accountancy accreditations and practising certificates, the claimant received an increase in his remuneration and ceased to be on the respondent's payroll and auto-enrolment pension scheme. Significantly, he was issued a P45, which he accepted and did not challenge. A draft associate agreement (albeit, in template form) was circulated between the respondent's equity partners. The claimant indicated that he wished to review the partnership accounts and agree all the terms before becoming a partner. There was no written agreement on remuneration, holidays, notice, or how his gross salary was to be paid. Nor was the claimant at any time given access to the partnership accounts, or expected to make any capital contribution. At the same time, however, his income tax and national insurance deductions ceased; something the claimant made no issue of, though he accepted in evidence that he understood the tax implications of becoming partner.

In May 2019, the claimant requested confirmation of his income, falsely stating that he needed this for a meeting with his bank in respect of his mortgage (in evidence, he described this as a 'white lie'). In subsequent correspondence, he sought further confirmation of his gross income and, in the absence of a partnership agreement, confirmation that the respondent would be paying his tax liability, as was its practice.

---

[16] *Watson v Wallwork Nelson Johnson and Johnson* [2024] EAT 105.

The respondent's evidence was that a difficult year, combined with poor administration, led to a delay in providing the claimant with a draft partnership agreement.

In November 2019, the claimant expressed dissatisfaction with the absence of partner meetings and the fact that he had never seen the partnership accounts. He complained that he and the other associate partners were 'still more like employees'. In response, a partnership meeting was scheduled, but was then cancelled and never rescheduled.

By January 2020, the claimant was raising concerns over the lack of any partnership agreement, or written confirmation that the respondent would pay his tax. He was subsequently provided with a draft partnership agreement, which he never accepted.

The employment tribunal found that some of the terms of the draft partnership agreement—such as the level of payment and the equity partners' obligation to pay his income tax and national insurance—reflected the arrangement under which the claimant had been working since April 2019. The parties failed to agree on a term that would have avoided the claimant sharing joint liability for the respondent's debts. In any event, the partnership agreement was never accepted or entered into, and so terms were never agreed.

In February 2020, the claimant commenced a period of ill-health absence, citing stress resulting from the situation with the respondent. The respondent agreed to his request that he be re-instated as an employee. The claimant expressed the view that since he had been removed from the respondent's payroll without a partnership agreement in place, his employment contract from 2018 was still effective and it was not necessary to sign another contract.

Thereafter, the relationship between the parties deteriorated, exacerbated by the onset of Covid-19, and culminating in the claimant's suspension. By this point, the respondent was of the view that the claimant's stance in asserting that he was an employee constituted a breach of his fiduciary duties as partner. For his part, the claimant accepted in cross-examination that this assertion represented a '180-degree turn'. The claimant was duly advised that his participation in the partnership would be treated as coming to an end, with effect from June 2020.

The employment tribunal did not find the claimant to be a credible witness and observed that his approach to his negotiations with the respondent 'were all about maximising his drawings'. It was telling that for almost 12 months, the claimant—a senior tax accountant—was paid and taxed as a self-employed partner, without raising any issues regarding his status. In short, the claimant had specialist insight into employment status and was 'quite prepared to work the system in order to minimise his tax exposure'.

As to the arrangement entered into by the parties in 2019, the tribunal rejected any suggestion that it had been anything other than genuine. It was satisfied that the claimant's appointment to associate partner was part of the respondent's succession planning, and that the intention was that the associates would ultimately progress to equity partners. While the respondent could have introduced the partnership deed much earlier, the employment tribunal accepted that its failure to do so did not betray a 'sham' appointment intended to reduce its national insurance costs.

The employment tribunal concluded that after his change in status to an associate partner, and after the essential terms were agreed, the claimant was no longer working for the respondent under a contract of employment, but was a self-employed partner. The tribunal gave particular weight to the claimant's new tax arrangement, and to what it found to have been the intention of the parties, given their particular expertise.

The EAT held that the employment tribunal was entitled to give weight to what it found to be the parties' genuine intention: that there was a partnership agreement, notwithstanding their failure to reach agreement on all of the terms proposed. The tribunal had had proper regard to the factors pointing in favour of and against a partnership, and had determined that the balance tipped in favour of a partnership.

The appeal was, accordingly, dismissed.

See also decision of UK Supreme Court in *Commissioners for Her Majesty's Revenue and Customs v Professional Game Match Officials Ltd*,[17] in **Ch 17**, Taxation at **[17.36]**.

FRIVOLOUS AND VEXATIOUS APPEALS

[4.14] *Novak v Intesa Sanpaolo Life DAC*[18]—*High Court—Simons J—appeal from Circuit Court—Unfair Dismissals Acts 1977 to 2015—appeal struck out as being frivolous and vexatious on a procedural motion*

The plaintiff appealed against the Circuit Court's dismissal of her statutory claim for unfair dismissal as being frivolous and vexatious. The proceedings, which had a protracted history, pre-dated the commencement of the Workplace Relations Act 2015, and so the Circuit Court matter was an appeal from the Employment Appeals Tribunal, albeit significantly delayed.

The defendant complained that the plaintiff was involved in separate litigation involving the Data Protection Commissioner and the Residential Tenancies Board, respectively. It was on this basis that the appeal was struck out as being frivolous and vexatious. This was done on the defendant's motion prior to the substantive matter being heard.

On appeal to the High Court, the defendant conceded that the Circuit Court appeal should not have been struck out as being frivolous and vexatious on the basis that the plaintiff was pursuing other litigation involving different parties. Thus, the appeal was allowed and the decision of the Circuit Court set aside.

Given that the Circuit Court had not exercised its appellate jurisdiction under the Unfair Dismissals Act 1977, the appeal was remitted to the Court below for a full hearing.

---

[17] *HMRC v Professional Game Match Officials Ltd* [2024] UKSC 29, in Chapter 17, Taxation at **[17.36]**. See *Arthur Cox Employment Law Yearbook 2020* at [5.10] for decision of Upper Tribunal (Tax and Chancery Chamber) in *Commissioners for Her Majesty's Revenue and Customs v Professional Game Match Officials Ltd* [2020] UKUT 147 (TCC).

[18] *Novak v Intesa Sanpaolo Life DAC* [2024] IEHC 262.

IDENTIFICATION OF EMPLOYER

[4.15]   *Metropolitan Films International Ltd v McCarthy[19]—Labour Court—appeal from Workplace Relations Commission—Terms of Employment (Information) Acts 1994 to 2014—respondent not the claimant's employer—no jurisdiction to hear substantive matter*

The respondent appealed against a WRC decision upholding a complaint under the Terms of Employment (Information) Acts 1994 to 2014.

The claimant, a stagehand in the film industry, did not attend to contest the appeal and conveyed that he would not be participating on health grounds. Nevertheless, the respondent applied to have the WRC decision set aside and contended that it was not the claimant's employer. The Court heard that, at all material times, the claimant's employment for tax purposes was with two entirely separate legal entities.

In light of there being no evidence that the respondent was the claimant's employer, the Court determined that it had no jurisdiction to hear the substantive matter. The complaint was not well founded and the decision of the WRC was set aside accordingly.

[4.16]   *Metropolitan Films International Ltd v Lyons[20]—Labour Court—appeal from Workplace Relations Commission—Protection of Employees (Fixed-Term Work) Act 2003, s 8—identification of employer*

The respondent appealed against the WRC's decision upholding a complaint under the Protection of Employees (Fixed-Term Work) Act 2003.

The claimant was engaged as a construction stagehand on different TV productions, including seasons 1–3 of 'Penny Dreadful' and season 3 of 'Into the Badlands'. He submitted that he was employed by the respondent on a succession of fixed-term contracts, none of which provided objective justification, neither for his further employment on a fixed-term basis, nor for not offering him a contract of indefinite duration.

It was common case that a separate Designated Activity Company ('DAC') was incorporated for each individual production, through which the claimant was employed as a PAYE worker. There was no documentary evidence before the Court that the claimant at any time entered into an employment agreement with the respondent. Nevertheless, the claimant submitted that each production was 'undertaken by the same producer company with both directors who are the shareholders in common with each DAC'.

The respondent submitted that the claimant was never in an employment relationship with the respondent, so that the complaint was unsustainable.

---

[19]   *Metropolitan Films International Ltd v McCarthy* TED2411.
[20]   *Metropolitan Films International Ltd v Lyons* FTD247.

The evidence before the Court established that the claimant was employed by Badlands Three TV Productions DAC at all material times. There was no evidence to support the claimant's assertion that he was employed at any time by the respondent.

The appeal therefore succeeded and the WRC's decision was set aside.

PRESS FREEDOM

[4.17] *Law Society of Ireland v Ellis*[21]—*High Court—Simons J—application to take up transcript of digital audio recording—press reporting on contents of affidavit not read aloud in open court*

This was an application to take up a transcript of the digital audio recording ('DAR') made by the respondent in the underlying proceedings and concerned a hearing in August 2022 in which the parties indicated that orders could be made on consent. These included orders suspending the respondent from practising as a solicitor and directing that funds held in the respondent's practice accounts be paid to the Law Society of Ireland for reimbursement to clients in anticipation of potential claims.

The respondent was concerned that the content of the applicant's grounding affidavit, which had not been read aloud in court, had since been referred to in the printed media. The suggestion was that the material had been provided to the media inappropriately. The respondent sought a transcript to demonstrate that the grounding affidavit was not read aloud in open court.

Emphasising that members of the media are typically entitled to report on the contents of affidavits, notwithstanding that they have not been read aloud in open court, Simons J was satisfied, given the gravity of the proceedings, that this was an appropriate case in which to grant access to the DAR. The Court decided against imposing any restrictions on the use of the transcript, being satisfied that the application was made *bona fide*. Thus, the order was granted, subject to the usual undertakings.

RES JUDICATA

[4.18] *Xerox (Ireland) Pension Scheme v Gavagan*[22]—*Labour Court—appeal from Workplace Relations Commission—Pensions Acts 1990 to 2014, s 81(1)—referral out of time—res judicata*

The claimant appealed against a decision of the WRC. He contended that he had been denied equal pension treatment in 2009, in breach of the Pensions Act 1990. The Adjudication Officer determined that the referral had been made out of time.

---

[21] *Law Society of Ireland v Ellis* [2023] IEHC 728.
[22] *Xerox (Ireland) Pension Scheme v Gavagan* PAT231.

The respondent employer submitted that the appeal was manifestly out of time and that the referral was *res judicata*, having regard to the fact that an identical complaint had been referred, and decided upon by the WRC in 2016 and 2017 respectively. The claimant did not dispute the fact of the identical referral.

The Court decided that the referral was manifestly out of time and the appeal therefore failed.

[4.19] *Parnell v Royal Mail Group Ltd*[23]—*UK Employment Appeal Tribunal—appeal from employment tribunal—Equality Act 2010, ss 15, 20 & 21—disability discrimination—unfair dismissal—issue previously determined by a different tribunal litigated in a separate claim*

The claimant appealed against an employment tribunal's dismissal of 10 complaints of disability discrimination and unfair dismissal. Earlier claims of disability discrimination (21 in total) involving the same parties, but relating to prior events, had previously been determined by a different tribunal.

The claimant was employed by the respondent as a postman from June 1999 until his dismissal in June 2020. From at least 2012, the claimant suffered anxiety and depression. This had a significant impact on his ability to carry out normal day-to-day activities. In May 2017, the claimant made a complaint of bullying and harassment against a manager. That complaint was investigated but not upheld. The respondent, taking the view that the allegations were made in bad faith, commenced a misconduct investigation against the claimant. In January 2018, the claimant went off work on sick leave; he did not return. The misconduct proceedings resulted in the issue of a two-year serious warning to the claimant, which was upheld on appeal. A second complaint of bullying and harassment in 2020 was also dismissed.

Following an absence management process, the respondent decided that the claimant's more than two-year absence was 'unsustainable', and that it could not be confident that the claimant had any intention of returning to work, or co-operating with management. There had been an irretrievable breakdown of trust and confidence and there was nothing the respondent could do to facilitate a return to work. The claimant would go on to bring 31 claims in two sets of proceedings.

The first employment tribunal, which was concerned solely with disability discrimination, concluded that the respondent was, or should have been, aware that the claimant was disabled with anxiety and depression from January 2012. It also found that the respondent failed to make reasonable adjustments in failing to remove the two-year serious warning from the claimant's record and to review the misconduct investigation. Otherwise, the claims were dismissed.

In the subsequent unfair dismissal hearing, the claimant attempted to re-litigate the respondent's refusal to remove the two-year serious warning. This was a departure from the agreed list of issues. All of those claims were dismissed, with the employment

---

[23] *Parnell v Royal Mail Group Ltd* [2024] EAT 130.

tribunal finding that the principal reason for the dismissal was a 'breakdown in employment relations/trust and confidence'. The respondent's conduct had not prevented the claimant from returning to work and it had acted reasonably, given the breakdown of the working relationship. The tribunal added that the two-year warning played no part in its decision.

On appeal, the claimant submitted that the second tribunal failed to consider the first tribunal's findings to support his argument that the failure to review the misconduct investigation and to remove the two-year warning exacerbated his anxiety and distrust in management, placing him at a substantial disadvantage.

The difficulty with the claimant's submission was that the first tribunal's decision in that regard was limited to a finding that the claimant was placed at a substantial disadvantage up to the start of 2020. The second tribunal was being asked to consider whether that was still the case in the months that followed, in particular after the warning had expired. The EAT did not consider that the second tribunal was bound to hold that there was a 'continuing link' between the earlier failure to review the two-year warning and the subsequent decision to dismiss. It was required to reach its own decision on the evidence before it in relation to the relevant events with which it was concerned, this included the reasonableness of the decision to dismiss at the time it was taken.

The second tribunal had permissibly found that there would be no efficacy in removing the two-year warning, which at the relevant time had expired, and so this would not have been a reasonable adjustment. The second tribunal had also permissibly found that any unfavourable treatment was a proportionate means of achieving a legitimate aim.

The appeal was, accordingly, dismissed.

SETTLEMENT AGREEMENTS

[4.20]   *North Leinster Citizens Information Centre v Gerety*[24]—*Labour Court—appeal from Workplace Relations Commission—Safety, Health and Welfare at Work Acts 2005 to 2014, s 29(1)—mediated settlement—action compromised*

The claimant appealed against the WRC's decision not to recommend concession of her claim under the Safety, Health and Welfare at Work Acts 2005 to 2014.

The respondent informed the Court that the claimant had entered into a mediated settlement with legal representation and compromised all claims and appeals. The claimant accepted that this was the case.

Accordingly, the Court did not have jurisdiction to hear the complaints and the appeal failed.

---

[24]   *North Leinster Citizens Information Centre v Gerety* HSD248.

[4.21] Abtran Unlimited v Sumaili[25]—Labour Court—appeal from Workplace Relations Commission—Employment Equality Acts 1998 to 2021, s 83(1)—legally binding mediated agreement—jurisdiction

The claimant appealed against the WRC's dismissal of her complaint under the Employment Equality Acts 1998 to 2021. The WRC held that it did not have jurisdiction to consider the complaint in circumstances where the substance of that complaint had been the subject of a binding mediation agreement between the claimant and the respondent.

The parties confirmed at the outset of the appeal hearing that a mediation agreement had concluded with the assistance of a mediation officer of the WRC. The matter forming the basis of the claim was covered by this agreement.

The Labour Court determined that it did not have jurisdiction to go behind a legally binding mediation agreement. Accordingly, the appeal was dismissed.

[4.22] Bathgate v Technip Singapore Pte Ltd[26]—Court of Session of Scotland—Clerk, Malcolm & Wise LJJ—appeal from UK Employment Appeal Tribunal—post-employment claim—settlement agreement—waiver in respect of future claims—whether such a waiver permitted by equality legislation—meaning of 'seafarer'—whether a statutory exception from discrimination protection continued to apply in respect of post-employment claims

The claimant brought a claim of post-employment age discrimination against his former employer before the employment tribunal. The matter was defended on jurisdictional grounds, of which, following an appeal to the UK EAT, two such grounds remained live before the Court of Session.

At issue in this appeal was, firstly, the proper interpretation of 'seafarer' under the Equality Act 2010 (the '2010 Act'), and secondly, whether a statutory exception from discrimination protection continued to apply in respect of post-employment claims under the 2010 Act. A cross-appeal by the respondent concerned whether the settlement agreement, which regulated the claimant's redundancy, ousted the tribunal's jurisdiction over the discrimination claim.

The claimant was employed by the respondent between 1997 and 2017 as chief officer aboard a number of vessels. From 2008 until 2016 he worked on a vessel registered in the Bahamas, which operated outside UK or EEA waters. The claimant would travel from his permanent residence in Scotland, serving a six-week tour of duty at a time on the vessel. When he ceased work on that vessel, the claimant undertook a variety of onshore tasks. In 2016, the respondent engaged in a redundancy scoring exercise with a view to reducing its fleet of chief officers. The claimant was placed at risk of redundancy and having received independent legal advice, he signed a settlement agreement

---

[25] *Abtran Unlimited v Sumaili* EDA2452.
[26] *Bathgate v Technip Singapore Pte Ltd* [2023] CSIH 48, [2024] IRLR 326.

with the respondent, part of which provided that he agreed not to pursue a long list of claims, including direct or indirect discrimination on the grounds of age.

The settlement agreement provided for two redundancy payments, including an 'additional payment', which the claimant was led to believe, from discussions with the respondent, that he would receive. At the date of redundancy, however, the claimant was 61 years of age. A clause in the agreement stated that the additional payment would apply to all officers 'who have not attained their 61st birthday'. Ultimately, the respondent decided that those over the age of 60 at the point of redundancy were ineligible for the additional payment.

The tribunal did not accept the claimant's submission that 'the particular complaint', a post-settlement claim, could not be waived. It concluded that the relevant clause covered claims 'whether or not in the contemplation of the parties' and that this had been expressed in 'plain and unequivocal terms' in the settlement agreement. On appeal, the EAT held that the 2010 Act did not permit a waiver of a future claim. At the very least, the circumstances giving rise to the complaint would need to have existed at the time of the agreement. However, the EAT went on to observe that 'seafarer' status attached to anyone who 'habitually' works aboard ships, rejecting the claimant's submission that he was only a 'seafarer' while on board a vessel. As the claimant had been a seafarer throughout his employment working on foreign vessels, the 2010 Act did not apply to him, and it followed that the tribunal had no jurisdiction to hear his claim.

The Court of Session did not find support for the EAT's approach in the words of the 2010 Act. The Court concluded that the 2010 Act does not exclude the settlement of future claims, provided this is sufficiently particularised in the terms of the settlement agreement. The complaint need not necessarily have been known of, or its grounds in existence, at the time of the agreement, and the task is to determine whether the complaint being made out is or is not covered by the terms of the agreement.

The jurisdiction of the tribunal was excluded by the terms of the settlement agreement and the claim was thus dismissed.

[4.23] *Clifford v IBM United Kingdom Ltd*[27]—*UK Employment Appeal Tribunal— appeal from employment tribunal—Equality Act 2010, ss 13, 15 & 19—disability discrimination—compromise agreement—legal advice*

The claimant appealed against an employment tribunal's striking out of his disability discrimination claim as having no reasonable prospect of success.

The claimant commenced employment with the respondent under a transfer of undertaking. From 2008, the claimant was continuously absent form work due to ill-health. In 2012, he raised a grievance, alleging disability discrimination in connection with a lack of salary increase and holiday pay. It was agreed that the claimant would be moved to the respondent's 'disability plan', allowing him to remain as an employee without an obligation to work. To that end, a settlement agreement was drawn up which

---

[27] *Clifford v IBM United Kingdom Ltd* [2024] EAT 90.

provided for a right to be paid 75% of agreed earnings at the date of transfer into the plan. Crucially, this was stated to be in settlement of any potential employment claims. The claimant signed the agreement having had the benefit of specialist legal advice.

This claim, presented in 2022, alleged unfavourable treatment as a result of 'something arising' from his disability. It was agreed that the claimant was a disabled person. The 'something arising' referred to his absences from work, his being placed on the disability plan, or in the alternative, his inability to perform his duties under his contract. The alleged unfavourable treatment referred to the following: his not having an annual salary review in the same way as those employees who were able to carry out their contractual duties; his not having a salary increase in line with his cohort, or in line with the average annual increases; and his annual leave payment having been at a rate of 75% of what was paid to those not on the disability plan.

The claimant also alleged indirect discrimination, claiming that the respondent's practice put disabled employees, including those on the disability plan, at a particular disadvantage, in that they were not given the benefit of an annual salary review and were not given equivalent annual salary increases.

Striking out the claim, the employment tribunal noted that the compromise agreement had been the result of a detailed negotiation, bringing to an end 'a lengthy process of grievance and appeal'. Future claims for holiday pay, and for not having had pay increases (the subjects of the 2012 grievance) were expressly settled. More generally, the compromise agreement was a 'consensual variation of a contract', whereby the claimant became an inactive employee, never again expected to work for the respondent. Accordingly, all the 'normal features' of an employment contract disappeared, leaving only the right to be paid 75% of previous salary. The claimant's reliance on a non-disabled person as a comparator was therefore flawed, since a person who did not have a disability could not receive 75% of their salary for their entire working life without having to do any work. The disability plan was a benefit available only to those with a severe disability. The transition to inactive employee status meant that there was no comparison with active employees, so that the inability to get a pay rise was not a detriment caused by something arising from disability.

On appeal, the EAT held that the employment tribunal was right to conclude that the disability discrimination claims were precluded by the compromise agreement, which came within the terms of waiver. Its analysis also concluded that the compromise agreement met the statutory requirements of a qualifying settlement agreement, and that the agreement 'related to the particular complaint'. A recent authority,[28] indistinguishable from this case, had held that future claims could be validly compromised by a qualifying settlement agreement where certain preconditions were met. While this was determinative of the appeal, none of the discrimination claims had any reasonable prospect of success in any event; the tribunal had correctly deduced that the comparator relied upon by the claimant was not a valid one.

The appeal was, accordingly, dismissed.

---

[28] *Bathgate v Technip Singapore Pte Ltd* [2023] CSIH 48, [2024] IRLR 326.

STRIKE OUT

[4.24] *Leeks v University College London Hospitals NHS Foundation Trust*[29]— UK Employment Appeal Tribunal—*appeal from employment tribunal—'lost' witness—whether a fair trial was possible—whether decision to strike out the claim was proportionate—whether refusal to engage in judicial mediation or assessment justified an award of costs*

The claimant appealed against an employment tribunal's decision to strike out her claim.

The claimant alleged that the respondent NHS trust offered her jobs conditionally but withdrew the offers. She brought claims of public interest disclosure detriment, and direct and indirect disability discrimination.

Following two adjournments of the substantive hearing at the claimant's request, the respondent applied to strike out the claim. That hearing too was adjourned, the claimant having apparently fallen off a chair outside the hearing room (she had refused to enter). Due to a delay in providing supporting medical evidence, the hearing took place some three months later. The employment Judge at that stage decided against striking out the claim, though she found that the claimant had acted unreasonably. Three years followed with no progress in preparation for the final hearing.

The respondent again applied to strike out the claim. By then, five years had passed since the events giving rise to the complaints. The employment Judge concluded that the claimant had not actively pursued the claims and that there had been an inordinate and inexcusable delay. It was no longer possible to have a fair trial because the respondent had lost access to a key witness. The strike out was therefore proportionate as the respondent would incur unacceptable prejudice if the matter were to proceed.

The claimant appealed on the ground that the employment tribunal misdirected itself in law in deciding that the loss of a key witness necessarily meant that there was no prospect of a fair hearing.

Allowing the appeal, the EAT observed that the employment tribunal was not told 'anything more of substance' at the strike out hearing, other than that the respondent intended to call three witnesses, one of whom was no longer in its employ, and therefore not 'compellable'. Unfortunately, this meant that the tribunal failed to consider important questions necessary to decide whether there was a risk that a fair hearing could not take place. Crucially, it was not the case that a witness who was no longer employed by one of the parties was 'lost'. Such a witness might still be willing to give evidence if requested, particularly where a former employer is accused of discriminatory conduct. Alternatively, a witness order could be sought. These matters were not considered by the tribunal. There was no suggestion that the respondent had lost contact with the witness in question, or that they were unwilling to give evidence.

---

[29] *Leeks v University College London Hospitals NHS Foundation Trust* [2024] EAT 134.

The decision to strike out the claim on the basis of a 'lost' witness could not stand. The matter was remitted to the same employment Judge, given her experience in managing the case.

The employment tribunal also erred in holding that a failure to engage in judicial mediation or assessment could 'never' result in an order for costs. The question of costs was also remitted.

TERRITORIAL JURISDICTION

[4.25] *The British Council v Beldica*[30]—*UK Employment Appeal Tribunal—appeal from employment tribunal—Employment Act 1996—Equality Act 2010—European Convention on Human Rights, art 6—Human Rights Act 1998—territorial reach of employment protections—jurisdiction*

The respondent appealed against an employment tribunal's decision on its jurisdiction to determine an extra-territorial employment claim.

The claimant was a Romanian national who had been living and working in Dubai from 2012. Between March 2016 and December 2020, she was employed by the respondent, the British Council, as its human resources business partner for the Middle East and North Africa region. The respondent, a public body overseen by the UK Foreign and Commonwealth Development Office, was considered 'an integral part of the British Embassy'. For her part, the claimant had no material involvement in the respondent's UK operations, and the employment tribunal described her as 'a local employee through and through'.

The claimant's employment was terminated in December 2020. When she raised a complaint about the dismissal, she was advised by the respondent that her employment was governed by Emirati labour law. She was, however, unable to register a complaint in the UAE Labour Court, as she had not been issued the requisite 'labour card', and the respondent did not fall under the purview of the issuing body. She therefore presented her claims for unfair dismissal, pregnancy or maternity discrimination, and redundancy pay before an employment tribunal in the UK. The respondent contested the tribunal's jurisdiction to hear the complaints.

Having found, in light of recent Emirati caselaw, that the claimant was not absolutely barred from submitting an employment claim in the UAE Labour Court, the employment tribunal proceeded to consider what would have happened had she done so. It concluded that the respondent would have successfully pleaded diplomatic immunity and the UAE Labour Court would have refused jurisdiction to hear the complaint. The respondent's immunity would have severed the territorial pull of Emirati law, frustrating the claimant's legitimate expectation to enforce her employment rights and breaching customary international law.

---

[30] *The British Council v Beldica* [2024] EAT 92.

However, the employment tribunal was satisfied that since the very act of claiming immunity was an activity of a diplomatic and consular agent, the Human Rights Act 1998 would apply extra-territorially. In the circumstances, the tribunal was satisfied that the claimant's art 6 ECHR rights were engaged and that the relevant UK employment legislation fell to be interpreted in a manner compatible with the Human Rights Act 1998.

The UK EAT found that the difficulty underlying the employment tribunal's decision was its foundation upon an 'exercise of hypothetical reasoning': the claimant never did submit a claim in the UAE Labour Court and the respondent never did assert immunity. This gave rise to conceptual difficulties that rendered the tribunal's reasoning flawed. The EAT pointed out that, crucially, the ECHR had no application in this case. No act or omission on the respondent's part could be described as an exertion of authority or control over the claimant's right to access court in the UAE. Entering a plea of immunity, or declining to waive that right, would still not amount to such an activity.

While this was determinative of the appeal, the EAT went on to find that there had been no relevant assessment as to whether the claimant's employment might amount to an exercise of sovereign authority, and so there was no basis for the tribunal's assumption that acceptance of a plea of immunity would breach customary international law. In any event, the authorities did not support the tribunal's contention that customary international law anticipates, 'in spirit if not in letter', that a plea of immunity must not result in lack of recourse in the employer's home state.

Accordingly, the appeal was allowed.

[4.26] *Stena Drilling Pte Ltd v Smith*[31]—*UK Employment Appeal Tribunal— appeal from employment tribunal—Employment Rights Act 1996—Equality Act 2010—Civil Jurisdiction and Judgments Act 1982, as amended—international jurisdiction—territorial jurisdiction—material error of law*

The respondent company appealed against a preliminary decision of an employment tribunal which ruled on the issue of jurisdiction in favour of the claimant.

The respondent was incorporated in Singapore where it also had a place of business. It was part of the global 'Stena Group' which owned and operated vessels involved in deep sea drilling. The claimant was employed by the respondent as a derrickman on vessels operated by the group between July 2011 and October 2012. His home address for tax purposes was Liverpool but in November 2012, he changed this to an address in France when he began working for another company in the Stena Group. The nature of the claimant's work did not change. In 2013, he was promoted to 'assistant driller' and in 2019 he became a 'junior driller'. Throughout this period, he was non-resident for the purpose of UK tax. He set up a bank account outside the UK and spent no more than 90 days per year in the UK.

---

[31] *Stena Drilling Pte Ltd v Smith* [2024] EAT 57.

In 2021, the claimant returned to his residential address in Liverpool and, owing to his changed tax residence status, entered into a new contract of employment with the respondent. When this contract commenced, the claimant was absent from work due to ill health. He undertook no further work for the respondent until his dismissal in October 2021.

The claimant's contracts of employment provided that they were to be governed and construed in accordance with Singaporean law. The contracts also stated that they were entered into in Singapore. The claimant was paid in sterling and, while employed by the respondent, was subject to UK income tax and national insurance. HR and payroll were administered by another company of the Stena Group with offices in Aberdeen. When he confirmed acceptance of his original employment offer in 2011, the claimant had done so in writing to the Aberdeen office.

The respondent submitted that the tribunal had failed to recognise the distinction between international jurisdiction and territorial jurisdiction. It submitted that the tribunal had correctly identified that the respondent was not domiciled in the UK, and that the claimant did not habitually work in the UK. It had also correctly rejected an argument that the Aberdeen-based administrator was an 'agent' of the respondent. Since no other route to international jurisdiction was apparent from the facts, the claims should have been dismissed at that point. Alternatively, the respondent asserted that the tribunal had erred in its conclusions as to territorial jurisdiction. It failed to recognise that the claimant 'plainly' did not work 'wholly or partly within Great Britain' and erroneously concluded that the parties had made no express choice of law.

The UK EAT concluded that the tribunal's reasons indicated that it had not appreciated that international jurisdiction and territorial jurisdiction fall to be considered separately. Specifically, the tribunal erred in law by proceeding as though rules on territorial jurisdiction could confer international jurisdiction. Since its conclusion as to jurisdiction was based on a material error of law, the tribunal's decision was set side.

However, the EAT refused to dismiss the appeal outright for lack of jurisdiction. Were it not for the involvement of the company in Aberdeen, to whom the claimant indicated his acceptance of the job offer, there could have been no argument that no other route to international jurisdiction was possible on the facts. At the very least, there was a possibility that a factual inquiry into the precise role of this company might yield to the conclusion that the business that engaged the claimant was situated in Aberdeen. The matter was therefore remitted to the tribunal to consider afresh the issue of jurisdiction.

TIME LIMITS—CLAIMS

[4.27] *TC v Firma Haus Jacobus Alten und Altenpflegeheim GmbH*[32]—*European Court of Justice—reference for a preliminary ruling from Germany—*

---

[32] *TC v Firma Haus Jacobus Alten und Altenpflegeheim GmbH* (Case C-284/23).

Directive 92/85/EEC[33]—safety and health of pregnant workers and workers who have recently given birth or are breastfeeding—prohibition of dismissal—worker who became aware of her pregnancy after the expiry of the time limit for bringing an action challenging her dismissal—request for leave to bring such an action out of time—right to effective judicial protection

This request for a preliminary ruling concerned the interpretation of Directive 92/85/EEC on the introduction of measures to encourage improvements in the safety and health at work of pregnant workers and workers who have recently given birth or are breastfeeding. The request was made in German proceedings between the applicant and the respondent company, concerning the dismissal of the applicant, who was pregnant at the time.

The applicant was employed by the respondent, a care home for the elderly, as a care assistant under a one-year employment contract. Her employment commenced on 1 August 2022. The applicant was dismissed with effect from 21 October 2022. On 9 November 2022, the applicant was medically certified as being seven weeks pregnant; she informed the respondent the following day.

On 13 December 2022, the applicant brought an action before the Labour Court in Mainz (the referring Court) against her dismissal on the ground that, on the date of the dismissal, she was pregnant. The referring Court noted the position in federal caselaw that, despite the prohibition of dismissal of a worker during her pregnancy, where an employer is informed of the employee's pregnancy after her dismissal, that dismissal is deemed valid after the expiry of a time limit of three weeks, unless a request for leave to bring an action out of time is lodged 'within two weeks of the removal of the obstacle to bringing an action'. Since no such request had been lodged, the action fell to be dismissed. The referring Court, however, had doubts as to the compatibility of the national law (itself the subject of criticism by legal commentators) with EU law. It therefore decided to stay the proceedings and to refer a question to the European Court of Justice ('ECJ') for a preliminary ruling.

The referring Court asked, in essence, whether arts 10 and 12 of Directive 92/85/EEC must be interpreted as precluding national legislation under which a pregnant worker, who only becomes aware of her pregnancy after the expiry of the time limit prescribed for bringing an action challenging the dismissal, is required to lodge a request for leave to bring an action out of time within two weeks.

The ECJ observed that arts 10 and 12 are a 'specific expression ... of the principle of effective judicial protection of an individual's rights under EU law'. Protective measures, once adopted, must have a genuine dissuasive effect on the employer and must be commensurate with the injury suffered. Procedural rules for the safeguarding of EU rights must be no less favourable than those governing similar domestic actions (principle of equivalence), and must not render the exercise of those rights practically impossible or excessively difficult (principle of effectiveness).

---

[33] Directive 92/85/EEC on the introduction of measures to encourage improvements in the safety and health at work of pregnant workers and workers who have recently given birth or are breastfeeding.

It was not apparent that the national law at issue did not comply with the principle of equivalence. As regards the principle of effectiveness, the ECJ noted that, in the interests of legal certainty, 'reasonable time limits' for bringing proceedings are compatible with EU law. It is for Member States to establish those limitation periods in light of, *inter alia*, the significance for the parties concerned of the decisions to be taken, the complexities of the procedures and the number of people who may be affected. The principle of effectiveness does not, therefore, preclude the setting of a relatively short limitation period in an action for unlawful dismissal. That said, procedural rules which are liable to make the exercise of art 10 rights excessively difficult for pregnant workers do not comply with the principle of effectiveness.

The two-week limit for a request for leave to bring an action out of time was 'particularly short' in view of 'the situation in which a woman finds herself at the start of her pregnancy'. It was also shorter than the ordinary time limit of three weeks for bringing an action challenging a dismissal. A worker who, for reasons not attributable to her, was not aware of her pregnancy before the expiry of the time limit, would have only two weeks in which to request leave to bring such an action—a 'considerable reduction' of the time limit in which to obtain effective advice, to draft and submit the request, and to bring the action itself (the national law requiring, in principle, that the action be lodged at the same time as the request).

The starting point of the two-week period—ie, the time when 'the obstacle to bringing an action is removed'—appeared ambiguous, potentially making the exercise of Directive 92/85/EEC rights more difficult. Further, the requirement in national law that the dismissed worker inform her employer 'without delay' of her pregnancy, coupled with the additional requirement that she submit a request for leave to bring an action out of time, demonstrated the complexity of the national legislation, which entailed 'competing obligations' to be fulfilled within 'separate overlapping periods'.

Procedural rules governing a request for leave to bring an action out of time could potentially infringe the principle of effective judicial protection. Accordingly, the referring Court's question was answered in the affirmative, in circumstances where those procedural rules give rise to problems liable to render the implementation of art 10 rights excessively difficult, thereby making them non-compliant with the requirements of the principle of effectiveness.

[4.28] *Xerox (Ireland) v Gavagan*[34]—Labour Court—appeal from Workplace Relations Commission—Pensions Act 1990, s 81E—alleged misrepresentation—complaint out of time

The claimant appealed against a WRC decision that his complaint under the Pensions Act 1990 was not well founded.

The claimant's employment with the respondent was terminated by reason of redundancy in July 2009. The complaint was made to the WRC in February 2022. It was

---

[34] *Xerox (Ireland) v Gavagan* PAT242.

common case that the complaint was identical to an earlier complaint against another Xerox entity, referred to the WRC in May 2016. In both instances, the claimant alleged that the delayed referral was due to misrepresentation by the respondent. The earlier complaint was dismissed for being out of time.

Here, the claimant submitted that, as a result of a decision of the Data Protection Commissioner, he became aware in June 2021 of certain matters, hitherto unknown to him, which he considered relevant to his contention that the respondent was guilty of misrepresentation to him in 2009 or before. He therefore asked for an extension of time to bring the complaint.

The Labour Court concluded that no alleged misrepresentation by the respondent, which became known to the claimant in 2021, could have delayed the referral of the complaint until 2022. The referral was therefore out of time and the appeal failed.

[4.29] *Galway and Roscommon Education Board v Moran*[35]—*Labour Court—appeal from Workplace Relations Commission —Industrial Relations Acts 1946 to 2019—Pensions Act 1990, s 81E, as amended—time limits—complaint made out of time*

The claimant appealed against a WRC decision that his complaint under the Pensions Act 1990 was out of time. On appeal, the issue of time limits was dealt with as a preliminary matter.

The claimant accepted that the complaint was lodged out of time. He urged the Court to set aside the statutory time limits 'and instead consider issues such as negligence, duty of care, contract law, natural justice, moral turpitude, and the imbalance of power'.

The respondent pointed out that the claimant's employment ended on 30 December 2018, with his pension entitlements beginning the following day. The complaint was submitted on 22 June 2022.

The claimant argued that the matter should never have been scheduled for hearing if it was statute-barred.

While sympathetic, the Court found that the complaint was not lodged within the time limits allowed under the Pensions Act 1990. As a creature of statute, the Court had no jurisdiction to hear the complaint.

[4.30] *Rose Hospitality Ltd v Scanlon*[36]—*Labour Court—appeal from Workplace Relations Commission—Unfair Dismissals Acts 1977 to 2015, s 8A—incorrect respondent named*

The claimant appealed against the WRC's award of €487.50 in upholding his complaint of unfair dismissal.

---

[35] *Galway and Roscommon Education Board v Moran* PAT241.
[36] *Rose Hospitality Ltd v Scanlon* UDD2429.

On the appeal form, the respondent was named as Jackson Hotel Ballybofey. When alerted to this, the claimant said that Rose Hospitality Ltd was not the lawful owner of Jackson Hotel, though he was still waiting to confirm who was. The claimant declined to lodge submissions, citing concern for the rain forest. Nor did he apply to the WRC for an order correcting the name of the respondent. The Labour Court determined that, as there was no Adjudication Officer decision against Jackson Hotel, there was no valid appeal before it.

The appeal failed.

[4.31] *Whelton t/a Whelton Dental v Corkery*[37]—*Labour Court—appeal from Workplace Relations Commission—European Communities (Protection of Employees on Transfer of Undertakings) Regulations 2003,*[38] *reg 11(1)—statutory time limit—complaint out of time*

The claimant appealed against a WRC decision that her complaint under the European Communities (Protection of Employees on Transfer of Undertakings) Regulations 2003 was out of time.

The claimant was employed as a dental nurse. Her employment transferred from the respondent to another party on 1 July 2021. The complaint was referred to the WRC on 21 February 2022. As this was outside six months of the alleged breach, with no justifiable basis for an extension of time, the Court did not have jurisdiction to hear the complaint, and so the appeal was rejected.

[4.32] *Rotunda Hospital v McNally*[39]—*Labour Court—appeal from Workplace Relations Commission—Employment Equality Acts 1998 to 2021, ss 77(6) & 83(1)—time limits—misrepresentation*

The claimant appealed against the WRC's dismissal of her complaint for being out of time.

The claimant was employed by the respondent hospital from March 2003 until 20 May 2019. Due to the volume of related cases (27 in total) in which time limits arose as a preliminary issue, a case management conference resolved to deal with the cases in blocks, focusing on the issue of time limits.

The claimant submitted that a misrepresentation had occurred on various dates and that the operative date in respect of time limits under the Employment Equality Acts 1998 to 2021 was the date on which she became aware of the misrepresentation. She referred to matters raised in other cases, as opposed to being relevant to these proceedings, without elaborating on how they constituted misrepresentation.

---

[37] *Whelton t/a Whelton Dental v Corkery* TUD247.
[38] European Communities (Protection of Employees on Transfer of Undertakings) Regulations 2003 (SI 131/2003).
[39] *Rotunda Hospital v McNally* EDA2416.

The Court determined that misrepresentation did not occur and the claimant could not benefit from the Employment Equality Acts 1998 to 2021 in that regard. The claims were therefore brought outside the statutory time limit and failed.

[4.33] *Care Choice v McCarthy*[40]—*Labour Court—appeal from Workplace Relations Commission—Unfair Dismissal Acts 1977 to 2015, ss 8(2) & 8A—time limits—complaint statute-barred—no reasonable cause for delay*

The claimant appealed against a WRC decision that his complaint under the Unfair Dismissal Acts 1977 to 2015 was out of time in circumstances where the claimant was dismissed for gross misconduct on 29 July 2021, but did not lodge his complaint until 15 February 2022, outside the six months allowed.

The claimant argued that, as the respondent's internal appeals process had not concluded until a later date, it was reasonable for him to believe—his contract being silent on the matter—that the lodging of an internal appeal 'acted as a stay on dismissal'. Alternatively, the claimant argued that it was reasonable to extend time in circumstances where he had reasonably and 'rightfully' availed of an internal appeals process.

The Court found no evidence of any 'procedure or practice' to indicate that the effective date of dismissal was the date on which the claimant's appeal against dismissal failed. His dismissal was therefore on 29 July 2021 and the complaint was out of time without reasonable cause. The appeal therefore failed.

[4.34] *IBM Ireland v Keane*[41]—*Labour Court—appeal from Workplace Relations Commission —Redundancy Payments Acts 1967 to 2014, s 24—time limits—complaint out of time*

The claimant appealed against a WRC decision that his complaint under the Redundancy Payments Act 1967 was out of time.

At a preliminary hearing, the respondent submitted that the claimant's employment terminated on 12 March 2021, following his written resignation on 11 February 2021. The complaint was lodged on 23 March 2023. These dates were not contested by the claimant.

It being apparent that the complaint was referred over 105 weeks after the claimant's termination, the claimant could not seek an extension of time for reasonable cause. Nor did the Court have any discretion to extend time beyond 104 weeks post-termination in the absence of a successful application under the Redundancy Payments Act 1967. The claimant had made no such application.

The complaint was therefore out of time and the appeal failed.

---

[40] *Care Choice v McCarthy* UDD2411.
[41] *IBM Ireland v Keane* RPD244.

[4.35] *Aronmar Plant Ltd v Brzezinski*[42]—*Labour Court—appeal from Workplace Relations Commission—Organisation of Working Time 1997, ss 11, 15(1)(a) & 17(1)—complaint out of time—reasonable cause—ignorantia juris non excusat*

The claimant appealed against the WRC's dismissal of his complaint under the Organisation of Working Time Act 1997 for being out of time.

There was a significant dispute before the Labour Court as regards the dates on which the claimant actually attended his workplace after June 2022. Hence, the Court decided to first hear from the parties on the applicable time limits.

The claimant did not dispute that his complaint was brought out of time. He submitted that he was a non-national whose first language was not English. A 'salient feature' of his complaint was that he was not given his contract and terms of employment, and so he could not have known what he was entitled to in law. Thus, he was in a 'uniquely vulnerable position' at the time of the working time contraventions giving rise to the complaint.

The respondent employer pointed out that the claimant had taken legal advice and initiated separate personal injuries proceedings against the respondent within the time limit for bringing the WRC complaint, demonstrating that he was aware he could make complaints against his employer if he so wished.

The Court concluded that the claimant's explanation fell short of demonstrating reasonable cause for the delay in bringing his complaint to the WRC. Even if the claimant had been unaware of his legal entitlements (despite his having taken legal advices in another matter), the principle of *ignorantia juris non excusat* applied. The complaint was therefore made outside the statutory time limit without reasonable cause and the appeal failed.

[4.36] *Flutter Entertainment Plc v Long*[43]—*Labour Court—appeal from Workplace Relations Commission—Unfair Dismissals Acts 1977 to 2015, s 8A—statutory time limits—appeal out of time*

The claimant appealed against the WRC's dismissal of his complaint of unfair dismissal against the respondent.

The claimant was employed by the respondent in a managerial capacity. His employment was terminated following findings of gross misconduct. The claimant contested the dismissal.

The primary issue before the Labour Court was whether the claimant's appeal had been lodged within the statutory time limit of six months or, alternatively, whether exceptional circumstances justified an extension of that time limit.

The claimant's employment with the respondent was terminated on 1 June 2023. He submitted his claim to the WRC on 22 December 2023, exceeding the six-month

---

[42] *Aronmar Plant Ltd v Brzezinski* DWT2422.
[43] *Flutter Entertainment Plc v Long* UDD2442.

statutory limit by 21 days. The claimant argued that the delay was due to personal and professional difficulties arising from the abrupt termination of his employment, which affected his ability to engage with the process earlier. The claimant submitted that these difficulties constituted 'exceptional circumstances' under the Unfair Dismissals Acts 1977 to 2015, which allow for an extension of up to 12 months in such cases.

The respondent contended that the statutory time limit was a fundamental aspect of the legislation, designed to ensure procedural fairness and efficiency in employment disputes, and that the claimant's circumstances, while unfortunate, did not meet the threshold for 'exceptional circumstances'. The respondent highlighted that the claimant had been aware of the time limits and failed to take timely action without providing a sufficiently compelling explanation.

The Labour Court upheld the WRC's decision. It found that the claimant had not established exceptional circumstances that would warrant the extension of the statutory time limit. The Court noted that while the claimant faced challenges following the dismissal, these did not amount to circumstances beyond his control preventing him from lodging the claim in time. Consequently, the complaint was out of time and could not proceed.

[4.37] *Bwg Foods Unlimited Company v Eldic*[44]—*Labour Court—appeal from Workplace Relations Commission—Unfair Dismissals Acts 1977 to 2015—complaint statute-barred—application to extend time*

The respondent appealed against the WRC's decision upholding a complaint under the Unfair Dismissals Acts 1977 to 2015.

The respondent submitted that the complaint was statute-barred. The claimant's employment terminated on 28 January 2022, but his complaint was not received by the WRC until 28 July 2022—one day outside the statutory six-month period.

The claimant accepted that this was the case and he sought an extension of time. He submitted that, following his dismissal, he availed of the respondent's internal appeals procedure, the outcome of which did not issue until 8 March 2022. Thereafter, the claimant cited a number of factors, including the need to allocate time to find alternative employment, to prepare for a WRC hearing of a separate complaint, and to await compliance with a GDPR data subject request. He also stated that he did not understand how the statutory time limit is calculated. The claimant admitted that he believed that he was within time when he submitted the complaint.

The Court noted that the claimant did not specify how any of the issues mentioned in support of his application 'both explained and afforded an excuse for the delay'. His misunderstanding of time limits did not afford him such an excuse. Moreover, his

---

[44] *Bwg Foods Unlimited Company v Eldic* UDD2433. See also related cases *Bwg Foods Unlimited Company, Unit D and E v Eldic* PWD2451 and *Bwg Foods Unlimited Company, Unit D and E v Eldic* UDD2434.

admission that he initially believed himself to be in time meant that he could not now logically seek to justify the delay on the basis of reasonable cause.

The application to extend time was refused and the appeal therefore succeeded.

[4.38] *Inspire Wellbeing v Conlon*[45]—**Labour Court—appeal from Workplace Relations Commission—Organisation of Working Time Act 1997, s 28(1)—complaint statute-barred—cognisable period**

The claimant appealed against a WRC decision that her complaint under the Organisation of Working Time Act 1997 was statute-barred.

The claimant was employed by the respondent company as a support worker between 22 August 2016 and *circa* 30 March 2021, when she was deemed to have resigned. By this time the claimant had been absent from the workplace for some two years and the respondent had received a reference request in respect of the claimant from another employer.

The respondent submitted that the cognisable period was 18 February 2020 to 17 August 2020, the date of referral. The claimant confirmed that she had not sought an extension of time to bring the complaint but was doing so now. The Labour Court explained that it had no discretion to accede to such an application, and even if it had, the claimant would not be permitted to go back in time earlier than 18 August 2019, by which date she had already been out of the workplace for four continuous months.

The complaint was therefore statute-barred and the appeal failed.

[4.39] *Pamukkale Trading Co Ltd v Turkay*[46]—**Labour Court—appeal from Workplace Relations Commission—Organisation of Working Time Act 1997—complaint out of time—vulnerable person—presumed victim of human trafficking—psychological stress—engagement with other agencies**

The claimant appealed against the WRC's dismissal of his complaint under the Organisation of Working Time Act 1997 for being out of time. The claimant referred his complaint to the WRC on 3 February 2023, some 11 months after he left his employment in February 2022.

On appeal, the respondent contended that the complaint was statute-barred.

The claimant claimed that there was reasonable cause for his failure to present the complaint within the statutory six-month period and sought an extension of time. It was submitted that the claimant was a vulnerable person with very little English and was identified as a 'presumed victim of human trafficking'. He suffered from 'moderate to severe psychological distress' and was not aware of his employment rights. He was dependent on the respondent for work, food, transportation and accommodation, and was assisted by An Garda Síochána to leave his position with the respondent and seek

---

45 *Inspire Wellbeing Ltd v Conlon* DWT2412.
46 *Pamukkale Trading Co Ltd Anatolia Café and Restaurant v Turkay* DWT2426.

safety. Thereafter, he was referred to the HSE's anti-human trafficking team and was assessed by a clinical psychologist. The claimant did not receive legal advice until after he had submitted his complaint.

The respondent denied that the claimant was a victim of human trafficking. It contended that the claimant was recruited having responded to an advert, and that the respondent followed a proper process of application for a visa and work permit. In February 2022, the claimant returned to Turkey on annual leave, where he was free to remain if he wished, but chose to return to Ireland. The claimant was provided with a summary of employment rights in Ireland when he received his work permit and was advised that further information was available on the WRC website. Any alleged breaches of his employment rights were denied and it was submitted that the claimant attended with the Legal Aid Board in March or April 2022, well within the cognisable period.

While the Labour Court accepted that the claimant had engaged with An Garda Síochána, the HSE and the Legal Aid Board during the relevant period for the allegation of human trafficking, it found that no adequate explanation was provided to explain what prevented him from lodging a complaint with the WRC during this time. No evidence other than hearsay was presented to show that mental health issues prevented the claimant from lodging the complaint in time. Further, no adequate explanation was given as to why the claimant was prevented from lodging the complaint within the statutory six-month period, when he could engage with other agencies during this time.

The Court held that no valid explanation properly accounted for the delay and the claimant had not met the threshold for extension of the statutory timeframe for reasonable cause. The claim was therefore statute-barred and the WRC's decision was upheld.

[4.40] *Holbrook v Cosgrove KC[47]—UK Employment Appeal Tribunal—appeal from employment tribunal—statutory time limits—application to extend time refused—valid reason for the delay—misunderstanding of the law*

The claimant appealed against the decision of an employment tribunal refusing to extend the time limit for his complaint of belief discrimination. His case centred on his expulsion from chambers due to a controversial tweet and his belief in social conservatism.

The claimant, a barrister with over 30 years' experience, was a tenant at Cornerstone Chambers until his expulsion in February 2021. His dismissal followed a tweet in which he criticised the Equality Act 2010, stating it empowered 'the stroppy teenager of colour'. The tweet attracted significant media criticism and allegations of racism. Cornerstone requested that he delete the tweet and apologise, asserting that it violated their social media policy and undermined public confidence in the Bar of England and Wales. The claimant refused to comply.

Following a chambers meeting on 31 January 2021, members resolved to expel the claimant. The claimant, who had already sought to resign from chambers—the

---

[47] *Holbrook v Cosgrove KC, Coppel KC, Findlay KC, Bhose KC, Townsend, Kohli, Green, Beglan, Williams and Bowes* [2023] EAT 168.

resignation not being accepted by management—voted in favour of the resolution, which took effect on 1 February 2021. He argued that his expulsion constituted belief discrimination under the Equality Act 2010, asserting that his views on social conservatism, focusing on community, family, and national values, amounted to a protected philosophical belief. However, he did not file his claim until September 2021, five months beyond the statutory three-month deadline.

The claimant argued that he initially believed his claim had little chance of success due to an earlier employment tribunal decision,[48] which found that gender-critical beliefs were not protected under the equality legislation. Although that decision was overturned by the EAT in June 2021,[49] the claimant stated that he did not read the judgment until August 2021 due to preoccupation with proceedings against him by the Bar Standards Board ('BSB') regarding other tweets. He submitted that once he became aware of the judgment, he acted promptly to bring his claim.

The employment tribunal rejected the claimant's application to extend time, finding that the delay was the result of a considered decision not to pursue a claim, based on the claimant's misunderstanding of the law. The claimant, as an experienced barrister, could easily have researched or sought advice on time limits. His preoccupation with the BSB proceedings did not excuse his failure to act, as there were no significant developments in those proceedings between June and August 2021. Extending time would unfairly prejudice the respondent members of chambers, given the passage of time and the number of individuals whose motivations would need to be examined. The tribunal concluded that the claimant had not provided a reasonable explanation for his delay, and the balance of probabilities favoured refusing the extension.

On appeal, the claimant argued that the employment tribunal failed to adequately assess the reasonableness of his delay, particularly his reliance on the tribunal's decision on gender-critical beliefs. He contended that the tribunal erred in dismissing his explanation that the BSB proceedings preoccupied him. Further, the tribunal placed undue weight on his responsibility for the delay, while disregarding the prejudice he would suffer if time was not extended.

The EAT upheld the employment tribunal's decision, dismissing all grounds of appeal. It found that the claimant's belief that his claim was precluded was not reasonable. The decision on gender-critical beliefs was substantively different and, in any event, non-binding in the first instance. Moreover, the principles protecting philosophical belief were longstanding and widely understood. The EAT rejected the claimant's contention that the BSB proceedings constituted a valid reason for his delay. It noted that the claimant had actively tweeted about June 2021 judgment, undermining his argument that he was unaware of its relevance. The EAT agreed with the tribunal that the delay caused significant prejudice to the respondents, as recalling events and motivations from early 2021 would be challenging for witnesses. It also upheld the tribunal's

---

[48] *Forstater v Centre for Global Development* [2019] UKET 2200909/2019.
[49] *Forstater v Centre for Global Development* [2021] EAT 87, see *Arthur Cox Employment Law Yearbook 2021* at [4.57] for decision of UK EAT.

finding that the claimant bore full responsibility for the delay, as he had chosen not to act within the time limit.

The EAT concluded that the employment tribunal had properly exercised its discretion in refusing to extend time. It emphasised that the claimant's misunderstanding of the law and failure to act promptly were insufficient grounds to justify the delay.

[4.41] *Jones v Secretary of State for Health and Social Care*[50]—*UK Employment Appeal Tribunal—appeal from employment tribunal—direct discrimination—limitation period—refusal to extend time—whether the decision of the employment tribunal was perverse*

The claimant brought a claim in which he alleged direct racial discrimination by the respondent, having been unsuccessful in his application for the role of assistant business development manager. The claim was dismissed on the merits and was found to have been brought out of time.

The claimant, who was of African-Caribbean descent, applied for the role on 8 March 2019, scoring the second highest of four candidates at the interview stage. The successful candidate was offered and accepted the role on 2 April 2019. The successful candidate was white, as were the candidates who came third and fourth. The tribunal found that, as a result of genuine error, the claimant and the other unsuccessful candidates were not informed of the outcome of the interviews until just over three months later.

The primary three-month limitation period expired on 1 July 2019. It was not until 3 July 2019, having already chased up the matter on a number of occasions, that the claimant was informed by an email that he had not been successful. On 24 July 2019, the claimant emailed the respondent enquiring as to the 'age, gender and ethnic origin' of the successful candidate, and whether any other candidates from minority groups were considered for the role. The respondent indicated that it could not disclose protected characteristics of other candidates due to GDPR concerns. It was suggested that the claimant instead make a freedom of information request. The tribunal found that the respondent had not refused to provide the information sought, as was asserted by the claimant, but had, rather, followed its own data protection procedure. The respondent, it was found, had a genuine concern that disclosure of information about the profiles of the other candidates in such a small pool would render them identifiable.

It was not until 30 September 2019 that the claimant commenced Acas early conciliation, with a certificate issuing on 14 October 2019. Given that conciliation occurred after the primary limitation period had expired, it was not possible to extend the period within which a claim could be submitted.

The claimant submitted a claim form indicating that he was bringing the claim 'primarily' based on comments made by the respondent in the email of 3 July 2019. The tribunal received this form on 29 October 2019.

---

[50] *Jones v Secretary of State for Health and Social Care* [2024] EAT 2.

On the time issue, the tribunal concluded that the claimant was aware in August 2019 that he had the 'raw material' to make a claim but had put off doing so until the end of October because he was on 'an information gathering exercise'. This was not a good enough explanation for the delay in presenting the claim and the tribunal concluded that it was not just or equitable to exercise its discretion to hear the claim outside the primary limitation period.

The claimant appealed. The claimant argued that the tribunal's refusal to extend time was perverse and that he was only notified of the outcome of the interview on 3 July 2019. Indeed, it was not until 19 June 2020 that he was notified of the date of the decision (which was claimed to be the discriminatory act) and he did not learn the race of the successful candidate until the day of first preliminary hearing. It was argued that it was unreasonable for the claimant to commence proceedings while not knowing the race of the successful candidate.

The EAT considered the difficulty with this argument was the manner in which the claimant put his case before the tribunal, specifically that he was bringing the claim 'primarily' based on comments made by the respondent in the email of 3 July 2019. This provided the context for the tribunal's findings and its decision. A further difficulty was that the claimant had brought the claim before he knew the race of the successful candidate. The main focus of the claimant's argument had been that the respondent's withholding of the race of the successful candidate was evidence of discrimination. The tribunal had also concluded that the claimant could have learned this information sooner, had he been prepared to follow the freedom of information procedure. The tribunal had been aware of its wide discretion and had considered the length of, and reasons for, the delay and the prejudice to the respondent resulting therefrom.

The EAT concluded that the claimant could not establish that the refusal to extend time was perverse, and so the appeal failed.

TIME LIMITS—APPEALS

[4.42] *Belfry Hospitality Services Ltd v McCaul*[51]*—Labour Court—appeal from Workplace Relations Commission—Organisation of Working Time Act 1997—Workplace Relations Act 2015, s 44*

The claimant appealed against a WRC decision that his complaint under the Organisation of Working Time Act 1997 was not well founded.

In the first instance, the Labour Court refused the claimant's application to anonymise its decision, finding there were no special circumstances within the meaning of the Organisation of Working Time Act 1997 for the hearing to be held otherwise than in public.

The claimant applied for an extension of time for late lodgment of the Labour Court appeal, which was submitted 85 minutes past the deadline, the statutory period being

---

[51] *Belfry Hospitality Services Ltd v McCaul* DWT2413.

42 days. He attributed this to his having been certified unfit to attend work during the relevant period.

The Court did not consider the claimant's explanation to fall within the 'exceptional circumstances' band. Since the claimant had not established the existence of exceptional circumstances, the Court was not permitted to direct an extension of time and the appeal failed.

[4.43] *St Vincent's Private Hospital v Pickford*[52]—*Labour Court—appeal from Workplace Relations Commission—Employment Equality Acts 1998 to 2021, s 83(1)—appeal lodged out of time—exceptional circumstances*

The claimant appealed against the WRC's dismissal of his complaint under the Employment Equality Acts 1998 to 2021.

The notice of appeal was received by the Labour Court outside of the 42-day period for bringing such an appeal. The claimant sought an extension of time due to exceptional circumstances. He submitted that he misunderstood emails and got confused about dates as he was preoccupied and under stress at the time. He submitted that the circumstances giving rise to the delay were exceptional to him, and so should be regarded as 'exceptional circumstances'.

The respondent denied the existence of exceptional circumstances and pointed out that the length of the delay in lodging the appeal, some 61 days after the WRC decision, was 'noteworthy' and required 'more cogent reasons' to explain it.

The Labour Court concluded that the existence of 'exceptional circumstances' had not been established by the claimant. The claim was therefore out of time and statute-barred.

The appeal was, accordingly, dismissed.

[4.44] *Ridley v HB Kirtley t/a Queen's Court Business Centre*[53]—*Court of Appeal of England and Wales—Baker, Davies & Laing LJJ—appeal from UK Employment Appeal Tribunal—Employment Appeal Tribunal Rules 1993—time limits—discretion to extend time to bring an appeal*

The appellants all wished to appeal to the UK EAT against decisions of employment tribunals.

In all three cases, the appellants lodged a notice of appeal within the prescribed 42-day time limit, but part of one of the documents necessary to institute the appeal was missing. Each sent the document to the EAT after the expiry of the time limit. They were required to apply for an extension of time for appealing. All three applications were refused, first by the registrar, then on appeal by an employment Judge.

---

[52] *St Vincent's Private Hospital v Pickford* EDA2448, see also related case *St Vincent's Private Hospital v Pickford* TED2420.

[53] *Ridley v HB Kirtley t/a Queen's Court Business Centre; Kostrova v McDermott International Inc and Anor; Taylor v Lloyds Pharmacy Ltd (In Liquidation)* [2024] EWCA Civ 884.

In an appeal on a point of law, the appellants submitted that the EAT erred in law in refusing to extend time to bring the appeals.

The Court of Appeal concluded that all three appeals should be allowed and each matter was remitted to the EAT to consider afresh the application to extend time. While it was entitled to enforce the time limit strictly, the EAT, in its discretion, failed to take into account that the appellants had substantially complied with the rules within the time limit. The Court agreed that the broad power to extend time had become 'encrusted by authority' in a way which had led to the emergence of 'rigid sub-rules which are not justified by the broad terms of [the EAT rules]'. This had created a tendency for employment Judges to rely on those sub-rules for 'automatic answers' as a substitute for looking closely at the facts of each case.

[4.45] *AB v University of East London and other cases[54]—UK Employment Appeal Tribunal—appeals from UK EAT registrar—practice and procedure—time limits—discretion to extend time*

This judgment concerned five appeals against decisions of the UK EAT registrar refusing to extend time for the lodgement of appeals.

In each case, the claimants lodged a notice of appeal within the prescribed 42-day time limit, but without all documents then required under the EAT rules. Each claimant rectified the omission after the expiry of the time limit. All applied for an extension of time for appealing. All five applications were refused by the EAT registrar.

Three appeals to the EAT were allowed, and extensions of time granted. The EAT was satisfied in each case that the circumstances, taken as a whole, warranted the 'exceptional' exercise of the EAT's discretion. Balancing the interest of the parties, and the interests of justice more generally, two appeals were refused, and the applications for extension of time dismissed.

WITHOUT PREJUDICE PRIVILEGE

[4.46] *Gallagher v McKinnon's Auto and Tyres Ltd[55]—UK Employment Appeal Tribunal—appeal from employment tribunal—unfair dismissal complaint—Employment Rights Act 1996, s 111A—pre-termination negotiations—protected conversations—improper behaviour—Acas Code of Conduct—without prejudice privilege—redundancy discussions—undue pressure—admissibility of evidence—settlement agreements—impropriety exception*

The claimant appealed against a ruling by the employment tribunal that evidence of pre-termination negotiations was inadmissible in his complaint of unfair dismissal.

---

[54] *AB v University of East London; Shina v Rendall and Rittner Ltd; Rehman v Healthbridge Direct; Adams v Power X Equipment Ltd; Samuels v Searcy Tansley and Co Ltd* [2024] EAT 157.
[55] *Gallagher v McKinnon's Auto and Tyres Ltd* [2024] EAT 174.

The claimant worked as a branch manager for the respondent for nearly five years before his dismissal in 2022. During June and July of that year, he was absent from work due to illness, including a Covid-19 infection and a broken foot. While covering for his role during his absence, the respondent's directors concluded that they could continue operations without a branch manager, effectively rendering the claimant's role redundant.

On 1 August 2022, one of the directors invited the claimant to what was described as a 'return to work' meeting. However, during the meeting, the director instead proposed an exit package involving redundancy, offering the claimant £10,000 in compensation. The claimant was told that if he did not accept the proposal within 48 hours a redundancy process would be initiated. Following this, he was invited to a formal meeting to discuss redundancy on 4 August 2022 and was ultimately dismissed. The claimant filed a complaint of unfair dismissal, seeking to rely on the discussions at the 1 August meeting as evidence of unfairness.

The employment tribunal determined that the discussions constituted 'pre-termination negotiations' as defined by the Employment Rights Act 1996, and were therefore inadmissible in an ordinary unfair dismissal claim unless impropriety could be demonstrated. The claimant alleged that the meeting involved undue pressure and misrepresentation. However, the tribunal found that the meeting was conducted calmly and without aggression, and that the director's actions, while unfair in some respects (for instance, describing the meeting as a 'return to work' discussion), did not amount to improper behaviour as defined by the Employment Rights Act 1996 or the Acas Code of Practice. The 48-hour timeframe to consider the proposal, while brief, did not constitute undue pressure given the circumstances. The tribunal concluded that the fact and content of the discussions were inadmissible and could not be relied upon in the claimant's unfair dismissal case.

On appeal, the claimant argued that the employment tribunal's decision was perverse in a number of respects. He contended that respondent's statement that his role was redundant, combined with the 48-hour deadline, exerted undue pressure on him, thus breaching the Acas Code. The claimant also argued that the meeting had been set up under false pretences as a 'return to work' discussion, which misled him and created further pressure. Finally, he maintained that the 48-hour timeframe to respond to the settlement proposal fell short of the Acas-recommended 10-day minimum for considering settlement agreements.

The EAT agreed with the employment tribunal that the redundancy discussions did not constitute improper behaviour. While the respondent presented the role as redundant, it did not convey that dismissal was inevitable if the claimant rejected the settlement offer. Instead, it stated that a redundancy process, including exploring alternative roles, would follow. The EAT distinguished between 'unfair behaviour', which is relevant to the overall unfair dismissal claim, and 'impropriety', which is the standard for lifting the confidentiality of pre-termination negotiations. The former does not necessarily equate to the latter.

The EAT noted that the Acas Code distinguishes between oral and written settlement proposals. The 48-hour deadline applied only to an initial verbal offer, and the claimant would have been given time to consider a formal written agreement had negotiations progressed. The tribunal's finding that this did not amount to undue pressure was not perverse.

The EAT considered the claimant's argument that the cumulative effect of the alleged redundancy—the misleading meeting purpose and the 48-hour deadline—constituted undue pressure. However, it concluded that the tribunal was entitled to find otherwise based on the evidence.

The appeal was dismissed. The pre-termination negotiations of 1 August 2022 were properly deemed inadmissible, and the substantive unfair dismissal complaint would proceed without reference to that evidence.

Chapter 5

Employment-Related Torts

INTRODUCTION

[5.01]

Defamation and Injurious Falsehood

In *George v Cannell*, decided by the UK Supreme Court, a disgruntled former employer was sued for defamation and injurious falsehood by reason of communications made to the new employer about the former employee's conduct.

Personal Injury

In *Maloney v Dunne*, the High Court declined to go along with the parties' attempt to insert an exclusion in a settlement order which would have the effect of depriving the Department of Social Protection of recoverable benefits.

In *Holmes v Poeton Holdings Ltd*, the Court of Appeal of England and Wales considered the appropriate test to be applied in determining causation in a case involving long term exposure to a hazardous substance which was claimed to have caused Parkinson's disease.

Vicarious Liability

In *C & S v Shaw and Live Active Leisure*, the vicarious liability of a sports centre operator for sexual abuse of children carried out by an employee caretaker in the children's homes and in the caretaker's employer-owned home, in circumstances where grooming occurred before the commencement of the employment, was considered by the Court of Session.

DEFAMATION AND INJURIOUS FALSEHOOD

[5.02] *George v Cannell[1]—UK Supreme Court—Leggatt, Hodge & Richards LJJ—appeal from Court of Appeal of England and Wales—Defamation Act 1952, s 3(1)—malicious falsehood—economic loss—damages for injured feelings*

The appellant was found to have maliciously published falsehoods about the respondent to two individuals. Neither publication caused the respondent any financial loss, so that only nominal damages were awarded. However, the respondent asserted that she sustained injury to her feelings for which she was entitled to compensation (ie, substantial damages) under the Defamation Act 1952, which the Court of Appeal of England and Wales accepted.

The appellant owned and operated a recruitment agency, LCA. The respondent was employed by the agency as a recruitment consultant. She resigned after eight months and then got a job at another agency, Fawkes & Reece. The respondent's contract of employment with LCA did not prohibit her from soliciting business from LCA's clients after her employment ended—although she gave the appellant verbal assurance that she would not do so. In fact, the respondent began actively targeting the appellant's clients right away.

The appellant threatened to take legal action against the respondent for breach of 'post-employment obligations … not to solicit business from LCA clients'. In an email, the appellant advised the respondent that she would be writing to the respondent's employer and LCA's clients to inform them of the respondent's actions and the 'violation' of the terms of her post-employment obligations. Although this email was only sent to the respondent, the appellant made similar statements to two other people, including the respondent's line-manager at Fawkes & Reece. The trial Judge found that when she did so, the appellant knew that the respondent's contract of employment contained no restriction on soliciting business from LCA's clients. She decided nevertheless to assert that there was such an obligation, hoping that the respondent would not realise the truth of the matter (in fact, the respondent had retained a copy of her employee handbook with LCA). The respondent resigned from Fawkes & Reece, incorrectly believing that the appellant had carried out her threat to contact other clients of LCA.

The respondent sued the appellant for both defamation and malicious falsehood. The tort of injurious falsehood is an economic tort. The respondent asserted, nonetheless, that she sustained injury to her feelings for which she was entitled to compensation (ie, substantial damages). Although not sustainable at common law, the claimant argued that statutory modifications made to the Defamation Act 1952 changed this—a change which, remarkably, had gone unnoticed for some 70 years. This was accepted by the Court of Appeal of England and Wales. The UK Supreme Court disagreed, concluding that it was 'neither the intention nor the effect of the 1952 Act to transform an economic tort into one which protects the claimant's emotional wellbeing'.

The appeal was dismissed.

---

[1] *George v Cannell* [2024] UKSC 19.

PERSONAL INJURY

[5.03] *Moloney v Dunne*[2]—*High Court—Twomey J—personal injuries—settlement order—refusal of application to insert a term*

A personal injuries matter settled before proceeding in the High Court. The defendants' insurance company applied to insert a term in the settlement order stating that there was no claim for loss of earnings in the proceedings. This would have had the effect of depriving the Department of Social Protection, and hence the taxpayer, of recoverable benefits to which it would otherwise have been entitled from the insurer. The Court refused to insert the term on the basis that its only purpose was to financially prejudice the Department, an unrepresented third party.

The Court went on to state that whether or not there was a claim for loss of earnings was a factual matter on which that Court had made no finding, the proceedings having settled out of Court. Such a term would not have been a finding of fact permissible in a Court order, but a statement agreed on by the settling parties in order to financially prejudice a third party.

[5.04] *Holmes v Poeton Holdings Ltd*[3]—*Court of Appeal of England and Wales—Stuart-Smith, Philips & Underhill LJJ—appeal from County Court at Cardiff—personal injury—causation—whether material contribution test appropriate—whether the evidence supported a finding of generic or individual causation*

The respondent was employed by the appellant between 1982 and 2020. In 2014, the respondent was diagnosed as suffering from Parkinson's disease and in 2020 he was forced to retire prematurely due to ill-health. He claimed damages from the appellant for exposing him to unsafe levels of trichloroethylene ('TCE') in the course of his employment from 1982 to 1997. The County Court at Cardiff found in favour of the respondent on the issues of breach of duty and causation. It concluded that 'the claimant was regularly exposed to levels significantly in excess of the short-term limit value and for a significant number of days a year in excess of the long-term value'.

The appellant submitted that the trial Judge adopted the wrong legal test for establishing causation of an 'indivisible disease' such as Parkinson's disease, and that the Judge failed to address whether the respondent's development of Parkinson's disease would have happened in any event, so that the exposure to TCE made no difference. It submitted that the evidence available to the Judge showed no more than that TCE may have caused an elevation of the risk of contracting Parkinson's disease.

The Court of Appeal, in referring to *Bonnington Castings Ltd v Wardlaw*,[4] rejected the appellant's submission that the 'material contribution' test relied upon by the trial

---

[2] *Moloney v Dunne* [2024] IEHC 84.
[3] *Holmes v Poeton Holdings Ltd* [2023] EWCA Civ 1377.
[4] *Bonnington Castings Ltd v Wardlaw* [1956] AC 613, [1956] 3 WLUK 6.

Judge was only applicable to cases of divisible injury. The material contribution test in *Bonnington* was held to be correctly applicable as the tortious exposure of TCE was found to have contributed to the onset the Parkinson's disease, as opposed to its severity and therefore a link between TCE and Parkinson's diseases must exist. The Court went on to observe that the trial Judge did not make specific findings about the duration or level of exposure to TCE; nor did he attempt to identify the extent to which any exposure had not fallen outside the accepted safety limits and was not tortious. Nevertheless, the trial Judge was fully entitled to reach certain conclusions in relation to the routine cleaning of a tank by the claimant without an adequate breathing apparatus. Indeed, on the information available to the trial Judge, there could be 'no doubt that [the appellant's] breaches of duty in relation to cleaning the tank led to operatives being exposed to very high levels of TCE that would have far-exceeded the short-term limits'.

However, it was observed that the evidence had 'significant limitations'. The trial Judge was merely entitled to conclude that a causative link between TCE and Parkinson's disease could not be disproved, 'so that, in a sense, it was *possible* that TCE was a cause of the condition'. Thus, the Court upheld the appellant's submission that the evidence before the trial Judge did not justify a finding of generic causation, ie, the respondent did not prove that the TCE to which he was exposed caused or materially contributed to his developing Parkinson's disease.

The appeal was, accordingly, allowed.

VICARIOUS LIABILITY

[5.05] *C & S v Shaw and Live Active Leisure*[5]—*Court of Session of Scotland—Clerk LJ, Malcolm & Pentland JJ—vicarious liability—sexual abuse—sufficiently close connection*

This appeal determined whether the respondent employer should be held vicariously liable for the sexual abuse of two children by its employee caretaker in the 1980s. Neither the employee's employment nor the fact of the sexual abuse were in dispute. Rather, the appeal turned on whether there was a sufficiently close connection between the employee and employer, and the abuse.

The issues at trial were restricted to the location of the abuse of the appellants. The trial Judge was satisfied the abuse occurred in both their home and the employee's home; the trial Judge did not make specific findings as to whether the abuse occurred in the employer's sports centre, though he went on to find that the employee had abused the appellants 'as specified in the claim'. Otherwise, the trial Judge rejected the 'close connection' stage of the test for vicarious liability. He found that, due to the employee's relationship with the appellants' family, grooming behaviour had already

---

[5] *C & S v Shaw and Live Active Leisure* [2023] CSIH 36.

taken place before the employee had commenced employment, and it was not clear that the employee's employment would have placed him in close isolated contact with children.

The appellants' submissions focused on the contractual obligation on the employee to reside in the caretaker's house, and the abuse perpetrated there, which, it was alleged, was of a significantly more serious nature, 'and thus severable from the previous abuse in the [appellants'] home'. The appellants submitted that the fact that previous abuse had occurred did not 'destroy' the subsequent close connection test.

The Court held that, while the crucial features of vicarious liability 'vary widely' from case to case, the trial Judge was fully entitled to conclude that, in this case, the close connection test had not been satisfied. The employee's contractual requirement to live in the caretaker's house could not be divorced from the whole circumstances in which the employee came to know the appellants and their mother before his employment by the respondent employer. These circumstances, pointed away from a conclusion that it would be fair, just and reasonable to attach vicarious liability to the abuse. Therefore, the appeal failed.

Chapter 6

European Law

INTRODUCTION

[6.01]

European Company—Employee Involvement

In *Konzernbetriebsrat der O SE & Co KG v Vorstand der O Holding SE*, the European Court of Justice considered the interpretation of Regulation (EU) 2157/2001 on the statute for a European company and Directive 2001/86/EC supplementing that statute with regard to employee involvement.

Free Movement of Workers

In *UL v URBSFA*, the European Court of Justice considered the UEFA rule, that required a minimum number of 'home grown players' in professional football leagues and its compatibility with free movement of workers provided for in the Treaty on the Functioning of the European Union.

Posting of Workers

In *SN*, the European Court of Justice considered the legality of a requirement on third-country posted workers to hold residence permits in the host Member State, in this case the Netherlands. In *Nord Vest Pro Sani Pro SRL*, the European Court of Justice considered national legislation that restricts the benefits of social security advantages only to employees of undertakings in the construction sector which carry on their activities in the territory of that Member State, as distinct from another Member State.

Recognition of Professional Qualifications

European Commission v Czech Republic concerned the alleged failure of the Czech Republic to properly implement EU Directive 2013/55/EU on the recognition of professional qualifications.

Social Security

XXXX v Sozialministeriumservice involved a challenge to the operation in Austria of Regulation (EC) No 883/2004 with reference to the resident's entitlement to social security benefits of the national Member State while residing and working in another Member State and caring for a family member in the first Member State.

Sports/Competition Law

In *FIFA v BZ*, the European Court of Justice considered whether FIFA's rules, which provide that a football club signing a professional footballer is, with the professional footballer concerned, jointly and severally liable in damages arising out of a breach of contract dispute between the footballer and their former club.

VAT Liability—Employee Fraud

In *P sp z oo v Dyrektor Izby Administracji Skarbowej w Lublinie*, the European Court of Justice considered the obligations of an employer relating to VAT under Directive 2006/1012/EC in circumstances where an employee issued fake VAT invoices without the employer's knowledge or consent.

EUROPEAN COMPANY—EMPLOYEE INVOLVEMENT

[6.02] *Konzernbetriebsrat der O SE & Co KG v Vorstand der O Holding SE*[1]*—European Court of Justice—reference for a preliminary ruling from Germany—Regulation (EC) 2157/2001,*[2] *art 12(2)—registration of a European company—involvement of employees—Directive 2001/86/EC, art 11—European company established and registered without employees but which became the parent company of subsidiaries with employees*

This request for a preliminary ruling concerned the interpretation of art 12(2) of Regulation (EC) 2157/2001 on the Statute for a European Company, and arts 3 and 7 of Directive 2001/86/EC[3] supplementing that Statute with regard to the involvement of employees. The referral was made in German proceedings concerning a request for the retrospective formation of a special negotiating body for the involvement of employees.

The respondent, O Holding SE, established two companies, in the UK and Germany respectively. Those companies had no employees and no subsidiaries with employees.

---

[1] *Konzernbetriebsrat der O SE & Co KG v Vorstand der O Holding SE* (Case C-706/22).
[2] Regulation (EC) 2157/2001 on the Statute for a European company.
[3] Directive 2001/86/EC supplementing the Statute for a European company with regard to the involvement of employees.

Accordingly, there were no negotiations on the involvement of employees prior to the establishment of those companies.

The respondent then became the sole shareholder of a company registered in Hamburg. That company had employees, whose representatives made up one-third of its supervisory board. The respondent converted the company into a limited partnership. Thereafter, employee involvement on the supervisory board came to an end.

Although the partnership had around 816 employees, as well as subsidiaries in several Member States with around 2,200 employees, neither of the two controlling companies—including the respondent—had employees.

The applicant, the group works council of the partnership, took the view that, since the respondent had subsidiaries with employees in several Member States, it was obliged retrospectively to create a special negotiating body and initiated proceedings.

Following the dismissal of those proceedings in the Labour Court and the High Labour Court, the dispute was brought before the Federal Labour Court in Hamburg (the referring Court). The referring Court requested an interpretation, first, of art 12(2) of Regulation (EC) 2157/2001, in conjunction with arts 3 to 7 of Directive 2001/86/EC, and, secondly, of art 6 of Directive 2001/86/EC. It observed that those provisions do not expressly provide that a retrospective negotiating procedure on the involvement of employees is to be conducted where such a procedure has not happened at the outset. Nevertheless, it considered that art 11 of Directive 2001/86/EC might carry such an obligation, particularly where the registration of a European company and the acquisition of subsidiaries take place within a very short period of time, as happened here. If the obligation did exist, the Court wondered as to its time limits and under whose national laws the process would be governed. The referring Court decided to stay the proceedings and to refer a number of questions to the ECJ for a preliminary ruling.

The referring Court asked, in essence, whether art 12(2) of Regulation (EC) 2157/2001, in conjunction with arts 3 to 7 of Directive 2001/86/EC, must be interpreted as requiring the opening of negotiations on the involvement of employees as contended in the main proceedings.

The European Court of Justice ('ECJ') referred to art 12(2) of Regulation (EC) 2157/2001, read with art 3(1)–(3) of Directive 2001/86/EC, from which it was apparent that the conclusion of an agreement for employee involvement (and therefore negotiations for the conclusion of that agreement) are to take place *before* the registration of the European company. While there is limited provision in Directive 2001/86/EC for the re-opening of a negotiation procedure at a later stage, its subsequent implementation in the case of a company already established is not envisaged. Nor could such an obligation be inferred from the recitals to Directive 2001/86/EC. Indeed, *travaux préparatoires* for the Directive were supportive of holding negotiations before registration in the interest of foreseeability for shareholders and employees, as well as the stability of the company. Article 11, which requires Member States to prevent 'misuse of procedures' leaves a margin of discretion to the State as regards the choice of appropriate measures to be taken.

Thus, the question was answered in the negative.

FREE MOVEMENT OF WORKERS

[6.03]   *UL v URBSFA*[4]—*European Court of Justice—reference for a preliminary ruling from Belgium—Treaty on the Functioning of the European Union, arts 45 & 101—competition—rules introduced by international and national sports associations—private law entities vested with regulatory control and sanctioning powers—rules requiring a minimum number of 'home-grown players'—restriction on freedom of movement of workers*

This request for a preliminary ruling concerned the interpretation of arts 45 and 101 of the Treaty on the Functioning of the European Union ('TFEU'). It was made in the context of proceedings between the applicant, UL, a professional football player for the Belgian club Royal Antwerp, and the respondent, the Royal Belgian Football Association. The dispute concerned an application to annul an arbitration award.

The applicant was a national of a third country. In February 2020, he brought an action before the Belgian Court of Arbitration for Sport in which he sought a declaration that rules adopted by UEFA and the respondent, which required a minimum number of 'home-grown players', were automatically void because they infringed arts 45 and 101 TFEU. That Court did not consider the rules to be the result of an 'agreement, decision, or concerted practice' between UEFA members (including the respondent) for the purposes of art 101 TFEU. The Court did not consider that the rules gave rise to any direct or indirect discrimination based on nationality. It held that the rules were justified by legitimate objectives and were proportionate to those ends. Further, the rules did not have 'either as their objective or their effect' the restriction of competition. The claims were, thus, rejected in part as being inadmissible and, in part, unfounded.

The applicant and his club brought proceedings against the respondent before the Brussels Court of First Instance (the referring Court) for the annulment of the arbitration award. They argued, first, that the rules on 'home-grown players' restricted competition within the meaning of art 101 TFEU, and second, that those rules interfered with the right to free movement under art 45 TFEU, in that they limited the possibility for a club to recruit players who do not have local or national roots, and limited the possibility for the applicant to be recruited by such a club. The referring Court decided to stay proceedings and to refer two questions to the ECJ.

By its first question, the referring Court asked, in essence, whether the rules on 'home-grown players' that were adopted by UEFA and the respondent could be categorised as 'agreements between undertakings', 'decisions by associations of undertakings' or 'concerted practices' within the meaning of art 101 TFEU. Second, it queried whether those rules complied with the prohibition of agreements, decisions and concerted practices laid down in art 101, and the freedom of movement for workers under art 45.

Having determined the request to be admissible, the European Court of Justice (the 'ECJ') addressed both questions together. It recalled that the practice of sport, in so far

---

[4]   *SA Royal Antwerp Football Club* (Case C-680/21).

as it constitutes an 'economic activity', is subject to EU law. Thus, rules governing paid work, or the performance of services by professional or semi-professional players (or rules having an indirect effect thereon), may come within the scope of art 45. Similarly, rules adopted by associations, and more broadly the conduct of those associations, fall within the provisions of the TFEU on competition law under certain conditions, meaning that those associations can be 'undertakings' within the meaning of art 101.

The rules at issue in the main proceedings were to be regarded as having a 'direct impact' on players' working conditions in that they imposed conditions, backed with sanctions, on the composition of the teams able to participate in inter-club football competitions, and thus the participation of the players themselves in those competitions. It was observed that, in the rules adopted by the respondent, the term 'home-grown players' was designated not only to players who were trained by the club which employed them, but also players who were trained by any Belgian club affiliated with the respondent. Hence, all of the rules at issue fell within the scope of arts 45 and 101.

The ECJ had regard to the wording of art 165 TFEU, read in the light of art 6 TFEU, which confers a 'supporting competence' on the EU, thereby allowing it to pursue an 'action' in a number of specific areas, including sport.

The ECJ found that art 101 applied to UEFA (an intervening party in the proceedings) and the respondent, since both associations have members or affiliate entities that can be categorised as 'undertakings', in that they are engaged in an economic activity. The 'decision by an association of undertakings' referred to those by which UEFA and the respondent adopted the rules on 'home-grown players' at issue in the main proceedings. The geographical scope of the decisions at issue, in turn, allowed the inference that they were 'capable of affecting trade between member states' in an appreciable manner. It was observed that the rules, by their very nature, limited the possibility of professional football clubs to include on their match sheets players not meeting 'home-grown' requirements. That limitation operated at the level of the association concerned (and therefore at a national level), as well as at the club level. It was apparent that the rules limited or controlled 'one of the essential parameters of the competition in which professional football clubs may engage, namely the recruitment of talented players, whatever the club or place where they were trained'.

It was for the referring Court to determine whether the rules, by their very nature, revealed 'a sufficient degree of harm to competition' to be regarded as having as their 'object' the prevention, restriction or distortion of competition, thus falling foul of art 101. Even so, not every such agreement between undertakings or decision of an association of undertakings is prohibited by art 101, and they can be justified by the pursuit of a legitimate objective which is not, *per se*, anti-competitive in nature. Furthermore, any agreement, decision or concerted practice shown to be contrary to art 101(1) TFEU, whether by its anti-competitive object or effect, can be exempted subject to conditions laid down in art 101(3).

The fact that the rules at issue in the main proceedings applied to all inter-club competitions governed by UEFA and the respondent 'and to all professional football clubs and to all players participating in those competitions' was not decisive. Indeed, this was inherent in associations with regulatory power in a given jurisdiction, to which all member undertakings and their affiliates are subject.

Accordingly, the answer to the first question was that art 101 is to be interpreted as precluding rules such as those at issue in the main proceedings, if it is established that the rules are liable to affect trade, and have either as their 'object' or 'effect' the restriction of competition between professional football clubs. Art 101(3), in turn, is to be interpreted as allowing such decisions which have been shown to be contrary to art 101(1) to benefit from an exemption, if it is demonstrated 'through convincing arguments and evidence' that all the requisite conditions are met.

Turning to the art 45 question, it was apparent that the rules at issue in the main proceedings were *prima facie* likely to disadvantage certain professional football players wishing to pursue an economic activity in a Member State other than their Member State of origin. To that extent, they were likely to give rise to indirect discrimination against players coming from another Member State. It followed that the rules *prima facie* infringed upon the right to freedom of movement of workers, subject to examination by the referring Court. The rules were thus precluded by art 45, unless it could be established that they were suitable for ensuring 'in a consistent and systematic manner, the attainment of the objectives of encouraging, at local level, the recruitment and training of young professional football players', not going beyond what was necessary to achieve that objective.

POSTING OF WORKERS

[6.04]   *SN v Staatssecretaris van Justitie en Veiligheid*[5]—*European Court of Justice—reference for a preliminary ruling from the Netherlands—freedom to provide services—Treaty on the Functioning of the European Union, arts 56 and 57—posting of third-country workers to an undertaking of one Member State to carry out works in another Member State—obligation of posted third-country workers to hold residence permits in host Member States—application fees—restriction on the freedom to provide services*

This request for a preliminary ruling concerned the interpretation of arts 56 and 57 TFEU (the right to the freedom to provide services). The request was made in Dutch proceedings between the applicants, who were third-country workers, and the respondent, the State Secretary for Justice and Security in the Netherlands.

The applicants were Ukrainian nationals who worked for a company in Slovakia (the 'employer'). They held temporary residence permits in Slovakia. The employer posted the applicants to a company in the Netherlands, where they then carried out work in the port of Rotterdam and the employer declared the nature and duration of the activity to which the applicants were being posted to the competent authorities, as required by Dutch legislation.

---

[5]   *SN v Staatssecretaris van Justitie en Veiligheid* (Case C-540/22).

The employer subsequently informed the authorities that the applicants' posting was being extended. The result of the extension was that the intended duration of the posting exceeded the three months afforded to aliens who hold residence permits issued by another Member State, as laid down in art 21(1) of the Convention implementing the Schengen Agreement. Accordingly, the employer applied to the authorities for ordinary fixed-term residence permits. Each application carried a processing fee of €290 or €320, depending on the applicants' circumstances.

The respondent issued the residence permits; however, their period of validity was limited to that of the Slovak temporary residence permits previously issued to the applicants—a period shorter than the duration of the activity for which the applicants were posted to the Netherlands.

The applicants lodged objections to the decisions granting them the residence permits. They challenged the obligation to hold such a permit in the first place, as well as the period of validity of those residence permits issued and the amount of the processing fees. The respondent's administrative hearings board dismissed the objections as unfounded.

The applicants brought an action before the District Court in The Hague (the referring Court) for annulment of that decision on the ground that it infringed arts 56 and 57 TFEU. In particular, they challenged their obligation as third-country workers to hold a residence permit in one Member State *in addition to* a residence permit in the Member State in which they supplied services. They maintained that this was a duplication of the declaration procedure required by national legislation. They also argued that the fact that the residence permits issued by the respondent were limited to the period of validity of the Slovak residence permits (and to a maximum of two years) was an unjustified restriction on the freedom to provide services. As regards the amount of the fees, the applicants contended that these were not consistent with EU law, in so far as they were significantly higher than the amount payable for certificates of lawful residence issued to EU citizens.

For its part, the referring Court questioned, in the light of existing caselaw, whether the right to the freedom to provide services under arts 56 and 57 TFEU confers a 'derived right of residence' on workers in the applicants' position. It also questioned whether requiring workers in the applicants' position to hold individual residence permits was inconsistent with the obligation to 'remove any restriction on the freedom to provide services', particularly where national legislation already required that the posting of third-country workers be declared to the authorities. It therefore decided to stay the proceedings and to refer three questions to the European Court of Justice ('ECJ') for a preliminary ruling.

By its first question, the referring Court asked, in essence, whether arts 56 and 57 TFEU were to be interpreted as meaning that third-country workers posted to a Member State by a service provider in another Member State must automatically be recognised as having a 'derived right of residence'.

The ECJ pointed out that the 'derived right of residence' referred to in the case law is the right enshrined in art 21(1) TFEU, ie, the right of an EU citizen, who is a *natural person*, 'to move and reside freely within the territory of the member states'. The right does not concern undertakings. Nor could it be said that a relationship between an undertaking and its employees is analogous to that of third-country nationals who are family members of an EU citizen. Third-country workers such as the applicants could not, therefore, be recognised as having a 'derived right of residence', either in the Member State in which they were employed or the Member State to which they were posted.

By its second question, the referring Court asked, in essence, whether art 56 TFEU is to be interpreted as precluding legislation, such as that at issue in the main proceedings, requiring not only the making of a declaration but the obtaining of a residence permit, where the duration of service exceeds three months.

Here, the ECJ observed that 'the entry to, and residence in, the territory of a member state by third-country nationals in connection with a posting by a service provider established in another member state' was a matter which had not been the subject of harmonisation at EU law level, and so the legislation at issue was capable of being assessed in the light of art 56.

The national legislation—while making no distinction between undertakings established in other Member States and those in the Netherlands as regards obligations *vis-à-vis* residence permits—imposed additional formal requirements in the case of activities exceeding three months in duration. The effect was that the provision of services between Member States was rendered more difficult than the provision of services purely within the Netherlands, such that there was a restriction on arts 56 and 57 freedoms.

However, the ECJ accepted the respondent's submission that the legislation might be justified by the objectives of 'increasing legal certainty for posted workers and of facilitating administrative checks'. For those purposes, the legislation was regarded as being proportionate. Similarly, the ECJ accepted that the objective of 'protecting public policy'—verifying that the worker concerned does not present a threat to public policy or public security—was capable of justifying the restriction, provided that the checks could not have been reliably carried out in the first place during the declaration procedure. That would be a matter for the referring Court to determine. Accordingly, art 56 was to be interpreted as not precluding legislation, such as that at issue in the main proceedings.

Finally, by its third question, the referring Court asked, in essence, whether art 56 TFEU precludes legislation whereby the period of validity of a residence permit issued by the host Member State may be shorter than the period needed to perform the service for which the worker was posted, and whether the issuing of residence permits requires the payment of fees greater than those payable for the issuing of a certificate of lawful residence.

The ECJ held that it could not be excluded that the supply of services, as in the circumstances in the main proceedings, might continue beyond the maximum period of validity assigned to a residence permit under national legislation. However, the fact of providing that the period of validity may not exceed a certain prescribed duration did not, itself, appear contrary to EU law, even if shorter than the period needed by the service provider. As to the question of fees, it was settled case law that such an amount could not be 'excessive or unreasonable'. This was to be assessed in light of the costs generated by the Member State in processing the application. The fact of those fees being greater than those payable for the issuing of a certificate of lawful residence, did not, in itself, establish that the amount was excessive or unreasonable. Accordingly, art 56 TFEU was to be interpreted as not precluding legislation containing such provisions.

[6.05] *Nord Vest Pro Sani Pro SRL v Administraţia Judeţeană a Finanţelor Publice Satu Mare and Anor*[6]—*European Court of Justice—reference for a preliminary ruling from Romania—art 56 TFEU—freedom to provide services—construction sector—posting of workers—tax and social security advantages granted to employees and construction undertakings—legislation seeking to preserve labour in the national territory—overriding reasons in the public interest—social security protection of workers—proportionality*

This reference for a preliminary ruling concerned the interpretation of arts 26 and 56 TFEU and of art 20 of Directive 2006/123/EC[7] on services in the internal market. The request was made in Romanian proceedings between the applicant, Nord Vest Pro, and the respondent tax authorities.

The applicant was a company incorporated under Romanian law and active in the construction sector. In the course of its activities, the applicant posted workers to Germany and Austria to carry out construction work. According to the respondents, because those workers were posted abroad, they were not entitled to benefit from certain tax and social security advantages provided for in Romanian law, and the applicant had erred in so finding. These advantages consisted of income tax rate exemptions, reduced social security contributions, and exemption from health insurance contributions. The applicant was notified of a tax liability shortfall of approximately €67,255.

The applicant unsuccessfully challenged the tax assessment notice before the Regional Directorate-General of Public Finances. Thereafter, it appealed to the Regional Court in Satu Mare (the referring Court), which noted that the disputed financial corrections emanated from emergency legislation whose aim was to support construction activity inside the territory of Romania. By limiting the benefit of tax advantages, the State legislature granted more favourable tax treatment to construction companies operating in Romania than those operating in other Member States. This appeared to run counter to the EU objective of creating an internal market. In those circumstances, the referring Court decided to stay the proceedings and to refer a question to the European Court of Justice ('ECJ') for a preliminary ruling.

The referring Court asked whether arts 26 and 56 TFEU must be interpreted as precluding national legislation 'that restricts the benefit of tax and social security advantages solely to employees of undertakings in the construction sector which carry on their activities in the territory of that member state'.

---

[6] *Nord Vest Pro Sani Pro SRL v Administraţia Judeţeană a Finanţelor Publice Satu Mare and Direcţia Generală Regională a Finanţelor Publice Cluj-Napoca* (Case C-387/22).
[7] Directive 2006/123/EC on services in the internal market.

The ECJ observed that the national legislation in question fell within the scope of 'freedom to provide services', and so that Court examined the request in the light of art 56 TFEU alone. It noted that, while the legislation applied in a non-discriminatory manner to all construction companies, both Romanian and foreign, provided that their workers carried out their duties in Romania, such legislation was capable of dissuading Romanian companies from posting workers to another Member State, and thus from providing construction services in that Member State. It appeared to the ECJ that Romanian companies providing construction workers in Romania and those posting workers to other Member States were in a comparable situation, in that they carried out the same activities and were subject to the same scheme under Romanian law. However, it would be for the referring Court to ascertain whether the difference in treatment resulting from the legislation reflected comparable situations objectively.

The ECJ accepted that the legislative objectives advanced by the respondents: the need to ensure the social security of construction workers, fair working conditions, and effective tax collection, while combating social welfare fraud, tax fraud and concealed employment, were all recognised as 'overriding interests in the public interest'. In addition, it recalled that TFEU rights on free movement are to be balanced against social policy objectives, including 'improved living and working conditions and proper social protection'. Purely 'economic' grounds, such as promotion of the national economy, could not justify obstacles to freedom of movement.

It would be for the referring Court to ascertain whether the legislation was appropriate for the purpose of ensuring, 'in a consistent, safe and sufficient manner', the social security protection of construction workers—by reducing the pay gap existing at EU level and, in particular, by ensuring that those tax advantages were actually reflected in the salaries of construction workers—while not going beyond what was necessary to attain those objectives

Thus, the legislation was capable of being TFEU-compliant, provided its measures were justified by overriding reasons in the public interest and compliant with the principle of proportionality.

RECOGNITION OF PROFESSIONAL QUALIFICATIONS

[6.06]   *European Commission v Czech Republic*[8]—*European Court of Justice—free movement of workers—Directive 2005/36/EC*[9]—*recognition of professional qualifications—failure to fulfil obligations*

The applicant sought a declaration from the European Court of Justice ('ECJ') that the Czech Republic had failed to fulfil its obligations under Directive 2005/36/EC on the recognition of professional qualifications.

---

[8]   *European Commission v Czech Republic* (Case C-75/22).
[9]   Directive 2005/36/EC on the recognition of professional qualifications.

Directive 2005/36/EC was amended, *inter alia*, by Directive 2013/55/EU, which had to be transposed no later than 18 January 2016 in accordance with art 3 thereof. By letter dated 25 January 2019, the applicant formally notified the respondent that it had taken the view that Czech legislation infringed a number of provisions of Directive 2005/36/EC (the 'Directive'). On 28 November 2019, having considered the response it received to be insufficient, the applicant sent the respondent a reasoned opinion. The respondent sent its observations in relation to the reasoned opinion in a communication dated 28 January 2020. On 18 February 2021, the applicant served a supplementary reasoned opinion on the respondent. Proceedings followed and eight complaints were presented to the ECJ.

The first complaint alleged that the respondent failed to fulfil its obligations under art 3(1)(g) and (h) of the Directive, which provides for the obligation on the host Member State to determine the 'status' of persons undergoing an adaptation period or preparing themselves for an aptitude test. It was apparent to the ECJ that the relevant national law did not contain any special provisions relating to the status of such persons, and thus the respondent had failed to fulfil its obligations.

The second complaint alleged that the respondent failed to fulfil its obligations under point (b) of the first paragraph of art 6 of the Directive concerning the exemption of service providers in another Member State from registration with a public social security body in the host Member State, as well as the obligations under the second paragraph of art 6 that service providers inform, in advance of, or in urgent cases, afterwards, the public social security body of the services he or she has provided. These provisions, it was alleged, had not been transposed into Czech law. The applicant's letter of formal notice only referred to point (b) of the first paragraph of art 6, while its reasoned opinion incorrectly attributed the obligation to provide prior information to point (b). Moreover, the complaint differed in its subject matter from the complaint initially referred—a failure to transpose—in that the complaint referred to a national law which was said to contravene point (b) of the first paragraph of art 6. The ECJ considered that the wording of the second complaint lacked coherence and precision. It was therefore declared inadmissible.

The third complaint alleged that the respondent failed to fulfil its obligations under art 7(3) of the Directive by failing to adopt the provisions necessary for veterinary surgeons and architects to provide services, within the framework of the freedom to provide services, under the professional title of the host Member State. The ECJ concluded that the respondent had failed to adopt those necessary provisions.

The fourth complaint alleged that the respondent failed to fulfil its obligations under arts 21(6) and 31(3) of the Directive by allowing in its national law the exercise of 'parallel' nursing professions, such that one was subject to lower qualification requirements than those required by the Directive. The ECJ agreed with the respondent that the subject matter of the fourth complaint was substantially altered at the application stage. The applicant's reasoned opinion related to the title of 'nurse practitioner', which it argued caused confusion with the title of 'general nurse', the latter corresponding with the profession of 'nurse responsible for general care' in art 21(6) of the Directive. By contrast, its application concerned the separate question of the compatibility of the very existence of a 'parallel' profession with the Directive. The fourth complaint was therefore rejected as inadmissible.

The fifth complaint alleged that the respondent failed to fulfil its obligations under art 45(2)(c), (f) and, in part, (e) of the Directive, by making the independent exercise of certain activities by pharmacists subject to 'special competence' requirements involving additional training. The applicant's letter of formal notice referred to a failure to fulfil obligations under art 45(2) on the ground that the relevant national law 'did not transpose at all' points (c), (f) and (h) to (j) of art 45(2), and that point (e) was transposed 'incompletely'. In its reasoned opinion, however, the applicant referred to non-compliance of the relevant national law with 45(2)(c), (f) and, in part, (e) of the Directive. Those provisions were again referred to in the applicant's supplementary reasoned opinion, but in order to claim that the respondent had failed to fulfil its obligations under art 45(2). Thus, new questions were raised concerning substantially different issues from that of whether the provisions were transposed into Czech law. The fifth complaint was therefore rejected as inadmissible.

The sixth complaint alleged that the respondent failed to fulfil its obligations under art 45(3) of the Directive relating to the conditions under which the supplementary professional experience required of pharmacists is recognised in the host Member State. The fifth complaint, having been declared inadmissible, the Court was unable to examine the sixth complaint. It was therefore rejected as unfounded.

The seventh complaint alleged that the respondent failed to fulfil its obligations under art 50(1) of the Directive, read in conjunction with point 1(d) and (e) of Annex VII thereto, as regards the obligation to send, within two months, documents relating, *inter alia*, to good character and repute which the host Member State may require an applicant to produce in order to take up a regulated profession. The ECJ accepted the applicant's argument that the Czech provisions were imprecise and did not appear to have transposed 'in a sufficiently clear and precise manner' the requirements of the two-month limit on the competent authority of the host Member State where a person requests one of the documents referred to in point 1(d) and (e) of Annex VII. However, the respondent was able to point to other measures and rules of national law, which, it argued, constituted sufficient transposition measures. The ECJ was satisfied that the applicant had failed to establish to the requisite standard why the measures relied upon by the respondent were not sufficient to transpose correctly the two-month period for providing the documents. The seventh complaint was therefore rejected as unfounded.

The eighth (and final) complaint alleged that the respondent failed to fulfil its obligations under art 51(1) of the Directive, in so far as it provides that the competent authority of the host Member State is to acknowledge, within one month, receipt of an application for recognition of professional qualifications and to inform an applicant of any missing document. The ECJ agreed that the respondent had failed to adopt the necessary provisions and had thereby failed to fulfil its obligations under art 51(1) of the Directive.

SOCIAL SECURITY

[6.07] *XXXX v Sozialministeriumservice*[10]—*European Court of Justice—reference for a preliminary ruling from Austria—Treaty on the Functioning of the European Union, art 18—Charter of Fundamental Rights of the European Union, art 7—social security—migrant workers—family benefits—Regulation (EC) No 883/2004,*[11] *arts 3, 4, 7 and 21—sickness benefits—scope—care leave allowance—national of a Member State residing and working in another Member State and caring for a family member in the first Member State—art 14—equality of treatment*

This reference for a preliminary ruling concerned the interpretation of art 18 TFEU, art 7 of the Charter of Fundamental Rights of the European Union ('the Charter'), arts 3, 4, 7 and 21 of Regulation (EC) No 883/2004 on the coordination of social security systems, and the principle of effectiveness. The request was made in Austrian proceedings between the anonymised applicant and the Department of the Ministry of Social Affairs relating to the Ministry's refusal to grant the applicant a care leave allowance.

The applicant was an Italian national, who had been residing and working in Austria since 2013. In 2022, it was agreed with his employer that he would take care leave for a period of several weeks in order to care for his father in Italy. The applicant applied to the Department of the Ministry of Social Affairs for a care leave allowance for the relevant period on the ground that his father required round-the-clock care. Were he habitually resident in Austria, the applicant's father would have been entitled to a 'level 3' care allowance owing to his state of health; he was in receipt of an Italian care allowance.

The applicant's father passed away and the respondent's decision duly followed. It rejected the application on the grounds that the applicant's father was not in receipt of the Austrian care allowance.

The applicant challenged the respondent's decision in the Federal Administrative Court (the referring Court). He argued that care leave allowance is not ancillary to care allowance but is a social benefit for the caregiver. Its grant should be determined by the caregiver's place of work, like a 'sickness benefit' within the meaning of art 3(1)(a) of Regulation (EC) No 883/2004. He submitted that, since he worked in Austria, the national legislation providing for the allowance was applicable to him in accordance with art 11(3)(a) of Regulation (EC) No 883/2004, and that he should receive the allowance, which is in the nature of a 'cash benefit' under art 21(1), even if staying in another Member State. He argued that the respondent's decision excluded, in essence, non-Austrian EU nationals from entitlement to the care leave allowance since, generally, only they are likely to have parents residing outside of Austria. This, he argued,

---

[10] *XXXX v Sozialministeriumservice* (Case C-116/23).
[11] Regulation (EC) No 883/2004 on the coordination of social security systems.

was indirect discrimination against migrant workers, or at least a restriction on the free movement of workers, contrary to art 45 TFEU and art 7(2) of Regulation (EU) No 492/2011 on freedom of movement for workers within the Union.

Though the parties agreed to classifying care leave allowance as a 'sickness benefit' within art 3(1)(a) of Regulation (EC) No 883/2004, the referring Court queried whether it was also conceivable that it could be treated as an allowance for temporary absence from work, and thus an 'unemployment benefit' within art 3(1)(b).

In the circumstances, the proceedings were stayed and a number of questions were referred to the European Court of Justice ('ECJ') for a preliminary ruling.

Taking a number of its questions together, the referring Court was understood to ask, in essence, whether the concept of 'sickness benefits' within art 3(1)(a) of Regulation (EC) No 883/2004 must be interpreted as covering a care leave allowance paid directly to an employee who is on unpaid leave in order to care for a close relative in receipt of a care allowance in another Member State.

The ECJ noted that a benefit may be regarded as a 'social security' benefit in so far as it is granted on the basis of a legally defined position without any assessment of personal needs. Being granted automatically, the care leave allowance at issue satisfied this condition. While it was true that the grant of care leave allowance arose from the caregiver's status as an employee, it was also subject to the condition that the person in need of care be in receipt of a care allowance pursuant to Austrian law. Further, it was clear that the care leave allowance, even if granted to compensate for the loss of the caregiver's wages, was intended, ultimately, to enable the caregiver to assist the person in need of care and was, thus, for the benefit of the latter person. In those circumstances, the ECJ found that the care leave allowance at issue was a 'sickness benefit' within art 3(1)(a). It was also satisfied that the allowance was a 'cash benefit', its caselaw holding that a payment of this kind must be categorised as a cash benefit, 'in so far as it is ancillary to the provision of proper care'.

Next, the referring Court was understood to ask, in essence, whether art 45(2) TFEU, art 5 of Regulation (EC) No 883/2004 and art 7(2) of Regulation (EU) No 492/2011 must be interpreted as precluding national legislation under which the grant of a care leave allowance is subject to the condition that the person in need of care be in receipt of care allowance of a certain level under the law of that Member State. The ECJ's analysis concluded that such national legislation is precluded, unless the condition can be 'objectively justified by a legitimate aim relating, in particular, to maintaining the financial balance of the national social security scheme, and is a proportionate means of achieving that aim'.

Finally, the referring Court asked, in essence, whether art 4 of Regulation (EC) No 883/2004 must be interpreted as precluding national legislation or caselaw that subjects the grant of care leave allowance and that of family hospice leave allowance to different rules, and does not allow an application for care leave to be reclassified as an application for family hospice leave. The ECJ noted that Regulation (EC) No 883/2004 'does not establish a common scheme of social security, but allows different national schemes to exist and its sole objective is to ensure the coordination of those schemes' in order to guarantee effective exercise of the right to free movement. Thus, Member States retain the power to organise their own social security schemes and any question of different rules applying to two social security benefits with different objectives is a matter for national law alone. It was therefore apparent that the different rules did not give rise to discrimination against persons who had exercised their right to freedom of movement.

SPORTS/COMPETITION LAW

[6.08] *FIFA v BZ*[12]—*European Court of Justice—reference for a preliminary ruling from France—competition—rules introduced by an international sports association—private law entities vested with regulatory, control and sanctioning powers—regulations on the status and transfer of players—art 45 TFEU—restriction on the freedom of movement of workers—justification—art 101 TFEU—decision of association of undertakings having as its object the prevention or restriction of competition*

This request for a preliminary ruling concerned the interpretation of arts 45 and 101 TFEU. The request was made in proceedings between the applicant, FIFA, and the respondent, BZ, concerning the latter's claim for compensation.

The applicant is the international self-regulatory governing body of association football, established in Switzerland. The respondent was a former professional footballer who resided in France.

In August 2013, the respondent signed a four-year contract with Lokomotiv Moscow, a professional football club in Russia. In August 2014, the club terminated that contract for reasons connected with the respondent's conduct. The club applied to the applicant's dispute resolution chamber (the 'DRC') for an order that the respondent pay it compensation of €20 million, alleging 'termination of contract without just cause' within the meaning of art 17 of the applicant's 2014 regulations on the status and transfer of players ('the regulations'). The respondent counterclaimed for unpaid wages and damages.

Meanwhile, the respondent's search for a new professional football club was hampered by the risk, borne by any club that might employ him, of incurring joint and several liability for any compensation due and owing to Lokomotiv Moscow. In February 2015, one such club, Royal Charleroi in Belgium, offered to employ the respondent on condition, first, that he be duly registered and eligible to play for its first team and, second, that the club get 'written and unconditional confirmation' that it could not be held jointly and severally liable to compensate Lokomotiv Moscow. The respondent sought those assurances from the applicant and the URBSFA, the representative body for Belgian football. However, he was informed that, while the breach of contract dispute was pending, his registration with Royal Charleroi was prohibited by the regulations. The respondent was therefore unable to take up the offer.

---

[12] *Fédération Internationale de Football Association v BZ* (Case C-650/22).

By decision in May 2015, the DRC upheld Lokomotiv Moscow's claim in part. The respondent was directed to pay the club compensation of €10.5 million and his counterclaim was dismissed. The DRC ruled that art 17(2) of the regulations (joint and several liability for terminating a contract without just cause) would not apply to the respondent in the future. That decision was upheld on appeal by the Court of Arbitration for Sport.

In December 2015, the respondent, employed by a French club, brought proceedings before the Commercial Court in Charleroi, Belgium seeking €6 million in compensation from the applicant and the URBSFA for alleged harm suffered as a result of their wrongful conduct. The Court declared that it had jurisdiction to hear the matter and determined the claim to be well founded in principle.

The applicant challenged that decision in the Court of Appeal in Mons (the referring Court), arguing that the claim was under the exclusive jurisdiction of the Court of Arbitration for Sport. At the very least, it argued, the claim did not come within the international jurisdiction of the Belgian Courts. The referring Court did not accept either point. The respondent, cross-appealing, submitted that arts 17 and 9(1) of the regulations, and art 8.2.7 of annex 3 thereof, infringed arts 45 and 101 TFEU. The applicant submitted that, even if the rules did give rise to a restriction on the freedom of movement of workers or competition, they were justified by the legitimate objectives of maintaining contractual stability and preserving the integrity of sporting competitions. The referring Court decided to stay the proceedings and to refer a question to the European Court of Justice ('ECJ') for a preliminary ruling.

The referring Court asked, in essence, whether arts 45 and 101 TFEU must be interpreted as precluding 'rules which were adopted by a private law association whose objectives include, *inter alia*, the regulation, organisation and control of football at world level', and which provide, first, that a new club is jointly and severally liable in damages for employing a professional player who is party to a breach of contract dispute with his or her former club, second, that the new club is to incur a sporting sanction preventing it from registering the new player during a specific period, unless it demonstrates that it did not induce the player to breach his or her contract, and third, that the existence of a breach of contract dispute prevents the former club's national football association from certifying the international transfer.

The ECJ found that all of the regulations in issue were contrary to EU law. They were such as to impede the free movement of professional footballers 'wishing to develop their activity by going to work for a new club' in another Member State. They imposed considerable legal risks, unforeseeable (and potentially very high) financial risks, as well as major sporting risks on those players and the clubs wishing to employ them. Subject to verification by the referring Court, it seemed to the ECJ that the regulations in issue went beyond what was necessary to pursue the objectives of ensuring the regularity of interclub football competitions.

The ECJ held that the regulations in issue had as their objective 'the restriction, and even prevention, of cross-border competition' in the EU. The possibility of competing by recruiting trained players was essential to the sporting sector. A rule 'immutably fixing the distribution of workers' between employers was similar to a 'no-poach' agreement. Again, subject to verification by the referring Court, the regulations in issue did not appear to be indispensable or necessary.

VAT LIABILITY—EMPLOYEE FRAUD

[6.09]   *P sp. z o.o. v Dyrektor Izby Administracji Skarbowej w Lublinie*[13]—*European Court of Justice—reference for a preliminary ruling from Poland—Directive 2006/112/EC,*[14] *art 203—common system of VAT—obligation to pay—person who enters VAT on an invoice—person liable to pay VAT—fake invoices issued by employee without employer's knowledge or consent—employer due diligence*

This request for a preliminary ruling from Poland concerned the interpretation of art 203 of Directive 2006/112/EC (the 'VAT Directive'). The request was made in proceedings between the applicant company and the respondent tax authority in Poland.

The applicant operated a petrol station for the period 2001 to 2014. From 2005, this was managed by an employee, PK. A tax audit showed that between January 2010 and April 2014, the applicant issued 1,679 invoices indicating a VAT amount that did not reflect the actual sale of goods. These invoices were sold by PK to third entities in order to fraudulently obtain VAT refunds. The invoices were accompanied by authentic sales receipts that falsely linked them to genuine transactions at the petrol station. They were not recorded in company accounts and the corresponding VAT was not reflected in the applicant's tax returns. All of this was done without the applicant's knowledge or consent, outside its computerised accounting system. In May 2014, PK's employment was terminated for misconduct.

The respondent upheld the amount of VAT payable as determined by the tax audit. It held that the applicant failed to exercise the requisite due diligence: the chair of the applicant's board knew that invoices were issued in relation to receipts issued by the petrol station, and that this occurred without accounting oversight. Accordingly, he 'could have and should have foreseen that that way of working would facilitate the issuance of invoices for fraudulent purposes'. There was still a budgetary loss to the respondent so that art 203 of the VAT Directive was applicable.

The Regional Administrative Court dismissed a challenge to the respondent's decision. The applicant appealed to the Supreme Administrative Court (the 'referring Court'), which encountered two contradictory lines of domestic caselaw with implications for the applicant's liability under art 203. The referring Court therefore decided to stay the proceedings and to refer two questions to the ECJ for preliminary ruling; these were examined together.

---

[13]   *P sp. z o.o. v Dyrektor Izby Administracji Skarbowej w Lublinie* (Case C-442/22).
[14]   Directive 2006/112/EC on the common system of value added tax.

The referring Court asked in essence whether art 203 must be interpreted as meaning that, where the employee of a 'taxable person' for VAT purposes issues a fake VAT invoice using the employer's identity without their knowledge or consent, that employee must be considered the person who 'enters the VAT' on the invoice and is thus liable to pay it.

The European Court of Justice ('ECJ') found that, according to settled caselaw, the issuer of the invoice is liable for the VAT amount, irrespective of any fault, where there is a risk of loss of tax revenue caused by the recipient of such an invoice exercising their right to deduct VAT. If there is no such risk, art 203 does not apply. In the present case, it was apparent that the invoices were issued for fraudulent purposes. There was still a risk of loss of tax revenue, bringing the present case within the scope of art 203.

The use of the expression 'any person' in art 203 signifies that this need not be a 'taxable person' within the meaning of art 9 but can, in theory, be a natural non-taxable person. The ECJ also noted that the prevention of fraud and potential abuse is an objective of the VAT Directive. It would be contrary to that objective to interpret art 203 so as to affix liability to an apparent issuer acting in good faith when the tax authority is aware of the identity of the person who actually issued the fake invoice.

On the question of due diligence, however, the ECJ noted that it was not contrary to EU law to require a trader 'to take every step which could reasonably be required of him or her to satisfy himself or herself that the transaction which he or she is effecting does not result in his or her participation in VAT fraud'. Where there are 'indications pointing to an infringement or fraud', a reasonable trader may be put on enquiry *vis-à-vis* another trader. A similar duty must therefore be owed by an employer to its employee, particularly one responsible for issuing VAT invoices. Thus, the employee's fraudulent conduct may be imputed to the employer so that the latter is considered the person who entered the VAT on the invoices at issue. It is for the tax authority or the Court to carry out 'an overall assessment of the relevant information' in order to determine whether the employer exercised the due diligence reasonably required to monitor the employee's conduct.

Chapter 7

Fixed-Term Work

INTRODUCTION

[7.01]

Contract of Indefinite Duration

AV v Ministero della Giustizia concerned the legal status of honorary judges and honorary deputy prosecutors in Italy and whether they had legal entitlements under Directive 1999/70/EC.

KT v Dirección General de la Función Pública Catalunya; HM v Departamento de Justicia de la Generalitat de Catalunya considered the entitlements of interim civil servants under Directive 1999/70/EC.

In *Lobo v University College London Hospitals NHS Foundation Trust*, the UK EAT considered the adequacy of the objective grounds relied on by the employer where there were ongoing delays on the employer's part in completing the selection process in order to fill the position on a permanent basis.

Less Favourable Treatment

In *KL v X sp. z o.o.*, the European Court of Justice considered, by reference to its compatibility with Directive 1999/70/EC, Polish law requiring an employer to state the reason for termination of a contract of indefinite duration but which did not require the employer to state the reason for termination of a fixed-term contract.

KV v Consiglio Nazionale delle Ricerche concerned the compatibility of Directive 1999/70/EC with Italian law in circumstances involving the reckonability of continuous service commencing in 1993 for the purpose of determining employee remuneration.

CONTRACT OF INDEFINITE DURATION

[7.02]   *AV v Ministero della Giustizia[1]—European Court of Justice—reference for a preliminary ruling from Italy—Directive 1999/70/EC,[2] clauses 2, 4 & 5—Directive 2003/88/EC,[3] art 7—principle of non-discrimination—equal treatment in employment and occupation—honorary and ordinary members of the judiciary—measures intended to penalise improper use of fixed-term contracts*

This request for a preliminary ruling concerned the interpretation of art 7 of Directive 2003/88/EC concerning certain aspects of the organisation of working time, as well as clauses 4 and 5 of the framework agreement annexed to Directive 1999/70/EC concerning the framework agreement on fixed-term work (the 'framework agreement'). The request was made in Italian proceedings between various applicants, who were 'honorary' members of the judiciary, and the respondent, Italy's Ministry of Justice.

The applicants bore the titles 'honorary deputy prosecutor' and 'honorary judge' (here, collectively referred to simply as 'honorary judges'). Having carried out those duties for more than 16 years, they brought an action before the Regional Administrative Court in Lazio, in which they sought to be accorded the same economic and legal treatment as 'ordinary' members of the judiciary. The action was dismissed and the applicants appealed to the Council of State (the referring Court).

The referring Court noted key differences in the regime applicable to honorary judges and ordinary members of the judiciary in terms of the rules governing their appointment, the nature of their judicial activity, rules of conduct, duration, remuneration, and social security entitlements. Despite these differences, it observed that honorary judges performed 'real and genuine services', which were 'neither purely marginal nor ancillary' and for which they received 'compensation representing remuneration'. Thus, they came within the concept of 'fixed-term worker'. Expressing doubt as to the compatibility of the regime with EU law, the referring Court decided to stay the proceedings and to refer two questions to the European Court of Justice ('ECJ') for a preliminary ruling.

By its first question, the referring Court asked, in essence, whether art 7 of Directive 2003/88/EC and clause 4 of the framework agreement were to be interpreted as precluding national legislation which does not confer entitlement on honorary judges to remuneration during court vacations, or compulsory social security and insurance protection, unlike the regime applicable to ordinary judges.

The ECJ concurred, in the first instance, that the applicants could, in principle, come within the concept of 'fixed-term worker', referred to in clause 2(1) of the framework agreement.

---

[1]   *AV, BT, CV and DW v Ministero della Giustizia* (Case C-41/23) (Peigli).
[2]   Directive 1999/70/EC concerning the framework agreement on fixed-term work concluded by ETUC, UNICE and CEEP.
[3]   Directive 2003/88/EC concerning certain aspects of the organisation of working time.

The ECJ stated that the concept of 'employment conditions' encompasses conditions relating to remuneration and to pensions which are consequent on the employment relationship. As regards a social protection and compulsory insurance scheme, such as that applicable to ordinary judges, it would be a matter for the referring Court to ascertain whether the scheme was contingent on the employment relationship of those judges so as to come within the concept of 'employment conditions' within the meaning of clause 4 of the framework agreement. As regards payment during vacation periods, it further stated that the concept of 'employment conditions' includes the right to paid annual leave.

Next, the ECJ held that it would be a matter for the referring Court to determine, on the facts, whether honorary judges were in a situation comparable to ordinary judges. If so, it would be necessary to ascertain whether objective reasons justified the different treatment complained of, and whether the unequal treatment 'responded to a genuine need, was appropriate for the purpose of attaining the objective pursued and was necessary for that purpose'. The objectives pursued by the Italian legislature, of reflecting the differences in practice between honorary and ordinary judges, might be considered to constitute an 'objective reason' within the meaning of clause 5, provided they satisfied those conditions. Similarly, the Italian Constitution hinted at the qualitatively different nature of the role of honorary members of the judiciary, setting them apart from ordinary judges.

That said, complete exclusion of honorary judges from any right to paid leave or from all forms of pension and social welfare protection could not be accepted in light of clause 4 of the framework agreement. Accordingly, it did not appear that the difference in treatment was justified. This, however, would be a matter for the referring Court to verify. Meanwhile the first question was answered in the affirmative.

By its second question, the referring Court asked, in essence, whether clause 5 of the framework agreement was to be interpreted as precluding national legislation under which the employment relationship of honorary judges could be renewed successively without provisions to limit the abuse of such renewals.

The Court stated that, while Member States have discretion in respect of measures to prevent the abuse of successive fixed-term employment contracts, they cannot compromise the objective or practical effect of the framework agreement. In particular, the concept of 'objective reasons' within the meaning of clause 5(1)(a) refers to 'precise and concrete circumstances' capable, in the context of the particular needs of a given activity, of justifying the use of successive renewals. Such needs must be temporary in nature, not fixed and permanent. Thus, compliance with clause 5 requires specific verification that the renewal of successive fixed-term employment contracts is intended to cover temporary needs, as opposed to an employer's fixed and permanent staffing needs.

The legislation at issue in the main proceedings introduced a derogation allowing for the renewal of the applicants' employment relationships on several occasions. 'Objective reasons', ie, the continuity of the administration of justice pending structural reform of the honorary judiciary, were cited by the Italian Government for the derogation.

While this was capable of constituting a legitimate objective, it was to be borne in mind that the applicants' fixed-term employment contracts had been renewed on several occasions, having entered service in 1995. Subject to an assessment of the facts by the referring Court, it did not appear that the legislation at issue could be justified by an 'objective reason'. Therefore the second question was also answered in the affirmative.

[7.03] *KT v Dirección General de la Función Pública Catalunya; HM v Departamento de Justicia de la Generalitat de Catalunya*[4]—*European Court of Justice—reference for a preliminary ruling from Spain—Directive 1999/70/EC*[5]—*framework agreement on fixed-term work, clause 5—fixed-term employment contracts in the public sector—interim civil servants—measures to prevent and penalise the improper use of successive fixed-term employment contracts or relationships*

These requests for a preliminary ruling concerned the interpretation of clause 5(1) of the framework agreement on fixed-term work (the 'framework agreement') annexed to Directive 1999/70/EC.

The requests were made in two sets of Spanish proceedings. The first concerned an applicant, KT, and the respondent, the Directorate General for the Civil Service attached to the Department of the Presidency of the Government of Catalonia. The second concerned applicants, HM and VD, and the respondent, the Ministry of Justice of the Autonomous Community of Catalonia.

The applicant in the first set of proceedings was an interim civil servant in Catalonia's administration. Between 2005 and 2015, she was the subject of several successive temporary appointments to her post, without any offer of employment. The respondent announced a public competition to fill a number of posts, including that of the applicant. The applicant was granted an interim order excluding her post from the selection procedure by an Administrative Court in Barcelona (the referring Court). She argued that she was entitled to the status of 'non-permanent worker of indefinite duration' in order to remedy the respondent's improper use of successive temporary appointments.

The first set of proceedings was initiated at a time when national law did not provide for any legal consequences for improper use of successive temporary appointments. While there were provisions laying down measures to reduce such improper use, the referring Court had doubts as to their compliance with the framework agreement.

The applicants in the second set of proceedings were interim civil servants in the justice administration in Catalonia, having served more than 37 and 17 consecutive years respectively. They argued before the referring Court that, throughout their years of employment with the respondent, they performed duties identical to civil servants in a comparable situation. Hence, they met needs that were not 'temporary, urgent and exceptional' but 'ordinary, lasting and permanent'. They too alleged improper use of

---

[4] *KT v Dirección General de la Función Pública Catalunya* (Case C-331/22); *HM v Departamento de Justicia de la Generalitat de Catalunya* (Case C-332/22).
[5] Directive 1999/70/EC concerning the framework agreement on fixed-term work concluded by ETUC, UNICE and CEEP.

successive temporary appointments and sought conversion of their employment relationships into relationships of indefinite duration.

The referring Court decided to stay both sets of proceedings and to refer a number of questions to the European Court of Justice ('ECJ') for a preliminary ruling.

First, the referring Court asked, in essence, whether clause 5 of the framework agreement must be interpreted as precluding national legislation under which successive fixed-term employment contracts in the public sector become 'abusive' where the public administrator concerned does not comply with time limits for filling the post occupied by the temporary worker, so that the needs of the administration are no longer temporary, but deemed fixed and permanent.

The ECJ considered that a measure which provides for the organisation of selection procedures to fill temporarily occupied posts within a deadline is, in principle, capable of preventing the abuse of successive fixed-term employment contracts. It would be for the referring Court to determine whether the requirements of clause 5 were met by the measure. Thus, clause 5 was to be interpreted as not precluding national legislation such as that at issue in the main proceedings.

Next, the referring Court asked, in essence, whether clause 5 of the framework agreement, read in light of the principles of equivalence, proportionality, and that damage suffered must be made good, must be interpreted as precluding national laws penalising the abuse of successive fixed-term employment contracts by providing for the continued employment of the temporary worker concerned pending the organisation and completion of selection procedures, as well as 'double ceiling' compensation on termination of the fixed-term contract.

The ECJ held that clause 5 does not lay down any specific penalties where misuse is established. It is therefore incumbent on Member States to adopt proportionate and sufficiently effective measures that act as a sufficient deterrent. It would be for the referring Court to determine to what extent those measures were appropriate for punishing misuse. Subject to verification by the referring Court, however, it did not appear that the organisation of selection procedures as a punitive measure in Spanish law was capable of duly penalising the improper use of successive fixed-term employment contracts. As regards compensation, the ECJ stated that payment of an end-of-contract compensation did not allow the purpose of clause 5 to be achieved. Limiting the compensation to 20 days' remuneration per year of service, capped at 12 monthly salary payments—as in Spanish law—did not make proportionate or effective compensation possible in cases of prolonged and excessive abuse. Compensation must be adequate, which is to say more than a purely nominal amount. Accordingly, clause 5 was to be interpreted as precluding national laws such as those at issue in the main proceedings.

Finally, the referring Court asked, in essence, whether clause 5 of the framework agreement, read in light of art 47 of the Charter, must be interpreted as meaning that, in the absence of adequate measures to prevent and penalise the abuse of successive fixed-term employment contracts, the offending contracts should be converted into employment contracts of indefinite duration, even if such a measure runs contrary to national law (as in Spain's case).

The ECJ found no general obligation on Member States to provide for the conversion of fixed-term contracts into contracts of indefinite duration, though it was clear that they have the power to do so in order to protect the stability of workers. In the case of a law preventing such a conversion, such as Spain's, another measure would be required to prevent and punish the abuse of successive fixed-term contracts. Failing that, national courts are bound to interpret domestic law, to the fullest extent possible, in conformity with EU law; in this instance, in a way which penalises abuse and nullifies the consequences of a breach of EU law. To that end, national courts can disapply established caselaw where necessary. They cannot, therefore, validly claim that it is impossible to interpret a national law in a manner consistent with EU law. Conversion of fixed-term contracts into contracts of indefinite duration is capable of constituting an effective penalty, provided it does not involve an interpretation that is *contra legem*.

[7.04] *Lobo v University College London Hospital NHS Foundation Trust*[6]—*UK Employment Appeal Tribunal—appeal from employment tribunal—renewal of fixed-term contract—justification on objective grounds*

The claimant appealed against an employment tribunal's finding that the renewal of her fixed-term employment contract was justified on objective grounds. She had sought a declaration that she was a permanent employee.

The claimant was employed by the respondent NHS trust as a locum consultant breast surgeon under a series of fixed-term contracts from February 2016, acquiring four years' continuous service in February 2020.

In 2019, the respondent commenced a service review, though the process was delayed by Covid-19. By 2021, the respondent resolved to appoint a 'substantive' consultant breast surgeon. It abided by a regulated process—to which it was not bound, but chose to follow—whereby a job description was drafted and the post advertised nationally. The interview was conducted by a specifically selected panel. The employment tribunal was satisfied that none of the substantive consultants were appointed without evidence of them having undergone this process. The claimant interviewed for the role but was unsuccessful. The tribunal recorded that she had twice previously applied for similar substantive consultant roles without success.

Locum consultants were typically appointed to cover temporary service gaps brought about by transition periods or leaves of absence. This was the case with the claimant. For administrative ease, contracts used for locum consultants were identical to those used for substantive consultants, though the roles were different in terms of day-to-day practice. In particular, locum consultants were not expected to carry out the wider managerial or governance work required of substantive consultants; nor were they expected to carry out teaching or research duties, and a lesser commitment to

---

[6] *Lobo v University College London Hospital NHS Foundation Trust* [2024] EAT 91.

'programmed activities' was required of them. The employment tribunal concluded that the roles were different.

The claimant contended that disputes between her and the other consultants played a part in her not being appointed to the role of substantive consultant. This was not considered relevant by the employment tribunal. Rather, the key question was whether, at the most recent renewal of her employment under a fixed-term contract, that decision was or was not justified on objective grounds. The tribunal accepted the respondent's evidence that, as at the renewal date, the respondent knew that the service review was finally complete, and that it needed to appoint a substantive consultant breast surgeon on a permanent basis. The claimant was reviewed through a prescribed process, but was not successful. The respondent was entitled to seek the best candidate for the job. The claimant was being interviewed for a substantive post; not to decide whether her locum contract should be made permanent. Moreover, it was appropriate to ensure the continued provision of clinical services pending the appointment of a substantive consultant, and to use fixed-term contracts to do so. The use of a fixed-term contract in the claimant's case had been the subject of mutual consultation, and was neither abusive nor discriminatory in the circumstances.

The EAT's analysis concluded that the employment tribunal made careful and detailed findings of fact, and that there was an 'impeccable' direction as to law. There was no error of law its approach to the question of justification on objective grounds, and it properly decided on the facts that the roles of 'substantive' and 'locum' consultant were genuinely different.

Accordingly, the appeal was dismissed.

LESS FAVOURABLE TREATMENT

[7.05] *KL v X sp. z o.o.*[7]—*European Court of Justice—reference for a preliminary ruling from Poland—social policy—Directive 1999/70/EC,*[8] *framework agreement on fixed-term work—principle of non-discrimination—difference in treatment in the event of dismissal—termination of a fixed-term employment contract—no obligation to state the reasons for termination—judicial review—Charter of Fundamental Rights of the European Union, art 47*

This request for a preliminary ruling from Poland concerned the interpretation of clause 4 of the framework agreement on fixed-term work (the 'framework agreement'), as well as arts 21 and 30 of the Charter of Fundamental Rights of the European Union (the 'Charter'). The request was made in proceedings between the applicant, KL, and their former employer, the respondent company.

---

[7] *KL v X sp z oo* (Case C-715/20).
[8] Directive 1999/70/EC concerning the framework agreement on fixed-term work concluded by ETUC, UNICE and CEEP.

The applicant was employed by the respondent on a fixed-term, part-time employment contract from November 2019 until his dismissal in July 2022. The applicant was not informed of the reason for his dismissal, and he brought an action before a District Court in Krakow, Poland (the 'referring Court'). He submitted that, even though the relevant law does not require employers to state the reasons for termination of a fixed-term contract of employment (unlike contracts of indefinite duration), the absence of such reasons is an infringement of the principle of non-discrimination enshrined in EU law.

The referring Court decided to stay the proceedings and to refer a question to the ECJ for preliminary ruling. Essentially, it asked whether clause 4 of the framework agreement must be interpreted as precluding legislation that obliges employers to give written reasons for termination only in the case of contracts of indefinite duration.

The European Court of Justice ('ECJ') noted that the principle of non-discrimination in clause 4 concerns the 'employment conditions' of workers. That concept covers, *inter alia*, the protection afforded to a fixed-term worker in the event of an unlawful dismissal, and so the legislation at issue fell under clause 4.

The ECJ observed that one of the objectives of the framework agreement is to improve the quality of fixed-term work by setting out minimum requirements to ensure non-discrimination. The principle must not be interpreted restrictively, and less favourable treatment must be justified on 'objective grounds' where the fixed-term worker and the permanent worker are engaged in similar work. It would be for the referring Court to assess the facts in that latter regard.

Less favourable treatment must be assessed objectively. Here, there was clearly a difference in treatment, which was liable to give rise to unfavourable consequences for a fixed-term worker, who might be deprived of the information required to assess *a priori* whether the dismissal was unjustified and the prospect of successful litigation. 'Precise' and 'specific' factors would be required in order to justify the difference in treatment entailed by the legislation. A 'national social policy aimed at full productive employment'—factors relied upon by the Polish Government—did not fit that requirement. An obligation to give reasons for early termination of a fixed-term contract would not threaten the flexibility inherent in that kind of employment.

The ECJ held that it would be for the referring Court to ascertain whether the legislation at issue could be interpreted in a manner consistent with clause 4 of the framework agreement, and to disapply any offending provision, provided this did not impose an additional obligation on an individual. The parties in the present case were private individuals, as opposed to State entities, meaning that EU law could not require the referring Court to disapply the offending provision solely on the basis that it was contrary to clause 4. That said, the affected worker had the right to an effective remedy, and, in that regard the difference in treatment undermined art 47 of the Charter. Accordingly, the referring Court could disapply a contrary provision to the extent necessary to give full effect to art 47.

[7.06] *KV v Consiglio Nazionale delle Ricerche*[9]—*European Court of Justice—reference for a preliminary ruling from Italy—social policy—Directive 1999/70/EC*[10]—*framework agreement on fixed-term work, clause 4—principle of non-discrimination—prohibition of less favourable treatment of fixed-term workers as compared with permanent workers—recruitment of a fixed-term worker as a permanent worker—determination of length of service*

This request for a preliminary ruling concerned the interpretation of clause 4.1 of the framework agreement on fixed-term work, annexed to Directive 1999/70/EC. The request was made in Italian proceedings between the applicant, KV, and the respondent, Italy's National Research Council. Those proceedings concerned the calculation of the applicant's 'length of service', having concluded an employment contract of indefinite duration with the respondent.

The applicant was a technologist and researcher, employed by the respondent under three successive fixed-term employment contracts spanning 1993 to 2001. From October 2001, the applicant was employed on a contract of indefinite duration. When calculating length of service for the purpose of determining his remuneration, however, the respondent did not recognise the fixed-term contracts that ended before the deadline for transposing Directive 1999/70/EC.

In February 2022, the applicant brought an action under clause 4 of the framework agreement before the Civil District Court in Padua (the referring Court) seeking recognition of the length of service he had accrued, and the associated salary increase acquired. The respondent contended that Directive 1999/70/EC did not have retroactive effect, and so the action should be dismissed.

In circumstances where the temporal application of clause 4 was in issue (and unresolved in Italian law) the referring Court decided to stay the proceedings and to refer the question to the European Court of Justice ('ECJ') for a preliminary ruling.

The referring Court asked, in essence, whether clause 4 was to be interpreted as precluding the length of service accrued by a worker under fixed-term employment contracts, performed in full or in part before expiry of the deadline date for transposing Directive 1999/70/EC, not being taken into account for the purposes of determining the worker's remuneration upon his or her recruitment on a permanent basis.

It was apparent to the ECJ that the applicant, when carrying out his duties for the respondent under the fixed-term contracts, was in a situation comparable to that of a permanent worker; the applicant performed tasks which could be performed by permanent workers. Had the applicant been on a contract of indefinite duration over the years, the respondent would have taken those years into account when calculating his overall length of service. The Court was therefore satisfied that the applicant's complaint was covered by the concept of 'employment conditions' within the meaning of clause 4.

---

[9] *KV v Consiglio Nazionale delle Ricerche* (Case C-439/23).
[10] Directive 1999/70/EC concerning the framework agreement on fixed-term work.

The ECJ compared this case to *O'Brien*,[11] which concerned taking into account periods of service before the deadline for the transposition of Directive 97/81/EC, required to qualify for a pension. The ECJ observed that a worker accrues length of service progressively, 'even if it is accrued under employment contracts that have come to an end' and the accumulated length of service must continue after the deadline for transposing Directive 1999/70/EC. The duration of individual employment contracts is irrelevant when calculating length of service. That being the case, the dispute in the main proceedings did not concern the retroactive application of clause 4 as the deadline for transposing the Directive had no bearing on the issue.

Thus, unless justified on objective grounds, clause 4.1 of the framework agreement is to be interpreted as precluding the exclusion of service accrued under fixed-term employment contracts, performed in full or in part before expiry of the deadline date for transposing Directive 1999/70/EC, from being taken into account when calculating length of service for remuneration purposes.

---

[11] *O'Brien* (Case C-432/17, EU:C:2018:879).

Chapter 8

Health and Safety

INTRODUCTION

[8.01]

Penalisation

Four decisions of the Labour Court on penalisation claims are noted. Those are *An Post v Dowling*, *LVX Remedies Holdings Ltd v Kelleher*, *University College Cork v Cooper* and *Wexford County Council v O'Connor*. In each of these cases, the claimant failed. Note also the WRC decision in *Ralph v Salvation Army*, in which the claim of penalisation did not succeed.

PENALISATION

[8.02] *An Post v Dowling[1]—Labour Court—appeal from Workplace Relations Commission—Safety, Health and Welfare at Work Acts 2005 to 2014, s 29(1)—protected disclosure—detriment in the form of penalisation or the threat of penalisation, s 27—failure to co-operate with employer's grievance procedure—causation*

The claimant appealed against the WRC's dismissal of her complaint of penalisation under the Safety, Health and Welfare at Work Act 2005 (the '2005 Act').

The claimant contended that she was penalised because she made a protected disclosure following an incident at work on 5 June 2020, in which her supervisor 'grunted aggressively' to 'serve the customer' and there was a 'resounding whack' on the armrest of her chair. The claimant felt alarm and shock. She reported the matter to her shop steward and her union official. A few days later, the claimant was given a verbal warning by her manager for 'slacking at the counter' on 5 June. When she told him about the incident

---

[1] *An Post v Dowling* HSD2410, see also related case *An Post v Dowling* EDA2451 at **[3.07]**.

with her supervisor, he was uninterested. This, she submitted, made the work environment unsafe and hostile.

The claimant submitted a formal grievance under the respondent's dignity at work policy, on foot of which she contended no steps were taken. In a meeting with her union official, the claimant was informed that her complaint could not be given to her supervisor as there was 'clear evidence' that he did not hit her chair. She was not allowed to watch the CCTV footage without her manager being present, something the claimant considered to be 'threatening'. In two letters, she requested a copy of the CCTV footage. She alleged that, in a replying email, the respondent's HR manager 'tried to force her to retract her statement and outlined several penalties that would be considered and taken against her', including withdrawal of her sick pay.

The claimant submitted a second grievance, reiterating her first complaint and claiming harassment and intimidation by the HR manager. She contended that no steps were taken to address that grievance and that her sick pay privilege was withdrawn in retaliation for pursuing the complaints.

The respondent accepted that the claimant made a 'complaint' within the meaning of the 2005 Act. Its position was that it responded speedily to the complaint and confirmed that the relevant CCTV footage would be available to her. In a remote meeting, the claimant was advised that the footage did not appear to corroborate her account of the incident of 5 June 2020. Arrangements were made for her to view the unredacted footage in the branch manager's office with her trade union representative; she refused to view it. In response to the claimant's second grievance, the respondent submitted that it applied its internal procedures 'in a fair, reasonable and transparent manner with a focus on resolution'. Due to lack of engagement from the claimant, the procedures were 'applied but not exhausted'. The claimant was moved from full pay to half pay following 92 days of absence within 12 months, as provided for in the relevant company circular. Employees have responsibilities to engage with investigations and reviews; the claimant elected not to do so. The decision to withdraw her sick pay was not a penalisation within the meaning of the 2005 Act.

The Labour Court found the respondent's policy restrictions on viewing unredacted CCTV footage reasonable. It accepted the respondent's explanation as to why the footage could not be released to the claimant in the manner she requested without compromising its security protocols. The claimant provided 'no cogent explanation' for her refusal to view the footage, having stated under cross-examination that she was not fearful of her supervisor or her other colleagues. The claimant also accepted that the reduction in her sick pay entitlements accorded with the terms and conditions of her employment. Therefore, the Court found that the making of the protected disclosure was not the 'operative cause' of the reduction in her sick pay, and so the claimant suffered no detriment during the relevant period.

Nor did the Court accept that the claimant was penalised because the respondent failed to address her grievance in accordance with its policies. The claimant herself accepted that she had 'no complaints' about the policies and procedures in place and that she had agreed to co-operate. The outcome of the grievance process had not concluded by the time the claimant referred her complaint to the WRC. Consequently, she could not claim to have been subject to adverse treatment in the way those policies were applied.

While the claimant was 'clearly dissatisfied' with her interactions with the HR manager, no evidence of any detriment arising from his replying email—whether by penalisation or the threat of penalisation—was presented to the Court. Though the tone and language of the email conveyed 'frustration', on balance the Court concluded that the threat to not uphold the claimant's grievance was in response to her having failed to co-operate with the process thus far, rather than her having made a protected act.

The complaint of penalisation was not well-founded and the appeal was therefore dismissed.

[8.03] LVX Remedies Holdings Ltd v Kelleher[2]—Labour Court—appeal from Workplace Relations Commission—Safety, Health and Welfare at Work Acts 2005 to 2014, s 29(1)—penalisation—protected act—constructive dismissal

The claimant appealed against a decision of the WRC dismissing her complaint of penalisation under the Safety, Health and Welfare at Work Act 2005 as not well founded.

The claimant, who worked at a branch of the respondent pharmacy, lodged a formal complaint of bullying by a colleague ('person A') in 2009. The complaint was upheld and person A was sanctioned and transferred to another branch. The claimant asserted that this arrangement formed the basis of an agreement between the parties. Following an extended period of absence due to illness, between 2017 and 2021, the claimant learned that person A had been re-assigned to the branch where the claimant worked. She raised concerns about the matter with the respondent and did not initially return to work, despite being fit to do so. Following a series of engagements between the parties, the claimant resigned from her employment in January 2022.

The claimant alleged that she suffered penalisation for having raised concerns about her health and safety in the workplace. She claimed that she suffered detriments, including transfer of duties, loss of pay, denial of due process, coercion and intimidation, and ultimately constructive dismissal.

The respondent denied the existence of an agreement in 2009, but confirmed that it was willing to assist the claimant in returning to work and that it had made proposals to minimise the claimant's working time with person A, but that these had been rejected. The claimant had also unilaterally terminated a mediation process with the respondent. Further, the respondent had facilitated the claimant in returning to work to engage in a grievance procedure, which was not upheld. The claimant refused a transfer to another branch. The respondent submitted that the decision to return person A to the claimant's branch was based on its 'operational needs' and nothing else.

---

[2] LVX Remedies Holdings Ltd v Kelleher HSD239.

The Court was satisfied that the communications from the claimant to the respondent in the period after she was certified fit to return to work constituted a protected act, in that they amounted to a representation in a matter concerning the claimant's safety, health or welfare at work. In addressing whether any penalisation had occurred during the cognisable period, the Court considered that the respondent had not acted unreasonably when it informed the claimant that she would be rostered at a different branch pending any agreed transfer. The claimant's contract of employment entitled the respondent to direct her to work in any branch where her services might be required. The claimant's pay was ceased because she failed to attend work at a different branch. Further, no evidence was presented to substantiate a claim that the claimant was denied due process, or that she was subject to coercion and intimidation. Finally, there was no basis for the claimant's assertion that she was constructively dismissed. Indeed, she was asked to reconsider her resignation and had the option of utilising the grievance procedure, but had chosen not to do so. The Court found that the respondent had acted reasonably in attempting to address the claimant's concerns.

The complaint of penalisation was not well founded and the decision of the Adjudication Officer was upheld.

[8.04] ***University College Cork v Cooper[3]—Labour Court—appeal from Workplace Relations Commission—Safety, Health and Welfare at Work Acts 2005 to 2014, s 27—penalisation—whether the employer's actions amounted to prohibited penalisation***

The claimant appealed against the WRC's dismissal, due to her non-attendance, of her complaint under the Safety, Health and Welfare at Work Act 2005 (the '2005 Act').

The claimant submitted that she carried out a protected act under the 2005 Act for which she was penalised. The respondent submitted that the claimant was not a safety representative and did not have any statutory role under the 2005 Act. The claimant, who had not been in work since March 2020, had not identified the 'immediate danger' that caused her to leave her workplace and refuse to return. The respondent had sought to engage with the claimant about her grievances, but to no avail and asserted that the claimant could not allege penalisation in those circumstances. A third party, and not the respondent, had refused the claimant's application under an income continuance policy, and so that detriment could not be attributed to the respondent.

The Labour Court found that, although the claimant made a complaint by letter in March 2022, and this was a protected act, she was not penalised when an occupational therapist certified her fit to attend a grievance meeting with the respondent, and no detriment arose from the letter.

The appeal therefore failed.

---

[3] *University College Cork v Cooper* HSD246.

[8.05] ***Wexford County Council v O'Connor***[4]—*Labour Court—appeal from Workplace Relations Commission—Safety, Health and Welfare at Work Acts 2005 to 2014, s 29(1)—protected act—penalisation—whether the employee was penalised*

The respondent County Council appealed against a WRC decision upholding a complaint of penalisation under the Safety, Health and Welfare at Work Acts 2005 to 2014 and awarding compensation of €20,000.

The claimant commenced employment with the respondent in March 2009. The claimant was a category A driver and alleged that he was penalised by having his variable overtime reduced for raising health and safety issues. He also alleged that he had become ostracised at work and that a complaint of bullying was not properly investigated.

The respondent accepted that the claimant had made a complaint, but disputed that he was penalised, or suffered a detriment for doing so. It argued, to the contrary, that the claimant's earnings had in fact increased and that his bullying complaint was formally investigated but not upheld. The claimant was the sole driver of a town road sweeper. He had been requested to drive for longer periods throughout the day to maximise efficient use of the vehicle.

The Labour Court concluded from the evidence that the claimant suffered no reduction in overtime during the relevant period. It noted that the claimant accepted that an investigation into his complaint occurred, but that he merely disagreed with the outcome. The claimant did not dispute that the respondent decided, prior to his making the complaint, that it wanted the sweeper driven for longer periods. The claimant had therefore failed to establish that he was penalised by the respondent.

The appeal succeeded and the WRC decision was set aside.

[8.06] ***Ralph v Salvation Army***[5]—*Workplace Relations Commission—Safety, Health and Welfare at Work Act 2005, s 28—penalisation for protected act—evidence of detriment—misconceived complaint*

The claimant alleged penalisation after presenting complaints of bullying to the respondent in February and April 2023.

In 2014, the claimant was employed by the respondent as a catering assistant. She submitted that she worked in an unsafe environment and was required to work alongside unqualified agency staff. She stated that, in addition to her catering duties, she was requested by the kitchen supervisor to cook for service users despite having no cookery qualification. This combined workload, she believed, was hazardous and compromised her health and safety and so, from Christmas 2022, she refused to do any cooking.

The claimant also described two instances of bullying arising from an incident where she was told that she was not allowed to leave the premises during a five-minute break, and another incident where she was issued an unwarranted verbal warning for arriving

---

[4] *Wexford County Council v O'Connor* HSD243.
[5] *Ralph v Salvation Army* ADJ-00046755.

late to work. She submitted complaints to the regional manager of the respondent, followed by the lodging of a grievance. Since doing so, she alleged that her extra shifts were reduced and that the respondent failed to offer her Sunday work. She heard nothing back in relation to her grievance.

The Adjudication Officer was satisfied that the claimant committed a protected act. However, it did not find the detriment identified by the claimant to be borne out by the evidence. She offered no specifics as to the number of extra shifts worked before and after the protected act and did not challenge evidence from the respondent that she was offered extra shifts at the material time. Her unhappiness with the pace of the response to her grievance did not fall within the range of responses to a protected act that would constitute a detriment.

The complaint was therefore found to be misconceived.

Chapter 9

Immigration

INTRODUCTION

[9.01]

Employment Permit

Employment permits were considered by the High Court in *Yoon*, where the Court considered the refusal to grant the applicant a general employment permit to work as a tattoo artist in the State.

Penalisation

Penalisation was considered by the Labour Court in *Ling*, which concerned the issue of an employee being dismissed on performance grounds after she refused to work extra hours to make up the increased minimum salary for a critical skills work permit from €55,000 to €64,000.

EMPLOYMENT PERMIT

[9.02] *Yoon v Minister for Enterprise, Trade and Employment*[1]—*High Court—O'Donnell J—judicial review—Employment Permits Act 2006 as amended, s 12(3)—Employment Permits Regulations 2017,[2] Schedule 4—judicial review of decision upholding refusal to grant a general employment permit—certain occupations ineligible for grant of a general employment permit—use of an external coding system as a 'tool'—whether the decision maker fettered their discretion—adequate reasons*

The applicant sought to challenge a decision made by an officer of the respondent Minister under the Employment Permits Act 2006 (the '2006 Act') and the Employment

---

[1] *Yoon v The Minister for Enterprise, Trade and Employment* [2024] IEHC 548.
[2] Employment Permits Regulations 2017 (SI 95/2017).

Permits Regulations 2017 (the '2017 Regulations'). The impugned decision upheld an earlier refusal to grant the applicant a 'general employment permit' to work as a tattoo artist in the State.

The 2006 Act provides that the respondent must refuse to grant an employment permit if the granting would contravene regulations made under that Act. The 2017 Regulations contain a schedule ('the schedule') setting out the occupations that are ineligible for grants of general employment permits. In the event of a refusal, the respondent is required to notify, in writing, the applicant of the decision and the reasons for it. The decision maker is guided by a coding system, the Standard Occupational Classification System 2010 (the 'SOC'), employed by the UK Office of National Statistics.

The applicant, a South Korean national, first came to Ireland on a student permission in September 2019. She was offered a permanent position as a tattoo artist, which required a work permit under the 2006 Act. In February 2022, the applicant applied for a general employment permit. Her application was accompanied by written submissions which argued that the position of 'tattoo artist' is not ineligible under the 2017 Regulations. Nevertheless, she was aware that 'tattooist' is identified in the SOC under the code 'beauticians and related occupations'. In anticipation of this, she submitted that its inclusion in the SOC is not sufficient to render it ineligible, since the occupation of 'tattoo artist' is not expressly listed in the schedule to the 2017 Regulations. She also submitted that 'beauticians and related occupations' are in substance very different to tattoo artists. Finally, the only other applicant for the job when it was advertised by Wildcat Ink was a Turkish resident, who also required an employment permit to work in the State.

In June 2022, the respondent refused the application for reasons connected with the applicant's working holiday authorisation. The applicant sought a review of that decision, which the respondent treated as an initial application. In September 2022, the respondent, again, refused the application, setting out its view that 'tattoo artist' is a scheduled occupation by reference to the SOC. In November 2022, the respondent's review officer upheld that refusal.

In the High Court, the applicant argued that the respondent fettered his discretion by not engaging with the substance of the reasons why the applicant said she was entitled to the permit, and that he failed to give adequate reasons for the decision.

The respondent submitted that Government policy is 'to meet Ireland's labour market needs primarily through the employment of Irish and EEA nationals'. Employment permits can be granted to non-EEA nationals where there is a 'labour or skills shortage which cannot be filled by Irish or EEA nationals'. The legislative framework is designed to facilitate that underlying policy.

The respondent strongly argued that the SOC system is not determinative but, rather, serves as a 'useful tool' in considering employment applications. Otherwise, the respondent carries out an individual assessment of each application. Here, he determined that the work proposed to be performed by the applicant was in the nature of 'beautician and related occupation'. That determination was supported by the fact that the occupation of 'tattooist' currently falls under the SOC. There was no labour market or skills shortage for persons in that field.

The Court was not satisfied, in the first instance, that much, if any, weight could be given to the respondent's use of the term 'all the circumstances of the application [have been considered]', which amounted to little more than 'administrative throat-clearing before proceeding to the substantive decision'. The Court went on to find that there had been no engagement with the applicant's submission that the SOC classification was not appropriate to the occupation of 'tattoo artist'. While not expected to engage seriatim with the applicant's submissions, more was required from the respondent than 'a simple assertion that SOC ... implicitly answered that submission'. Even if the reasons given had been adequate, they did not demonstrate any exercise of judgment or discretion. Indeed, the reasons 'taken on their own terms' suggested that the SOC was treated as binding and determinative.

The Court was satisfied that the respondent failed to exercise 'the limited discretion required' in reviewing the refusal decision, although this was in no way to suggest that any ultimate finding of ineligibility would be unreasonable. The Court made an order of *certiorari* quashing the decision of November 2022 and remitted the matter for consideration by a different officer.

PENALISATION

[9.03] *The Square Dental Services Ltd v Ling*[3]—*Labour Court—appeal from Workplace Relations Commission—Employment Permits Act 2006, Schedule 2—penalisation*

The respondent appealed against the WRC's finding that the claimant had been penalised under the Employment Permits Act 2006 and awarding her compensation of €14,378.

The claimant was a Canadian national and a qualified dentist. In August 2021, she was offered employment by the respondent on an agreed salary of €55,000 for a 39-hour week. The respondent subsequently learned that a minimum salary of €64,000 for a 39-hour week would be required in order for the claimant to qualify for a critical skills work permit. The claimant's terms of employment were revised accordingly, however, €1,000 was erroneously and illegally deducted from her salary to cover the cost of the work permit application. The amount was repaid only when the matter came before the Labour Court.

In October 2021, the claimant was requested to work 'extra hours' in order to 'make up' the €64,000 salary. She countered that her employment permit was granted on the basis of her working a 39-hour week. In November 2021, the respondent purported to issue the claimant a further revised contract stating the claimant's salary to be €55,000 per annum. The claimant was directed to sign the revised contract and to return it immediately. The claimant queried the salary amount. The following day she received notice

---

[3] *The Square Dental Services Ltd v Ling* EPD241.

of dismissal, purportedly linked to her performance in her role. The claimant obtained alternative work as a dentist in February 2022.

Having heard evidence from respondent witnesses, described as 'lacking in credibility', 'contradictory' and 'unconvincing', the Labour Court rejected allegations made about the claimant's performance, her purported clinical practice shortcomings, and debts accrued to the dental practice arising from the claimant's failure to explain the respondent's treatment plan to her patients. The 'clear evidence' was that no disciplinary process or performance improvement plan was ever initiated with the claimant as a result of these concerns. In the Court's view, the most likely explanation underlying the dismissal was the claimant's refusal to sign the revised contract, which had been falsely described to her as 'mandatory'.

The Court found that the claimant was penalised within the meaning of the Employment Permits Act 2006. Compensation was measured at €30,000 and the decision of the WRC was varied accordingly.

Chapter 10

Industrial Relations and Trade Unions

INTRODUCTION

[10.01]

Defamation of a Trade Union

In *Prospect v Evans*, the High Court of England and Wales dismissed an application to strike out defamation proceedings instituted by a trade union, where it was contended that a trade union, by reason of its legal status, cannot institute proceedings for defamation.

European Works Council

In *HSBC European Works Council v HSBC Continental Europe*, the UK EAT was called upon to interpret the HSBC European Works Council Agreement with reference to the exclusion of HSBC's Europeans Operations post-Brexit.

The employer's obligation to pay the fees of experts engaged by a Works Council was considered by the Labour Court in *Verizon Ireland Ltd v Charpentier*.

Industrial Relations Act 1969

In *Ryanair Holdings Limited v A Worker*, a dispute relating to dismissal was the subject of a compensation recommendation.

In *Three Ireland Limited v A Worker*, the Labour Court noted that legal proceedings based on the same or similar facts were in being, as a consequence of which there was no reality to the parties reaching a voluntary agreement on the basis of a non-legally binding decision; the Court therefore recommended the parties consider their industrial relations trade dispute to be resolved.

In *Microsoft v A Job Offeree*, the Labour Court considered whether an applicant was a worker, in circumstances where the dispute concerned the treatment of the applicant's application for employment with the respondent.

In *South Dublin County Council v A Worker*, the Labour Court considered the scope of the statutory time limit in respect of applications made by retired workers under s 20(1) of the Industrial Relations Act 1969.

Penalisation for Taking Part in Industrial Action

The UK Supreme Court in *Secretary of State for Trade and Business v Mercer* considered, with reference to art 11 of the European Convention on Human Rights, the absence of any provision in UK law protecting workers against detriment for participating in lawful strike action.

Rectification of Collective Agreements

In *National Union of Rail, Maritime and Transport Workers v Tyne and Wear Passenger Transport Executive t/a Nexus*, the UK Supreme Court, in the context of an action for rectification of a non-legally binding collective agreement which was incorporated into the contracts of employment of relevant employees, concluded that the proper defendants in a rectification claim of that type instituted by the employer are the employees, as distinct from the union.

Sectoral Employment Orders

In *Martompol v Tomiak*, the Labour Court considered the scope of the Construction Sectoral Employment Order.

Trade Union Recognition

Decotek Automotive v 60 Siptu Members concerned a recognition dispute which was the subject of a Labour Court recommendation under s 20(1) of the Industrial Relations Act 1969.

Trade Unions—Interference with the Right to Organise

In *ASTI v Ireland*, the European Committee of Social Rights considered whether the Irish Government's distinction, in the context of austerity measures, between public servants who were members of a union that had entered into a collective agreement and those who were members of unions who had not entered into a collective agreement, was compatible with the revised European Social Charter.

DEFAMATION OF A TRADE UNION

[10.02] *Prospect v Evans[1]—High Court of England and Wales—Steyn J—application to strike out proceedings—defamation—whether a trade union has the right to sue in defamation*

The claimant trade union brought claims in defamation and malicious falsehood against the respondent, who was a member of that trade union at the time of the publication. In a preliminary hearing, the respondent sought a declaration that the Court had no jurisdiction to hear the claim because a trade union has no standing to sue in defamation. Submissions turned on the interpretation of the Trade Union and Labour Relations (Consolidation) Act 1992 (the '1992 Act').

Broadly, the respondent's contention was that a trade union is a group of people, not a natural or juridical person, and so cannot be libelled as it has no reputation distinct from that of its members.

The claimant's broad position was that it is not necessary for a body to have corporate or quasi-corporate personality to sue in defamation, provided it has the necessary character to pursue such an action. This was evidenced by the fact that a partnership, which has no separate legal personality, can sue in its own name.

In finding for the claimant, the Court considered that the 1992 Act, in its natural meaning, revealed no ambiguity, and that Parliament conferred on trade unions the rights to enter into contracts, to sue in any cause of action, and to be prosecuted in their own name. It was plain that 'the attributes of a trade union are such that it has a separate reputation, distinct from its members'. While not a body corporate, trade unions were conferred 'sufficient personality', in the manner of a quasi-corporation, such as to be entitled to bring an action in libel in order to protect that reputation.

Accordingly, the respondent's application to strike out was dismissed.

EUROPEAN WORKS COUNCIL

[10.03] *HSBC European Works Council v HSBC Continental Europe[2]—UK Employment Appeal Tribunal—appeal from Central Arbitration Committee—European Works Council Agreement—Directive 2009/38/EC[3]—change of location of central management—Brexit*

---

[1] *Prospect v Evans* [2024] EWHC 1533 (KB).
[2] *HSBC European Works Council v HSBC Continental Europe* [2024] EAT 104, see *Arthur Cox Employment Law Yearbook 2021* at [11.12] for original decision of CAC in *HSBC European Works Council and HSBC Continental Europe*, Central Arbitration Committee Case No. EWC/38/2021.
[3] Directive 2009/38/EC on the establishment of a European Works Council or a procedure in Community-scale undertakings and Community-scale groups of undertakings for the purposes of informing and consulting employees.

The claimant appealed against a decision of the Central Arbitration Committee ('CAC') which had dismissed its complaints.

The claimant and the respondent employee were party to a European Works Council Agreement (the 'agreement') under which the central management was located in the UK. Following Brexit, the respondent took the view that, for the purposes of Directive 2009/38/EC, the UK could no longer be the location of central management. In December 2020, the respondent gave notice that it would be designating a representative agent in Ireland to assume the role of central management, excluding its UK business from the scope of the agreement and excluding UK representatives as members of the European Works Council ('EWC').

The claimant objected and brought a complaint to the CAC. That complaint was dismissed as not well founded. The CAC was satisfied that the agreement clearly and unambiguously confined the respondent's operations to the EEA Member States. It did not accept the claimant's argument that references in the agreement to 'the EEA member states' should, post-Brexit, be read as 'the relevant states' (thus including the UK within its scope), in the absence of an express amendment to that effect. Although some form of prior consultation would have been 'good industrial relations practice', it was not required under the agreement. The UK's exclusion followed automatically from Brexit.

Further complaints concerning the respondent's compliance with certain terms of the agreement were also dismissed, with the CAC observing that the claimant did not dispute the choice of HSBC Ireland as the representative agent, but nevertheless sought to argue that amendments to reflect this change constituted a breach of the agreement. The CAC concluded that it would have been 'anomalous' for the agreement to continue to state, in its unamended form, that central management was situated in the UK, and so the amendments were necessary consequences of the change of representative agent.

The EAT rejected the claimant's appeal. The terms of the Directive were clear that the powers and competences of a EWC shall 'cover all establishments ... located within member states'. Where a State ceases to be a Member State, the obligations under Directive 2009/38/EC do not extend to operations in that State, and would not do so unless the parties expressly so agreed. The agreement, for its part, expressly envisaged *automatic* amendment of the list of operations where operations expanded or contracted as a result of a commercial decision by HSBC. The EAT took the view that the same would apply if the expansion or contraction resulted from a change in EEA membership. The parties had expressly agreed that the agreement should only cover EEA operations and had clearly made provision for automatic changes to the list of operations. Other changes, such as the applicable regulations and choice of law, followed from that change and were consistent with the terms of the agreement.

[10.04] *Verizon Ireland Ltd v Charpentier*[4]—*Labour Court—appeal from Workplace Relations Commission—Transnational Information and Consultation of Employees Act 1996, s 17B—Directive 2009/38/EC*[5]—*European Works Council—compensation—whether redress provisions under Irish legislation apply to individual EWC members—costs associated with procurement of an expert and attendance at a training event*

The claimant appealed against the WRC's dismissal of his complaint under the Transnational Information and Consultation of Employees Act 1996 (the '1996 Act').

The claimant chaired the European Works Council (the 'EWC') of Verizon Communications Inc, for which he appeared in a representative capacity. The respondent was the company's representative agent in the EU following Brexit. The EWC's select committee (of which the claimant was also a member) engaged an expert from the EWC Academy in Hamburg to provide advisory and research services on a number of occasions in 2021. While Verizon's central management took no issue with the nominated expert or his rates, it disputed certain items on the invoice which had been subsequently raised (totaling €11,200).

In this appeal, the claimant sought a direction that the respondent make full payment of the disputed invoice plus interest and VAT. Crucially, he also sought compensation under the 1996 Act, plus his legal costs.

The Labour Court heard that the Academy did not furnish the invoice to the respondent—though it had been provided with its address and VAT number—but instead issued it to the claimant at his business address. The claimant submitted that he was entitled to be indemnified by the respondent. The respondent accepted that the EWC was entitled to procure necessary and reasonable expert assistance, for which purpose it was entitled to receive funding from central management.

The dispute lay in relation to whether the redress provisions under the 1996 Act were applicable in that context. The respondent submitted that those provisions did not concern the respondent's funding of the EWC's expert and, in any event, were concerned with the protection of *individual* EWC members, as opposed to the collective.

The Court found that the claimant's submission that he was acting for the EWC in a representative capacity was 'effectively a concession' that the issues in dispute were collective in nature and not particular to him as an individual. The legislation was framed so as to afford statutory protection to individual members of EWCs *qua* individuals, as opposed to being a means of progressing collective disputes.

---

[4] *Verizon Ireland Ltd v Charpentier* TID241; TID242. See *Arthur Cox Employment Law Yearbook 2023* at [10.05] for decision of Workplace Relations Commission in *Charpentier v Verizon Ireland Ltd* ADJ-00034402.

[5] Directive 2009/38/EC on the establishment of a European Works Council or a procedure in Community-scale undertakings and Community-scale groups of undertakings for the purposes of informing and consulting employees.

It followed that that appeal failed and the Court did not consider it necessary to examine each of the items in the disputed invoice.

In a separate appeal, heard in tandem, the claimant sought a direction that the respondent indemnify him the costs of his attendance at a two-day training event for EWC members in Hamburg, including the conference fee and his travel expenses. He also sought his legal costs.

The respondent's position was that adequate training was provided at its expense to the claimant and his fellow EWC members at an online training event, and that the Hamburg event had been unnecessary. The respondent had therefore fulfilled its obligations under the 1996 Act. Further, the claimant had been instructed, in advance of his attendance at the Hamburg event, that the respondent would not be funding it. As to the question of costs, the respondent submitted that the Court lacked jurisdiction to make such an award, there being no such statutory basis in either the 1996 Act or Directive 2009/38/EC.

For his part, the claimant criticised the online training event as being 'too general', for not sufficiently addressing the subject of confidentiality as it applies to an EWC, and for lacking practical exercises and case studies. There had also been very little time for questions and answers. The claimant told the Court that he attended the Hamburg conference without taking annual leave, contrary to the respondent's instructions, and, indeed, had himself been a speaker at the event.

Having viewed the material covered in the online presentation, the Court was satisfied that this met the dictionary definition of 'training', ie, a 'process providing … instruction' to participants relevant to their 'occupation' as Verizon EWC members. The Court did not find the respondent liable for the claimant's costs of attending the Hamburg conference 'in circumstances where he had been unequivocally informed in advance that the company would not fund his attendance'. The claimant's decision to attend the conference had been unilateral, 'in the full knowledge' that it would not be supported by the respondent. The issue of who should determine the training to be provided to EWC members should be 'a collaborative activity' with input from both EWC members and management. To that end, a company could not be required under Directive 2009/38/EC to furnish its EWC with a 'blank cheque'.

That appeal therefore failed and the question of costs was rendered moot.

INDUSTRIAL RELATIONS ACT 1969

[10.05] *Ryanair Holdings plc v A Worker[6]—Labour Court—appeal from Workplace Relations Commission—Industrial Relations Act 1969, s 20(1)—dismissal—misconduct—trade dispute referral—goodwill gesture*

---

[6] *Ryanair Holdings plc v A Worker* LCR23002.

The worker referred a trade dispute to the Labour Court under the Industrial Relations Act 1969 and agreed to be bound by the Court's recommendations. The employer did not attend the hearing, which proceeded in its absence.

It was common case that the worker was dismissed by the employer following an investigation into alleged misconduct, a disciplinary hearing and an appeal. The worker appeared to dispute the conclusions reached at each stage of the disciplinary procedure.

The Court concluded that, in all of the circumstances, the trade dispute could best be resolved by a goodwill gesture in the form of an *ex gratia* payment to the worker without prejudice to the position of either party. It therefore recommended payment of €3,000 in full and final settlement of the trade dispute.

[10.06] *Three Ireland Ltd v A Worker*[7]—*Labour Court—appeal from Workplace Relations Commission—Industrial Relations Acts 1946 to 2015—Industrial Relations Act 1969, s 13(9)*

The employer appealed against an Adjudication Officer's recommendation under the Industrial Relations Act 1969.

Having heard from the parties that there were legal proceedings based on the same or similar facts, the Labour Court determined that there was no reality to the parties reaching a voluntary agreement on the basis of a non-legally binding decision. The Court therefore recommended that the parties consider their industrial relations trade dispute resolved. The recommendation of the Adjudication Officer was set aside.

[10.07] *Microsoft v A Job Offeree*[8]—*Labour Court—appeal from Workplace Relations Commission—Industrial Relations Act 1969, s 13—whether the claimant was a 'worker'—conditional offer of employment—whether a contract of employment was entered into*

The claimant, a job offeree, appealed against an Adjudication Officer's recommendation to the Labour Court in accordance with the Industrial Relations Act 1969. The Adjudication Officer declined jurisdiction, having concluded that the contract of employment between the parties was not entered into.

The respondent made a conditional offer of employment to the claimant. That offer was expressly stated to be conditional on, *inter alia*, verification of the claimant's qualifications. The respondent subsequently wrote to the claimant to advise that it was revoking the conditional offer of employment, having determined that the claimant had misrepresented her educational history and achievements.

In all of the circumstances, the Court was satisfied that no contract of employment ever came into being between the parties. It followed that the claimant did not work 'under a contract with the employer', and therefore she was not a 'worker' within the Industrial

---

[7] *Three Ireland Ltd v A Worker* LCR22926.
[8] *Microsoft v A Job Offeree* LCR23018.

Relations Act 1969, nor was her dispute with the respondent a 'trade dispute' for the purposes of that Act.

The Court accordingly had no jurisdiction to investigate the matters in dispute and the Adjudication Officer's recommendation was affirmed.

[10.08] *South Dublin County Council v A Worker*[9]—*Labour Court—Industrial Relations Act 1969, s 20(1)—statutory time limit—complaint out of time—justification*

A worker referred a trade dispute to the Labour Court concerning the inclusion of overtime in the worker's reckonable pensionable pay.

The worker retired from his employment with South Dublin County Council on 7 June 2023. The complaint was submitted to the Labour Court on 6 February 2024, outside the statutory six-month time limit. The worker indicated that this was due to efforts to resolve matters directly with the Council.

While commending the worker for those efforts, the Court did not find that the reasons offered—exhausting an alternative means to resolve the dispute—provided a justifiable excuse for a delay. Accordingly, it had no jurisdiction to hear the complaint and it was rejected.

PENALISATION FOR TAKING PART IN INDUSTRIAL ACTION

[10.09] *Secretary of State for Trade and Business v Mercer*[10]—*UK Supreme Court—Simler, Lloyd-Jones, Hamblen, Burrows & Richards LJJ—Trade Union and Labour Relations (Consolidation) Act 1992, s 146—European Convention on Human Rights, art 11—absence of worker protection against detriment for participation in lawful strike action—compatibility with art 11—declaration of incompatibility*

The appellant was employed as a support worker in the care sector. She was also a union representative and was involved in planning and taking part in lawful strike action at her workplace. She was suspended by her employer and received her normal pay, but nothing for the overtime she would normally have worked. The effect of the suspension was to remove the appellant from the workplace during the strike.

The appellant complained to an employment tribunal that the sole or main purpose of the suspension was to prevent her from taking part in independent trade union activities 'at an appropriate time', or to penalise her for having done so. The employer maintained

---

[9] *South Dublin County Council v A Worker* LCR22963.
[10] *Secretary of State for Trade and Business v Mercer* [2024] UKSC 12. See *Arthur Cox Employment Law Yearbook 2022* at [10.05] for the decision of the Court of Appeal of England and Wales in *Mercer v Alternative Future Group Ltd and Pritchard* [2022] EWCA Civ 379; see also *Arthur Cox Employment Law Yearbook 2021* at [11.07] for the decision of the UK EAT in *Mercer v Alternative Future Group Ltd and Pritchard* UKEAT/0196/20/JOJ.

that the appellant was suspended for abandoning her shift and having spoken to the press without authorisation.

The words 'at an appropriate time' in s 146 of the Trade Union and Labour Relations (Consolidation) Act 1992 (the '1992 Act') do not include working time, unless the activities are permitted by the employer. Hence, this legislation has been interpreted as not providing protection to workers engaged in lawful strike action from a detriment short of dismissal. Protection is, thus, limited to activities outside working time and/or not consistent with primary duties to the employer. The appellant argued that art 11 ECHR and the Human Rights Act 1998 made it imperative to expand this protection.

The UK EAT held that a compatible interpretation with art 11 was 'both necessary and possible' by qualifying the definition of 'appropriate time' in the 1992 Act to include time within working hours when the worker is taking part in industrial action. The Court of Appeal of England and Wales held that lawful industrial action was not included in the relevant section 'as a matter of legislative design'. To interpret the section compatibly with art 11 'would result in impermissible judicial legislation'. Because the case involved a *lacuna* in the law, a declaration of incompatibility would not be appropriate.

The UK Supreme Court recognised that the State's positive obligations under art 11 do not require it to confer 'universal protection in all circumstances to all workers against any detriment (however slight)' intended to dissuade or penalise participation in a lawful strike. That said, it did not follow that the State had no positive obligations at all. While recognising that Parliament had likely made deliberate choices in legislating as it had, the Court did not accept that the absence of any protection against detriment for participation in lawful industrial action was justified. In the Court's judgment, the right of an employer 'to impose any sanction at all short of dismissal' for participation in lawful strike action nullified the right to take lawful strike action. If a worker could only take strike action by exposing themselves to detrimental treatment, the right dissolved. The failure to legislate at all for such protection, including in the private sector, placed the UK in breach of art 11.

The Supreme Court found that the Court of Appeal was correct to hold that the legislation could not be interpreted to be compatible with the ECHR. The Supreme Court held that it seemed that there was 'no single, obvious legislative solution' that would ensure compliance with art 11, balancing the competing rights of employers while not contradicting a fundamental feature of the 1992 Act. Additional legislation would be required.

The Supreme Court held that it would not have been inappropriate for the Court of Appeal to have made a declaration of incompatibility. The impugned provision had the implicit effect of legitimising sanctions short of dismissal for participation in a lawful strike. It put the UK in breach of art 11 and was inherently objectionable as it stood. The Supreme Court declared the impugned provision, s 146 of the 1992 Act, incompatible with art 11 ECHR.

RECTIFICATION OF COLLECTIVE AGREEMENTS

[10.10] *National Union of Rail, Maritime and Transport Workers v Tyne and Wear Passenger Transport Executive t/a Nexus*[11]—*UK Supreme Court—Lloyd-Jones, Sales, Leggatt, Burrows & Simler LJJ—appeal from Court of Appeal of England and Wales—collective agreements, rectification—Employment Rights Act 1996, ss 13 & 24—incorporation into individual contracts—Trade Union and Labour Relations (Consolidation) Act 1992, s 179(1)—proper defendants, individual employees—estoppel, cause of action and issue estoppel—abuse of process, finality of litigation—unauthorised deductions from wages—employment tribunal jurisdiction—unilateral and common mistake*

The UK Supreme Court addressed the issue of rectification of collective agreements, particularly where such agreements are not legally enforceable but have been incorporated into individual employment contracts.

The appellant entered into a 2012 collective agreement with two trade unions (RMT and Unite) to consolidate a 25.5% 'productivity bonus' into employees' basic pay. A dispute later arose as to whether this consolidation also increased the shift allowance, which was calculated as a percentage of basic pay. The appellant argued that it was never intended to increase the shift allowance, while the unions claimed otherwise.

The dispute led to multiple employment tribunal claims by employees, beginning in 2015 (the 'Anderson decision'). The employment tribunal, and later the Court of Appeal of England and Wales, ruled in favour of the employees, holding that the shift allowance was properly calculated on the increased basic pay. The appellant, having exhausted its appeals on interpretation, filed a fresh claim in the High Court seeking rectification of the collective agreement to reflect its original understanding.

The High Court dismissed preliminary objections from the unions, allowing the appellant's rectification claim to proceed. It held that the absence of legal enforceability of the collective agreement did not preclude rectification and rejected arguments of estoppel and abuse of process.

The Court of Appeal reversed the High Court decision. It ruled that the appellant had issued proceedings against the wrong defendants by naming the unions instead of the employees, whose contracts would be affected by rectification. The unenforceability of collective agreements under the Trade Union and Labour Relations (Consolidation) Act 1992 barred rectification of such agreements. The appellant was estopped from raising rectification claims that sought to overturn the outcome of the Anderson decision.

---

[11] *National Union of Rail, Maritime and Transport Workers and Anor v Tyne and Wear Passenger Transport Executive t/a Nexus* [2024] UKSC 37, see *Arthur Cox Employment Law Yearbook 2022* at [10.07] for the decision of the Court of Appeal of England and Wales in *Tyne and Wear Passenger Transport Executive t/a Nexus v National Union of Rail, Maritime and Transport Workers* [2022] EWCA Civ 1408.

On appeal, the UK Supreme Court held that while the Court of Appeal erred on some points, its ultimate conclusion was correct. The Supreme Court rejected the notion that the lack of legal enforceability under the Trade Union and Labour Relations (Consolidation) Act 1992 precludes rectification. It held that a collective agreement can be rectified if its terms, once incorporated into individual contracts of employment, affect legal rights. The aim of rectification is to align the document with the parties' shared intention.

The Supreme Court affirmed that the proper defendants in a rectification claim are the employees whose individual contracts incorporate the terms of the collective agreement. The unions, as non-parties to these contracts, were not the appropriate defendants. The appellant was barred from raising rectification claims in a way that would undermine the Anderson decision, given the public interest in finality of litigation. While rectification could have been raised as a defence in those proceedings, the appellant had failed to do so. The Supreme Court noted that employment tribunals lack the power to order rectification but can treat documents as if they were rectified to resolve disputes over unauthorised deductions under the Employment Rights Act 1996.

The appeal was dismissed. The Supreme Court upheld the principle that rectification must directly involve those whose legal rights would be affected and emphasised the importance of procedural justice. The appellant could pursue rectification against the employees in separate proceedings but could not do so in order to overturn the Anderson decision.

SECTORAL EMPLOYMENT ORDERS

[10.11]   *Martompol v Tomiak*[12]—*Labour Court—appeal from Workplace Relations Commission—Industrial Relations (Amendment) Act 2015, s 23—Sectoral Employment Order (Construction Sector) 2019*[13]—*construction industry—statutory rates of pay for skilled workers*

The claimant claimed that the respondent employer had not paid him the rate of pay for an experienced construction worker, and had instead paid him an hourly rate of €10.50 throughout his employment. The claimant submitted that he was a category A worker as defined by the Construction Industry SEO. He sought €41,905, representing underpayments between 2016 and 2022.

The claimant appealed against a WRC decision that his complaint under the Industrial Relations (Amendment) Act 2015 was not lodged in time and that no reasonable cause was demonstrated to warrant an extension.

The claimant lodged his complaint on 25 August 2022, over six months after his employment with the respondent ended on 22 February 2022. He argued that the date of

---

[12]   *Martompol v Tomiak* LCR22943.
[13]   Sectoral Employment Order (Construction Sector) 2019 (SI 234 of 2019).

the alleged contravention, 10 March 2022, which was the date of his final payslip, fell within the cognisable period. The Court accepted that the complaint was lodged in time.

The respondent disputed that the claimant was employed in any construction capacity and submitted that he worked as a maintenance operative, 'cleaning windows, gutters and general power washing'. The claimant's role did not meet the criteria for inclusion in the SEO and he was not a skilled general operative. The respondent accepted that it operated in a sector encompassed by the SEO and that the claimant worked on construction sites for it.

The claimant's evidence was that he was recruited by the respondent as a qualified worker but ended up working as a 'helper'. He accepted that he did not have the required qualifications or certifications for a category A worker.

The Court's assessment was limited to the statutory period from 26 February to 25 August 2022, the date of the alleged contravention being 10 March 2022. It had 'serious difficulty' with the respondent's assertion that the claimant was not employed in any construction capacity encompassed by the SEO given 'clear evidence' that he undertook construction work while working on construction sites for the respondent. The claimant was therefore a worker encompassed by the SEO when he worked for the respondent, though he was held not to be a category A, but a category B, worker. The applicable rate of pay for the relevant period was €18.47 per hour, rather than the €10.50 actually paid. The underpayment was calculated at €270.66 and compensation of €5,000 was awarded for failure to pay the statutory rate of pay applicable.

TRADE UNION RECOGNITION

[10.12] *Decotek Automotive v 60 Siptu Members*[14]—*Labour Court—referral under Industrial Relations Act 1969, s 20(1)*

Siptu (the 'union') referred a dispute to the Labour Court on behalf of 60 workers, who were employees of Decotek Automotive. The union asked the Court to recommend that the employer enter into meaningful negotiations with the union on behalf of the workers.

The employer submitted that it had never recognised trade unions for collective bargaining purposes and maintained that it had a strong relationship with its employees, with whom it had engaged directly over the years. It claimed, without elaborating, that the union's complaint was in retaliation for the employer setting up a staff association.

The Court, noting that the employer was not opposed to using external expertise, recommended that the employer recognise the union as the workers' representative and engage with it on matters concerning their employment.

---

14 *Decotek Automotive v 60 Siptu Members* LCR23011.

TRADE UNIONS—INTERFERENCE WITH THE RIGHT TO ORGANISE

[10.13] *ASTI v Ireland*[15]—*European Committee of Social Rights—Revised European Social Charter, art 5—complaint of interference with the right to organise—austerity—pay restoration measures for public servants—allegation of favourable treatment for another trade union—failure to follow prescribed dispute resolution procedure*

The claimant trade union alleged that the Irish Government interfered with the right to organise guaranteed by art 5 of the Revised European Social Charter (the 'Charter') by according favourable treatment as regards pay and increments to a rival trade union, the TUI. In doing so, the claimant alleged that the respondent influenced the choice of teachers as to which union they should join or in which they should remain. The respondent, for its part, asked the Committee to find that there was no violation of art 5.

Following the financial crisis in 2008, the respondent introduced fiscal austerity measures through a series of Financial Measures in the Public Interest ('FEMPI') Acts. These measures included reductions in public services pay, a pensions levy and the freezing of increments. As the financial situation improved, the respondent engaged in gradual pay restoration through Public Service Stability Agreements ('PSSAs') and amendments to the FEMPI Acts.

While initially applicable to all public sector workers, irrespective of trade union, the claimant stated that, by 2013 the FEMPI Acts 'were reflecting government cognisance of the fact that different unions might adopt different attitudes/approaches to FEMPI measures'. Thus, the FEMPI Act 2013 differentiated between public servants 'to whom a collective agreement relates' and those to whom no such agreement related, providing that suspension of increments and pay scales should apply to the former 'only to the extent specified in the agreement or ... with such modification as are specified in the agreement'. The claimant asserted that, as regards teachers, this distinction was first made in the Department of Education and Skills ('DES') circular letter of 22 April 2016 (CL0030/2016). The claimant alleged that although the circular drew no express distinction between members of different trade unions, incremental progression was to resume on 1 July 2017 for those teachers covered by the PSSA 2013–2018 (the 'Lansdowne Road Agreement'), and was to be suspended until 1 July 2018 for those who were not.

The claimant indicated that, subsequently, the Public Service Pay and Pensions Act 2017 (the '2017 Act') went on to distinguish between public servants who were covered by the 2013–2018 agreements ('covered public servants') and those who were not ('non-covered public servants'). The 2017 Act provided for the further restoration of the basic salaries of public servants. However, s 3 of the 2017 Act provided that, where a recognised trade union had not notified the WRC of its assent to be bound by the Lansdowne Road Agreement, its members would be treated as non-covered

---

[15] *ASTI v Ireland* 180/2019.

public servants, securing the same progression as their covered counterparts but at a much slower rate. The claimant alleged, essentially, that teachers who did not engage in industrial action were 'covered', while those who engaged in industrial action were 'not covered', and were treated less favourably.

Under the Croke Park Agreement and further PSSAs, an additional 33 hours per annum were required of teachers (the 'Croke Park hours'). In May 2016, the claimant's members voted against the Croke Park hours and to engage in industrial action from 11 July 2016.

It was against this background, the claimant argued, that 'an explicit distinction was drawn between its members and those of the TUI' in a DES circular letter of 14 July 2016 (CL0045/2016). The claimant submitted that, by virtue of this circular letter, only TUI members were to receive payroll adjustments provided for in the Lansdowne Road Agreement. The TUI had agreed to be bound by the relevant PSSAs, and as such were deemed to be encompassed by its terms. Insofar as the claimant's members were concerned, however, incremental progression was suspended.

On 10 June 2017, the claimant's members voted to suspend the industrial action and, consequently, have been treated as 'covered public servants' since that date. In spite of this, the claimant claimed that its members are subjected to continuing disadvantage insofar as their incremental dates are concerned.

In May 2017, the DES, in response to a question relating to increment payment dates in future years, indicated that the question 'would fall to be considered in the context of the [claimant's] formal entry to the applicable collective agreement' (for example, the PSSA 2018–2020). According to the claimant, in November 2017 a commitment was secured from the DES to enter discussions on increment dates before any formal ballot took place. However, it subsequently became clear that only formal entry into a PSSA would lead to the outcome of the negotiations being implemented.

The claimant alleged that the comparatively favourable treatment afforded to the TUI 'was not based on any objective criteria other than a desire to punish [the claimant] for exercising its right not to be forced into agreeing to be bound by a national agreement which it believed to be inimical to the interests of teachers'. The respondent had, thus, 'influenced the choice of teachers' as to which trade union they should join, or in which they should remain, contrary to art 5 of the Charter.

The Committee noted that, in voting not to fulfil the Croke Park hours and engaging in industrial action, the claimant did not follow the dispute resolution procedure provided for in the Lansdowne Road Agreement. The rejection by the claimant of the Lansdowne Road Agreement 'meant that the financial and other benefits provided by that agreement no longer applied to [the claimant's] members', until its members voted to suspend industrial action and were again treated as covered public servants. The Committee noted the respondent's position that several invitations to engage in negotiations were refused by the claimant, and that the claimant was notified of the implications of its decision, including the loss of benefits accruing under the PSSA in force. The claimant did not contest that, prior to the strike action, the DES proposed to delay the implementation of the impugned measures.

Once the claimant withdrew from the Lansdowne Road Agreement, without following the dispute resolution procedure therein, the FEMPI Act 2013, which drew a distinction between covered and non-covered public servants, became applicable to its members. The situation was 'at all times objectively known to the parties'. The evidence provided by the claimant did not demonstrate 'any specific or targeted actions on the part of the [respondent] which might have been intended to influence teachers' choice regarding the trade union to which they belong'. Conversely, the loss for the claimant's members of benefits to public servants bound by a collective agreement derived from 'the deliberate choice of the [claimant] to withdraw from the agreement in force, while being aware of the effects of such withdrawal'.

The Committee found no compelling evidence of favourable treatment or action by the respondent that was intended to 'exert pressure, impose restraints or influence the choice of teachers in joining the TUI'. It followed that there was no violation of art 5 of the Charter.

See also decision of Irish Supreme Court in *HA O'Neil Ltd v Unite the Union*,[16] relating to picket injunctions at **[11.14]**.

---

[16] *HA O'Neil Ltd v Unite the Union* [2024] IESC 8.

Chapter 11

Injunctions

INTRODUCTION

[11.01] Applications for interlocutory injunctions restraining disciplinary processes, dismissal, unknown defendants, post-termination competition with the previous employer, and picketing are all noted, as is an application to restrain stalking and harassment.

Disciplinary Process

An application to restrain a disciplinary process was considered successively by the High Court, the Court of Appeal and the Supreme Court in *Rajpal v HSE*.

Dismissal

Applications to restrain dismissal were considered by the High Court in *Campbell v The Irish Prison Service*, *Nolan v Science Foundation Ireland* and *Durnin v Horse's Mouth Ltd*.

The UK Supreme Court considered an application to restrain a fire and re-hire policy in *USDAW v Tesco Stores Ltd*.

Non-compete

Numerous post-termination non-compete injunction applications are noted: *Creganna Ltd v Cullen and Lake Region Medical Ltd* in the High Court, *Derma Med Ltd v Ally* in the Court of Appeal in England and Wales, and *Sparta Global Ltd v Hayes* and *Literacy Capital plc v Webb* are decisions of the High Court of England and Wales.

Picket Injunctions

The crucially important decision of the Supreme Court in *HA O'Neil Ltd v Unite the Union* (which concerned an interlocutory application for an injunction restraining a picket) is noted, as is the decision of the High Court in *Carey Glass UC v Unite the Union*.

Stalking

Finally, an application to restrain stalking and harassment was considered by the High Court of England and Wales in *RBT v YLA*.

Unknown Defendant Injunctions

Whether an interlocutory injunction can restrain unnamed and unknown newcomers was considered by the UK Supreme Court in *Wolverhampton City Council v Londan Gypsies and Travellers*.

DISCIPLINARY PROCESS

[11.02] *Rajpal v HSE*[1]—*High Court—Egan J—interlocutory injunction—prohibitory order—disciplinary process—fair question to be tried—unlawful delegation of authority—balance of convenience*

The applicant was a consultant surgeon in Cavan General Hospital (the 'hospital'). He sought an injunction restraining the respondent employer from taking any further steps in an investigation against him for alleged misconduct.

The applicant had been employed at the hospital since 1999. He was employed on a 1998 contract with the then North Eastern Health Board. That board's functions were transferred to the respondent in 2005, and the applicant remained on legacy contract terms. Nevertheless, some 200 HSE consultants were employed on terms similar to those of the applicant.

In August 2022, a complaint of sexual assault against the applicant was made by a staff member to the hospital general manager and to An Garda Síochána. The applicant was subsequently notified that the matter had been referred to the respondent's CEO in line with the applicant's contract. By letter in September 2022, the general manager furnished the complainant's Garda statement to the CEO, it having been agreed by the complainant and An Garda Síochána that it could be shown to the applicant.

A subsequent letter in September 2022 informed the applicant of a second allegation concerning the potential abuse by the applicant of prescription medication (arising from medical prescription forms which had been signed by two non-consultant hospital doctors reporting to him). The prescription forms were sent anonymously to the general manager, who informed the applicant of her intention to 'establish the facts relating to the matter'. This complaint was also passed to the CEO.

---

[1] *Rajpal v HSE* [2024] IEHC 70; see *Rajpal v HSE* [2024] IECA 194 at **[11.03]**; and *Rajpal v HSE* [2024] IESCDET 121 at **[11.04]**.

By letter dated 21 October 2022, the CEO formally notified the applicant of the two allegations. The CEO advised that he was considering requiring the applicant to take administrative leave and invited him to make representations. The applicant denied the sexual assault allegation in full. He accepted that he had asked junior colleagues to sign prescription forms, but maintained that the medication was legitimately required by his parents and himself. The applicant suggested that there was a clear agenda against him at the hospital and accused management of intimidation and harassment.

In January 2023, the CEO advised the applicant that an investigation regarding the allegations was warranted and that a suitably qualified investigator would be appointed for that purpose. A meeting took place in February 2023, during which (and without prior notice) the CEO put to the applicant a third allegation; namely that he had disclosed to multiple colleagues CCTV footage from the date and location of the alleged sexual assault showing the complainant leaving the applicant's car after the alleged assault. The applicant expressed no recollection of having done so (but later made certain admissions at the appeal hearing of this matter). Later in February 2023, the CEO informed the applicant of his intention to engage an independent investigator in respect of the three allegations.

In March 2023, the applicant was furnished with the investigator's terms of reference. The investigator was tasked with considering 'the concerns and allegations identified below and [making] findings on the balance of probabilities'. Any such findings would be set out in a final report to the CEO 'by reference to the evidence gathered by [the investigator] during the course of the investigation process'. No particular procedures were specified in the terms of reference and the investigator was free to 'adopt his own procedures', subject to the provisions of the applicant's contract and the requirements of natural justice and fair procedures. The investigator would have the final say on which witnesses were relevant and the 'general thrust' of the terms of reference seemed to envisage that witnesses would be interviewed by him, rather than there being a separate hearing.

The High Court, in the first instance, accepted that the applicant was not seeking to compel the respondent to perform any action 'which may be difficult to undo or may cause it irremediable prejudice'. It was therefore satisfied that the 'substance' of the order sought was prohibitory, and not mandatory, as the respondent contended. Hence, the applicant needed only to demonstrate that there was a fair question to be tried (as opposed to a strong case likely to succeed at trial). In the context of disciplinary proceedings, this would entail proving at trial that the process had gone irremediably wrong.

The decision to suspend or not to suspend the applicant was solely a matter for the CEO. To this end, and in order to carry out such 'further examination' as he considered necessary, the CEO had a discretion to commission external investigators to assist him, including in the collecting, collating and presenting of the essential facts to the CEO for his adjudication. This was a valid exercise. However, here, the terms of reference required the investigator to make findings of fact themselves. The Court agreed that such findings would inevitably be central to a finding of misconduct and it was not clear on what basis the CEO could decide not to accept those findings of fact. Applying the test as to whether there was a fair question to be tried, the High Court stated that the applicant was 'entitled to nothing less than that the CEO would make such findings of fact himself', and that the procedure envisaged in the sexual assault investigation 'resulted in a failure by the CEO to perform his decision-making function'. A 'crucial aspect' of his decision-making function would be delegated to the investigator, so that there would be 'nothing left for the CEO to decide'. Accordingly, there was a fair question to be tried as to the lawfulness of the delegation of the CEO's authority. Such a procedural defect, if made out, would not be capable of rectification later in the process, since the identity of the decision maker was not something that could easily be altered once the process had commenced, without starting the process from scratch.

In view of the potential for irreparable harm to the applicant's reputation and livelihood in the event of a finding against him in the investigation, the Court was satisfied that the balance of convenience weighed in the applicant's favour, notwithstanding the importance of progressing the disciplinary process. The Court's order would not restrain the disciplinary process absolutely, but rather the investigation in its current shape. It was notable that the applicant was continuing to work in the hospital and that the CEO had not instigated the administrative leave provisions of the applicant's contract of employment. This indicated that the CEO was of the view that there was no unacceptable risk to patients or staff requiring any such action.

Accordingly, the Court granted an interlocutory order restraining the respondent's investigation 'as presently convened'.

[11.03] *Rajpal v HSE*[2]—*Court of Appeal—Butler J—appeal from High Court—interlocutory reliefs—order restraining a disciplinary procedure—whether the trial Judge applied the correct test—whether a fair question to be tried had been established—delegation of contractual functions to an independent third party*

The hospital appealed the High Court's decision to grant the respondent consultant surgeon an interlocutory injunction restraining the holding of the disciplinary inquiry into him pending further order. Much of the appeal concerned the extent of the powers of the appellant's CEO to delegate significant investigative functions to an independent investigator, including powers to make findings on disputed issues of fact as part of that procedure. The interpretation of the relevant provisions of the respondent's employment contract had further potential impact beyond this case.

The appellant challenged the High Court's finding that the applicable test was whether the respondent had established a fair question to be tried (as opposed to a strong case likely to succeed at trial) regarding whether it was permissible for the CEO to delegate contractual functions in the manner complained of. The Court of Appeal considered the trial Judge to have 'crossed the line', going further than was necessary to decide whether a fair question arose and 'purporting to make definitive findings'. Were those findings to be upheld at trial, the CEO's ability to establish an independent investigation would be reduced.

---

[2] *Rajpal v HSE* [2024] IECA 194; see *Rajpal v HSE* [2024] IEHC 70 at **[11.02]**; and *Rajpal v HSE* [2024] IESCDET 121 at **[11.03]**.

However, the interlocutory reliefs sought by the respondent required no positive action on the appellant's part. At most, the disciplinary investigation would be stalled pending the trial. The order sought was therefore prohibitory, and not mandatory, as the appellant sought to argue.

The appellant pointed to jurisprudence establishing that 'a Court should be very reluctant to intervene in an ongoing disciplinary process and should only do so if the process has gone irremediably wrong'. The Court of Appeal, however, took the view that a complaint as to whether the decision maker can contractually delegate a fact-finding exercise to an independent investigator is undoubtedly serious; fatal to the investigative process if decided in the respondent's favour. The respondent had therefore met the threshold for establishing a fair question to be tried, which, if successful, would be capable of supporting the grant of a permanent injunction.

The Court of Appeal dismissed the appeal and affirmed all orders.

[11.04] *Rajpal v HSE*[3]—*Supreme Court—Charleton, Collins & Donnelly JJ—determination on application for leave to appeal from Court of Appeal—Constitution of Ireland, Art 34.5.3—leave refused*

The hospital sought leave to appeal to the Supreme Court against the Court of Appeal judgment.

The appellant submitted that the intended appeal raised matters concerning the extent to which the appellant's CEO was personally obliged to undertake various steps in the disciplinary process, and whether he could delegate significant investigative functions (including fact-finding powers) to independent third parties, as well as the conduct of the appellant, its disciplinary procedure, and workplace investigations generally. These matters did not amount to a fair question to be tried at a full hearing of the case and the lower Courts had erred in so finding. Further, it was in the interests of justice that the intended appeal proceed, given the serious nature of the allegations against the respondent.

The respondent argued that the application was premature, arising as it did from an interlocutory injunction.

The Supreme Court saw no apparent reason why a full substantive hearing in the High Court 'ought not to take place in the near future'. There, the appellant would be able to fully ventilate its case, so that it was not necessary in the interests of justice that the issue be appealed to the Supreme Court. The intended appeal also related to the construction of the respondent's contract and relevant provisions of the Health Act 1970 and its regulations. An appeal in an interlocutory matter was not the appropriate avenue for determining those issues.

The application for leave was therefore refused.

---

[3] *Rajpal v HSE* [2024] IESCDET 121; see *Rajpal v HSE* [2024] IEHC 70 at **[11.02]**; and *Rajpal v HSE* [2024] IECA 194 at **[11.03]**.

DISMISSAL

[11.05] *Campbell v The Irish Prison Service*[4]—*High Court—Mulcahy J—interlocutory injunction—disciplinary procedure—allegation of procedural unfairness—whether there was a strong case likely to succeed*

The applicant, a recruit prison officer, was notified that his employment with the respondent was to be terminated on 20 June 2023. On 16 June 2023, the applicant obtained an *ex parte* High Court order restraining his dismissal until after 20 June 2023 or further order.

In this interlocutory application, the applicant sought an injunction restraining his dismissal and reinstating him to full duties pending the determination of the proceedings.

The applicant's dismissal was based on a finding of serious misconduct against him in a disciplinary process following the discovery, on 9 June 2022, of three plastic bags containing a white powdery residue (later identified as cocaine) in the bedside locker of a room that had been previously occupied by the applicant. The applicant denied any wrongdoing and alleged deficiencies in the investigative, disciplinary and appellate phases of the process, which amounted to breaches of fair procedure.

The applicant argued that, having regard to the seriousness of the allegations, which were criminal in nature, a standard higher than the balance of probabilities should have been applied by the respondent when it reached its conclusions. Although not persuaded by that argument, the Court was satisfied that, in principle, it was possible that the applicant could secure a permanent injunction restraining any disciplinary action grounded on a flawed process at the hearing of the action. Accordingly, interlocutory injunctive relief 'should be available' to the applicant.

However, in the circumstances, the Court concluded that the applicant had not met the threshold for a strong case likely to succeed in order to obtain an injunction to restrain his dismissal. Despite an apparent procedural misstep in the manner in which the disciplinary process had commenced, the respondent had 'mended its hand', and 'the process hadn't gone so irredeemably wrong that the procedure couldn't be completed without affording the [applicant] the benefit of the procedure to which he was entitled'. In any event, the applicant did not advance any argument that the incorrect procedure had been applied, and there was no basis for concluding that the relevant procedure had not been complied with. The Court did not consider that any strong case had been made in those respects.

There was no 'exceptional feature' or indeed anything 'sufficiently out of the ordinary' resulting in the applicant's contract being inadequate to ensure fair procedures. Nor had the applicant made out a strong case that he has been left without 'adequate representation' at the disciplinary hearing. The Court held that the failure to provide legal representation at the disciplinary hearing was not the relevant issue, notwithstanding the serious nature of the allegation. The allegation itself did not give rise to 'complex legal

---

[4] *Campbell v The Irish Prison Service* [2023] IEHC 706.

issues,' nor did it rest on disputed evidence, or the credibility of a particular witness, none of whom purported to have witnessed any action by the applicant which he wished to dispute. More importantly, it was not clear that the applicant was prevented from calling witnesses by the respondent.

There was no 'want of fair procedures' in the respondent's reliance on its review of CCTV footage, and it seemed to the Court, 'at this stage', that the approach taken by the respondent was a reasonable one. The applicant's complaint that a motion sensor was not sufficiently calibrated was 'wholly speculative'. Similarly, the suggestion that the applicant should have been provided with the plastic bags in order to independently test them seemed to be 'somewhat fanciful'.

The reliefs were therefore refused.

[11.06] *Nolan v Science Foundation Ireland[5]—High Court—Mulcahy J—mandatory injunction—dismissal—fair procedures—whether employee dismissed for misconduct, or whether dismissed under employment contract—strong case likely to succeed at trial*

On 27 May 2024, the respondent's board took the decision to dismiss the applicant from his post as director general. The applicant was notified of the decision that evening.

Although there had been an investigation into allegations of misconduct against the applicant and a decision had been made to conduct a disciplinary hearing, the applicant had been given no prior notice that the respondent board was meeting to discuss his position, or that any such decision was being contemplated. The applicant sought and obtained an interim injunction restraining the respondent from taking any further steps towards his dismissal.

In these proceedings, the applicant sought a mandatory injunction restraining his dismissal. He claimed that the decision to dismiss him was a response to allegations of misconduct, and that the decision had been reached without affording him fair procedures. The respondent's position was that the applicant had been dismissed in accordance with the provisions of his employment contract. As he had not been dismissed for misconduct, the respondent was not required to afford the applicant fair procedures.

The parties agreed that his dismissal for misconduct would have entitled the applicant to fair procedures, and, conversely, that the respondent retained a contractual entitlement to terminate the applicant's employment on a 'no fault' basis, without recourse to fair procedures.

The applicant alleged that certain protected disclosures, all of which were made within the space of three days—and which included complaints of bullying and breaches of corporate governance—were made on a 'co-ordinated basis' and were part of a larger 'orchestrated attempt' to frustrate his efforts to deliver considerable change and reform to the respondent's organisation, whether by securing his dismissal or making

---

[5] *Nolan v Science Foundation Ireland* [2024] IEHC 368.

it impossible for those changes to be implemented. He argued that damages would be an inadequate remedy in circumstances where his reputation would likely be irreparably damaged if the respondent were permitted to dismiss him in the absence of fair procedures.

The respondent contended that, as it had complied with the relevant provisions of his contract of employment, the applicant's complaint was not made out. It asserted that, if the applicant thereafter contended that his dismissal was unfair, the appropriate remedy would be to pursue an unfair dismissal claim before the WRC. In any event, given the refusal voiced by some of its members of staff to work with the applicant, his return to work pending the outcome of a High Court trial would not be sustainable.

Mulcahy J had regard to a number of matters, including that the respondent's board, having adopted the recommendations of a report prepared by a specially constituted sub-committee, concluded that there were allegations against the applicant 'which merited and would be brought to a disciplinary hearing', though that disciplinary hearing had not yet convened. The letter purporting to terminate the applicant's employment 'clearly illustrated' that these allegations were part of the respondent's considerations when taking the decision to dismiss him. While it was true that the letter also referenced the contractual provisions entitling the respondent to dismiss the applicant without fault on his part, it did not make clear that there were no extant allegations of misconduct against the applicant, who, on receiving it, clearly understood his dismissal to relate to allegations against him. Matters did not conclude there, however.

Despite the lack of clarity in the respondent's letter, there was no evidence of a decision having been made to dismiss the applicant because of misconduct, so that it could not be said that misconduct was the 'stated reason' for dismissal. While the respondent had clearly resolved that a disciplinary hearing was warranted, the evidence did not suggest that it determined the disciplinary issue prematurely, deciding then to terminate the applicant's employment. It might be argued at trial that the reasons for the applicant's dismissal and the allegations could not be 'decoupled'; however, at this stage, the applicant had not established a strong case likely to succeed that the respondent's decision to dismiss him was based on its conclusion that he was guilty of misconduct.

In the circumstances, the applicant had not met the necessary standard for the grant of mandatory relief and the application was refused.

[11.07] ***Durnin v Horse's Mouth Ltd[6]—High Court—Stack J—interlocutory injunction—suspension followed by summary dismissal—conflicting business interests—strong case likely to succeed at trial as to lawfulness of the suspension and summary dismissal—balance of convenience***

The applicant sought an interlocutory injunction restraining the respondent from taking any steps to terminate his employment. He also sought an order compelling the respondent to continue to pay his salary and other entitlements as they fell due, and to return him to his position within the respondent company.

---

[6] *Durnin v Horse's Mouth Ltd trading as Sportcaller* [2024] IEHC 532.

The applicant was an expert within the software development gaming industry. He set up a company, with another individual, trading as The Unit, which designed and developed 'free-to-play games' (interactive games or quizzes). These games were distributed to other companies (including the respondent), who would licence them to well-known betting companies.

In 2017, the respondent recruited the applicant to provide consultancy services. The applicant and his co-founder of The Unit each held a 50% shareholding in that company and were directors from the outset. Crucially, the applicant informed the then managing director of the respondent of his interest in The Unit. The respondent saw no difficulty with this and, in fact, considered the arrangement potentially advantageous as The Unit would provide necessary services to the respondent.

In February 2021, Bally's Corporation ('Bally's'), a major US-based online betting company and casino operator, acquired the respondent's shareholding through a wholly-owned subsidiary. The applicant, who had signed a contract of employment with the respondent in 2017, signed a fresh contract in largely similar terms.

In July 2022, the applicant and his co-founder of The Unit incorporated another company, The Unit Digital Service Ltd (for simplicity's sake, still referred to here as 'The Unit'), of which they were each directors and 38.7% shareholders. The reduced shareholding was accounted for by the fact that two investors (one of whom was the former managing director of the respondent) loaned monies to the new company in exchange for a 10% shareholding.

In March 2024, the applicant was summarily suspended from his employment on the basis that The Unit appeared to be a competitor of the respondent. The respondent apparently believed that the applicant was using his position as an employee of the respondent to poach its staff and direct business to The Unit. Notwithstanding those suspicions, an investigator from Bally's appointed to investigate the applicant's role in The Unit, rejected that suggestion. Indeed, it was clear to the Court that the investigator made no finding against the applicant that The Unit was a competitor business and that there was 'no material loss of business from the respondent to The Unit'. Rather, the investigator's findings related to the applicant's directorship and shareholding of The Unit and a potential conflict of interest. The decision to summarily dismiss the applicant arose from a finding of gross misconduct.

According to the respondent, it was not until September 2023 that Bally's learned that the applicant—by then appointed head of 'business to business' within the respondent— was a co-founder of The Unit, with whom the respondent was transacting business. Thereafter, no action was apparently taken. In was only in March 2024, when further enquiries were made, that it came to light that the applicant was a substantial shareholder and director of The Unit.

The applicant challenged the lawfulness of both his suspension and his ultimate dismissal.

In the Court's view, the applicant had not established a basis for interlocutory relief relating to the lawfulness of the initial suspension. The respondent's investigation was established on the basis that it would consider the 'entire question' of whether the applicant's involvement with The Unit breached his contract of employment. The respondent had not strayed outside the broader issue and the applicant was given an opportunity to address specific issues which emerged in the course of the investigation.

However, the applicant had a strong case, likely to succeed at trial, that his dismissal was unlawful, having regard to the terms of his contract of employment. The dismissal was based on alleged breaches of clauses relating to promoting the respondent's interests, restrictions on outside business interests and adherence to the 'group code of conduct'. The applicant had an unblemished record within the respondent with no prior warnings. More importantly, he had openly disclosed his interest in The Unit to the respondent years before. While it was true that the applicant did not have the written consent of the parent company's board to pursue his activities with The Unit, those activities had been obvious for years without any objection being raised. It was therefore unclear why, after years of apparently accepting the applicant's activities with The Unit, the respondent suddenly sought to strictly enforce those contractual provisions, without offering the applicant an opportunity to address or rectify the issues.

The group code of conduct, on which the respondent relied, was deemed 'non-contractual' by the applicant's own contract of employment. The code could not legally form the basis for summary dismissal. It did not have the force of contract, and so its contravention did not constitute 'serious misconduct' under the contract's dismissal terms. This important detail had not been considered by the respondent, despite the seriousness of the decision to dismiss. The Court held that the respondent's attempt to 'elevate' the significance of the code of conduct was unlawful as it constituted 'an attempt to unilaterally alter the applicant's contract of employment'.

Otherwise, certain allegations, such as the sending of a single email on behalf of The Unit during working hours, were patently trivial in nature and did not constitute serious misconduct. The Court noted a lack of proportionality and due consideration in treating such a minor infraction as grounds for summary dismissal.

Collectively, these defects pointed to a dismissal that was procedurally and substantively flawed. Balancing the relatively small values involved and the fact that the managing director of the day was at all times fully aware of the applicant's involvement in The Unit, as well as the potential damage to the applicant's reputation, the Court decided that the balance of convenience favoured the applicant being allowed to return to work immediately.

[11.08] *USDAW v Tesco Stores Ltd*[7]—*UK Supreme Court—Burrows & Simler LJJ—appeal from Court of Appeal of England and Wales—Trade Union and*

---

[7] Union of Shop, Distributive and Allied Workers and Ors v Tesco Stores Ltd [2024] UKSC 28. See *Arthur Cox Employment Law Yearbook 2022* at [1.18] for the decision of the Court of Appeal of England and Wales in *Tesco Stores Ltd v USDAW, Webb, Singh and Kumar* [2022] EWCA Civ 978; see also *Arthur Cox Employment Law Yearbook 2022* at [1.19] for the decision of the High Court of England and Wales granting the declaration in *Union of Shop, Distributive and Allied Workers and Ors v Tesco Stores Ltd* [2022] EWHC 201 (QB).

Labour Relations (Consolidation) Act 1992—permanent right to retained pay subsequently incorporated into contract of employment—necessity to imply a term preventing 'fire and re-hire' tactics to remove right to retained pay—business efficacy test—obviousness

The appellant was the relevant trade union recognised for collective bargaining purposes by the respondent. This appeal concerned the correct interpretation of an express term concerning 'retained pay' agreed in a collective agreement. It was common case that the retained pay term was incorporated into the workers' contracts of employment.

In 2007, the respondent embarked on an expansion programme involving the closure of certain existing distribution centres and the expansion or restructuring of others. Retained pay was negotiated by the parties to incentivise workers at a distribution centre at Crick in Northamptonshire to relocate to other sites. Accordingly, those workers were receiving retained pay from September 2007, when they were moved from Crick to distribution centres at Daventry and Lichfield. The retained pay clause was formally agreed in a collective agreement some two years later in 2009 and signed in February 2010. It was only shortly thereafter that the express term became incorporated into the workers' individual contracts of employment. Subject to certain conditions—notably change by 'mutual consent'—this term provided that retained pay 'will remain a permanent feature of an individual's contractual eligibility'.

Retained pay constituted approximately 32% to 39% of the affected workers' wages. Each took out a mortgage on the basis of their overall income, including retained pay, which on their evidence, they had no reason to believe would be withdrawn.

In January 2021, the respondent formally announced its intention to remove retained pay, having notified the appellant on an embargoed basis. Workers on retained pay were offered an advance payment of 18 months in exchange for voluntary forfeiture of their retained pay rights. They were informed that failure to agree would result in their 'firing and re-hiring' on the same terms but with their retained pay rights removed. Proceedings issued.

The High Court of England and Wales decided upon the nature and extent of the employees' contractual entitlement to retained pay and granted an injunction restraining the respondent from removing the contractual entitlements to retained pay through firing and re-hiring tactics. That decision was overturned by the Court of Appeal.

The 'judicial task' for the UK Supreme Court was to interpret the full retained pay provision, taking into account the 'pre-contractual material' that preceded the moves in September 2007. In a joint lead judgment, Burrows LJ and Simler LJ considered the word 'permanent' in the retained pay term to convey a right which was not time limited in any way and would continue to be paid to the workers for as long as their employment in the same role continued. Such a term would, naturally, qualify the respondent's otherwise unrestricted contractual right to terminate the employment contracts on notice in order to remove the right to permanent retained pay. The real question was whether such a term was implied by fact.

The Supreme Court agreed with the appellant that it was necessary for business efficacy to imply a term qualifying the respondent's right to dismiss on notice. The implied term was necessary—or, alternatively, so obvious that it went without saying—'in order not to undermine the promise that retained pay would be a "permanent" feature of contractual entitlements for the relevant employees', subject only to the qualifications specified in that term. The circumstances in which the right to retained pay was agreed made clear that the offer of permanent retained pay 'was intended as an inducement to employees to accept terms of the collectively negotiated agreement and make permanent changes to their lives by relocating to the new distribution centres rather than accepting redundancy'. The respondent needed experienced workers to relocate and wished to retain them at the new sites. Relocation would not have been palatable without such an inducement and it was 'inconceivable' that the mutual intention of the parties was that the respondent would retain a 'unilateral right' to terminate the contracts of employment in order to bring retained pay to an end 'whenever it suited Tesco's business purposes to do so'.

The Supreme Court therefore allowed the appeal and reinstated the injunction granted by the High Court.

NON-COMPETE

[11.09] *Creganna Ltd v Cullen and Lake Region Medical Ltd*[8]*—High Court—Quinn J—interlocutory injunction—non-compete clause—issue to be tried—validity of non-compete clause—inducement to breach of contract—balance of convenience*

The applicant employer sought an interlocutory injunction restraining the defendant employee from taking up a job offer with another company, Lake Region Medical (also a defendant), on the strength of what it contended was a valid 'non-compete' clause applicable for 12 months from the date of termination of the employee's contract. The defendants disputed the validity of the clause and asked the Court to make a definitive ruling on that issue. They also claimed that the applicant was guilty of delay in bringing its application.

The applicant specialised in the design and manufacture of medical devices for its international clients and was part of a global business, TE Connectivity. Lake Region Medical was also part of a global group, Integar, and was engaged in largely similar business. The defendant was a senior employee, initially employed by the applicant as its European sales manager in 2015, and being promoted over the years until reaching the level of director for product management in 2022. In January 2024, the defendant, having signed an offer of employment from Lake Region Medical, handed in his resignation to the applicant, who in February 2024 placed him on garden leave.

The applicant claimed that the defendant continued to maintain relationships with 'key decision makers' in global companies, who were customers of the applicant, and that

---

[8] *Creganna Ltd v Cullen and Lake Region Medical Ltd* [2024] IEHC 231.

he was privy to 'highly sensitive commercial information'. The extent of these claims was disputed by the defendant.

The defendant's 2015 contract of employment contained clauses headed 'non-compete' and 'confidentiality', and the applicant claimed that he had signed an additional document headed 'staff member confidentiality agreement'. The parties were in dispute as to whether or not each promotion involved a new contract of employment or a formal variation of the existing contract. The applicant contended that, with every promotion, the terms of the non-compete clause were incorporated into the varied contract.

The Court was not persuaded that there had been any substantial delay to justify refusing relief. Indeed, progress in the matter had been 'reasonably prompt', the interlocutory hearing taking place within two months of the defendant making his position clear to the applicant. A brief interregnum to facilitate without prejudice discussions did not visit any prejudice upon the defendant, and he had yet to start working for his new employer. The Court refused the defendants' request for a 'definite and final decision' on the validity of the non-compete clause at that interlocutory stage.

It was apparent to the Court that there was a dispute as to the relevant factual background to the non-compete clause, as well as to its validity. In particular, the applicant had identified a serious question that the clause was necessary to protect its legitimate business interests. As against the defendant company, there was the question as to its awareness of the non-compete clause, if valid.

The Court was also satisfied, given the confidential and sensitive information acquired by the defendant employee in his roles and the 'nature of the competitive business' between the two companies, that damages would probably not be an adequate remedy for the applicant if the injunction were refused and the non-compete clause was later found to be valid. Conversely, damages would be an adequate remedy for the defendant if he were successful at trial. It was not clear that the job offer would be withdrawn, as the defendant asserted, and the likelihood was that he would merely be delayed taking up his new job, while still receiving his salary from the applicant.

Even if mistaken on the unlikelihood of withdrawal of the job offer, the Court was of the view that the balance of convenience had been adequately addressed by the applicant agreeing to continue paying the defendant his salary. The Court would fix an early trial date.

The application for interlocutory relief succeeded.

[11.10] *Derma Med Ltd v Ally*[9]—*Court of Appeal of England and Wales—Bean, Males & Lewis LJJ—appeal from High Court of England and Wales—ex parte injunction—duty of full and frank disclosure—whether the trial Judge erred in setting aside ex parte orders for failure to disclose relevant matters*

The respondent was a high-profile medical practitioner specialising in cosmetic procedures. He and his wife built up a successful business which, in March 2022, they sold

---

[9] *Derma Med Ltd and Peal Athena Ltd v Ally, Zackally Ltd and Qasemzahi* [2024] EWCA Civ 175.

to Pearl Athena Ltd in consideration of a substantial sum, together with a shareholding in the purchasing company. The sale and purchase agreement included terms that the respondent would not compete with the applicant for a period of two years, including dealing with any of its clients, enticing away any supplier, or using any of the applicant's intellectual property; and that he would observe the confidentiality of information relating to the applicant's business, clients and suppliers. In view of his reputation, which was considered important for attracting business, the respondent was to remain a director of the applicant and would continue to work for it.

The applicant came to suspect that the respondent was dishonestly diverting business from it, using confidential information in order to do so. The respondent was suspended in May 2023, as a result of which he resigned as a director and an employee, alleging constructive dismissal. The applicant applied *ex parte* for an injunction in order to enforce the non-compete and confidentiality obligations. The injunction was granted by the High Court (Constable J), which was satisfied that there was a strong *prima facie* case that: the respondent was breaching those obligations; the balance of convenience favoured the grant of an injunction pending a return date; and it was appropriate to grant the injunction *ex parte* in view of a 'strong inference' that the respondent would take steps to cover his tracks if forewarned.

On the return date, however, Bourne J (the 'trial Judge') set aside the injunction on the ground that there had been 'significant and culpable' failures of disclosure on the applicant's part at the earlier hearing. The trial Judge was critical of the making of the *ex parte* application. While it was logical to seek orders preserving devices and images without notice, the same logic did not apply to the non-compete and confidentiality injunctions, and there was 'no good reason' to seek those orders *ex parte*. The trial Judge also criticised the applicant's failure to disclose a letter dated 31 May 2023 suspending the respondent pending an investigation. Further, the applicant had failed to disclose that the definition of 'confidential information' in the order—'including but not limited to … any information that would reasonably be regarded as confidential'—was too wide. Finally, there was a failure to disclose the applicant's non-payment of the final instalment due to the respondent under the sale and purchase agreement.

The trial Judge refused to grant a fresh injunction, being satisfied that damages would provide an adequate remedy to the applicant if they succeeded in their claim, given that the respondent was a 'person of means'. The applicant appealed against the decision.

The Court of Appeal was satisfied that the applicant made 'conscientious efforts' to comply with its duty of full and frank disclosure. Having identified the test for an *ex parte* application, it made submissions that it satisfied that test. It was a matter for Constable J to evaluate whether a non-compete injunction without notice was justified for a short period until the return date, or whether it would be preferable to hear that aspect of the application on notice. The trial Judge was wrong to characterise this as a failure of disclosure by the applicant.

While it was true that Constable J had not been shown the suspension letter at the *ex parte* hearing, a chain of correspondence was furnished in which the applicant expressed concerns that the respondent was divulging confidential information and enticing suppliers and employees away from the applicant. The applicant's letter expressly reserved the right to seek 'urgent injunctive relief' if certain undertakings were not forthcoming. The correspondence included a replying letter from the respondent's solicitor characterising those concerns as 'paranoia'. Accordingly, it was expressly drawn to Constable J's attention that there had been correspondence between the parties in which the respondent was notified of complaints against him, and that an urgent injunction was a real possibility. There was therefore no failure of disclosure by the applicant in this respect.

The applicant accepted that there had been a 'want' of full and frank disclosure in failing to draw Constable J's attention to problems inherent in the words 'including but not limited to'. Nevertheless, the Court of Appeal considered this to be of relatively limited significance. The omission was clearly not deliberate.

As regards the failure to disclose the applicant's non-payment of the final instalment, the trial Judge was entitled to regard this as a 'culpable, albeit not deliberate', failure of disclosure by the applicant.

The Court of Appeal was left in no doubt that the injunction should not have been set aside. Constable J had rightly held that there was a strong *prima facie* case that the respondent had committed serious breaches of his obligations under the sale and purchase agreement, and had taken extensive steps to conceal his wrongdoing. Nothing the respondent said suggested that the grant of an injunction was wrong in principle. The failures of disclosure were not deliberate and a 'sense of proportion' was needed.

The appeal was therefore allowed and a fresh injunction granted.

[11.11] *Sparta Global Ltd v Hayes*[10]—*High Court of England and Wales—Dias KC—interim injunction—non-compete clause—enforceability of restrictive covenants—serious issue to be tried—adequacy of damages as a remedy—balance of convenience—bargaining power*

The applicant carried on business in a niche area in the technology sector. The respondent worked for the applicant as the sales director of its financial services division, beginning in November 2020 and tendering his resignation in September 2023. As such, he had access to, and gained knowledge of, confidential and commercially sensitive information. Following his resignation, he signed a contract to work for another company, Kubrick, a market competitor of the applicant. The respondent's contract of employment contained post-termination restraints and he gave full undertakings to abide by same, though the applicant was not assuaged.

During his employment with the applicant, the respondent also signed an investment agreement ('IA'). While both documents contained non-compete and non-solicitation clauses, the scope of the IA went beyond that of the contract of employment in that there was no 'carve out' for undertaking a different role for a competitor. It also contained a non-compete clause of a longer duration: 12 months, as opposed to the

---

[10] *Sparta Global Ltd v Hayes* [2024] EWHC 100.

six months provided for by the contract of employment. Accordingly, the applicant sought to enforce the 'better protection' provided by the IA.

The Court did not accept the respondent's submission that there was not a serious issue to be tried by virtue of his having given appropriate undertakings and by the 'sheer extensiveness' of the IA, which he argued rendered it unenforceable. In the Court's view there was clearly a serious issue about whether the prohibitive clauses in the IA were reasonable and enforceable.

The Court agreed that damages would not be an adequate remedy for the applicant if successful at trial: the loss of a client might lead to the loss of repeat business, making it very difficult to calculate damages, which could be substantial. Similarly, in the respondent's case, enforcement of the covenants would 'damage [his] standing and attractiveness in the marketplace', making damages inadequate in view of the unquantifiable impact on his future employment prospects in a highly technical field.

In assessing where the balance of convenience lay, the Court observed that there was sufficient material (beyond what was factually in dispute) to allow for a preliminary view as to the likely merits of the IA's enforceability. It was satisfied that the respondent was bound by the IA and that the covenants therein prevented the respondent from taking a non-competing role with Kubrick. It further noted that at the time the respondent became bound by the IA, he was still subject to a six-month probationary period which could be unilaterally extended by the applicant, and during which he could be dismissed with a week's notice. The Court judged that the respondent's vulnerability to being dismissed with a week's notice was to be weighed against the IA's 12-month restriction. From the evidence before the Court, there was nothing to indicate that there were meaningful, or any, negotiations of the IA covenants, which were apparently presented to the respondent as a *fait accompli*. Nor did the applicant contradict the respondent's assertion that he was never given a copy of the IA despite repeated requests. Thus, on a preliminary view, there was a clear inequality of bargaining power.

The IA was 'more akin to a contract of employment' and intricately connected to the respondent's employment; thus, the covenants fell to be assessed by their reasonableness. Given that the restrictions extended to activity beyond that which the respondent previously undertook for the applicant, it was likely that the trial Judge would hold the IA restrictions to be an unlawful restraint of trade unless shown to be justified.

The Court was not persuaded by the applicant's suggestion that the respondent might 'inadvertently' let slip commercially sensitive information in his new (unrelated) role. There was no evidence before the Court to suggest any misuse of such information by the respondent and it was not reasonably arguable that there was a material risk of future disclosure since the respondent would not be working in a client-facing role. Indeed, he was specifically 'ringfenced' in a staff recruitment role with Kubrick and it was difficult to envisage a situation in which the respondent could make damaging inadvertent disclosures. The Court judged that there was 'a real and serious risk' of the respondent losing his job if the IA covenants were enforced, preventing him from working for Kubrick in any capacity.

Hence, the Court judged the risk of prejudice and injustice to the respondent to significantly outweigh that of the applicant. The covenants in the contract of employment provided sufficient protection for the applicant's business interests and the respondent had given undertakings in respect of same. Thus, the balance of convenience lay 'decisively' against granting the injunction sought and the application was dismissed.

[11.12] *Literacy Capital plc v Webb[11]—High Court of England and Wales—Ritchie J—interlocutory injunction—restrictive covenant—non-compete—restraint on trade—whether the duration and scope of the covenant rendered it unenforceable*

The applicant sought an interim injunction to restrain the respondent from trading in competition with a group of subsidiary companies owned by the applicant. The applicant relied on a restrictive covenant.

The applicant was an investment company with controlling shareholdings in other companies. The respondent was a businesswoman who, with a partner, ran and grew Mountain Healthcare Ltd ('Mountain'), a company providing medical services to sexual assault referral centres.

In 2018, the respondent sold her 25% shareholding in Mountain to the applicant through various subsidiary companies for around £4.7 million. This was partly paid up front, with the balance on a deferred loan. The respondent stayed on as a director of Mountain. When she decided to resign in 2021, the respondent renegotiated the sale of her shares, then valued at approximately £7 million. The new agreement with the applicant contained restrictive covenants, one of which prevented her from competing with any of the applicant's subsidiaries anywhere in the UK for 10 years.

The respondent went on to co-found Nurture Health and Care Ltd ('Nurture'). Nurture started to deliver sexual assault referral services and, in 2024, successfully tendered for a contract with the South Wales Police.

The applicant asserted a breach of the restrictive covenant in the 2021 agreements. The respondent contended that the covenant was void. It was far too long to protect any legitimate interest, and too wide in scope, covering all activities engaged in by the applicant's subsidiaries and going far wider than the services Mountain provided. The applicant therefore had no arguable prospect of succeeding at trial.

The Court was satisfied that common law restraint of trade provisions applied in this case. The restrictive covenants arose from the respondent's status as an employee of the applicant and the architect and vendor of Mountain. No evidence was put forward to justify the necessity of the 10-year covenant. The covenant was nationwide, notwithstanding the applicant's evidence that Mountain had only contracted with Norfolk and Suffolk police in 2020 and 2021. The applicant offered no justification for the covenant's scope, other than to say it had 'nationwide ambition'. While protecting Mountain made sense (to a point), protecting the other different subsidiaries made no legitimate

---

[11] *Literacy Capital plc v Webb* [2024] EWHC 2026 (KB).

sense because the respondent did not have expertise in those fields. It appeared that the restrictive covenants arose because of the respondent's special expertise, having successfully grown Mountain.

The restrictive covenant was drafted so widely and of such long duration that it was 'plainly unenforceable at common law for breaching the public policy of restraint against trade'. The application was therefore rejected.

PICKET INJUNCTIONS

[11.13] *HA O'Neil Ltd v Unite the Union*[12]—*Supreme Court—O'Donnell CJ, Hogan & Murray JJ—right of workers to engage in industrial action—limitations on employers seeking injunctions*

On 6 March 2024, the Supreme Court fundamentally changed the approach that the High Court should take in considering any application for an interlocutory injunction so as to restrain picketing and industrial action that is sanctioned or supported by a trade union. It has done so by emphasising the constitutional foundation of the right of association and has given effect to the clear meaning of s 19(2) of the Industrial Relations Act 1990 (the '1990 Act').

The applicant was a mechanical engineering firm engaged in the construction industry. The respondent union organised workers in the mechanical engineering industry, including employees of the company. In February 2023, the respondent, having balloted its members employed by the applicant, wrote to the applicant giving notice of the industrial action due to take place 10 days later. The industrial action involved targeted strikes taking place on a rolling basis at third-party sites where company employees were working. The applicant brought an application for an interlocutory injunction restraining the respondent and named employee respondents from picketing the third-party sites and sought certain ancillary orders. The injunction was granted and the Supreme Court permitted a leapfrog appeal on the basis that the case raised important issues of law relating to the grant of injunctions in respect of industrial disputes, with particular reference to s 19(2) of the 1990 Act and related matters.

Section 19(2) of the Industrial Relations Act 1990 is in the following terms:

> '(2) Where a secret ballot has been held in accordance with the rules of a trade union as provided for in section 14, the outcome of which or, in the case of an aggregation of ballots, the outcome of the aggregated ballots, favours a strike or other industrial action and the trade union before engaging in the strike or other industrial action gives notice of not less than one week to the employer concerned of its intention to do so, a court shall not grant an injunction restraining the strike or other industrial action where the respondent establishes a fair case that he was acting in contemplation or furtherance of a trade dispute'.

---

[12] *HA O'Neil Ltd v Unite the Union* [2024] IESC 8.

The Supreme Court noted that in order to secure an interlocutory injunction it is necessary for the applicant to establish that:

— s 19 does not bar the grant of an injunction, noting that this is for the union to establish;
— the statutory immunities and protections in s 10 (acts in contemplation or furtherance of a trade dispute), s 11 (peaceful picketing), and s 12 (removal of liability for certain acts) of the 1990 Act do not apply in relation to the respondent, noting that this is for the employer to establish;
— s 13 (restriction of actions of tort against trade unions) does not apply in respect of the claim against the trade union, again noting that this is for the employer to establish; and
— an interlocutory injunction should otherwise be granted by reference to the well-established criteria for the grant of an interlocutory injunction, again a matter for the employer to establish.

The Supreme Court also held that the existence of a 'no strike' clause in a collective agreement or in a Sectoral Regulation Order does not disapply s 19(2) and, accordingly, is not a basis upon which an injunction can be granted. That is so because the Supreme Court concluded that s 19(2) is not confined to injunction applications based on the law of tort but extends also to injunction applications based on the law of contract. The Supreme Court also held that the existence of a 'no strike' clause does not prevent employees to whom it applies from participating in the required secret ballot, nor does such participation create circumstances in which it cannot be contended that there is a trade dispute.

The Supreme Court concluded that it was not correct for the courts to approach this area of law:

'[O]n the basis that industrial action is presumptively wrongful and tortious, and that the 1906 and 1990 Acts should be viewed as providing islands of immunity which are exceptions to the general rule, and which must accordingly be strictly construed. This, in my view, would be to ignore the clear objective of the legislation, the history against which it is to be understood, and indeed, the constitutional context in which it is to be read. It is true that both the 1906 and 1990 Acts are framed as providing immunities from actions, principally for tort, against unions and their members. But it must be recognised that those torts were created by the Victorian common law in response to the activities of trade unions, which were regarded as criminal and tortious'.[13]

The Supreme Court's approach was also grounded in the Constitution and in particular the right to form associations and unions. The Court noted that:

'The right to form unions would be of little benefit if the activities of the union and its members were to be regarded as presumptively unlawful. Whereas the common law insisted on seeing employment as the exercise of the freedom of contract between an individual and his or her employer, and thus ignoring the inequality of bargaining power, the organisation

---

[13] *HA O'Neil Ltd v Unite the Union* [2024] IESC 8 at [57], *per* O'Donnell CJ.

of employees in a trade union offered the possibility of balancing the collective power of the employees and the economic power of their employer, allowing issues in relation to contract to be resolved by collective bargaining and disputes to be pursued, if necessary, by collective action ... The 1990 Act should not, therefore, be read narrowly or restrictively, but should be read to give effect to the protection of unions and their members which the Acts were clearly intended to provide ...

If anything given the constitutional context just discussed, it would be appropriate to read the provisions of the Act generously to give full effect to the rights sought to be protected'.[14]

The Supreme Court concluded that, with reference to s 19(2), an interlocutory injunction must not be granted if the trade union respondent establishes four things, namely that:

— a secret ballot has been held in accordance with the rules of the trade union as provided for in s 14 of the 1990 Act;
— the outcome of the ballot favoured a strike or other industrial action;
— not less than one week's notice has been given to the employer concerned of the intention to engage in the strike; and
— the trade union respondent to the injunction application has established a fair case that they were acting in contemplation or furtherance of a trade dispute. That fair case must be established by the trade union respondent on the balance of probabilities.

The Supreme Court made it clear that it is not the law that the prohibition on the granting of interlocutory injunctions, contained in s 19(2), can be disapplied if the applicant employer can establish a fair case to the contrary.

On the facts of this particular case, there was no issue with the holding of the ballot (it was not within the scope of the appeal); there was no question that the outcome of the ballot favoured the taking of the industrial action; and there was no question that notice of not less than one week was provided. The union succeeded in establishing a fair case that the industrial action was in contemplation or furtherance of a trade dispute.

The Supreme Court concluded:

'Where it was once easy to obtain an interlocutory injunction, it should now be extremely difficult to, even where an employer may have an arguable, indeed strong case, that the industrial action is unlawful. The uncertainty of the application of the law to the facts of a case which was a factor weighing strongly in favour of the grant of an injunction, has now been neutralised in the hands of the employer, and instead becomes a factor which weighs strongly against the grant of an injunction. For example, if it is only arguable that this is not a trade dispute, it follows, as a matter of logic, that it is also, at least arguable, that it is. If so, it must also follow that the respondent to the application can establish a fair case that he was acting in contemplation or furtherance of a trade dispute. The uncertainty in relation to the legal argument, which hitherto had been capable of being exploited on behalf of a party seeking an interlocutory injunction, now leads to its refusal'.[15]

---

14   *HA O'Neil Ltd v Unite the Union* [2024] IESC 8 at [59], *per* O'Donnell CJ.
15   *HA O'Neil Ltd v Unite the Union* [2024] IESC 8 at [64], *per* O'Donnell CJ.

Finally, and tellingly, the Supreme Court concluded that even if s 19(2) did not operate to prohibit the granting of an interlocutory injunction, in this case an injunction should not have been granted, even applying the normal criteria (namely arguable case and balance of convenience). Traditionally, in considering the balance of convenience, the courts have favoured the employer by reason of likely disruption of the employer's business and the inadequacy of damages. The Supreme Court however, emphasised the importance to employees of being permitted to engage in industrial action and the loss that they would suffer by being wrongly restrained, stating:

> 'The ability to engage in lawful industrial action is an important right in civic, societal, legal and constitutional terms (and one which is much valued by employees and trade unionists). An important part of the value of any such right is that the individuals concerned choose when to exercise it. It is not, for example, an answer to a person who seeks to exercise their right to free speech in public on a given occasion, to tell them that they cannot express their views now or here and to those they wish to address, but may be allowed to speak much later in a different place and perhaps in private or at least to a different audience. The loss of that opportunity to exercise a lawful entitlement when one chooses to do so is at the level of principle precisely the type of loss which cannot be compensated for by the award of monetary damages, or indeed, even assessed in monetary terms. In the context of an industrial dispute there is the additional consideration that the postponement of an ability to engage in industrial action may empty that right, not just of theoretical, but also practical value. In my view, it was possible to resolve this case on the balance of convenience alone, and by concluding, at a minimum, that it had not been demonstrated that the balance of convenience favoured the grant of the injunction.'[16]

The Supreme Court also noted that:

> 'The default position in applications for injunctions restraining industrial action should be therefore, that it should be assumed that the case will not go to trial, and the *NWL/Merck* criteria should apply, unless there are particular features in the claim which may make it probable that the case will proceed to trial on the issue, and in relatively early course. It should be a matter for the party seeking the injunction to displace that presumption'.[17]

In summary, the *NWL*[18]/*Merck*[19] criteria require a court, in considering an application for an injunction, to make its best estimate at this point of the respective parties' cases. This will normally make it more difficult for an employer applicant to secure an injunction, even if it successfully contends that s 19(2) does not apply.

[11.14] ***Carey Glass UC v Unite the Union*[20]—*High Court—Nolan J—injunction prohibiting unlawful picketing—trade dispute in another jurisdiction not covered by the Industrial Relations Act 1990—serious issue to be tried—balance of convenience—adequacy of damages***

---

[16] *HA O'Neil Ltd v Unite the Union* [2024] IESC 8 at [72], *per* O'Donnell CJ.
[17] *HA O'Neil Ltd v Unite the Union* [2024] IESC 8 at [69], *per* O'Donnell CJ.
[18] *NWL Ltd v Woods (The Nawala) (No. 2)* [1979] 3 All E.R. 614.
[19] *Merck Sharp & Dohme Corporation v Clonmel Healthcare Ltd* [2019] IESC 65, [2020] 2 IR 1.
[20] *Carey Glass UC v Unite the Union* [2023] IEHC 705.

This *ex tempore* judgment followed an application by the applicant glass manufacturers for injunctions preventing the respondent union from carrying out what the applicant alleged was unlawful picketing at the applicant's premises in Tipperary.

Following a ballot, the respondent proceeded to take strike action against an employer at an applicant-owned facility in Northern Ireland. The applicant was alerted in the local media that there may be a demonstration by those workers outside its Tipperary premises the following day. The article quoted the respondent, which indicated that it was calling for the applicant, as 'parent company', to intervene and put an end to the dispute at the facility in Northern Ireland. The applicant wrote to the respondent to say that it was not the employers of any of the striking workers, which was a separate legal entity in another jurisdiction, and that, accordingly, the protest would appear to be illegal. In a subsequent letter, the respondent indicated that, contrary to 'inaccurate' media reporting, it would be hand-delivering a letter addressed to the applicant seeking the applicant's intervention in an ongoing trade dispute. The respondent indicated that it had 'no intention' to picket the Tipperary premises.

The applicant alleged that, on 16 August 2023, the respondent's members, having delivered the letter, set up a picket at the approaches to the applicant's premises in Tipperary and stayed there for about 90 minutes, during which time they handed out leaflets. Thereafter, they attended the car park of a local supermarket and canvassed members of the public to sign a petition. The applicant alleged that, on 25 August 2023, the respondent's members again attended at the applicant's premises carrying banners and attempting to distribute leaflets. Proceedings issued on 17 August 2023.

The applicant further alleged that, on 21 September 2023, despite the matter having already been before the Court on a number of occasions, the respondent's members turned up at the applicant's premises wearing themed facemasks and carrying a placard, which alleged that the applicant was seeking to 'silence them through an injunction in the south'. The respondent's members were photographed in the local newspaper and gave an interview in which that allegation was re-asserted.

The applicant submitted that the Industrial Relations Act 1990 does not apply to trade disputes outside of the jurisdiction and that, 'unless specifically identified in very limited circumstances', legislation must be presumed not to have extra-territorial effect. The applicant argued that the respondent's conduct constituted picketing, and not protesting as the respondent claimed.

The Court found that the trade dispute in question was not in this jurisdiction and, was therefore not covered by the Industrial Relations Act 1990. On the evidence, the respondent's members had been picketing and not protesting, and were doing so on a premises which was not that of their employer. Accordingly, the picket was not lawful and there was clearly a serious issue to be tried regarding their activities on the three occasions they attended at the applicant's premises, and in particular the third visitation. The balance of convenience clearly rested with the applicant, given the potential for 'incalculable' damage to the applicant's name and reputation. Damages would therefore not be an appropriate remedy and it followed that the applicant was entitled to the orders sought.

STALKING

[11.15] *RBT v YLA*[21]—High Court of England and Wales—Eardley KC—application for continuation of an interim injunction—harassment

The applicant was the founder and chairman of an asset management company ('the business'). In 2023, the business appointed the respondent to a management position. A number of complaints were made about the respondent's conduct at work and the business decided to dismiss him before the end of his probationary period. The respondent brought a complaint of unfair dismissal before an employment tribunal but was unsuccessful as he had not been employed for the minimum period necessary.

At some point after his dismissal, the respondent turned up at the applicant's home unannounced and blocked the driveway for some three hours. The applicant invited the respondent into his home, where the respondent pleaded for his job back, but was told that this was a matter for the HR department and had nothing to do with the applicant.

In May and June 2024, the respondent sent communications in the form of emails and WhatsApp messages to the applicant and to two individuals closely involved with the applicant and the business. In explicit and intimidating terms, these communications demanded money and threatened to discredit the applicant and the business. The communications linked the applicant and the business to online material that either had nothing to do with them or which contained falsehoods. The communications also made threats of physical violence and covert surveillance.

The applicant applied for an interim injunction, which was granted *ex parte*. The respondent was prohibited from physically approaching, or directly contacting the applicant, his family, business and staff, or from publishing, communicating or disclosing any information to any third party about the applicant, his family, business and staff. The respondent was also directed to serve on the applicant copies of all such information, and any material obtained by the respondent from the business that was in his possession or in the possession of third parties (the 'mandatory orders').

The respondent refused to hand over the material he had removed from the business, stating that he needed it to act as a whistleblower and to bring a counterclaim. He did not attend court on the return date—giving an inconsistent account in an email about having Covid-19—and the hearing proceeded in his absence.

The Court was satisfied that the applicant was more likely than not to obtain at trial a final injunction preventing the respondent from communicating with him and from carrying out his threat to publish material to third parties. The emails and WhatsApp messages were likely to be found to be 'deliberate, unacceptable, oppressive, highly objectionable and of a gravity that would sustain criminal liability'. They were clearly targeted at the applicant and were clearly persistent. It was likely, moreover, that the respondent would be found to have engaged in blackmail. It appeared that the

---

[21] *RBT v YLA* [2024] EWHC 1855 (KB).

allegations made by the respondent were largely false, and there was a strong case that the respondent knew, or ought to have known, that his conduct amounted to harassment. The applicant was genuinely frightened of the actions the respondent could take to harm him and the business. The respondent, for his part, had not filed any evidence to substantiate his allegations.

The threshold having been met, the injunction would continue until the trial of the action.

UNKNOWN DEFENDANT INJUNCTIONS

[11.16] *Wolverhampton City Council v London Gypsies and Travellers*[22]—*UK Supreme Court—Reed, Hodge, Lloyd-Jones, Briggs & Kitchin LJJ—appeal from Court of Appeal of England and Wales—newcomer injunctions—whether a court can grant an injunction against unidentifiable persons—on what basis and subject to what safeguards can a court grant an injunction against unidentifiable persons*

These proceedings concerned a number of conjoined cases in which local authorities sought to vary or extend, without notice, existing injunctions preventing unauthorised encampments by Roma and Travellers who were not capable of being identified and were described as 'persons unknown'. Having reviewed those injunctions, the High Court of England and Wales concluded that only interim injunctions could be granted against persons unknown, while final injunctions would only be granted against identified parties who had had an opportunity to contest the final order sought. The Court of Appeal held that the trial Judge was wrong to hold that a court could not grant final injunctions preventing persons unknown from occupying and trespassing on land.

At issue in this UK Supreme Court appeal was whether, and if so, on what basis and subject to what safeguards, a court has the power to grant an injunction against unidentifiable persons, who have not at the time committed or threatened to commit an infringement, but who may do so in the future as 'newcomers'. Submissions were heard from the appellants, comprising bodies representing the interests of Roma and Travellers, and the respondents, comprising various local authorities; and intervening parties with a particular interest in the law relating to protests.

While it agreed with the order made by the Court of Appeal, the Supreme Court expressed dissatisfaction with its reasoning, ie, that persons to whom an injunction is addressed can be described by reference to the behaviour prohibited by the injunction—so that effectively those persons identify themselves by the very act of disobeying the injunction and are then bound by it. The Supreme Court reasoned that 'newcomer injunctions' are analogous to other orders which operate *contra mundum*, and, while newcomers

---

[22] *Wolverhampton City Council v London Gypsies and Travellers* [2023] UKSC 47.

should be described as precisely as possible, in these circumstances, 'they potentially embrace the whole of humanity'.

The Supreme Court's analysis concluded that there was 'no immoveable obstacle in the way of granting injunctions, on an essentially without notice basis', whether interim or final. This did not necessarily mean that newcomer injunctions ought to be granted. The Supreme Court stated that such a 'novel exercise of equitable discretionary power' is only likely to be justified by a 'compelling need' for the protection of civil rights or the prevention of anti-social behaviour in the locality, not adequately met by any other measures available, and in circumstances where there are adequate procedural safeguards in place for affected newcomers; and local authorities are seen to strictly comply with their disclosure duties to the Court. Newcomer injunctions should be constrained by appropriate geographical and temporal limits and the Court should be satisfied that they are just and convenient on the particular facts.

While principally concerned with their application in Roma and Traveller cases, the Supreme Court also reasoned that newcomer injunctions could, in appropriate circumstances, where proportionate, and subject to a 'full and careful assessment' of their justification, target protestors engaged in direct action, such as blocking motorways or occupying motorway gantries.

The appeals were thus dismissed.

Chapter 12

Judicial Review

INTRODUCTION

[12.01]

Conduct of Hearing

In *O'Reilly*, which began as an Equal Status Act 2000 complaint and which related to members of the Traveller community attempting to book emergency accommodation, the High Court considered whether the Circuit Court appeal hearing was unfair by reason of there being an objective apprehension of bias and alleged 'excessive intervention' from the Judge.

Discharge from Defence Forces

In *Donoher*, the High Court considered the lawfulness of a decision to discharge a member of the Irish Permanent Defence Forces on medical grounds.

Employment Equality

In *Holland*, the High Court refused an application for the judicial review of a decision where the applicant consultant was taken off salary upon reaching the age of 71.

Garda Disciplinary Process

In *Ivers*, the issue before the High Court was whether the decision of the Commissioner of An Garda Síochána to appoint a second disciplinary board of inquiry into allegations against the applicant should be quashed under the principle of *res judicata*.

CONDUCT OF HEARING

[12.02] *O'Reilly v Atlantic Troy Ltd[1]—High Court—O'Donnell J—application for judicial review—certiorari of Circuit Court orders—Equal Status Act 2000—apprehension of bias—fairness of procedure—excessive intervention by trial Judge*

This judgment concerned two related sets of proceedings in which the applicants sought to quash orders made by the Circuit Court in October 2022. The respondent company, Atlantic Troy Ltd, owned and operated the Charleville Park Hotel in Cork (the 'hotel'). The applicants were members of the Traveller community.

In September 2018, the applicants were in need of emergency accommodation. Cork City Council declared them homeless for the purposes of the Housing Act 1988. Their community welfare officer ('CWO') approached the respondent but was informed that there was no availability at the hotel. Using a booking website, the applicants saw that there was in fact accommodation available at the hotel and made a booking using a debit card.

The applicants attended at the hotel with the CWO, who had a cheque for the full amount of a three-day stay. They were refused accommodation on the stated basis that the hotel's policy was that a credit card should be provided in the name of one of the guests at the time of check-in. The applicants sought the assistance of a solicitor at the Free Legal Aid Centre in Dublin. Contacting the hotel, this solicitor offered the use of her own credit card to complete the booking but was told that the credit card had to be in the name of the person staying in the hotel. The applicants were unable to use the hotel and returned to their existing residence.

A complaint of discrimination on the grounds that the applicants were Housing Assistance Payment recipients and members of the Traveller community was upheld by the WRC, which awarded compensation and directed the respondent to revise its credit card policy so that it did not infringe the Equal Status Act 2000.

The respondent appealed against that decision to the Circuit Court and a hearing occurred in October 2022. In an *ex-tempore* judgment, that Court allowed the appeal and vacated the WRC's order.

Despite having simultaneously embarked upon a separate statutory appeal, which would in time be struck out, the High Court permitted the applicants to proceed with an application for judicial review, being satisfied that the case raised 'very significant issues in relation to the fairness of the procedure before the Circuit Court', which was a matter clearly appropriate to judicial review proceedings.

The applicants claimed that the Circuit Court hearing was unfair by reason of there being an objective apprehension of bias, and by the overall conduct of the hearing, which was characterised by 'excessive intervention' from the Judge.

---

[1] *O'Reilly and O'Neill v Atlantic Troy Ltd* [2024] IEHC 541.

While not accepting the bias claim, the High Court gleaned 'a number of themes or patterns of concern' from a consideration of the transcript of the hearing. In particular, 'the extent of the interventions by the learned judge were such that it is impossible to conclude that the hearing was fair'. This level of intervention was 'excessive' and 'went far beyond any need to clarify points or to keep the case on track'. Indeed, the trial Judge's intervention in the examination and cross-examination of witnesses was such as to give 'the appearance of having entered the fray to a substantial extent'.

Having been informed that there were four claimants, the trial Judge expressed a preference to hear from just one witness 'to short circuit matters'. When one of the applicants was called, the trial judge 'effectively took over the examination in chief', and 'despite having asked the bulk of the questioning', expressed considerable scepticism that the burden of proof under the Equal Status Act 2000 had been discharged. Thereafter, the trial Judge 'continued to interrupt' the applicant's counsel in making her submissions. 'Strikingly', all of the questions in the respondent's examination-in-chief were asked by the trial Judge. Most were leading questions directed towards explaining and justifying the hotel's booking policy. Again, the respondent's cross-examination was 'continually interrupted'.

In all of the circumstances, the objective impression of the hearing was that it was unfair. The High Court therefore quashed the Circuit Court orders and remitted the matter for a fresh hearing before a different judge.

DISCHARGE FROM DEFENCE FORCES

[12.03] *Donoher v Minister for Defence*[2]—*High Court—Simons J—judicial review—decision to discharge a member of the Permanent Defence Forces—lawfulness of decision-making process—prescribed procedure*

The applicant sought leave to apply for judicial review. He challenged the respondent's decision to discharge him from the Irish Defence Forces, ostensibly on medical grounds, and sought to restrain the implementation of that decision.

The applicant relied on the respondent's written procedure for discharging a member of the Permanent Defence Forces. This procedure required that the member concerned be informed: (a) of the statutory reason for the proposed discharge; and (b) of the grounds upon which the proposed discharge was based. The decision maker would then be required to consider any representations made by the member concerned within seven days. It was not apparent to the High Court that the procedure had been properly followed in this instance.

The applicant had arranged for his own medical examination and the ensuing report indicated no significant health impairment. The applicant averred that he submitted this report to the military authorities a number of months after lodging an appeal against the

---

[2] *Donoher v Minister for Defence, Ireland and the Attorney General* [2024] IEHC 370.

proposed discharge. When, subsequently, the authorities informed him of the Deputy Chief of Staff's decision to approve his discharge, they gave no indication that the Deputy Chief of Staff had had an opportunity to review the report.

The High Court was satisfied, given the Deputy Chief of Staff's requirement to follow the prescribed procedure, that there were arguable grounds that the decision-making process may have been unlawful. In particular, there was 'no contemporaneous explanation as to what status had been afforded to the [medical] report'. Accordingly, the applicant had met the threshold for leave to apply for judicial review.

EMPLOYMENT EQUALITY

[12.04] *Holland v HSE[3]—High Court—Bolger J—application for judicial review—age-based retirement—Public Service Superannuation (Miscellaneous Provisions) Act 2004, s 3A—claim of unlawful exclusion from HSE pension scheme—claim of entitlement to contract of indefinite duration—Protection of Employees (Fixed-Term Work) Act 2003*

The applicant was a consultant psychiatrist. He was informed in a letter from his clinical director, dated 2 November 2022, that he had reached the maximum retirement age of 70 and was asked to fill out a retirement form. The applicant was taken off salary in January 2023, when he was a week short of 71 years of age, but did not notice until he read the letter in March 2023.

The applicant, who was self-represented, alleged age discrimination and asserted that he was entitled to be paid his salary up to age 72 and a half years of age and sought damages calculated accordingly. He did not challenge the State's right to implement and apply appropriate age-based retirement legislation. Nor did he challenge the respondent's contention that he was a 'relevant public servant' for the purposes of the legislation and therefore was lawfully retired at age 71. The Court held that, since the applicant had continued to work until age 71, despite the public service retirement age of 70, there were no grounds to support his claim for age discrimination.

The applicant also claimed that he was unlawfully excluded from the respondent's superannuation pension scheme. He was not, and never was, a member of the respondent's pension scheme, and although he was entitled to a non-pensionable gratuity payment, this had not yet been paid as the applicant had not completed and returned the necessary forms. The applicant asserted that he had a legitimate expectation to a gratuity and membership of a pension scheme. He maintained that he was consistently offered admission to the wrong scheme.

The respondent averred that its (only) pension scheme was offered to the applicant on a number of occasions from 2009 but that the offers were not taken up. In 2016, the applicant was given a final deadline to join the pension scheme (which would have

---

[3] *Holland v HSE and Midland Louth Meath Mental Health Services* [2024] IEHC 533.

required him to pay contributions back to the commencement of his employment) but he did not respond.

The Court found that the applicant was clearly aware that he was not in any HSE pension scheme 'throughout his long period of employment', though he had taken steps to try to address that situation 'as he perceived it'. Any claim of unlawful exclusion from the pension scheme was undoubtedly out of time under the Rules of Court relating to judicial review. In any event, the Court was satisfied that the applicant had not been unlawfully excluded from the pension scheme.

The applicant also sought to rely on an entitlement to a contract of indefinite duration and to equal treatment with a comparable permanent employee. These were statutory claims, however, and in this instance were not amenable to judicial review. Any concern the applicant had about his treatment as a fixed-term employee should have been brought before the WRC.

The application for judicial review was therefore refused.

GARDA DISCIPLINARY PROCESS

[12.05]   *Ivers v Commissioner of An Garda Síochána*[4]—*High Court*— *Simons J*—*judicial review*—*disciplinary proceedings*—*res judicata*—*finality of decisions*—*cause of action estoppel*—*Henderson v Henderson rule*—*insufficient evidence*—*disciplinary boards*—*inquisitorial process*—*Garda Síochána (Discipline) Regulations 2007*[5]—*certiorari*

The applicant sought an order quashing the decision of the respondent to appoint a second disciplinary board of inquiry into allegations against him.

The dispute stemmed from an incident in January 2020, when the applicant removed items, including a Bluetooth speaker and cables, from an impounded vehicle. The applicant claimed he took the items home for safekeeping, intending to return them. However, allegations emerged that his actions were improper and motivated by personal gain. While the DPP decided not to bring criminal charges, GSOC recommended disciplinary proceedings against the applicant for alleged discreditable conduct, neglect of duty, and misuse of property.

In March 2023, a board of inquiry was convened under the Garda Síochána (Discipline) Regulations 2007. During its first hearing in June 2023, the board concluded that it could not proceed due to insufficient evidence and documentation, as no supporting file or witness statements accompanied the GSOC report. The board issued its statutory report in July 2023, formally stating that the evidential deficit prevented it from properly dealing with the allegations. Instead of adjourning to gather further evidence, the board concluded its inquiry, effectively bringing the proceedings to an end. Despite

---

[4]   *Ivers v Commissioner of An Garda Síochána* [2024] IEHC 626.
[5]   Garda Síochána (Discipline) Regulations 2007 (SI 214/2007).

this, in October 2023, the respondent established a second board of inquiry to address the same allegations. The applicant contended that the first board's decision barred the establishment of a second inquiry under the principle of *res judicata*.

The High Court emphasised that *res judicata* prevents individuals from facing repeated proceedings on the same matter, safeguarding the finality of decisions and protecting against vexatious litigation. The doctrine applies not only to court cases but also to disciplinary proceedings. It encompasses three forms: cause of action estoppel (prohibiting the re-litigation of a resolved cause of action); issue estoppel (barring re-litigation of specific issues decided in earlier proceedings); and the rule in *Henderson v Henderson* (precluding matters that could have been raised in earlier proceedings). Central to this case was whether the first board's decision not to proceed due to evidential insufficiency constituted a determination on the merits, thereby evoking *res judicata*.

The Court found that the first board's conclusion did amount to a final determination on the merits. The Garda Síochána (Discipline) Regulations 2007 require breaches of discipline to be proven on the balance of probabilities. By stating that there was insufficient evidence to proceed, the board implicitly determined that the allegations were unproven. The decision not to call oral evidence or use its powers to obtain further documentation underscored the board's view that the evidential deficit was irreparable. The Court rejected the respondent's argument that the absence of a full hearing or oral evidence negated the *res judicata* effect, noting that disciplinary boards under the An Garda Síochána framework operate with an inquisitorial element. The board had access to presumptive evidence, including the GSOC report, and could have sought additional evidence but chose not to, rendering itself *functus officio*.

The Court also noted that *res judicata* can arise even from procedural dismissals if they involve substantive engagement with the merits. For example, a dismissal based on excessive delay or insufficient evidence qualifies as a decision on the merits because it resolves the allegations in a substantive way. Here, the first board's decision met this threshold by concluding that the evidence did not support the allegations. The Court noted that allowing a second inquiry would undermine the principles of fairness and finality, subjecting the applicant to repetitive and vexatious proceedings.

The Court granted an order quashing the respondent's decision to establish a second board of inquiry. It held that the first board's conclusion represented a final and binding determination on the allegations, barring further disciplinary proceedings relating to the same matter.

Chapter 13

Legislation 2024

INTRODUCTION

[13.01]

Acts

Notable legislation published this year included the Automatic Enrolment Retirement Savings System Act 2024, which provides that employees aged between 23 and 60, who earn in excess of €20,000 per year and are not already enrolled in an occupational pension scheme, be automatically enrolled into the new automatic enrolment system.

The Employment (Collective Redundancies and Miscellaneous Provisions) and Companies (Amendment) Act 2024 amends legislation in the areas of employment and company law dealing with collective redundancies following company insolvency, and enhances the rights of workers in such circumstances.

The employment permits regime was changed with the introduction of the Employment Permits Act 2024, which repeals prior employment permit laws and introduces a new type of permit, the seasonal employment permit, among other notable changes.

The Maternity Protection, Employment Equality and Preservation of Certain Records Act 2024 introduces a number of changes to the law in relation to maternity leave, the use of non-disclosure agreements in discrimination, victimisation and harassment claims, and the preservation of certain records relating to the Mother and Baby Homes.

The Social Welfare (Miscellaneous Provisions) Act 2024 amends the manner in which employment contributions are to be calculated for the purposes of the Social Welfare Consolidation Act 2005; it also provides for a new 'jobseeker's pay-related benefit' and removes certain notification requirements in respect of the delivery of a notice of attachment to persons subject to certain investigations.

Code of Practice on Determining Employment Status (October 2024)

The updated Code of Practice takes account of the Supreme Court decision in Karshan and should be read in conjunction with the Revenue Commissioners' guidelines on the same topic noted at **[17.13]**.

A selection of 2024 Statutory Instruments affecting employment are also noted.

ACTS

[13.02] *Automatic Enrolment Retirement Savings System Act 2024*[1]

The Automatic Enrolment Retirement Savings System Act 2024 (the 'Automatic Enrolment Act') completed its passage through the Oireachtas and the legislation was signed into law by the President of Ireland on 9 July 2024.

The Automatic Enrolment Act provides for employees aged between 23 and 60, who earn in excess of €20,000 per year from all employments and who are not already enrolled in an occupational pension scheme, to be automatically enrolled into the new automatic enrolment system.

On 30 September 2024, the Minister for Social Protection signed a commencement order in respect of the Automatic Enrolment Act, as part of Budget 2025; the Government referred to the Auto-Enrolment Retirement Savings Scheme as 'My Future Fund', which it is understood will be the name of the system once formally launched. The commencement order provides for a commencement date of 30 September 2025—this is considerted to be an optimistic implementation date given the extent of the system still to be created.

Employers should begin preparing for automatic enrolment. The main initial step is to undertake a gap analysis of the workforce to see who is covered by a pension arrangement and who is not. Employers will then need to decide whether: (i) they wish to maximise the number of employees that are included in their occupational pension scheme; or (ii) they want the automatic enrolment system to apply to all employees; or (iii) they want to operate both systems in tandem for different cohorts of employees.

Depending on the size and make up of a workforce, it may be impractical or unachievable to include all employees in any existing occupational pension scheme so that they are not caught by the automatic enrolment system. To minimise the impact of automatic enrolment, amendments to certain provisions of the trust deed and rules of the existing pension scheme (eg, eligibility provisions; removal of waiting periods;

---

[1] See **Ch 15**, Pensions at **[15.02]**.

contribution rules) will be required. Where such amendments require trustee consent, trustees should consider the employer's request and all relevant factors relating to it before giving their consent, taking legal advice where necessary.

[13.03] *Employment (Collective Redundancies and Miscellaneous Provisions) and Companies (Amendment) Act 2024*[2]

On 1 July 2024, the Employment (Collective Redundancies and Miscellaneous Provisions) and Companies (Amendment) Act 2024 (the '2024 Act') was commenced in full and is now law.[3]

In June 2020, the coalition parties committed, in the Programme for Government, to review whether the legal provisions surrounding collective redundancies and the liquidation of companies effectively protect the rights of workers.

As a result, a Plan of Action was published in May 2021 outlining the following decisions that had been taken:

— to amend legislation in the areas of employment law and company law dealing with matters relating to collective redundancies following company insolvency;

— to develop a guidance document for employees facing a collective redundancy situation following a company insolvency; and

— to establish a statutory expert Employment Law Review Group ('ELRG').

In December 2021, the Department of Enterprise, Trade and Employment published an Information Handbook—Rights and Remedies Available to Employees Facing a Collective Redundancy Situation. The 2024 Act reflects the changes to employment law and company law, and the establishment of the ELRG, as set out in the Plan of Action.

Collective redundancies are redundancies that are effected by an employer where, in any period of 30 consecutive days, the number of dismissals falls within certain thresholds set out in the Protection of Employment Acts 1977 to 2014 (the 'Acts').

The 2024 Act introduces the changes outlined below to the Acts to enhance employee protections.

(a) Responsible person: The 2024 Act inserts into the Acts the definition of responsible person, which will include: a liquidator; a provisional liquidator; a receiver; or any other person appointed by the court where they assume full control of the business.

(b) Obligations of responsible person:

   (i) Consultation

---

[2] See also **Ch 16**, Redundancy.
[3] Commenced by the Employment (Collective Redundancies and Miscellaneous Provisions) And Companies (Amendment) Act 2024 (Commencement) Order 2024 (SI 303/2024).

Where a responsible person proposes to create collective redundancies, they are required to, with a view to reaching an agreement, initiate consultations with employees' representatives.

Consultations should be at the earliest opportunity and, in any event, at least 30 days before the first notice of dismissal is given.

Where an employer has initiated consultations with employees' representatives, a responsible person may continue that consultation.

    (ii) *Information*

For the purposes of consultations, the responsible person is required to supply employees' representatives with all relevant information relating to the proposed redundancies.

The Acts set out a non-exhaustive list of the information that should be provided in writing to employees' representatives. The Minister for Enterprise, Trade and Employment (the 'Minister') must be provided with copies of all such information as soon as possible.

    (iii) *Notification*

Where a responsible person proposes to create collective redundancies, they are required to notify the Minister in writing of their proposals at the earliest opportunity and in any event at least 30 days before the first dismissal takes effect.

(c) Defence: It is a defence for a responsible person to show that, having exercised all reasonable professional care and skill, they had reasonable grounds for believing that the employer had complied with its information and consultation obligations and obligation to notify the Minister.

(d) Removal of exemption: Collective redundancies must not take effect before the expiry of the period of 30 days beginning on the date of the relevant notification to the Minister. Previously, this protection for employees did not apply in an insolvency situation. Under the 2024 Act, this exemption in insolvency situations has been removed. The prohibition on effecting redundancies before the expiry of the period of 30 days beginning on the date of the relevant notification to the Minister now applies to all collective redundancies.

The Government's Plan of Action noted that an employee may be placed on temporary layoff by the liquidator for the duration of the 30-day notification period (with the employment termination date to coincide with the expiry of the statutory 30-day period). It noted in the Plan of Action that, in these circumstances, the employee would be eligible for a jobseeker's payment during the layoff period. There is, however, no provision in the 2024 Act that addresses this point.

(e) New avenue of redress: An employee is entitled to take a claim to the Workplace Relations Commission where they are dismissed prior to the expiry of the 30-day period following the notification to the Minister. The maximum award of compensation that can be awarded to an employee will be four weeks' remuneration.

(f) Notification by e-mail: The 2024 Act amends the Acts so that the notification to the Minister can be sent by 'electronic means' and not just by registered post as was the previous position.

Failure to comply with the consultation, information and notification obligations is a criminal offence, and the responsible person may be liable on summary conviction to a fine up to €5,000. Failure to comply with the obligation not to effect redundancies prior to the expiry of 30 days following notification to the Minister is a criminal offence, and the responsible person may be liable on indictment to a fine up to €250,000. Under the 2024 Act, the outlined obligations on the responsible person, and the corresponding penalties, are similar to those of an employer proposing and/or effecting collective redundancies.

The 2024 Act amends the Companies Act 2014 to improve the dissemination of information to employees as creditors in a corporate insolvency situation.

The Companies Act 2014 is amended to introduce an obligation on company directors to notify all employees and employees' representatives of a winding-up petition 'at the time that petition is presented or as soon as reasonably practicable after such presentation'. In deciding whether to grant the winding-up order, the court will be obliged to have regard to whether this notification was made.

Further, a provisional liquidator will be ordered by the court to inform employees (and, where applicable, employees' representatives) of their appointment, the date of their appointment, the liquidation process (so far as it is applicable to employees), the fact that employees or their representatives can provide the provisional liquidator with information, and any other matter the provisional liquidator considers relevant. A liquidator or provisional liquidator will also be obliged, where a copy of a statement of affairs is served on them, to notify the employees and their representatives of this, and to send such a person a copy of this statement if requested to do so.

The Companies (Rescue Process for Small and Micro Companies) Act 2021 amended the Companies Act 2014 in December 2021 to reflect a number of proposals in the Government's Plan of Action. These changes included:

1. providing a liquidator with the power to bring or defend legal proceedings on behalf of a company before the Workplace Relations Commission and Labour Court;
2. obliging the liquidator and director to ensure creditors are made aware they have the right to form and participate in a Committee of Inspection; and,
3. where a Committee of Inspection is appointed it must include at least one employee creditor member.

The 2024 Act also strengthens certain ancillary sanctions in the Companies Act 2014 that may apply in the context of a winding-up.

Firstly, it will no longer be a prerequisite to making a contribution order (against a company related to one being wound up) that the court would be satisfied that the circumstances that give rise to the winding-up are attributable to acts or omissions of the related company; rather, this will just be a factor to which the court shall have regard.

Secondly, in deciding whether a creditor has been given an unfair preference, the court will be permitted to look back further than the six-month period currently specified, where it considers it just and equitable to do so.

Finally, the test for reckless trading has become an objective one, in that where a person is a party to the carrying on of business in a reckless manner, it is no longer a requirement that they 'knowingly' did so. Moreover, it is no longer a defence in this regard that the person acted honestly and responsibly; instead, they need to show that they took all reasonably practicable steps with a view to minimising loss.

In lowering the threshold for such sanctions to be applied, it is anticipated that this will result in a greater focus on compliance in advance of winding-up.

The 2024 Act provides for the establishment of a statutory expert Employment Law Review Group (the 'ELRG') to assess, on an ongoing basis, all aspects of employment and redundancy law to ensure it is fit for purpose. It will be similar to the existing Company Law Review Group.

The ELRG will act independently, with the chair appointed by the Minister. Its members will have expertise and an interest in the development of employment law, including legal practitioners, businesses and unions, implementation and enforcement bodies (Workplace Relations Commission, Labour Court) and representatives from Government departments as well as the Revenue Commissioners and the Office of the Attorney General. Terms of reference and an annual work programme will be agreed with the Minister for Enterprise, Trade and Employment. The forum will act as an independent advisory expert group to help with the formulation of policy and legislation impacting employees.

The Employment (Collective Redundancies and Miscellaneous Provisions) and Companies (Amendment) Act 2024 (Commencement) Order 2024[4] appointed 1 July 2024 as the date on which the entire Act came into operation.

[13.04] *Employment Permits Act 2024*[5]

The Employment Permits Act 2024 (the '2024 Act'), which was enacted on 25 June 2024, commenced on 2 September 2024.[6] The new legislation repeals prior employment permit laws. The following is a summary of some of the main provisions of the 2024 Act.

The requirement on employers to place the adverts for vacancies in print media has been removed. The 2024 Act now provides for the publication of these adverts to be placed 'on one or more online platforms'. Online platforms can be an electronic system for the online publication of information that are easily accessible by Irish/EEA

---

4 Employment (Collective Redundancies and Miscellaneous Provisions) And Companies (Amendment) Act 2024 (Commencement) Order 2024 (SI 303/2024).
5 See also **Ch 9**, Immigration.
6 Commenced by Employment Permits Act 2024 (Commencement) Order 2024 (SI 443/2024).

citizens including websites, software or any other electronic technology that provides for the online publication of information. Online platforms can include the newspapers' websites or dedicated employment websites. The requirement for vacancies to be published with the Jobs Ireland and EURES websites remains.

The 2024 Act introduces a new provision allowing certain employment permit holders to change their permit employer to another employer after a period of nine months has passed since commencing their first employment permit in the State. The Change of Employer provision applies to the General Employment Permit ('GEP') and the Critical Skills Employment Permit ('CSEP').

The holder of a GEP can apply to change to an employer within the type of employment for which they have been granted a permit. For example, a meat processing operative can move to another meat processing role. The holder of a CSEP can change to an employer across a broader category of employments, for example, different engineering roles.

The 2024 Act upholds the option for employment permit holders to seek employment in another eligible role and apply for a new employment permit, whether with their current employer or a new employer. The time restriction—where the permit holder is expected to remain with their first employer on the first employment in the State for a certain period—remains, but is reduced from 12 months to a period of at least nine months before a new application can be made.

The 2024 Act contains a provision which allows for promotion and internal transfer in the same company where a permit holder would use the same skills and the employment remains eligible. This removes the requirement for the permit holder to undergo a new employment permit application process where they remain with the current employer but have been granted a promotion or uplift. At renewal, this situation will now be assessed on the basis of what would previously have been considered a change of employment permit.

Upon the grant of an employment permit, the Minister will cancel any other permit which is in force for that foreign national, ensuring only one permit per foreign national can be in place at one time. The Minister will notify the foreign national and the employer identified on that employment permit in writing that the permit is canceled with effect from a date specified. A new provision also requires that the foreign national must commence employment within a period of six months from when the permit is granted or comes into force.

The Dependant/Partner/Spouse Employment Permit has been revised to cater for the dependants of Critical Skills Employment Permit holders and Researchers under Directive 2005/71/EC.[7]

---

[7] Directive 2005/71/EC on a specific procedure for admitting third-country nationals for the purposes of scientific research.

The new Seasonal Employment Permit ('SEP') is a short-term employment permit for a non-EEA national to work for a maximum of seven months per calendar year in a seasonally recurrent employment. The Department states that the permit will be first introduced under a limited pilot scheme later in 2024 with the intention that it commence in early 2025.

Employers wishing to apply for the new SEP will be required to apply annually to become registered, pre-approved seasonal employers in order to access the scheme. Applications will be considered based on relevant criteria including the need for the employment to be in a seasonally recurrent employment and the size of the employer. Eligible employers will be granted approved status for a period of 12 months and issued with a certificate of approval as an approved seasonal employer. Seasonal employment permit holders will have the option to transfer their SEP to another approved seasonal employer under the scheme through a simplified notification procedure.

The Employment Permits Regulations 2024[8] were commenced on 2 September 2024. These Regulations are made under the 2024 Act and set down the qualifying criteria, application process, fees and other general provisions in respect of employment permits. They replace the Employment Permit Regulations 2017, which were revoked by the 2024 Act.

[13.05] *Maternity Protection, Employment Equality and Preservation of Certain Records Act 2024*[9]

This Act:

1. allows for the postponement of maternity leave in the event of a serious health condition;
2. amends the Employment Equality Acts 1998 to 2021 to provide for restriction on the use of non-disclosure agreements in respect of allegations of discrimination, victimisation, harassment and sexual harassment, whereby such agreements will be null and void, unless certain conditions are met;
3. provides for maternity leave for members of the Houses of the Oireachtas; and
4. provides for the preservation of certain records broadly relating to Mother and Baby Homes.

In relation to the postponement of maternity leave in the event of a serious health condition, the Act provides:

1. A relevant employee (ie, someone who is pregnant or on maternity leave and has a serious health condition) can notify their employer that they intend to postpone the commencement of all or part of their maternity leave for up to 52 weeks from the

---

[8] Employment Permits Regulations 2024 (SI 444/2024).
[9] See also **Ch 3**, Employment Equality.

date on which the postponement commences. A serious health condition means a health condition that entails a serious risk to the life or health, including the mental health, of the employee and in order to address the risk, requires necessary medical intervention that is ongoing for a period of time.
2. The notification to the employer must: specify the date on which the postponement is to commence and end (which must be at least five weeks from the commencement of the postponement) and be accompanied by a medical certificate which specifies those dates.
3. The notification must be made at least two weeks before the postponement is due to commence.
4. Where a notification is made in accordance with the above, the relevant employee will be entitled to the maternity leave (or any untaken part thereof) to be taken in one continuous period on the day immediately after the end date.
5. The entitlement to resumed leave is subject to the employee, in writing, notifying the employer of their intention to commence the leave as soon as reasonably practicable but no later than on the day on which the leave begins.
6. Where the employee has already postponed their leave, they may notify the employer in writing of their intention to postpone the commencement of the leave one further time only. Again, this postponement can be for a maximum of 52 weeks from the date on which the first postponement was due to commence.
7. The requirements for this second notification are the same as the first.
8. An employee cannot postpone their maternity leave under both this provision and under s 14B (ie, in the event of the hospitalisation of a child) in respect of the same birth.

In relation to the restriction on the use of non-disclosure agreements, the 2024 Act adds a new s 14B to the Employment Equality Acts 1998 to 2021, which provides:

1. An employer must not enter into a non-disclosure agreement and, if they do, the agreement will be null and void.
2. A non-disclosure agreement is defined as an agreement, or provision thereof, whether or not in writing and howsoever described, between an employer and an employee that purports to preclude the making of a relevant disclosure by the employer or the employee or both.
3. A relevant disclosure means a disclosure of information relating to either or both of the following:
    (a) the making by the employee of an allegation that he or she was discriminated against, or subjected to victimisation, harassment or sexual harassment, in relation to his or her employment (or potential employment) by the employer;
    (b) any action taken by the employer or employee in response to the making of such an allegation, including any action taken in relation to any complaint made, or proceedings taken, by the employee in relation to the subject matter of the allegation.

4. However, an employer may enter into an 'excepted non-disclosure agreement' only where the employee requests the employer to do so and, prior to entering into the agreement, the employee has received independent legal advice in writing from a legal practitioner in relation to the implications of entering into an agreement.
5. The employer must also pay the reasonable legal costs and expenses of obtaining the legal advice.
6. In addition, such an agreement must:
   a. be in writing;
   b. be of unlimited duration, unless the employee decides otherwise;
   c. be in clear language that is easily understood and a format that is easily accessible (including by any party with a disability);
   d. provide that the employee has a right to withdraw from the agreement without penalty within 14 days of entering into it; and
   e. include a provision that the agreement does not prohibit the making of relevant disclosure, to one or more of the following persons, where at the time of the making of the disclosure, the person concerned is acting in the course of their office, employment, business, trade or profession: garda, lawyer, medical practitioner, mental health professional, Revenue, Ombudsman, trade union official or such individual as may be specified in the agreement.

[13.06]   *Social Welfare (Miscellaneous Provisions) Act 2024*

This Act provides changes to the manner in which employment contributions are to be calculated for the purposes of the Social Welfare Consolidation Act 2005. It provides for a new benefit to be known as 'jobseeker's pay-related benefit'. It further removes the need for certain notifications to be provided to persons who are the subject of certain investigations before a notice of attachment may be given to such persons.

CODE OF PRACTICE ON DETERMINING EMPLOYMENT STATUS (OCTOBER 2024)[10]

The updated Code of Practice on Determining Employment Status (the 'Code') has been published, after a review conducted by an interdepartmental group comprising the Department of Social Protection, the office of the Revenue Commissioners and the Workplace Relations Commission ('WRC') to reflect the 2023 judgment of

---

[10] See also **Ch 4**, Employment Litigation (Employment Status) and Chapter 17, Taxation.

the Supreme Court in *The Revenue Commissioners v Karshan (Midlands) LTD t/a Domino's Pizza*.[11]

The Code's stated aim is to assist employers, employees, independent contractors and legal, financial and HR professionals, along with decision makers in the interdepartmental groups, in determining the employment status of individuals, taking into account current labour market practices and developments in legislation and caselaw. The Code's aim is to ensure that workers are correctly classified in a way that matches the reality of the relationship between the worker and the business.

The Code acknowledges that there is no single, clear definition of the terms 'employed' and 'self-employed' in Irish or EU law. Therefore, decision makers are required to look at any formal contracts that may exist, consider how the work is actually carried out and assess the relationship between the worker providing the service and the business paying for that service in line with the five-step framework set out in the *Karshan* judgment. The Code is designed to help with this assessment.

This Code is in addition to the Revenue Guidelines for Determining Employment Status for Taxation Purposes which was published by the Revenue Commissioners earlier this year.[12]

The Questions to be Considered

The five-step framework set out in the *Karshan* judgment provides a clear decision-making model to determine the employment status of each worker, taking account of the facts and circumstances. The Code follows this framework and states that the question of whether a worker is an employee can be resolved by firstly having regard to the following three 'filter' questions (whereby if any one of these questions is answered negatively, no contract of employment can exist):

(a) Does the contract involve the exchange of wage or other remuneration for work?
(b) If so, is the agreement one where the worker is agreeing to provide their own services, and not those of a third party, to the business?
(c) If so, does the business exercise sufficient control over the worker to render the agreement one that is capable of being an employment agreement?

If those three requirements are met, the decision maker must go onto consider:

(d) All of the circumstances of the arrangement/agreement/contract. In other words, whether the terms of the arrangement/agreement/contract between the business

---

[11] *Revenue Commissioners v Karshan (Midlands) Ltd t/a Domino's Pizza* [2023] IESC 24, see *Arthur Cox Employment Law Yearbook 2023* at [4.14].
[12] See **Ch 17**, Taxation at **[17.13]–[17.14]** for a full consideration of the Revenue Guidelines for Determining Employment Status for Taxation Purposes, contained in Part 05-01-30 of the *Tax and Duty Manual*.

and the worker, interpreted in light of the practical/real conditions of engagement (the 'factual matrix'), are consistent with a contract of employment or with some other form of contract, having regard, in particular, to whether the arrangements point to the worker working for themselves or for the business/employer.

(e) Whether there is anything in the particular legislative regime under consideration that requires a particular approach to be taken, eg, a person might be an employee for social insurance purposes but self-employed for employment law or tax purposes.

The Code confirms that all the relevant considerations established by applying the framework as a whole are to be taken into account in determining the employment status of a worker in any given case. The Code goes on to give additional guidance on each of the five questions contained in the framework.

Exchange of Wage or Other Remuneration for Work

The first question a decision maker must consider is whether the parties have entered into a contract at all (whether expressed or implied). For a contract of employment to exist, there has to be an offer of work, acceptance of that offer, and resulting payment or 'consideration'.

Provided there is payment by a business to a worker for a service directly or indirectly for the provision of the worker's labour, whether agreed in writing or not, and whether the work is carried out on a once-off basis or on a continuous basis or anything in between, there is a contract which is capable of being an employment contract.

Personal Service

This question considers whether and to what extent the worker has agreed to provide their services to the business personally, ie, the 'substitution test'. Substitution concerns a worker's right to appoint someone else as a substitute if he or she is unable, unwilling or never intended, to personally undertake to do all or part of the work. The Code states that, in applying this test, the Department of Social Protection, the Revenue Commissioners and the WRC will always ask the following question: who does the work when the worker is absent and who selects, arranges and remunerates the replacement worker? Even where the worker arranges the substitute, an important factor in assessing the level of substitution available is whether, and if so to what extent, the person/business who is offering the work has a say in who the worker hires. Other important factors to consider are whether and to what extent the substitute is controlled and/or paid directly by the business/person offering the work or the worker. The more restrictions imposed on the freedom of a worker to appoint a substitute, the more indicative the arrangement is that of a contract of employment, eg where prior approval of substitutes is required, payment of substitutes is made directly by the business rather the person they are providing cover for, or where substitutes are from a pool of pre-approved workers.

Control

This question considers the ability, authority, or right of a business to exercise control over a worker concerning what work should be done, and how, when and where it should be done. When assessing the degree of control held by the business and the degree of independence held by the worker, it should be borne in mind that the right of the business to exercise control is more relevant than whether they actually exercise this right.

The Code states that, when considering the issue of 'control', a decision maker may also have regard to the issues of 'enterprise' and 'integration' as follows:

Enterprise: The extent to which the worker carries risk and their ability to make financial gain through their own ingenuity/efficiency.

Integration: The extent to which a worker is an integral part of the operations of the business/person engaging their services, as opposed to carrying out work that, although done for the business, is peripheral or accessory to it.

All of the Circumstances of the Engagement

Only where the first three 'filter' questions are answered affirmatively do decision makers need to consider the entire factual matrix of the engagement. The question to be considered is whether the facts indicate that the worker is providing services on his or her own account, or whether the facts indicate that the worker is providing the services on behalf of the business.

The Legislative Context

Consideration also needs to be given to any legislation that requires an adjustment or supplement to any of the foregoing questions in the particular circumstances of the relationship being considered. The Code notes, in the context of the WRC determining employment status under the relevant employment legislation, that the definitions of 'contract of employment', 'employee' and 'employer' differ from one employment enactment to another. As a result, each case lodged with the WRC is different and is decided on its own facts by an Adjudication Officer.

Typical Characteristics of an Employee

While noting that not all the following factors may apply to every case, the Code also outlines the typical characteristics of an employee:

— is under the control of another person who directs them as to how, when and where the work is to be carried out;
— supplies labour only;
— receives a fixed hourly/weekly/monthly wage;
— cannot subcontract the work;
— does not supply materials for the job;
— does not provide equipment other than the small tools of the trade;
— is not exposed to personal financial risk in carrying out the work;
— does not assume any responsibility for investment and management in the business;
— does not have the opportunity to profit from sound management in the scheduling of engagements or in the performance of tasks arising from the engagements;
— works set hours or a given number of hours per week or month;
— works for one person or for one business;
— receives expense payments to cover subsistence and/or travel expenses; and
— is entitled to sick pay or extra pay for overtime.

The Code also contains a number of 'caveats' to the above criteria, namely:

— If the work can be subcontracted and 'paid on' by the person subcontracting the work, it is possible the employer/employee relationship may simply be transferred on.
— It is possible that the provision of tools or equipment will not have a significant bearing on the determination of employment status, having regard to all the circumstances of a particular case.
— An individual could have considerable freedom and independence in carrying out work and still be an employee.
— An individual with specialist knowledge might not be directed as to how the work is to be carried out and still be an employee.
— An individual who is paid by commission, by share, or by piecework, or in some other atypical fashion may still be regarded as an employee.
— Some individuals work for more than one employer at the same period of time, and may still be regarded as employees.
— Some individuals may also be self-employed in respect of other work being performed by him or her, and may still be regarded as employees of another business.

— Some individuals work remotely or otherwise not on the business premises and are still regarded as employees.
— Employees may work in a range of ways, including, but not limited to, part-time work, temporary work, seasonal work or occasional work.
— Some employees are paid by reference to contracted hours, while others may be paid by reference to the amount of work actually done.
— The hours of work or remuneration of an employee may be uncertain.

Typical Characteristics of Self-Employment

The Code also outlines the following typical characteristics of self-employment but notes that all the factors may not apply to every case:

— own their own business;
— are exposed to financial risk by having to bear the cost of making good any faulty or substandard work carried out;
— assume responsibility for the investment in and management of their work activities;
— have the opportunity to profit from sound management in the scheduling and performance of engagements and tasks;
— have control over what is done, how it is done, when and where it is done and whether they or another person does the work;
— are free to hire other people, on terms they specify, to do the work which has been agreed to be undertaken;
— can provide the same services to more than one person or business at the same time;
— provide the materials for the job;
— provide equipment and machinery necessary for the job, other than the small tools of the trade or equipment which in an overall context would not be an indicator of a person in business on their own account;
— have a fixed place of business where materials, equipment etc can be stored;
— costs and agrees a price for the job;
— provide their own insurance cover, eg, public liability cover, etc;
— control the hours of work in fulfilling the job obligations.

The Code also contains a number of 'caveats' to the above criteria, namely:

— The fact that an individual has registered for income tax or VAT under the principles of self-assessment does not automatically mean that he or she is self-employed.

- A person who is a self-employed contractor in one job is not necessarily self-employed in another job. It is also possible to be employed and self-employed at the same time in different jobs.
- In the construction sector, for health and safety reasons, all individuals, regardless of employment status, are under the direction of the site foreman/overseer.

Special Circumstances and Developments in the Labour Market

Helpfully, the Code considers the special considerations that may apply when dealing with the following scenarios:

- PRSI classification for people who own or control companies—employed persons who control, either directly or indirectly, 50% or more of the shareholding of the company that they work for cannot normally be an employee of that company for PRSI purposes under social welfare legislation. They must be classified as self-employed and are liable to pay PRSI at Class S.
- Agency workers—who the employer is will depend on the relevant employment, social welfare or tax legislation.
- Use of intermediary arrangements, including personal services companies and managed service companies—notwithstanding the use of intermediary structures, the same five-step framework will be used to determine the employment status of these workers.
- Workers in the digital/gig economy—notwithstanding the method of engagement of these workers, the same five-step framework will be used to determine the employment status of these workers.

False/Bogus Self-Employment and PRSI Arrears

The Code reiterates that false/bogus self-employment is a criminal offence giving rise to a loss of PRSI and taxation income and subject to significant sanctions under the Social Welfare Acts. Where a determination by the Department of Social Protection is made that a worker has been incorrectly classified as being self-employed for PRSI purposes, the employer will be required to pay the relevant PRSI contributions for the employee(s) for the full period in question and may be subject to a range of penalties under the Social Welfare Consolidation Act 2005. There is no limitation on the period of retrospection.

Health and Safety Matters

Finally, the Code notes that the Safety, Health and Welfare at Work Act 2005 applies to all workers on a premises, regardless of their employment status.

STATUTORY INSTRUMENTS

2023

[13.07] **SI 602/2023—The Solicitors Acts 1954 to 2015 (Apprentices' Fees) Regulations 2023**

Effective from 1 January 2024, these Regulations outline the specific fees payable to the Law Society of Ireland in respect of courses and examinations provided for in The Solicitors Acts 1954 to 1994 (Apprenticeship and Education) Regulations 2001[13] and The Solicitors Acts 1954 to 2011 (Apprenticeship and Education) (Amendment) Regulations 2019.[14]

[13.08] **SI 611/2023—Garda Síochána (Admissions and Appointments) (Amendment) Regulations 2023**

These Regulations amend the eligibility requirements for garda trainee applicants, increasing the maximum age of applicants so individuals must be at least 18 years of age but not yet 50 years of age at midnight on Thursday, 8 February 2024. The previous age limit was 35 years of age.

[13.09] **SI 617/2023—Personal Injuries Assessment Board Rules 2023 (No 2)**[15]

These Regulations outline the rules established by the Personal Injuries Assessment Board (the 'Board') in accordance with the Personal Injuries Assessment Board Act 2003 (the '2003 Act'), effective from 14 December 2023. The key points are as follows:

(a) Application process: details the requirements for making an application under s 11 of the 2003 Act, including submission formats, required information, and accompanying documents.
(b) Charge for application: specifies that an application must be accompanied by a charge imposed by the Board.
(c) Confirmation by claimant: requires a confirmation from the claimant affirming the accuracy of the information provided and acknowledging the obligation to provide truthful information.
(d) Notice to respondents: describes the format for serving notice to respondents alleged to be liable for the claim.
(e) Supply of records: allows the Board to supply relevant records or documents to involved parties as necessary.
(f) Authorisation for proceedings: outlines conditions under which the Board may issue authorisation for claimants to bring proceedings against respondents.

---

[13] The Solicitors Acts 1954 to 1994 (Apprenticeship and Education) Regulations 2001 (SI 546/2001).
[14] The Solicitors Acts 1954 to 2011 (Apprenticeship and Education) (Amendment) Regulations 2019 (SI 503/2019).
[15] See also **Ch 5**, Employment Torts.

(g) Mediation: introduces mediation for certain types of claims, detailing procedures, confidentiality requirements, and the appointment of mediators.
(h) Revocation of previous Rules: revokes the Personal Injuries Assessment Board Rules 2023[16] upon the commencement of these rules.

[13.10] SI 626/2023—Personal Injuries Resolution Board Act 2022 (Commencement of Certain Provisions) (No 3) Order 2023

This Order outlines the date on which specific provisions of the Personal Injuries Resolution Board Act 2022 become operational.

[13.11] SI 627/2023—Personal Injuries Resolution Board Act 2022 (Change of Name of Board) Order 2023

This Order provides for, effective from 14 December 2023, the amendment of the name of the 'Personal Injuries Assessment Board' to the 'Personal Injuries Resolution Board'.

[13.12] SI 633/2023—Social Welfare (Temporary Provisions—Increase for Qualified Child) Regulations 2023

These Regulations provide for a once-off bonus payment of €100 to a beneficiary in respect of a qualified child or children and to recipients of certain social welfare payments, paid in the week commencing 27 November 2023.

[13.13] SI 634/2023—Social Welfare (Temporary Provisions) (No 3) Regulations 2023

These Regulations provide for the payment of a bonus to recipients of social welfare payments and to recipients of domiciliary care allowance during the months of December 2023 and January 2024, and also set out requirements for minimum payment and rounding of payments.

[13.14] SI 687/2023—Social Welfare (Consolidated Occupational Injuries) Regulations 2023

These Regulations provide for increased rates of benefits and pensions under the Occupational Injuries Benefits Scheme (the 'Scheme'), with provisions relating to injury benefit coming into effect from 1 January 2024, and provisions that relate to disability pension and disablement gratuity from 5 January 2024.

The Social Welfare (Miscellaneous Provisions) Act 2023 (the '2023 Act') provides for an increase in the maximum rate of benefits payable under the Scheme where the

---

[16] The Personal Injuries Assessment Board Rules 2023 (SI 425/2023).

degree of disablement ranges from 20% to 100%, and/or where the beneficiary is over the age of 16. These Regulations supplement the 2023 Act by extending the increased benefits to beneficiaries where

(a) the degree of disablement ranges from 1% to 18% in cases where the disablement arose prior to 1 January 2012;
(b) the degree of disablement is greater than 14% for disablements which occurred after 1 January 2012; and
(c) the beneficiary is under the age of 16.

[13.15] SI 688/2023—Social Welfare (Consolidated Contributions and Insurability) (Amendment) (No 1) (Credited Contributions) Regulations 2023

Part 4 of the Social Welfare (Miscellaneous Provisions) Act 2023 amends the Social Welfare Consolidation Act 2005 to facilitate *inter alia*:

— the introduction of flexibility to the State pension (contributory) to allow a person to defer claiming the State pension (contributory) up to the age of 70; and
— continued access to specified weekly social welfare payments after reaching the State pensionable age and during pension deferral.

These Regulations make consequential changes to the Social Welfare (Consolidated Contributions and Insurability) Regulations 1996[17] restricting the extent to which employment contributions can be credited to an insured person who has attained the State pensionable age and:

(a) whose entry into insurance had not occurred prior to attaining the State pensionable age;
(b) is claiming illness benefit, partial capacity benefit, jobseeker's benefit or jobseeker's benefit (self-employed);
(c) is attending certain approved courses of education or training;
(d) is employed as a volunteer development worker.

These restrictions take effect from 1 January 2024.

The Regulations also allow for credited contributions in respect of periods during which an insured person is in receipt of parent's benefit or is availing of parent's leave—similar to the credits already available in respect of periods of health and safety benefit, maternity benefit/leave, adoptive benefit/leave, paternity benefit/leave or carer's benefit/leave. Such credits will be deemed to be available in respect of any periods beginning on or after 1 November 2019, the date on which the provisions of the Parent's Leave and Benefit Act 2019 came into force which created entitlements to parent's benefit and parent's leave.

---

[17] Social Welfare (Consolidated Contributions and Insurability) Regulations 1996 (SI 312/1996).

[13.16]   SI 689/2023—Social Welfare (Consolidated Claims, Payments and Control) (Amendment) (No 13) (Notifications Where Claimant Wishes For Certain Payments to Continue After Attaining Pensionable Age) Regulations 2023

Illness benefit, partial capacity benefit, jobseeker's benefit, jobseeker's benefit (self-employed) or back to work family dividend ordinarily cease to be paid to a person upon that person attaining the State pensionable age. The Social Welfare (Miscellaneous Provisions) Act 2023 amends the Social Welfare Consolidation Act 2005 to provide that, subject to meeting the conditions specified in that Act, a person born on or after 1 January 1958 who is in receipt of illness benefit, partial capacity benefit, jobseeker's benefit, jobseeker's benefit (self-employed) or back to work family dividend immediately before attaining the State pensionable age, may notify the Minister that they wish to continue to receive that payment past the State pensionable age, for any remaining period in which they would be entitled to it.

These Regulations amend specified articles of the Social Welfare (Consolidated Claims, Payments and Control) Regulations 2007[18] relating to notifications where a claimant wishes for these payments to continue after attaining the State pensionable age, and specify the manner and time limits which will apply to such a notification.

[13.17]   SI 690/2023—Social Welfare (Consolidated Claims, Payments and Control) (Amendment) (No 12) (State Pension (Contributory)—Long Term Carer's Qualifying Contribution) Regulations 2023

These Regulations amend provisions of the Social Welfare (Consolidated Claims, Payments and Control) Regulations 2007[19] and the Social Welfare (Consolidated Claims, Payments and Control) (Amendment) (No 2) (State Pension (Contributory)) Regulations 2019[20] relating to the terms and conditions to be satisfied in order to qualify for long-term carer's qualifying contributions, and to help long-term carers access the State pension (contributory) when they reach the State pensionable age.

These Regulations confirm the classes of persons in respect of whom a long-term carer may provide care, the circumstances in which a long-term carer may be regarded as providing full-time care and attention to a relevant person or qualified child, the requirements in relation to applications to be regarded as a long-term carer, the evidence demonstrating the nature, extent and duration of long-term caring, and the contributions to be satisfied by non-resident long-term carers.

[13.18]   SI 705/2023—Workplace Relations Act 2015 (Fixed Payment Notice) Regulations 2023[21]

These Regulations consolidate new and existing fixed payment notices for employment law offences and introduce 'on the spot' fines that can be imposed by WRC inspectors.

---

18   Social Welfare (Consolidated Claims, Payments and Control) Regulations 2007 (SI 142/2007).
19   Social Welfare (Consolidated Claims, Payment and Control) Regulations 2007 (SI 142/2007).
20   Social Welfare (Consolidated Claims, Payments and Control) (Amendment) (No 2) (State Pension (Contributory)) Regulations 2019 (SI 40/2019).
21   See also **Ch 4**, Litigation.

The Regulations also set out the form of a fixed payment notice to be issued by a WRC inspector. The Regulations provide for the following fines for each specified offence:

(a) €2,000, in circumstances where:
  (i) the employer fails in a collective redundancy situation to consult with employees' representatives and to provide them with mandatory specified information;
  (ii) the employer fails, without reasonable cause, to provide an employee with their terms of employment within one month of their commencement date or provides false or misleading information to the employee; or
  (iii) the employer fails to provide an employee with a written statement of wages and the nature and amount of any deductions from wages.
(b) €1,500, in circumstances where the employer does not provide an employee with a statement of the average hourly rate of pay for a pay reference period at the employee's request.
(c) €750, in circumstances where the employer does not provide employees with a written statement on the distribution of tips and gratuities or fails to treat a service charge as a tip.
(d) €500, in circumstances where the employer does not display a 'tips and gratuities notice' or a 'contract workers tips and gratuities notice'.

Where the fine is not paid within 42 days, the employer will be referred to the WRC's internal Legal Affairs Committee which will then decide whether to proceed with prosecution of the offence. If an employer is convicted on summary conviction of any of the above offences, it may be liable to a Class C fine (currently €2,500).

2024

[13.19]   SI 1/2024—*Income Tax (Employments) Regulations 2024*[22]

These Regulations amend the Income Tax (Employments) Regulations 2018[23] which prescribed the manner in which the deduction of tax from salaries and wages under the PAYE system operates.

These Regulations introduce a new category of 'reportable benefits', which extends to 'small benefits', 'remote working day allowances' and 'travel and subsistence payments', all as defined in s 897C of the Taxes Consolidation Act 1997.

[13.20]   SI 8/2024—*Employment Permits (Amendment) Regulations 2024*

These Regulations amend the Employment Permits Regulations 2017[24] by deleting reg 29(2) thereof, which sets out minimum annual and hourly rates of remuneration in the case of renewals of employment permits for specified categories of employment as set out in the 2017 Regulations.

---

[22] See also **Ch 17**, Taxation.
[23] Income Tax (Employments) Regulations 2018 (SI 345/2018).
[24] Employment Permits Regulations 2017 (SI 95/2017).

[13.21] SI 10/2024—Sick Leave Act 2022 (Increase of Statutory Sick Leave Days) Order 2024

These Regulations increase the number of statutory sick leave days to which an employee is entitled in a year from three to five, as set out in the Sick Leave Act 2022. These Regulations are effective from 1 January 2024.

[13.22] SI 12/2024—Employment Permits (Amendment) (No 2) Regulations 2024[25]

These Regulations amend the Employment Permits Regulations 2017[26] by adjusting the minimum annual and hourly rates of remuneration payable in the case of employees who are granted General Employment Permits for specified categories of employment (ie, health care assistant, care worker, home carer, horticulture worker or meat processor operative) and confirms a minimum annual and hourly rate of remuneration for any other category of employment.

[13.23] SI 24/2024—European Union (Workers on Board Seagoing Fishing Vessels) (Organisation of Working Time) (Share Fishermen) (Amendment) Regulations 2024

These Regulations amend the European Union (Workers on Board Seagoing Fishing Vessels) (Organisation of Working Time) (Share Fishermen) Regulations 2020,[27] which relate to share fishermen, by clarifying that the calculation of hours for the average working week over the relevant reference period should not include periods of paid annual leave or sick leave.

[13.24] SI 25/2024—European Union (International Labour Organisation Work in Fishing Convention) (Working Hours) (Amendment) Regulations 2024

These Regulations amend the European Union (Workers on Board Seagoing Fishing Vessels) (Organisation of Working Time) (Share Fishermen) Regulations 2020,[28] which relate to fishermen, by clarifying that the calculation of hours for the average working week over the relevant reference period should not include periods of paid annual leave or sick leave.

[13.25] SI 29/2024—Joint Labour Committees (Statutory Review) Order 2024[29]

This Order confirms the terms of the Labour Court's recommendations made on 12 April 2023 and the maintenance of the establishment of the following listed Joint Labour Committees in their current form:

(a) Agricultural Workers Joint Labour Committee (SI 198/1976);

---

[25] See also **Ch 9**, Immigration.
[26] Employment Permits Regulations 2017 (SI 95/2017).
[27] European Union (Workers on Board Seagoing Fishing Vessels) (Organisation of Working Time) (Share Fishermen) Regulations 2020 (SI 585 of 2020).
[28] European Union (Workers on Board Seagoing Fishing Vessels) (Organisation of Working Time) (Share Fishermen) Regulations 2020 (SI 585 of 2020).
[29] See also **Ch 10**, Industrial Relations and Trade Unions.

(b) Catering Joint Labour Committee (SI 591/2018);
(c) Contract Cleaning Joint Labour Committee (SI 626/2007, as amended by SI 25/2014);
(d) Hairdressing Joint Labour Committee (SI 212/1964, as amended by SI 26/2014);
(e) Hotels Joint Labour Committee (SI 81/1965, as amended by SI 28/2014);
(f) Retail, Grocery and Allied Trades Joint Labour Committee (SI 58/1991);
(g) Security Industry Joint Labour Committee (SI 377/1998, as amended by SI 30/2014);
(h) Early Years' Service Joint Labour Committee (SI 292/2021); and
(i) English Language Schools Joint Labour Committee (SI 24/2020).

[13.26] *SI 34/2024—Social Welfare (Consolidated Contributions and Insurability) (Amendment) (No 1) (Employment Contributions—Miscellaneous Amendments) Regulations 2024*

Part 4 of the Social Welfare (Miscellaneous Provisions) Act 2023 amends the Social Welfare Consolidation Act 2005 to facilitate:

(a) access to the State pension (contributory), in certain circumstances, for long-term carers;
(b) the introduction of flexibility to State pension (contributory) to allow a person to defer claiming the State pension (contributory) up to the age of 70;
(c) continued access to specified weekly social welfare payments after reaching the State pensionable age and during pension deferral; and
(d) the phased transition to the total contributions approach, in the calculation of the State pension (contributory).

These Regulations make consequential changes to arts 31 and 88 of the Social Welfare (Consolidated Contributions and Insurability) Regulations 1996[30] arising from changes to the system of PRSI which follow from the 2023 Act.

[13.27] *SI 35/2024—Social Welfare (Consolidated Claims, Payments and Control) (Amendment) (No 2) (Days not to be treated as days of unemployment) Regulations 2024*

Section 62(9) of the Social Welfare Consolidation Act 2005 provides that the Minister may make Regulations prescribing circumstances whereby certain work-type situations are, or are not, to be treated for the purposes of jobseeker's benefit as days of unemployment or of incapacity for work.

Article 44(1)(b) of the Social Welfare (Consolidated Claims, Payments and Control) Regulations 2007[31] specifies certain work-type situations which, despite being analogous to employment, may allow a person to qualify for jobseeker's benefit. In other words, the person is treated as unemployed.

---

[30] Social Welfare (Consolidated Contributions and Insurability) Regulations 1996 (SI 312/1996).
[31] Social Welfare (Consolidated Claims, Payments and Control) Regulations 2007 (SI 142/2007).

The Social Welfare (Consolidated Claims, Payments and Control) (Amendment) (No 8) (Days not to be treated as days of unemployment) Regulations 2023[32] amended art 44 to add another work-type situation whereby a person may qualify for jobseeker's benefit. This is the situation where, under an agreement sponsored by the Workplace Relations Commission or the Labour Court, that person is retained without any undertaking of work for that person in their occupation, and that person's income from that retention of employment does not exceed €144 a week for a period of 13 weeks.

The Social Welfare (Consolidated Claims, Payments and Control) (Amendment) (No 10) (Days not to be treated as days of unemployment) Regulations 2023[33] extended this period for another 13 weeks.

These Regulations allow that period to continue for an indefinite period subject to a review every 13 weeks.

[13.28] SI 56/2024—Industrial Training (Beauty Therapy Industry) Order 2024

This Order defines the activities of the beauty therapy industry in relation to which An tSeirbhís Oideachais Leanúnaigh agus Scileanna ('SOLAS') shall exercise its functions in the creation of statutory apprenticeships. The Order declares that the provision of beauty or spa treatments to persons in a non-medical setting are designated industrial activities for the purposes of the Industrial Training Act 1967.

[13.29] SI 64/2024—Garda Síochána (Reserve Members) Regulations 2024

These Regulations provide for improvement in the recruitment, support and supervision of reserve members of An Garda Síochána.

[13.30] SI 90/2024—Work Life Balance and Miscellaneous Provisions Act 2023 (Commencement) Order 2024[34]

This Order appoints 6 March 2024 as the day on which Pt 3 (Requests for remote working arrangements), Pt 4 (Code of Practice) and s 40 (Amendment of Workplace Relations Act 2015) of the Work Life Balance and Miscellaneous Provisions Act 2023 shall come into operation.

[13.31] SI 91/2024—Work Life Balance and Miscellaneous Provisions Act 2023 (Commencement) (No 2) Order 2024[35]

This Order appoints 6 March 2024 as the day on which the following provisions of the Work Life Balance and Miscellaneous Provisions Act 2023 shall come into operation:

(a) s 8 (requests for flexible working arrangements for caring purposes);

---

[32] Social Welfare (Consolidated Claims, Payments and Control) (Amendment) (No 8) (Days not to be treated as days of unemployment) Regulations 2023 (SI 362/2023).
[33] Social Welfare (Consolidated Claims, Payments and Control) (Amendment) (No 10) (Days not to be treated as days of unemployment) Regulations 2023 (SI 512/2023).
[34] See also **Ch 22**, Working Time.
[35] See also **Ch 22**, Working Time.

(b) s 12(a); and
(c) ss 13 and 14 (in relation to disputes under Pt 2 of the Work Life Balance and Miscellaneous Provisions Act 2023 regarding flexible working arrangements).

[13.32] *SI 92/2024—Work Life Balance and Miscellaneous Provisions Act 2023 (Workplace Relations Commission Code of Practice on the Right to Request Flexible Working and the Right to Request Remote Working) Order 2024*[36]

This Order declares the Code of Practice, set out in the schedule to this Order, to be an approved Code of Practice for the purposes of the Work Life Balance and Miscellaneous Provisions Act 2023. The Code of Practice is for the purpose of practical guidance to employers, employees and any other persons as to the steps that may be taken for complying with one or more provisions of Pt 2 of the 2023 Act, in relation to flexible working arrangements, and Pt 3 of the 2023 Act, in relation to requests for remote working arrangements.

[13.33] *SI 120/2024—Public Service Pay and Pensions Act 2017 (Section 42) Payments to General Practitioners) (Amendment) Regulations 2024*

These Regulations amend the Public Service Pay and Pensions Act 2017 (Section 42) (Payments to General Practitioners) Regulations 2019,[37] to provide a fee for GPs for the provision of MMR vaccinations.

[13.34] *SI 122/2024—Safety, Health and Welfare at Work (Carcinogens, Mutagens and Reprotoxic Substances) Regulations 2024*[38]

These Regulations give effect to Directive (EU) 2022/431[39] on the protection of workers from the risks related to exposure to carcinogens or mutagens at work.

Directive 2022/431 amends Directive 2004/37/EC[40] by introducing reprotoxic substances as a group of chemicals to be regulated. Reprotoxic substances are chemicals which affect fertility, sexual function or have adverse effects on the offspring of workers. Reprotoxins were previously regulated under Directive 98/24/EC[41] (the 'Chemical Agents Directive'), but it was determined that it was more appropriate to regulate them under the stricter requirements of Directive 2004/37/EC.

These Regulations also introduce allowances for biological monitoring for those companies who wish to carry it out.

---

[36] See also **Ch 22**, Working Time.
[37] Public Service Pay and Pensions Act 2017 (Section 42) (Payments to General Practitioners) Regulations 2019 (SI 692/2019).
[38] See also **Ch 8**, Health and Safety.
[39] Directive (EU) 2022/431 amending Directive 2004/37/EC on the protection of workers from the risks related to exposure to carcinogens or mutagens at work.
[40] Directive 2004/37/EC on the protection of workers from the risks related to exposure to carcinogens or mutagens at work.
[41] Directive 98/24/EC on the protection of the health and safety of workers from the risks related to chemical agents at work.

[13.35] SI 124/2024—Occupational Pension Schemes (Revaluation) Regulations 2024

These Regulations provide for changes in the percentage by which the amount of a preserved benefit is to be increased or decreased in a specified year.

These Regulations confirm there shall be a 4% revaluation of preserved benefits under s 33 of the Pensions Act 1990 for 2023.

[13.36] SI 177/2024—Industrial Training (Social Work Industry) Order 2024

This Order defines the activities of the social work industry in relation to which SOLAS shall exercise its functions in the creation of statutory apprenticeships. This Order confirms that, for the purposes of the Industrial Training Act 1967, the following are designated industrial activities:

(a) the conduct of social work assessments of risk and protective factors impacting the safety and welfare of children and adults;
(b) the design, management, supervision and review of care and/or intervention plans;
(c) the delivery of social work interventions for individuals, families and communities; and
(d) the preparation of reports regarding the protection and welfare of children and adults at risk or in need of social services.

[13.37] SI 255/2024—Employment Regulation (Amendment) Order (Contract Cleaning Industry Joint Labour Committee) 2024

Effective from 1 June 2024, this Order fixes the statutory minimum rates of remuneration and other conditions of employment for workers employed in the contract cleaning industry, providing cleaning and janitorial services in or on the exterior of establishments including hospitals, offices, shops, stores, factories, apartment buildings, hotels, airports and similar establishments.

[13.38] SI 259/2024—Employment Equality Act 1998 (Section 20A) (Gender Pay Gap Information) (Amendment) Regulations 2024[42]

These Regulations insert additional definitions into the Employment Equality Act 1998 (Section 20A) (Gender Pay Gap Information) Regulations 2022.[43] The Regulations amend the definition of 'relevant employer' to include an employer who employs at least 150 employees on the relevant date. The previous number of employees required to be a 'relevant employer' was 250.

---

[42] See also **Ch 3**, Employment Equality.
[43] Employment Equality Act 1998 (Section 20A) (Gender Pay Gap Information) Regulations 2022 (SI 264/2022).

[13.39] SI 262/2024—Social Welfare (Consolidated Claims, Payments and Control) (No 8) (Child Maintenance and Liable Relatives) Regulations 2024

The Social Welfare and Civil Law (Miscellaneous Provisions) Act 2024 gives legislative effect to two changes to the social welfare system. It provides for changes to the social welfare means tests so that child maintenance payments will no longer be assessed as means, and the discontinuation of the 'Liability to Maintain Family' provisions. These Regulations provide consequential amendments to the Social Welfare (Consolidated Claims, Payment and Control) Regulations 2007.[44] With respect to child maintenance, the Regulations provide:

(a) a definition of 'maintenance payment made to or in respect of a qualified child';
(b) consequential changes to the 'calculation of income limited' and 'maintenance arrangements'; and
(c) amendments to the 'sums disregarded in determining weekly family income' so that child maintenance payments will not be assessed for working family payment. The 'liable relatives' provisions are so revoked.

[13.40] SI 263/2024—Social Welfare and Civil Law (Miscellaneous Provisions) Act 2024 (Part 2) (Commencement) Order 2024

This Order provides for the commencement of Pt 2 of the Social Welfare and Civil Law (Miscellaneous Provisions) Act 2024. The purpose of Pt 2 is to change the means tests for social welfare payments so that child maintenance payments will no longer be assessed as means and to remove the liable relatives provisions from the social welfare codes.

[13.41] SI 267/2024—Registered Employment Agreement (Overhead Powerline Contractors Group) Order 2024

This Order sets out the agreed terms and conditions to apply to the workers specified who are engaged by an overhead powerline contractor.

[13.42] SI 296/2024—Employment Regulation (Amendment) Order (Early Years' Service Joint Labour Committee) Order No 1 2024

This Order amends the Employment Regulation Order (Early Years' Service Joint Labour Committee) No 1 2022[45] and fixes the statutory minimum rates of remuneration and other conditions of employment for the following category of workers:

(a) early years educators; and
(b) school age childcare practitioners.

---

[44] Social Welfare (Consolidated Claims, Payment and Control) Regulations 2007 (SI 142/2007).
[45] Employment Regulation Order (Early Years' Service Joint Labour Committee) No 1 2022 (SI 457/2022).

[13.43] SI 297/2024—Employment Regulation (Amendment) Order (Early Years' Service Joint Labour Committee) Order No 2 2024

This Order amends the Employment Regulation Order (Early Years' Service Joint Labour Committee) No 2 2022[46] and fixes the statutory minimum rates of remuneration and other conditions of employment for the following category of workers:

(a) lead educators (room leaders) and school age childcare coordinators (including graduate rate);
(b) deputy/assistant managers; and
(c) centre manager (including graduate rate).

[13.44] SI 300/2024—Parent's Leave and Benefit Act 2019 (Extension of Periods of Leave) Order 2024

This Order provides for the amendments of s 5(1) and s 16(1) of the Parent's Leave and Benefit Act 2019, to increase the entitlement of parent's leave from seven weeks to nine weeks during the first two years of a child's life, or in the case of adoption, within two years of the placement of the child with the family.

[13.45] SI 319/2024—Employment Regulation Order (Security Industry Joint Labour Committee) 2024

This Order replaces the Employment Regulation Order (Security Industry Joint Labour Committee) 2023[47] and fixes the statutory minimum rates of remuneration and other conditions of employment for security industry workers.

[13.46] SI 324/2024—Protection of Employment Act 1977 (Notification of Proposed Collective Redundancies) Regulations 2024[48]

These Regulations prescribe the particulars to be specified by an employer or responsible person in a notification to the Minister for Enterprise, Trade and Employment of proposed collective redundancy under s 12 of the Protection of Employment Act 1977. An employer proposing a collective redundancy must notify the Minister at least 30 days before the first redundancy occurs. The notification to the Minister must contain the certain information outlined in these Regulations.

[13.47] SI 328/2024—Employment Permits (Amendment) (No 3) Regulations 2024[49]

These Regulations amend the Employment Permits Regulations 2017[50] to provide for employment permits for sea fishers in the Irish fishing fleet and make other minor amendments to the schedules thereto.

---

46 Employment Regulation Order (Early Years' Service Joint Labour Committee) No 2 2022 (SI 458/2022).
47 Employment Regulation Order (Security Industry Joint Labour Committee) 2023 (SI 424/2023).
48 See also **Ch 16**, Redundancy.
49 See also **Ch 9**, Immigration.
50 Employment Permits Regulations 2017 (SI 95/2017).

[13.48] SI 335/2024—Immigration Act 2004 (Visas) (Amendment) (No 2) Order 2024[51]

This Order amends the Immigration Act 2004 (Visas) Order 2014.[52] It imposes a requirement for nationals of Botswana and South Africa both to obtain a visa in order to be granted authorisation to land in the State, as well as to obtain a transit visa in order to be granted authorisation to arrive at a port in the State for purposes of passing through the port in order to travel to another State.

This Order also allows for an exception to the visa requirement for South African nationals who are holders of a diplomatic passport and holders of a service passport or public affairs passport who arrive in the State in the company of a Minister of the Government where that Minister is on an official visit.

[13.49] SI 336/2024—European Union (Corporate Sustainability Reporting) Regulations 2024[53]

These Regulations were made on 5 July 2024 and came into operation on 6 July 2024. The Regulations transpose the Corporate Sustainability Reporting Directive ('CSRD')[54] (which amended the: Accounting Directive, Transparency Directive, Audit Regulation and Statutory Audit Directive).

The CSRD requires in-scope companies to report annually on environmental, social, human rights and governance matters. These Regulations, in transposing the CSRD into Irish law, make amendments to the Companies Act 2014 and the Transparency Regulations 2007. The Regulations require all large companies, and all listed companies (except listed micro-enterprises) to provide information on sustainability and ESG matters, including human rights matters. Sustainability reporting will become gradually applicable across the period 2024 to 2028.

Key features of the Regulations include:

— New Pt 28: Sustainability Reporting is inserted into the Companies Act.

— Companies in Scope: defined in Pt 28 by reference to 'applicable companies'. As per the CSRD, exemptions are available for subsidiaries included in the group report of a holding company, subject to certain conditions.

— Amendments to the Transparency Regulations: brings certain issuers listed on an EU regulated market within scope of sustainability reporting obligations under the Accounting Directive (as amended by the CSRD).

— Timeframes are as per the CSRD:

— FY 2024 (reporting 2025) for large public interest entities ('PIEs') with more than 500 employees;

---

[51] See also **Ch 9**, Immigration.
[52] Immigration Act 2004 (Visas) Order 2014 (SI 473/2014).
[53] See also **Ch 6**, European Union Law.
[54] Directive (EU) 2022/2464 amending Regulation (EU) No 537/2014, Directive 2004/109/EC, Directive 2006/43/EC and Directive 2013/34/EU, as regards corporate sustainability reporting.

- FY 2025 (reporting 2026) for large companies;
- FY 2026 (reporting 2027) for listed SMEs (opt-out available until 2028); and
- FY 2028 (reporting 2029) for subsidiaries and large branches of non-EU companies with a net turnover of EUR 150 million in the EU.
— Key Intangible Resources: The directors' report must include information on 'key intangible resources' in relation to the company, and an explanation of how the business model fundamentally depends on such resources and how such resources are a source of value creation for the company.
— Sustainability Reporting:
  - Section 1590 (s 1596 for consolidated reporting) sets out the information to be included in a clearly identifiable dedicated section of the directors' report.
  - Sections 1590(1)/1596(1) set out the double materiality obligations. The directors must also report on the materiality assessment process (for financial and impact materiality).
  - Sections 1590(2)/1596(2) set out the sustainability information to be reported from a double materiality perspective and in accordance with the European Sustainability Reporting Standards.
  - Reporting must contain information about the company's value chain, in addition to its own operations, subject to a three-year phase-in period in the event that not all necessary information regarding the value chain is available.
  - As per the Non-Financial & Diversity Reporting Directive ('NRFD') Regulations,[55] information relating to impending developments or matters in the course of negotiation may be omitted.
  - Where applicable, the sustainability information shall also contain references to, and additional explanations of, the other information included in the directors' report and the amounts reported in the company's statutory financial statements.
— Consultation with Employee's Representatives: The directors must provide information to and consult with employees' representatives at the appropriate level in relation to the sustainability information to be reported and the means of obtaining and verifying such information.
— Single Electronic Reporting Format: The directors' report must be in electronic (XHTML) format with sustainability reporting (including disclosures under art 8 of the Taxonomy Regulation) 'tagged' in accordance with the European Single Electronic Format ('ESEF').
— Assurance Report:
  - A statutory auditor/audit firm shall carry out assurance of the sustainability reporting—it can be different from the statutory auditors appointed to carry out a statutory audit.
  - The assurance report shall state clearly the statutory auditors' opinion, based on a limited assurance engagement, as regards the compliance of the sustainability

---

[55] European Union (Disclosure of Non-Financial and Diversity Information by certain large undertakings and groups) Regulations 2017 (SI No 360/2017).

reporting of the applicable company with the requirements of Pt 28 including compliance with the European Sustainability Reporting Standards and the reporting requirements under art 8 of the Taxonomy Regulation.
— Section 1616 sets out the responsibilities of the PIE Audit Committee in relation to the assurance of sustainability reporting.

— Non-Financial & Diversity Reporting Regulations 2017:

— The Regulations do not repeal the NFRD Regulations. As a result, companies who fall within scope of non-financial reporting obligations under the NFRD Regulations, but do not fall within scope of the Pt 28/CSRD reporting obligations until FY 2025, appear to remain subject to the obligations under the NFRD Regulations for FY 2024.

— The Regulations do not deal with the CSRD amendment regarding the annual diversity report, which large traded companies are required to include in their corporate governance statement.

[13.50] SI 420/2024—Local Government Act 2001 (Retirement of Firefighters) Regulations 2024

These Regulations provide for the retirement of firefighters (full time and retained) at age 55, but allows firefighters who are medically fit to continue to serve as firefighters up to age 62.

These Regulations do not apply to firefighters whose existing terms and conditions of service provide for a minimum retirement age in excess of 65 years or a mandatory retirement age in excess of 62 years.

[13.51] SI 421/2024—Local Government (Superannuation) (Consolidation) (Amendment) Scheme 2024

This Scheme amends the Local Government (Superannuation) (Consolidation) Scheme 1998 to provide for changes to pension entitlements for fire brigade officers and fire brigade employees, which limit the age at which fast accruals apply to 60.

[13.52] SI 437/2024—Garda Síochána (Retirement) Regulations 2024

These Regulations provide for a member of the Garda Síochána who was appointed as a new entrant to the Garda Síochána on or after 1 April 2004 and who holds a rank below the rank of Garda Commissioner to retire on attaining the age of 62 years.

The following statutory instruments were introduced to amend the previously existing legislation to confirm the new retirement age of 62:

— Garda Síochána Act 2005 (Retirement) (Amendment) Regulations 2024[56] provide for the amendment of reg 2(b) of the Garda Síochána Act 2005 (Retirement) Regulations 2018[57] by the substitution of retirement age of '62' for '60';

---

[56] Garda Síochána Act 2005 (Retirement) (Amendment) Regulations 2024 (SI 438/2024).
[57] Garda Síochána Act 2005 (Retirement) Regulations 2018 (SI 28/2018).

— Garda Síochána (Retirement) (Amendment) Regulations 2024[58] amend reg 6 of the Garda Síochána (Retirement) (No 2) Regulations 1951[59] with the substitution of 'sixty-two' for 'sixty' and of 'three years' for 'five years'; and

— Garda Síochána (Retirement) (Amendment) (No 2) Regulations 2024[60] provide that reg 3 of the Garda Síochána (Retirement) Regulations 1996[61] is amended by the substitution of '62' for '60'.

[13.53] *SI 563/2024—National Minimum Wage Order 2024*[62]

This Order sets out that the national minimum hourly rate of pay be €13.50 effective from 1 January 2025.

[13.54] *SI 598/2024—Employment Permits (Amendment) (No 4) Regulations 2024*

These Regulations have extended the employment permit quotas for car mechanics, motor mechanics, auto electricians, and motor vehicle technicians by 200 general employment permits.

[13.55] *SI 620/2024—Sectoral Employment Order (Construction Sector)*

This Order provides for statutory minimum pay, pension and sick pay entitlements for craft persons, construction workers and apprentices employed in the construction industry.

[13.56] *SI 632/2024—Social Welfare (Consolidated Occupational Injuries) Regulations 2024*

These Regulations provide for increases in the rate of disablement gratuity and the weekly rates of disablement pension where the degree of disablement ranges from 1 to 19 per cent. The Regulations also provide for an increase in the rate of injury benefit payable to those under 16 years of age. If, in such cases, there is what amounts to full-time employment the rate will be increased by €12. In all other cases, the rate will increase by €5.70. The rate increases come into effect on 6 January 2025 in the case of injury benefit and on 3 January 2025 in the case of disablement gratuity and disablement pension.

[13.57] *SI 633/2024—European Union (Adequate Minimum Wages) Regulations 2024*

These Regulations transpose Directive (EU) 2022/2041[63] on adequate minimum wages into Irish law. The Regulations provide for the Low Pay Commission to carry out annual

---

[58] Garda Síochána (Retirement) (Amendment) Regulations 2024 (SI 439/2024).
[59] Garda Síochána (Retirement) (No 2) Regulations 1951 (SI 335/1951).
[60] Garda Síochána (Retirement) (Amendment) (No 2) Regulations 2024 (SI 440/2024).
[61] Garda Síochána (Retirement) Regulations 1996 (SI 16/1996).
[62] See also **Ch 20**, Wages.
[63] Directive (EU) 2022/2041 on adequate minimum wages in the European Union.

examinations of the national minimum hourly rate of pay and make recommendations to the Minister for Enterprise, Trade and Employment on same.

[13.58] *SI 635/2024—Social Welfare (Consolidated Claims, Payments and Control) (Amendment) (No 15) (Jobseeker's Pay-Related Benefit) Regulations 2024*

These Regulations allow for the commencement of a new social insurance scheme entitled jobseeker's pay-related benefit from 31 March 2025. Key features of the new scheme include, that the weekly rate of payment for those who have at least five years paid PRSI contributions will be set at 60% of previous earnings, subject to a maximum of €450 for the first three months, the rate will then reduce to 55%, up to a maximum of €375 for the next three months. A further three months will be paid at the rate of 50%, up to a maximum of €300.

These Regulations also provide for a number of consequential amendments to the Social Welfare (Consolidated Claims, Payments and Control) Regulations 2007[64] following the introduction of the jobseeker's pay-related benefit scheme.

[13.59] *SI 636/2024—Social Welfare (Consolidated Claims, Payments and Control) (Amendment) (No 16) (Jobseeker's Pay-Related Benefit) Regulations 2024*

These Regulations provide for the commencement of a new social insurance scheme under the Social Welfare (Miscellaneous Provisions) Act 2024. These Regulations insert a new chapter, Chapter 5AA, into Pt 2 of the Social Welfare (Consolidated Claims, Payments and Control) Regulations 2007.[65] These Regulations, which will commence on 31 March 2025, provide for circumstances in which a person is considered to be engaged in casual employment and include provisions in relation to how a person may re-qualify for jobseeker's pay-related benefit. These Regulations also provide that jobseeker's benefit will not be available to persons eligible to apply for jobseeker's pay-related benefit from 31 March 2025.

[13.60] *SI 640/2024—Maternity Protection, Employment Equality and Preservation of Certain Records Act 2024 (Section 6) (Commencement) Order 2024*

This Order provides for the commencement of s 6 of the Maternity Protection, Employment Equality and Preservation of Certain Records Act 2024. This section amends s 47 of the Social Welfare Consolidation Act 2005 to enable the Minister for Social Protection to make Regulations to allow for the postponement of the payment of maternity benefit in the event of the person who is entitled to that benefit having a serious health condition within the meaning of s 14C of the Maternity Protection Act 1994.

---

[64] Social Welfare (Consolidated Claims, Payments and Control) Regulations 2007 (SI 142/2007).
[65] Social Welfare (Consolidated Claims, Payments and Control) Regulations 2007 (SI 142/2007).

Chapter 14

Part-Time Work

INTRODUCTION

[14.01] Two UK EAT decisions involving less favourable treatment afforded to part-time workers are noted, namely *Augustine v Data Cars Ltd* and *Clayson v Ministry of Justice*.

LESS FAVOURABLE TREATMENT

[14.02] *Augustine v Data Cars Ltd*[1]—*UK Employment Appeal Tribunal—appeal from employment tribunal—Part-Time Workers (Prevention of Less Favourable Treatment) Regulations 2000*[2]—*causation—intention*

The claimant appealed against an employment tribunal's dismissal of his complaint of less favourable treatment as a part-time worker.

The claimant was a private-hire driver and an employee of the respondent. The claimant paid the respondent a 'circuit fee' of £148 per week. This was a flat fee that gave drivers access to the respondent's booking system and applied irrespective of whether they were full time or part time. The claimant, who worked an average of 34.8 hours a week, argued that the circuit fee amounted to less favourable treatment of part-time workers, contrary to the Part-Time Workers (Prevention of Less Favourable Treatment) Regulations 2000.

The employment tribunal found that the claimant was a part-time worker (his comparator worked an average of over 90 hours a week). However, it went on to dismiss the complaint, holding that the claimant was not less favourably treated as regards the terms of his contract. Alternatively, he was not less favourably treated on the ground that he was a part-time worker: the claimant and his comparator were treated 'in exactly the same way', and, in any event, the charging of the circuit fee was not 'on the sole ground' that he was a part-time worker.

---

[1] *Augustine v Data Cars Ltd* [2024] EAT 117.
[2] Part-Time Workers (Prevention of Less Favourable Treatment) Regulations 2000 (SI 2000/1551).

The EAT accepted the claimant's submission that there was a need to adopt a *pro rata* analysis in this case. The employment tribunal had not done so and, hence, failed to take into account that the claimant was paying a higher circuit fee as a proportion of hours worked than his full-time comparator. To the extent that the tribunal found that the circuit fee did not constitute less favourable treatment of the claimant, that ground of appeal was upheld.

The employment tribunal was also found to have erred in that it considered the respondent's intention, or lack thereof, to be a relevant consideration when determining causation. The EAT stated that the authorities are clear that, when determining the reason why the treatment in question occurred, the intention of the relevant actor is not relevant. That said, the tribunal was not bound to say that the charging of the flat-rate circuit fee was on the sole ground that the claimant was a part-time worker. The respondent's drivers worked a wide range of hours. The less favourable treatment identified by the claimant arose from the failure to apply the circuit fee on a *pro rata* basis. And yet, had the claimant worked above the employee average of 43.17 hours a week (and thus been treated as working full-time), he would still have been treated less favourably than his comparator on the flat-rate circuit fee. The ground of appeal was therefore upheld in part.

The issue of causation was remitted to the employment tribunal for re-hearing.

[14.03] *Clayson v Ministry of Justice*[3]—*UK Employment Appeal Tribunal—appeal from employment tribunal—Judicial Pensions and Retirement Act 1993—judicial pensions—difference in treatment—less favourable treatment on the ground of being part-time workers—causative factor*

The claimants appealed against an employment tribunal's finding that the respondent 'did not treat the claimants less favourably than comparable full-time workers on the ground that the claimants were part-time workers', and its dismissal of their claims.

The claimants were full-time salaried circuit judges, representing a larger cohort of active and retired circuit judges appointed on or after 31 March 1995—the date of introduction of a new judicial pension scheme (the 'judicial pension scheme'). Before that date, they were part-time recorders or (in the claimants' case) assistant recorders. They were not entered into a pension scheme because, at the time, there was no such scheme for part-time, fee-paid judges, though that office retrospectively became pensionable.

The claimants contended that, by virtue of their part-time status, they fell to be treated less favourably in respect of their pension rights than their comparators, full-time circuit judges, who were appointed when the claimants were appointed assistant recorders. The comparators were given a right to elect to join the new judicial pension scheme or to remain in their existing scheme. When the claimants were appointed full-time circuit judges, they were compulsorily enrolled in the new scheme without a right of election.

---

[3] *His Honour Judge Clayson, His Honour Judge Wollman and His Honour Judge Griffith-Jones v Ministry of Justice, Lord Chancellor and Secretary of State for Justice* [2024] EAT 99.

It was not disputed that the work done by the claimants and their comparators was comparable. They performed 'essentially the same activity', conducting trials and applying the law, though recorders are more flexible and itinerant, 'responding to the short terms needs of the court'. This supported the employment tribunal's conclusion that recorders who subsequently become circuit judges are appointed to a different judicial office. If, when the claimants were assistant recorders, there had been a pension scheme for fee-paid judges, the tribunal reasoned that it would have been a different scheme to that of full-time salaried judges.

While it was true that the claimants were treated less favourably than their comparators once they became full-time circuit judges, the comparison was between two groups of full-time workers, not between part-time and full-time workers. Had the claimants continued as recorders and not accepted a full-time appointment they would (with their retrospective pension rights) have been treated in the same way as their comparators. The difference in treatment only started when they ceased to be part-time workers. A circuit judge appointed before 31 March 1995 would not have been required to leave the old judicial pension scheme, whether or not they had previously served part time. A circuit judge appointed to that office on the same day as the claimants, but who had never served part-time, would have been treated in the same way as the claimants regardless. This suggested that the date of the appointment, as opposed to the fact of the claimants having been part-time workers, was the causative factor.

While sympathetic to the claimants' grievance, the EAT did not consider the employment tribunal's reasoning to have beeen flawed. It had been right to conclude that the treatment in respect of pension entitlements was (other than the discrimination which had been remedied by the introduction of retrospective pension entitlements) not caused by their part-time working as recorders before being appointed full-time circuit judges. The claimants' 'misfortune was that their pensions were less favourable than those of their predecessors', including those who had never been recorders at all. Nevertheless, the appeal was not well founded.

Chapter 15

Pensions

BUDGET 2025

[15.01] Budget 2025 was announced on 1 October 2024. The budget included a permanent increase of €12 in most weekly State social welfare payments. It was also announced that pensioners in receipt of the living alone allowance are to receive a separate once-off €200 lump-sum payment. Pensioners also received a cost-of-living bonus in October 2024 in addition to the Christmas bonus in December 2024.

For the first time since 2014, there will be an increase to the Standard Fund Threshold ('SFT') which is currently set at €2 million. There will be a phased increase to the SFT to €2.8 million; to increase by €200,000 p/a from 2026 to 2029, thereafter increasing in line with applicable wage growth. The threshold for the higher rate of taxation to apply to a pension lump sum is to be limited to €500,000; as opposed to changing by reference to the SFT, which is currently the case. The rate of tax applicable to any chargeable excess over and above the SFT is to remain unchanged; a specific review of the rate is to take place in 2030.

The budget provided further clarity on the Auto-Enrolment Retirement Savings Scheme, noting that the most recent proposed commencement date is 30 September 2025, further detail in relation to which is set out below.

IRISH UPDATES

Automatic Enrolment Retirement Savings System Act 2024

[15.02] The Automatic Enrolment Retirement Savings System Act 2024 (the 'Automatic Enrolment Act') completed its passage through the Oireachtas and the legislation was signed into law by the President of Ireland on 9 July 2024.

The Automatic Enrolment Act provides for employees aged between 23 and 60, who earn in excess of €20,000 per year from all employments and who are not already enrolled in an occupational pension scheme, to be automatically enrolled into the new automatic enrolment system.

On 30 September 2024, the Minister for Social Protection signed a commencement order in respect of the Automatic Enrolment Act as part of Budget 2025; the

Government referred to the Auto-Enrolment Retirement Savings Scheme as 'My Future Fund', which it is understood will be the name of the system once formally launched. The commencement order provides for a commencement date of 30 September 2025—an optimistic implementation date given the extent of the system still to be created.

Employers should begin preparing for automatic enrolment. The main initial step is to undertake a gap analysis of the workforce to see who is covered by a pension arrangement and who is not. Employers will then need to decide whether: (i) they wish to maximise the number of employees that are included in their occupational pension scheme; or (ii) they want the automatic enrolment system to apply to all employees; or (iii) they want to operate both systems in tandem for different cohorts of employees.

Depending on the size and make up of a workforce, it may be impractical or unachievable to include all employees in any existing occupational pension scheme so that they are not caught by the automatic enrolment system. To minimise the impact of automatic enrolment, amendments to certain provisions of the trust deed and rules of the existing pension scheme (eg eligibility provisions; removal of waiting periods; contribution rules) will be required. Where such amendments require trustee consent, trustees should consider the employer's request and all relevant factors relating to it before giving their consent, taking legal advice where necessary.

State Pension

[15.03] Following the enactment of the Social Welfare (Miscellaneous Provisions) Act 2023, with effect from 1 January 2024, an employee can choose to start claiming their State pension (contributory) anytime between the ages of 66 and 70. If an employee chooses to defer their State pension beyond age 66, they can continue to work and make PRSI contributions to increase their personal rate of payment.

Whether or not the change to the State pension regime will impact on a given occupational pension scheme turns on the precise language used in the provisions relating to calculation and payment of benefits which are linked to the State pension. For example, a State pension offset calculated by reference to the date on which payment of the State pension commences may now potentially differ from member to member, whereas if a State pension offset is calculated by reference to the date on which a member becomes first eligible for payment of a State pension there may be no change. Similarly, a supplementary pension (also known as a bridging pension) may be payable until the age at which the State pension commences to be payable, which may now be as late as age 70 under the new legislation. In addition, the treatment and calculation of any State pension offset in the event of late retirement may require clarifying amendments to avoid uncertainty in the application of late retirement factors and the correct determination of the amounts of State pension to be included in a State pension offset in these circumstances.

Employers and trustees should review their scheme rules to assess whether scheme amendments are required to address the changes to the State pension on foot of the deferral options brought about by the Social Welfare (Miscellaneous Provisions) Act 2023.

Financial Services and Pensions Ombudsman (Amendment) Bill 2023

[15.04] On 19 December 2023, the Government published the Financial Services and Pensions Ombudsman (Amendment) Bill 2023 (the 'FSPO Bill'). At the date of writing it has not been enacted. The main purpose of the FSPO Bill is to amend the legislation underpinning the Financial Services and Pensions Ombudsman (the 'FSPO') in light of the decision of the Supreme Court in the *Zalewski*[1] case, which found the Workplace Relations Commission is engaged in the permissible administration of justice.

In order to align the practices of the FSPO with the decision in *Zalewski*, the FSPO Bill introduces the following main changes to FSPO proceedings:

— enabling the FSPO to hold oral hearings in public where the 'interests of justice' require and following consultation with the parties to the complaint;

— allowing individuals appearing before the FSPO to be cross-examined (on oath or affirmation); and

— making it an offence for an individual to give evidence on oath or affirmation which they know to be false.

The FSPO Bill also confirms that the services and protections currently afforded to consumers by the FSPO extend to financial service and pension providers who no longer operate in the Irish market.

Occupational Pension Schemes (Fees) (Amendment) Regulations 2023

[15.05] On 20 December 2023, the Occupational Pension Schemes (Fees) (Amendment) Regulations 2023 (the 'Fee Regulations') were introduced by the Minister for Social Protection.

The Fee Regulations alter the method of calculating the fees payable to the Pensions Authority (the 'Authority') for pension schemes with 20 or more participating employers on 31 December in the preceding calendar year, so are likely to be of most relevance to master trusts. Previously the fees payable by such schemes were calculated on the basis of the number of active members in the scheme on the commencement date of the scheme year preceding the year of account. Following the introduction of the Fee Regulations, the fees payable must be calculated on the basis of the number of active members in the scheme on 31 December of the scheme year preceding the year of account.

There is no change to the Authority's fee rates for the 2024 year of account.

---

[1] *Zalewski v Adjudication Officer, the WRC, Ireland and the Attorney General* [2021] IESC 24, see *Arthur Cox Employment Law Yearbook 2021* at [5.02].

EUROPEAN LEGISLATION

Digital Operational Resilience Act ('DORA')

[15.06] DORA is an EU Regulation which aims to create a harmonised regulatory framework strengthening the Information and Communication Technology ('ICT') security of financial entities (which includes pension schemes). Its objective is to achieve a high common level of digital operational resilience across all EU Member States so that financial entities are able to effectively respond to unplanned disruption while minimising the impact on their business and customers.

DORA will be directly effective across the EU from 17 January 2025, so it is important that pension scheme trustees now begin to take steps towards compliance with its requirements.

On 29 July 2024, the Authority published guidance on how it expects pension schemes and trustees to comply with DORA. The guidance provides that it is trustees who will be responsible for ensuring the scheme's compliance with the DORA requirements, even in situations where there are outsourcing arrangements in place.

In its guidance on DORA, the Authority has summarised the main requirements for trustees under DORA to include:

— Documenting and maintaining a comprehensive ICT risk management framework to include ICT business continuity plans and other policies and controls, as part of the overall risk management system.

— Identifying all sources of ICT risk and cyber threats on a continuous basis together with ongoing monitoring of the security and functioning of ICT systems relied on.

— Effective management of ICT third-party risks ensuring that key contractual provisions are in place with service providers as set out in art 30 of DORA.

— Maintaining a register of information on all contractual arrangements on the use of ICT services provided by third-party providers.

— Managing and reporting major ICT-related incidents to the Authority and keeping a record of significant cyber threats.

— Testing ICT systems supporting critical or important functions at least yearly.

The compliance deadline was 17 January 2025. Trustees of pension schemes are generally advised to take the following steps to ensure DORA compliance:

— undertaking trustee training to understand your responsibilities under DORA;

— preparing a list of any scheme activities that are supported by ICT systems and services and identifying any third parties providing those ICT services;

— preparing the main documents required (or appropriate additions to existing documents) to include an ICT risk management framework document and ICT business continuity plans as well as a register of information on all contractual arrangements in place with third-party service providers;

— appointing a relevant person to take ownership of ensuring compliance with DORA; and
— putting in place DORA compliant contractual terms with all ICT service providers (which may include sponsoring employers, particularly where scheme administration is undertaken in-house).

REGULATORY UPDATES

Authority Publishes Investment Strategy (Liquidity Risk) Guidance for Trustees

[15.07] On 18 June 2024, the Authority published guidance for trustees on investment strategies that may give rise to significant liquidity risks. The Authority has previously noted that there are lessons to be learned from the issues that arose in Autumn 2022 for UK defined benefit pension schemes that were exposed to liability driven investments ('LDIs'), requiring intervention from the Bank of England to stabilise the UK pensions and gilts markets.

The Authority identifies investments that may give rise to significant risks as including LDIs, leveraged LDIs, sale and repurchase agreements (repos), swaps, currency hedging, and inflation hedging. The Authority noted that such strategies involve more complexity than traditional strategies and may incur losses requiring the liquidation of scheme assets. It stated that, as a result, greater understanding and proactivity is required on the part of trustees in managing the risk.

The Authority's guidance states that trustees pursuing an investment strategy, which includes such investments, should:

— ensure that their investment strategy complies with the requirements of the Pensions Act 1990, the Occupational Pension Schemes (Investment) Regulations 2021, and the Authority's Code of Practice;
— set out detailed information on the investment strategy in their Statement of Investment Policy Principles ('SIPP');
— satisfy themselves that their investment managers have the necessary expertise and operational capability to manage such investments;
— acting in conjunction with their advisers, establish a target level of liquidity and have a liquidity preparedness plan in place to restore the target level of liquidity following adverse market movements or during periods of decreased market liquidity;
— have operational arrangements in place that ensure that the scheme's decision-making process can cope with rapid market movements; and
— closely monitor the risks and performance of their investment strategy and include information on these in the trustee annual report.

FSPO Publishes Overview of 2023 Complaints

[15.08] On 27 March 2024, the Financial Services and Pensions Ombudsman ('FSPO') published its overview of the complaints it received in 2023. The FSPO received a total of 6,182 complaints in 2023, of which 336 related to pensions. This represented a 44% increase in pensions complaints compared to 2022.

Of the 336 pension complaints received by the FSPO, 71% related to occupational pension schemes and 20% related to PRSAs, with the balance relating to Retirement Annuity Contracts or other pension products. The most common ground for complaints was maladministration (46%), followed by miscalculation of pension benefits (22%) and failure to provide correct information (10%).

EIOPA Quarterly Updates of Occupational Pensions Risk Dashboard

[15.09] The European Insurance and Occupational Pensions Authority ('EIOPA') has published three editions of its Occupational Pensions Risk Dashboard. The Dashboard is designed to summarise the main risks and vulnerabilities facing occupational pension schemes in the European Economic Area.

The first Risk Dashboard on Institutions for Occupational Retirement Provisions ('IORPs') was published on 1 February 2024. This showed IORPs' exposure to market and asset return risks at a high level due to high volatility in bond markets while macro and liquidity risks were at a medium level.

EIOPA published the second edition of its Dashboard on 2 May 2024. This also highlighted that the exposure of IORPs to market and asset return risks remained at a high level, caused by vulnerabilities in the real estate market in addition to market volatility. Macro and liquidity risks remained at a medium level.

On 29 July 2024, EIOPA published the latest edition of its Occupational Pensions Risk Dashboard. This shows that exposure to market and asset returns risk remains at a high level due to increased volatility in the fixed income and equity markets at the end of Q2 2024 and a continued decline in real estate prices across the Euro Area, mainly driven by commercial real estate. Concentration risks are considered to have decreased over the quarter due to lower sectorial and geographical concentration in pension schemes' investment portfolio. All other risk categories remain unchanged at a medium level, although it remains the case that digitalisation and cyber risks are likely to increase over the next 12 months.

Authority Launches Consultation on Revised Code of Conduct for PRSA Providers

[15.10] Under the Pensions Act 1990, the Authority is required to prepare and, from time to time, amend a code of conduct in relation to the producing, marketing and selling of PRSA products by PRSA providers (the 'PRSA Code'). It is a condition of the approval of PRSA products by the Authority that the product and PRSA provider are compliant with the PRSA Code. On 20 September 2024, the Authority published a draft revised PRSA Code.

The PRSA Code includes requirements on PRSA providers to: co-operate with the Authority; put in place a written conflicts of interest policy; provide risk warnings to PRSA contributors where appropriate; identify the target market for its PRSA products; and take steps to ensure that its products are being distributed to the identified target market. A particular focus of the revised draft PRSA Code is to ensure that PRSA providers are providing sufficient information to PRSA contributors about the risks arising from unregulated investment products.

Following a review of the submissions received by the closing deadline of November 2024, it is anticipated that the revised PRSA Code will be published in Q1 2025 and will come into effect six months after its publication date.

REVENUE UPDATE—NO MORE RETIREMENT ANNUITY CONTRACTS

Revenue to no longer approve new Retirement Annuity Contracts ('RACs')

[15.11] Section 17 of the Finance (No 2) Act 2023 amends s 784 of the Taxes Consolidation Act 1997 (the 'TCA') and provides that, from 1 January 2024, the Revenue Commissioners will not approve any RACs under s 784 except where the application for approval has been made before 1 January 2024. This means that one-person self-employed arrangements will now have to be set up using a PRSA. For employees, there remains a choice between a PRSA and an occupational pension scheme (or a one-member section of a Master Trust).

CASE LAW

Ireland

Interpretation of Trust Deed and Rules

[15.12] *Vodafone Ireland Ltd and Trustees of Vodafone Ireland Pension Plan*[2]*— High Court—Roberts J—pension increases—interpretation of trust deed and rules*

The applicant, Vodafone Ireland Ltd ('Vodafone'), applied to the High Court to secure a decision on the correct interpretation of a clause in the Vodafone Ireland Pension Plan ('VIPP'), which was formerly the pension scheme of Eircell Ltd. The defendants

---

[2] *Vodafone Ireland Ltd v Farrell* [2024] IEHC 280.

were the trustees of the VIPP, as well as a second-named defendant, Mr Fahy, who was appointed to represent the interests of affected VIPP members (the 'affected members').

The contextual background is that, in the early 1980s, the responsibility for telecommunications services were transferred from the Department of Posts and Telegraphs to Bord Telecom Éireann ('BTÉ'). BTÉ was required by the Postal and Telecommunications Services Act 1983 to establish a pension scheme for its employees on no less favourable conditions than had applied to employees immediately before the transfer to BTÉ. Eircell was established as a subsidiary of BTÉ in 1996 and introduced the Eircell Scheme for its employees with effect from 27 May 1996. BTÉ was privatised in 1999 and became Eircom. Vodafone then acquired Eircell in 2001 and replaced Eircell as the principal employer of the Eircell scheme, which was renamed the VIPP. On Vodafone's acquisition of Eircell, the affected members (some of whom had previously been seconded to Eircell) transferred employment from Eircom to Vodafone and became members of the Eircell scheme.

The VIPP is a defined benefit occupational scheme with four schedules that relate to different cohorts of employees. Scheme C was the relevant schedule in this case as it related to those Vodafone employees who transferred from Eircom on Vodafone's acquisition of Eircell and who were previously members of the Eircom pension scheme. The VIPP was subject to six amending deeds from 1999 to 2005. The provision at the centre of this case was rule 10 of Schedule III of the 2005 Trust Deed and Rules ('rule 10, 2005 Deed'), which governed increases to pensions in payment and preserved pensions for Scheme C members and stated that:

> 'All Pensions under this Scheme C will increase in no less favourable a manner than had the Member remained as a Member of the Eircom Scheme and will increase in line with the percentage increase in the relevant grade for that Member'.

The directions sought were split into two distinct issues. The first concerned the interpretation of rule 10, 2005 Deed (the 'interpretation issue'). The central question was whether rule 10, 2005 Deed, when properly interpreted, provided for guaranteed 'pay parity' pension increases for Scheme C members. Vodafone contended that rule 10, 2005 Deed gave them ultimate discretion related to pension increases and did not provide for guaranteed 'pay parity' increases. The defendants argued that Scheme C members were entitled to guaranteed pension increases aligned through retirement with increases in salaries for the grade and point at which they retired.

The second issue related to who or what the appropriate comparator was for calculating any pension increases under rule 10, 2005 Deed (the 'comparator issue'). Vodafone contended that an increase of the prior year's annual increase in CPI inflation up to a maximum of 4% per annum ('capped CPI') was appropriate. The defendants disagreed, stating that capped CPI increases would break the guaranteed pay parity link, and was not what rule 10, 2005 Deed or related legislation permitted.

In giving judgment, the Court utilised the 'text in context' approach from *Law Society of Ireland v Motor Insurers Bureau of Ireland*,[3] as it is considered the leading authority

---

[3] *Law Society of Ireland v Motor Insurers Bureau of Ireland* [2017] IESC 31.

on contractual interpretation. The 'text in context' approach establishes that the meaning of a relevant provision of an agreement must be determined from the consideration of that agreement as a whole and in its wider context. Contextual factors which the Court considered relevant to the interpretation issue included: the general employment history of the relevant members (almost all of whom were formerly employed in the civil service prior to transferring to Vodafone); legislative provisions in relation to the transfer of members to private sector employment; the manner in which the VIPP was operating at the time rule 10, 2005 Deed was drafted; and any stated reasons or objectives for introducing rule 10, 2005 Deed.

The Court acknowledged that the clause was not straightforward and there was scope for ambiguity. However, it did not agree with Vodafone that the increases for Scheme C members were discretionary. Therefore, the correct interpretation of rule 10, 2005 Deed was that it provided Scheme C members with guaranteed entitlement to pension increases on a 'pay parity' basis in line with a percentage increase in salary in the relevant grade to that member. This did, however, present a complication in the comparator issue. With the abolition of grades in 2013, pension increases were calculated in line with average general salary increases in Vodafone. In 2017, Vodafone determined the new reference population were to be active members of Scheme C, rather than the entire population. This meant that, as the size of the Scheme C cohort shrunk, there would be a negative effect on the calculation of pension increases for Scheme C members, with no further increases once the population reduced to zero active employees.

In respect of the comparator issue, the Court ruled that, for the purpose of calculating any pension increase under rule 10, 2005 Deed, the comparator should be the average percentage salary increase across the general Vodafone staff, excluding payments related to increments, promotions or any variable or *ex gratia* payments such as bonuses. The Court further stipulated that the parties would be free to agree on any other comparator that would be acceptable to all other stakeholders.

[15.13] *Masterson and Others v Córas Iompair Éireann*[4]—*High Court—Sanfey J—superannuation scheme—statutory interpretation—scheme solvency*

The High Court was asked to interpret Rule 20 of the Córas Iompair Éireann Superannuation Scheme 1951 (the 'Scheme') which provides for the liability of Córas Iompair Éireann ('CIÉ') to contribute to the Scheme. Rule 20 states that:

> 'In every year the Board shall contribute to the Fund such sum as the Board after consulting the Actuary determines to be necessary to support and maintain the solvency of the Fund'.

The applicants were members of the committee responsible for the administration of the Scheme. The questions put to the High Court included whether Rule 20 placed an obligation on CIÉ to pay employer contributions sufficient to ensure that the Scheme met the statutory minimum funding standard ('MFS') and the funding standard reserve, each as provided for in the Pensions Act 1990.

---

[4] *Masterson and Others v Córas Iompair Éireann* [2024] IEHC 222.

The High Court held that an assessment of 'solvency' in this context required that the Scheme must satisfy the MFS and the funding standard reserve buffer. Based on a construction of the rules of the Scheme as a whole, the Court held that the obligation on CIÉ to determine the contribution 'necessary to support and maintain the solvency of the fund' required a determination as to the adequacy of the assets to meet liabilities, to include the liabilities for which provision must be made to satisfy the MFS.

The Court went on to note that where there were liabilities, whether relating to future benefits such as those arising from projected wage increases, which did not come within the terms of the MFS, these must also be taken into account. However, the Court also found that the obligation on CIÉ to contribute to the fund was not absolute and pointed out, in particular, that the rules of the Scheme explicitly referred to the right of the committee to vary members' contributions in certain circumstances where the CIÉ contribution required to support and maintain the solvency of the fund exceeded a certain threshold.

UK

[15.14] **BBC v BBC Pension Trust Ltd**[5]—*Court of Appeal of England and Wales—Lewison LJ, Falk LJ & Sir Floyd—appeal from High Court of England and Wales—construction of scheme wording—pension scheme*

In July 2024, the Court of Appeal of England and Wales upheld the ruling of the High Court that a restriction in an amending power which refers to the 'interests' of members should be read to include both past and future service rights but that this will be considered on a case-by-case basis, with reference to the context in which the members' 'interests' are examined.

This case concerned the BBC pension scheme (the 'Scheme') which provided defined benefit retirement benefits for employees who had joined the Scheme before December 2010. The BBC, in an effort to reduce costs, sought to limit future service benefits which had not yet been earned by the members of the Scheme. The amendment power under which the change to benefits was sought was subject to the limitation that no alteration could take effect in relation to active members unless the following criteria were fulfilled: (1) the actuary certified that the alteration or modification did 'not substantially prejudice the interests of such members'; (2) the actuary certified that, to the extent to which such members' interests were prejudiced, 'substantially equivalent benefits' were provided; and (3) the alteration was approved by resolution adopted at a duly convened meeting of such members.

The High Court held that this restriction to members' interests was not limited to protecting rights earned by past service, before the date of the proposed amendment but also covered the ability of current active members of the Scheme to earn future service benefits. This finding was upheld by the Court of Appeal who confirmed that the

---

[5] *BBC v BBC Pension Trust Ltd* [2024] EWCA Civ 767.

true construction of 'interests' should be read as untethered to any composite phrase, as it was used in this context in a deliberate, simple, broad and open-textured fashion. The Court held that the High Court was correct to hold that 'interests' did not have to have the same precise meaning in every context within which it appeared and that a liberal approach could be taken to the construction of words, taking into consideration the context in which they are used. The Court of Appeal also noted that one of the most valuable interests that an active member has is their ability to build benefits as their duration of pensionable service increases and that this interest is covered by the language of the amendment power.

[15.15] *Re abrdn (SLSPS) Pension Trustee Co Ltd, Petitioner*[6]—*Scottish Court of Session—Tyre, Malcolm & Doherty LJJ—occupational pension scheme—de-risking of defined benefit scheme*

This case concerned an application for directions by abrdn (SLSPS) Pension Trustee Company Limited (the 'trustee') in its capacity as trustee of the abrdn SLSPS (the 'Scheme'). Directions were sought as to whether the trustee was entitled to make a decision to enter into an arrangement in relation to a 'de-risking' process regarding the Scheme.

The defined benefit section of the Scheme was in surplus and, as there was no guarantee that this would remain the case, it was proposed to secure accrued benefits with an insurance company initially by entering into a 'buy-in' contract and to convert in due course to a 'buy-out' contract. Following negotiations between the employer and trustee, the proposed arrangement was also to involve an augmentation of defined benefit members' benefits, financed by part of the 'surplus' assets of the Scheme, and also the replacement of discretionary pension increases with guaranteed CPI-linked increases on buy-out. Finally, it was proposed that the remaining surplus would be paid to the employer. However, the Scheme rules made no specific provision for what should be done with any surplus.

The trustee sought directions from the Court in respect of certain matters including: (i) whether it was entitled to enter into the buy-in and buy-out agreement, including securing fixed increases and if doing so was in accordance with the Scheme Rules and trustee's fiduciary duties; (ii) whether surplus assets were the subject of a resulting trust; (iii) if the resulting trust operated in favour of the last participating employers or also former participating employers; and (iv) did the surplus, which was the subject of a resulting trust, only operate following buy-out and sufficient provision having been made for wind-up expenses? In short, the Court answered in the affirmative in relation to all questions.

Power to enter into the de-risking arrangements and the trustee's fiduciary duties

As a preliminary point, the Court noted it was not being asked to express an opinion on whether the trustee's discretion should be exercised in the manner proposed. The Court

---

[6] *Re abrdn (SLSPS) Pension Trustee Co Ltd, Petitioner* [2023] CSIH 31.

noted a trustee may not surrender to the Court a discretion that has been vested in the trustee by the trust deed. Rather the Court was being asked if the trustee was entitled to enter the proposed arrangements. In respect of whether the trustee was entitled to enter the buy-in and buy-out transactions, the Court looked at this question from two perspectives.

First, it agreed that the decision was one the trustee was entitled to make under the powers vested in the trustee by the trust deed and rules of the Scheme.

Second, the Court considered whether it could interfere with the exercise of a trustee's discretion in entering into such arrangements and confirmed there was no basis for it doing so. As the trustee had sought appropriate professional advice and taken into consideration all material matters, the Court was satisfied that entering into the buy-in and buy-out was a decision that a pension trustee, acting reasonably, was entitled to make. The Court noted that the arrangement as a whole benefited the members by removing the risk that, at some future date, the fund might come to be insufficient to meet the full cost of pensions. In addition, the Court referred to the fact that enhanced benefits had been secured for members following lengthy negotiation in which the trustee acted in members' interests.

Are surplus assets the subject of a resulting trust?

This aspect of the decision turned on the particular circumstances of the Scheme governing documentation which did not contain a provision regarding what would happen to surplus assets on wind up. The Court agreed that a resulting trust in favour of the employer arose as a matter of law. The Court stated that:

> 'the essence of the emergence of a resulting trust is that the purpose of the trust has been fulfilled, leaving a surplus of funds in the hands of the trustee which is not required for the trust purposes. In those circumstances the truster becomes entitled to have the unused funds returned to him'.

In whose favour does the resulting trust operate?

In principle, the Court held that any surplus that is held on resulting trust is for those who provided it. The Court was satisfied that this was to be held for those who were participating employers immediately before the date when no members remained in pensionable service under the scheme. The Court was also satisfied that no other former participating employers whose participation has terminated retained any entitlement to share in the surplus.

When does a surplus which is the subject of a resulting trust arise?

The surplus only emerges once all the members' benefits have been secured on buy-out and all other liabilities and winding-up costs have been provided for, and until then, a surplus has not emerged.

[15.16] *Campbell v NHS Business Services Authority*[7]—*Court of Appeal of England and Wales—Asplin LJ—appeal from decision of Pensions Ombudsman—National Health Service Pension Scheme Regulations*[8]—*pension entitlement—whether employee died within pensionable employment*

The appellant's wife had been employed by an NHS trust and had been a member of the NHS Pension Scheme. Having been informed that she had limited life expectancy, she applied to commute ill-health retirement benefits and sought a lump sum payment. Her application was approved by her employer and her employment was terminated on the grounds of capability due to ill health. She died shortly thereafter on 6 June 2018.

The respondent refused to authorise the payment of the commuted ill-health benefits. The appellant (acting as the administrator of his wife's estate) complained to the Pensions Ombudsman, who dismissed the complaint on the basis that, taking into account the appellant's wife's outstanding annual leave, she had technically died in service because she was still in pensionable employment until 20 June 2018. The appellant appealed the decision, arguing that the phrase 'retires from pensionable employment' in the National Health Service Pension Scheme Regulations 1995 (the '1995 Regulations') only required that the member retire in the ordinary sense of having ceased to work.

The Court of Appeal of England and Wales dismissed the appeal. The words 'retires' and 'retirement' were not defined in the 1995 Regulations. The Court therefore held that the natural meaning of the words, when read in context, was that pensionable employment was treated as continuing until the end of the period of untaken leave for which payment was made. As such, despite the fact that the appellant's wife's employment had terminated as a result of ill health, under the 1995 Regulations, she had not retired from pensionable employment at the date of her death.

[15.17] *Avon Cosmetics Ltd v Dalriada Trustees Ltd*[9]—*High Court of England and Wales—Davis-White KC—pension scheme—validity of amendment to scheme*

This case concerned the validity of an amendment made by the defendants to a pension scheme, of which the claimant was the principal employer. The effect of the amendment was to close the final salary section of the scheme to future accrual and introduce career average revalued earnings ('CARE') for future service benefits. It also severed the final salary link for then active members of the scheme who were members of that section.

However, the amendment power in the trust deed prohibited any changes which would prejudicially affect the accrued rights of members. Although the impact of the changes on the accrued rights of members would only be clear once the benefits crystallised, members could be categorised into two categories: those who would be worse off as

---

[7] *Campbell v NHS Business Services Authority* [2023] EWCA Civ 1377.
[8] National Health Service Pension Scheme Regulations (SI 1995/300).
[9] *Avon Cosmetics Ltd v Dalriada Trustees Ltd* [2024] EWHC 317 (Ch), see also related judgment *Avon Cosmetics Ltd v Dalriada Trustees Ltd* [2024] EWHC 34.

a result of the amendment and those who would be better off, depending on salary increases and the rate at which their deferred salary benefits were to be revalued.

A compromise was reached with those members who would be worse off, with an underpin providing that, if a calculation based on final salary provided a greater sum than that achieved by the revaluation, that final salary method of calculation would be accepted. This compromise having been reached, the Court was asked to consider only the validity of the amendment regarding those members in light of the restriction contained in the amendment power.

It was submitted by the defendants that the effect of the restriction in the amendment power was to invalidate the amendment in its entirety and that it was not possible to sever the impact of the amendment regarding different categories of members. The claimant submitted that the impact of the restriction on amendment only had the potential to invalidate the amendment with regard to those members whose accrued benefits were negatively impacted.

The Court concluded that, in the case of an excessive execution of power, it would incline to uphold validity as far as possible. Where the exercise of power can be conceptually separated into two parts, the valid and the invalid, the valid part can be preserved either through severance or by an implication of limitation of the terms. To do so, the Court had to be satisfied that the defendants, having understood the limitations to their exercise of power, would still have exercised it in the same way.

Determining this required an objective assessment of the defendants' intention which, per *Re Hastings-Bass*,[10] did not entail an investigation into the defendants' actual state of mind. Rather, the Court was to determine whether the power had been exercised in order to give effect to the substantial purpose of the amendment. If the substantial purpose had been to give effect to the part which could be considered valid, the exercise of power resulting in invalidity was considered incidental. Confirming that two categories of members were sufficiently distinct categories, it was held that the substantial purpose of the amendment had been to sever the link to the final salary and benefits by a move toward the CARE basis. As this could not be done fully in the case of the members negatively impacted, the amendment was invalid insofar as they were concerned. However, the other members still fell within the substantial purpose of the amendment, and it was valid in so far as it related to those members.

---

[10] *Re Hastings-Bass* [1975] Ch 25.

Chapter 16

Redundancy

INTRODUCTION

[16.01]

Collective Redundancy

Two collective redundancies decisions are noted. In *CL v DB*, the European Court of Justice considered the concept of redundancy for the purpose of the application of Directive 98/59/EC, and in *Debenhams Retail (Ireland) Ltd v Crowe*, the Labour Court considered whether the collective redundancy consultation process commenced in good time in the context of the liquidation of Debenhams.

Redundancy Payments—Layoff

Two Labour Court decisions involving the triggering of a redundancy situation by reason of layoff are noted, namely *Northway Personnel Ltd v Nacu* and *Parnells GAA Club v Fogarty*.

Statutory Redundancy

Whether a redundancy dismissal occurred was considered by the Labour Court in *Frank McHale t/a Stacks Bar v Joyce*.

COLLECTIVE REDUNDANCY

[16.02] *CL v DB*[1]—*European Court of Justice—reference for a preliminary ruling from Spain—social policy—Directive 98/59/EC,*[2] *arts 1(1)(a) and*

---

[1] *CL, GO, GN, VO, TI, HZ, DN and DL v DB and Fondo de Garantía Salarial (Fogasa)* (Case C-196/23) [Plamaro].
[2] Directive 98/59/EC on the approximation of the laws of the Member States relating to collective redundancies.

2—collective redundancies—obligation to inform and consult workers' representatives—scope—termination of employment contracts on the ground of the employer's retirement—Charter of Fundamental Rights of the European Union, arts 27 and 30

This request for a preliminary ruling concerned the interpretation of Directive 98/59/EC on the approximation of the laws of the Member States relating to collective redundancies. The request was made in Spanish proceedings between the applicant workers and their former employer, the respondent.

In June 2020, the eight applicants were notified that their employment contracts were to be terminated due to the respondent's impending retirement. The respondent's company owned eight establishments. As a result of the respondent's retirement, some 54 contracts of employment in those establishments were terminated, including those of the applicants.

The applicants brought an action before the Social Court of Barcelona, challenging what they claimed were unlawful dismissals. That action was dismissed and the applicants appealed to the High Court of Justice of Catalonia (the referring Court), arguing that the dismissals were null and void due to the failure to consult the workers' representatives. The referring Court noted that the consultation procedure provided for in Spanish legislation did not envisage dismissals resulting from the retirement of the 'natural person' employer. It wondered, however, whether such a position was compliant with Directive 98/59/EC, and, if not, whether the applicants might rely on that Directive, even though it had not been correctly implemented in domestic law. In those circumstances, the referring Court decided to stay the proceedings and to refer two questions to the European Court of Justice ('ECJ') for a preliminary ruling.

By its first question, the referring Court asked, in essence, whether arts 1(1) and 2 of Directive 98/59/EC, read together, must be interpreted as precluding a national law in which the termination of the employment contracts of a number of workers—greater than that provided for in art 1(1)—as a result of the employer's retirement is not classed as a 'collective redundancy' and does not give rise to an obligation to inform and consult the workers' representatives.

The respondent submitted that an employer who is a natural person should, in the same way as his or her workers, be able to legitimately retire and thus bring all of the employment contracts to an end. An employer's retirement is a foreseeable event and a consultation procedure is irrelevant where the dismissals are connected with the employer's inevitable retirement.

The ECJ, however, found that the concept of 'redundancy' in art 1(1)(a) of Directive 98/59/EC cannot be given a narrow definition. The concept does not require that the underlying causes of the termination of employment reflect the employer's wishes; nor can a termination escape the application of the Directive just because it depends on external circumstances not contingent on the employer's will. The purpose of consulting workers is not only to avoid or reduce collective redundancies, but to mitigate their consequences. Such consultations therefore were held to 'remain relevant where the foreseen terminations are connected with the employer's retirement'. The employer contemplates those terminations in the light of his or her retirement and, in principle, is capable 'of conducting consultations seeking, *inter alia*, to avoid those terminations or to reduce their numbers or, in any event, to mitigate their consequences'. These circumstances are to be differentiated from the death of an employer, where it has previously been held that the Directive does not apply.

The ECJ stated that it 'mattered little' that situations such as those at issue in the main proceedings were not classified as 'redundancies' in Spanish law. They were 'in point of fact' terminations of the contract of employment against the will of the worker, and were therefore redundancies for the purposes of Directive 98/59/EC. To interpret the national law as narrowly as was suggested would 'alter the scope' of the Directive, and thus 'deprive it of its full effect'. Accordingly, arts 1(1) and 2 of Directive 98/59/EC were to be interpreted as precluding such legislation.

By its second question, the referring Court asked, in essence, whether EU law must be interpreted as requiring a national Court to disapply a national law such as that as issue in the main proceedings, in the event that it is contrary to arts 1(1) and 2 of Directive 98/59/EC.

The ECJ observed that the national Court's obligation to refer to EU law when interpreting and applying relevant domestic law is limited by general principles of law, and cannot produce a *contra legem* interpretation. It would be for the referring Court to decide whether the national law at issue in the main proceedings could be interpreted in a manner compliant with the Directive. However, arts 1(1) and 2 could not of themselves be relied upon in a dispute between individuals to require a national Court to disapply a national law held to be contrary to those provisions. Nor could arts 27 and 30 of the Charter of Fundamental Rights be invoked, either on their own or with arts 1(1) and 2 of Directive 98/59/EC, in a dispute such as that in the main proceedings, to require a national Court to set aside a non-compliant law.

Accordingly, EU law was not to be interpreted as requiring national Courts to disapply a non-Directive compliant national law, such as that at issue in the main proceedings.

[16.03] *Debenhams Retail (Ireland) Ltd v Crowe[3]—Labour Court—appeal from Workplace Relations Commission—Protection of Employment Act 1977—collective redundancies—consultation process—commencement date—whether the consultation process commenced in good time and/or at the earliest opportunity*

The respondent employer, which was in liquidation, appealed against a WRC decision upholding a complaint under the Protection of Employment Act 1977.

The claimant commenced work in 1996 as a shop assistant with the respondent, working 20 hours per week. She alleged that the respondent breached its consultation obligations when it was contemplating collective redundancies.

The complaints named the respondent and the respondent 'in liquidation' separately. The claimant argued that both entities existed over the cognisable period and both had

---

[3] *Debenhams Retail (Ireland) Ltd v Crowe* PED241.

responsibilities towards her. There was a dispute as to when the consultation process commenced and whether it did so 'in good time' or at the earliest opportunity.

On 9 April 2020, staff were informed in an email from the respondent's director of its decision to cease trading. The email explained that Debenhams UK, the respondent's sole shareholder, would no longer be in a position to fund its Irish operation. The email expressed regret over the decision and thanked staff for their service and loyalty. In the claimant's submission, this was a clear indication that the respondent was contemplating redundancies on 9 April 2020 and the consultation should have commenced no later than that date.

In a letter to the employees' representative dated 14 April 2020, the respondent's HR director advised of proposed redundancies but made no reference to a requirement for consultation with the employees. On 16 April 2020, staff were advised that a liquidator had been appointed that day and that a consultation with union representatives was scheduled for the following day, 17 April. It was on that date that the consultation process started, according to the claimant. At this first consultation meeting, the respondent acknowledged that there had been a lack of communication over a number of days and apologised for the delay.

A letter from the provisional liquidators on 23 April 2020 advised workers that the respondent would enter into a 30-day consultation period with union representatives. A second consultation meeting was suggested to the union, which took place on 28 April 2020. There, representatives pointed out that their members required information as to the assets that would form part of the liquidation, such as stock, leases and profits from the online site. The liquidators indicated that they were still in talks with the UK company and that these issues would be clarified.

In a letter of 5 May 2020, the union highlighted the shortfall in information to date and sought an extension of the 30-day consultation period. A third consultation meeting took place on 7 May 2020 and the union raised concerns about the paucity of information received, now two-thirds of the way through the consultation process. The liquidators indicated that they were still in discussions with the UK company regarding the division of revenue from the website, but the position was that the UK company owned the property leases in Ireland and was asserting ownership of stock in the Irish stores; nor did the UK company intend to support its Irish operation going forward. The liquidators did not see a basis for extending the consultation period. In a letter dated 11 May 2020, the union put the liquidators on notice that workers were now in dispute with the respondent.

At a fourth consultation meeting on 15 May 2020, the liquidators advised that discussions concerning the legal ownership of the stock were ongoing. Again, the liquidators saw no basis for extending the consultation period and expressed the view that to do so would be irresponsible. By letter of 20 May 2020, the liquidators informed workers that the consultation period had come to an end and that they were being made redundant.

The respondent submitted that it was only one legal entity and that the second set of complaints were duplicates.

While not disputing the timeline of events, the respondent submitted that it would have been known to the union that the respondent had been loss making for years and that it was placed in examinership in 2016. The respondent was itself caught unawares when it received word that its funding from the UK was being withdrawn. Once provisional liquidators were appointed, management of the respondent lost its authority.

Overall, the respondent argued, the chronology of events did not suggest any breach of the Protection of Employment Act 1977. The respondent was alerted to the withdrawal of its funding on 8 April 2020 and the consultation process, in its submission, commenced on 14 April 2020, when the sole shareholder consented to seeking the appointment of a liquidator. It submitted that the claimant was reading an 'urgency' into the legislation that was not in fact there.

The Court, in the first instance, decided that there were two cases properly before it since the legal personality of a company, once dissolved, continues for the limited purpose of fulfilling its legal obligations. The adding of the words 'in liquidation' to the title of the respondent in the second case was a requirement in company law.

The Court noted that the respondent's letter of 14 April 2020, referencing the proposed redundancies, made no mention of consultations within the meaning of the Protection of Employment Act 1977 and correspondence from the liquidators acknowledged that consultations began on 17 April 2020, as contended by the claimant. The Court concurred.

It was also apparent that the respondent was aware of its responsibilities under the Protection of Employment Act 1977 and, indeed, from the minutes of its board meeting on 9 April 2020, it was aware that collective redundancies were a real possibility. The Court concluded that the consultation did not commence in good time, or at the earliest opportunity. By delaying the process until after liquidators had been appointed, the respondent, already in a precarious position, limited the options available for coming to an agreement with union representatives. The consultation should have started on 9 April 2020 and the respondent was in breach of the Protection of Employment Act 1977.

The Court awarded compensation of four weeks' pay and the WRC decision was upheld.

REDUNDANCY PAYMENTS—LAYOFF

[16.04] *Northway Personnel Ltd v Nacu*[4]—*Labour Court—appeal from Workplace Relations Commission—Redundancy Payments Acts 1967 to 2014, s 12—redundancy by reason of layoff—notice*

The claimant appealed against the WRC's dismissal of his complaint under the Redundancy Payments Acts 1967 to 2014.

---

[4] *Northway Personnel Ltd v Nacu* RPD2418.

The respondent was a licensed employment agency supplying construction workers. The claimant commenced employment as an agency worker with the respondent on 21 November 2016 and was assigned to a client's worksite. When that job was complete, the claimant was placed on layoff with effect from 5 May 2023. By letter dated 29 June 2023, he received an offer of alternative employment in Kilkenny, to commence the following morning. The claimant resided some 120km from Kilkenny and, lacking private means of transport, declined the respondent's employment offer.

The claimant initiated a claim for redundancy by reason of layoff on 30 June 2023. He did so using Form RP77. When no response was forthcoming from the respondent, he referred a complaint to the WRC.

The respondent's solicitor contended that the claimant should have used Form RP9; because the claimant had submitted the wrong form, he was not entitled to a redundancy payment by reason of layoff. The respondent also submitted that it made a further offer of employment to the claimant on 17 August 2023. Otherwise, no one appeared to give evidence on behalf of the respondent.

The Labour Court took the view that it would be unjustly harsh on the claimant to determine that he had not put the respondent on notice of his intention to claim redundancy simply because he had used an incorrect form, neither RP77 nor RP9 being 'statutory forms'. The respondent was clearly aware that it had placed the claimant on layoff on 5 May 2023. That period of layoff had continued for more than four consecutive weeks by the time the respondent received the claimant's RP77.

In the absence of any evidence that the respondent did not regard the RP77 as notice of the claimant's intention to claim redundancy, the Court found that the claimant was entitled to seek a redundancy payment following a period of layoff by the respondent. The respondent did not avail itself of the opportunity to make a counter-notice to the claimant within one week of the claimant's notice. It followed that the claimant's appeal succeeded and he was entitled to a redundancy lump sum payment, calculated at €945 per week for the relevant period of employment: 21 November 2016 to 5 May 2023.

[16.05] *Parnells GAA Club v Fogarty*[5]—*Labour Court—appeal from Workplace Relations Commission—Redundancy Payments Acts 1967 to 2014—no notice of layoff provided—employment relationship not terminated by reason of redundancy*

The claimant appealed against the WRC's dismissal of his complaint under the Redundancy Payments Acts 1967 to 2014.

The respondent closed its premises on 12 March 2020, due to the Covid-19 pandemic. From that date, the claimant was not provided with work or wages by the respondent. He confirmed that no notice of layoff or termination was given to him at the time, or at any time since. He served an RP9 form on the respondent on 4 May 2020, though there was no substantive response. The respondent chose not to attend the appeal hearing.

---

[5] *Parnells GAA Club v Fogarty* RPD2419, RPD2420.

The Labour Court concluded that, in the absence of notice from the respondent that he was being laid off or terminated, the claimant's employment did not cease by reason of layoff or termination on 12 March 2020, or at any other time. It followed that the serving of a notice to claim redundancy on 4 May 2020 could have no meaning because the claimant was not at that time, or at any time, laid off within the meaning of the Redundancy Payments Acts 1967 to 2014. The employment relationship therefore remained in being, albeit the respondent had, since March 2020, ceased to pay the claimant's wages in accordance with the terms of his employment and to provide him with work.

Because the claimant had not been dismissed from his employment by reason of redundancy, the complaint was not well founded and the appeal failed.

STATUTORY REDUNDANCY

[16.06] *Frank McHale t/a Stacks Bar v Joyce*[6]—*Labour Court—appeal from Workplace Relations Commission—Redundancy Payments Acts 1967 to 2014, s 19—statutory redundancy payment*

The claimant appealed against the WRC's dismissal of his complaint under the Redundancy Payments Act 1967 as being out of time and statute barred. The respondent did not attend the appeal hearing.

The claimant commenced full-time employment with the respondent in 2007. He was laid off during the Covid-19 pandemic in March 2020 but returned to work in March 2022, by which time the pub premises was under new ownership. He was then informed that the pub would be closing. The claimant submitted that he was entitled to a statutory redundancy payment, having been made redundant when the pub closed.

Having regard to the unchallenged facts, the Court found that the claimant's position was made redundant. He was therefore entitled to a redundancy payment in respect of his service from 2007 to 2022, calculated on the basis of his weekly rate of pay of €600 per week.

The claim was therefore well founded and the WRC's decision was set aside.

---

[6] *Frank McHale t/a Stacks Bar v Joyce* RPD2416.

Chapter 17

Taxation

INTRODUCTION

[17.01]

Karshan

The various changes to the Irish tax regime that affect employers and employees are considered below, including, most notably, the changes relating to the classification of employment status in Ireland for tax purposes following the landmark Supreme Court judgment last year in *Revenue Commissioners v Karshan (Midlands) Ltd t/a Domino's Pizza*[1] (the '*Karshan* judgment'). The Irish Revenue ('Revenue') issued updated guidance on the classification of employment status for tax purposes in May 2024. In order to determine whether a worker is an employee or self-employed for taxation purposes, the new Revenue Guidelines describe the applicable decision-making framework as consisting of five questions. Details of this new decision-making framework are set out below.

Enhanced Reporting for Employee Benefits

Another notable development was the introduction of the enhanced reporting obligations ('ERR') for employee benefits. The enhanced reporting requirement came into operation on 1 January 2024, with employers required to report from this date. However, Revenue has been operating what is known as 'Service for Compliance', whereby no penalties are due for non-compliance until the end of 2024, with the aim of giving employers time to fully implement the new measures and put the necessary procedures in place. Details of the obligations are also set out below.

Tax Costs

Employment tax cases are also noted. Irish High Court cases this year include a case on the interpretation of the term 'proprietary director' under s 472(1)(a) of the Taxes

---

[1] *Revenue Commissioners v Karshan (Midlands) Ltd t/a Domino's Pizza* [2023] IESC 24, see *Arthur Cox Employment Law Yearbook 2023* at [4.14].

Consolidation Act 1997 ('TCA 1997') in the context of a claim for transborder workers relief by the taxpayers.[2] The High Court also handed down a judgment that gives much needed clarity on the application of s 192A of the TCA 1997 to the tax treatment of *ex gratia* termination payments in an employment-related dispute context.[3]

Key Determinations of the first-tier Tax Appeal Commission ('TAC') are also considered. The TAC is the first-tier tribunal whose role is to hear and determine appeals against decisions and determinations of the Revenue Commissioners concerning taxes and duties. Appeals from the TAC can be made on a point of law to the High Court, from which another appeal on a point of law can be made to the Court of Appeal.

The UK courts have also been grappling with the determination of employment status and we have included the recent UK Supreme Court judgment in *Professional Game Match Officials Ltd*,[4] which ruled that football referees may be employees on a match-by-match basis. We also examine other notable cases before the UK Upper Tribunal dealing with the question of employment status, and the application of the intermediaries legislation ('IR35').

REVENUE eBRIEF UPDATES

[17.02] Revenue eBriefs are short articles produced by the Irish Revenue Commissioners which highlight the latest changes and updates to the Irish tax regime and practice set out in Revenue Tax and Duty Manuals ('TDM'). Tax and Duty Manuals are documents that contain the rules, guidelines, procedures and practices that cover the whole range of Revenue activities.

The various changes this year are set out below, including changes relating to remote working relief, the income tax return for 2023, the guidelines on the statutory time limits for making or amending PAYE assessments on employers, the code of practice on determining employment status, and a new enhanced employer reporting obligations regime for certain employee benefits.

Relief for Key Employees Engaged in Research and Development Activities

[17.03] On 27 August 2024, Revenue issued *eBrief 228/24* stating that TDM Part 15-01-40 has been updated to reflect the provisions of s 766C of the TCA 1997. Section 766C was introduced in the Finance Act 2022 and was subsequently amended in the Finance Act (No.2) 2023. From 1 January 2023, a key employee may avail of a reduction in their income tax liability as a result of the surrender by their employer

---

2   *Revenue Commissioners v Aidan Hennessy and Gerard Hennessy* [2024] IEHC 245, at **[17.34]**.
3   *Siddiqi v The Revenue Commissioners* [2024] IEHC 195, at **[17.35]**.
4   *Commissioners for His Majesty's Revenue and Customs v Professional Game Match Officials Ltd* [2024] UKSC 29, at **[17.36]**.

company of some or all of the research and development corporation tax credit to which that company was entitled under s 766C.

The manual has been updated throughout to reflect how s 766C interacts with this relief. In addition, the examples in the manual have been refreshed to account for tax credits and tax bands applicable for the 2023 and 2024 years of assessment.

Employer-Provided Vehicles

[17.04] On 20 August 2024, Revenue published *eBrief 219/24* stating that TDM Part 05-01-01b was updated. They updated para 4.1 to outline the current treatment pertaining to the cash equivalent calculation at the start of the para for clarity.

Further to the Finance (No 2) Act 2023, para 4.1.3 was updated to reflect the extension of the temporary reduction to open market value ('OMV') and para 6.3 was updated to reflect the extension of relief available in respect of battery electric vehicles to 2027. The table at para 6.3.2, which summarises the battery electric vehicle regime, was also updated.

A new para 6.3.1 has been added to show the combined effect of the temporary reduction to OMV and relief available in respect of battery electric vehicles. Example 10, which demonstrates the combined effect, was also updated.

In Appendix A, a table has been included showing the business mileage applicable from 1 January 2023.

Guidelines on PAYE Assessments

[17.05] On 30 July 2024, Revenue issued *eBrief 206/24* stating that TDM Part 42-04-72—Guidelines on PAYE Assessments was updated, both in the Introduction and by the addition of para 6.2, to reflect amendments made by the Finance (No 2) Act 2023, introducing a statutory time limit on the making or amending of PAYE assessments on employers. Additional guidance on how to appeal a PAYE assessment is included.

The Employers' Guide to PAYE from 1 January 2019

[17.06] On 17 July 2024, Revenue published *eBrief 201/24* stating that TDM Part 42-04-35A was updated as follows:

— updated list of applicants who can submit a paper application to register as an employer;
— updated contact information for Revenue offices throughout;
— details of employer obligations under enhanced reporting requirements;
— updated guidance in relation to service charges (tips) paid out by/on behalf of an employer;

- updated guidance in relation to annual membership fees paid to a professional body;
- notification regarding the eSARP portal available in ROS; and
- detailed guidance in relation to employer obligations throughout the income tax year.

Revenue Guidelines for Determining Employment Status

Updates to Other Relevant TDMs

[17.07] On 15 July 2024, Revenue issued *eBrief 194/24* setting out the TDMs which have been updated in light of the publication of TDM Part 05-01-30—Revenue Guidelines for Determining Employment Status for Taxation Purposes.

The following TDMs were updated:

- Part 04-01-07 Taxation of Couriers;
- Part 04-01-17 Code of Practice on Determining Employment Status (Employed or Self-Employed);
- Part 05-01-11 Part-time Lecturers/Teachers/Trainers;
- Part 05-01-15 Agency Workers;
- Part 05-01-20 Individuals described as 'locums' engaged in the fields of medicine, health care and pharmacy;
- Part 05-01-24 Taxation of Exam Setters, Exam Correctors, Exam Attendants, Invigilators, etc; and
- Part 42-04-55 National Co-op Farm Relief Service Operators.

Special Assignee Relief Programme

[17.08] On 12 July 2024, Revenue published *eBrief 189/24* stating that TDM Part 34-00-10 was updated to provide guidance on the calculation of special assignee relief programme ('SARP') relief in re-grossed net pay/benefit cases.

Schedule E Basis of Charge

[17.09] On 1 July 2024, Revenue issued *eBrief 181/24* stating that TDM Part 05-01-08 Schedule E, Basis of Charge was updated to improve ease of reference to relevant guidance, to include additional hyperlinks, and to update examples where relevant.

PAYE Reviews Where Week 53 Applies

[17.10] On 19 June 2024, Revenue published *eBrief 170/24* stating that TDM Part 42-04-07 was updated to reflect the 2024 tax rate bands and tax credits in the examples provided.

Tax Treatment of the Reimbursement of Expenses of Travel and Subsistence to Office Holders and Employees

[17.11] On 04 June 2024, Revenue issued *eBrief 151/24* stating that TDM Part 05-01-06 was updated as follows:

Paragraph 1.4

Paragraph 1.4 was reviewed to include guidance regarding the mandatory reporting by employers under enhanced reporting requirements ('ERR'). The payment of travel and subsistence expenses free of tax comes within the scope of the ERR.

Appendix 1

Appendix 1 was updated to reflect the increases in the civil service subsistence rates that apply from 14 December 2023.

Returns by Employers in Relation to Reportable Benefits—Enhanced Reporting Requirements

[17.12] On 1 July 2024, Revenue published *eBrief 179/24* stating that TDM Part 38-03-33 was updated in para 1, to confirm that, in relation to the period 01 July 2024 to 31 December 2024, Revenue will continue to support employers in relation to enhanced reporting requirement ('ERR') obligations and will not seek to apply penalties for non-compliance.

The ERR came into operation on 1 January 2024, with employers required to report from this date. However, Revenue have been operating what is known as 'Service for Compliance' whereby no penalties are due for non-compliance until the end of 2024, with the aim of giving employers time to fully implement the new measures and put the necessary procedures in place. From 1 January 2025, ERR will form part of employer interventions, with normal sanctions and penalties for non-compliance applying.

The new s 897C of the TCA 1997 requires an employer to notify Revenue on or before the provision to an employee of any of the three reportable benefits:

— the remote working daily allowance of €3.20;

- the payment of travel and subsistence expenses; and
- the small benefit exemption.

It is up to the employer to determine, in advance of the benefit being given, whether the conditions for tax-free payment have been satisfied.

In relation to the remote working daily allowance, an administrative practice operated by Revenue allows an employer to make payments up to €3.20 to employees, for each day worked from home, subject to certain conditions being satisfied, without the need to deduct income tax, USC or PRSI.

Revenue requires employers to report the following details:

- total number of remote working days;
- amount paid; and
- date paid to the employee/director.

In respect of travel and subsistence payments, expenses of travel (and subsistence relating to that travel) incurred by an office holder or employee in the performance of their office or employment can, subject to conditions, be reimbursed without deduction of income tax, USC and PRSI. The expense would then be subject to ERR. However, an advance payment to an office holder or employee in respect of expenses is subject to tax via the payroll and as such would not fall within the scope of ERR.

To alleviate the practical issues for employers in complying with these ERR requirements, Revenue has implemented an optional administrative practice in respect of advance travel and subsistence payments. This practice allows advance travel and subsistence payments to be treated as not being subject to tax via the payroll and therefore subject to ERR reporting if certain conditions are met. When the expense is incurred and claimed by the employee, the employer must then reconcile their ERR submission to Revenue in a timely manner to reflect the actual travel and subsistence expense amount.

Reporting under ERR is not required where untaxed payments for travel and subsistence expenses are reimbursed to individuals who work on a voluntary and unpaid basis for organisations which operate on a not-for-profit basis.

Revenue requires employers to report the following details:

- amount paid; and
- date paid to the employee/director.

In respect of the small benefit exemption, employers may offer tax-free benefits to employees in the form of vouchers or other benefits within the remit of s 112B of the TCA 1997.

Revenue requires employers to report the following details:

- value of the benefit; and
- date provided to the employee.

There are three reporting mechanisms available to employers:

1. *Direct reporting software packages:* direct reporting software packages can integrate with Revenue systems via a dedicated Application Programming Interface channel to allow for the reporting of non-taxable payment information.
2. *ROS File upload:* employers also have the option to input the required information to a file which they can upload directly to their Revenue Online Service ('ROS') account.
3. *ROS Online Form:* using the online form, employers can input the required information directly into ROS.

Determining Employment Status for Taxation Purposes[5]

[17.13] On 21 May 2024, Revenue published *eBrief 140/24* stating that a new TDM was created to outline the implications for determining employment status for taxation purposes arising from the Supreme Court *Karshan* judgment.[6] In that case, the Supreme Court examined the difference in treatment between employees and self-employed persons engaged as independent contractors and, ultimately reformulated and restated the law in this area in Ireland. Overturning the decision of the Court of Appeal, the Supreme Court held that delivery drivers were properly categorised by Revenue as employees and not as independent contractors.

The Revenue Guidelines for Determining Employment Status for Taxation Purposes, contained in Part 05-01-30 of the *Tax and Duty Manual*, were issued to provide guidance on the tax implications of the *Karshan* judgment. The guidelines set out the key elements of the decision and the effect it will have on employers, which is illustrated through an exploration of several practical examples.

In order to determine whether a worker is an employee or self-employed for taxation purposes, the guidelines describe the applicable decision-making framework as consisting of five questions which can be summarised as relating to:

1. the work/wage bargain;
2. personal service;
3. control;
4. all the circumstances of the employment; and
5. the legislative context.

According to the guidelines, the first three questions should be viewed as a 'filter', meaning that all three must be answered affirmatively if the possibility of an employment contract is to exist. If this requirement is satisfied, questions four and five will be considered to determine if an employment contract exists in the circumstances.

---

[5] See also **Ch 4**, Employment Litigation.
[6] *Revenue Commissioners v Karshan (Midlands) Ltd t/a Domino's Pizza* [2023] IESC 24, see *Arthur Cox Employment Law Yearbook 2023* at [4.14].

The first question asks whether the contract involves the exchange of wages or other remuneration for work, which is necessary if a working arrangement is to be categorised as an employment contract. Arrangements which lack consideration, or which are truly casual or domestic in nature will not meet this requirement. However, the guidelines note that there need not necessarily be continuity of obligation—in other words, an individual 'can be considered an employee in respect of one '"job"'.

The second question considers whether the worker has agreed to provide their services to the employer personally. This is known as the 'substitution test' as it concerns the worker's right to subcontract or appoint a third party to carry out all or part of the work. The more restrictions imposed on a worker's freedom to appoint a substitute, the more likely it is that the arrangement is that of an employment contract.

The third question considers 'the ability, authority, or right of a business to exercise control over a worker' regarding the nature of their work and the manner in which it is conducted. The guidelines explain that this part of the test is a 'gateway' which considers the minimum level of control necessary for a relationship to be an employment contract; this will differ according to the nature of the employment. Matters to be considered include the 'enterprise test' (which examines where the economic risk lies as between the parties to the arrangement), the question of integration, notice periods, and control over payment and working hours. Finally, the guidelines emphasise that it is the right of the employer to exercise control which is relevant, rather than whether they actually exercise that right in practice.

The fourth question, namely all the circumstances of the employment, is a broad one which the guidelines describe as an examination of 'the entire factual matrix of the engagement'. Factors to be considered include: the factual matrix in which the contract was concluded; and the actual dealings between the parties. The guidelines also note that this part of the inquiry is free standing (in other words, it does not depend on the findings made in the other parts) and that, if the finding is that the contract is not one of employment, the matter should be resolved by identifying what it actually is.

The fifth and final question looks to the legislative context, and involves a consideration of whether any legislation requires 'an adjustment or supplement to any of the foregoing questions in the particular circumstances'. In other words, the guidelines affirm that certain legislative schemes might require modification of the test or, indeed, the approach taken to the relationship between the written contract and the parties' dealings in practice.

[17.14] The guidelines include the following diagram:

Decision Tree from Revenue Guidelines for Determining Employment Status for Taxation Purposes

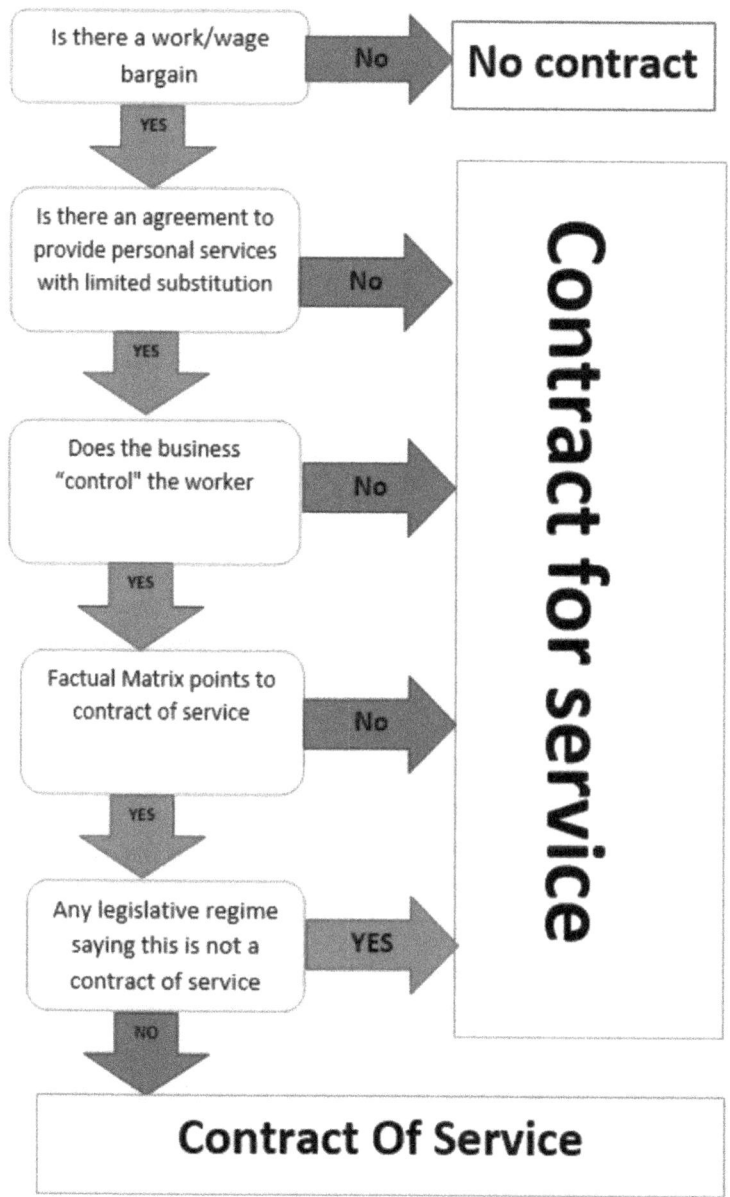

TDM Part 05-01-30—Revenue Guidelines for Determining Employment Status for Taxation Purposes, Figure 1[7]

---

[7] Information provided courtesy of the Revenue Commissioners under a Creative Commons Attribution 4.0 International (CC BY 4.0) licence.

The guidelines contain commentary on workers engaged in particular sectors, such as workers engaged in the construction, telecommunications, information technology, healthcare, courier, and entertainment industries—as well as part-time, casual or seasonal workers, public sector workers and platform workers.

The guidelines also provide commentary on the provision of workers through a company and through an employment agency. It confirms the existing view that an engagement of companies by businesses cannot constitute contracts of service, or employment, for taxation purposes; however, it notes that the status of those workers contracting with the company should be analysed.

In addition to the commentary, several practical examples designed to assist businesses by illustrating the manner in which the *Karshan* judgment may be applied to certain working arrangements are included.

From the perspective of businesses, Revenue's interpretation of the *Karshan* judgment as contained in the Guidelines provides welcome clarity on the determination of the employment status of workers for taxation purposes.

Provision of Miscellaneous Benefits

[17.15] On 21 May 2024, Revenue published *eBrief 139/24* to confirm changes to TDM Part 05-01-011. The main updates relate to the following:

Paragraph 8.1

Paragraph 8.1 provides additional guidance regarding the tax treatment of examination awards.

Paragraph 21

Paragraph 21 offers guidance on pension contributions to note that, since 1 January 2023, an employer's contribution to an employee's personal retirement savings account ('PRSA') is not treated as a benefit-in-kind.

Returns by Employers in Relation to Reportable Benefits—Enhanced Reporting Requirements

[17.16] On 20 May 2024, Revenue published *eBrief 138/24* to confirm that TDM Part 38-03-33 has been updated in a new para 4.2.2 to provide guidance in regard to unpaid volunteers and enhanced reporting requirements ('ERR').

Revenue do not require reporting under ERR regarding unpaid volunteers whose only payments are for travel and subsistence expenses incurred in the performance of their volunteer duties in not-for-profit organisations.

Pension Manual Chapter 14 Amended

[17.17] On 1 March 2024, Revenue issued *eBrief 056/24* to confirm changes to Chapter 14 of the Pension Manual which deals with Discontinuance of Schemes.

It has been updated to add a new para 8 containing contact details for Pensions Branch in Large Cases—High Wealth Individuals' Division.

Employee (PAYE) Tax Credit

[17.18] On 20 February 2024, Revenue issued *eBrief 044/24* updating TDM Part 15-01-07 in order to reflect the increase to the credit as provided for in the Finance Act 2023, together with a new table inserted at para 1 to show the credit amount for prior years.

Income Tax Credits and Reliefs for Individuals Over 65 and Individuals Caring for Those Over 65

[17.19] On 1 February 2024, Revenue published *eBrief 034/24* updating TDM Part 15-01-26, largely to reflect information pertaining to the 2024 year of assessment.

Remote Working Relief

[17.20] On 20 February 2024, Revenue issued *eBrief 042/24* stating that TDM Part 05-02-13 has been updated.

The main changes are as follows:

In para 4, to confirm that the remote working daily allowance applies in the case of directors, (including proprietary directors), where the director has incurred and defrayed relevant expenses 'out of the emoluments' of the office or employment of profit, that are subject to tax under the PAYE system. The relevant expenses must be 'out of' the relevant emoluments and all other conditions must be met.

In para 5, to include guidance regarding the mandatory reporting by employers under enhanced reporting requirements of the payment of a remote working daily allowance of up to €3.20.

Revenue Documentation to Verify Personal Addresses for Non-Revenue Purposes

[17.21] On 9 February 2024, Revenue published *eBrief 038/24* stating that TDM Part 37-00-16 had been updated to provide further information on updating personal name or address details in myAccount to appear on Revenue documentation.

Paragraph 2.2—Employment Detail Summary

To request an employment detail summary ('EDS'), an individual needs to be in employment or in receipt of an occupational pension. The EDS can be viewed, printed, or downloaded in MyDocuments in myAccount in a pdf format. It is important to note that once the EDS has been created for a past year it cannot be re-created with an updated change in name or address. The only time that a customer can re-request an EDS with updated personal details is if the pay and tax details have been subsequently amended by the employer/pension provider.

Customers who are non e-enabled can request their EDS from Revenue and will receive a paper copy of their EDS by post. The EDS document can be used as proof of income or proof of address where required by third parties such as financial institutions.

Paragraph 2.3—Summary of Pay and Tax Details

The customer can create this summary as a secure document (pdf) in myAccount. It can include an employee's or occupational pension recipient's:

— pay and statutory deductions for the current year as reported by the employer or pension provider; or
— full details of any payments received as submitted by the employer(s)/pension provider(s) for the last three months; or
— statements of liability for the last year or the last four tax years, where statements of liability have already been requested and issued.

A customer can select which information to include on the summary, which can be viewed, printed or downloaded in MyDocuments in myAccount. A secure, password-protected copy can be created in pdf format.

A customer can amend their own name and address. It will take overnight processing for these details to be updated on the summary. It is important to ensure all details are up to date if the customer is providing the summary to a financial institution, a solicitor or local authority as proof of income or tax paid for the purposes of applying for a loan, mortgage, grants etc.

Loss Relief for Self-Employed Individuals Adversely Impacted by Covid-19 Restrictions

[17.22] On 12 January 2024, Revenue issued *eBrief 021/24* to update TDM Part 12-01-03. The guidance confirms that a claim for relevant loss relief under s 395A of the TCA 1997 or relevant allowances under s 304(3A) can no longer be made due to the time limits provided for in the legislation. The last possible date by which a final claim could be made under s 395A or s 304(3A) was the due date for the Form 11 tax return for 2021, which was 31 October 2022.

The guidance also includes references to s 1077F and the Code of Practice for Revenue Compliance Interventions.

Income Tax Return 2023—ROS Form 11

[17.23] On 10 January 2024, Revenue issued *eBrief 015/24* to confirm changes to TDM Part 38-01-04H.

The changes are as follows:

— Information is provided on rental income paid to non-resident landlords (para 4.1) and the removal of references to s 97(2)K (para 4.2).

— The guidance provides updates to the non-refundable foreign tax panel (para 5.4).

— The guidance has been updated in respect of 'employments not subject to PAYE' panel (para 6.1).

— A reminder has been added about the amount of expenses (30%) that can be claimed as 'allowable deductions incurred in employment' (para 6.2).

— The guidance provides updates regarding social welfare payments (para 6.3) to advise that the annual amount will be shown in the summary table, filers are reminded to fill in the fields in the return in order for the income to be declared and included in the summary calculation of tax due, and social welfare payments information is prefilled from late January, so returns submitted before then should include welfare payments even if the table is not populated with information at that time.

— The guidance includes an advisory message about new questions to be added to the 'Lump sums from relevant (foreign) pension arrangements' panel to reflect the new s 200A of the TCA 1997 (para 6.4).

— The 'transborder relief' panel has been updated regarding the dropdown country field (para 7.1).

— The tax credits panel (para 8) has been updated to reflect increased values.

Income Tax (Employments) Regulations 2024

[17.24] On 9 January 2024, Revenue published *eBrief 011/24* which confirmed changes to TDM Part 42-04-71 to reflect the changes made to the Income Tax (Employments) Regulations 2018[8] as a result of the Income Tax (Employments) Regulations 2024 (the '2024 Regulations').[9]

The amendments, which are operational from 4 January 2024, are specific to the particulars which an employer must report in a notification to Revenue on or before the provision of a reportable benefit to an employee, commonly referred to as enhanced reporting requirements or 'ERR'.

The changes are as follows:

---

[8] Income Tax (Employments) Regulations 2018 (SI 345/2018).
[9] Income Tax (Employments) Regulations 2024 (SI 1/2024).

Regulation 2(1)

Regulation 2(1) is amended to include the following definitions:

— relevant particulars;
— remote working daily allowance;
— reportable benefit;
— small benefit; and
— travel and subsistence payment.

Regulation 10(1)

Regulation 10(1) has been amended to provide that where an employer has sent a prior notification in respect of a reportable benefit, the employment identifier used on that prior notification should be used, or in cases where no prior notification has been sent, an employment identifier, being a unique identifier, should be assigned to the employment of the employee where the employee's PPSN is available.

Regulation 10A

A new reg 10A is inserted which provides that, on or before the provision of any reportable benefit to an employee, an employer shall send a notification containing the relevant particulars relating to the provision of such a benefit to Revenue.

Regulation 23

The provisions of reg 23 have been extended to provide that employers must retain all documents and records relating to the provision of a reportable benefit to an employee for a period of six years after the end of the year to which they refer, or for such shorter period as Revenue may authorise and make such information available to an authorised officer.

Salary Sacrifice Arrangements

[17.25] On 4 January 2024, Revenue published *eBrief 008/24* stating TDM Part 05-01-01k-Chapter 11 has been updated, largely to refresh the examples.

Arrears of Pay Being Paid to an Employee Who Has Left an Employment

[17.26] On 3 January 2024, Revenue issued *eBrief 006/24* to confirm changes to TDM Part 42-04-24B to include the following:

Paragraph 2.1—Definition of Revenue Payroll Notification

A revenue payroll notification ('RPN') is defined in reg 2 of the 2024 Regulations as the latest notification issued or made available to an employer in respect of an employee. Employers are required to use the latest RPN available, and it must be for the tax year in which the payment is being made.

Paragraph 2.2—Link to 'The Employers' Guide to PAYE with Effect from January 2019'

Link to Part 42-04-35A—'The Employers' Guide to PAYE with effect from January 2019'—at para 2.2:

> 'in any other circumstances, tax must be deducted at the higher rate of tax applicable on the date the payment is made. Part 42-04-35A-'The Employers' Guide to PAYE with effect from January 2019' provides information on post cessation payments incorporating arrears of pay at Chapter 8.9.3'.

Removal of Material—PAYE on Arrears of Pay Prior to 2019

Removal of material regarding the operation of PAYE on arrears of pay prior to 2019.

Road Haulier Drivers Employees—Subsistence Rates

[17.27] On 3 January 2024, Revenue published *eBrief 005/24* stating that TDM Part 05-02-10 has been updated as follows:

Paragraph 4

Paragraph 4 includes guidance regarding the mandatory reporting by employers under enhanced reporting requirements ('ERR'). The payment of subsistence allowances free of tax by road haulier firms (employers) to road haulier drivers (employees) falls within the scope of the ERR.

Paragraph 5

Paragraph 5 is updated to reflect the increases in the civil service subsistence rates that apply from 14 December 2023.

Taxation of Couriers

[17.28] On 3 January 2024, Revenue published *eBrief 004/24* confirming that TDM 04-01-07 is being reviewed as part of the development of detailed guidance on the implications of the Supreme Court *Karshan* judgment. TDM 04-01-07 has been updated and published in conjunction with the detailed guidance relating to the *Karshan* judgment.[10]

Code of Practice on Determining Employment Status (Employed or Self-Employed)

[17.29] On 3 January 2024, Revenue published *eBrief 003/24* confirming that TDM Part 04-01-17 is being reviewed to reflect the judgment of Supreme Court in *Karshan*.[11]

The following TDMs that have a reference to the Code have also been updated:

— TDM 05-01-11 Part-time Lecturers/Teachers/Trainers;

— TDM 05-01-15 Agency Workers;

— TDM 05-01-20 Individuals described as 'locums' engaged in the fields of medicine, health care and pharmacy;

— TDM 05-01-24 Taxation of Exam Setters, Exam Correctors, Exam Attendants, Invigilators, etc;

— TDM 18-02-04 Relevant Contracts Tax for Principal Contractors;

— TDM 42-04-35A Employers Guide to PAYE; and

— TDM 42-04-55 National Co-op Farm Relief Service Operators

In addition to changes to the Code, Revenue will also be issuing separate guidelines to address the implications of the *Karshan* judgment.

These Guidelines were issued on 21 May and are discussed in the context of the relevant eBrief above.

EMPLOYMENT TAX CASES

IRISH TAX APPEALS COMMISSION

[17.30] *Determination 85TACD2024[12]—CT, DWT & PREM—Tax Appeals Commission— conferring of a credit to a director by means of a director's loan account falls within the definition of an emolument under Taxes Consolidation Act 1997, Sch E*

---

[10] *Revenue Commissioners v Karshan (Midlands) Ltd t/a Domino's Pizza* [2023] IESC 24, see *Arthur Cox Employment Law Yearbook 2023* at [4.14].

[11] *Revenue Commissioners v Karshan (Midlands) Ltd t/a Domino's Pizza* [2023] IESC 24, see *Arthur Cox Employment Law Yearbook 2023* at [4.14].

[12] 85TACD2024.

This case involved an appeal brought on behalf of the appellant, whose principal business activity was taxation services, in relation to a notice of amended assessment to corporation tax; a notice of assessment to dividend withholding tax; and a notice of estimation of amounts due employer PAYE/PRSI, each for the period ending 31 December 2012.

Following a settlement in December 2012, an employment benefit trust ('EBT') was established between the settlor (a third-party entity) and the original trustee. According to the appellant, it borrowed money under a loan facility, which it paid to the settlor in order to acquire the pre-existing and pre-funded EBT.

The appellant contended that the purpose of the EBT was to reward and incentivise employees and that the settlor was a third-party entity unconnected to the appellant. The EBT was renamed to remove potential beneficiaries other than employees of the appellant and the protector of the EBT was changed to a director of the appellant (the 'director'). The appellant contended that the trustees of the EBT then agreed to advance a loan to the director so that the director could repay, on behalf of the appellant, the loan facility acquired.

The facts, as accepted by the Commissioner, were that the director's loan account showed a credit sum in December 2012. In February 2013, that credit was met and the loan repaid by the appellant. The Commissioner accepted that there was no evidence of a loan agreement between the trustees of the EBT and the director, nor any evidence that any payment was paid to the settlor of the EBT.

The Commissioner considered the following preliminary matters as part of the decision: the admission of documentary evidence; the applicability of a time limit in respect of the notice of estimation; and the jurisdiction of an Appeals Commissioner in relation to alternative assessments.

The Commissioner then considered the applicability of s 112 of the TCA 1997. Under that section, income tax under Schedule E is charged for each year of assessment on every person having or exercising an office or employment of profit mentioned in that Schedule, and in respect of every annuity, pension or stipend chargeable under that Schedule. The charge to tax covers all salaries, fees, wages, perquisites or profits whatever derived from the office, employment or pension for the year of assessment.

The appellant argued that the payment to the settlor of the EBT did not represent the payment of an emolument to which s 112 of the TCA 1997 applies. It argued that the payment merely facilitated a mechanism for providing future benefits to potential beneficiaries, but that it was not the provision of benefits to beneficiaries in itself, nor the payment of emoluments. Revenue argued that the conferring of a credit to the director by means of his director's loan account, albeit an indirect payment, came within the definition of an emolument for Schedule E and related to his employment with the appellant.

Due to an evidential deficit in respect of documentation submitted to support the appellant's arguments, the Commissioner held that the credit to the director's loan account was not for the purpose of enabling the director to discharge a debt on behalf of the appellant. Accordingly, the amount credited to the director's loan account was an emolument paid to the director, who was an employee of the appellant. The appellant was therefore obliged to deduct the appropriate PAYE/PRSI.

Revenue, citing *McKeown (Inspector of Taxes) v Roe*,[13] also argued that, as the liability was earned and accrued in 2012 it was therefore subject to tax for that period. This was upheld by the Commissioner.

The Commissioner then considered the applicability of s 436A of the TCA 1997. Under that section, any amount which is settled by a close company in connection with a relevant settlement shall be deemed to be a distribution by the company to the trustees of the settlement. The appellant argued that the payment to the settlor of the EBT could not be regarded as a settlement and therefore did not constitute a distribution. As the credit to the director's loan account was held to be an emolument under the provisions of Schedule E of the TCA 1997, the Commissioner held that the amounts were not captured by the provisions of s 436A of the TCA 1997.

Lastly, the Commissioner dealt with the applicability of s 81 of the TCA 1997. The appellant argued that the payment to the settlor of the EBT was made wholly and exclusively for the purposes of its trade and it was therefore entitled to treat the payment as a deductible expense. As the credit to the director's loan account was held to be an emolument under the provisions of Schedule E of the TCA 1997, the Commissioner held that s 81 of the TCA 1997 was not applicable.

Accordingly, the appeal was denied.

[17.31] Determination 63TACD2024[14]—Tax Appeals Commission—income tax—amounts drawn down from a credit to a director's loan account fall within the definition of an emolument under Taxes Consolidation Act 1997, Sch E

The appellant was a businessman who carried on a sole trade. The appellant was also registered as an employee of a limited liability company in which, at its date of incorporation, he had a 99% shareholding, with his wife having the other 1%. (the 'company'). They were both also directors of the company.

The appellant transferred his sole trade business to the company and, subsequently, €250,000 was credited to the appellant's director's loan account in the company. This was drawn down by €205,502. The company invoiced the appellant for administrative and secretarial services provided to the sole trading business prior to the sale to the company. This included VAT at a rate of 23%.

The appellant and his wife resigned as directors of the company and their three children were appointed. Additionally, they transferred their shares in the company to the same children in 2016, with valuation of €1. The appellant remained as an employee of the company.

---

[13] *McKeown (Inspector of Taxes) v Roe* ITR 214.
[14] 63TACD2024.

In November 2015, the appellant and the company were issued with a notification of revenue audit following which Revenue issued, *inter alia*, notices of amended assessment to income tax to the appellant. Notices were also issued to the company. However, these were not dealt with in this judgment and are themselves the subject of another appeal.[15]

It was the respondent's case that there was no transfer of goodwill from the sole trade business to the company and, therefore, the creation of a €250,000 credit to the appellant was an emolument under Schedule E of the TCA 1997, or a distribution under Schedule F of the TCA 1997.

The appellant argued that there was a transfer of goodwill from the sole trade business to the company to the value of €250,000. They further argued that the appellant made a CGT return where the transfer of €250,000 was reported. Therefore, the assessments as to income tax made by the respondent should be reduced to nil. The appellant also submitted that there were additional amended assessments issued by the respondent in the period of actual repayment of the loan, which amounted to double taxation of the appellant.

The Commissioner found that the material facts at issue in the appeal were whether a sale of the goodwill of the sole trade business to the company took place and what the appropriate valuation of the goodwill of the sale trade business was.

The Commissioner first considered whether a sale of the goodwill of the sole trade business to the company took place. The Commissioner quoted from *Inland Revenue Commissioners v Muller & Co's Margarine Ltd*,[16] which states that 'goodwill has no independent existence. It cannot subsist by itself. It must be attached to a business'. The Commissioner stated that they were satisfied on the evidence that the sole trade business was a specialist business with a reputation built for specialist knowledge and excellence. They noted that the business had continuing and repeat customers.

The Commissioner accepted that the sole trade business had built up goodwill over the years and that this was then transferred to the company, as the financial statement for that year noted that intangible fixed assets in the form of goodwill were acquired by the company in the amount of €250,000 and this was also reflected in subsequent years. Further, the Commissioner accepted the appellant's evidence that he wanted to place the company in a position to allow his children to become part of it, deducing from the evidence that it was also the children's intention to do so.

The Commissioner then considered what was the appropriate valuation of the goodwill of the sole trade business. It was accepted that no valuation of the sole trade business was undertaken at the time of its transfer. The Commissioner therefore found that it fell on them to make a historic valuation for these purposes. In this assessment, the Commissioner looked to ascertain the future maintainable profits and appropriate multiple to apply. They noted that it was open to them to stray from the expert witness's

---

[15] M180/18.
[16] *Inland Revenue Commissioners v Muller & Co's Margarine Ltd* [1901] A.C. 217.

assessment in this regard, citing *Donegal Investment Group Plc v Danbywiske and Others*.[17]

The Commissioner did not consider the transfer of shares in the business for €1 as relevant to the valuation, as this took place two years later. The Commissioner ultimately found, as a material fact, that the value of the goodwill of the sole trade business was €41,225 at time of transfer.

The Commissioner then considered the question of alternative assessments. The respondent submitted that the assessments raised were alternative assessments, which do not amount to double taxation, and made it clear that they were only seeking to recover the appropriate tax once. The respondent argued that it is long established that the raising of alternative assessments is permissible, citing *Bye (Inspector of Taxes) v Coren*,[18] in which the trial Judge dismissed the argument that alternative assessments are unfair and noted that it 'has long been accepted as being a sensible and proper way of dealing with difficult cases' and that they were merely a 'variety of routes' by which the taxpayer 'could avoid any problems of unfairness'. This was cited by the Court of Appeal in *Bird v IRC*.[19]

The Commissioner found that their role was not to grapple with these concepts, but rather to focus on the assessment and tax charge, citing *Lee v Revenue Commissioners*,[20] in which it was stated that the jurisdiction of the Commissioner does not extend to 'the distinct issue of whether as a matter of public law or private law there are additional facts and/or other legal principles which preclude enforcement' of the assessment at issue. They further noted that the appellant was allowed to bring judicial proceedings against the respondent on the validity of the notices which they did not do. The Commissioner therefore found it open to them to focus on what the correct charge to tax in the appeal was, rather than undergo an assessment on the validity of the notices issued.

Lastly, the applicability of Schedule E of the TCA 1997 was considered. The Commissioner noted that there was no dispute between the parties as to the correct operation of Schedule E contained in s 19 of the TCA 1997, which provides that tax under this schedule is to be paid 'in respect of all public offices and employments of profit in the State'. The extent of chargeability is then provided for in s 112 of the TCA 1997:

> 'for each year of assessment on every person having or exercising an office or employment of profit mentioned in that Schedule, or to whom any annuity, pension or stipend chargeable under that Schedule is payable, in respect of all salaries, fees, wages, perquisites or profits whatever therefrom'.

The Commissioner found that the appellant did not put forward any alternative explanation as to the credit of €250,000 to the director's loan in the company other than

---

[17] *Donegal Investment Group Plc v Danbywiske and Others* [2017] IESC 14.
[18] *Bye (Inspector of Taxes) v Coren* [1986] STC 393.
[19] *Bird v IRC* [1989] A.C. 300.
[20] *Lee v Revenue Commissioners* [2021] IECA 18.

the transfer of goodwill of the sole trade business, and thus that the appellant did not discharge the burden of proof to prove that the amounts drawn down, other than €41,225 relating to the goodwill of the sole trade, were not emoluments under the provisions of Schedule E.

Further, the respondent submitted that it was the amounts that the appellant drew down from the director's loan that were to be taxed as emoluments. The Commissioner found that, as there were no submissions arguing that it was rather the creation of the director's loan that amounted to emoluments under Schedule E, they must agree with the respondent in this regard.

The Commissioner found that the amounts drawn down were emoluments under Schedule E of the TCA 1997 and, therefore, they could not fall under Schedule F of the TCA 1997.

[17.32] *Determination 60TACD2024[21]—Tax Appeal Commission—income tax—redundancy payments not tax exempt in case of de facto continuation of employment in a successor company*

Revenue contested the treatment of certain payments as tax exempt redundancy payments in circumstances where there was a *de facto* continuation of employment, albeit in a successor company. Revenue assessed these payments to income tax, USC and PRSI. This assessment was upheld and affirmed by the TAC on the basis that the positions of the employees were not terminated but continued in the successor company.

The appellant company operated a food supply business. The appellant company had two directors, the 'first director' and his daughter (the 'second director') (together, the 'directors'). At the time of incorporation (1999), the second director was 19 years old and her inclusion as director was largely to satisfy the two-director requirement of Irish company law. The first director served as the appellant company's managing director and was its sole shareholder from 2012 onwards. However, the second director's role within the appellant company grew over time and she became more active in the management of the appellant company. Aside from the directors, management activities were also performed by one of the appellant company's employees who had significant experience in the food industry (the 'experienced employee'). The appellant company had 12 employees.

The first director made the decision to retire in early 2017 due to his declining health. A strategic review of the business was conducted by the second director and the experienced employee, which found the profitability of the business was falling.

The appellant company ceased trading on 4 August 2017. A separate company (the 'successor company'), of which the second director was the sole shareholder and sole director, commenced operating a food supply business on 5 August 2017.

---

[21] 60TACD2024.

The successor company:

— executed employment contracts with all staff of the appellant company (save for the first director) on 5 August 2017, on the same terms (with the exception that the new contracts provided for one day less annual leave than the original contracts) and in the same positions as their previous contracts;

— entered into a month-to-month lease of the same factory premises that the appellant company had operated from;

— utilised the same plant, equipment, and machinery already *in situ* at the premises (the second director gave evidence that this equipment had been purchased from the appellant company for the sum of €30,000, though no documentary evidence of this payment was furnished);

— had the same suppliers as the appellant company;

— had the same customers as the appellant company;

— produced the same food products as the appellant company; and

— operated under a name and logo similar to those of the appellant company.

Shortly after its cessation of trade, the appellant company paid the sum of €276,758 in purported redundancy payments to the directors and employees of the appellant company. The appellant company considered that these payments fell under s 123 of the TCA 1997 and so benefited from tax exemptions under ss 201, 203 and Schedule 3 of the TCA 1997. The €276,758 was comprised of: (a) statutory amounts payable to the employees under the Redundancy Payments Act 1967 in the event of their redundancy; and (b) increased amounts paid to the first director, second director and experienced employee equal to the maximum non-taxable sum allowed under Schedule 3 of the TCA 1997.

The appellant company entered into a members voluntary liquidation process in 2019. On 15 December 2021, as part of an audit, Revenue notified the appellant company it was treating the redundancy payments (with the exception of the payment made to the first director who did not resume employment in the successor company) as Schedule E remuneration, chargeable to tax under s 112 of the TCA 1997. The appellant company's liability in respect of income tax, PRSI, and USC was assessed to be €140,545. The appellant company appealed this assessment.

The appellant company, and the directors giving evidence, submitted that what had occurred was a genuine redundancy of the employees. To support this argument, it was submitted that:

— the appellant company and the successor company were entirely separate entities;

— the first director controlled the appellant company, and it was the first director's decision to cease the activities of the appellant company based on the findings of the strategic review and his ill health;

— the successor company was controlled by the second director, it was her decision to establish this company, commence trading and hire staff;

— there was no evidence of any assurance having been given to the employees they would be offered new employment in the successor company; and
— there was no agreement between the appellant company and successor company to rehire the employees post-cessation of trade in the appellant company.

It was argued that in a 'firing and rehiring' scenario, both acts must be carried out by one entity and that in these circumstances, where there were clearly two entities with no bridging employment agreements, the redundancies must be genuine.

Revenue submitted that the employees had not been made redundant, that the successor company had taken over the business of the appellant company, and that the positions the employees occupied in the successor company were identical to those they occupied in the appellant company.

Revenue relied on *Spijkers v Gebroeders Benedik Abbatoir CV*[22] (*'Spijkers'*) to support its argument that the business of the appellant company had been transferred to the successor company. In the *Spijkers* case, the European Court of Justice (the 'ECJ') set out factors to be considered in determining whether a business/undertaking has been transferred. The ECJ stated that the decisive criterion in such cases was 'whether the business in question retains its identity'. The ECJ went on to state that it is necessary to consider:

> 'whether the business was disposed of as a going concern, as would be indicated, inter alia, by the fact that its operation was actually continued or resumed by the new employer, with the same or similar activities'.

Finally, the ECJ stated, in determining whether those conditions are met, all the facts of the transaction must be examined, including: the type of undertaking or business in question; whether or not the tangible assets of the business are transferred; the value of its intangible assets at the time of the transfer; whether or not the majority of its employees are taken over by the new employer; whether or not its customers are transferred; the degree of similarity between the activities carried on before and after the transaction; and any period for which the activities of the business were suspended.

On this basis, Revenue argued that the business of the appellant company had clearly transferred to the successor company. The obligations owed by the appellant company to the employees therefore also transferred, such that, with the exception of the first director, the positions of the employees never ceased to exist and the employees were never made redundant. The payments would therefore fall to be taxed under s 112 of the TCA 1997 and should not benefit from the tax exemptions available under ss 201, 203 and Schedule 3 of the TCA 1997.

The Commissioner determined that the payments could only be regarded as redundancy payments if the positions of the employees ceased to exist on the termination of their employment. The Commissioner referred to *Spijkers* and the 'decisive factual

---

[22] *Spijkers v Gebroeders Benedik Abbatoir CV* (Case C-24/85), [1986] ECR 119.

criterion' in determining whether a transfer of a business/undertaking had taken place being 'whether the business in question retains its identity'. The Commissioner determined that, having regard to all the relevant facts, there was no doubt the appellant company's business was not brought to an end, but taken over and continued by the successor company.

The Commissioner referred to the following indicia of a continuation of the appellant company's business:

— the continued leasing of the same factory premises;
— all plant and machinery necessary for the operation of the business was taken over and operated by the successor company;
— all staff of the appellant company (with the exception of the first director) made a seamless transition to the successor company, and performed exactly the same roles as they had in the appellant company on almost identical terms;
— the successor company inherited the appellant company's single major customer;
— the evidence of the directors, which indicated that it was critical to the successor company to preserve the goodwill built up by the appellant company;
— the striking similarities in the logo and name of the successor company and those of the appellant company further indicated it was intended that the goodwill of the appellant company be preserved and transferred to the successor;
— submissions that there was no agreement between the appellant company and the successor company on the rehiring of the employees was not credible—the seamless transition between employments clearly indicated advance co-ordination between the persons controlling each company;
— the evidence of the directors evinced a clear plan for the second director to continue the business following the exit of the first director, including the first director's statement that it was always his intention that the second director would inherit the business; and
— the reasons the second director provided for the creation of the successor company were commercial and provided the best chance of success for the business—this indicated an intention to continue the business of the appellant company rather than the commencement of a new business.

The Commissioner found that the findings of the strategic review were not relevant. Though it had been argued that the findings of the review should cause the Commissioner to determine the business was failing and needed to be terminated, it concluded those same issues necessarily impacted the business as operated by the successor company the day after the appellant company's cessation of trade.

The Commissioner thus found that the successor company took over a going concern in the appellant company's food production business and that those in control of the appellant company would have been aware at the time of terminating the employees' contracts that their positions were to be retained in the successor company.

In those circumstances, the appellant company could not be said to have made redundancy payments to its employees, and Revenue's assessment was upheld and affirmed.

[17.33] *Determination 148TACD2024[23]—Tax Appeals Commission—income tax—determining employment status for taxation purposes[24]—did amounts drawn from a company account by a person who was the sole director and shareholder amount to employment status or a director's loan*

Background

This case concerned whether payments totaling €290,468 made in 2021 by an Irish company (the 'second appellant') to its UK-resident director and sole shareholder (the 'first appellant') (together the 'appellants') constituted a director's loan, as claimed by the appellants, or disguised salary payments, as claimed by Revenue, the respondent.

Facts

The first appellant is a UK-based entrepreneur who established the second appellant company in Ireland and is its sole director and shareholder. The first appellant utilised an outsourcing company to run the day-to-day business of the second appellant. The first appellant did not have an employment contract with the second appellant. He was not in receipt of pension entitlements or health insurance benefits from the second appellant. He had no work-for-wage bargain with the second appellant; he had not agreed to provide services to it personally; and was not subject to its control.

In 2021, the first appellant withdrew amounts totaling €290,468.22 from the bank account of the second appellant. The first appellant intended to repay the monies to the second appellant, and did so by way of offset from a dividend payment to him from the second appellant in December 2022. No loan documentation was provided by the appellants showing the terms and conditions of the loan afforded to him. There was no interest charged by the second appellant though the transactions were recorded on the second appellant's trial balance and in its financial statements.

Tax was paid on the benefit-in-kind accruing to the first appellant from the monies advanced to him by the second appellant. The first appellant paid dividend withholding tax in the UK on the dividend payment made to him by the second appellant.

On 24 February 2023, Revenue raised an assessment to PREM against the second appellant of €296,314.96 and on 25 February 2023, Revenue raised an assessment to income tax against the first appellant for €213,852.44. The appellants appealed against the assessments to the Tax Appeals Commission on 23 March 2023 and the appeals were heard together on 18 June 2024.

---

[23] 148TACD2024.
[24] See also Chapter 4, Employment Litigation.

Revenue had raised alternative assessments against both appellants, treating the payments as salary subject to income tax, USC and PRSI. The appellants argued the payments were a director's loan that was later offset by a portion of a €990,000 dividend payment the first appellant received in 2022.

The key issues to be determined were whether the first appellant was an employee of the second appellant, and whether the payments constituted a loan or taxable emoluments/perquisites. Revenue argued the first appellant was an 'employee director' as he controlled the company. The appellants contended there was no employment relationship based on the Supreme Court's test in the *Karshan* judgment.[25]

Tax Appeal Commission Legal Analysis

It was noted that the burden of proof in the appeal rested on the appellants to show the alternative assessments made against them were incorrect, as set out in *Menolly Homes*.[26] The Commissioner agreed with Revenue's submission that he fact that the first appellant had been using monies from the second appellant for day-to-day living expenses did not in itself determine that the monies constituted a loan or emolument. Making reference to s 112 of the TCA 1997, which states: 'Income tax under Schedule E shall be charged ... on every person having or exercising an office or employment of profit mentioned in that Schedule ... in respect of all salaries, fees, wages, perquisites or profits whatever therefrom', the Commission noted that, for the monies received by the first appellant to be subject to Schedule E income they must constitute 'salaries, fees, wages, perquisites or profits whatever' from an 'office or employment of profit'.

The Tax Appeal Commissioner then referenced the five-step test, as set out in *Karshan*, which must be assessed in order to determine if the first appellant was engaged as an employee, noting that the first three tests must be answered in the affirmative. The first step is that there is a work-for-wage bargain between the individual and the business, the second is that the worker has agreed to provide services personally to the business, and the third is that the business is able to exercise control over the worker. The Commissioner stated that, based on the evidence presented, none of those three tests were met. In addressing each limb of the test, the Commissioner noted that the first appellant had no salary arrangement with the second appellant, had no employment contract, was not entitled to health or pension benefits, and had not undertaken to provide any services to the second appellant. Indeed, it was acknowledged that the first appellant had engaged an outsourcing company to run the second appellant's day-to-day business, and the second appellant could not exercise any control over him.

The Tax Appeal Commissioner considered that the Revenue had not engaged with the test set out in the *Karshan* case at all, but rather asserted that the first appellant was an 'employee director' and pointed to a different test for ascertaining if someone

---

[25] *Revenue Commissioners v Karshan (Midlands) Ltd t/a Domino's Pizza* [2023] IESC 24, see *Arthur Cox Employment Law Yearbook 2023* at [4.14].
[26] *Menolly Homes Ltd v Appeal Commissioners* [2010] IEHC 49.

is an 'employee director' as compared to an ordinary employee. The Commissioner stated that they considered the appropriate test to be applied was the one set out in the *Karshan* case.

Regarding the loan, the Commissioner noted that the most fundamental indicium of a loan of money is that it is to be repaid, adding that s 122 of the TCA 1997 defines a loan broadly as 'any form of credit' and does not limit the definition to, for example, a loan with a specified term or amount. The Commissioner was satisfied that the monies advanced to the first appellant were repaid by him as evidenced in the second appellant's financial statements for the period ending 31 August 2021, which recorded that an unsecured loan to the first appellant in the amount of €204,790 (at that stage) was outstanding. The financial statements for the period ending 31 December 2022 showed that the loan was paid off by means of a dividend payment to the first appellant. The Commissioner found that it was the intention of the appellants that the monies paid to the first appellant would be repaid, and they were in fact subsequently repaid. While the first appellant had the use of the monies for a period of time, they were not taxable as an emolument, as they could not be 'converted by him into money or money's worth', as per *Tennant v Smith*.[27] Therefore, the monies did not constitute a perquisite taxable under s 112 of the TCA 1997.

Decision

The Tax Appeal Commissioner found the first appellant was not an employee, as there was no work-for-wage bargain, no agreement to provide services personally, and no control by the company. While there was limited loan documentation, the Tax Appeal Commission accepted the payments were intended to be, and were in fact, repaid and were recorded as a loan in the company's accounts. As such, they did not constitute a taxable perquisite.

The Tax Appeal Commissioner determined the payments were a loan, not taxable as salary/emoluments. The assessments were reduced to nil and the appeal was successful.

IRISH HIGH COURT

[17.34] *Revenue Commissioners v Hennessy and Hennessy*[28]—*High Court—Quinn J—appeal from Tax Appeals Commission—interpretation of 'proprietary director' under Taxes Consolidation Act 1997, s 472(1)(a)—whether transborder workers relief applies to the taxpayers*

This was an appeal by Revenue against a decision of the Tax Appeals Commission ('TAC') in favour of the respondent taxpayers. The TAC determined that taxes were not due by the respondents by virtue of s 825A of the TCA 1997. This decision primarily

---

[27] *Tennant v Smith (Surveyor of Taxes)* [1892] A.C. 150.
[28] *The Revenue Commissioners v Aidan Hennessy and Gerard Hennessy* [2024] IEHC 245.

concerned the interpretation of 'proprietary director' under s 472(1)(a) of the TCA 1997 and whether the respondents fell within that definition.

The respondents were directors, shareholders, and full-time employees of a Donegal company (the 'company') and claimed Transborder Workers Relief ('TWR') under s 825 of the TCA 1997, which provides for a reduction in income tax for income due outside the State. The respondents were Irish residents living in Donegal, the company's offices were in Strabane and their employment duties were exclusively carried on in the UK. The respondents paid UK income taxes.

The ordinary share capital of the company was made up of 5,000 shares in the form of 1,000 'ordinary shares' and 4,000 'A ordinary shares'. The 4,000 A ordinary shares were held by the respondents' brother and, under the Articles of Association of the company, the holder of the A ordinary shares had no voting rights.

The Articles of Association did not impose any such limitations on the ordinary shares held by the respondents and, as holders of such shares, the respondents had voting rights in addition to other rights as assigned by the Articles of Association. The respondents were not beneficial owners of more than 15% of the ordinary share capital of the company.

Revenue claimed that the respondents were not entitled to relief because s 825A(2)(c) of the TCA 1997 provides that relief is not available to a person who is a 'proprietary director' of the employing company. Revenue's position was that each respondent was such a director. Section 825A of the TCA 1997 provides that 'proprietary director' has the meaning set out in s 472(1)(a) of the TCA 1997.

Three questions were stated to the High Court for determination and they can be distilled into one core question, namely whether the respondents fell within the definition of 'proprietary directors' under the legislation.

Revenue submitted that:

— the respondents had control over the business and the owner of the A ordinary shares had no such control because those shares had no voting rights;

— 'control' meant a power of decision-making and the purpose of s 825A (2)(c) was to prevent relief being afforded to those who had a real measure of control over the company's shares and was intended to provide relief to a company's 'ordinary employees' rather than to employees who were also directors who exercised real control over the company;

— the respondents had control 'in reality' over the A ordinary shares notwithstanding that they were not the owners of those shares but, as owners of the voting shares, had control over the A ordinary shares for the purposes of the legislation; and

— s 472 of the TCA 1997 distinguished ownership of shares from control of the shares and this distinction was significant. The TAC accepted that the purpose of the distinction in the legislation was to delineate between ordinary employees and proprietary directors. Revenue argued that the respondents, as persons in control of the business were the type of persons intended not to benefit from TWR.

The respondents submitted that Revenue's analysis of the statutory provision conflated control of the business with control of the ordinary shares. The respondents further submitted that the statutory provisions clearly concerned control of 'ordinary share capital' and the question to be determined was whether the respondents had control over the A ordinary shares.

The High Court endorsed the respondent's position and the conclusion and reasoning of the TAC, finding that:

— the term 'control' in the definition of 'proprietary director' was not a free-floating concept in the legislation, noting that it was linked by the words 'in the ordinary share capital' of the company;

— control of shares without voting rights associated with them will not involve controlling voting powers and if Revenue's submission was accepted, the holders of the majority of shares with voting rights would almost always control the ordinary share capital of other shareholders where that capital did not have voting rights attached;

— control of a measure of ordinary share capital is not equivalent to power over the company and control had to be understood by considering to what the statutory definition of 'control' connects. Control, in this context, is of a particular measure of ordinary share capital. If the rights associated with that capital are limited, as envisaged as possible by the Statute, the nature of the power flowing from that control will therefore also be, necessarily, limited;

— the respondents did not control their brother's A ordinary shares, the raft of contractual and statutory rights attaching to the A ordinary shares were in his control and he could not be directed as to how such rights should be exercised even though the respondents had control of the majority of the share capital with the voting rights;

— it was irrelevant to the question of control that the respondents' brother had no control of the dividend to be declared for the A ordinary shares;

— it was incorrect to say that the foregoing analysis failed to distinguish adequately between 'ownership' and 'control' as the distinction between the two concepts arises in the statutory context of s 472(1) (a) of the TCA 1997 and this distinction is maintained by the TAC decision; and

— the legislation provides a definition of 'proprietary director' that arises in two contexts; one where the director is the beneficial owner of more than 15% of the 'ordinary share capital' of the company or, where the director exercises control, directly or indirectly, over more than 15% of the 'ordinary share capital' of the company.

The conclusion of the High Court was that the TAC's determination was correct and that the respondents did not fall within the definition of 'proprietary directors' for the purposes of the legislation. The provisions of s 825A of the TCA 1997 applied to the respondents and they were entitled to TWR.

[17.35] Siddiqi v The Revenue Commissioners[29]**—High Court—Quinn J—appeal from Tax Appeals Commission—interpretation and application of Taxes Consolidation Act 1997, s 192A to termination payments in the context of employment-related disputes**

In April 2024, the High Court delivered a judgment concerning the application of s 192A to termination payments in the context of employment-related disputes. This was an appeal by the taxpayer, Mr Siddiqi, of a Tax Appeals Commission ('TAC') determination, contesting the tax treatment of an *ex gratia* payment of approximately €85,000 from the appellant's former employer that had been taxed as a termination payment.

The appellant was an accountant, originally from Pakistan, who had been working and living in Ireland with his family since 2000. As part of a compromise agreement entered into in March 2014, an *ex gratia* payment of €84,903.76, together with a statutory redundancy payment of €4,416, had been provided to the appellant by his employer, a car rental company. Revenue held that it had treated the *ex gratia* payment as connected with the termination of the appellant's employment, the wording of the compromise agreement expressly described the *ex gratia* sum as being a termination payment and that it should therefore be subject to tax of approximately €22,000. The agreement was entered into while the appellant was out on sick leave (due to stress suffered from racial discrimination, harassment and alleged victimisation) and there was a claim for racial discrimination against the employer, together with a potential claim for personal injuries to his mental health caused by the discrimination, pending before the Equality Tribunal. The agreement required that claim be withdrawn. The appellant argued that the payment was, in reality, consideration for the settlement of the pending claim before the Equality Tribunal and therefore should not be liable to tax under s 192A the TCA.

The appellant appealed the Revenue's decision in February 2019 and this was upheld by the TAC in 2022.

The points raised before the High Court were, first, whether the Revenue Commissioners were correct in their interpretation of the written agreement as one made in consequence of, or otherwise in connection with, the termination of the appellant's employment with the employer within the meaning of s 123(1) of the TCA 1997; and second, if not, whether the Revenue Commissioner was correct in finding that the *ex gratia* sum paid to the appellant was one not made in settlement of a relevant claim under a relevant act falling under s 192A of the TCA 1997, with the effect that he was not entitled to an exemption from income tax.

Revenue submitted that the TAC had been correct in its interpretation of the compromise agreement and was therefore correct to treat the *ex gratia* payment as a termination payment within the meaning of s 123 of the TCA 1997, stating that once an *ex gratia* payment is seen as a termination payment, then it is to be excluded from the complete relief available under s 192A or s 201(2)(a) of the TCA 1997. Furthermore, the TAC had found that provisions of s 192A made it plain that it is only payments arising from

---

[29] *Siddiqi v The Revenue Commissioners* [2024] IEHC 195.

issued proceedings under one of the relevant acts that can be exempt. Accordingly, the payment should not get the benefit of s 192A of the TCA 1997 in respect of claims where no proceedings had issued. Finally, the Revenue pointed to the fact that the compromise agreement itself, on its face, proposed the payment be treated as a termination payment and the appellant had received legal advice from an experienced employment solicitor.

The High Court held that the TAC was incorrect in its interpretation and application of s 192A of the TCA 1997. While s 192A(2) and (3) involve scenarios where proceedings are issued in a set number of venues earlier outlined in the section, s 192A(4) clearly outlines that issuing a claim is not a prerequisite to having a payment come within the section.

In terms of the documents that should have been reviewed in order to better understand the background context of the ongoing claims, the Court acknowledged that the use of the phrase 'statement of claim' at various points in s 192A(4) of the TCA 1997 had created some uncertainty and held that the meaning of 'statement of claim' in that section does not mean a 'statement of claim' in the sense meant in the Rules of the Superior Courts. The Court referred to the relevant Revenue guidance, which noted that a statement of claim is not a single document but can include documentation that discloses the nature of the claim between the parties. In this regard, he referred to certain correspondence from the appellant's former solicitors, which referenced an 'employment dispute' being settled.

While the TAC had concluded that this correspondence did not override the contemporaneous terms of the compromise agreement entered into by the appellant and his former employer, the High Court, citing the interpretive principles set out by the Supreme Court in *Analog Devices B.V. v Zurich Insurance Company*[30] and *Law Society v MIBI*[31] disagreed with that position. The Court referred to those principles, namely that 'the one overarching principle when interpreting a legal document is to ascertain the meaning which the document would convey to a reasonable person having all of the background knowledge which would have been reasonably available to the parties in the situation at the time of making the agreement', and that that background knowledge or 'matrix of fact' includes anything which would have affected the way in which the language would be understood by a reasonable person. The Court stated that the documents provided were clearly relevant as they referred back to the context of the settlement, and at the very least should have been considered by the TAC when establishing the matrix of fact to the agreement.

The judgment also noted that, although the agreement provided for a payment of a net sum of €65,000 plus the statutory redundancy, the real question that the TAC should have considered was the true substance of the *ex gratia* payment, which is the intention of s 192A of the TCA 1997.

The labels included by the parties for the payment in the agreement were not determinative, and the High Court held that it could look behind the face of the agreement and

---

[30] *Analog Devices B.V. v Zurich Insurance Company* [2005] 1 I.R. 274.
[31] *Law Society v MIBI* [2017] IESC 31.

consider the entire context in which the settlement was entered into. Citing *Menolly Homes*,[32] the Court stated that the dictum of Charleton J, 'revenue law has no equity', is a double-edged sword for Revenue. The High Court held that the following conditions need to be met, in order for s 192A of the TCA 1997 to apply:

— there must be a genuine *bona fide* employment claim;
— it must be evidenced in writing;
— the claim must have been likely to lead to an award if it had not been settled;
— the amount paid as part of the settlement must be no more than would have been awarded by the statutory body; and
— the employer must retain copies of the relevant documents for six years, which must be made available to Revenue to inspect.

The High Court held that all of these factors indicated that the focus should be on the true substantive nature of the payment rather than the labels designated by the parties.

The Court concluded as follows:

— there was no basis for inferring that the claim was other than a *bona fide* claim;
— the existence of the claim was evidenced in writing;
— although it was not clear whether the claim was likely to lead to an award in favour of Mr Siddiqi, the former employer had agreed to pay him an additional €85,000 on top of his statutory redundancy;
— the *ex gratia* amount was significantly over a year's pay for the employee but less than two years, which is the typical statutory maximum; and
— the relevant documents included correspondence between the employer and employee, and documents filed with the Equality Tribunal, and provided background context to interpret the agreement in a reasonable manner.

Accordingly, the High Court overturned the decision of the TAC, holding that the payment should have been examined under s 192A, and concluding that if the payment fell within the definition of s 192A(4) of the TCA 1997, even if labeled a 'termination payment' and was higher than envisaged, it should qualify as tax-exempt.

UK CASE LAW

Determination of Employment Status

[17.36] *HMRC v Professional Game Match Officials Ltd*[33]—*UK Supreme Court—Richards, Hodge, Leggatt, Stephens & Rose LJJ—appeal from Court of Appeal of England and Wales—employment status—referees may be employees for individual arrangements—part-time referees—mutuality of obligation—control*

---

[32] *Menolly Homes Ltd v Appeal Commissioners* [2010] IEHC 49.
[33] *HMRC v Professional Game Match Officials Ltd* [2024] UKSC 29.

This UK Supreme Court judgment considers whether part-time football referees were employees of the appellant company. The judgment provides more certainty on crucial concepts underpinning the determination of employment status and determining whether a contract of employment exists, ie: the mutual obligation involved in the provision of services personally by the putative employee and the obligation of the putative employer to pay remuneration for those services; and the requirement for a sufficient degree of control by the putative employer over the provision by the putative employee of his or her services.

The issues in this case arose in the context of taxation and national insurance payments. The relevant legislation adopts employment under a contract of employment or under a contract of service as the criterion for determining the treatment of income for the purposes of income tax and national insurance contributions. The legislation contains no definition of a contract of employment or a contract of service but leaves them to be determined in accordance with common law principles.

The appellant, Professional Game Match Officials Ltd ('PGMOL'), is a company limited by guarantee which provides referees and other match officials for the most significant football competitions, including the Premier League, the FA Cup and the English Football League. It is funded by its members and is intended to be run on a not-for-profit basis. The Football Association ('FA') is the governing body of English football, including match officials. It is effectively their regulator. Referees must be registered with the FA if they are to officiate at any match in any affiliated competition and they must comply with the FA's rules and regulations.

The FA classifies match officials according to nine levels, the highest of which is Level 1 (the National List). PGMOL's role relates to the training and provision of referees, primarily at Level 1, which comprises two sub-sets. The first is a group of full-time referees, who principally officiate at Premier League matches and who are employed under written contracts of employment (the 'select group'). The second is a larger group (the 'national group') comprising those who referee in their spare time and who usually have other full-time employment or occupations. They primarily officiate at matches in the Championship League and the FA Cup and may also act as fourth official in some matches, including in the Premier League.

PGMOL treated the national group as self-employed and therefore did not treat the fees paid to them as employment income. The system for engaging referees involved match appointments being offered to referees via a computer system. A National Group referee could refuse an appointment but, in such circumstances, PGMOL would want to know the reason for the refusal. Once a referee had accepted an appointment, he or she could back out of it before arriving at the ground on match day; this generally only happened in a situation where they were off injured, ill or had work commitments. When a referee accepted a match appointment offered by PGMOL, a contract was formed under which the referee agreed to officiate and submit a match report and PGMOL agreed to pay the appropriate fee.

The First-Tier Tribunal ('FTT') found in favour of PGMOL on the basis that the right to cancel shifts meant there was no mutuality of obligation, nor was there sufficient control over the referees. The Upper Tribunal agreed with the FTT that there was no mutuality of obligation (although disagreed on the control point) and dismissed the appeal.

The Court of Appeal of England and Wales found in favour of HMRC, holding that there was sufficient mutuality of obligation and control in respect of the contracts between the referees and PGMOL, which were formed in respect of each individual match. PGMOL appealed to the Supreme Court on the two elements of the test outlined above.

At the outset, the UK Supreme Court noted that, in arrangements of this kind, there are two contracts of employment: (i) the overarching annual contract between the referee and PGMOL, which, by virtue of the referees passing fitness tests, adhering to the code of conduct etc, enabled them to be part of the cohort to whom matches were offered; and (ii) the contracts which arose in respect of each individual match a referee chose to accept. The Supreme Court noted that, in this case, it was only analysing the contracts which arose for individual matches.

The Supreme Court found that there was sufficient mutuality of obligation in the period from the acceptance of the assignment by national group referees, through to officiating the game, and subsequently concluding upon the referee submitting their match report, for which they were paid.

The Supreme Court found that there was control exerted in the contractual obligations imposed on the national group referees by PGMOL whereby they had to meet relevant standards through a match-day procedure document and the code of conduct. If these standards were not met, PGMOL demonstrated control through disciplining referees by denying them the opportunity to officiate future matches, thereby reducing their share in an end-of-year performance bonus payment.

The Supreme Court held that:

> 'mutuality of obligation and control are regarded as largely determinative, with only a minor role for other considerations, courts may be led to apply an unduly restrictive interpretation of control in order to prevent relationships which overall are not suggestive of employment from being characterised as such. Conversely, by according a real significance to the 'totality of the provisions ... and all the circumstances of the relationship created by' the contract, a realistic approach can be taken to the issue of control. In other words, the bar to the existence of control need not be set at an unduly high level'.

The Supreme Court referred to *Uber BV v Aslam*,[34] where the ride-sharing technology company was deemed to exert a 'form of control' over its drivers on the basis that it had the ability to monitor trip acceptance rates and customer ratings. Where a driver was found to fall below a certain prescribed standard, Uber was able to discipline them.

The Supreme Court held that two essential elements for the test for employment status—namely, mutuality of obligation and a sufficient degree of control—were met in respect of part-time referees engaged by PGMOL under contracts to officiate individual professional football matches.

---

[34] *Uber BV v Aslam* [2021] UKSC 5, see *Arthur Cox Employment Law Yearbook 2021* at [5.08].

The case was remitted to the FTT to determine the larger question of whether these contracts are contracts of employment. The First-Tier Tribunal will look at the final limb of the test, which requires a global assessment of the other provisions of a contract and the relationship between the parties to determine whether it is consistent with an employer-employee relationship.

[17.37] *HMRC v RALC Consulting Ltd[35]—Upper Tribunal Tax and Chancery decision—Richards & Greenbank JJ—appeal from First-Tier Tribunal—Income Tax (Earnings and Pensions) Act 2003—IR35 appeal remitted to FTT as FTT had failed to follow self-direction on how to determine existence of contract of employment*

The case involves the employment status of an IT contractor named Mr Alcock who provided his services via a company called RALC Consulting Ltd (the 'company'), and who was its sole director and shareholder. The company faced an HMRC 'intermediaries' legislation' rules challenge in relation to three contracts in which it was engaged. The contracts were entered into through an employment agency, which added a further layer of legal complexity. IR35 legislation was enacted to prevent a situation whereby an intermediary is used to engage an employee on behalf of an employer to prevent an employment relationship being created, thus creating an adverse tax consequence for HMRC. Under IR35, if applicable, the above-described relationship should be taxed as an employment relationship rather than allowing a situation whereby the use of a service company could prevent the payment of employer and employee national insurance contributions ('NICs').

HMRC used IR35 to challenge three specific contracts in which the company was engaged; two with Accenture and one with the Department for Work and Pensions ('DWP'). The contracts spanned five tax years: (i) contract one with Accenture spanning 20 months, followed by a three-month break, before a further six-month stint; (ii) contract two with Accenture spanning nine months; and (iii) contract three with the DWP lasting just over 12 months, capturing two Christmas periods.

Each of the contracts was not between the intermediary and the client but rather through an employment agency. While this does not prevent IR35 rules from applying, it was an added complication for legal analysis. HMRC determined that Mr Alcock, via the company, was in fact an employee of Accenture and DWP for the periods in which he was contracted to them. The company appealed this decision to the First-Tier Tribunal ('FTT'), which concluded that the company and the contracts were outside the scope of the IR35 rules. The FTT came to this conclusion on the basis that there was insufficient mutuality of obligation in the hypothetical contracts between the worker and the end clients, so that those contracts would not have represented employment, but would instead have amounted to self-employment. HMRC appealed that decision to the Upper Tribunal ('UT') on the basis that the FTT had made errors in law in reaching that conclusion.

---

[35] *HMRC v RALC Consulting Ltd* [2024] UKUT 99.

The UT found that the FTT had failed to properly follow the three-stage process outlined by the Court of Appeal in *Atholl House*:[36]

— Stage 1: Find the terms of the actual contractual arrangements and relevant circumstances within which the individual worked.
— Stage 2: Ascertain the terms of the hypothetical contract postulated by s 49(1)(c)(i) of the Income Tax (Earnings and Pensions) Act 2003 and the counterpart legislation as applicable for the purposes of NICs; and
— Stage 3: Consider whether the hypothetical contract would be a contract of employment.

The UT considered that the FTT had correctly directed itself to follow the procedure as set out in *Atholl House*, but then had not properly done so. The UT decided that the FTT had failed to fully construct the terms of the hypothetical contracts before applying the common law tests for employment status. The FTT had instead prematurely applied the common law tests, particularly the test regarding mutuality of obligation, to certain aspects of the actual contracts. The result of this error was that some aspects of the fully constructed hypothetical contracts had not been properly taken into account.

It was common ground that the question as to whether any contract amounted to an employment contract should be addressed by reference to a three-stage test as laid down by the High Court of England and Wales in the case of *Ready Mixed Concrete*,[37] as supplemented by later caselaw. HMRC's complaint was that, despite the FTT's direction as to the approach it should take, the tribunal did not actually follow its own ruling. The UT agreed.

The UT then conducted an analysis of whether these errors in law had a material effect on the outcome of the case and if so, whether it should set aside and/or remake the decision. In this process, the UT determined that the FTT had placed too great an emphasis on the mutuality of obligation test. It held that, while mutuality of obligation is a requirement in order for employment to exist, its existence does not of itself prove employment. It is necessary but not sufficient. The UT added that the FTT had incorrectly found the lack of any guaranteed minimum hours and the right of the putative employer to terminate the arrangement without notice to be inconsistent with mutuality of obligation. The UT held this finding was contrary to jurisprudence, particularly the *Quashie*[38] case. It added that the putative employer is not obliged to offer more work in the future; and this does not prevent mutuality of obligation existing during the period that work is offered, the offer is accepted, and for which the worker is paid as set out by the Court of Appeal in *Professional Game Match Officials*.[39]

---

[36] *R & C Commrs v Atholl House Productions Ltd (Kaye Adams)* [2022] EWCA Civ 501, [2022] BTC 12, see *Arthur Cox Employment Law Yearbook 2022* at [18.34].
[37] *Ready Mixed Concrete (South East) Ltd v Minister of Pensions and National Insurance* [1968] 2 QB 497.
[38] *Quashie v Stringfellows Restaurant Ltd* [2012] EWCA Civ 1735.
[39] *R & C Commrs v Professional Game Match Officials Ltd* [2021] EWCA Civ 1370; [2021] BTC 27.

The UT held, based on the above facts, that there was sufficient evidence to set aside the finding of the FTT. There was, however, an insufficient finding of facts which would require further evidence and witnesses for the UT to remake the decision. On that basis they remitted the case to the FTT for the appeal to be heard by a new panel.

[17.38] *HMRC v S&L Barnes*[40]—*Upper Tribunal Tax and Chancery*—*Scott & Baldwin JJ*—*appeal from First-Tier Tribunal*—*income tax and national insurance*—*First-Tier Tribunal erred in its application of the third stage of the Ready Mixed Concrete test*

This case involves the employment status of Stuart Barnes, a former England international rugby player. Upon retirement from rugby, he began working as a freelance writer, television presenter and pundit. He provided these services via S&L Barnes Ltd, his own personal service company through which he provided the above services to various media organisations.

The company had two separate contracts with Sky from 6 April 2013 to 5 April 2019, while separately having engagements with other broadcasters and newspapers during this period. HMRC determined that the two Sky contracts fell within the meaning of IR35 and issued determinations for income tax and notices of decision for national insurance contributions for the relevant tax years. The company appealed HRMC's determinations and decisions to the FTT.

The FTT found that, due to the presence of mutuality of obligation and exercise of control, there was the suggestion of a contract of employment as per *Ready Mixed Concrete*.[41] In consideration of the other factors presented to them as part of the third test in *Ready Mixed Concrete*, the FTT held that Mr Barnes was in business on his own account. HMRC was refused permission to appeal the decision by the FTT, but was granted a right to appeal by the UT on two grounds:

(i) that the FTT erred in its construction of the hypothetical contract concerning Sky's right of first call over Mr Barnes and purported variations to the contract ('the first ground'); and
(ii) that the FTT erred in its interpretation and/or application of the third stage of the test from the *Ready Mixed Concrete* case by taking account of irrelevant factors while ignoring other relevant factors ('the second ground').

HMRC posited that the FTT had incorrectly assumed that a key term in both Sky contracts, which gave them first call on Mr Barnes' time, had been varied such that he could deal with standing commitments he had to newspaper columns he worked on. HMRC argued that there had been no evidence presented to the FTT to substantiate this variation and it was only that Sky had not, in practice, needed to exercise this right that implied a change in terms. HMRC argued that this made the FTT's decision irrational.

---

[40] *HMRC v S&L Barnes* [2024] UKUT 262.
[41] *Ready Mixed Concrete (South East) Ltd v Minister of Pensions and National Insurance* [1968] 2 QB 497.

The UT noted that Mr Barnes had given oral evidence that he always gave priority to his newspaper columns at various times of the sporting calendar, which amounted to sufficient evidence for the FTT to make the determination that they did, even if it was flawed. Therefore, the UT dismissed the appeal under the first ground.

HMRC challenged the FTT's conclusions regarding the overall analysis as part of the third and final stage of the employment status test in *Ready Mixed Concrete*. HMRC argued that the FTT had considered 12 separate factors under the third *Ready Mixed Concrete* stage. The UT noted that, while it could not apply a weighting to any single factor which had been considered by the FTT, the FTT took into account factors which were, as a matter of principle, irrelevant or failed to take into account factors that were, as a matter of principle, relevant. On that basis, the UT determined that the FTT did not err in law in considering six of the factors which they did, however it did err in law in considering the other six. The UT concluded that the FTT had taken into account irrelevant factors and treated factors as inconsistent with employment which were, in fact, consistent. The UT added that the weight applied to these factors was not known but they nonetheless concluded that this error may have affected the FTT's decision and it was thus set aside. In considering the third *Ready Mix Concrete* stage the UT noted that no single factor was decisive, stating that it was, 'about painting a picture from an accumulation of detail and then standing back to make an informed qualitative assessment'.

The UT concluded that the FTT had failed to weigh all the factors and had erred in law in doing so. The UT opined that the FTT had, in particular, ignored the terms of the hypothetical contract and instead looked at the circumstances of the operation of that contract in practice. The UT further noted that the FTT had failed to explain in its decision which terms acted for or against employment status.

On the basis of the above analysis, the UT overturned the FTT's decision, and rather than remitting to the FTT, the UT used its power to remake the decision itself. In making this decision, the factors which the UT determined were in favour employment were:

— The FTT's findings on the terms of the hypothetical contract and its conclusions on mutuality and control were unchanged.
— The hypothetical contract would be for a fixed term of four years, extendable by two years and subject to further renewal by mutual agreement. It could be terminated by Sky with immediate effect at any time but only if, in Sky's reasonable opinion, specific conditions applied.
— Mr Barnes, via the company was contractually obliged to perform the service himself without a right of substitution.
— Sky had a right of first call on Mr Barnes' services for up to 228 days per annum, varied by arrangements regarding availability.
— Sky had UK exclusivity for Mr Barnes' services as a broadcaster. Prior written consent was required to engage in new commercial activities with any media outlet.
— Mr Barnes' annual fee (which ranged from £235,000 and £265,000) was payable monthly and fixed in advance. It was not linked to actual days of airtime. Sky provided all necessary studio equipment and related travel and accommodation bookings such that the company had very little financial risk.

The factors which the UT determined were contrary to a contract of employment were:

— The company's use of its intellectual property was not restricted by Sky. Mr Barnes was permitted to reuse material from his work with Sky in his newspaper columns with Sky's full knowledge.

— The variation in the hypothetical contract identified by the FTT allowed Mr Barnes to make himself unavailable for match commentaries during various tournaments.

The UT held that on balance, the relationship between the company and Sky under the hypothetical contract would have been one of employment. The long duration of the contract, the absence of a right of substitution, the right of first call for 228 days a year (as varied), the rights of exclusivity and the absence of financial risk were collectively the factors with the greatest weight and indicative of a contract of employment. The UT furthered that, 'The evaluation of all relevant admissible factors required at the Third RMC Stage leads us to conclude that the relationship would have been one of employment'.

The UT found in favour of the HRMC's appeal with respect to the second ground, setting aside the FTT's decision, and dismissing the company's original appeal.

[17.39] *HMRC v Basic Broadcasting[42]—Upper Tribunal Tax and Chancery—Meade & Scott JJ—appeal from First-Tier Tribunal—income tax and national insurance—appropriate test to be applied in assessing whether certain contracts come within the IR35*

Mr Chiles was a well-known radio and television presenter. During the relevant period, he provided services to ITV and BBC through his company Basic Broadcasting Ltd ('BBL'). HMRC issued determinations in respect of income tax and notices of decision in respect of national insurance contributions to BBL for the relevant period, on the basis that Mr Chiles was an employee of ITV and BBC pursuant to the IR35.

The purpose of IR35 is to ensure individuals who ought to be subject to income tax and social insurance payments are not reducing or deferring liabilities by virtue of a corporate structure. HMRC found Mr Chiles' renumeration under the relevant contracts fell under this legislation and was subject to tax. BBL appealed to the First-Tier Tribunal (Tax Chamber) ('FTT'), which allowed the appeal in February 2022.

The FTT found that the relevant facts satisfied s 49(1)(a) and (b) of the IR35 ie, there was an individual who personally performed, or was under an obligation to personally perform, services for another person and these were under an arrangement with a third party.

Under the IR35, the services provided must also be such that, if provided under a contract directly between the client and the worker, the worker would be regarded as an employee for income tax purposes. The UT noted that the test for this requirement was

---

[42] *HMRC v Basic Broadcasting* [2024] UKUT 165.

set out in *Ready Mixed Concrete (South East) Ltd v Minister of Pensions and National Insurance*[43] ('RMC') and summarised in *Kickabout Productions Ltd v HMRC*[44] as being:

— establish the actual contractual arrangements and relevant circumstances in which the individual worked;
— establish the terms of the 'hypothetical contract' (ie, the contract should it have been made with the individual rather than a third party); and
— consider whether the hypothetical contract would be a contract of employment or a contract for services (the 'third RMC stage').

The grounds of HMRC's appeal centred on the FTT's assessment of the third RMC stage as they argued that the correct test for the assessment of this limb was not adopted, and that the FTT decision was undermined by the recent judgment in *HMRC v Atholl House Productions Ltd*[45] ('*Atholl House CA*'), which had been decided in the intervening period as it had provided that additional factors in relation to actual or constructive knowledge of third parties should be taken into account.

The FTT considered the Upper Tribunal's decision in *HMRC v Atholl House Productions Ltd*[46] ('*Atholl House UT*') as outlining the correct test to be applied in the assessment of the hypothetical contract under the third RMC stage. Consequently, the FTT noted that the most significant factor that might displace the *prima facie* case that Mr Chiles was an employee was whether he was in business on his own account.

HMRC firstly argued that, as noted by *Atholl House CA*, *Atholl House UT* made an error, which the FTT then reproduced in its assessment of this case. HMRC noted the finding in *Atholl House CA* that the Upper Tribunal erred in law in applying an approach that depended on the relationship between the services performed by the individual in question both within and outside the contract.

The UT found that the FTT took the same flawed approach in the instant case. In this regard the UT pointed to the fact that the FTT approach centred on the fact that Mr Chiles was carrying on a business on his own account outside the contract. The UT stated: 'Put simply, that approach does not answer the question ... how to characterise the terms of the contract in point, but a different question, which is the relationship between the activities under that contract and the individual's other activities'.

Additionally, HMRC criticised the FTT for focusing unduly on the business on own account test instead of keeping the terms of the hypothetical contracts central to the assessment. In this regard, the UT found that the business on his own account test

---

[43] *Ready Mixed Concrete (South East) Ltd v Minister of Pensions and National Insurance* [1968] 2 QB 497.
[44] *Kickabout Productions Ltd v HMRC* [2022] EWCA Civ 502, see *Arthur Cox Employment Law Yearbook 2022* at [18.35].
[45] *R & C Commrs v Atholl House Productions Ltd (Kaye Adams)* [2022] EWCA Civ 501, [2022] BTC 12, see *Arthur Cox Employment Law Yearbook 2022* at [18.34].
[46] *HMRC v Atholl House Productions Ltd* [2021] UKUT 37.

may be used in two different ways. Firstly, it may be used to assess that status of the contracts in question. In this use, the UT noted that it is one way of approaching the third RMC stage, rather than a separate test and that the use of this approach may be helpful or unhelpful depending on the facts of the case. Secondly, the UT found that this test may be used to describe the individual's working practices outside of the contract. In this regard, the test is a relevant factor to be taken into account and the weight to be attached to it is up to the FTT.

The UT therefore found that the FTT erred in law in its approach to the third RMC stage, in both looking at the relationship between the activities under the contract and the other activities performed by the individual, and unduly focusing on the business on own account test to the exclusion of all other factors. The decision with regard to the third RMC stage was set aside by the UT.

BBL argued that the FTT did not to take into account the finding in *Atholl House CA*, ie, that whether certain matters were within the actual or constructive knowledge of BBC and ITV was a factor to be considered.

BBL tried to argue that the actual or constructive knowledge of the third parties did not form part of the test in *Atholl House CA* and thus should not be considered by the UT. Additionally, BBL argued that its inclusion conflicted with previous cases which did not identify it as a factor. The UT found this not to be the case noting that, regardless of whether the knowledge formed part of the *ratio*, it was intended to set out general guidance in law. The UT also found that it was incumbent on it to follow the Court of Appeal's guidance regardless of whether it conflicts with previous jurisprudence.

BBL also argued that it would be unfair for HMRC to rely on this ground as it had not been raised in pleadings or evidence. While BBL pointed to *HMRC v Ritchie*[47] (TCC) in this regard, the Court distinguished the facts in the instant case as they accepted that it was not a deliberate or tactical choice of either party not to raise this point before the FTT.

Indeed, the UT found that the reason for the delay in raising the argument was the decision of *Atholl House CA*. Based on this, and the fact that the FTT's decision in the third RMC stage was being set aside in any event and so must be remitted, the UT found that the argument could be submitted and did succeed.

The UT therefore remitted the decision for reconsideration by the FTT.

[17.40]   HMRC v Marlborough DP Ltd[48]—Upper Tribunal Tax and Chancery—Johnson & Brannan JJ—appeal from First-Tier Tribunal—income tax—Income Tax (Earnings and Pensions) Act 2003, Pt 7A—loans from remuneration trust to director/shareholder were disguised remuneration

This was an appeal to the Upper Tribunal ('UT') to consider whether loans made to a company's sole shareholder and director from an offshore remuneration trust ('RT')

---

[47]   *HMRC v Ritchie* [2019] UKUT 71.
[48]   *HMRC v Marlborough DP Ltd* [2024] UKUT 98.

funded by contributions from the company were disguised remuneration subject to tax under Pt 7A of the Income Tax (Earnings and Pensions) Act 2003.

A dentist ('D') set up the respondent company, Marlborough DP Ltd ('MDPL'), through which he carried out his dental practice. MDPL entered into a tax avoidance scheme, whereby it made payments through Baxendale-Walker ('BW') remuneration trust arrangements, which were paid to D by way of loans, with the objective that MDPL would obtain a corporation tax deduction for the payments and D would avoid the income tax on the loan amounts. The scheme was not effective and the question arose as to the correct tax treatment of the various payments.

The UT had to consider whether the First-Tier Tribunal ('FTT') was correct to find that the payments did not constitute employment income in D's hands, such that they were taxable as distributions in respect of his shareholding in MDPL. The HMRC argued that the payments made by MDPL to RT and the subsequent loans to D constituted payments from D's office as a director of MDPL. The HMRC considered it relevant that D had drawn no minimal salary from MDPL during the years in question, but had previously taken drawings, which represented the fruits of D's labour and thus represented earnings in the form of loans which were never intended to be repaid. The HMRC mounted effectively an *Edwards v Bairstow*[49] challenge regarding some of the FTT's findings of fact in relation to whether the contributions to RT were distributions in respect of shares.

The UT stated that the essential question in this appeal was whether the source of the payments made by MDPL to RT was either the office of D as director of MDPL or his shareholding in MDPL.

The UT found the fact that the payments from MDPL to D represented income for labour did not lead to the conclusion that the payments constituted income. The fact that the contributions had been authorised by D in his capacity as a director did not mean that they were employment payments. The UT confirmed that the FTT had applied the correct legal principles in finding that the source of the payments was the director's shareholding, not his office as director, and were not general earnings. It was reasonable for it to reach this conclusion and it did not fail to take account of relevant evidence.

However, the UT held that the FTT had erred by concluding that, for Pt 7A to apply, employment had to be part of the reason for the reward. The test in s 554A(1)(c) of the Income Tax (Earnings and Pensions) Act 2003 (broadly requiring it to be reasonable to suppose that the relevant arrangement was a means of providing rewards, recognition or loans in connection with employment) was held to be objective and drafted expansively to catch a wide range of arrangements where benefits were provided 'in connection with' (rather than 'from') an employment. It was held that Parliament's intention was to give s 554A of the Income Tax (Earnings and Pensions) Act 2003 a wider scope than to charge income tax on general earnings. It followed that a loan could be provided in connection with an employment even if it was not 'from' an employment.

---

[49] *Edwards v Bairstow* [1956] A.C. 14.

The UT considered that the purpose of Pt 7A of the Income Tax (Earnings and Pensions) Act 2003 was to tax, as employment income, payments provided through third parties and there had to be a relatively strong or direct nexus between the employment/directorship and the contribution/loans. It was not Parliament's intention to catch loans where the relationship between the loan and the employment were merely peripheral and the emphasis on the 'essence' of the arrangements reinforced that conclusion.

It was held that the FTT had erred in law in stating that the statutory test was that employment had to be part of the reason for reward.

MDPL's profits were profits of the dental practice that D was actively engaged in. D was the sole director of MDPL and the 'guiding mind' of the company business from which the profits were derived. It was held that the test in s 554A(1c) was wider than the tax charge on general earnings, so was not confined to schemes involving a redirection of earnings. However, a relatively strong or direct nexus between the employment (office) and benefit had to exist. The director's resolutions to make contributions to the trust and loan requests were insufficiently connected to his office to satisfy the test. However, his sole responsibility for the conduct and direction of MDPL's business resulted in a sufficient direct and close connection between the loans and the directorship such that Pt 7A applied. As a relevant step occurred between 9 December 2010 and 5 April 2011, the Pt 7A anti-forestalling provisions deemed it to occur on 6 April 2012, so HMRC's determination could be increased.

The UT noted that the contributions made by MDPL were not deductible as planned tax efficiency had been the objective of the scheme, in addition to rewarding D. The twin objectives had been to empty MDPL of profit, and to advance that profit via a trust to D by way of non-taxable loans. There had been no intention to benefit MDPL's trade by doing so. The loans were caught by the anti-avoidance provisions of Pt 7A as being connected with D's directorship. It was impossible for the UT to conclude that because the sums were caught within Pt 7, that they were expensed wholly for the purpose of MDPL's trade, and HMRC's appeal on that ground was allowed.

[17.41] *Atholl House Productions and Revenue and Customs Commissioners*[50]*—First-Tier Tribunal—case remitted to FTT from UT—income tax and national insurance—Income Tax (Earnings and Pensions) Act 2003—intermediaries legislation—IR35—personal service company—if contracts in question had been directly between the end user and the individual, would they have been contracts of employment*

This case deals with the applicability of the intermediaries legislation ('IR35') to the arrangements between the appellant, a personal service company, Atholl House Productions Ltd, and the British Broadcasting Corporation ('BBC') regarding the services provided by Ms Kaye Adams. This legislation seeks to address tax avoidance

---

[50] *Atholl House Productions and Revenue and Customs Commissioners* [2024] UKFTT 37, see further *R & C Commrs v Atholl House Productions Ltd (Kaye Adams)* [2022] EWCA Civ 501, [2022] BTC 12, *Arthur Cox Employment Law Yearbook 2022* at [18.34].

through the use of intermediaries, such as limited companies, by individuals providing services akin to employment. This is the fourth decision by the First-Tier Tribunal ('FTT'), in the long-running case involving broadcaster Ms Adams, and arose from a remittance of the case back to the FTT from the Upper Tribunal ('UT'). HMRC (the respondent) raised determinations of just under £125,000 for income tax and national insurance. These related to status determinations under the intermediaries/IR35 rules (Income Tax (Earnings and Pensions) Act 2003, ss 48–61; Social Security Contributions (Intermediaries) Regulations 2000,[51] regs 5 and 6).

HMRC's initial enquiry began in July 2014. The *Atholl House* case concerned a headline tax figure of £124,000, which was likely to have been reduced to around £70,000 once taxes already paid by Atholl House and Ms Adams were considered.

Ms Adams applied to the FTT in March 2018 and was successful in her first hearing in April 2019. HMRC claimed the FTT had made errors in law and was granted permission to appeal to the UT. While the UT noted certain mistakes in the FTT's rationale, the UT reached the same conclusion as the FTT. HMRC claimed further errors in law were made and appealed the UT's decision to the Court of Appeal of England and Wales for a third hearing. The Court of Appeal's decision in April 2022 concluded that certain errors were made and remitted the case to the UT.[52] The UT made an order to remit the case back to the FTT as the more appropriate forum to deal with the case, the order of the UT sanctioned the introduction of new factual evidence to be laid before the FTT.

The key issue was whether, had Ms Adams been contracted directly with the BBC, would she have been considered an employee for income tax and national insurance contribution purposes under IR35. The FTT reviewed the contractual arrangements and determined that if Ms Adams's services had been provided directly to the BBC, they would not have constituted a contract of employment but a contract for services, indicating self-employment.

The FTT considered various factors, including the written contract terms, the extent of control exercised by the BBC, the ability to provide substitutes, and the practical behaviour of the parties. An emphasis was placed on the holistic perspective of the relationship rather than isolating certain elements.

The hearing focused on the correct application of the three-stage test using the *Ready Mixed Concrete*[53] case framework, being mutuality of obligation (3A), control (3B), and other factors consistent with a contract of service (3C).

The FTT noted that Stage 3A requires a contract of service whereby the employer is to provide work or a retainer and the employee to perform work or services personally.

---

[51] Social Security Contributions (Intermediaries) Regulations 2000 (SI 2000/727).
[52] *R & C Commrs v Atholl House Productions Ltd (Kaye Adams)* [2022] EWCA Civ 501, [2022] BTC 12, Arthur Cox Employment Law Yearbook 2022 at [18.34].
[53] *Ready Mixed Concrete (South East) Ltd v Minister of Pensions and National Insurance* [1968] 2 QB 497.

Stage 3B requires the employer to have control over what the worker does and how, when, and where they do it.

The FTT further noted that Stage 3C requires an examination of any other terms of the contract to determine if they are indicative of an employment relationship. The factors which the FTT considered when analysing if the requirements of Stage 3C were met were:

— the financial risk undertaken by the putative employee;
— dependence on or independence of the putative employee from the putative employer;
— the existence of similar engagements and the overall way of carrying out professional activities;
— provision of own equipment;
— length and continuity of the relationship;
— the degree to which the putative employee is part and parcel of the employer's organisation;
— custom and practice in the industry concerning employment or self-employment status;
— contractual statements regarding employment status;
— whether other benefits typical of employment are absent; and
— the employee's inclusion or exclusion from internal business opportunities.

The FTT noted that the position was 'finely balanced'; however it believed the factors pointing towards employment were outweighed by the factors pointing in the direction of a self-employment relationship. In doing so, the FTT added that the BBC did not treat Ms Adams as an employee in any way.

The FTT found that, despite Ms Adams being able to provide a substitute for her services, the dominant feature of her contract signified personal performance, fulfilling the mutuality of obligation criteria. The FTT allowed the appeal, stating the engagements fell outside IR35 provisions and Ms Adams was not an employee of the BBC.

The FTT further found that the hypothetical contracts were indicative of self-employment, considering factors like the absence of traditional employment benefits, the ability to work for other clients, and the nature of the control exercised by the BBC.

[17.42] *Aramark Ltd v HMRC*[54]—**First-Tier Tribunal—appeal against HMRC decision—whether company liable for NIC under the 'host employer' provisions**

In this case, the FTT found that the appellant company, Aramark, was liable to account for employer's NIC under the so-called 'host employer' provisions in the Social Security (Categorisation of Earners) Regulations 1978,[55] Sch 3 para 9 (as they applied before 6 April 2014).

---

[54] *Aramark Ltd v HMRC* [2024] UKFTT 00832 (TC).
[55] Social Security (Categorisation of Earners) Regulations 1978 (SI 1978/1689).

The appellant was a UK company and part of a group headed by a US corporation. Its business included providing catering and hospitality services to the operators of offshore oil and gas installations located in the North Sea on the UK Continental Shelf. In 2004, around 700 of its employees were transferred to another group company, Aramark US Offshore Services LLC (OSI), and immediately subcontracted back to Aramark. The intention was to eliminate the cost of secondary Class 1 NIC to ensure that Aramark remained competitive. This was believed to be effective because the contractual employer, OSI, did not have a place of business in the UK and therefore could not be liable for UK NICs.

HMRC raised determinations on the basis that Aramark should be treated as the secondary contributor under the 'host employer' provisions. Aramark was appealing in respect of those determinations.

A host employer, under UK law, is a business in the UK to which the employee's services are supplied by a foreign employer. The host employer provisions state that a host employer is made liable for secondary Class 1 contributions if an employee works in the UK under a contract with a foreign employer (ie who has no UK place of business) and where three conditions are met:

1. the personal service of the employee is made available to the host employer;
2. the personal service is rendered for the purposes of the host employer's business; and
3. the personal service for the host employer begins on or after 6 April 1994.

The FTT was asked to determine whether the host employer provisions applied to the appellant in respect of the employees provided by OSI. This required that there be a supply of staff and that the personal service of the staff was rendered for the purposes of the appellant's business.

Aramark argued that the host employer provisions were intended to cover workers who had been 'seconded' to someone other than their contractual employer as *de facto* employees, but in this case, OSI continued to exercise the control and management of staff through the unit manager.

HMRC argued that while OSI might retain a contractual right of control, it was Aramark that exercised control over workers on the offshore installations. The unit manager, although ostensibly an OSI employee, reported to Aramark's operations manager, so that directions to the unit manager from Aramark cascaded down to all members of the offshore crew.

The FTT held that the purpose of the host employer provisions was to impose a secondary NIC liability where a worker is contractually employed by a foreign employer, but where the host acts as an employer in terms of the substantive day-to-day control of the worker. The FTT stressed that day-to-day control was not the same as the 'ultimate control' needed to establish an employment relationship (if the same test was applied there would be no need for the host employer provisions, as the host employer would be the actual employer).

In this case, the FTT concluded that OSI was little more than a contractual shell. Its decisions were limited to formal HR/contractual and certain financial decisions following recommendations by Aramark. The FTT found that the appellant exercised day-to-day control of the relevant employees of the US company, such that they were 'seconded' to the appellant for this purpose. This meant that the personal service of the employees was 'made available' to the appellant and 'rendered' for the purposes of the appellant's business as host employer. As the conditions of the host employer provisions were met, the appeal was dismissed.

The FTT's conclusion was consistent with the recent decision in *Bilfinger Salmis UK Ltd v HMRC*,[56] concerning the operation of the host employer regulations. Both cases dealt with the provisions of the legislation as it was until 2014. From 6 April 2014, the Social Security (Categorisation of Earners) Regulations 1978 were amended to include (among others) an anti-avoidance provision (reg 5A). Cases such as these are unlikely to arise again in respect of years later than 2014–2015.

---

[56] *Bilfinger Salmis UK Ltd v HMRC* [2024] UKFTT 736 (TC).

Chapter 18

Transfer of Undertakings

INTRODUCTION

[18.01]

Dismissal

In *Lewis v Dow Silicones UK Ltd*, the UK EAT considered whether a dismissal was transfer-connected and accordingly prohibited.

Post-Transfer Changes

The permissibility of post-transfer changes to terms of employment was considered by the Labour Court in *Trinity Motors Ltd v Breslin*.

Transfer?

In *Ballymun Regional Youth Resource v Davis*, the Labour Court considered whether there was a transfer of undertaking in the first place.

The transfer of tortious liability from the old employer to the new employer was considered by the UK EAT in *Sean Pong Tyres Ltd v Moore*.

In *Mansfield Care Ltd v Newman*, the UK EAT considered whether there was a transfer of undertakings in circumstances where a care home closed and each resident was transferred to one of two other care homes. In *Bicknell v NHS Nottingham and Nottinghamshire Integrated Commissioning Board*, the UK EAT considered whether a transfer of undertakings occurred in circumstances where there was a reorganisation of the public health service in the region concerned.

DISMISSAL

[18.02] *Lewis v Dow Silicones UK Ltd*[1]—*UK Employment Appeal Tribunal— appeal from employment tribunal—Employment Rights Act 1996, s 95(1)(c)— Transfer of Undertakings (Protection of Employment) Regulations 2006,*[2] *reg 4(9)—unfair dismissal—transfer of undertaking sole or principle reason for the dismissal—whether economic, technical or organisational reason for dismissal made out*

The claimant appealed against an employment tribunal's dismissal of his complaint of constructive automatic unfair dismissal as a result of a transfer of undertakings. His appeal succeeded and the matter was remitted to a tribunal.[3] The second hearing concluded that, while the transfer 'would have involved a substantial change in working conditions to the material detriment of the claimant', it was neither the sole nor principal reason for the dismissal. The claim for unfair dismissal was therefore not well founded. This was the appeal against that second decision.

The claimant commenced work for the company Npower as an operations technician at its combined heat and power plant in Wales in 1999. In 2013, the respondent, Dow Silicones UK Ltd, purchased the plant and outsourced operations and maintenance to another company, Engie. In 2017, the respondent insourced operations and maintenance. This amounted to a service provision change under the Transfer of Undertakings (Protection of Employment) Regulations 2006. The respondent sought to introduce changes, including to standby/call-out arrangements and responsibility for issuing safety permits. The claimant, who had all along raised health and safety concerns, resigned.

It was clear from the employment tribunal's conclusions that there were pre-existing problems with the respondent's standby/call-out arrangements as well as the need for a single system of safe work permits. According to the tribunal, the need to address these problems, and thereby ensure the safety of those onsite or living nearby, was the sole or principal reason for the claimant's dismissal, and not the transfer of undertakings.

The UK EAT found no basis for this determination, which was not the respondent's pleaded case to begin with. From a reading of the respondent's defence, there had been a failure to adequately plead its case at all and the appeal would succeed on that basis alone. The tribunal's finding was not supported by any of the respondent's evidence, witness or documentary, at either hearing. Rather, it had come from something said by the claimant under cross-examination, which was not evidence of the respondent's reason for dismissal. This was fatal to the tribunal's finding that the respondent had established an 'economic, technical or organisational' reason for the dismissal.

---

[1] *Lewis v Dow Silicones UK Ltd* [2024] EAT 51.
[2] Transfer of Undertakings (Protection of Employment) Regulations 2006 (SI 2006/246).
[3] See *Lewis v Dow Silicones UK Ltd* UKEAT/0155/20/LA in *Arthur Cox Employment Law Yearbook 2021* at [21.05].

The appeal was allowed and a decision substituted that the claimant was unfairly dismissed because the sole or principle reason for dismissal was the transfer; no economic, technical or organisational reason for the dismissal had been made out.

POST-TRANSFER CHANGES

[18.03] *Trinity Motors Ltd v Breslin*[4]—*Labour Court—appeal from Workplace Relations Commission—European Communities (Protection of Employees on Transfer of Undertakings) Regulations 2003,*[5] *reg 11(1)—transfer of undertakings—complaint of unlawful variation to terms of employment contract post-transfer—complaint of diminution of contractual entitlements—information and consultation, reg 8—absence of employee representatives—measurable change to employment contract post-transfer*

The respondent employer, a Volkswagen franchisee, appealed against two WRC decisions which upheld complaints under the European Communities (Protection of Employees on Transfer of Undertakings) Regulations 2003 (the '2003 Regulations'), awarding the claimant compensation of €5,120 and €35,840, respectively.

The claimant transferred to the respondent's employment under a transfer of undertakings on 4 January 2021, having been employed by his previous employer (the 'transferor') since 1996. He complained that the respondent did not consult him in relation to the transfer and that it failed to observe the terms and conditions transferred from his previous employment.

In December 2020, the transferor confirmed in writing to the claimant that his employment would transfer to 'the Trinity Motor group' on 4 January 2021 and that there would be no change to his employment terms. Following the transfer, the claimant was provided with a copy of the respondent's employment handbook which, he asserted, differed from his old handbook in material respects. It was agreed there were some differences between the manner in which the transferor and the respondent carried on their business, including in their opening hours. This was by request of sales staff who, post-transfer, wished to increase their commission earnings. Sales staff were therefore given the option of changing their working hours to reflect the new opening hours or to remain on their existing hours.

The claimant, who had been brand manager and head of sales, stated that he agreed to change his work hours in order to 'fit in', having been asked on several occasions to do so. As a result, he claimed that his days off were more restricted and his annual leave was reduced by 10 days post-transfer. He now reported to a 'director' instead of a 'principal', with the result that he was no longer part of the senior management team. His job title changed to 'sales manager', he no longer arranged car finance for clients,

---

[4] *Trinity Motors Ltd v Breslin* TUD249, TUD2410.
[5] European Communities (Protection of Employees on Transfer of Undertakings) Regulations 2003 (SI 131/2003).

was no longer in charge of vehicle valuations, no longer had sole authority over pricing trade-ins, and was not included in management meetings. Due to a streamlining of sales personnel at the time, there was an increased workload, though the claimant accepted that this was due to the Covid-19 pandemic.

In April 2021, the claimant sought a meeting with the respondent to raise a number of issues, chief among them how busy the sales department had become. He subsequently went on sick leave, during which period he submitted a written grievance stating that there had been an unlawful variation in his terms and conditions of employment post-transfer. Believing his role to be diminished, the claimant tendered his resignation.

The Labour Court was in no doubt that a transfer of undertakings had taken place. Nevertheless, it was not argued that there were no employee representatives, and so there was no breach of reg 8 of the 2003 Regulations, as submitted. Nor was it disputed that the claimant was notified by the transferor of the date of the proposed transfer, the reason for the transfer, and its implications for employees. It concluded 'there were no changes to the claimant's terms and conditions linked to the transfer, therefore, there were no measures that the employee needed to be informed of'. The claimant accepted that he was not placed on probation, was never asked to move location, and was never refused annual leave or told that his annual leave entitlement was being reduced. The claimant's evidence, in the round, could not be considered a diminution of his rights and obligations arising from his contract in existence at the time of the transfer. The only 'measurable change' was the introduction of new working hours, to which the claimant voluntarily signed up.

The appeals were thus upheld and the decisions of the Adjudication Officer were set aside.

TRANSFER?

[18.04] *Ballymun Regional Youth Resource v Davis*[6]—*Labour Court—appeal from Workplace Relations Commission—Redundancy Payments Acts 1967 to 2014—European Commission (Protection of Employees on Transfer of Undertakings) Regulations 2003*[7]—*whether a transfer of undertaking occurred*

The respondent appealed against a WRC decision upholding a complaint under the Redundancy Payments Act 1967. The Adjudication Officer held that the claimant had been dismissed by reason of redundancy on 31 December 2021 and that he was entitled to a lump sum payment.

The claimant was employed by the respondent as a youth outreach worker between April 2002 and December 2021. His was one of four positions out of six in the outreach team that were funded by the HSE. Between May and November 2021, the respondent

---

[6] *Ballymun Regional Youth Resource v Davis* RPD249.
[7] European Communities (Protection of Employees on Transfer of Undertakings) Regulations 2003 (SI 131/2003).

was actively considering whether to retain the outreach team or relocate it, either as a standalone service or within another larger organisation. It appears that the HSE was strongly supportive of relocation by means of a transfer of undertakings. Ultimately, the respondent took the decision to move the team to another organisation.

Following a period of considerable indecision on the issue, the respondent took the view that the move would not give rise to a transfer of undertaking. Notices of dismissal issued to all of the HSE-funded outreach workers and the claimant was duly offered employment with the Star Project in Ballymun, commencing in January 2022. The claimant was advised by the Star Project that his employment with it would not be regarded as giving rise to a transfer of undertaking. However, in March 2022 the respondent again changed its position, advising the claimant that a transfer of undertaking had indeed occurred, though the position of the Star Project remained unchanged.

The Court found that, from May 2021 onwards, the respondent conducted itself 'generally in a most unreasonable manner'. It engaged in neither a redundancy consultation process nor in a transfer of undertakings information consultation process, despite having vacillated on the issue. It appeared to the Court that this behaviour could only be explained by the respondent's desire to retain the HSE funding it had been in receipt of to support the claimant's work. Nevertheless, the Court found that the transfer of the majority of the outreach team, along with essential funding from the HSE, was a transfer of undertaking. The claimant formed part of that transfer and he was not therefore dismissed by reason of redundancy.

The appeal succeeded and the decision of the WRC was set aside.

[18.05] *Sean Pong Tyres Ltd v Moore[8]—UK Employment Appeal Tribunal—appeal from employment tribunal—refusal of application to amend pleadings—transfer of undertakings—whether tortious liability transferred from the transferor to the transferee*

The respondent appealed against the employment tribunal's refusal of its application to amend its response in order to plead that liability had transferred to another company. The tribunal went on to uphold the claimant's complaints of unfair constructive dismissal, age and race-related discrimination and harassment. The claimant did not participate in the appeal.

The perpetrator of the discriminatory conduct in question transferred to another company (the 'putative transferee') in July 2021, by which point the claimant had resigned in response to that conduct, in April 2021.

In rejecting the appeal, the UK EAT concluded that even if there was a transfer from the respondent to the putative transferee, and the perpetrator's employment transferred, the respondent's primary liability to the claimant under the relevant legislation would not have transferred to the putative transferee.

---

[8] *Sean Pong Tyres Ltd v Moore* [2024] EAT 1.

Even if this was not a correct statement of the law, the tribunal had not erred in refusing the amendment application in that it had properly recognised it as an amendment designed to alter the basis of an existing claim by substituting a new respondent for the discrimination claim. If the respondent's statement of the law was correct, on the other hand, any prejudice to the respondent would be significantly lessened because its remedy would lie against its representative for failing to identify the potential defence to the proceedings at an earlier stage.

The appeal was accordingly dismissed.

[18.06] *Mansfield Care Ltd v Newman*[9]—*UK Employment Appeal Tribunal—appeal from employment tribunal—Transfer of Undertakings (Protection of Employment) Regulations 2006,*[10] *reg 3—transfer of undertakings—business transfer—redundancy—Trade Union and Labour Relations (Consolidation) Act 1992—employment status—contract of employment—Employment Rights Act 1996, s 230(1)*

The respondent companies appealed an employment tribunal's finding that there had been a relevant transfer of undertakings from one company to the other and that there was a failure to consult staff.

The respondents operated care homes. In 2021, one respondent entered into discussions for the sale of its business to the second respondent. The employment tribunal found that, at some point in June 2021, a discussion took place between the respondents regarding continuity of care for the elderly residents, who would be moving from one facility to another. Although the respondents did not commit their agreement to writing, the tribunal was satisfied that during this discussion, assurances were made that 'the staff would also be looked after'.

Staff were subsequently informed that the care home in which they worked would be closing. They raised concerns through their union representative about the respondents' precise intentions for the staff, which remained unclear. It was suspected that there was a collective redundancy situation involving over 20 employees such as to give rise to consulting obligations. These concerns were put in a letter to the care home manager, whose evidence was that she did not see that communication.

In a meeting, it was explained that all staff that would be transferring to one of two homes, that they would be looking after residents from their current facility and would be able to choose which location they preferred. The lead claimant, Ms Smith, was a registered general nurse who had worked at the closing facility for over 20 years. She worked two night shifts per week on a regular basis over an extensive period, with an expectation that this would continue. Although described as a 'bank contract',[11] the claimant was treated as an employee for tax and national insurance purposes, and in respect of holiday entitlement and pension deductions. She received her P45 in July

---

[9] *Mansfield Care Ltd v Newman and Ors and Rollandene Ltd* [2024] EAT 128.
[10] Transfer of Undertakings (Protection of Employment) Regulations 2006 (SI 2006/246).
[11] 'Bank staff' are skilled healthcare professionals who provide temporary and short-term cover at care facilities in the UK.

2021 and was offered a position at one of the two homes, having been interviewed. She worked there for four weeks but finding the new facility too big, decided to leave.

The proceedings before the employment tribunal arose from multiple claims: one seeking protective awards for a failure to consult on collective redundancies, the other alleging unfair dismissal, unpaid holiday pay, wrongful dismissal, unpaid wages and redundancy pay.

The 'selling' respondent argued that there had been a relevant transfer in accordance with the Transfer of Undertakings (Protection of Employment) Regulations 2006 ('TUPE'), such that there was no redundancy situation. Alternatively, it contended that the employees at the relevant time numbered less than 20, as those who worked as 'bank staff' were not to be included in the relevant headcount.

The 'buying' respondent, having been joined to the proceedings, denied there was a relevant transfer. Alternatively, it contended that it had offered each of the claimants employment but they had objected to being transferred.

The employment tribunal was satisfied that the selling respondent was a 'going concern', notwithstanding its contention that it could no longer afford to look after its residents to the standard required. This did not alter the fact that, as at June 2021, the selling respondent was still caring for its residents. The tribunal was also satisfied that the going concern transferred to the buying respondent, which paid a purchase price calculated by reference to the number of residents who transferred to its care.

The employment tribunal found that there had been a service provision change in respect of the care home residents for the purposes of TUPE. Accordingly, the staff should have transferred to the employment of the buying respondent.

Having found that the claimant was an employee of the selling respondent as at the date of transfer, the employment tribunal extended that finding to the other 'bank staff'—a group comprising more than 20 employees. The tribunal noted that the term 'bank staff' in the context in which it was used was unhelpful and not determinative of employment. Having determined that more than 20 employees were to be affected by the closure of the nursing home, the tribunal went on to find that there had been no consultation on the part of either respondent.

On appeal, the EAT concluded that the employment tribunal had made no error of law in its approach to the question of employment status, and permissibly found that the lead claimant had a continuing contractual relationship (as opposed to a series of contracts for each assignment) with the selling respondent.

However, the employment tribunal was found to have erred in finding that there had been a failure to consult. Its conclusion that there had been a relevant transfer would suggest that the employees should have been dismissed, rather than simply transferring to the buying respondent. That conclusion could not stand, given the tribunal's finding that the respondents had contemplated the continued employment of the staff. The tribunal had made no finding that there was any proposal for collective redundancies.

The appeal was therefore part-allowed.

[18.07] Bicknell v NHS Nottingham and Nottinghamshire Integrated Commissioning Board[12]—UK Employment Appeal Tribunal—appeal from employment tribunal—Transfer of Undertaking (Protection of Employment) Regulations 2006[13]—dismissal—whether there was a relevant transfer—commissioning entity—whether employer engaged in economic activity—public administrative function

The claimant appealed against an employment tribunal's dismissal of his complaints of automatic unfair dismissal and dismissal because of a transfer of undertakings. In reaching its conclusions, the tribunal found that there was not a 'relevant transfer' from the claimant's employer to the body that would be succeeded by the respondent, the NHS Nottingham and Nottinghamshire Integrated Commissioning Board.

Following a statutory restructure of the NHS, clinical commissioning groups ('CCGs') were established with responsibilities for different geographical areas. In 2020, six CCGs in Nottinghamshire (one of which was the claimant's employer) merged to form what would subsequently be replaced by the respondent.

The employment tribunal's analysis was concerned only with the merging of the claimant's employer with the other Nottinghamshire CCGs, and whether there was a transfer of undertaking at that point. It explained that the 'core function' of CCGs was for the commissioning of healthcare services. As this did not entail the supply of goods or services on the market, the claimant's employer was not undertaking an 'economic activity', and so there was no relevant transfer of undertaking. It followed that the claimant was not unfairly dismissed. Had there been such a transfer, the dismissal would have been automatically unfair.

The UK EAT rejected the claimant's submission that the tribunal misunderstood the test of an economic activity. The leading authority[14] was unequivocal that, for commissioning to be an economic activity, the commissioner also had to supply goods or services to the market. Commissioning by itself could not be an economic activity. That reasoning was not obviously or manifestly wrong, and so there was no reason to disturb it. Nor did the EAT find that the tribunal had misunderstood the test of public administration functions. Having satisfied itself that the activities of CCGs did not constitute an economic activity, it was not necessary for the tribunal to go on to examine whether they exercised public administrative functions. Finally, the EAT was satisfied that the tribunal made sufficient findings with respect to the relevant activities of a CCG and gave adequate reasons for why it fell to be treated as a commissioning entity. The tribunal's findings were set out with reference to the underlying statutory framework.[15] All other functions or activities of the CCG were 'clearly ancillary' to that function.

The appeal was, accordingly, dismissed.

---

[12] *Bicknell and The British Medical Association v NHS Nottingham and Nottinghamshire Integrated Commissioning Board* [2024] EAT 103.
[13] Transfer of Undertakings (Protection of Employment) Regulations 2006 (SI 2006/246).
[14] *Nicholls v London Borough of Croydon* [2019] ICR 542.
[15] Health and Social Care Act 2012.

Chapter 19

Unfair Dismissal

INTRODUCTION

[19.01]

Agency Workers

Liability for unfair dismissal affecting agency workers was considered by the European Court of Justice in *LM v Omnitel Comunicaciones SL*.

Capability

Dismissal on the grounds of capability was the subject of the decision of the UK EAT in *Kikwera-Akaka v Salvation Army Trading Co Ltd*.

Choice of Employer

The importance of the identification of the employer in unfair dismissal proceedings is illustrated by the decision of the Labour Court in *Element Pictures v Arkins*, where the claimant was successively employed by a number of special purpose vehicles but the claimant issued proceedings against the parent company.

Compensation

The manner in which compensation for unfair dismissal should be calculated was addressed by the Labour Court in *Waterford Health Park Pharmacy Ltd v Foley* and by the UK EAT in *Astha Ltd and Chakraborty v Grewal*.

The UK EAT in *N Notaro Homes Ltd v Keirle* considered whether compensation should be reduced by reason of a finding of contributory conduct.

Conduct

A number of decisions relating to dismissal for conduct reasons are noted, namely the decisions of the Labour Court in *Aer Lingus v Linehan* and *Ringsend Community Services Forum Clg v Moore* and of the UK EAT in *Greater Glasgow Health Board v Mullen*.

Conduct—Freedom of Expression

Dismissal for having disclosed confidential information to a journalist and whether same constituted misconduct or whether dismissal as a reaction to same constituted an infringement of the employee's entitlement to freedom of expression was considered by the European Court of Human Rights in *Aghajanyan v Armenia*.

Constructive Dismissal

A number of constructive dismissal decisions are noted, namely *DHL Supply Chain (Ireland) Ltd v McAndrew* and *Forte Healthcare Ltd v Duffy* (Labour Court), and *Leaney v Loughborough University* and *Nelson v Renfrewshire Council* (UK EAT).

Dismissal or Resignation?

Whether there was a dismissal or a resignation was considered by the Labour Court in *St John of God Community Services v Oyegoke*.

Notice

The Labour Court, in *Ringsend Community Services Forum Clg v Moore*, considered whether the employer had discharged its obligation to give pay in lieu of notice.

Other Substantial Grounds—Refusal to be Vaccinated

One 'other substantial grounds' case is noted, namely whether a refusal to be vaccinated justified dismissal—*Masiero v Barchester Healthcare Ltd* (UK EAT).

Redundancy

The redundancy defence and the adequacy of the consultation process in a claim of unfair dismissal was considered by the Court of Appeal of England and Wales in *De Bank Haycocks v ADP RPO UK Ltd*.

Re-engagement

The Supreme Court in *An Bord Banistíochta, Gaelscoil Moshíológ v The Labour Court* considered circumstances in which the remedy of re-engagement is appropriate.

Retirement

In *Presentation Secondary School Board of Management v Murphy*, the impact of retirement on a constructive dismissal claim was considered by the Labour Court.

Trade Union Activities

Finally, *Doyle Shipping Group v Troy* (Labour Court) is a rare example of a claim of dismissal for trade union activities and whether it operated to allow the claim to proceed notwithstanding the fact that the claimant did not have 12 months' service.

AGENCY WORKERS

[19.02]   *LM v Omnitel Comunicaciones SL*[1]—*European Court of Justice— reference for a preliminary ruling from Spain—social policy—Directive 2008/104/ EC,*[2] *art 3(1)—temporary agency work—user undertaking—definition—contract for the provision of services—principle of equal treatment—Directive 2006/54/EC,*[3] *art 15—maternity leave—invalid or unfair dismissal—declaration that the temporary-work agency and the user are jointly and severally liable*

This request for a preliminary ruling concerned the interpretation of art 3(1) and art 5(1) of Directive 2008/104/EC on temporary agency work and art 2(2) and art 15 of Directive 2006/54/EC on the implementation of the principle of equal opportunities and equal treatment of men and women in matters of employment and occupation. The request was made in Spanish proceedings between the applicant, LM, and the respondent companies, Omnitel Comunicaciones SL and others, concerning the applicant's dismissal following maternity leave.

The applicant completed an occupational traineeship at Microsoft from September 2010 to June 2011. Following this, she entered into successive employment contracts with the respondents between August 2011 and August 2017. These companies provided services to Microsoft under agreements that required the applicant to perform specific contractually agreed services. Under her final contract, dated August 2017, the applicant was employed as a sales consultant for Microsoft's original equipment

---

[1]   *LM v Omnitel Comunicaciones SL and Ors* (Case C-441/23).
[2]   Directive 2008/104/EC on temporary agency work.
[3]   Directive 2006/54/EC on the implementation of the principle of equal opportunities and equal treatment of men and women in matters of employment and occupation (recast).

manufacturer ('OEM') department. Her duties primarily involved providing marketing services exclusively for Microsoft, which were not performed by any of its employees.

In 2020, while the applicant was pregnant, Microsoft informed the respondents that their service contract would terminate on 30 September 2020, citing budgetary constraints. Shortly thereafter, on 22 September 2020, the applicant was temporarily unable to work, and following the birth of her child on 8 December 2020, she took maternity leave. This was immediately followed by parental leave and annual leave. Upon her return on 29 April 2021, the applicant received a letter from the respondent terminating her employment, effective 27 April 2021. The dismissal was justified on the grounds of a reduction in demand, attributed to the cancellation of planned projects.

The applicant challenged her dismissal before the Social Court in Madrid, seeking a declaration that her dismissal was invalid or unfair. She also sought joint and several liability for the respondents, including Microsoft. The Court ruled that Microsoft bore no liability, as the respondents had retained responsibility for organising the applicant's work schedule, processing her salary, providing training, and managing her leave, including maternity leave. While it declared the applicant's dismissal invalid, the Court rejected her claim for maternity-related discrimination, concluding that the dismissal was based exclusively on budgetary reasons. Nonetheless, the Court ordered the respondents to compensate the applicant for unpaid salary and untaken leave.

The applicant appealed the decision to the High Court of Justice in Madrid (the referring Court). She argued that her employment with the respondent constituted an 'assignment' to Microsoft, thereby implicating Microsoft in her dismissal. She sought reinstatement to her role and joint and several liability for Microsoft.

The referring Court expressed uncertainty regarding the applicability of Directive 2008/104/EC to this case, particularly concerning its application to undertakings not recognised under national law as temporary-work agencies due to a lack of administrative authorisation. It raised questions about whether the applicant's employment arrangement constituted an 'assignment' to Microsoft and whether the supervision and direction of her work rested with Microsoft or the respondents. The Court highlighted that the applicant had performed daily tasks for Microsoft, was provided with a computer by Microsoft, worked remotely to assist Microsoft's customers, regularly communicated with Microsoft managers, and accessed Microsoft's premises weekly. Conversely, the respondents retained administrative functions, such as approving her leave, setting her hours, and submitting monthly reports on her activities.

Finally, the referring Court questioned the implications of the invalid dismissal ruling for the applicant's reinstatement. It noted that the role the applicant held prior to her dismissal no longer existed with the respondent, raising the issue of whether Microsoft, as the user undertaking, bore any obligation to reinstate her under art 5(1) of Directive 2008/104/EC. The referring Court queried whether, under the Directive 2008/104/EC, Microsoft could be jointly and severally liable with the respondents for the consequences of her dismissal, including reinstatement, back pay, and compensation.

In those circumstances, the referring Court decided to stay the proceedings and to refer a number of questions to the European Court of Justice ('ECJ') for preliminary ruling.

The first question addressed whether Directive 2008/104/EC applies to entities that are not recognised as temporary-work agencies under national law due to the absence of administrative authorisation. The ECJ held that Directive 2008/104/EC applies to any undertaking that enters into employment contracts or employment relationships with workers for the purpose of assigning them to a user undertaking to work under its supervision and direction. The lack of recognition under national law does not preclude the application of Directive 2008/104/EC. The Court reasoned that limiting Directive 2008/104/EC's scope to formally recognised temporary-work agencies would undermine its purpose, which is to provide uniform protections for temporary agency workers across the EU.

The second question related to the definition of 'temporary agency work' and whether the applicant's employment relationship fell within the scope of Directive 2008/104/EC. The Court noted that temporary agency work involves a 'triangular' relationship: the worker has a contract with the agency; the agency assigns the worker to a user undertaking; and the user undertaking supervises and directs the worker.

In this case, although the respondents retained administrative control over the applicant's leave and hours, the Court found that Microsoft had significant supervisory authority. The applicant's daily activities were integrated into Microsoft's operations, and she worked under its instructions and guidance. The Court emphasised that such a relationship qualifies as temporary agency work, provided the user undertaking exercises supervision and direction over the worker.

In response to the third question, the Court held that art 5(1) of Directive 2008/104/EC requires that temporary agency workers receive the same basic working and employment conditions, including pay, as they would have received if directly recruited by the user undertaking. Therefore, the applicant was entitled to a salary equal to that of Microsoft employees performing comparable roles for the duration of her assignment.

The fourth and fifth questions concerned whether the dismissal protections under Directive 2006/54/EC applied to the applicant's situation and whether Microsoft, as the user undertaking, could be held jointly and severally liable for the consequences of her dismissal. The Court deemed these questions inadmissible, as the contractual relationship between Microsoft and the respondents had ended before the applicant's dismissal. The absence of an active relationship between Microsoft and the applicant rendered the questions hypothetical, preventing the Court from ruling on them.

CAPABILITY

[19.03]   *Kikwera-Akaka v Salvation Army Trading Co Ltd*[4]—*UK Employment Appeal Tribunal—appeal from employment tribunal—unfair dismissal—capability and performance—fairness of dismissal—adequate warning of the risk of dismissal*

The claimant appealed against an employment tribunal's dismissal of his complaints of unfair dismissal, failure to provide written reasons for the dismissal, race discrimination,

---

[4]   *Kikwera-Akaka v Salvation Army Trading Co Ltd* [2024] EAT 49.

harassment and victimisation. The tribunal concluded that the reasons for dismissal were 'capability and performance'.

The claimant worked for the respondent, which is the trading arm of the Salvation Army, from 2016 until his dismissal in April 2019. The respondent operates a number of charity shops which are staffed by a combination of volunteers and employees. In July 2018, when he was working at the Beckenham store, the claimant was issued with a final written warning for a staff discount he had applied. This was reduced to a written warning on appeal. By the end of 2018, a number of other issues had arisen. In particular, the claimant was criticised for his attitude, for rudeness to customers, avoiding tasks, walking off during tasks and failing to carry out tasks with due diligence. For his part, the claimant did not perceive any problems with his work.

In January 2019, the respondent received a complaint about the claimant from a store volunteer who was described as vulnerable, with significant learning difficulties and special needs. The claimant accepted that he had threatened to punch her in the face. The incident led to disciplinary proceedings, which found the claimant guilty of gross misconduct. However, he was issued with a final written warning because the respondent wanted to give him another chance. The final written warning was to remain live for 12 months. Crucially, it advised that further misconduct during that period was likely to result in a further disciplinary hearing that may lead to dismissal.

The claimant was placed on a four-week performance improvement plan ('PIP') but when the PIP was discussed with the claimant in a meeting, he walked out. The employment tribunal accepted that training was offered to the claimant at review meetings, which he refused. The PIP lasted only three-and-a-half weeks before a decision was made that the matter should proceed to a capability review. In a letter, the claimant was invited to attend a performance capability hearing. The tribunal noted that this letter expressly warned him of the possibility of dismissal. The claimant told the hearing that he received no meaningful training, while insisting that he did not require further training and that there were no areas in which he needed to improve. He attributed many of his problems at the store to the volunteers, whom he alleged were envious of him.

The respondent decided to dismiss the claimant. It set out the reasons for that decision in a letter of 24 April 2019. The claimant appealed unsuccessfully, the decision maker found that his performance had not improved to an acceptable standard, and it was reasonable to believe that there was 'unlikely to be any further improvement'. The claimant had decided not to engage with volunteers, which was essential to the respondent's business model and ethos.

The employment tribunal found that the final written warning played a part in the decision to put the claimant on a PIP. The final written warning was for conduct but also 'went to performance in relation to working with volunteers, in a store with many volunteers, of whom a number were vulnerable'. The claimant's conduct was therefore an element of his performance and the two were interlinked. The final written warning was justified; the claimant's conduct was serious and he was 'entirely unrepentant'. There was no reason to think that he would threaten a vulnerable volunteer again. The decision to put the claimant on a PIP was not also reasonable and the decision to cut it short was not enough to take the procedure 'outside the reasonable range'. Finally, the decision to dismiss was itself reasonable.

For the avoidance of doubt, the employment tribunal concluded that, had the PIP been extended by half a week, it would have made no difference; the claimant would not have changed. Even a finding of unfair dismissal would have resulted in a 100% reduction to compensation.

On appeal, the claimant contended that the employment tribunal erred in ruling that his dismissal by reason of capability or performance was fair, in circumstances where he had not been given a fair warning of the risk of dismissal. He also challenged the tribunal's ultimate finding, which was based entirely on what would have happened had the PIP run to completion, rather than what would have happened if the claimant had been given a fair warning.

The EAT was satisfied that the employment tribunal properly considered the question of adequate warning. The tribunal recorded that when the final written warning issued, the claimant was specifically informed about the respondent's concerns regarding his interactions with volunteers. It also found that these concerns were a specific and important part of the PIP, following which the claimant was expressly warned about the possibility of dismissal ahead of the performance capability hearing. The tribunal had properly considered all aspects of fairness in the claimant's dismissal and there was no error of law.

The appeal was, accordingly, dismissed.

CHOICE OF EMPLOYER

[19.04] *Element Pictures v Arkins*[5]—*Labour Court—appeal from Workplace Relations Commission—Unfair Dismissals Acts 1977 to 2015, s 8(A) —identity of employer*

The claimant appealed against the WRC's rejection of his unfair dismissal complaint. The claimant alleged that he was dismissed by the respondent when he was not offered a job in April 2019. The fact of the dismissal was in dispute.

The claimant was a supervising stagehand who had worked in film production since 1994. He submitted that the respondent was one of several Irish film production companies of a similar scale, all part of a single organisation, which appeared to operate as a cartel. He claimed that no production company would give him work after he appeared before a committee of the then Department of Culture, Heritage and Gaeltacht in 2018, which was looking into working conditions in the Irish film industry.

An issue arose as to whether the respondent was indeed the entity against whom the claimant was taking his complaint.

---

[5] *Element Pictures v Arkins* UDD2414.

The Court found that the claimant failed to establish that he was at any time employed by the respondent in any capacity and his appeal failed.

COMPENSATION

[19.05] *Waterford Health Park Pharmacy Ltd v Foley*[6]—*Labour Court—appeal from Workplace Relations Commission—Unfair Dismissal Acts 1977 to 2015, s 7—quantum of compensation—financial loss—just and equitable*

The respondent appealed against a WRC decision that the claimant had been unfairly dismissed and awarding compensation of €14,000. The appeal was limited to the quantum of compensation.

The claimant initially worked 43.5 hours per week at €12 per hour. The respondent proposed reducing her hours from mid-February 2021. The claimant queried the proposal and this led to her dismissal.

The claimant submitted that she was without work for some 11 weeks following her dismissal, before she secured fixed-term employment at €15.65 per hour. She then secured permanent employment elsewhere at €15.47 per hour.

The respondent submitted that the claimant's 'actual loss' was €5,742 and that she could not have any future losses in circumstances where she secured employment at a higher rate than she would have been paid by the respondent. The respondent also submitted that the claimant had not accrued sufficiently long service to bring her within the scope of the Redundancy Payments Act 1967, and so the Court was asked not to have regard for 'loss of statutory rights' in that respect.

The Court observed that a key feature of the case was that there had been 'not a scintilla of procedural fairness in the manner in which the [claimant] was dismissed from her employment' (a point conceded by the respondent). It was clear from the Unfair Dismissal Acts 1977 to 2015 that the amount of compensation payable is that which the Court 'deems just and equitable having regard to all the circumstances', and that 'financial loss' is not curtailed by an exhaustive definition and includes actual loss and estimated prospective loss.

The Court concluded that the appropriate level of compensation payable to the claimant was €14,000 and the decision of the WRC was upheld. The appeal therefore failed.

[19.06] *Astha Ltd and Chakraborty v Grewal*[7]—*UK Employment Appeal Tribunal—appeal from employment tribunal—Employment Rights Act 1996—unfair dismissal and discrimination—remedy—reduction in compensation otherwise payable—chain of causation—joint and several liability*

---

[6] *Waterford Health Park Pharmacy Ltd v Foley* UDD2412.
[7] *Astha Ltd and Chakraborty v Grewal* [2023] EAT 170.

Both respondents initially appealed against the decision on remedy of the employment tribunal, following the claimant's successful claim for disability discrimination.

The respondents were found jointly and severally liable to compensate the claimant for disability discrimination, though it became apparent at the appeal stage that the tribunal's decision suggested that the respondents collectively were liable for the basic award, which included compensation for unfair dismissal and a failure to provide written particulars of employment. The Employment Rights Act 1996 does not make provision for individual liability for unfair dismissal, which can only attach to the employer. The position is similar in the Employment Act 2002, and an award for failure to provide written particulars of employment. Astha Ltd therefore withdrew its appeal and Ms Chakraborty proceeded as the sole respondent for the purpose of this appeal, which was successful in the above respects.

The tribunal applied a 75% reduction in the compensation otherwise payable to the claimant on the basis that he was 'highly likely in any event to have been dismissed from his employment … in particular due to his conduct', which 'probably amounted to gross misconduct'. The UK EAT did not accept the respondent's argument that the authority on which the tribunal relied for not making any further deduction was wrong in law. The EAT noted that the tribunal had discussed other aspects of the claimant's relationship with the respondent and had set out reasons why dismissal might not have occurred or might have been unfair had it occurred. The claimant's conduct clearly formed 'at least part' of the reason for the 75% reduction and there would be a serious risk of 'double counting' if a further deduction were applied.

The EAT did not accept the respondent's argument that the tribunal failed to address whether the chain of causation for the claimant's loss of earnings was broken by the fact that he gained new employment as a minibus driver at a lower wage, from which he was subsequently dismissed. Among the tribunal's findings of fact was that the claimant had incurred a 'modest partial weekly loss', which was substantially mitigated by his new employment. The respondent was given full credit for earnings during that period, and it followed that the new employment did not eliminate the loss entirely and did not break the chain of causation. The claimant lost his new employment in consequence of the Covid-19 pandemic. It seemed to the EAT that there was 'no scope' for excluding loss of earnings after the claimant had lost that employment through no fault of his own. Accordingly, that did not provide a basis for concluding that the chain of causation had been broken.

The appeal was therefore allowed in part.

[19.07] *N Notaro Homes Ltd v Keirle[8]—UK Employment Appeal Tribunal—appeal from employment tribunal—Employment Rights Act 1996, s 123—unfair dismissal—protected disclosures—social media policy*

The respondent operated care homes. The claimant employees alleged unfair dismissal for making multiple protected disclosures. Of five such claims, four were upheld.

---

[8] *N Notaro Homes Ltd v Keirle, Nash, Owens and Mead* [2024] EAT 122.

The four successful claimants were dismissed by the same person, purportedly for breaches of the respondent's social media policy. The employment tribunal found that protected disclosures were the *real* reason for the dismissals, though the claimants' social media activity was a contributory reason.

The respondent argued that the compensation awards should be reduced by a suggested 10%, reflecting the tribunal's finding that the claimants' social media posts were culpable and blameworthy. The tribunal found that, the claimants' conduct notwithstanding, it was not just and equitable to make any reductions to the award. The respondent challenged that decision.

Dismissing the appeal, the EAT concluded that, while in most cases some reduction to a compensatory award will follow from a finding of contributory conduct, it is not the law that this need necessarily be the case. The employment tribunal did not err in deciding not to make a reduction on the facts of the case.

CONDUCT

[19.08] *Aer Lingus v Linehan*[9]—*Labour Court*—*appeal from Workplace Relations Commission*—*Unfair Dismissals Acts 1977 to 2015, s 8A*—*gross misconduct*—*whether dismissal fell within the band of reasonable responses*

The claimant appealed against a WRC decision that her complaint under the Unfair Dismissals Acts 1977 to 2015 was not well founded.

The claimant commenced employment as a customer service agent with the respondent in July 2009. Her employment was terminated in May 2021 following a disciplinary and appeal process brought about by an incident in July 2019 (the 'incident'). The claimant alleged that she was unfairly dismissed. She submitted that her behaviour on the day had been the result of stress, though she accepted it was unacceptable in the workplace.

The respondent submitted that the claimant was dismissed for gross misconduct, ie, her verbally abusive and aggressive conduct towards colleagues. Fair procedures were followed in the internal investigation, the disciplinary process and the appeal process. The claimant was represented by her union at every stage. The incident was captured on CCTV and witnessed by several colleagues who each gave statements. Based on the information available, dismissal was within the range of reasonable responses available to the respondent.

The Court noted that no issue was taken with the process, and that the claimant accepted that her behaviour on the day was unacceptable. A medical certificate provided by a GP, to whom the claimant presented following the incident, simply stated that she 'presented in a distressed state' and went no further. Taking into account the claimant's conduct on the day and the fact that she was employed in a public facing role, the Court found that the decision to dismiss fell within the band of reasonable responses. The dismissal was therefore not unfair and the appeal failed.

---

[9] *Aer Lingus v Linehan* UDD2418.

[19.09] Ringsend Community Services Forum Clg v Moore[10]—Labour Court—appeal from Workplace Relations Commission—Unfair Dismissals Acts 1977 to 2015, s 8A—allegation of gross misconduct—absence of disciplinary procedure—summary dismissal

The respondent appealed against a WRC decision upholding a complaint of unfair dismissal. The respondent did not attend the hearing at first instance.

The claimant was a former employee of the respondent. The respondent submitted that she terminated her own employment on 31 May 2021, having refused to come to work for a prolonged period. The respondent asserted that it was entitled to consider the employment relationship to be terminated. The situation was confirmed in writing to her in a letter on 31 May, as the respondent could not ignore the claimant's continued breach of her contract. It submitted that there was no need for a disciplinary process in the circumstances and no dismissal occurred in that instance.

The claimant contended that she was summarily dismissed without notice in a letter from the respondent dated 31 May 2021. The dismissal was unfair, without any recourse to due process for an allegation of gross misconduct. The claimant was never made aware of the allegation and was never put on notice that her job was at risk.

The Labour Court noted that the letter of 31 May 2021 expressly stated that the respondent considered the claimant's actions—not reporting to her line manager and failing to take directions from the board—to constitute gross misconduct. This letter contained all the ingredients of a dismissal letter and the Court concluded that the claimant was dismissed for gross misconduct. No disciplinary procedure, or indeed any procedure, was utilised by the respondent in advance of the dismissal. It followed that the claimant was unfairly dismissed and the complaint was well founded. The claimant was awarded four weeks' salary, being €2,300.

[19.10] Greater Glasgow Health Board v Mullen[11]—UK Employment Appeal Tribunal—appeal from employment tribunal—unfair dismissal—gross misconduct—deficiencies in disciplinary procedure—whether dismissal fell within the band of reasonable responses

The claimant complained of unfair dismissal by the respondent health board.

The employment tribunal found that the respondent's reason for summarily dismissing the claimant was its genuinely held belief that he had shouted at and threatened one of his line managers and was therefore guilty of gross misconduct. The respondent's conclusion followed a reasonable investigation and the tribunal considered that the respondent had reasonable grounds for finding that the misconduct had occurred. Nevertheless, the tribunal accepted some of the claimant's submissions on deficiencies in the disciplinary process, including a delay in informing the claimant of the allegation against him, and a 'lack of transparency' by the respondent as to the policy it was

---

[10] *Ringsend Community Services Forum Clg v Moore* UDD2432.
[11] *Greater Glasgow Health Board v Mullen* [2023] EAT 122.

following. The tribunal considered that dismissal did not fall within the band of reasonable responses, and it upheld the complaint. The respondent appealed.

The UK EAT considered the tribunal's reasoning to be inconsistent, basing its decision (in whole or in part) on fairness, despite having 'unequivocally' established the principal reason for the dismissal. The tribunal fell into error in failing to recognise that 'not every departure from an agreed disciplinary procedure will necessarily render a dismissal unfair'. In this instance, the deficiencies in the process had no bearing at all on whether the reason to dismiss was sufficient.

The finding of unfair dismissal was therefore set aside and the appeal succeeded.

CONDUCT—FREEDOM OF EXPRESSION

[19.11] *Aghajanyan v Armenia*[12]—*European Court of Human Rights—European Convention on Human Rights, art 10—freedom of expression—positive obligation on State to protect art 10 rights from interference by private individuals—publication of 'commercial secrets' in the public interest—domestic courts' failure to give relevant and sufficient reasons*

The applicant was dismissed from his employment in a private factory on the grounds that he had disclosed sensitive information to a journalist concerning his employer. He relied on art 10 ECHR.

Since 2003, the applicant had been working as a senior researcher at the Nairit chemical plant (the 'factory'), of which the Armenian government (the respondent) had minority ownership. In 2007, the factory directed that information about the salary levels of its employees was to be considered a fundamental commercial secret. Employee contracts were duly varied to include a confidentiality clause regarding salary levels. In 2009, the factory adopted internal regulations, defining 'commercial secret' so as to include information concerning the factory's production capacity, the nature of scientific work, ongoing experiments, storage of raw material, and technological processes in development.

On several occasions between 2006 and 2010, the applicant filed reports with his management about the need to properly handle 'lacquer', a harmful chemical waste that was stored in the plant. The applicant proposed an experiment to produce a type of paint, which could be used to coat pipes and equipment and guard against corrosion. The proposal was tested in 2007, but produced unsatisfactory results. The applicant complained that the experiment had not been carried out properly. It appears that, in 2009, the applicant was again permitted to carry out the experiment, but was later prohibited from doing so on threat of dismissal.

In April 2010, a local newspaper featured an interview with the applicant in which he discussed certain shortcomings in the running of the factory. In May 2010, the applicant was dismissed without notice for disclosing commercial secrets—'a gross violation of

---

[12] *Aghajanyan v Armenia* App No 41675/12.

labour discipline'—in breach of his employment contract and the factory's labour code. The dismissal order stated that the information divulged by the applicant was 'false' and 'unfounded'.

The applicant challenged his dismissal in the civil courts. The Shengavit District Court of Yerevan found that the dismissal was unlawful. That judgment was quashed by the Civil Court of Appeal. The matter was remitted to the District Court where, this time, it was dismissed. The applicant appealed, relying on his right to freedom of expression and the fact that he had attempted on numerous occasions to bring the issues reported upon— matters of human health and environmental protection—to the attention of his superiors, but in vain. He had a duty to make such information public, given the lack of preventative measures by the factory. The Civil Court of Appeal dismissed his appeal as unsubstantiated. An appeal on points of law was declared inadmissible by the Court of Cassation.

Before the European Court of Human Rights, the applicant argued that his dismissal following publication of the newspaper article breached his art 10 rights.

The Court recalled that art 10 applies to the workplace in general, and that in certain cases the State has a positive obligation to protect the right to freedom of expression from interference by private individuals. It observed that the domestic judgments contained 'very little reasoning' and failed to address any of the applicant's arguments concerning the lawfulness of his dismissal. In particular, the approach taken by the domestic courts—describing the applicant's statements as 'commercial secrets' while simultaneously accepting that they were 'false' and 'unfounded'—was contradictory. More importantly, the domestic courts failed to assess the case before them in light of the art 10 caselaw. No attempt was made to specify which of the applicant's statements was found to be inaccurate or defamatory. No consideration was given to the applicant's arguments about his repeated attempts to alert his superiors of his concerns. The domestic courts also failed to verify the applicant's motive, and whether the information disseminated was in the public interest. There was no mention of any harm sustained by the factory as a result of the newspaper article. The measure imposed on the applicant, summary dismissal, was 'the heaviest one possible'.

The domestic courts had failed to strike a fair balance between the competing interests at stake and failed to adduce 'relevant and sufficient' reasons for their decisions. There had therefore been a violation of art 10.

CONSTRUCTIVE DISMISSAL

[19.12] *DHL Supply Chain (Ireland) Ltd v McAndrew*[13]—*Labour Court—appeal from Workplace Relations Commission—Unfair Dismissal Acts 1997 to 2015— failure to exhaust all available internal procedures*

The claimant appealed against a decision of the WRC dismissing his claim for constructive unfair dismissal.

---

13 *DHL Supply Chain (Ireland) Ltd v McAndrew* UDD2341.

The claimant resigned with immediate effect from his employment with the respondent very shortly after being notified that his request for a two-year career break could not be accommodated. The claimant had been employed as a HGV driver, working both day and night shifts. Following illness-related absences from work, the claimant was rostered on day shifts only. He submitted that his motivation for resigning was to protect his mental and physical well-being.

The Court stressed that a claimant in a constructive dismissal case faces a 'high bar' and is expected to exhaust all available internal procedures so that the employer has an opportunity to address any reasonable concerns. The claimant afforded the respondent no such opportunity. The Court found that the claimant was 'very familiar' with the respondent's grievance procedure, having used it himself on a number of occasions. He offered 'no evidence' as to why he did not do so before taking the drastic step of resigning from his employment. Thereafter, he refused to engage with the respondent, having been invited to do so.

It followed that the complaint of constructive dismissal was not made out and the appeal failed.

[19.13] *Forte Healthcare Ltd v Duffy*[14]—*Labour Court—appeal from Workplace Relations Commission—Unfair Dismissals Acts 1977 to 2015, ss 1 & 8A—constructive dismissal—resignation—grievance procedures—reasonableness test—employee conduct—employer conduct—repudiatory breach*

The claimant appealed against the WRC's dismissal of his complaint of constructive dismissal.

The claimant worked as a territory manager for the respondent from June 2016 until his resignation in November 2018. He alleged that his resignation amounted to constructive dismissal, citing the respondent's conduct as unreasonable and claiming he had no choice but to terminate his employment. The respondent denied the claim, maintaining that the claimant resigned voluntarily and failed to utilise internal grievance procedures to address his concerns.

The claimant's role involved selling animal healthcare products in the northwest of Ireland. Issues arose in 2018, including disputes over the safety of a company-provided car; his placement on a performance improvement plan ('PIP'); and his exclusion from a sales conference. Following a period of parental and sick leave, the claimant submitted his resignation on 30 November 2018, effective 31 December 2018, while simultaneously seeking to return to work temporarily. The respondent engaged with the claimant and offered him the opportunity to withdraw his resignation, which he declined. The resignation was formally accepted on 17 December 2018.

The Labour Court considered whether the circumstances of the claimant's resignation amounted to constructive dismissal as defined under the Unfair Dismissals Acts 1977 to

---

14 *Forte Healthcare Ltd v Duffy* UDD2440.

2015. The claim rested on three primary issues raised by the claimant: concerns about the car; the PIP; and the conference exclusion.

Regarding the car, the claimant argued that repeated power failures made it unsafe to drive, and he had lost confidence in the vehicle. The Court found that the respondent had acted reasonably by returning the car to the dealership for inspection on multiple occasions and by arranging an independent assessment, which confirmed the car was safe. The claimant was provided with an alternative car during these investigations. The Court determined that the respondent's reliance on professional advice and efforts to address the issue did not amount to unreasonable conduct.

As regards the PIP, the claimant contended that its implementation in July 2018 was a form of undue pressure. The respondent argued that the PIP addressed legitimate concerns about the claimant's technical knowledge and use of a customer management system. The Court noted that while the claimant was informed of the concerns and given support, the PIP was never fully implemented due to his subsequent parental and sick leave. In any event, introducing the PIP was not unreasonable behaviour and fell within the scope of standard performance management practices.

As for the sales conference, the claimant claimed he was excluded without explanation. The Court found that, while the communication regarding his exclusion could have been clearer, the claimant was on certified sick leave during the relevant dates and would not have been able to attend the event, even if invited. The exclusion, therefore, did not constitute unreasonable conduct by the respondent.

The claimant's resignation letter mentioned several concerns, but he did not utilise the respondent's grievance procedures to resolve these issues. The respondent made multiple efforts to engage with him and provided an opportunity to withdraw his resignation, which he declined. The Court found that the claimant's decision to resign without exhausting available remedies was unreasonable.

Ultimately, the Court held that the claimant's resignation did not meet the definition of constructive dismissal, which requires either a repudiatory breach of contract by the employer or conduct so unreasonable that the employee could not remain in employment. Neither threshold was satisfied on the evidence presented.

The Court therefore affirmed the WRC's decision, rejecting the appeal and concluding that the complaint was not well founded.

[19.14] *Leaney v Loughborough University*[15]—*UK Employment Appeal Tribunal—appeal from employment tribunal—affirmation of contract*

The claimant resigned from his employment of some 40 years with the respondent and claimed constructive unfair dismissal, alleging a cumulative breach of the implied duty of trust and confidence. His claim was dismissed by an employment tribunal which found that between the 'last straw' date (29 June 2020) and the date of his resignation (28 September 2020), the claimant had affirmed the contract.

---

[15] *Leaney v Loughborough University* [2023] EAT 155.

This appeal challenged the employment tribunal's decision on affirmation only. The wider background to the case was an incident in 2018 in which a student living in a hall of residence, of which the claimant was then warden, self-harmed. A concern was raised by the student in relation to how the claimant handled the matter and, while a disciplinary investigation concluded that there was no formal case to answer, the respondent indicated that it had concerns about the claimant's judgement, which it wished to discuss with him informally. This led to the claimant raising a grievance that was partially, though not wholly, successful.

The claimant sought to appeal the outcome of the grievance procedure but, the tribunal found, no steps were taken by the respondent to convene an appeal panel. The claimant resigned from his position as warden, referring to the failure to convene an appeal panel. Thereafter, he was encouraged by the respondent to draw a line under the matter. The tribunal accepted that following a conversation with the respondent on 29 June 2020, the claimant decided that there was no point in raising the issue again as the respondent was not going to help him. Negotiations followed, which came to nothing, and the claimant regarded the date those negotiations ended (7 September 2020) as the 'last straw' date leading to his resignation from his employment.

The UK EAT found the tribunal erred in its approach to affirmation. It found that, in its self-direction as to the law, the tribunal's reasoning had not fully demonstrated that it is not the passage of time, as such, that gives rise to affirmation, 'but conduct or other circumstances occurring in that period from which affirmation may be inferred'. The authorities make the point 'very broadly' that an employee with long service 'might reasonably need longer to make up his mind', and that length of service may give context for other factors, such as whether the employee would be abandoning a secure and stable job or losing valuable benefits.

The tribunal did not signal a finding that the claimant's work, in itself, constituted affirmation for the relevant period, or that he was paid during that time. Indeed, the tribunal noted that it did not have any evidence about what, if any, work the claimant was doing. The relevant period was largely taken up by negotiations and, although the claimant was signed off sick for the last three weeks leading up to his resignation, these factors were not given sufficient attention by the tribunal in the context of affirmation.

The matter was thus remitted to the same tribunal for fresh consideration of affirmation.

[19.15] *Nelson v Renfrewshire Council*[16]—*UK Employment Appeal Tribunal— appeal from employment tribunal—Employment Rights Act 1996, s 95(1)(c)— constructive unfair dismissal—whether the tribunal's decision was perverse—whether the tribunal misapplied the test for breach of implied term of trust and confidence*

The claimant appealed against an employment tribunal's dismissal of her claim for constructive unfair dismissal.

The claimant was employed as a teacher by the respondent, Renfrewshire Council, from February 2012 until November 2022, when she resigned with immediate effect.

---

[16] *Nelson v Renfrewshire Council* [2024] EAT 132.

The initiating event came about during a discussion between the claimant and the head teacher, in which the latter was said to have behaved in an aggressive and intimidating way towards the claimant. Witnesses saw the head teacher point at the claimant and say, 'if you have anything to say to me, say it to my face'.

The claimant lodged a grievance that was not upheld, with the investigator concluding, 'I do not find evidence' that the head teacher treated the claimant in a manner that was 'threatening, insensitive and aggressive'. The employment tribunal found this outcome 'curious', given that there was at least partial-corroboration of the claimant's account. No evidence was gathered formally from the head-teacher and it appears that she gave her account in an informal discussion. In a subsequent internal appeal, which was also not upheld, the employment tribunal found that, the decision maker 'summarised the sources of evidence without explaining even in the broadest terms why he gave more or less weight to any particular piece of evidence'.

The claimant did not exercise her right to appeal that outcome, saying that she no longer had faith in the system. She resigned with immediate effect, citing a 'serious material breach' of contract and constructive dismissal.

While the employment tribunal agreed that the head teacher acted in a way that was aggressive and intimidating, it concluded that the incident on its own 'did not come close' to breaching the implied term of trust and confidence. The tribunal was roundly critical of the grievance procedure, which it found to be of poor quality and, in certain respects, biased against the claimant. Nevertheless, the final appeal stage (in which the claimant did not engage) remained a viable option with a 'realistic chance of righting the wrongs' of the earlier stages. For those reasons, it dismissed the claim. The claimant argued that the tribunal's decision was perverse.

The EAT held that, 'despite the significant findings in the claimant's favour', the threshold for perversity had not been reached. However, the employment tribunal erred in drawing the conclusion that the relationship had not been damaged to the necessary extent because of the claimant's failure to exhaust the grievance process; that the claimant might eventually have been successful in the grievance process was an irrelevant consideration in that context. The tribunal also failed to apply the correct test for repudiatory breach of contract, its language belying an error of law, rather than mere semantics.

The appeal was upheld in part.

DISMISSAL OR RESIGNATION?

[19.16] **Saint John of God Community Services v Oyegoke[17]—Labour Court—appeal from Workplace Relations Commission—Unfair Dismissal Acts 1977 to 2015, s 8A—blanket policy of refusing to allow an employee to retract a resignation—special circumstances**

---

17 *Saint John of God Community Services v Oyegoke* UDD2415.

The respondent appealed against a WRC decision upholding a complaint of unfair dismissal and ordering reinstatement of the claimant.

The claimant had been employed by the respondent as a social care worker since 2004. In January 2022, she tendered her resignation, but a short time later, on foot of medical advice, sought to retract it. The respondent refused, apparently due to an unwritten policy of not allowing staff to retract a letter of resignation in any circumstances.

The claimant had an unblemished work record and suffered a personal tragedy in 2019. In November 2021, the respondent proposed to transfer the claimant. She resisted the transfer for health reasons linked to smoke inhalation and provided a medical certificate from her GP in respect of same. The claimant sought an occupational health assessment, though this was not facilitated by the respondent. The claimant also enquired about giving up her permanent job and moving to the relief panel. She was certified unfit for work, and, while on sick leave tendered her resignation. It was on the advice of her GP that the claimant resolved to retract her resignation during her notice period.

It was clear to the Court that the WRC had taken into account a number of factors, including the claimant's state of mind when she tendered her resignation. These were enough to suggest that there may have been 'special circumstance' at play when the claimant tendered her resignation, which the respondent should have considered before applying a 'blanket policy' of refusing to allow her to retract her resignation. At a minimum, there should have been some 'follow up' by the respondent to understand why the proposed transfer was triggering such a response from the claimant. The Court would not give weight to the respondent's 'blanket policy' as this did not accord with existing caselaw.

The Court found that the claimant was unfairly dismissed and considered reinstatement the appropriate form of redress. Accordingly, the decision of the WRC was upheld.

NOTICE

[19.17] *Ringsend Community Services Forum Clg v Moore*[18]—*Labour Court—appeal from Workplace Relations Commission—Minimum Notice and Terms of Employment Acts 1973 to 2005—notice of termination—whether payment in lieu of notice was made*

The respondent appealed against a WRC decision which upheld a complaint under the Minimum Notice and Terms of Employment Acts 1973 to 2005. The respondent did not attend the hearing at first instance.

In a linked appeal, the Labour Court found that the claimant was unfairly dismissed.[19]

The respondent submitted that the claimant had no entitlement to notice of termination of her employment as she terminated her own employment on 31 May 2021. She had

---

[18] *Ringsend Community Services Forum Clg v Moore* MND249.
[19] See *Ringsend Community Services Forum Clg v Moore* UDD2432 at **[19.09]**.

no entitlement to notice in circumstances where she refused to work. Regardless, the respondent had paid the claimant a notice payment of €1,218.71 as a goodwill gesture.

The claimant contended that she was dismissed in a letter dated 31 May 2021. She was dismissed without notice and, under her contract of employment, was entitled to six weeks' notice.

Having seen the claimant's final payslip, the Court did not accept the respondent's submission that a payment recorded as 'holiday pay' was in fact a payment in lieu of notice. The respondent could not rely on the claimant's refusal to attend the workplace prior to her dismissal in order to negate her entitlement to statutory notice. No notice of termination was served on the claimant. That said, the claimant was only entitled to the statutory four weeks' paid notice, as opposed to the six weeks she sought.

The claimant was awarded compensation of €2,300, being four weeks' notice pay. The complaint was well founded and the appeal failed.

OTHER SUBSTANTIAL GROUNDS—REFUSAL TO BE VACCINATED

[19.18] *Masiero v Barchester Healthcare Ltd*[20]—*UK Employment Appeal Tribunal—appeal from employment tribunal—unfair dismissal—religion and belief discrimination—Covid-19 vaccination policy—ECHR, arts 2, 5 and 8— justification—substantive fairness*

The five claimants appealed against an employment tribunal's rejection of their complaints of unfair dismissal and direct and indirect religion and belief discrimination.

The claimants were dismissed by the respondent care home provider for refusal to comply with its then newly introduced policy requiring all staff to be vaccinated against Covid-19 unless medically exempt. The policy preceded UK regulations to that effect.

The respondent was the second-largest provider of care home services in the UK, with around 12,600 residents and more than 17,000 employees. The employment tribunal found that the respondent had increased death rates during the pandemic, with Covid-19 recorded as a cause of death for some 1,250 residents and six staff members during 2020. The residents were more susceptible to infection and were particularly vulnerable to Covid-19 due to age and other medical conditions. The respondent took measures such as PPE, enhanced hygiene practices, PCR testing of staff and refusing to accept sick patients discharged from hospital until they showed a negative Covid-19 test. These measures were only partly effective, however, and the respondent was also struggling to maintain staffing levels.

During the onset of the more transmissible Alpha variant of Covid-19 in 2021, the respondent introduced its first vaccine policy, requiring new employees to be vaccinated

---

[20] *Masiero, Hussain, Chadwick and Dimitrova v Barchester Healthcare Ltd* [2024] EAT 112.

and restricting promotion and discretionary bonuses to vaccinated staff. Following a consultation with employees, residents and unions, a second-stage policy was introduced. Staff were given two months' notice that they needed to be vaccinated in order to continue to work for the respondent. The unions, while supportive of the national vaccine rollout, did not support the respondent's policy, which they viewed as being 'at odds with the vast majority of employers in the sector and good practice being urged by government'. That said, by March 2021 more than 90% of the respondent's staff had been vaccinated.

The claimants maintained their refusal to be vaccinated and were dismissed in May and June 2021. One claimant asserted that his decision not to get vaccinated stemmed from a protected belief under equality legislation.

The employment tribunal concluded that the reason for the introduction of the respondent's vaccine policy was 'to reduce the risk of spread of Covid infection in its homes and, therefore, death and serious illness amongst primarily its residents, but also its staff and any visitors'. The tribunal found this to be a 'genuine and substantial [reason] which could justify dismissal of care home workers'. It went on to consider the substantive fairness of the dismissals in light of the claimants' human rights. In doing so, it noted that the right to life is 'absolute', whereas those relied upon by the claimants were 'qualified rights' which may be interfered with in order to protect the rights of another or the wider interest. The respondent was reasonable in considering that its vaccination policy minimised the risk of death to residents. The policy did not interfere with the claimants' art 5 ECHR rights; they retained the autonomy to decide whether to be vaccinated or not and the respondent's policy imposed a consequence depending on that choice. The tribunal accepted that the claimants' art 8 ECHR rights were engaged, though it concluded that the interference was justified by the legitimate aim of minimising the risk of death and serious illness among residents and staff. Dismissal was, in principle, a proportionate measure necessary in a democratic society to achieve that aim. The dismissals themselves were substantively fair.

On appeal, the EAT found no error of law in the employment tribunal's decision. It had properly applied the relevant employment legislation and properly concluded that the claimants' dismissals were compatible with their art 5 and art 8 ECHR rights. The respondent's policy did not involve the imposition of a mandatory requirement to submit to medical treatment and the interference with the claimants' art 8 rights was justified. It did not accept that the tribunal's decision on the procedural fairness of the dismissals was perverse, despite 'some shortcomings' in the process.

The appeal was, accordingly, dismissed.

REDUNDANCY

[19.19] *De Bank Haycocks v ADP RPO UK Ltd*[21]—*Court of Appeal of England and Wales—Underhill, Singh & Baker LJJ—appeal from UK EAT—unfair*

---

[21] *De Bank Haycocks v ADP RPO UK Ltd* [2024] EWCA Civ 1291.

dismissal—redundancy—consultation, meaningful engagement—procedural fairness—selection criteria and scoring—employment tribunal remedy—EAT procedural failings—consultation obligations—finality of decision making—limited compensation for procedural unfairness

The respondent appealed a decision by the UK EAT regarding the fairness of the claimant's redundancy dismissal and the adequacy of the consultation process.

The claimant was employed by the respondent, a recruitment process outsourcing company providing services to clients, including Goldman Sachs. Due to a reduction in client needs caused by the Covid-19 pandemic, the respondent decided in May 2020 to make redundancies within its team. This decision affected the claimant's team of 16 employees based in London and four employees in Warsaw.

The redundancy process began with a scoring exercise undertaken by the claimant's manager in June 2020, using a matrix of 17 criteria. The claimant received the lowest score. Although the decision to implement redundancies was not finalised until later, the claimant was placed 'at risk' on 30 June 2020, with a consultation process scheduled to last 14 days. During the initial consultation, the claimant was informed of the redundancy situation and the matrix criteria but was not told his own score. Nor was he informed that the scoring exercise had already taken place. On 14 July 2020, the claimant was dismissed after being informed of his redundancy. At his dismissal meeting, he raised concerns about the fairness of the process but received no substantive response. He subsequently appealed the decision, raising issues around the consultation process and the fairness of the scoring. The appeal, which lasted 45 minutes, was dismissed on 17 August 2020.

In his appeal, the claimant argued that the redundancy was procedurally unfair. Specifically, he raised concerns about not being consulted before the scoring exercise was conducted, a lack of transparency around how he was assessed, and inadequate consultation on how redundancies might have been avoided. Additionally, the claimant alleged that his scoring may have been influenced by a prior falling-out with a senior Goldman Sachs recruiter which, he contended, unfairly affected his performance evaluation.

The claimant brought proceedings for unfair dismissal before the employment tribunal. The tribunal considered whether redundancy was the true reason for dismissal; whether the redundancy decision was unduly influenced by the claimant's earlier conflict with Goldman Sachs personnel; and the fairness of the selection and consultation process. The tribunal found that redundancy was the genuine reason for dismissal and that the scoring process had not been manipulated. While it acknowledged shortcomings in the consultation process, particularly the failure to disclose the claimant's scores before dismissal, it concluded that the overall process was fair. Importantly, the tribunal found that the appeal process had been 'conscientious' and addressed the claimant's concerns about scoring, rendering the redundancy decision reasonable. As such, the tribunal rejected the claimant's claim for unfair dismissal.

The claimant appealed to the EAT, challenging the employment tribunal's findings on the consultation process and procedural fairness. The EAT ruled in his favour, holding that the dismissal was procedurally unfair due to the lack of meaningful consultation at the formative stage. The EAT highlighted that consultation should occur when proposals are still open to change and employees can realistically influence the outcome. It criticised the respondent's decision to conduct the scoring exercise before consultation, which it said gave the appearance of 'pre-selection'. The EAT further ruled that deficiencies in the consultation process were not remedied by the appeal process and found the redundancy dismissal unfair. The case was remitted to the tribunal to determine remedies.

The respondent appealed to the Court of Appeal. It argued that the EAT had mis-characterised the consultation process and had incorrectly elevated procedural guidance into rigid legal standards. The Court considered whether the scoring exercise amounted to pre-selection, the adequacy of the consultation process, and whether any procedural flaws were cured by the appeal process.

The Court of Appeal upheld the employment tribunal's original decision, finding no error of law in its reasoning. It accepted that the respondent's decision to score employees before consultation was poor practice, but rejected the EAT's conclusion that this amounted to pre-selection. The Court noted that the consultation process provided the claimant with an opportunity to challenge his scores and argue against redundancy, even if this occurred later than was ideal. The Court also endorsed the tribunal's finding that the appeal process addressed any remaining deficiencies in consultation. Specifically, the appeal allowed the claimant to review and contest his scores, and the respondent conducted a thorough review of his concerns before upholding its decision.

The Court of Appeal further criticised the EAT for introducing a novel requirement for 'workforce-level consultation' as part of good industrial relations practice. The EAT had suggested that employers in non-unionised workplaces should consult employees collectively about redundancy criteria and alternatives. The Court found no legal basis for this requirement, emphasising that the adequacy of consultation must be assessed on a case-by-case basis. It reiterated that procedural fairness does not require strict adherence to rigid rules but should instead consider whether the overall process was reasonable in the circumstances.

Ultimately, the Court of Appeal concluded that the respondent's redundancy process, while imperfect, fell within the range of reasonable responses available to an employer. It held that the consultation and appeal processes, taken together, provided the claimant with a fair opportunity to engage with the redundancy decision. The Court acknowledged that redundancy decisions often involve difficult choices and reiterated that procedural flaws do not automatically render a dismissal unfair unless they have a material impact on the outcome.

The respondent's appeal was allowed. The Court of Appeal restored the employment tribunal's original decision, and rejected the claim for unfair dismissal.

RE-ENGAGEMENT

[19.20] *An Bord Banistíochta, Gaelscoil Moshíológ v The Labour Court*[22]— Supreme Court—O'Donnell CJ, O'Malley, Hogan, Murray & Collins JJ— appeal from High Court—Unfair Dismissals Acts 1977 to 2015, s 6—remedy of re-engagement—failure to give consideration to whether re-engagement practicable in the circumstances

This Supreme Court appeal arises out of a dispute concerning the conduct of the principal of Gaelscoil Moshíológ in the management of enrolment in the school for the school year 2009–2010. The principal was initially placed on administrative leave in January 2012 and later suspended on full pay on 29 May 2013. Following a disciplinary hearing over three separate days between November 2014 and June 2015, he was dismissed with effect from 30 November 2015. The dismissal of the principal by the board of management was upheld by a disciplinary appeal panel established under the Education Act 1998, with the dismissal taking effect on 30 November 2015.

The principal initiated a complaint to the WRC on 8 February 2016. In July 2016, an existing teacher at the school was appointed principal of the school. The WRC found that the dismissal was unfair and, considering that compensation was an inadequate remedy, concluded that re-engagement, with effect from 1 January 2018 on the same terms and conditions as he held prior to dismissal, was a more appropriate remedy. This meant that the principal would recover arrears of salary for the period from that date, but not for the period between dismissal and 1 January 2018.

This decision was appealed by the board of management. The Labour Court dismissed the appeal, finding that the principal was unfairly dismissed and directed re-engagement with effect from 1 September 2017 (being four months earlier than the date set by the WRC), with the period from the date of dismissal to that date being regarded as a period of unpaid suspension. The board of management appealed to the High Court.

The High Court dismissed the appeal and concluded that the Labour Court had erred in directing re-engagement from September 2017, and instead initially directed reinstatement of the principal with effect from 30 January 2013, being the date on which it was considered the administrative leave should have ended. After subsequent hearings, the High Court delivered a further judgment directing that the principal:

— be put back on the payroll with effect from 1 August 2023;
— be deemed to be re-engaged as principal with effect from 30 November 2015 (being the date of his dismissal) and restored to his duties with effect from 4 August 2023;

---

[22] *An Bord Banistíochta, Gaelscoil Moshíológ v The Labour Court* [2024] IESC 38. See also *Arthur Cox Employment Law Yearbook 2023* for the decisions of the High Court in *An Bord Banistíochta, Gaelscoil Moshíológ v Labour Court (No 1)* [2023] IEHC 484 at [19.08] and *An Bord Banistíochta, Gaelscoil Moshíológ v Labour Court (No. 2)* [2023] IEHC 497 at [19.09]. See also *Arthur Cox Employment Law Yearbook 2022* at [20.11] for the decision of the Labour Court in *An Bord Banistíochta Gaelscoil Moshíológ v Ó Súird* UD/18/102.

— be paid arrears of salary from 30 November 2015; and
— have all previous entitlements restored from 30 November 2015.

In effect, this decision removed any period of unpaid suspension imposed by the Labour Court. The High Court refused an application for a stay on the order pending appeal and directed that all arrears be paid by 15 September 2023. The High Court also ordered that the board of management should pay the principal's legal costs.

On 31 October 2023, the Supreme Court granted leave to appeal, identifying the following issues as matters to be considered in the appeal:

'1. In an appeal on a point of law against the dismissal and reengagement of an employee, is the High Court at large when assessing the reasonableness of the dismissal and thus entitled to take a view on the actions of the employer in the investigation of the alleged misconduct, in the disciplinary proceedings and in the procedures before the relevant statutory employment bodies?
2. In assessing the reasonableness of a dismissal of a school principal in circumstances of an admitted overstatement of pupil enrolment figures to the Department of Education, what are relevant factors that ought to be taken into account?
3. What are the principles to be applied when deciding to order reengagement rather than reinstatement?
   a) To what extent, if any, does an employer's asserted lack of trust in an employee whom they have unfairly dismissed factor into the consideration as to whether the remedy of reengagement ought to be ordered?
   b) What, if any, relevance to the remedy of reengagement has the fact that, following the dismissal but prior to the conclusion of the employment law proceedings, the employer has appointed another person to the post on a permanent basis?
4. In what circumstances ought the High Court make an order for costs against an employer and in particular the circumstances in which costs on a legal practitioner and client basis ought to be made?'.[23]

The Supreme Court, in a judgment written by the Chief Justice, upheld the decision of the Labour Court that the dismissal of the principal was unfair, finding that it was a conclusion which, on the evidence, the Labour Court was entitled to come. However, it found that the decision of the Labour Court that the principal should be re-engaged in his position as principal with effect from 1 September 2017 was erroneous in law, stating:

'No proper consideration was given to the exceptional nature of the remedy, the practicability of such reengagement, or the impact upon the school or on the principal who had been appointed. Any decision on the exceptional remedy of reinstatement or, as here, reengagement in the original position, requires that it be reasoned and justified by reference to the circumstances of the case'.[24]

The Supreme Court was of the view that it would not be appropriate in the particular circumstances of this case to set aside the order of the Labour Court directing re-engagement in the position of principal.

---

[23] An Bord Banistíochta, Gaelscoil Moshíológ v The Labour Court [2023] IESCDET 128.
[24] An Bord Banistíochta, Gaelscoil Moshíológ v The Labour Court [2024] IESC 38 at [v], per O'Donnell CJ.

On 11 January 2012, an incident occurred at the school, described as 'the single child incident'. The principal was teaching first class, and had just disciplined a pupil, who then returned to his seat and deliberately stamped his feet. The principal lost his temper, approached the pupil, banged the table in front of him and physically pulled the child towards him by his jumper, and/or lifted him and put him back down. A number of parents of children in the class made written complaints to the board of management. The principal met with the parents of the child in question, who accepted his apology and said that they considered the incident a minor one. The chairperson of the board of management sought advice and the principal was put on administrative leave, which meant that he continued to carry on administrative duties but did not attend the school in person during the school day. The incident was referred to the HSE. At that point, the solicitors for the parents of the child wrote to the board of management stating that they were satisfied that the incident was a minor one, and that they were alarmed that their son had been referred to in complaints made by others and that the matter had been referred to the HSE.

The HSE wrote to the board of management stating that they did not consider that any child protection intervention was warranted. The letter also stated that 'the HSE will now be writing to the school Board of Management requesting that a comprehensive and thorough investigation of the incident be completed with a view to ensuring prevention of other incidents'. The principal's administrative leave was extended until 31 January 2013.

In January 2013, after a board meeting, the chairperson of the board was approached by teachers in the school, including the acting principal, who raised a number of concerns regarding the absence of policies within the school, including child protection policies. The acting principal also expressed concerns about the enrolment practices at the school and what she described as the overstatement of numbers enrolled in annual returns to the Department of Education, and consequent additional funding received by the school. The chairperson of the board of management sought access to the school's roll books and associated documentation and became concerned by a number of matters including the use of Tipp-Ex on the roll books, and the removal of names from the roll books at different points in time. The board wrote to the principal's trade union representatives stating that 'serious issues have arisen which require to be investigated by the Board of Management. The chairperson Ms. Melanie Ní Dhuinn is preparing a comprehensive report on the issues of concern which will be forwarded to the Board of Management for investigation under the disciplinary procedures'. The letter stated that the principal would remain on administrative leave pending the outcome of the investigation. The chairperson then wrote to INTO, informing the union that she had decided to initiate the agreed disciplinary proceedings in relation to a serious matter which she said 'has just recently come to my attention', ie, the enrolment issues.

While the principal was initially placed on administrative leave arising out of the single child incident, no inquiry into that incident was ever concluded. The disciplinary hearing which proceeded, and also subsequent hearings and reviews were confined to the question of enrolment for the school year 2009/2010. The essential response of the principal was to argue that the question of deliberate inclusion of pupils who would not attend the school in that academic year in the roll was a grey area, that other schools adopted similar practices, and that the board of management in place as of September 2009 was aware of the practice adopted.

The commencement of the disciplinary procedure meant a change in the status of the principal from that of administrative leave to suspension on full pay. Following the disciplinary hearing, he was dismissed with effect from 30 November 2015.

The Supreme Court found that where a dismissal is challenged by an employee, the relevant test is whether the decision is within the range of responses open to a reasonable employer, the onus in this respect being on the employer. The Labour Court found that, notwithstanding the misconduct of the principal in the falsification of documents relating to enrolment in the school, the sanction of dismissal in this case had not been shown to be proportionate in all the circumstances of the case. When a decision of the Labour Court is appealed to the High Court on a point of law under s 46 of the Workplace Relations Act 2015, the Supreme Court reiterated that such an appeal is not a rehearing on the merits. The test to be applied is whether there was evidence supporting conclusions of facts arrived at by the Labour Court; whether any inferences drawn from such facts were justified; and whether the decision exhibits any error of law.

The Supreme Court upheld the Labour Court's decision that the principal's dismissal was unfair. The Labour Court was entitled, based on the evidence before it, to conclude that it had not been established that dismissal was a proportionate response to the wrongdoing.

However, the Supreme Court found that the decision of the Labour Court that the principal should be re-engaged in his position as principal with effect from 1 September 2017 was erroneous in law. The Supreme Court stated that, in the normal course, the appropriate order would be to set aside the decision of the Labour Court in this regard and remit the matter to the Labour Court to consider the appropriate remedy in all the circumstances of the case in the light of this judgment. However, the Court stated that, given the inordinate amount of time which had already elapsed, and the fact that the consequence of the High Court order, and the refusal of a stay in that Court, was that the principal had been back in the position for almost one year and the replacement principal had left the school. Therefore, the Supreme Court was of the view that it would not be appropriate in the circumstances to set aside the order of the Labour Court directing re-engagement in the position of principal.

The Supreme Court also found that the decision of the High Court that the Labour Court had erred in ordering re-engagement from 1 September 2017, and substituting an order of re-engagement with effect from 30 November 2015, being the date of dismissal, was itself erroneous, and in excess of the proper jurisdiction of the High Court in an appeal on a point of law and must be set aside. The Supreme Court ordered that the arrears of salary which were ordered by the High Court to be paid to the principal by the board of management in respect of the period between 30 November 2015 (being the date of dismissal) and 1 September 2017 (being the date of re-engagement under the order of the Labour Court) must now be repaid by the principal. It stated that the refusal of the High Court to put a stay on that order was also erroneous.

Therefore, the Supreme Court allowed the appeal to the extent that the order of the High Court should be set aside and the order substituted simply dismissing the board of management's appeal on a point of law against the decision of the Labour Court, to order re-engagement of the principal with effect from 1 September 2017, and making a special order awarding the principal his costs of the appeal on a party and party basis.

RETIREMENT

[19.21] *Presentation Secondary School Board of Management v Murphy*[25]*—Labour Court—appeal from Workplace Relations Commission—Unfair Dismissals Acts 1977 to 2015, s 8A—complaint of constructive dismissal—behaviour of employer*

The claimant appealed against the WRC's dismissal of her complaint of constructive dismissal.

The claimant was formerly employed by the respondent, the board of management of Presentation Secondary School. In November 2019, she raised a grievance against the principal of the school. The grievance was subsequently resolved by independent mediation. The claimant's case was that she decided to retire from her employment due to the subsequent behaviour of the chairperson of the board of management which, she alleged, undermined her trust in the respondent. She submitted that her decision to retire amounted to an unfair dismissal.

The claimant had been absent from work due to illness in the weeks prior to November 2019 and had not received any contact from the chairperson during that period. The chairperson had emailed the principal seeking guidance as to how the claimant's continued absence from work, and the fact that a grievance had been raised by her, should be brought to the respondent's attention in its upcoming meeting. These behaviours were the cause of the claimant's decision to terminate her own employment.

The respondent submitted that it behaved reasonably and compassionately towards the claimant at all times. The claimant retired from her employment before exhausting available internal procedures. Her decision to retire was not caused by a fundamental breach of the contract of employment by the respondent, nor did it result from conduct which was so unreasonable that the claimant could not be expected to tolerate it any longer. The chairperson had allowed the claimant privacy and space to recover from her illness, as was normal practice in the education sector. No aspect of the engagement between the chairperson and the principal could fairly be said to amount to unreasonable behaviour or behaviour which undermined the contract of employment.

---

[25] *Presentation Secondary School Board of Management v Murphy* UDD2437.

The Labour Court could find no basis to conclude that the respondent's behaviour during the relevant period was so unreasonable as to mean that the claimant could not be expected to continue in her employment, or that any behaviour of the respondent was such as to undermine the contract of employment. It followed that the complaint of constructive dismissal was not well founded and the appeal was dismissed.

TRADE UNION ACTIVITIES

[19.22] *Doyle Shipping Group v Troy*[26]—*Labour Court—appeal from Workplace Relations Commission—Unfair Dismissal Acts 1977 to 2015, s 8A—trade union membership or activities—whether the claimant came within the exemption outlined in the Acts*

The claimant appealed against a decision of the WRC in an unfair dismissal claim against his employer. The Adjudication Officer held that the claimant did not have the requisite 12 months of service (which was accepted by the parties), and that he had not demonstrated that he came within the exceptions set out in the Unfair Dismissal Acts 1977 to 2015.

The claimant submitted that his dismissal fell within the exception under s 6(2)(a) of the Acts in that it arose wholly or mainly from his trade union activities. The respondent denied that the claimant carried out any trade union activities, or that they were aware of same. The Labour Court found that a letter submitted by the claimant purporting to assert that he was a trade union official over a certain period was 'completely contradicted and undermined' by his oral evidence, so that it could not attach any credence to the letter.

The Court determined that the claimant failed to establish that his dismissal arose wholly or mainly from his trade union membership or activities and the appeal failed.

---

[26] *Doyle Shipping Group v Troy* UDD2342.

Chapter 20

Wages

INTRODUCTION

[20.01]

Covid-19—Pay Cuts

The impact of Covid-19 on wages and temporary reductions in pay during the pandemic was considered by the Labour Court in *Aer Lingus v Fennell*.

National Minimum Wage

Commissioners for Revenue and Customs v Lees of Scotland Ltd, a case before the UK EAT, concerned whether a voluntary company-operated savings scheme for employees was unlawful having regard to national minimum wage requirements.

Payment of Wages

In *Ringsend Community Service Forum Clg v Moore*, the Labour Court considered whether an employee's refusal to attend the workplace justified removal from payroll.

Payment of Wages Act—Bonus

The payment of bonuses was the topic at issue in the Labour Court's decision in *Natus Manufacturing Ltd v Callanan* and the UK EAT's decision in *Moon v Slater & Gordon UK Ltd*.

Payment of Wages Act—Deductions

The Labour Court considered claims of unlawful deductions from wages in *Doherty, Serao, McMahon, Porter* and *Cannon*. The same topic was considered by the UK EAT in *Mendy* and *Al-Naimi*.

COVID-19—PAY CUTS

[20.02] *Aer Lingus v Fennell[1]—Labour Court—appeal from Workplace Relations Commission—Payment of Wages Act 1991, s 7(1)—unlawful deductions—Covid-19*

The claimant appealed against a WRC decision under the Payment of Wages Act 1991.

The claimant had been employed by the respondent since 1995 and was a permanent senior cabin crew member. In March 2020, the respondent implemented temporary reductions in pay and short-term working. This was in order to avoid mass redundancies and unpaid layoffs during the Covid-19 pandemic. The claimant received a 50% pay cut followed by a 30% cut. Cuts were applied across the respondent's workforce.

The claimant referred her complaint on 7 September 2020, and so the cognisable period was 8 March 2020 to 7 September 2020. She argued that her contract of employment made no provision for short-term working or for unilateral reductions in pay and that the reductions imposed by the respondent were unlawful.

The respondent submitted that the circumstances of this case were on all fours with those of a previous Labour Court decision,[2] in which it was held that the amount of compensation that was reasonable in the circumstances was nil, in light of the employer's efforts to mitigate the disruptive effects of the pandemic.

The Court found no material facts to distinguish this matter from its previous decision. Though the complaint was well founded, the amount of compensation payable to the claimant was nil.

NATIONAL MINIMUM WAGE

[20.03] *Commissioners for Revenue and Customs v Lees of Scotland Ltd[3]—UK Employment Appeal Tribunal—appeal from employment tribunal—voluntary deductions—national minimum wage—whether deductions were for the company's use and benefit*

The claimant appealed against an employment tribunal's decision to rescind a notice of underpayment.

The respondent company operated a savings scheme, whereby its workers made voluntary contributions into a fund to help them save for holidays. The respondent retained the deducted sums in its main trading account, paying them on request. In the case of some of the workers, the deductions pushed their wages below the UK's national minimum wage. It was in those circumstances that the claimant served a notice of underpayment, requiring the respondent to pay minimum wage arrears to certain workers.

---

1 *Aer Lingus v Fennell* PWD2426.
2 *Jones v Aer Lingus* PWD2248, see *Arthur Cox Employment Law Yearbook 2022* at [21.07].
3 *Commissioners for Revenue and Customs v Lees of Scotland Ltd* [2024] EAT 120.

The respondent appealed the notice to the employment tribunal, which decided that the deductions were not for the respondent's 'own use and benefit' for the purposes of national minimum wage regulations.

However, the EAT concluded that, because the deductions were held in the respondent's main trader account, they were at the respondent's disposal, and so *were* for its use and benefit. The notice of underpayment was thus restored.

PAYMENT OF WAGES

[20.04] *Ringsend Community Service Forum Clg v Moore*[4]—*Labour Court—appeal from Workplace Relations Commission—Payment of Wages Act 1991, s 7(1)—employee's refusal to attend the workplace—whether disputed wages were properly payable*

The respondent, Ringsend Community Services Forum, appealed against a WRC decision which upheld a complaint under the Payment of Wages Act 1991. In linked appeals, the Labour Court upheld complaints under the Unfair Dismissals Acts 1977 to 2015 and the National Minimum Wage Acts 2000 to 2015. The claimant did not attend the hearing at first instance.

The claimant contended that she worked her full hours from home in the period from 10 May to 31 May 2021 and did not receive any payment for the work. The respondent's position was that the claimant refused to attend her workplace during that period, despite repeated instructions to do so. She was notified that her continued failure to comply with the terms of her contract would result in her removal from payroll. The respondent also disputed that the claimant worked from home.

The claimant had a contractual entitlement to €575 gross during the relevant period. It was accepted that she did not attend her contracted place of work during that period. It was clear from her contract that the right to payment of wages was contingent on her attending and working from her place of work, subject to any agreement to the contrary, which the Court held was clearly not the case here. No evidence suggested that the claimant had, in fact, carried out her contractual duties from home, nor did any evidence suggest that she was entitled to absent herself from the workplace, or to work from home for the relevant period. In the circumstances, the respondent was not obliged to pay the claimant's wages when she failed to attend for work as instructed.

Accordingly, no wages were properly payable to her for the relevant period and the appeal succeeded. The WRC's decision was overturned.

---

[4] *Ringsend Community Service Forum Clg v Moore* PWD2450, see further *Ringsend Community Services Forum Clg v Moore* UDD2432 at **[19.09]** for the decision of the Workplace Relations Commission.

PAYMENT OF WAGES ACT—BONUS

[20.05]   *Natus Manufacturing Ltd v Callanan[5]—Labour Court—appeal from Workplace Relations Commission—Payment of Wages Act 1991—discretionary bonus scheme—whether non-payment of a bonus was an unlawful deduction*

The respondent appealed against the WRC's decision, upholding a complaint under the Payment of Wages Act 1991. It found that the claimant suffered an unlawful deduction from her wages when she was not paid a bonus in 2022. The respondent was not in attendance at the first-instance hearing.

The claimant was a former employee of the respondent; her employment ended in August 2022. Her final salary payment was processed later that month; this did not include a bonus payment of €640 to which the claimant submitted she was entitled for work undertaken during a six-month period. The claimant had understood from a meeting with her supervisor that she would receive the bonus payment the next month. She pursued the matter with HR and was advised that she was not eligible to receive the bonus payment as she had left her employment prior to the pay-out date.

The respondent refuted the complaint. It submitted that its global bonus plan was entirely discretionary and that participants were required to be employed on the pay-out date. The claimant received all payments properly payable to her and no unlawful deduction was made. The claimant should have been on notice that her resigning might make her ineligible for that year's bonus pay-out. The position was explained to her during her exit interview.

It was clear to the Labour Court that the respondent's bonus plan operated as a discretionary scheme based on company performance. There was a rule stating that participants in the scheme had to be employed on the pay-out date. The claimant accepted that she had no contractual entitlement to participate in the scheme.

The Court found that no bonus payment was properly payable to the claimant. The complaint was not well founded and the appeal was allowed.

[20.06]   *Moon v Slater & Gordon UK Ltd[6]—UK Employment Appeal Tribunal—appeal from employment tribunal—Employment Rights Act 1996—unlawful deduction of wages—discretionary bonus scheme—harassment—unfair dismissal—redundancy*

The claimant appealed against an employment tribunal's dismissal of his complaints of unlawful deduction from wages, harassment, and certain aspects of his complaint of unfair dismissal.

The claimant was employed by the respondent law firm as a costs resolution manager ('CRM') in the Cardiff office. His responsibilities included overseeing a small team of six costs professionals. In contrast, other CRMs in the respondent's wider operations

---

5   *Natus Manufacturing Ltd v Callanan* PWD2447.
6   *Moon v Slater & Gordon UK Ltd* [2024] EAT 144.

managed significantly larger teams. Over time, the claimant became dissatisfied by how he was treated at work. Central to his complaints were issues surrounding his bonus entitlements, the respondent's handling of his ill-health (including anxiety and depression), and the circumstances of his dismissal.

The claimant raised concerns regarding his bonus payments for the financial years ending in 2017 and 2018. Having received a significant bonus in 2016 (£20,830), this was reduced to £3,400 the following year. By 2018, his entitlements had been further pro-rated, due to absences. The claimant argued that the respondent failed to properly exercise its discretion in determining his bonuses and that the reduction amounted to an unlawful deduction of wages. The respondent maintained that its bonus scheme was discretionary and non-contractual, and that it had acted within its rights.

The claimant also struggled with depression and anxiety, conditions which he linked to the pressures of his role. Following periods of sick leave in late 2017 and early 2018, he attempted to return to work but found the environment increasingly challenging. His relationships with senior managers also became strained. In a meeting in February 2018, the claimant alleged that two managers made derogatory remarks about his alleged insubordination and history of sending inappropriate communications. The claimant felt that this meeting was conducted in an insensitive manner, violating his dignity and creating a hostile environment. For the respondent's part, the managers asserted that they were simply trying to address concerns and ensure the claimant's wellbeing. This meeting formed the basis of the harassment complaint.

In October 2018, the respondent undertook a restructuring exercise aimed at reducing costs within its personal injury division, including the costs team to which the claimant belonged. His role was identified as potentially redundant due to the lower team-to-manager ratio in Cardiff compared to other offices. During this period, the claimant had also raised grievances related to his bonuses and general treatment at work. Ultimately, the claimant's position was made redundant in early 2019. The claimant contended that the redundancy was a sham, orchestrated in retaliation for his grievances, absences, and legal claims. He argued that the true reason for the redundancy was personal animosity from senior management.

The employment tribunal found in favour of the respondent but upheld one element of the claimant's unfair dismissal complaint. The tribunal concluded that the claimant's entitlement to bonuses was discretionary and non-contractual. While the respondent's bonus scheme allowed for significant awards, it did not guarantee fixed sums. The tribunal noted that the claimant failed to establish any entitlement to an identifiable or quantifiable sum that could be claimed as unpaid wages. As regards the February 2018 meeting, while accepting that it was upsetting for the claimant, the tribunal determined that the managers' conduct did not have the purpose or effect of creating a hostile or offensive environment. The tribunal found that the managers acted with good intentions, albeit without fully understanding the claimant's mental health condition. It upheld the redundancy as the genuine reason for dismissal, supported by evidence of organisational restructuring and an independent consultation process. However, the dismissal was found to be procedurally unfair due to the respondent's failure to offer the claimant an appeal mechanism.

On appeal, the claimant challenged the employment tribunal's analysis of his claims. The respondent cross-appealed on aspects of the unlawful deduction claim.

The EAT acknowledged errors in the tribunal's approach to the definition of 'wages' but held that they were immaterial. Even if properly analysed, the claimant's bonus entitlement remained discretionary and unquantifiable, precluding a valid claim under employment rights legislation.

The claimant contended that the employment tribunal wrongly focused on the managers' intentions rather than the broader circumstances of his workplace. The EAT rejected this argument, affirming that the tribunal had appropriately considered both the claimant's perception and the objective reasonableness of the conduct.

The claimant argued that the redundancy was a pretext and that the EAT failed to properly scrutinise the decision-making process. The EAT found no error, emphasising the independence of the decision maker and the clear evidence supporting redundancy as the principal reason for dismissal.

The respondent's cross-appeal succeeded, with the EAT confirming that the bonus claims fell outside the scope of the employment tribunal's jurisdiction. Otherwise, the appeal was dismissed.

See also decision of High Court of England and Wales in *Gupta v DB Group Services Ltd*,[7] relating to a bonus in the context of a claim for breach of employment contract, at **[1.03]**.

PAYMENT OF WAGES ACT—DEDUCTIONS

[20.07] *Department of Justice v Doherty*[8]—*Labour Court—appeal from Workplace Relations Commission—Payment of Wages Act 1991, s 7(1)—unlawful deductions—suspension pay—member of An Garda Síochána serving a custodial sentence—whether suspension allowance properly payable for period following member's release from prison in run up to their dismissal*

The claimant appealed against the WRC's dismissal of her complaint of unlawful deduction from her wages.

The claimant was a member of An Garda Síochána. During the relevant period (24 January 2019 to 2 July 2019), she was on unpaid suspension as she was serving a 20-month prison sentence.

The claimant submitted that she commenced her term of imprisonment on 31 October 2017 but that she was paid suspension pay until 30 August 2018, at which time the payment stopped. Because she had continued to be paid initially, she contended that An Garda Síochána's policy on suspension pay did not apply to her. On her release from prison on 2 July 2019, the claimant was not returned to suspension pay in the run up to

---

[7] *Gupta v DB Group Services Ltd* [2024] EWHC 2297 (KB).
[8] *Department of Justice and An Garda Síochána v Doherty* PWD2454.

her dismissal from the force. She submitted that suspension pay was properly payable to her for that period.

The respondent submitted that the decision to cease paying the claimant suspension pay with effect from August 2018 was clearly permitted by the Payment of Wages Act 1991 as it was authorised by the relevant policy document and An Garda Síochána's disciplinary regulations, due to the fact that the claimant was serving a custodial sentence.

The respondent accepted that no review of the claimant's entitlement to suspension pay occurred for the period 3 July to 23 July 2019.

The Labour Court determined that, during part of the cognisable period (24 January 2019 to 2 July 2019) the claimant was detained and therefore not entitled to a suspension allowance. For the period 3 July to 23 July 2019, however, the claimant did not fall into any of the excluded categories in the disciplinary regulations, and so the suspension allowance was properly payable. It followed that non-payment of the suspension allowance for that period was an unlawful deduction.

The respondent was directed to pay the claimant the suspension allowance for the period 3 July to 23 July 2019. Thus, the appeal succeeded and the decision of the WRC was set aside.

[20.08] *Crystal Valet Centre Ltd v Serao*[9]—*Labour Court—appeal from Workplace Relations Commission—Payment of Wages Act 1991—complaint of unlawful deduction—sick pay—properly payable*

The claimant appealed against the WRC's dismissal of his complaint of unlawful deduction from his wages.

The claimant commenced employment with the respondent, Crystal Valet Centre Ltd, on 22 September 2021 and went out sick on 9 October 2021. The claimant was on sick leave for the full cognisable period.

The claimant accepted that there was no contractual or statutory obligation to pay him while he was absent on sick leave. His complaint was that the respondent would not sign a form that would entitle him to illness benefit from the Department of Social Protection.

The respondent's position was that no monies were properly payable to the claimant for the cognisable period. The form to which the claimant referred was in respect of an accident in the workplace, of which the respondent was not on notice.

The Labour Court determined that as no payment was properly payable during the relevant period, the appeal failed.

[20.09] *HSE v McMahon*[10]—*Labour Court—appeal from Workplace Relations Commission—Payment of Wages Act 1991, s 7(1)—payment of wages—deduction—Covid-related special leave—overtime averaging—properly payable wages*

The claimant appealed against the WRC's dismissal of his complaint under the Payment of Wages Act 1991. The claimant alleged that his wages, paid on 27 January 2022, were

---

[9] *Crystal Valet Centre Ltd v Serao* PWD2455.
[10] *HSE v McMahon* PWD2460.

incomplete due to the omission of €75.02, which he argued should have been included as an average of overtime earnings during his Covid-19-related special leave from 3 to 9 January 2022.

The claimant, who was rostered to work 39 hours per week, was absent on Covid-19-related special leave with pay. Under an agreement between the respondent and trade unions, employees on such leave were entitled to their regular wages, including an average of any overtime payments earned during the six weeks preceding the leave. The claimant argued that, in accordance with this agreement, he was entitled to an additional €75.02. The respondent countered that the claimant had not worked or received any overtime in the six weeks before his leave, and so no such payment was due. The respondent further asserted that the claimant had received his full wages for the period in question.

The Labour Court first considered whether a deduction had occurred. It found that the claimant had received no overtime pay during the six-week period preceding his leave and was therefore not entitled to an additional payment. Consequently, the wages paid to him on 27 January 2022 represented his full entitlement, with no shortfall.

Although the claimant's arguments before the Labour Court differed from those presented to the WRC, which were general in nature, the Court chose to proceed with the case as the relevant timeframe was covered, and neither party objected. It concluded that the claimant's complaint was misconceived, as no deduction had occurred, and no additional payment was properly due.

The appeal was, accordingly, rejected and the WRC's decision affirmed.

[20.10] *Excel Roofing Systems Ltd v Porter*[11]—*Labour Court—appeal from Workplace Relations Commission—Payment of Wages Act 1991, s 7(1)—unpaid layoff—Covid-19 restrictions—lawfulness of deduction to wages—whether deductions to the employee's wages were required or authorised by a contract term*

The claimant appealed against the WRC's dismissal of his complaint for non-attendance.

The claimant was employed by the respondent. He was laid off from his employment on 2 January 2021 and resigned on 25 March that year. The claimant contended that the layoff was not linked to the Covid-19 pandemic and that he was not paid his normal weekly wages for the relevant period.

The respondent submitted that any deduction to the claimant's wages was 'required or authorised' by a term in his contract in force at the time. While it accepted that there was no written contract of employment in place between the parties at the relevant time, the claimant acquiesced to unpaid layoffs as a term of his contract when he accepted a three-month unpaid layoff in 2020. He had not sought redress at the time and availed of the pandemic unemployment payment.

The claimant accepted that he had not objected to being laid off without pay during the first lockdown. He also accepted that, on this occasion, he received a retrospective payment for the initial days that he was laid off.

---

[11] *Excel Roofing Systems Ltd v Porter* PWD2444.

The Labour Court held that wages were properly payable to the claimant for the relevant period. Given the exceptional circumstances that prevailed during the Covid-19 pandemic, the Court did not accept that a 'custom or practice' of unpaid layoffs had developed that was 'so notorious and well known that an employee was certain of its existence', such that it could be taken to be a term of the contract, absent written terms. The respondent had not shown that the contract was varied by custom and practice and, hence, the deductions were unlawful. Notwithstanding emergency measures in place at the time, nothing affected the application of the Payment of Wages Act 1991.

Although the complaint was well founded, an award of no compensation was deemed reasonable in the circumstances.

[20.11] *Kostal Ireland Gmbh v Cannon[12]—Labour Court—appeal from Workplace Relations Commission—Payment of Wages Act 1991, s 7(1)—reduced weekly working hours—lawfulness of deductions to wages—whether deductions were mandated by a term of the contract of employment or collective agreement*

The respondent appealed against the WRC's decision, upholding a complaint under the Payment of Wages Act 1991.

The respondent's plant shut down from 25 March 2020 until 27 April 2020, during which time employees were not paid and were advised that they would be entitled to State support. Shut-downs were a regular feature of the plant, especially at Christmas, and on such occasions workers were invited to avail of annual leave or unpaid leave. As the pandemic progressed, employees were regularly updated in relation to the difficulties facing the respondent.

The claimant submitted that in May 2021 she was placed on a shorter working week than her contracted 39 hours. Her weekly pay was adjusted. The claimant submitted that there were deductions from her wages on four dates in 2021. No term of her contract of employment, or the collective agreement between the respondent and the claimant's union, permitted these changes. Short-time working was implemented by the respondent in an attempt to avoid layoffs and redundancies. The rosters were forced upon the employees, who had objected to short-time working, and the claimant participated under protest.

The respondent pointed out that the plant was shut down on one of the four dates in question. Otherwise, it accepted that wages actually paid to the claimant during the relevant period were less than the amount properly payable. The Labour Court was satisfied that this difference was a deduction within the meaning of the Payment of Wages Act 1991. The Court concluded that while 'shut-downs' were a regular and accepted event in the employment, the deductions on the other three dates were not mandated by the contract of employment; nor were they agreed by the claimant.

It followed that the deductions, cumulatively €555.16, were unlawful. The Court directed compensation of €277.50, which it considered reasonable in the circumstances. The appeal was dismissed.

---

[12] *Kostal Ireland Gmbh v Cannon* PWD2452.

[20.12] *Mendy v Manchester City Football Club Ltd*[13]—*UK employment tribunal—Employment Rights Act 1996, s 13—unauthorised deductions from wages—ready, willing, and able to work—FA suspension—custody and bail conditions—avoidable vs unavoidable impediments—breach of bail conditions—professional football contract—gross misconduct—safeguarding measures*

The claimant, a professional footballer formerly employed by the respondent, brought a claim for unauthorised deductions from wages under the Employment Rights Act 1996. The case revolved around whether the club was entitled to withhold his wages during periods of suspension, bail conditions, and custody, arising from serious criminal allegations of which he was ultimately acquitted.

The claimant was employed by the respondent from 2017 under a contract guaranteeing an annual salary of £6 million. In August 2021, following allegations of sexual offences, he was remanded in custody. The respondent subsequently suspended him without pay from September 2021 until his contract expired in June 2023. The Football Association ('FA') also imposed a safeguarding suspension on the claimant, barring him from football-related activities due to allegations involving a minor. Despite being acquitted of all criminal charges by July 2023, the respondent refused to pay his wages for the periods of custody and bail, claiming his inability to work was avoidable and resulted from his own actions.

The claim was split into four key periods: the 'first custody period' (September 2021 to January 2022), the 'first bail period' (January 2022 to December 2022), the 'second custody period' (December 2022 to January 2023), and the 'second bail period' (January 2023 to June 2023).

The key question was whether the wages were 'properly payable' under the contract and whether the respondent had contractual or statutory authority to withhold them. The employment tribunal's analysis considered whether the claimant was able to perform his contractual obligations and whether impediments were avoidable or unavoidable. It found no express or implied terms permitting the respondent to withhold wages during suspension or bail conditions unless there was gross misconduct or other specific contractual provisions.

The employment tribunal held that, for the first custody period, the respondent was entitled to withhold wages as the claimant had breached bail conditions, contributing to his remand in custody. Similarly, the respondent was entitled to withhold wages for the second custody period, which also arose from an admitted breach of bail conditions. For the first and second bail periods, the tribunal found that the FA suspension, and not the bail conditions, was the effective cause of the claimant's inability to work, making the impediment unavoidable. The respondent was therefore ordered to pay wages for those periods.

The employment tribunal awarded the claimant approximately £9.45 million in unpaid wages for the periods where his inability to work was deemed unavoidable. It upheld

---

[13] *Mendy v Manchester City Football Club Ltd* 2411709/2023.

the respondent's right to withhold wages during the custody periods due to the claimant's culpable breaches of bail conditions.

[20.13] **Buildmaster Construction Services Ltd v Al-Naimi**[14]—*UK Employment Appeal Tribunal—appeal from employment tribunal—Employment Rights Act 1996—unlawful deductions from wages—properly payable—lack of written agreement—oral variation of contract of employment—adequate reasoning*

The respondent appealed against an employment tribunal decision awarding the claimant £9,750 for unlawful deductions from wages.

The claimant was employed by the respondent on a monthly salary of £2,400. During the period from October 2021 to May 2022, her salary payments were significantly reduced, without prior written agreement or explanation, totaling £9,450 instead of the agreed £19,200. The claimant maintained that her contract guaranteed a fixed monthly salary of £2,400, while the respondent argued that her wages were subject to workload and company profits, as verbally agreed during the Covid-19 pandemic. The respondent contended that the claimant had consented to a reduction in pay due to financial difficulties caused by the pandemic. However, no written agreement or documentation confirming this variation was provided.

The employment tribunal concluded that the claimant's agreed monthly salary was £2,400, as established by the payslips and her original employment terms. There was no credible evidence to suggest that her wages were contingent on workload or company profits. The respondent failed to provide documentation or written consent from the claimant authorising the salary reduction. The tribunal found that any contractual variation must meet the requirements of the Employment Rights Act 1996, which necessitates written agreement for wage deductions. The tribunal determined that the difference between the claimant's salary and the amount she received constituted an unauthorised deduction. Consequently, the claimant was awarded £9,750.

On appeal, the respondent argued that the employment tribunal conflated the determination of 'properly payable' wages under the Employment Rights Act 1996 with the formalities required for lawful deductions under that Act. The respondent contended that oral agreement was sufficient to vary the claimant's contract and that the tribunal had erred by requiring written evidence. The respondent also claimed that the tribunal failed to adequately explain why the claimant's evidence was preferred and why the respondent's assertion of an oral variation was rejected.

The EAT found no evidence that the employment tribunal conflated the two stages of analysis under the Employment Rights Act 1996. The tribunal correctly identified that wages 'properly payable' were determined by the contractual terms and that the absence of written agreement invalidated any claimed variation. The EAT rejected the respondent's assertion that the tribunal improperly dismissed the oral variation argument. The tribunal's judgment clearly indicated that it considered this claim but

---

[14] *Buildmaster Construction Services Ltd v Al-Naimi* [2024] EAT 101.

found it unsupported by evidence, particularly given the absence of contemporaneous documentation. More generally, the tribunal's judgment provided sufficient clarity and explanation. The decision outlined the factual findings, legal principles, and reasoning that led to its conclusion, enabling the respondent to understand the decision. The EAT agreed with the tribunal that the claimant's monthly salary of £2,400 was properly payable and that deductions from this amount were unauthorised under the Employment Rights Act 1996.

The appeal was, accordingly, dismissed.

Chapter 21

Whistleblowing

INTRODUCTION

[21.01]

Compensation

The assessment of compensation in a case involving dismissal for having made a protected disclosure was considered by the UK EAT in *SPI Spirits (UK) Ltd & Shefler v Zabelin*.

Criminal Justice Act 2011

A rare example of a whistleblowing claim under the Criminal Justice Act 2011 is that of *Department of Justice & An Garda Síochána v Doherty*, decided by the Labour Court.

Detriment—Penalisation

A number of detriment/penalisation UK EAT decisions are noted, namely *Sullivan v Isle of Wight Council, First Greater Western Ltd v Moussa*, and *Erhard-Jensen Ontological/Phenomenological Initiative Ltd v Rogerson*.

The absence of a causal link between the detriment and the protected disclosure was considered by the UK EAT in *Dowding v The Character Group plc*.

Dismissal

Whether a dismissal was connected to a protected disclosure was considered by the Labour Court in *Madigan's Pharmacy Kilkenny Ltd v Murphy* and by the UK EAT in *Ritson v Milan Babic Architects Ltd*.

Employer's Knowledge

Whether the employer was aware of the protected disclosure was the subject of the decision of the UK EAT in *Nicol v World Travel and Tourism Council*.

Protected Disclosure?

In *Moorehall Disability Services t/a Moorehall Living v Novak*, the Labour Court had to consider whether there was in fact a protected disclosure in the first place. That question was also the subject of the UK EAT decision in *William v Lewisham and Greenwich NHS Trust*.

Relevant Wrongdoing/Reasonable Belief

Whether there was a reasonable belief that there was relevant wrongdoing on the part of the claimant was considered by the Labour Court in *Moorehall Disability Services t/a Moorehall Living v Novak*.

Vicarious Liability

Whether there can be vicarious liability for detrimental treatment in the context of a protected disclosure was considered by the UK EAT in *Treadwell v Barton Turns Development Ltd*.

Worker

Finally, whether the claimant was or was not a worker was the subject of the UK EAT decision in *MacLennan v The British Psychological Society*.

COMPENSATION

[21.02] *SPI Spirits (UK) Ltd & Shefler v Zabelin*[1]—*UK Employment Appeal Tribunal—appeal from employment tribunal—protected disclosure—damages—contractual clause purporting to put a cap on damages—failure to follow Acas Code on disciplinary and grievance procedure—decision to award uplift to damages against respondents jointly and severally*

---

[1] *SPI Spirits (UK) Ltd & Shefler v Zabelin* [2023] EAT 147.

The claimant was employed by the respondent, and the second respondent was held by the employment tribunal to be the respondent's agent. In a decision on liability, the tribunal found that, in a telephone conversation, the second respondent subjected the claimant to detriment and dismissed him on the ground that he had made a protected disclosure. In a subsequent remedy decision, the tribunal made joint and several awards against both respondents. The respondents appealed against certain aspects of the remedy.

Before the tribunal, the respondents relied upon contractual clauses, which they contended capped the amount of compensation to which the claimant would be entitled on dismissal, at £270,000 net. These clauses, they argued, had been freely negotiated and were relevant to the tribunal's assessment of damages. The UK EAT was satisfied that the tribunal had not 'failed' to consider that argument, and, in any event, was correct not to uphold it. The clauses were in substance an unenforceable contractual cap on the tribunal's awards.

The tribunal uplifted its award of compensation on the basis of the respondents' failure to follow the Acas Code on disciplinary and grievance procedure. The EAT held that it had not erred in rejecting an argument that the procedure did not apply in this case on the basis that, when written grievances were first raised, the claimant had yet to raise them in the form of a protected disclosure, and only did so orally subsequently. The tribunal was entitled to conclude that the underlying matter remained the same and the uplift arose in circumstances where the provisions of the Acas Code applied.

Finally, the tribunal did not err in applying the uplift against the individual agent as well as against the corporate employer. The circumstances were such that the tribunal found that the agent was responsible for the employer's failure to comply with the Acas Code.

The appeal was, accordingly, dismissed.

CRIMINAL JUSTICE ACT 2011

[21.03] *Department of Justice & An Garda Síochána v Doherty[2]—Labour Court—appeal from Workplace Relations Commission—Criminal Justice Act 2011, s 20(2)—complaint of penalisation for making a protected disclosure—failure to make a complaint to a member of An Garda Síochána*

The claimant appealed against a decision of the WRC dismissing a claim that her employer, An Garda Síochána, penalised her for making a protected disclosure under the Criminal Justice Act 2011. During the relevant period, the claimant was on unpaid suspension as she was serving a 20-month prison sentence. She submitted that, by placing her on unpaid suspension as it did, the respondent had penalised her.

The Court determined that the claimant did not make a complaint to a member of An Garda Síochána as required by the Act.

Accordingly, the appeal failed.

---

[2] *Department of Justice & An Garda Síochána v Doherty* CJD231.

DETRIMENT—PENALISATION

[21.04] *Sullivan v Isle of Wight Council*[3]—*UK Employment Appeal Tribunal—appeal from employment tribunal—protected disclosure—complaint of less favourable treatment—external applicant—inadmissible complaint—European Convention on Human Rights, arts 10 & 14—whether tribunal's findings contravened job applicant's arts 10 and 14 rights—comparator group*

The claimant contended that, as a job applicant, she had been subjected to detriments on the ground that she had made protected disclosures in the public interest. The employment tribunal found that it lacked jurisdiction to consider the whistleblowing complaints and dismissed them. The claimant appealed against that finding and argued that the tribunal's findings were in contravention of her rights under arts 10 and 14 of the European Convention on Human Rights ('ECHR').

The UK EAT took no issue with the tribunal's finding that the facts, taken at their highest, fell within the ambit of art 10 ECHR. However, it did not accept the claimant's argument that her situation was analogous to that of an internal applicant for the purpose of determining whether she had been treated less favourably regarding her art 10 rights. While it was true that, unlike those applicants, the claimant had been denied the possibility of bringing proceedings before an employment tribunal, an internal applicant's entitlement to statutory protection would derive from his or her status as a worker in an existing role. Further, the claimant's disclosure came about some months after the application process, it related to matters unconnected with that process (or indeed the respondent itself), and had been made through a channel available to members of the public.

The EAT did not accept that the claimant's situation was analogous to that of applicants for non-clinical roles who are protected by NHS regulations prohibiting discrimination against whistleblowers: the claimant was 'not even indirectly' concerned with patient safety in a non-clinical capacity, nor was a 'sound evidence-base' provided to the tribunal indicating the existence of issues of a similar nature and extent outside the NHS.

Finally, the EAT did not accept that 'external job applicant' constituted 'some other status' for the purposes of art 14, and the treatment which the claimant alleged she suffered was not suffered '*qua* external applicant'.

The tribunal had been entitled to draw the above conclusions, and, while it erred in its approach to proportionality when considering the issue of justification, this had no material effect in light of those conclusions. The appeal was therefore dismissed.

[21.05] *First Greater Western Ltd v Moussa*[4]—*UK Employment Appeal Tribunal—appeal from employment tribunal—Equality Act 2010, s 27—victimisation—protected acts—detriments—protected disclosures*

---

[3] *Sullivan v Isle of Wight Council* [2024] EAT 3.
[4] *First Greater Western Ltd v Moussa* [2024] EAT 82.

The respondent appealed against an employment tribunal's decision which upheld complaints of victimisation for having done a protected act and detriments for having made protected disclosures.

The claimant had been employed by the respondent railway company since 2006. In 2012, when he was working at Ealing Broadway Station, a dispute arose when a new health and safety representative was appointed with the support of a local union leader. The appointment was opposed by the claimant and others, who believed that the correct process was not followed. The claimant raised a grievance, alleging that the union leader had threatened and abused him. Matters escalated and the claimant and three others were dismissed in 2013 for having acted in an intimidating manner towards the union leader. An unfair dismissal complaint was settled and the claimant was reinstated and transferred to Paddington, where he became the station manager.

In 2018, an incident occurred in which a member of the public was escorted away from the ticket barriers by the claimant, and the police were called. The man was arrested and it was later suggested that he was carrying a knife and drugs and had attempted to push his way onto the platform without a ticket. The claimant and his colleague, both of whom were on duty at the ticket barrier, filled in an 'assault report form'. The claimant, who was not a native English speaker, was assisted in doing so. The colleague also gave a police statement, though the claimant did not. Having considered the evidence, the station police commander complained verbally to the respondent that it appeared the claimant and his colleague had made false allegations of assault. The matter was left with the respondent to handle internally. Based on that verbal complaint, the claimant and his colleague were suspended pending an investigation, a measure reserved for allegations of gross misconduct. The stated reason in the letter of suspension was providing a false statement; there was no mention of gross misconduct. The respondent was provided with a written statement from the station police commander. This statement was unsigned and undated, and it was not clear to which employee it referred, simply stating that 'he' had been 'pushed'.

The respondent appointed an investigator. This person had never conducted such an investigation before and lacked experience. Indeed, he failed to interview three employee witnesses. Having viewed the CCTV footage, he then sought to add a further allegation that the claimant had assaulted or physically restrained a member of the public. The employment tribunal concluded, having viewed the same footage, that the claimant appeared to shepherd the man away from the scene, and saw no clear evidence of physical restraint or assault. Nonetheless, this formed part of one of the recommended charges set out in the investigator's findings. Although this letter made no mention of gross misconduct, the claimant remained suspended pending investigation, contrary to the respondent's disciplinary rules. His colleague, having withdrawn his statement and issued an apology 'of sorts', was permitted to return to work. The tribunal found that the investigation was 'poorly conducted, unfair and unreliable'.

The claimant was signed off work by his doctor on grounds of sickness. He submitted a complaint to the respondent's managing director through his solicitors. The complaint was passed to a human resources worker who then sent an email to colleagues using language which the employment tribunal found 'trivialised' the claimant's concerns.

The tribunal also considered the email prejudicial and suggestive of a 'received wisdom and collective memory relating to the claimant as being an agitator and a malign influence'. The tribunal linked this to the events of 2012 and 2013.

An occupational health doctor, who assessed the claimant, advised the respondent that he was suffering from work-related mental health problems and that he should not be contacted directly. The respondent replied to the claimant's solicitors in what amounted to a cursory acknowledgement, not engaging with the substance of the issues raised.

The disciplinary hearing, when it did take place, dismissed the allegation of making a false statement and did not uphold the allegation of laying hands on a customer unnecessarily.

The employment tribunal identified the bringing of the unfair dismissal claim in 2013 as a protected act. The 2012 written complaint and collective grievance against the union leader were identified as protected disclosures. The detriments to which the claimant was subjected were as follows: accusing the claimant of making a false statement about the 2018 incident; suspending him; conducting an inadequate and biased investigation; adding two extra allegations at the end of the investigation; deciding to convene a disciplinary hearing; failing to address the claimant's formal written complaints; failing to follow the recommendations of the occupational health doctor; and failing to liaise with the claimant's solicitor about the disciplinary process.

The EAT's analysis concluded that the employment tribunal's decision in relation to detriments was adequately reasoned and revealed no perverse findings of fact. The tribunal was also entitled to its finding that 'management lore', encouraged by HR, had perpetuated a culture of prejudice and ill-will towards the claimant, which in turn had fed into the investigation. There was no procedural unfairness in making such a finding against the HR worker in question—whom the respondent decided against calling as a witness—since no liability attached to the investigator personally.

The appeal was, accordingly, dismissed.

[21.06] *Erhard-Jensen Ontological/Phenomenological Initiative Ltd v Rogerson*[5]— *UK Employment Appeal Tribunal—appeal from employment tribunal—judicial proceedings immunity—whether immunity applied to arbitration proceedings alleged to be a detriment*

The respondent appealed against an employment tribunal decision that judicial proceedings immunity did not apply to an alleged detriment relied upon by the claimant for having made protected disclosures.

The respondent was a Singapore-based charity. In 2016, the claimant, who was based in London, entered into a confidentiality agreement with the respondent. This contained an arbitration clause providing for an arbitration seated in Singapore.

---

[5] *Erhard-Jensen Ontological/Phenomenological Initiative Ltd v Rogerson* [2024] EAT 135.

After the claimant resigned in 2019, he made a number of allegations of mistreatment of members of staff in London. In 2021, the respondent brought arbitration proceedings against the respondent in the ICC International Court of Arbitration in Singapore.

The claimant alleged that he suffered a detriment when he was put to the trouble and expense of having to face arbitration proceedings, which he claimed were groundless and were brought maliciously. The respondent argued that the arbitration proceedings were 'quasi-judicial proceedings' and that the alleged detriment was barred as it was privileged.

The tribunal held that although the arbitration process in Singapore was a 'quasi-judicial exercise; judicial proceedings immunity did not extend 'to the mere bringing of a claim' and, in any event, the immunity did not apply generally to overseas bodies. The respondent challenged that decision.

The EAT held that the employment tribunal failed to focus upon the way that the detriment was pleaded by the claimant, instead approaching the issue of immunity as a 'broad generic one'. In doing so, the tribunal wrongly considered that the question was simply whether the immunity prevented a second set of proceedings from being brought, irrespective of whether the second set of proceedings was founded upon an aspect of the first proceedings.

The employment tribunal also erred in concluding that judicial proceedings immunity does not apply 'generally to overseas bodies'.

The EAT concluded that the pleaded detriment fell within the established parameters of judicial proceedings immunity and, as such, there was no interference with the claimant's art 6 ECHR rights.

The appeal was therefore allowed.

[21.07] *Dowding v The Character Group plc*[6]—*UK Employment Appeal Tribunal—appeal from employment tribunal—detriment and unfair dismissal for making a public interest disclosure—relevant wrongdoing—subjective belief that the disclosure was in the public interest—causal link between alleged detriments and the asserted protected disclosures—credibility—ordinary unfair dismissal*

The claimant appealed against an employment tribunal's dismissal of his complaint of ordinary unfair dismissal. A complaint of unfair dismissal for making protected disclosures was also dismissed.

The claimant was employed by the respondent, a producer and distributor of toys, from 2012 until his dismissal in September 2021. In 2016, the claimant was appointed group financial director and company secretary. At his request, the claimant was provided with a draft director service agreement and copies of the service agreements of his fellow directors. He was invited to submit comments on the terms of his draft service agreement by 29 June 2017.

---

[6] *Dowding v The Character Group plc* [2024] EAT 153.

On 14 June 2017, the claimant emailed the respondent's board of directors advising that all directors' service agreements would need to be available for inspection by shareholders at the respondent's registered office. The claimant was told by the director to whom he reported, Mr Shah, that this would be sorted in a few weeks and that there was 'no urgency'. His evidence to the employment tribunal—which he introduced for the first time—was that Mr Shah then told him not to discuss the matter with the other two founding directors.

The claimant, again, emailed the board on 3 and 10 July, referring to a 'technical breach' of the Companies Act 2006. At this time, the claimant was also seeking an increase to his basic salary. On 14 July 2017, the respondent's remuneration committee made the claimant an improved offer, stated to be open for 14 days. Meanwhile, the claimant asked for more time to respond to his service agreement terms. He was told by Mr Shah that his request would be referred to the remuneration committee, that he should in any event respond by 7 August with a tracked-change Word document, and that the financial offer of 14 July had lapsed. The claimant replied on 8 August to say that this was unfair. He asked to deal directly with the remuneration committee but Mr Shah maintained his position.

The claimant was on leave from 10 to 24 August 2017. Following his return, he emailed Mr Shah accusing him of being 'insidious'. On 29 August, the claimant provided a pdf version of his service agreement with several hand-written changes and deletions.

Meanwhile, in August 2017 the claimant instructed two firms to assist in a matter relating to the respondent's corporation tax returns, due at the end of that month. The employment tribunal found that this was done without the knowledge or consent of Mr Shah. In an email exchange with the claimant, Mr Shah made repeated requests for the email correspondence with the firms, only some of which was ultimately provided. On 24 August 2017, there was a meeting between the claimant and Mr Shah which became heated and voices were raised. In a subsequent email to the claimant, Mr Shah wrote: 'Your behaviour was inappropriate and unprofessional'. He accused the claimant of pointing a pen in his face in a threatening manner. The claimant apologised for raising his voice but said that this was the 'only' thing he had done.

By letter of 4 September 2017, the claimant was invited to a disciplinary hearing to consider allegations of misconduct, which included: 'unprofessional and threatening behaviour'; failing to respond to the draft service agreement 'in a timely and professional manner'; and not providing emails with external consultants, until asked to do so six times, without an explanation. More generally, the claimant was accused of conduct that was 'aggressive, unhelpful, adversarial and unproductive'. The claimant was informed that he was being placed on a performance improvement plan. Later that day, the respondent proposed a mutually agreed 'parting of the ways', enclosing a draft settlement agreement. The claimant returned a marked-up Word copy of his draft service agreement.

Following a disciplinary hearing on 6 September 2017, the claimant was dismissed with notice. Appealing that decision, the claimant alleged for the first time that he had made a protected disclosure. He made various allegations against Mr Shah. That appeal was rejected.

The employment tribunal specifically addressed the claimant's credibility. It found that the claimant dishonestly claimed that he did not have certain emails referred to in his witness statement (he admitted under cross-examination to having copies). His evidence on the particular detriment he suffered was rejected out of hand as 'entirely unsatisfactory'. The claimant also made 'a serious and unambiguous' allegation of fraud and dishonesty against a named person, the making of which triggered an investigation by the Financial Conduct Authority; the allegation was maintained at hearing and not withdrawn, despite the investigation having exonerated that person. An allegation that the respondent altered or falsified information was withdrawn mid-hearing. The tribunal did not believe the claimant's evidence, introduced for the first time, that Mr Shah told him that he did not want the other directors to know about the requirement for directors' service agreements to be available for inspection.

The employment tribunal concluded that the claimant did not believe that his disclosures were made in the public interest. The claimant acknowledged not being aware of any shareholder having exercised the right to inspect directors' service agreements. He was not aware of any prosecutions for failing to provide those documents for inspection and, in his own words, considered the breach 'technical' in nature. Indeed, it was not until his appeal against dismissal that the claimant alleged for the first time that he had made a protected disclosure. If he did hold such a subjective belief, it was not reasonably held. There was no causal link between the alleged detriments, such as they were, and the asserted protected disclosures ('each issue had their own triggering events'). It was 'inevitable' that the claimant's 'insubordination' would lead to a matters escalating and he was 'the author of his own misfortune'. It concluded that there had been a fatal undermining of the necessary trust and confidence, such that dismissal was within the band of reasonable responses.

On appeal, the UK EAT rejected the contention that the tribunal 'failed to give adequate reasons for its conclusion that the respondent's investigation and procedure were fair'. It was clear the claimant's 'general stance' was that the appeal process was a 'sham' and 'pre-ordained'. The tribunal's reasoning conveyed that it considered the process was conducted independently and thoroughly, and therefore was not a sham. It did not need to say any more in this case. The EAT also rejected that the tribunal erred 'by substituting its own view for that of the respondent' when deciding on the question of reasonable belief that the claimant's conduct gave rise to a loss of trust and confidence. The tribunal not only stated and understood the test it had to apply, but did so. Its reasons were sufficient and its conclusion was certainly not perverse.

The appeal on liability was, accordingly, dismissed.

DISMISSAL

[21.08] *Madigan's Pharmacy Kilkenny Ltd v Murphy*[7]—*Labour Court—appeal from Workplace Relations Commission—Unfair Dismissals Acts 1977 to 2015,*

---

[7] *Madigan's Pharmacy Kilkenny Ltd v Murphy* UDD2424.

s 8A—protected disclosures—causative link—whether dismissal wholly or mainly from having made protected disclosures

The claimant appealed against the WRC's decision that it had no jurisdiction to hear her complaint under the Unfair Dismissals Acts 1977 to 2015.

The claimant was employed by the respondent from September 2020 until her dismissal some 10 months later. She contended that her dismissal was wholly or mainly due to a series of protected disclosures she had made to the respondent and that the 12 months' service requirement had no application. The respondent submitted that the claimant's dismissal was wholly due to concerns about her performance and that a replacement pharmacist was recruited prior to the alleged protected disclosures having been made. Indeed, the respondent's case was that it began looking for a direct replacement very shortly after recruiting the claimant. It was not disputed that the respondent encountered significant difficulty in its efforts to recruit a pharmacist, owing in part to the location and nature of the business. It was also common case that the claimant took up new employment soon after her dismissal.

The Court concluded that, on the balance of probabilities, the respondent was, over a period of several months, engaged in efforts to replace the claimant. It followed that the claimant's dismissal resulted from the recruitment of a replacement pharmacist and was not a result of her making protected disclosures. This meant that the Unfair Dismissals Acts had no application to the complaint and the appeal failed.

[21.09] *Ritson v Milan Babic Architects Ltd*[8]*—UK Employment Appeal Tribunal—appeal from employment tribunal—Employment Rights Act 1996, ss 47B, 103A & 105—automatic unfair dismissal—protected disclosure—likely breach of legal obligation*

The claimant appealed against an employment tribunal's dismissal of his complaints of automatic unfair dismissal for having made protected disclosures, unfair selection for redundancy, and other detriments.

The claimant was employed as an architect by the respondent from 2018 until his dismissal by reason of alleged redundancy in 2020. He had less than two years' service when his employment was terminated.

In March 2020, by reason of Covid-19, the respondent informed its staff that they were all being furloughed and placed on the UK job retention scheme. In an email, the claimant accepted furlough and stated that he would undertake no further work. At the time, the claimant was involved in an ongoing project. In two text messages to the respondent, which he claimed were protected disclosures, the claimant said that he was not allowed to work while on furlough, and would not be undertaking further work on the project for the duration. The claimant appeared to express concern for breaking the rules of the job retention scheme.

---

[8] *Ritson v Milan Babic Architects Ltd* [2024] EAT 95.

The employment tribunal was satisfied that the redundancies which followed arose from anticipated cash flow issues while awaiting the receipt of furlough money. The respondent acted on advice from its accountant and decided that the best solution was to make its highest earners (including the claimant) redundant. In the developing circumstances, this was a reasonable position for the respondent to adopt.

In an email, the claimant raised concerns about redundancy but made no mention of a concern about being dismissed for whistleblowing or making protected disclosures. The employment tribunal concluded that the protected disclosures relied upon by the claimant were not qualifying disclosures. The claimant had no subjective belief that rules were likely to be breached, such that the disclosures would be made in the public interest; the only interests the claimant had in mind were those of himself and the respondent. None of the proven detriments were linked to protected disclosures. The claim therefore failed.

The EAT rejected the appeal, finding no proper basis to intervene with the employment tribunal's decision. The tribunal rejected the case on the facts and made permissible findings that the protected disclosures were not qualifying disclosures. There was no error of law and adequate reasons were given.

EMPLOYER'S KNOWLEDGE

[21.10] *Nicol v World Travel and Tourism Council*[9]—*UK Employment Appeal Tribunal—appeal from employment tribunal—Employment Rights Act 1996, ss 103A & 47B—unfair dismissal—protected disclosure*

The claimant appealed against an employment tribunal's dismissal of his complaints of unfair dismissal and detriment as a result of making protected disclosures.

The claimant was a consultant for the respondent from 2011. On 1 May 2019, he became vice-president of communications and PR. He was dismissed on 14 October 2019. The employment tribunal found that, by the end of May/beginning of June 2019, the claimant had decided that he was not willing to work with the CEO of the respondent as a full-time employee.

On 12 June 2019, the CEO sent a series of angry WhatsApp messages to a member of the claimant's team following an error in setting up a conference call with some journalists. On 14 June, that team member complained to HR about the CEO. In two WhatsApp messages dated 12 and 14 June, the claimant warned the CEO of the dangers of communicating with junior staff members by WhatsApp, citing the risk of resignation and 'legal challenge'. The respondent accepted that these were protected disclosures ('PD1' and 'PD2').

On 18 July 2019, another member of the claimant's team was signed off sick with stress for four weeks. That team member reported concerns about the claimant's behaviour,

---

[9] *Nicol v World Travel and Tourism Council, Guevara and Gracia* [2024] EAT 42.

which were shared with HR consultants engaged by the respondent specifically to improve staff morale. The claimant was informed, although he was not told that the concerns related to allegations of sexual harassment. The claimant alleged that he made a third protected disclosure ('PD3') to HR in a conversation on 14 August 2019. He said that the team member in question had been signed off sick because the CEO had repeatedly sent her messages in the evenings and at weekends. Meanwhile, the CEO was informed by HR that the claimant had behaved inappropriately towards that team member on a number of occasions.

In a meeting between the CEO and the claimant on 21 August 2019, the claimant alleged that he made a fourth disclosure ('PD4') to the effect that he was being 'bullied and harassed' and that the CEO's behaviour towards his team members was unacceptable. The claimant also told the CEO that he had taken legal advice on his situation and that he no longer wished to be an employee of the respondent, and wanted to work as a consultant instead. After the meeting, the claimant was informed of the sexual harassment allegations against him. An investigation ensued.

In an email on 27 August 2019, the claimant complained to HR that the CEO had called a meeting to discuss issues which the claimant said had been raised in a team member's exit interview, including allegations of bullying and harassment against the CEO. The claimant complained that it was entirely inappropriate to discuss these matters in front of others, and that this amounted to further bullying and harassment. This email was the fifth alleged protected disclosure ('PD5'). Although the CEO was made aware of PD5, she did not have an opportunity to read the email.

On 28 August 2019, the CEO, who by this time was considering whether to terminate the claimant's employment, alerted HR to material available through a Google search alleging that the claimant had abused a free flights benefit when he was a director of EasyJet in 2010. The CEO said that the allegations were previously unknown to her and she now considered that the claimant 'needed to be out of the organisation'.

On 2 September 2019, the claimant wrote a letter to the CEO (the sixth alleged protected disclosure, 'PD6') citing employment rights infringements and proposing a consultancy arrangement on terms which included an *ex gratia* payment of £40,000 and the same salary as he was currently earning, all while working three days per week for the remainder of 2019, and two days per week thereafter. The CEO believed that the claimant was blackmailing her.

The investigation into the sexual harassment allegations concluded that the claimant could be 'laddish, lewd and inappropriate' at work but that there was 'no case for him to answer at this time'. The respondent made the claimant a without prejudice offer of settlement but negotiations failed. The claimant was dismissed, purportedly for redundancy.

Among the employment tribunal's findings of fact were that the claimant did make 'inappropriate sexualised comments' as alleged. With respect to PD3, the tribunal found that the claimant did not disclose that the reason for the team member's absence was repeated evening and weekend calls from the CEO, and so on balance that disclosure was not actually made on 14 August 2019. PD5 was upheld, though its 'primary motivating factor' was found to be 'to strengthen the claimant's position in the forthcoming negotiations and to safeguard his position against disciplinary action'. Nevertheless, the email of 27 August 2019 was not brought to the CEO's attention, so that she was not aware of a protected disclosure having been made on that occasion. PD6 did not provide any more information about how the claimant's employment rights had been infringed and was merely 'a broad statement of opinion of the claimant's solicitor'. Nor did it contain a disclosure of information which the claimant reasonably believed to be in the public interest. It too was found to be a 'carefully considered negotiation tactic relating to the claimant's request for more favourable terms and a financial settlement'.

The employment tribunal found that there was no genuine redundancy, and that the label was a 'cover' for the breakdown in the relationship with the claimant. It also concluded that the respondent never considered the claimant to be a whistleblower, and therefore that consideration played no part in the decision to dismiss. The claimant was not dismissed for making 'disclosures' and PD1, PD2 and PD5 did nothing more than 'trivially influence' the respondent.

The EAT accepted that the employment tribunal erred in reaching a decision on a point that had not been argued; namely that PD3 had not been made on or around 14 August 2019. Nevertheless, the error was immaterial to the tribunal's conclusion, so that remittal was not required. The tribunal also erred in finding that the claimant made inappropriate sexualised comments towards an employee. This was not part of the case which the claimant understood he had to meet and he was not cross-examined on that point. The EAT held this error did not infect the decision as a whole as it was a 'standalone point'.

The employment tribunal did not err in deciding that, in order to be fixed with liability personally, the CEO needed to have some knowledge of what the claimant had disclosed in PD5. It was not sufficient that she knew that the claimant had made a disclosure to HR. The claimant's argument in that regard was rejected.

The appeal was therefore allowed in part and dismissed in part.

PROTECTED DISCLOSURE?

[21.11] *Moorehall Disability Services t/a Moorehall Living v Novak[10]—Labour Court—appeal from Workplace Relations Commission—Unfair Dismissals Acts 1977 to 2015, s 8A—protected disclosures—whether the employee made protected disclosures*

The claimant appealed against the WRC's dismissal of his complaint of being unfairly dismissed by the respondent for having made protected disclosures.

The respondent provided community care services for adults with disabilities. The claimant was employed as a care assistant from February until June 2018, when he was dismissed. The claimant argued that he was penalised during and after his employment, and that it was terminated because he raised health and safety irregularities.

---

[10] *Moorehall Disability Services t/a Moorehall Living v Novak* UDD2419.

The respondent contended that no such protected disclosures were made. The claimant was fairly dismissed during his probationary period because of his inability to engage effectively with the residents.

The Labour Court, having already decided on the issue in a linked case,[11] concluded that the claimant had failed to establish that he made protected disclosures during his employment. In addition, he had accrued less than 12 months of service when his employment ended. He could not avail of the Protected Disclosures Act 2014 and the Court had no jurisdiction to hear his unfair dismissal complaint.

The appeal was dismissed and the WRC decision upheld.

[21.12]   *William v Lewisham and Greenwich NHS Trust*[12]*—UK Employment Appeal Tribunal—appeal from employment tribunal—Employment Rights Act 1996, s 47B—whistleblowing—protected disclosure—reasonable belief that the disclosure tended to suggest a threat to health and safety—whether the detriment was motivated by the protected disclosure*

The claimant appealed against an employment tribunal's dismissal of her complaint. She alleged that she was subjected to detriments by the respondent NHS trust because she had made a protected disclosure.

The claimant was a consultant paediatrician and neonatologist at the University Hospital Lewisham, operated by the respondent. There were found to be serious issues within the neonatology department, including 'some dysfunctional working relationships between consultants', and evidence of a 'particularly poor' relationship between the claimant and a Dr Ezzati. Each had filed incident reports about the other's clinical practice.

On 30 July 2019, a confrontation erupted between the two in the lead-up to a complex procedure. Dr Ezzati recorded some of what took place on her phone and later criticised the claimant in a consultant's WhatsApp group. On 2 August 2019, the claimant made two complaints to the divisional director, Dr Lawrence, and a third complaint through the respondent's safeguarding system against Dr Ezzati. Among the allegations was that, on 13 July 2019, Dr Ezzati failed to do a handover to the claimant, which negatively impacted on patient care (the 'handover disclosure'). The claimant also referred to an audit she had supervised, which she claimed showed that the rate of necrotising enterocolitis ('NEC') in the hospital was higher than average national rates. Guidelines for feeding pre-term infants, prepared by the claimant for the neonatology department, were effectively dismissed by the department manager.

The incident of 30 July became the subject of a professional standards investigation and the claimant was suspended from site until 30 September, when she was told that her first clinic would be on 11 October. On 2 October, a further incident report was filed. This was mistakenly recorded as having come from the claimant and the lead investigator, Dr Harding, believing the claimant to have entered the premises in breach of her suspension, extended and widened the scope of the investigation to include that

---

11   See *Moorehall Disability Services t/a Moorehall Living v Novak* PDD242 at **[21.13]**.
12   *William v Lewisham and Greenwich NHS Trust* [2024] EAT 58.

incident. The claimant submitted a grievance. By 25 November it was apparent that the claimant had not filed the further incident report; nevertheless, the suspension was not lifted until 7 January 2020.

The investigation produced a report on 25 January 2020. It found that, while no allegations against the claimant were made out, the claimant had provided an incorrect account of events on 30 July 2019, though she had not intended to mislead as she was upset at the time. Nevertheless, on 12 February the claimant was informed by Dr Harding that there was a case to answer on the charge that she had provided misleading information and that there would be a disciplinary hearing. The claimant updated her grievance to include allegations of bullying and harassment. The disciplinary hearing took place on 22 April 2020 and the claimant was issued with a written warning for 12 months. That decision was upheld on appeal.

On 9 September, the claimant was advised that part of her grievance had been upheld, including an allegation that Dr Ezzati had called her a liar. The claimant appealed but that decision too was upheld.

The tribunal found that the handover disclosure was a protected disclosure, but that the complaint about the rejection of her feeding guidelines and her allegation about NEC rates were not. This was because the claimant 'did not reasonably believe that [the disclosures] tended to show that health and safety had been, was being or was likely to be endangered'. It held that the force of the guidelines complaint was that her contribution had been unjustifiably dismissed, as opposed to that the adopted guidelines endangered health and safety. The audit conducted by the claimant in fact found that the respondent's NEC rate was higher than rates 'in higher income countries generally', as opposed to being higher than average national rates. The audit was thus at odds with the claimant's disclosure.

The UK EAT considered these to be fair points, providing a logical 'basis for the view that the disclosure did not tend to suggest any threat to health and safety'. It did not accept the claimant's argument that distinguishing national rates of NEC from rates in a group of higher income countries was nit-picking.

The tribunal found that the respondent subjected the claimant to a detriment by its decision to suspend her, and not lift the suspension until 7 January 2020, and to subject her to investigation. Although these decisions were not reasonable, they were not motivated 'to any extent' by the fact that the claimant had made the handover disclosure. Dr Harding was much more focused on the incident of 30 July 2019 and his decision to proceed to disciplinary hearing, while harsh in the light of the report's findings, was motivated by his wish 'for someone else to take ownership of the decision'. While the decision to issue a written warning was a 'bad decision', the decision maker had no links with the handover and was only concerned with the incident of 30 July. The detriment was therefore not motivated 'to any extent' by the protected disclosure.

The EAT made no criticism of the tribunal's approach. Its reasons showed that it was 'fully aware of the scope of the defects' in the respondent's decision making. The tribunal explicitly asked itself whether it should draw an inference in favour of the claimant and gave logical reasons for not doing so.

The tribunal had also correctly applied EAT caselaw supporting the dictum that a decision maker who inflicts a detriment but did not know of protected disclosures, and therefore could not have been influenced by them, cannot be ascribed the knowledge and motivation of another individual who influenced the decision maker.

The appeal was accordingly dismissed.

RELEVANT WRONGDOING/REASONABLE BELIEF

[21.13] *Moorehall Disability Services t/a Moorehall Living v Novak*[13]—*Labour Court—appeal from Workplace Relations Commission—Protected Disclosures Act 2014, s 12(2)—protected disclosures—penalisation—reasonable or objective belief that relevant wrongdoings occurred*

The claimant appealed against the WRC's dismissal of his complaint of being penalised and dismissed by the respondent for having made protected disclosures.

The claimant did not attend the Labour Court hearing when due to be cross-examined, citing illness in an email to the Court. That was the second such occurrence, with no medical certification, so the hearing proceeded in his absence.

The respondent provided community care services for adults with disabilities. The claimant was employed as a care assistant from February until June 2018, when he was dismissed. The claimant alleged that he was penalised during and after his employment, and that it was terminated because he raised various health and safety irregularities. These included his lack of training in medication management and money handling, and the neglect of residents in his own care. He also maintained that it was dangerous and contrary to HIQA guidelines to allow HIQA personnel access to the premises at any time of day or night.

The respondent contended that no such protected disclosures were made, and so there could be no penalisation. The claimant was fairly dismissed during his probationary period because of his inability to engage effectively with the residents. He could not reasonably have believed that the alleged protected disclosures indicated any wrongdoing on the respondent's part. The claimant himself had unlawfully removed medical records belonging to residents without authorisation, and had fraudulently created documents to support the making of 'disclosures' after the fact. One such document was made by piecing post-it notes together; others were blatantly doctored by the claimant, belied by grammatical errors.

The Labour Court observed, in the first instance, that expressing strong opinions or disagreeing with the way work should be carried out does not amount to a protected disclosure. The Court was struck by inconsistencies and anomalies in the claimant's

---

[13] *Moorehall Disability Services t/a Moorehall Living v Novak* PDD242.

evidence, which called into question his credibility. It concluded that the claimant did not have a reasonable or objective belief that relevant wrongdoings occurred.

The complaints were not well founded and the decision of the WRC was upheld.

VICARIOUS LIABILITY

[21.14] *Treadwell v Barton Turns Development Ltd[14]—UK Employment Appeal Tribunal—appeal from employment tribunal—Employment Rights Act 1996, s 103A—dismissal for having made protected disclosures—application to amend claim to add vicarious liability—whether the amendment should have been allowed*

The claimant appealed against an employment tribunal's refusal of an amendment to her complaint to add a claim of vicarious liability.

The claimant was employed as an events manager by the respondent between January and June 2022, when she was dismissed by one of its directors. She complained that the true reason for her dismissal was that she had made protected disclosures to that director, and so her dismissal was automatically unfair. In a preliminary hearing, the claimant sought an amendment to her claim, adding that the director subjected the claimant to a detriment by dismissing her. That amendment was refused, with the employment Judge holding that a dismissal cannot be a 'detriment' under UK employment rights legislation. The claimant appealed against that decision.

The EAT concluded that it was bound by a Court of Appeal authority holding that an individual co-worker may be sued vicariously for being 'a party to the decision to dismiss', and that this can constitute a detriment.[15] It is the act of dismissal which is excluded from the definition of 'detriment'. The amendment should therefore have been allowed and the EAT made an order to that effect.

The appeal succeeded.

WORKER

[21.15] *MacLennan v The British Psychological Society[16]—UK Employment Appeal Tribunal—appeal from employment tribunal—Employment Rights Act 1996, s 47B—protected disclosures—detriment—whether the claimant was a 'worker'—intention to enter into a contractual relationship—European Convention on Human Rights, art 10 read in conjunction with art 14*

The claimant appealed against an employment tribunal's dismissal of his complaint of detriment on the grounds of making protected disclosures. The tribunal held that the

---

[14] *Treadwell v Barton Turns Development Ltd* [2024] EAT 137.
[15] *Timis and Sage v Osipov* [2018] EWCA Civ 2321.
[16] *MacLennan v The British Psychological Society* [2024] EAT 166.

claimant was not at any time a worker of the respondent and so it had no jurisdiction to hear the complaint.

The claimant was a psychologist and a trustee of the respondent, a charity incorporated by Royal Charter. He was elected to the role of 'president-elect' on the understanding that he would assume the full responsibility of the presidency after a year. His role included 'deputising for the president if required' and required a minimum of 16 days per year with a further four days allocated for 'preparation and correspondence'. The president was entitled to limited compensation for demonstrable loss of earnings. This was subject to a maximum daily rate of £519, payable for 25 out of the 35 days per year required to fulfil his or her duties. Not all presidents chose to claim for loss of earnings and the respondent's charter provided that the provision 'must be interpreted narrowly and restrictively'. Accordingly, compensation was not guaranteed and appointees were expected to operate on a *pro bono* basis.

The claimant had concerns about the manner in which the respondent was run. He campaigned for president-elect on a promise to address those concerns. On 4 May 2020, he was told that he had been elected but that this would remain confidential until the result was ratified at the AGM on 30 June 2020, and he took up the role of president-elect. In that time, the claimant contended that he made four protected disclosures. Following ratification of his appointment, the claimant contended that he made a further nine protected disclosures.

At a board meeting on 19 March 2021, the claimant confirmed he would not be seeking any compensation as president. As it happened, he never did become president. Relations between the claimant and the respondent's senior management team became strained, resulting in a grievance against the claimant. Following an investigation, on 4 May 2021, the claimant was expelled from membership of the respondent and his role was terminated.

The employment tribunal made no determination on the fairness of the expulsion, or whether the claimant had made protected disclosures or suffered detriments as a result, including his expulsion. Such considerations were deemed not to be within the scope of its judgment as there was no contractual relationship between the parties. The claimant also relied on art 10 read in conjunction with art 14 ECHR. While it was agreed that the facts fell within the ambit of the ECHR, the tribunal did not consider that the claimant had been treated less favourably than others in an analogous situation, or that the reason for that less favourable treatment was because of some 'other status'.

The EAT concluded that the employment tribunal was entitled to its finding that there was no intention to enter into a contractual relationship. It had formed its conclusion 'on an overall assessment of the facts' and had addressed the correct questions. However, on the ECHR point, the tribunal had not adequately considered the relevant circumstances, and had not conducted the 'broad-brush assessment' necessary to decide whether there was an 'analogous situation' between the claimant and an employee; or whether, being a charity trustee, a president-elect or a president was an 'other status'.

The appeal was therefore allowed in part and remitted to the employment tribunal for hearing on that point.

Chapter 22

Working Time

INTRODUCTION

[22.01]

Annual Leave

The European Court of Justice, in *TF*, considered the right to carry over paid annual leave in the context of the Covid-19 quarantine in 2020. In *BU*, the European Court of Justice balanced the right of a public servant to receive an allowance in lieu of leave not taken at the end of the employment relationship with the organisational needs of a public employer and control of public expenditure.

Holiday Pay

Holiday pay was the issue at play in *British Airways plc v De Mello*, a decision of the UK EAT which looked at whether allowances paid to cabin crew members counted as normal pay for the purposes of calculating statutory holiday pay.

Maternity Leave

In *CCC*, the European Court of Justice considered maternity leave and the balance between working life and the private life of parents.

Night Workers

The obligation on employers of night workers to properly assess the health of night workers was considered by the European Court of Justice in *EA*.

Parent's Leave

In *Emagine*, the question before the Labour Court was whether the refusal of a parent's leave request was for legitimate reasons.

Public Holiday Pay

In *Mater Misericordiae University Hospital v Stefan*, the Labour Court considered whether being 'on call' meets the definition of 'working time' as set out in European caselaw.

Remote Working

In *Karabko*, the WRC considered an employee's right to request remote working under the Work Life Balance and Miscellaneous Provisions Act 2023.

Standby

The High Court in *Walsh* considered whether the Labour Court had erred in failing to take account of the restrictions on an employee who was not working for his employer during 'standby' periods.

ANNUAL LEAVE

[22.02] *TF v Sparkasse Südpfalz[1]—European Court of Justice—reference for a preliminary ruling from Germany—protection of the safety and health of workers—organisation of working time—Charter of Fundamental Rights of the European Union—Directive 2003/88/EC,[2] art 7—right to paid annual leave—SARS-Cov-2 virus—quarantine measure—carrying over of paid annual leave for period coinciding with Covid-19 quarantine*

This request for a preliminary ruling concerned the interpretation of art 7(1) of Directive 2003/88/EC concerning certain aspects of the organisation of working time, and of art 31(2) of the Charter of Fundamental Rights of the European Union (the 'Charter'). The request arose out of proceedings between the applicant, TF, and his employer, the respondent bank. The dispute concerned the carry-over of paid annual leave days granted for a period while the applicant was in quarantine.

The applicant was granted paid annual leave for the period 3 to 11 December 2020. On 2 December, following exposure to Covid-19, he was ordered by a public authority to

---

[1] *TF v Sparkasse Südpfalz* (Case C-206/22).
[2] Directive 2003/88/EC concerning certain aspects of the organisation of working time.

quarantine until 11 December 2020. The respondent refused a request that those leave days be carried over and the applicant issued proceedings before a German Labour Court (the referring Court).

The referring Court questioned whether domestic law, which required an employer to carry over leave days granted where workers could demonstrate 'incapacity', excluding quarantine, for work during the leave period, was compatible with art 7(1) of Directive 2003/88/EC. It decided to stay proceedings and refer the matter to the European Court of Justice (the 'ECJ') and asked, in essence, whether art 7(1) of Directive 2003/88/EC and art 31(2) of the Charter must be interpreted as precluding national laws that do not permit the carry-over of days of paid annual leave granted in the circumstances.

The ECJ noted that the right to paid annual leave must be regarded as a particularly important principle of EU social law, to be implemented within the limits laid down by Directive 2003/88/EC. The right is enshrined in the Charter, to which Directive 2003/88/EC gives 'concrete expression', and cannot be interpreted restrictively. Settled caselaw states that the right to paid annual leave serves the purpose of allowing the worker to rest and enjoy a period of relaxation and leisure. In that regard, workers must be able to have the 'actual benefit' of the minimum paid annual leave and other rest periods provided for in the Directive. In particular, the ECJ has held that the right to paid annual leave is different from that of sick leave, which is to enable the worker to recover from illness. Thus, the Court has previously concluded that a worker who is on sick leave during a period of previously scheduled annual leave 'has the right, at his or her request, and in order that he or she may actually use his or her annual leave, to take that leave during a period which does not coincide with the period of sick leave'. During minimum rest periods, workers must not be subject to any obligation *vis-à-vis* their employers 'which may prevent them from pursuing freely and without interruption their own interests in order to neutralise the effects of work on their safety and health'.

Here, the applicant was not incapacitated for work during his quarantine and his situation was different to that of a worker on sick leave. It could not therefore be found that the purpose of quarantine was comparable to that of sick leave and a period of quarantine could not, in itself, 'present an obstacle to the attainment of the purpose of paid annual leave'. Consequently, an employer could not be required to compensate for the disadvantages arising from an unforeseeable event and the national legislation was held to not be precluded by the Charter or by Directive 2003/88/EC.

[22.03] ***BU v Commune di Copertino***[3]*—European Court of Justice—reference for a preliminary ruling from Italy—Directive 2003/88/EC,*[4] *art 7—Charter of Fundamental Rights of the European Union, art 31(2)—allowance in lieu of leave not taken at the end of the employment relationship—national legislation prohibiting payment of such an allowance in the event of voluntary resignation of a public servant—control of public expenditure—organisational needs of public employer*

---

[3] *BU v Commune di Copertino* (Case C-218/22).
[4] Directive 2003/88/EC concerning certain aspects of the organisation of working time.

This reference for a preliminary ruling concerned the interpretation of art 7 of Directive 2003/88/EC, concerning certain aspects of the organisation of working time, and art 31(2) of the Charter of Fundamental Rights of the European Union (the 'Charter'). The request was made in proceedings between the applicant, BU, a public servant formerly employed by the respondent, the Municipality of Copertino in Italy.

The applicant was an administrative officer for the respondent until his voluntary resignation in 2016. He brought an action before the District Court of Lecce (the referring Court) in which he sought an allowance in lieu of the 79 days' paid annual leave he had accrued between 2013 and 2016. Opposing his action, the respondent pointed out that the applicant had taken leave in 2016, showing that he was aware of his obligation under national law to use the leave days before the end of his employment relationship.

The referring Court expressed doubts as to the compatibility with EU law of the national law, which provided, subject to exceptions, that no financial compensation may be paid to public servants for untaken paid leave. Thus, it decided to stay the proceedings and refer two questions to the European Court of Justice ('ECJ') for preliminary ruling.

Having determined the questions to be admissible, the ECJ examined both together. The referring Court was asking, in essence, whether art 7 of Directive 2003/88/EC and art 31(2) of the Charter must be interpreted as precluding national legislation which, 'for reasons relating to the control of public expenditure and the organisational needs of the public employer', prohibits the payment of an allowance in lieu of paid annual leave days acquired but not taken, as in the circumstances of the applicant.

The ECJ found that under art 7(2) of Directive 2003/88/EC, a worker, who has not been able to take all of his entitlements to paid annual leave before his employment relationship has ended, is entitled to an allowance in lieu thereof, and, in that respect, the reason for which the employment relationship ended is not relevant. Therefore, the fact that a worker has voluntarily resigned has no bearing on that entitlement to an allowance where appropriate. Article 7(2) precludes national legislation or practices which provide that, upon termination of the employment relationship, no allowance is to be paid to a worker who has been unable to take all the annual leave to which he was entitled before the end of that employment relationship, in particular in cases of sickness.

Article 7(1) of Directive 2003/88/EC does not in principle preclude national legislation which sets conditions for the right to paid annual leave, 'including even the loss of that right at the end of the year or of a carry-over period', provided the affected worker has actually had the opportunity to exercise that right.

It was apparent that the national law at issue in the main proceedings was intended to put an end to the uncontrolled use of 'financial compensation' for leave not taken by public servants. Thus, its purpose was to ensure that the 'actual taking of leave' is prioritised over payment of an allowance in lieu. That objective was found to be consistent with Directive 2003/88/EC, the overarching purpose of which is to ensure that workers are entitled to 'actual rest'. However, the national law introduced a condition going beyond those expressly laid down in art 7(2). In particular, the prohibition covered the last year of employment and the reference period during which the employment relationship ended. The national law at issue therefore limited the right to an allowance in lieu of annual leave not taken on termination of the employment relationship. The ECJ observed that the limitation complied with art 52(1) of the Charter, insofar as it was provided for by law and pursued the objectives of controlling public expenditure and meeting the organisational needs of the public employer.

In circumstances where a worker had deliberately refrained from taking his paid annual leave 'in full knowledge of the ensuing consequences', having been given the opportunity actually to exercise that right, art 32(2) of the Charter does not preclude the loss of that right, or the absence of an allowance in lieu of paid annual leave not taken. Nevertheless, the employer is required, in view of the mandatory nature of art 7 of Directive 2003/88/EC, to ensure, 'specifically and transparently, that the worker is actually given the opportunity to take the paid annual leave to which he or she is entitled, by encouraging him or her, formally if need be, to do so', and by informing the worker 'accurately and in good time' of the consequences of not so doing. The burden of proof is on the employer to show that it has exercised all due diligence in that respect.

It followed that art 7 of Directive 2003/88/EC and art 31(2) of the Charter must be interpreted as precluding national legislation such as that at issue in the main proceedings.

HOLIDAY PAY

[22.04] *British Airways plc v De Mello[5]—UK Employment Appeal Tribunal—appeal from employment tribunal—Directive 2000/79,[6] clause 3—paid annual leave—air crew—whether allowances paid to cabin crew members counted as part of normal pay for purposes of calculating annual leave—employer power to designate certain leave days as statutory leave days*

These appeals related to the statutory holiday pay entitlements of members and former members of British Airways cabin crew, who were the claimants.

The respondent, British Airways plc, had a complex pay system during the relevant period. This provided for multiple supplementary allowances for cabin crew members, payable in a variety of circumstances. The dispute arose as to which of these allowances—29 in total—should be reckoned-in to the calculation of holiday pay. Both parties challenged aspects of the employment tribunal's decision.

The respondent appealed against the tribunal's conclusion that meal allowances formed part of normal pay, and therefore fell be included for the purposes of calculating statutory holiday pay.

The UK EAT found that the tribunal fell into error, adopting an approach that was 'too rigid and compartmentalised', rather than weighing all the relevant facts and

---

[5] *British Airways plc v Mello and Ors* [2024] EAT 53.
[6] Directive 2000/79/EC concerning the European Agreement on the Organisation of Working Time of Mobile Workers in Civil Aviation concluded by the Association of European Airlines (AEA), the European Transport Workers' Federation (ETF), the European Cockpit Association (ECA), the European Regions Airline Association (ERA) and the International Air Carrier Association (IACA).

circumstances and deciding on 'which side of the line' the meal allowances fell. Here, the tribunal addressed payments which were intended exclusively to cover expenses as a matter for the respondent to prove, then decided the issue on the basis that the respondent had failed to discharge that burden of proof. In reality, the tribunal was not confined to evidence from the respondent on this issue and it should have considered what proper inference could be drawn 'from the *overall* constellation of relevant facts'. The respondent's appeal was therefore allowed and the question was remitted to the tribunal for fresh determination.

The claimants cross-appealed on a number of points, including that the tribunal erred in concluding that the respondent was entitled in law to designate—as it did—the first 20 or 28 days of each leave year as statutory, as opposed to contractual leave (the 'designation ground'). They also argued that the tribunal erred by interpreting a 'series' of deductions as broken where there was a time gap between them of more than three months (the 'series of deductions ground'). Finally, the claimants challenged the tribunal's conclusion that commission on duty-free sales and a so-called 'back-2-back' allowance should not count as part of normal pay.

On the series of deductions ground, the EAT concluded that the tribunal would have been bound to hold that there was sufficient similarity of subject matter between the impugned deductions, 'because they were linked by the common fault or vice that holiday pay was not calculated by reference to normal pay'. This was so, even though the particular allowances varied as between occasions. The EAT substituted a conclusion to that effect. While there was no 'three month rule' as far as time gaps between deductions were concerned, the question of a sufficient *temporal* nexus between the deductions remained open to the tribunal.

Turning to the designation ground, the EAT agreed that the Civil Aviation (Working Time) Regulations 2004[7] do not appear to confer power on an employer to designate which leave days are to be treated as statutory, although it pointed out that a recent decision by the UK Supreme Court did not entirely preclude a contract from granting such a power,[8] provided it does not make a worker's position less favourable on a time point. In any event, the EAT found that the tribunal erred in concluding that the respondent had made such a designation. Even if a worldwide agreement gave the respondent the power to so designate, the evidence did not support a finding that it generally did so. This ground was upheld.

The tribunal was mistaken in relying on its finding that excluding commission from holiday pay was 'highly unlikely' to deter cabin crew members from taking annual leave. In doing so, the tribunal made a principled error. The caselaw of the European Court of Justice has held that holiday pay must 'correspond exactly' to normal pay. The worker must not suffer 'any disadvantage', including financial loss, as a result of exercising the right to annual leave. This ground, too, was upheld.

---

[7] Civil Aviation (Working Time) Regulations 2004 (SI 756/2004).
[8] *Chief Constable of the PSNI v Agnew* [2023] UKSC 33, see *Arthur Cox Employment Law Yearbook 2023* at [23.02].

The tribunal had incorrectly used a reference period of 12 months for its conclusion that three payments of the back-2-back allowance in that period was insufficient for the allowance to count as normal pay for that year. The underlying principle, to which the tribunal ought to have attended, was that there should be a 'sufficiently representative reference period'.

The matter was remitted to the employment tribunal for fresh determination.

MATERNITY LEAVE

[22.05] *CCC v Tesorería General de la Seguridad Social[9]—European Court of Justice—reference for a preliminary ruling from Spain—social policy—Directive (EU) 2019/1158[10]—balance between working life and private life of parents—single-parent family—equal treatment—extension of maternity leave—art 5—parental leave—inadmissibility of request for preliminary ruling*

This request for a preliminary ruling concerned the interpretation of art 5 of Directive (EU) 2019/1158 on the work-life balance for parents and carers. The request was made in Spanish proceedings between the applicant and the respondent, Spain's social security administration.

The applicant, a single mother, applied to the respondent for maternity benefit, following the birth of her child in November 2021. This was granted for the duration of her 16-week maternity leave. The applicant then applied for a 16-week extension of that leave with cover. She argued that Spanish legislation discriminates against single-parent families who do not have the benefit of a second parent to look after the child during the second 16-week period. This application was rejected by the respondent, who pointed out that entitlement to parental leave is assessed on an individual basis and its grant is subject to compliance with statutory conditions. As such, in two-parent families, each parent must satisfy those conditions and the right to parental leave is not automatically recognised in their case.

The applicant brought an action against the respondent before Seville's Social Court (the referring Court) in order to obtain an extension of her maternity leave with allowances to cover a 32-week period. That Court was uncertain whether the Spanish legislation on parental leave complies with Directive (EU) 2019/1158, in so far as the legislation does not take account of the specific situation of single-parent families. It therefore stayed the proceedings and referred two questions to the ECJ for a preliminary ruling, essentially querying whether the absence of an assessment mechanism for the needs of single-parent families in the area of work-life balance is compatible with the Directive, and whether the existing eligibility criteria should be interpreted flexibly.

---

[9] *CCC v Tesorería General de la Seguridad Social & Instituto Nacional de la Seguridad Social* (Case C-673/22).
[10] Directive (EU) 2019/1158 on the work-life balance for parents and carers.

The ECJ did not consider the referring Court to have sufficiently clarified the relationship between the dispute in the main proceedings—an application for extension of maternity leave—and the interpretation of art 5 of Directive (EU) 2019/1158, which confers on each parent an individual right to parental leave and specifies the rules governing same. Article 5 does not concern maternity leave and, accordingly, does not govern the question of extending maternity leave in the case of a single-parent family. Because the referring Court had not demonstrated the material relevance of art 5 to the dispute in the main proceedings, the request for a preliminary ruling was deemed inadmissible.

NIGHT WORKERS

[22.06] *EA v Artemis Security SAS*[11]—*European Court of Justice—reference for a preliminary ruling from France—Directive 2003/88/EC,*[12] *art 9(1)(a)—protection of the safety and health of workers—organisation of working time—obligation to assess the health of night workers—employer's failure to comply with that obligation—right to compensation—need to establish the existence of specific harm*

This request for a preliminary ruling concerned the interpretation of art 9(1)(a) of Directive 2003/88/EC, concerning certain aspects of the organisation of working time (the 'Directive'). The request was made in French proceedings between the applicant worker and the respondent employer concerning the latter's alleged failure to comply with its obligations to assess the health of night workers.

The applicant was employed by the respondent as a fire safety and personal assistance service officer. He brought an action before the Labour Tribunal in Compiègne seeking judicial termination of his employment contract and damages. The applicant complained that by transferring him from day work to night work, the respondent had not only unilaterally amended his employment contract, but in doing so had failed to provide the enhanced medical check-ups to which he was entitled as a night worker. The action was dismissed and the dismissal was upheld by the Court of Appeal in Amiens on the ground that the applicant had not proved the existence and nature of the alleged harm suffered as a result of his not receiving the enhanced medical check-ups.

On appeal to the Court of Cassation (the referring Court), the applicant argued that a finding of a failure to comply with the protective provisions on enhanced medical check-ups for night workers, by itself, entitled him to damages. The referring Court decided to stay the proceedings and to refer a question to the European Court of Justice ('ECJ') for a preliminary ruling. It asked, in essence, whether art 9(1)(a) of Directive 2003/88/EC must be interpreted as precluding national legislation under which the right to compensation for an infringement of that provision is conditional on the affected worker proving the harm suffered by him or her as a result of the infringement.

---

11   *EA v Artemis Security SAS* (Case C-367/23).
12   Directive 2003/88/EC concerning certain aspects of the organisation of working time.

The ECJ observed that Directive 2003/88/EC does not provide for sanctions in the event that the minimum requirements it lays out are infringed; nor is there a specific rule governing reparation for loss or damage caused by an infringement. In the absence of such provisions, it is for the Member States to lay down the conditions under which a worker may recover damages for an infringement of art 9(1)(a) by an employer, provided those conditions are compliant with the principles of equivalence and effectiveness.

There was nothing before the ECJ to suggest that the legislation at issue was at odds with the principle of equivalence. As regards the principle of effectiveness, it would be for the referring Court to determine whether the rules relating to proof of harm suffered made it 'impossible in practice' or 'excessively difficult' to exercise the rights conferred by art 9(1)(a). The fact that the worker could, in the event of the employer's failure to meet its obligations under that provision, obtain 'adequate' compensation contributed to ensuring such 'effectiveness', in that it was likely to discourage reoccurrence of the unlawful conduct. On the other hand, the national Court would be in a position to take steps to prevent the unjust enrichment of the rights-holder. It was further noted that the legislation at issue contained specific rules for imposing fines on errant employers which were essentially punitive in nature and not conditional on the existence of harm.

It was therefore not apparent that the national legislation at issue was capable of undermining the effectiveness of the rights derived from art 9(1)(a), and so that provision was to be interpreted as not precluding legislation such as that at issue in the main proceedings.

PARENT'S LEAVE

[22.07]   *Emagine v Teke*[13]—*Labour Court—appeal from Workplace Relations Commission—Parent's Leave and Benefit Act 2019, s 19—request for parent's leave refused—misconceived complaint of penalisation*

The claimant appealed against the WRC's dismissal of her complaint under the Parent's Leave and Benefit Act 2019.

The claimant was employed by the respondent as a service lead between 1 July 2022 and her dismissal on 26 May 2023. She successfully passed her six-month probation. On 21 March 2023, the claimant formally requested parent's leave from 12 to 28 June 2023 to care for her young son, for whom she had been unable to locate a creche. On 3 April 2023, the respondent replied, informing the claimant she could only have her choice to two weeks' leave in the period 1 June to 28 July 2023 'due to business reasons concerning the role [she was] fulfilling'. The claimant queried the decision. In a HR meeting on 19 April 2023, she was informed, without any prior notice, that due to 'performance issues', the client to whom she had been assigned by the respondent was requesting that her contract end early. The claimant was told that the respondent would

---

[13]   *Emagine v Teke* PLBD241.

endeavour to find her an alternative role. No such role emerged and the claimant was given notice of termination.

Critically, the claimant submitted that her dismissal was an act of 'penalisation' under the Unfair Dismissals Acts 1977 to 2015. No such claim was brought at first instance.

On the facts, the Labour Court accepted that the rationale offered by the respondent for refusing the parent's leave request ('business needs'), coupled with the 'subsequent haste' with which the respondent concluded that no alternative role could be found for her, 'raised many questions ... about the respondent's *bona fides vis-à-vis* the claimant'. Nevertheless, the claimant had not initiated an unfair dismissal claim at first instance and the Court had no option but to dismiss the claim.

PUBLIC HOLIDAY PAY

[22.08] *Mater Misericordiae University Hospital v Stefan*[14]—*Labour Court—appeal from Workplace Relations Commission—Organisation of Working Time Act 1997, s 28(1)*

The respondent hospital appealed against a WRC decision in which a complaint under the Organisation of Working Time Act 1997 was upheld.

The claimant contended that, because he was required to be 'on call' for two public holidays during the cognisable period, he was entitled to holiday pay. He argued that this time spent on call was 'working time' within the meaning of the Organisation of Working Time Act 1997.

The respondent pointed out that the claimant was not 'called out' or otherwise contacted by the respondent on either of the dates concerned. He was not actually working while on call and was free at all times to carry out his own activities.

In the Court's view, the claimant had not demonstrated 'that he was in any way constrained in terms of how he chose to spend his time on the two occasions or where he chose to locate himself'. It concluded that the fact of the claimant being on call on the two occasions did not meet the definition of 'working time' as set out in European Court of Justice jurisprudence. The decision of the WRC was set aside accordingly.

REMOTE WORKING

[22.09] *Karabko v TikTok Technology Ltd*[15]—*Workplace Relations Commission—Work Life Balance and Miscellaneous Provisions Act 2023—right to request remote working—employee's individual needs*

---

[14] *Mater Misericordiae University Hospital v Stefan* DWT2415.
[15] *Karabko v Tiktok Technology Ltd* ADJ-00051600.

The claimant was employed by the respondent. At the outset of her employment, she was required to work from home due to the Covid-19 pandemic. After that, the respondent introduced a 'return to office' policy, though the claimant was permitted, on a discretionary basis, to remain working from home full time. The respondent then commenced a planned return to office for all employees. This new policy required a minimum of three days a week in the office. The claimant did not return to the office at all, and, following a disciplinary process, she was issued a verbal warning for failure to follow company guidelines. The claimant applied to the respondent for fully remote working arrangements. The request was denied.

The claimant queried the decision but was not satisfied with the response she received. The respondent suggested that the claimant start a grievance procedure; the claimant instead referred a complaint to the WRC.

The claimant did not live in Dublin and asserted that her accommodation issues were not taken into consideration by the respondent. She alleged that her remote working request was not considered in line with the Work Life Balance and Miscellaneous Provisions Act 2023 (the '2023 Act') and the Code of Practice on the Right to Request Remote Working. In particular, she alleged that the respondent disregarded her needs when deciding on her request, and did not consider the request 'in an objective, fair and reasonable manner'.

The respondent submitted that the complaint was misconceived; it had assessed the claimant's application in good faith, and made a decision, based on objective reasons, weighing up both the needs of the company and those of the claimant. No actionable breach could arise from their refusing a remote working request. The claimant had not identified any problem with the process; she was simply disappointed with the outcome.

The WRC was precluded by the 2023 Act from considering the merits of the respondent's decision. Provided the respondent could show that it considered and responded to the claimant's request, there was no basis for the complaint. The respondent had done so. The complaint was therefore misconceived in law and held to be not well founded.

STANDBY

[22.10] *Walsh v Kerry County Council*[16]—*High Court—Barr J—appeal from Labour Court—working time—finding that employee was not working for his employer during standby periods—whether the Labour Court erred in failing to take into account the overall impact of restrictions on him while on standby*

This was an appeal on a point of law from a decision of the Labour Court which held that the appellant, a retained firefighter attached to Ballybunion Fire Station, was not 'working' for his employer during periods when he was on standby. The appellant

---

[16] *Walsh v Kerry County Council* [2023] IEHC 719.

submitted that in so finding, the Labour Court erred in failing to take into account the overall impact of the constraints on him while on standby.

In its decision, the Labour Court noted that the appellant was on call 168 hours a week, 52 weeks of the year. He was required to attend the fire station within five minutes of receiving an alert, so that he was obliged to live in close proximity to the station. In practice, the appellant would still be paid the full amount if he arrived at the station within 10 minutes of the alert. Although the requirement was to attend all alerts, the appellant would not be sanctioned, provided he attended a minimum of 75% alerts, this 75% turnout minimum was the only point of factual dispute between the parties. The appellant ran a bed and breakfast with his partner and was engaged in other professional activities, such as organising golf tours. In the previous six years, the average number of calls to the fire station was 52 calls per year; calls averaged two hours and twenty minutes in duration and the appellant was, on average, obliged to attend 84 hours per annum at fire incidents, averaging 1.7 hours per week.

The High Court was satisfied there was 'ample evidence' to support the findings made by the Labour Court, and there was no basis to set aside any of the primary findings of fact, or the inferences drawn therefrom. It was obvious from its decision as a whole that the Labour Court had had regard to all the relevant facts and had applied the correct test. It followed that the Labour Court had been entitled to conclude that the constraints on the appellant were not such as to 'objectively and very significantly' affect the appellant freely managing his time and pursuing business and social interests while on standby.

The Court was thus satisfied that there was no basis on which to set aside the decision and the appeal was dismissed.

Chapter 23

Northern Ireland—2024 in Outline

INTRODUCTION

[23.01] Following a two-year political impasse, the laws of Northern Ireland have made little legislative progress since 2022. Many of the Orders passed by the Northern Ireland Assembly prior to the deadlock remain unenacted. This legislative inertia has been particularly notable in the area of employment law, given that it is entirely devolved. Consequently, while legislation would previously have followed the precedent set in the neighbouring jurisdictions of England and Wales, and occasionally the Republic of Ireland, employment law in Northern Ireland has remained stagnant. For instance, several provisions of the Employment Act (Northern Ireland) 2016 have not yet been commenced, such as the laws in relation to gender pay gap reporting.[1]

However, in February 2024, after a 24-month hiatus, devolved Government returned to Stormont, sparking a push to update and modernise Northern Ireland's employment law to meet the needs of modern workers and employers. At the top of the Northern Ireland Assembly's agenda was an ambition to rejuvenate the economy, alongside an increased drive to improve working conditions and opportunities in Northern Ireland.

As a result, throughout 2024, the Department for the Economy in Northern Ireland has sought public feedback on a range of legislative proposals.

LEGISLATIVE DEVELOPMENTS

The 'Good Jobs' Employment Rights Bill Consultation

[23.02] One of the most highly anticipated public consultations of 2024 has been the 'Good Jobs' Employment Rights Bill (the 'Good Jobs Bill'). Spearheaded by the Economy Minister, the 12-week public consultation period (which concluded on 30 September 2024) was widely welcomed by employers across Northern Ireland, who were eager to contribute to the direction of employment law in the jurisdiction—particularly in light of the sweeping changes set to take place in Great Britain.

---

[1] Employment Act (Northern Ireland) 2016, s 19.

Key Great Britain proposals include: improvements to workers' rights; enhanced work-life balance provisions to facilitate the needs of modern families; and economic reforms to stimulate growth. Having pledged to introduce legislation in Parliament within the first 100 days of entering Government (which concluded on 12 October 2024), the Labour party in Great Britain published the proposed Employment Rights Bill on 10 October 2024. The Bill will need to go through the parliamentary process and could result in amendments or require further consultations and secondary legislation to bring some of the provisions into force. Consequently, it could take quite some time before the full legislative provisions can be realised.

Meanwhile in Northern Ireland, the pace of legislative reform in Great Britain seemed to inspire many of the proposals outlined in the 'Good Jobs' Employment Rights Bill consultation papers. However, some notable provisions have been omitted from the local Bill. For example, the Northern Ireland proposals do not include the Great Britain equivalent to the 'day one' right to claim unfair dismissal or the two-year limitation period for claims for unfair deductions from wages. In summary, the proposals outlined in the Good Jobs Bill consultation focus on four key areas, based on the Carneige Trust's definition of a 'Good Job'[2]:

i. satisfactory terms of employment;
ii. fair pay and benefits;
iii. voice and representation; and
iv. promotion of a healthy work-life balance.

Some of the key provisions include: enhanced minimum wage standards; additional health benefits; and new types of paid leave for employees, in conjunction with reinforced protections against unfair dismissal and discrimination. One of the prominent themes throughout the consultation papers is a drive for greater job security across all employment types. For example, the consultation explores the impact of abolishing zero-hours contracts, imposing stricter regulations on 'fire and re-hire' practices and banning pay disparity between agency and non-agency workers.

It can be expected that the outcome of the Great Britain Employment Rights Bill is likely to have a major influence on Northern Ireland's legislative trajectory. Therefore, it is anticipated that Northern Irish employees will enjoy improved flexible working provisions such as 'day one' maternity, paternity and parental leave entitlements; as well as reduced qualifying periods for unfair dismissal claims. Whether Northern Ireland will follow the lead of Ireland, where zero-hours contracts were abolished in 2019, or adopt Great Britain's approach of regulating such contracts, is unclear at present.

What is certain is that businesses operating within the jurisdiction will need to prepare for the impact the reforms may have on their operations and adapt accordingly. It is likely that small- and medium-sized enterprises may face the biggest challenges.

---

[2] Measuring Good Work: The final report of the Measuring Job Quality Working Group, Carneige UK Trust and the RSA, 2018.

Domestic Abuse—Safe Leave Consultation

[23.03] Prior to the dissolution of the Northern Ireland Assembly in 2022, the Domestic Abuse (Safe Leave) Act (Northern Ireland) 2022 was passed, with the aim of entitling victims of domestic abuse to up to 10 days of paid 'safe leave' each year. This safe leave is intended to support employees suffering domestic violence by providing some time away from work to deal with issues linked to the abuse.

The Department for the Economy launched a public consultation to gather views on certain practical aspects of the Domestic Abuse (Safe Leave) Act (Northern Ireland) 2022 that need to be addressed through regulations. The consultation covers key questions, such as whether a single incident of abuse should merit an individual qualifying for safe leave and clarification on the appropriate definitions for key terms such as 'issues linked to domestic abuse' and 'abusive behaviour'.

The overall aim of the legislation is not only to provide greater workplace protections for employees, but also to educate employers on how they can support employees suffering domestic abuse. While the commencement date has not yet been legislated for, employers could begin to prepare for its introduction by implementing domestic violence policies and fostering open and confidential communication channels with employees to create a 'safe space' within the workplace environment.

The Fair Employment (School Teachers) Act (Northern Ireland) 2022

[23.04] The Fair Employment (School Teachers) Act (Northern Ireland) 2022, which was passed before the Northern Ireland Assembly's dissolution, extended the protection against religious discrimination of teachers. Prior to this, teachers were expressly excluded from the statutory protection against religious discrimination in art 71 of the Fair Employment and Treatment (NI) Order 1998.[3] While the Act was partially enacted in 2022, certain crucial provisions did not come into force until 12 May 2024. This date marked the full coming into force of the Act, and made it illegal to discriminate, based on religion, in recruitment, selection and treatment of teachers.

Unfair Dismissal

[23.05] As of 6 April 2024, the limit for compensatory awards in unfair dismissal claims increased from £105,915 to £115,341, due to the rise in the maximum weekly pay limit used to calculate such awards (from £669 to £729).

---

[3] Fair Employment and Treatment (NI) Order 1998 (SI 1998/3162 (NI 21)).

CASELAW HIGHLIGHTS

[23.06] Throughout 2024, the Tribunals have continued to deal with a backlog of holiday pay claims in the wake of last year's landmark UK Supreme Court ruling in *Chief Constable of the Police Service of Northern Ireland v Agnew*.[4] Unlike Great Britain, which has a two-year limitation on holiday pay claims, no such restriction exists in Northern Ireland. This means that holiday pay claims made against employers operating in Northern Ireland have the potential to date back to the earlier of the introduction of the Working Time Regulations in 1998,[5] or the commencement of the claimant's employment.

Unfair Dismissal

[23.07]   *Colhoun v Royal Mail*[6]*—Northern Ireland Court of Appeal—O'Hara J—Employment Rights (Northern Ireland) Order 1996,*[7] *Pt XI—Tribunal's rejection of unfair dismissal overturned and retrial ordered*

In this case, the Northern Ireland Court of Appeal's decision was handed down in December 2023 and provides a valuable lesson for employers on the level of thoroughness required when considering dismissing a long-serving employee.

The appellant had been employed by Royal Mail as a postman on a part-time contract for 15 years prior to his dismissal on the grounds of gross misconduct. The allegations arose from the appellant's failure to deliver three rounds of unaddressed mail in the form of flyers for third-party businesses with whom Royal Mail had entered into 'Door-2-Door' contracts, promising to deliver in exchange for payment. At the time of the incident in March 2021, the appellant failed to report that he had not delivered the mail. However, the appellant later admitted that he had not completed the task, citing an overwhelming workload and lack of time required to carry out the work. A disciplinary hearing decided that, despite the appellant's blemish-free disciplinary record, his actions constituted gross misconduct punishable by summary dismissal with immediate effect, in line with Royal Mail's disciplinary policy.

In the initial hearing, the Industrial Tribunal upheld Royal Mail's decision to dismiss the appellant, concluding that the appellant had failed to complete a fundamental duty of his role, as required under his contract of employment without any reasonable excuse and that his summary dismissal fell within the band of reasonable responses of a reasonable employer.

---

[4]   *Chief Constable of the Police Service of Northern Ireland v Agnew* [2023] UKSC 33, see *Arthur Cox Employment Law Yearbook 2023* at [23.02]; see also *Arthur Cox Employment Law Yearbook 2019* at [25.02] for decision of NI Court of Appeal in *Chief Constable of the Police Service of Northern Ireland and Northern Ireland Policing Board v Agnew* [2019] NICA 32.
[5]   Working Time Regulations (Northern Ireland) 1998 (SI 1998/386).
[6]   *Colhoun v Royal Mail Group Ltd* [2023] NICA 88.
[7]   Employment Rights (Northern Ireland) Order 1996 (SI 1996/1919 (NI 16)).

On appeal, the Northern Ireland Court of Appeal allowed the appellant's appeal and quashed the Tribunal's decision. The Court of Appeal found that the dismissal was highly disproportionate. Notably, the appellant's line managers, who were responsible for overseeing his work and who had failed to identify and address the issue at the time, avoided discipline. It was determined that one of the fundamental principles of fairness in employment law—that there must be 'some equivalence between the treatment of employees whose misconduct or failings overlap' was entirely absent from the Tribunal's assessment of the case.[8]

Furthermore, the Northern Ireland Court of Appeal rebuked the Tribunal's view that they did not need to assess whether the appellant's workload at the time of the incident was achievable in order to reach their judgment. As regards this 'fundamental error', O'Hara J stated:

> 'To put it colloquially, there is no suggestion that [the appellant] was skiving ... That fact immediately brings into question the issue of how blameworthy his conduct actually was. Should he have told his employer that he was under pressure and just could not add the [Door-2-Door] mail to his existing workload? Yes, he should. Should the managers who oversaw his work every day have noticed day after day that this mail was going undelivered? Yes, they should have ... but they did not ... One way of interpreting this is that while the appellant was busy on the job (if not on the full job) his line managers were asleep on (part of) their job. Yet it was the appellant who was sacked summarily while the line managers went entirely unpunished'.[9]

The Tribunal's decision was quashed on the basis that Royal Mail's decision to dismiss the appellant 'was a gross over reaction to [his] very limited wrongdoing'.[10] The Northern Ireland Court of Appeal determined that this was in direct contravention of the appellant's right not to be unfairly dismissed under Pt XI of the Employment Rights (Northern Ireland) Order 1996 and ordered that the case be remitted to the Tribunal for a fresh hearing.

Equal Pay

[23.08] ***Boyle v Caterpillar*[11]*—Industrial Tribunal of Northern Ireland—Employment Judge Wimpress—Sex Discrimination (Northern Ireland) Order 1976[12]—sex discrimination—equal pay—landmark award for individual claim in Northern Ireland***

The claimant was first employed by Caterpillar (NI) Ltd ('Caterpillar') as a graduate electronic engineer in January 2003 and, by the time she brought her claim in 2018, she had worked her way up the company's hierarchy to become a grade 23 sigma black

---

[8] 'Summary of Judgment—Robert Martin Colhoun & Royal Mail Group Ltd', Judicial Communications Office, 7 December 2023.
[9] *Colhoun v Royal Mail Group Ltd* [2023] NICA 88, [20(iii)].
[10] *Colhoun v Royal Mail Group Ltd* [2023] NICA 88, [21].
[11] *Boyle v Caterpillar (NI) Ltd* [2024] NIIT 9826/18.
[12] Sex Discrimination (Northern Ireland) Order 1976 (SI 1976/1042 (NI 15)).

belt engineer. She brought a claim to the Tribunal on the grounds of sex discrimination, as she contended that the duties she carried out should be regraded to the higher grade SG24, while some of her male colleagues were being paid at grade SG24 level for what should be classed as SG23 duties.

The claimant presented evidence of three male comparators, each of whom carried out similar duties to her but were paid a higher salary. The Industrial Tribunal determined that the claimant was, and continued to be, engaged in like work to her comparators and that any differences in the work undertaken were of minimal practical importance, concluding that Caterpillar was unable to justify the pay disparity between the claimant and her male comparators by any factor other than gender.

The Tribunal awarded the claimant £305,719 as a compensatory award, which accounted for back pay for the period for which she was underpaid and loss of benefits such as employer pension contributions, car allowance and share contributions that her male comparators had received while she was on the lower salary. This ruling represents the highest individual equal pay award in Northern Ireland to date.

Index

[*all references are to paragraph number*]

Abuse of process
  multiple claims concerning same issue, 4.02
  re-litigation of decided issue, 4.02
  res judicata, 4.02
Accent
  race discrimination, 3.43
Adequate minimum wage
  transposition of EU law, 13.57
Adequacy of damages
  non-compete covenants, 11.12
  picket injunctions, 11.15
Adjournment application
  capacity of witness, 4.05
  error in refusal, 4.04–4.05
  ill-health of claimant, 4.04
Adverse treatment
  race discrimination, 3.42
Affirmation of contract
  breach of duty of trust and confidence, 19.14
Affirmative action
  sex discrimination, 3.28
Aggravated damages
  race discrimination, 3.41
Age discrimination
  burden of proof, 3.08
  compensation calculation, 3.09
  harassment, 3.07
  ill-health retirement, 3.09
  judicial review
    unlawful exclusion from pension scheme, 12.04
  legitimate aim, 3.03, 3.05
  less favourable treatment, 3.08
  mandatory retirement, 3.03–3.05
  objective justification, 3.05
  occupational qualification, 3.02
  person with disabilities, 3.02
  post-retirement employee benefits, 3.06
  provision, criterion or policy, 3.06
  res judicata, 3.04
  ridicule by colleagues, 3.07

Agency workers
  dismissal
    joint and several liability of agency and user, 19.02
    maternity leave, 19.02
    parental leave, 19.02
    supervisory authority by user, 19.02
    'temporary agency work', 19.02
  status of claimant, 1.02
  temporary work, 1.02
Airbnb
  investigations, decisions and fines
    identity verification, 2.27
Annual leave
  carrying over period of quarantine, 22.02
  prohibition on allowance in lieu for untaken period prior to resignation of public servant, 22.03
Annual reports
  Data Protection Commission (2023), 2.22
Anonymity orders
  dishonest and untruthful evidence, 4.03
Apple Inc
  investigations, decisions and fines
    retention of data in hashed form, 2.28
Arrears of pay
  employee who has left employment, 17.26
Artificial intelligence (AI)
  Data Protection Commission
    statement on large language models, 2.42
  European Data Protection Board
    report on ChatGPT Taskforce, 2.43
    statement on DPAs role in AI Act framework, 2.44
  introduction, 2.41
Associate partners
  employment status, 4.13
Associative discrimination
  race discrimination, 3.44

Index

Autism spectrum condition
 disability discrimination, 3.24
Automatic enrolment retirement savings system
 legislation, 13.02
 pension schemes, 15.02

Baby and mother homes records
 legislation, 13.05
Balance of convenience
 disciplinary process, 11.02
 dismissal, 11.07
 non-compete covenants, 11.10, 11.12
 picket injunctions, 11.15
Balancing fundamental rights
 freedom of expression and information, 2.29
Band of reasonable responses
 conduct, 19.08, 19.10
 redundancy, 19.19
Bathrooms
 guidance on use of CCTV, 2.20
Beauty therapy industry
 industrial training, 13.28
Behavioural advertising
 consent or pay model, 2.25
Benefit payments
 bonus to recipients, 13.13
 child maintenance and liable relatives
  means tests, 13.39–13.40
 consolidated claims, payments and control
  child maintenance and liable relatives, 13.39
  days not to be treated as days of unemployment, 13.27
  jobseeker's pay-related benefit, 13.58–13.59
  long term carer's qualifying contribution, 13.17
  payments to continue after pensionable age, 13.16
 consolidated contributions and insurability
  credited contributions, 13.15
  employment contributions, 13.26
 consolidated occupational injuries
  disablement gratuity, 13.56
  increase of benefits and pensions, 13.14
 credited contributions, 13.15
 days not to be treated as days of unemployment, 13.27
 domiciliary care allowance, 13.13
 employment contributions, 13.26

Benefit payments – *contd*
 EU law
  care leave allowance, 6.08
  equality of treatment, 6.08
  family benefits, 6.08
  migrant workers, 6.08
 jobseeker's pay-related benefit
  engaged in casual employment, 13.59
  key features, 13.58
 legislation, 13.05
 liable relatives
  child maintenance, 13.39–13.40
  long term carer's qualifying contribution, 13.17
 means tests
  child maintenance, 13.39–13.40
  payments to continue after pensionable age, 13.16
 qualified child bonus payments, 13.12
 temporary provisions, 13.12–13.13
Bias
 conduct of hearing, 12.02
Bills in 2024
 See also **Legislation in 2024**
 introduction, 13.01
Biometric data
 guidance on use of CCTV, 2.19
 inadequate notification, 2.07
Bonuses
 affordability, 1.03
 discretionary scheme, 1.03
 exercise of power to award, 1.03
Botswanan nationals
 immigration visas, 13.48
Breach of confidence
 confidential information, 1.04
Breach of duty of trust and confidence
 affirmation of contract, 19.14
Budget 2025
 pension schemes, 15.02
Bullying
 health and safety, 8.03, 8.05, 8.06
Burden of proof
 age discrimination, 3.08
 disability discrimination, 3.13
 race discrimination
  accent, 3.43
  comparators, 3.39
  disparate impact, 3.39
  general, 3.38, 3.40
  harassment, 3.43
  procedural bias, 3.43
  provision, criterion or policy, 3.39
  remuneration of outsourced workers, 3.39
 sex discrimination, 3.29

Capability
  fairness of dismissal, 19.03
  interaction with conduct of employee, 19.03
  performance improvement plan, 19.03
  warning of risk of dismissal, 19.03
Capacity of witness
  adjournment application, 4.05
Car mechanics, electricians and technicians
  employment permits, 13.54
Carcinogens
  protection of workers from exposure risks, 13.34
Cause of action estoppel
  Garda disciplinary proceedings, 12.05
CCTV
  access to footage by data subjects, 2.17
  accountability for use, 2.13
  areas of increased expectation of privacy, in, 2.20
  biometric data, 2.19
  covert surveillance, 2.18
  data protection by design and default, 2.14
  disclosure of footage to third parties, 2.16
  DPC Guidance on use
    access to footage by data subjects, 2.17
    accountability for use, 2.13
    areas of increased expectation of privacy, in, 2.20
    biometric data, 2.19
    covert surveillance, 2.18
    data protection by design and default, 2.14
    disclosure of footage to third parties, 2.16
    facial recognition, 2.19
    introduction, 2.11
    legitimate interests assessments, 2.21
    mitigation of risks, 2.21
    pre-installation considerations, 2.12
    third party data processors, 2.15
    toilets and rest rooms, in, 2.20
  facial recognition, 2.19
  legitimate interests assessments, 2.21
  mitigation of risks, 2.21
  pre-installation considerations, 2.12
  third party data processors, 2.15
  toilets and rest rooms, in, 2.20
Change in working pattern
  health and safety, 8.05
Change of workplace
  penalisation for protected act, 8.04
Civil servants
  contracts of indefinite duration, 7.03

Codes of Conduct
  PRSA providers consultation process, 15.10
Codes of Practice
  employment status, 13.06, 17.29
  flexible and remote working, 13.32
Collective agreements
  failure to provide information as pay increases, 1.08
  rectification, 10.10
  unauthorised deductions from wages, 10.10
Collective redundancies
  commencement date of consultation process, 16.03
  legislation, 13.03
  obligation to inform and consult, 16.02
  notification of proposals to the Minister for ETE, 13.46
  termination of contracts at retirement, 16.05
Comparators
  disability discrimination, 3.15
  race discrimination, 3.39
  sex discrimination
    equal pay, 3.29
    interview process, 3.26
    'like work', 3.29
    recruitment process, 3.26
Compensation
  age discrimination, 3.09
  conduct of employee, 19.06
  dismissal
    conduct of employee, 19.06
    financial loss, 19.05
    joint and several liability, 19.06
    just and equitable, 19.05
    protected disclosures, 19.07
    quantum, 19.05
    reduction in sum otherwise payable, 19.06–19.07
    social media activity, 19.07
  financial loss, 19.05
  joint and several liability, 19.06
  just and equitable, 19.05
  protected disclosures
    contractual cap on damages, 21.02
    social media activity, 19.07
    uplift of award, 21.02
  quantum, 19.05
  reduction in sum otherwise payable
    conduct of employee, 19.06
    social media activity, 19.07
  social media activity, 19.07

Index

Competition law
  agreements between undertakings, 6.05
  concerted practices, 6.05
  sports associations
    'home-grown' player rules, 6.05
    player transfer rules, 6.06
Conditional offer of employment
  meaning of 'worker', 10.07
Conduct of hearing
  apprehension of bias, 12.02
  excessive intervention by judge, 12.02
  fairness of procedure, 12.02
  Traveller community members, 12.02
Conduct of parties
  absence of disciplinary procedure, 19.09
  band of reasonable responses, 19.08, 19.10
  deficiencies in disciplinary procedure, 19.10
  fair procedures, 19.08
  freedom of expression, 19.11
  gross misconduct, 19.08–19.10
  interaction with capability of employee, 19.03
  publication of 'commercial secrets', 19.11
  stress-related behaviour, 19.08
  summary dismissal, 19.09–19.10
Confidential information
  files, folders and spreadsheets, 1.04
Conflict of interest
  misuse of corporate opportunities, 1.06
Construction sector
  sectoral employment order, 13.55
Constructive dismissal
  See also **Unfair dismissal**
  affirmation of contract, 19.14
  breach of duty of trust and confidence
    affirmation of contract, 19.14
    failure to exhaust internal procedures, 19.15
  conduct of parties, 19.13
  failure to exhaust internal procedures
    breach of duty of trust and confidence, 19.15
    resignation due to employer conduct, 19.13
    resignation to protect mental health, 19.12
  penalisation for protected health and safety act, 8.03
  performance improvement plan, 19.13
  perverse decision of tribunal, 19.15
  repudiatory breach, 19.13
  resignation due to employer conduct, 19.13
  resignation to protect mental health, 19.12
  sex discrimination, 3.35

Contract cleaning industry
  Joint Labour Committee, 13.37
Contract for services
  employment status, 4.11
Contracts of employment
  agency work
    status of claimant, 1.02
    temporary work, 1.02
  bonuses
    affordability, 1.03
    discretionary scheme, 1.03
    exercise of power to award, 1.03
  breach of confidence
    confidential information, 1.04
  collective agreements
    failure to provide information as pay increases, 1.08
  confidential information
    files, folders and spreadsheets, 1.04
  conflict of interest
    misuse of corporate opportunities, 1.06
  corporate governance
    fiduciary duty, 1.06
  employee benefit trusts
    entitlement after termination, 1.05
  failure to provide written statement of terms
    basic information, 1.09
    'day-5 statement', 1.10
  fiduciary duty
    conflict of interest, 1.06
    misuse of corporate opportunities, 1.06
  introduction, 1.01
  right to silence
    privilege against self-incrimination, 1.07
    refusal to comply with instruction to answer questions, 1.07
  status of claimant
    agency work, 1.02
  temporary work
    purpose and nature of work, 1.02
  terms of employment
    failure to provide written statement, 1.09–1.10
    pay increases arising from collective agreements, 1.08
Contracts of indefinite duration
  equal treatment, 7.02
  honorary members of judiciary, 7.02
  interim civil servants, 7.03

Index

Contracts of indefinite duration – *contd*
  judicial review
    age-based retirement, 12.04
  justification, 7.04
  locum surgeons, 7.04
  non-discrimination principle, 7.02
  public sector workers, 7.03
  successive contracts, 7.02–7.04
Contracts of service
  employment status, 4.11
Corporate governance
  fiduciary duty, 1.06
Corporate sustainability reporting
  key features, 13.49
Costs
  unrepresented unsuccessful party, against, 4.06
Couriers
  impact of *Karshan* judgment, 17.28
Covert surveillance
  guidance on use of CCTV, 2.18
Covid-19
  deductions from wages
    reasonableness, 20.02
    special leave, 20.09
  race discrimination, 3.41
  self-employed individuals, 17.22
Criminal Justice Act 2011
  whistleblowing
    failure of suspended Garda officer to make complaint, 20.03
Customer verification process
  lawfulness and transparency, 2.24

Data controllers
  guidance on use of CCTV
    access to footage by data subjects, 2.17
    accountability for use, 2.13
    areas of increased expectation of privacy, in, 2.20
    biometric data, 2.19
    covert surveillance, 2.18
    data protection by design and default, 2.14
    disclosure of footage to third parties, 2.16
    facial recognition, 2.19
    introduction, 2.11
    legitimate interests assessments, 2.21
    mitigation of risks, 2.21
    pre-installation considerations, 2.12
    third party data processors, 2.15
    toilets and rest rooms, in, 2.20

Data minimisation
  financial reporting, 2.28
  identity verification, 2.27
Data protection
  See also **Data Protection Commission; European Data Protection Board; European Data Protection Supervisory Authority**
  accountability of comptroller
    processing of personal data principles, 2.60
  artificial intelligence
    DPC, 2.42
    EDPB, 2.43–2.44
    introduction, 2.01
  breach of data privacy
    personal injury assessment, 2.62
  case law
    ECHR decisions, 2.61
    EU decisions, 2.48–2.60
    Irish decisions, 2.62–2.63
    UK decisions, 2.64–2.65
  compensation
    effectiveness principle, 2.56
    identity theft or fraud, 2.55
    introduction, 2.52
    'non-material damage', 2.54–2.56, 2.59
    publication without consent of data subject, 2.59
    seriousness of damage, 2.54
    theft of personal data, 2.55
    unauthorised transfer of data to third party, 2.58
    unlawful processing of data, 2.56
  'controller'
    corrective powers, 2.51
    development of IT application, 2.50
    role of supervisory authority, 2.51
  corrective powers
    role of supervisory authority, 2.49, 2.51
  Data Protection Commission
    Annual Report 2023, 2.22
    artificial intelligence statement, 2.42
    guidance on use of CCTV, 2.11–2.21
    investigations, decisions and fines, 2.23–2.30
  data minimisation principle
    online social networks, 2.48
    personalised advertising, 2.48
  data subjects
    capacity to work, 2.53
  derogating regulations
    immigration exemption, 2.64
    personal-household exemption, 2.65
    'rights of others' exemption, 2.65

Data protection – *contd*
  development of IT application
    processing of personal data, 2.50
  ECHR case law
    ongoing retention of data about a
      penalty, 2.61
    right to private life, 2.61
  effectiveness principle
    compensation for 'non-material
      damage', 2.56
  EU case law
    accountability of comptroller,
      2.60
    compensation, 2.52, 2.54–2.56,
      2.58–2.59
    'controller', 2.50–2.51
    corrective powers, 2.49, 2.51
    data subject's capacity to work,
      2.53
    data minimisation principle, 2.48
    development of IT application,
      2.50
    effectiveness principle, 2.56
    identity theft or fraud, 2.55
    non-compulsory personal data,
      2.57
    'non-material damage', 2.54–2.57,
      2.59–2.60
    online social networks, 2.48
    personalised advertising, 2.48
    'processing', 2.50
    Processing of personal data
      principles, 2.60
    protection of natural persons,
      2.48–2.51, 2.54–2.55, 2.58
    publication without consent of data
      subject, 2.59
    purpose limitation principle, 2.48
    right to compensation, 2.52,
      2.54–2.56, 2.58–2.59
    right to erasure, 2.57
    role of supervisory authority, 2.49,
      2.51
    security of processing, 2.60
    seriousness of damage, 2.54
    sexual orientation, 2.48
    special category processing, 2.48
    theft of personal data, 2.55
    unauthorised transfer of data to
      third party, 2.58
    unlawful processing of data, 2.56
  EU-US Data Privacy Framework
    FAQ for European individuals,
      2.47
    generally, 2.45

Data protection – *contd*
  European Data Protection Board
    artificial intelligence, 2.42–2.43
    guidance on processing of personal
      data, 2.31–2.32
    Information Note, 2.46
    Opinions, 2.33–2.39
    Strategy 2024–2027, 2.40
  European Data Protection Supervisory
    Authority
    biometric data, 2.07
    employee data, 2.05–2.06
    facial recognition, 2.10
    introduction, 2.02
    job applicant data, 2.04
    surveillance of employees, 2.05
    transfer of personal data, 2.03
    video surveillance, 2.08
    work returns, 2.09
  failure to account for erasure
    video recording of employee
      off-premises, 2.63
  identity theft or fraud
    right to compensation, 2.55
  immigration exemption
    derogating regulations, 2.64
  introduction, 2.01
  Irish case law
    breach of data privacy, 2.62
    failure to account for erasure, 2.63
    'personal injury', 2.62
    video recording of employee
      off-premises, 2.63
    'wrong', 2.62
  non-compulsory personal data
    lack of consent, 2.57
  'non-material damage'
    effectiveness principle, 2.56
    lack of consent, 2.57
    processing of personal data principles,
      2.60
    publication without consent of data
      subject, 2.59
    right to erasure, 2.57
    seriousness of damage, 2.54
    theft of personal data, 2.55
    unlawful processing of data, 2.56
  online social networks
    personalised advertising, 2.48
  personal-household exemption
    voice recordings, 2.65
  personalised advertising
    online social networks, 2.48
  'processing'
    development of IT application, 2.50

Data protection – *contd*
processing of personal data principles
'non-material damage', 2.60
publication without consent of data subject
'non-material damage', 2.59
purpose limitation principle
personalised advertising, 2.48
right to compensation
effectiveness principle, 2.56
identity theft or fraud, 2.55
introduction, 2.52
'non-material damage', 2.54–2.56, 2.59
publication without consent of data subject, 2.59
seriousness of damage, 2.54
theft of personal data, 2.55
unauthorised transfer of data to third party, 2.58
unlawful processing of data, 2.56
right to erasure
'non-material damage', 2.57
right to private life
ongoing retention of data about a penalty, 2.61
'rights of others' exemption
voice recordings, 2.65
security of processing
'non-material damage', 2.60
seriousness of damage
'non-material damage', 2.54
sexual orientation
personalised advertising, 2.48
special category processing
personalised advertising, 2.48
theft of personal data
'non-material damage', 2.55
trans-Atlantic transfers
EDPB Information Note, 2.46
EU-US Data Privacy Framework, 2.45, 2.47
UK case law
derogating regulations, 2.64
immigration exemption, 2.64
personal-household exemption, 2.65
'rights of others' exemption, 2.65
voice recordings, 2.65
unauthorised transfer of data to third party
right to compensation, 2.58
unlawful processing of data
'non-material damage', 2.56
video recording of employee off-premises
failure to account for erasure, 2.63
voice recordings
personal-household exemption, 2.65

Data protection by design and default
guidance on use of CCTV, 2.14
Data Protection Commission
Airbnb
identity verification, 2.27
Annual Report 2023, 2.22
Apple
retention of data in hashed form, 2.28
artificial intelligence
introduction, 2.41
large language models, 2.42
balancing fundamental rights
freedom of expression and information, 2.29
behavioural advertising
consent or pay model, 2.25
customer verification process
lawfulness and transparency, 2.24
data controllers
guidance on use of CCTV, 2.11–2.21
data minimisation
financial reporting, 2.28
identity verification, 2.27
erasure request
failure to inform of ability to review refusal, 2.26
requests for copies of identity, 2.27
retention of data in hashed form, 2.28
freedom of expression and information
balancing fundamental rights, 2.29
guidance
use of CCTV, 2.11–2.21
identity verification
requests for copies of ID, 2.27
investigations, decisions and fines
Airbnb, 2.27
Apple, 2.28
introduction, 2.23
Mediahuis, 2.29
Meta Platforms, 2.25, 2.30
Microsoft, 2.26
Ryanair, 2.24
legitimate interests
financial reporting, 2.28
Mediahuis
freedom of expression and information, 2.29
Meta
behavioural advertising, 2.25
visibility of passwords, 2.30
Microsoft
erasure request, 2.26
Ryanair
customer verification process, 2.24

Data Protection Commission – *contd*
  Statements
    Artificial intelligence, 2.42
  use of CCTV
    access to footage by data subjects, 2.17
    accountability for use, 2.13
    areas of increased expectation of privacy, in, 2.20
    biometric data, 2.19
    covert surveillance, 2.18
    data protection by design and default, 2.14
    disclosure of footage to third parties, 2.16
    facial recognition, 2.19
    introduction, 2.11
    legitimate interests assessments, 2.21
    mitigation of risks, 2.21
    pre-installation considerations, 2.12
    third party data processors, 2.15
    toilets and rest rooms, in, 2.20
  visibility of passwords
    employees of social platform, to, 2.30
Death
  pensionable employment, 15.16
Declaration of incompatibility
  art 11 ECHR
    penalisation for involvement, 10.09
Defamation
  damages for injured feelings, 5.02
  economic loss refused, 5.02
  trade unions, 10.02
Defence forces, discharge from
  lawfulness of decision-making process, 12.03
  prescribed procedure, 12.03
Demeanour of employee
  disability discrimination, 3.16
De-risking
  defined benefit pension schemes, 15.15
Detriment
  protected disclosures
    external job applicant, 21.04
    judicial proceedings immunity, 21.06
    less favourable treatment, 21.04
    making protected acts and disclosures, 21.05
    penalisation, 21.04–21.06
    victimisation, 21.05
  sex discrimination, 3.36
Digital Operational Resilience Act (DORA)
  pension schemes, 15.06

Diplomatic immunity
  application of correct test, 4.07
  psychiatric injury exception, 4.07
  waiver, 4.07
Director's loan accounts
  amounts drawn down from a credit, 17.31
  conferring a credit, 17.30
Disability discrimination
  'arising in consequence of disability', 3.16
  autism spectrum condition, 3.24
  burden of proof, 3.13
  conflicting medical opinion, 3.13, 3.17
  demeanour of employee in investigative meeting, 3.16
  disability at relevant time, 3.13
  factual features of the disability, 3.22–3.23
  failure to engage with substantive case, 3.19
  harassment, 3.18
  hypothetical comparator, 3.15
  inference of occurrence of discriminatory act, 3.12
  knowledge of the disability, 3.11, 3.22–3.25
  legitimate aim, 3.21
  medical opinion, 3.13, 3.17
  provision, criterion or policy, 3.21–3.22, 3.25
  reasonable accommodation, 3.10–3.13
  reasonable adjustments, 3.14–3.15, 3.19–3.20, 3.22, 3.24–3.25
  redeployment, 3.20
  refusal to void previous unsuccessful exam attempts, 3.14
  restricted duties, 3.19
  stammer, 3.23
  substantial disadvantage test, 3.15, 3.22
  vicarious liability, 3.17
  victimisation, 3.10, 3.18
Disabled person
  age discrimination, 3.02
Discharge from defence forces
  lawfulness of decision-making process, 12.03
  prescribed procedure, 12.03
Disciplinary process
  Garda
    cause of action estoppel, 12.05
    finality of decisions, 12.05
    Henderson v Henderson rule, 12.05
    insufficient evidence, 12.05
    res judicata, 12.05

Index

Disciplinary process – *contd*
  injunctions
    balance of convenience, 11.02
    fair question to be tried, 11.02–11.04
    hospital surgeon, 11.02–11.04
    irreparable harm to reputation, 11.02
    procedural unfairness, 11.05
    unlawful delegation of investigations, 11.02–11.04

Disclosure orders
  iniquity exceptions, 4.08
  privilege, 4.08
  relevance of material disclosed, 4.09

Discretion to extend time limits
  'exceptional circumstances', 4.45
  missing supporting information or documents, 4.44–4.45
  perverse refusal, 4.41
  substantial compliance with rules within limit, 4.44–4.45

Discretionary bonus scheme
  deductions from wages
    employment on pay-out date, 20.05
    non-contractual and unquantifiable, 20.06

Discrimination
  See **Employment equality**

Disguised remuneration
  loans from trust to director/shareholder, 17.40

Dishonest evidence
  anonymity orders, 4.03

Dismissal
  See also **Constructive dismissal; Unfair dismissal**
  protected disclosures
    cashflow issues during furlough, 21.09
    causative link, 21.08
    insufficient qualifying employment, 21.08–21.09
    likely breach of legal obligation, 21.09
    non-qualifying disclosures, 21.09
  refusal by employer to allow retraction of resignation, 19.16

Dismissal-related injunctions
  balance of convenience, 11.07
  business efficacy test, 11.08
  conflicting business interests, 11.07
  contract of employment, under, 11.06
  director-general, 11.06
  fair procedures, 11.06
  'fire and re-hire' process, 11.08
  procedural unfairness, 11.05
  retained pay provisions, 11.08

Dismissal-related injunctions – *contd*
  strong case likely to succeed, 11.05–11.07
  summary dismissal, 11.07
  want of fair procedures, 11.05

Duty of full and frank disclosure
  non-compete covenants, 11.11

Early years' service
  Joint Labour Committee, 13.42–13.43

Economic loss
  defamation, 5.02

Emoluments
  amounts drawn down from a credit to director's loan account, 17.31
  conferring a credit to director's loan account, 17.30

Employee benefit trusts
  entitlement after termination, 1.05

Employee data
  excessive collection, 2.05
  unauthorised sharing, 2.06

Employee relief
  research and development activities, 17.03

Employee tax credit
  generally, 17.18

Employer-provided vehicles
  generally, 17.04

Employer returns
  generally
  reportable benefits, 17.12

Employment conditions
  fixed-term contracts
    contracts of indefinite duration, 7.02
    less favourable treatment, 7.05

Employment detail summary (EDS)
  generally, 17.21

Employment equality
  age
    burden of proof, 3.08
    compensation calculation, 3.09
    harassment, 3.07
    ill-health retirement, 3.09
    judicial review, 12.04
    legitimate aim, 3.03, 3.05
    less favourable treatment, 3.08
    mandatory retirement, 3.03–3.05
    objective justification, 3.05
    occupational qualification, 3.02
    person with disabilities, 3.02
    post-retirement employee benefits, 3.06
    provision, criterion or policy, 3.06
    res judicata, 3.04
    ridicule by colleagues, 3.07

Employment equality – *contd*
  disability
    'arising in consequence of disability', 3.16
    autism spectrum condition, 3.24
    burden of proof, 3.13
    conflicting medical opinion, 3.13, 3.17
    demeanour of employee in investigative meeting, 3.16
    disability at relevant time, 3.13
    factual features of the disability, 3.22–3.23
    failure to engage with substantive case, 3.19
    harassment, 3.18
    hypothetical comparator, 3.15
    inference of occurrence of discriminatory act, 3.12
    knowledge of the disability, 3.11, 3.22–3.25
    legitimate aim, 3.21
    medical opinion, 3.13, 3.17
    provision, criterion or policy, 3.21–3.22, 3.25
    reasonable accommodation, 3.10–3.13
    reasonable adjustments, 3.14–3.15, 3.19–3.20, 3.22, 3.24–3.25
    redeployment, 3.20
    refusal to void previous unsuccessful exam attempts, 3.14
    restricted duties, 3.19
    stammer, 3.23
    substantial disadvantage test, 3.15, 3.22
    vicarious liability, 3.17
    victimisation, 3.10, 3.18
  gender pay gap information, 13.38
  gender recognition
    binary concept of 'gender', 3.31
    change of legal status, 3.31
    non-binary status in California, 3.31
  introduction, 3.01
  judicial review
    age-based retirement, 12.04
    entitlement to contract of indefinite duration, 12.04
    unlawful exclusion from pension scheme, 12.04
  legislation, 13.05
  pregnancy and maternity leave
    issue of P45, 3.33
    substantial grounds for dismissal, 3.33

Employment equality – *contd*
  race
    abuse by prisoners to officers, 3.37
    accent, 3.43
    adverse treatment, 3.42
    aggravated damages, 3.41
    associative discrimination, 3.44
    burden of proof, 3.38–3.40, 3.43
    cognisable 6-month period, 3.42
    comparators, 3.39
    continuing discrimination, 3.42
    contradictory findings, 3.37
    Covid-19 quarantine, 3.41
    disparate impact, 3.39
    failure to give reasons, 3.37
    harassment, 3.41, 3.43
    person not having same protected characteristic but suffers same disadvantage, 3.44
    procedural bias, 3.43
    provision, criterion or policy, 3.39
    rationality of decision, 3.37
    remuneration of outsourced workers, 3.39
    substantial disadvantage, 3.41
  religion
    anti-Muslim views, 3.47
    conflict between beliefs and professional duties, 3.45
    English nationalism as a protected belief, 3.47
    ethos of school known to pupil, 3.46
    Grainger criteria, 3.47
    legitimate aim, 3.46
    professional duties and misconduct, 3.45
    prohibition of pupils' prayer rituals on secular school premises, 3.46
    teachers' standards, 3.45
  sex
    additional overtime pay for full-time workers, 3.25
    affirmative action, 3.28
    ambit of protected characteristic, 3.27
    burden of proof, 3.29
    comparators, 3.26, 3.29
    constructive dismissal, 3.35
    detriment, 3.36
    equal opportunity measures, 3.28
    equal pay, 3.29, 3.34–3.35
    evidence linking behaviour to protected characteristic, 3.30
    firefighters, 3.35
    gender identity, 3.36
    gender recognition, 3.31

Index

Employment equality – *contd*
  sex – *contd*
    harassment, 3.27, 3.30
    holding protected beliefs, 3.36
    inducing a discriminatory act, 3.36
    interview process, 3.26
    less favourable treatment, 3.25
    'like work', 3.29
    occupational benefit scheme, 3.32
    part-time work, 3.25
    pregnancy and maternity leave, 3.33–3.34
    procedural fairness, 3.30
    recruitment process, 3.26
    redundancy, 3.34
    selection process, 3.26
    unfair dismissal, 3.27, 3.34

Employment litigation
  abuse of process
    multiple claims concerning same issue, 4.02
    re-litigation of decided issue, 4.02
    res judicata, 4.02
  adjournment application
    capacity of witness, 4.05
    error in refusal, 4.04–4.05
    ill-health of claimant, 4.04
  anonymity orders
    dishonest and untruthful evidence, 4.03
  capacity of witness
    adjournment application, 4.05
  costs
    unrepresented unsuccessful party, against, 4.06
  diplomatic immunity
    application of correct test, 4.07
    tort exception for psychiatric injury, 4.07
    waiver, 4.07
  disclosure orders
    iniquity exceptions, 4.08
    privilege, 4.08
    relevance of material disclosed, 4.09
  employment status
    associate partners, 4.13
    contract of service vs contract for services, 4.11
    fixed-term contracts, 4.16
    identification of employer, 4.15–4.16
    intention of parties, 4.13
    invoicing as self-employed contractor, 4.11
    Karshan (Midlands) test, 4.10
    mutuality of obligation test, 4.10
    protected disclosures dismissal, 4.10

Employment litigation – *contd*
  employment status – *contd*
    rescue services, 4.12
    separate legal entities, 4.15–4.16
    series of fixed-term contracts, 4.16
    statutory service requirement, 4.10
    vexatious appeals, 4.14
    volunteers, 4.12
    'worker', 4.12–4.13
  frivolous proceedings
    multiple applications to different tribunals, 4.14
  ill-health of claimant
    adjournment application, 4.04
  international jurisdiction
    material error of law, 4.26
  introduction, 4.01
  legal advice privilege
    disclosure orders, 4.08
  litigation privilege
    disclosure orders, 4.08
  press freedom
    reporting on affidavit not read aloud in open court, 4.17
    transcript of digital audio recording, 4.17
  protected disclosures dismissal
    statutory service requirement, 4.10
  res judicata
    identical referral made out of time, 4.18
    issue previously determined by different tribunal in separate claim, 4.19
  seafarers
    ouster of jurisdiction over discrimination claim, 4.22
  settlement agreements
    action compromised by mediated settlement, 4.20
    binding mediation between parties, 4.21
    consensual variation of a contract, 4.23
    legal advice on transfer to 'disability plan', 4.23
    waiver in respect of future claims, 4.22
  state immunity
    territorial reach of employment protections, 4.25
  striking out
    fair trial possible after five year delay and 'lost' witness, 4.24
    proportionality of decision, 4.24
  substantial disadvantage
    failure to review two-year warning, 4.19

Index

Employment litigation – *contd*
  territorial jurisdiction
    extra-territorial employment protections, 4.25
    material error of law, 4.26
    state immunity, 4.25
  time limits
    alleged misrepresentation by employer, 4.28, 4.32
    cognisable period, 4.38
    delay of three and a half years, 4.29
    determination that misrepresentation did not occur, 4.32
    discretion to extend, 4.41–4.44
    engagement with other agencies, 4.39
    'exceptional circumstances', 4.41, 4.42
    extension of time, 4.31, 4.34–4.41
    ignorance of the law is no excuse, 4.35
    incorrect respondent named, 4.30
    internal appeals process delayed, 4.33, 4.37
    missing supporting information or documents, 4.44–4.45
    misunderstanding of emails, 4.43
    misunderstanding of the law, 4.40
    one-day late, 4.37
    personal and professional difficulties, 4.36
    perverse refusal of extension, 4.41
    psychological stress, 4.39
    reasonable cause, 4.35, 4.37, 4.39
    substantial compliance with rules within limit, 4.44–4.45
    vulnerable person, 4.39
    worker becoming aware of pregnancy after dismissal, 4.27
  vexatious proceedings
    multiple applications to different tribunals, 4.14
  without prejudice privilege
    improper behaviour, 4.46
    pre-termination negotiations, 4.46
    protected conversations, 4.46

Employment permits
  car and motor mechanics, electricians and technicians, 13.54
  coding system used for decision-making, 9.02
  dentists, 9.03
  ineligible occupations, 9.02
  introduction, 9.01
  legislation, 13.04
  remuneration rates, 13.20, 13.22
  review of refusal to grant, 9.02

Employment permits – *contd*
  sea fishers in Irish fishing fleet, 13.47
  statutory instruments, 13.20, 13.22, 13.47, 13.54
  tattooists, 9.03

Employment-related torts
  defamation
    damages for injured feelings, 5.02
    economic loss refused, 5.02
  injurious falsehood
    damages for injured feelings, 5.02
    economic loss refused, 5.02
  introduction, 5.01
  loss of earnings claims
    refusal to insert term in settlement order, 5.03
  personal injury
    evidence of generic or individual causation, 5.04
    material contribution test, 5.04
    terms of settlement order, 5.03
  settlement orders
    refusal to insert no loss of earnings claim, 5.03
  vicarious liability
    abuse of children by employee caretaker, 5.05
    sufficiently close connection, 5.05

Employment status
  amounts drawn down from a company account by sole director, 17.33
  associate partners, 4.13
  Code of Practice on determination, 13.06, 17.29
  contract of service vs contract for services, 4.11
  fixed-term contracts, 4.16
  identification of employer
    fixed-term contracts, 4.16
    separate legal entities, 4.15–4.16
  intention of parties, 4.13
  invoicing as self-employed contractor, 4.11
  Karshan (Midlands) test, 4.10, 17.13–17.14
  mutuality of obligation test, 4.10
  protected disclosures dismissal, 4.10
  referees, 17.36
  rescue services, 4.12
  Revenue Guidelines, 17.07
  separate legal entities
    fixed-term contracts, 4.16
    generally, 4.15
  series of fixed-term contracts, 4.16
  sports commentators, 17.38
  statutory service requirement, 4.10

Employment status – *contd*
  taxation
    amounts drawn down from a company
      account by sole director, 17.33
    application of *RMC* test, 17.38
    Code of Practice on determination, 17.29
    generally, 17.07
    Karshan judgment, 17.13–17.14
    referees as employees, 17.36
    Revenue Guidelines, 17.07
    sports commentator, 17.38
    television presenters, 17.39, 17.41
  television presenters, 17.39, 17.41
  transfer of undertakings
    care home staff, 18.06
  vexatious appeals, 4.14
  'worker'
    associate partners, 4.13
    volunteers, 4.12
Enforceability
  non-compete covenants, 11.12–11.13
Enhanced reporting obligations
  generally, 17.12, 17.16
  introduction, 17.01
Equal opportunity measures
  sex discrimination, 3.28
Equal pay
  burden of proof, 3.29
  comparators, 3.29
  constructive dismissal, 3.35
  firefighters, 3.35
  'like work', 3.29
  redundancy, 3.34
  unfair dismissal, 3.34
Equal treatment
  fixed-term contracts, 7.02
  social security benefits, 6.08
Erasure request
  failure to inform of ability to review
    refusal, 2.26
  requests for copies of identity, 2.27
  retention of data in hashed form, 2.28
EU-US Data Privacy Framework
  trans-Atlantic transfers
    FAQ for European individuals, 2.47
    generally, 2.45
European company
  employee involvement, 6.04
  parent company of subsidiaries with
    employees, 6.04
European Data Protection Board
  artificial intelligence
    ChatGPT Taskforce, 2.43
    DPAs role in AI Act framework, 2.44
    introduction, 2.41

European Data Protection Board – *contd*
  co-ordinated enforcement action, 2.32
  data protection officers
    designation and position, 2.32
  guidance
    processing of personal data, 2.31
  Information Note
    trans-Atlantic transfers, 2.46
  main establishment of a controller
    in the EU
      article 4(16)(a) GDPR, under, 2.39
  Opinions
    introduction, 2.33
    main establishment of a controller in
      the EU, 2.39
    reliance on processors and
      sub-processors, 2.34–2.38
  processing of personal data
    guidance, 2.31
  reliance on processors and sub-processors
    identification of sub-processors, 2.35
    introduction, 2.34
    processing personal data to comply
      with third country law, 2.38
    processor to sub-processor international
      transfers, 2.37
    verification of guarantees of
      sub-processors, 2.36
  reports
    ChatGPT Taskforce, 2.43
    co-ordinated enforcement action,
      2.32
    designation and position of DPOs,
      2.32
  statements
    DPAs role in AI Act framework, 2.44
  Strategy 2024–2027, 2.40
  trans-Atlantic transfers
    redress mechanism for EU/EEA
      individuals, 2.46
European Data Protection Supervisory
Authority
  See also **Data protection**
  biometric data
    inadequate notification, 2.07
  employee data
    excessive collection, 2.05
    unauthorised sharing, 2.06
  facial recognition
    use to monitor attendance at work,
      2.10
  job applicant data
    unjustified collection, 2.04
  surveillance of employees
    excessive collection of data, 2.05

European Data Protection Supervisory Authority – *contd*
  transfer of personal data
    failing to appropriately safeguard, 2.03
  video surveillance
    unlawful distribution, 2.08
  work returns
    unlawful monitoring, 2.09
European Insurance and Occupational Pensions Authority
  Risk Dashboard, 15.09
European law
  See also **EU regulations**
  competition law
    agreements between undertakings, 6.05
    concerted practices, 6.05
    player transfer rules, 6.06
    sports associations, 6.05–6.06
  equality of treatment
    social security benefits, 6.08
  European company
    employee involvement, 6.04
    parent company of subsidiaries with employees, 6.04
  free movement of workers
    legitimate aims, 6.05
    number of 'home-grown' players, 6.05
    proportionality, 6.05
    restrictions, 6.05
    sports association rules, 6.05
  freedom to provide services
    obligation to hold residence permits, 6.02
    posting of workers, 6.02–6.03
    proportionality, 6.03
    restrictions, 6.02
    social policy objectives, 6.03
  introduction, 6.01
  posting of workers
    duration of work longer than permit allowed, 6.02
    obligation to hold residence permits, 6.02
    tax and social security advantages, 6.03
  recognition of professional qualifications
    failure of member State to fulfil obligations, 6.07
  restriction on free movement of workers
    number of 'home-grown' players, 6.05
    sports association rules, 6.05
  restriction on freedom to provide services
    obligation to hold residence permits, 6.02
    social policy objectives, 6.03

European law – *contd*
  social security
    care leave allowance, 6.08
    equality of treatment, 6.08
    family benefits, 6.08
    migrant workers, 6.08
  sports associations
    competition law, 6.05–6.06
    'home-grown' player rules, 6.05
    player transfer rules, 6.06
  VAT liability
    due diligence by employer, 6.09
    fake invoices issued by employee, 6.09
European Works Council
  change of location of central management, 10.03
  funding of external training event, 10.04
  impact of 'Brexit', 10.03
  procurement of expert services, 10.04
  protection of individual members qua individuals, 10.04
Ex gratia termination payments
  employment-related disputes, 17.35
Ex parte orders
  non-compete covenants, 11.11
Examination awards
  generally, 17.15
'Exceptional circumstances'
  internal appeals process delayed
    one-day late, 4.37
    reasonable cause, 4.37
  misunderstanding of emails, 4.43
  one-day late, 4.37
  personal and professional difficulties, 4.36
  reasonable cause, 4.37
  substantial compliance with rules within limit, 4.45
  unfitness to attend work, 4.42
Extension of time
  belief that claim precluded, 4.40
  cognisable period, 4.38
  discretion to extend
    'exceptional circumstances', 4.45
    missing supporting information or documents, 4.44–4.45
    perverse refusal, 4.41
    substantial compliance with rules within limit, 4.44–4.45
    engagement with other agencies, 4.39

Index

Extension of time – *contd*
'exceptional circumstances'
internal appeals process delayed, 4.37
misunderstanding of emails, 4.43
one-day late, 4.37
personal and professional difficulties, 4.36
reasonable cause, 4.37
substantial compliance with rules within limit, 4.45
unfitness to attend work, 4.42
generally, 4.31
ignorance of the law is no excuse, 4.35
internal appeals process delayed
one-day late, 4.37
reasonable cause, 4.37
missing supporting information or documents, 4.44–4.45
misunderstanding of emails, 4.43
misunderstanding of the law
belief that claim precluded, 4.40
one-day late, 4.37
personal and professional difficulties, 4.36
perverse refusal of extension, 4.41
psychological stress, 4.39
reasonable cause
engagement with other agencies, 4.44
ignorance of the law is no excuse, 4.35
one-day late, 4.37
psychological stress, 4.39
vulnerable person, 4.39
substantial compliance with rules within limit, 4.44–4.45
unfitness to attend work, 4.42
vulnerable person, 4.39
External job applicant
protected disclosures, 21.04

Facial recognition
guidance on use of CCTV, 2.19
use to monitor attendance at work, 2.10
Failure to give reasons
race discrimination, 3.37
Failure to provide written statement of terms
basic information, 1.09
'day-5 statement', 1.10
Fairness of procedure
conduct of hearing, 12.02

Fiduciary duty
conflict of interest, 1.06
misuse of corporate opportunities, 1.06
Finality of decisions
Garda disciplinary proceedings, 12.05
Financial Services and Pensions Ombudsman (FSPO)
complaints overview (2023), 15.08
legislative update, 15.04
Firefighters
retirement age, 13.32
sex discrimination, 3.35
superannuation, 13.51
Fitness to attend meeting
health and safety, 8.04
Fixed-term contracts
contracts of indefinite duration
equal treatment, 7.02
honorary members of judiciary, 7.02
interim civil servants, 7.03
justification, 7.04
locum surgeons, 7.04
non-discrimination principle, 7.02
public sector workers, 7.03
successive contracts, 7.02–7.04
employment conditions
contracts of indefinite duration, 7.02
less favourable treatment, 7.05
employment status, 4.16
equal treatment, 7.02
framework agreement
contracts of indefinite duration, 7.02–7.04
less favourable treatment, 7.05–7.06
honorary members of judiciary, 7.02
interim civil servants, 7.03
introduction, 7.01
justification, 7.04
less favourable treatment
in event of dismissal, 7.05
length of service, 7.06
non-discrimination principle, 7.05–7.06
locum surgeons, 7.04
non-discrimination principle
contracts of indefinite duration, 7.02
less favourable treatment, 7.05–7.06
public sector workers, 7.03
reasons for termination, 7.05
renewal, 7.04
successive contracts, 7.02–7.04
termination, 7.05
Flexible working
Code of Practice, 13.32

Football referees
employment status, 17.36
Free movement of workers
legitimate aims, 6.05
number of 'home-grown' players, 6.05
proportionality, 6.05
restrictions, 6.05
sports association rules, 6.05
Freedom of expression and information
balancing fundamental rights, 2.29
obligation to protect rights from interference by individuals, 19.11
publication of 'commercial secrets' in public interest, 19.11
Freedom to provide services
obligation to hold residence permits, 6.02
posting of workers, 6.02–6.03
proportionality, 6.03
restrictions, 6.02
social policy objectives, 6.03
Frivolous proceedings
multiple applications to different tribunals, 4.14
Full-time workers
sex discrimination, 3.25

Garda
admissions and appointments, 13.08
disciplinary proceedings
  cause of action estoppel, 12.05
  finality of decisions, 12.05
  Henderson v Henderson rule, 12.05
  insufficient evidence, 12.05
  res judicata, 12.05
reserve members, 13.29
retirement age, 13.52
Gender identity
sex discrimination, 3.36
Gender pay gap information
'relevant employer', 13.38
Gender recognition
See also **Sex discrimination**
binary concept of 'gender', 3.31
change of legal status, 3.31
non-binary status in California, 3.31
General Practitioners
MMR vaccination payments, 13.33

Harassment
age discrimination, 3.07
disability discrimination, 3.18
interim injunctions
  application for continuation, 11.16

Harassment – *contd*
race discrimination
  accent, 3.43
  Covid-19 quarantine, 3.41
  procedural bias, 3.43
  substantial disadvantage, 3.41
sex discrimination
  ambit of protected characteristic, 3.27
  evidence linking behaviour to protected characteristic, 3.30
  procedural fairness, 3.30
  unfair dismissal, 3.27
Health and safety
bullying, 8.03, 8.05, 8.06
changes in working pattern, 8.05
fitness to attend grievance meeting, 8.04
introduction, 8.01
penalisation for protected act
  constructive dismissal, 8.03
  failure to attend work as directed, 8.03
  failure to co-operate with grievance procedure, 8.02
  failure to identify 'immediate danger', 8.04
  lack of evidenced detriment, 8.06
  reduction of variable overtime, 8.05
refusal of payment under income continuance policy, 8.04
refusal to change workplace, 8.03
***Henderson v Henderson* rule**
Garda disciplinary proceedings, 12.05
Holding protected beliefs
sex discrimination, 3.36
Holiday pay
cabin crew allowances to be treated as normal pay, 22.04
requirement to be 'on call', 22.08
Honorary members of judiciary
contracts of indefinite duration, 7.02
Host employer provisions
liability for NICs, 17.42
Human rights
declaration of incompatibility with art 11 ECHR
penalisation for involvement in industrial action, 10.09
Hypothetical comparator
disability discrimination, 3.15

Identification of employer
fixed-term contracts, 4.16
separate legal entities, 4.15–4.16

Identity verification
  requests for copies of ID, 2.27
Ill-health of claimant
  adjournment application, 4.04
Ill-health retirement
  age discrimination, 3.09
Immigration
  employment permits
    coding system used for
      decision-making, 9.02
    dentists, 9.03
    ineligible occupations, 9.02
    review of refusal to grant, 9.02
    tattooists, 9.03
  introduction, 9.01
  visas for nationals of South Africa
    and Botswana, 13.48
Income continuance policy
  penalisation for protected act, 8.04
Income tax credits
  individuals over 65 and carers, 17.19
Income tax return (2023)
  ROS Form 11, 17.23
Indefinite duration contracts
  equal treatment, 7.02
  honorary members of judiciary, 7.02
  interim civil servants, 7.03
  justification, 7.04
  locum surgeons, 7.04
  non-discrimination principle, 7.02
  public sector workers, 7.03
  successive contracts, 7.02–7.04
Income tax
  reportable benefits, 13.19
Inducement to breach of contract
  non-compete covenants, 11.10
Inducing a discriminatory act
  sex discrimination, 3.36
Industrial action
  penalisation for involvement, 10.09
Industrial relations
  collective agreements
    rectification, 10.10
    unauthorised deductions from wages,
      10.10
  conditional offer of employment
    meaning of 'worker', 10.07
  declaration of incompatibility with
    art 11 ECHR
    penalisation for involvement, 10.09
  defamation of a trade union
    right of union to sue, 10.02
    striking out proceedings, 10.02
  dismissal of claimant for misconduct,
    10.05

Industrial relations – *contd*
  European Works Council
    change of location of central
      management, 10.03
    funding of external training event,
      10.04
    impact of 'Brexit', 10.03
    procurement of expert services, 10.04
    protection of individual members qua
      individuals, 10.04
  exhaustion of alternative means of
    resolution, 10.08
  industrial action
    penalisation for involvement, 10.09
  interference with right to organise
    distinction between covered and
      non-covered public servants, 10.13
    favourable treatment given to rival trade
      union, 10.13
    withdrawal from Lansdowne Road
      Agreement, 10.13
  introduction, 10.01
  outstanding proceedings between employee
    and employer
    trade dispute considered resolved, 10.06
  sectoral employment orders
    construction industry, 10.11
    rates of pay for skilled workers, 10.11
  trade dispute referral
    dismissal of claimant for misconduct,
      10.05
    exhaustion of alternative means of
      resolution, 10.08
    outstanding proceedings between
      employee and employer, 10.06
    withdrawal of conditional offer of
      employment, 10.07
  trade union recognition
    recommendation to employer, 10.12
  trade unions
    defamation, 10.02
    interference with right to organise, 10.13
    recognition, 10.12
  unauthorised deductions from wages
    rectification of collective agreements,
      10.10
  'worker'
    conditional offer of employment, 10.07
Industrial training
  beauty therapy industry, 13.28
  social work industry, 13.36
Information and consultation
  collective redundancy
    date of commencement, 16.03
    generally, 16.02

Index

Injunctions
adequacy of damages
  non-compete covenants, 11.12
  picket injunctions, 11.15
balance of convenience
  disciplinary process, 11.02
  dismissal, 11.07
  non-compete covenants, 11.10, 11.12
  picket injunctions, 11.15
disciplinary process
  balance of convenience, 11.02
  fair question to be tried, 11.02–11.04
  hospital surgeon, 11.02–11.04
  irreparable harm to reputation, 11.02
  procedural unfairness, 11.05
  unlawful delegation of investigations, 11.02–11.04
dismissal
  balance of convenience, 11.07
  business efficacy test, 11.08
  conflicting business interests, 11.07
  contract of employment, under, 11.06
  director-general, 11.06
  fair procedures, 11.06
  'fire and re-hire' process, 11.08
  procedural unfairness, 11.05
  retained pay provisions, 11.08
  strong case likely to succeed, 11.05–11.07
  summary dismissal, 11.07
  want of fair procedures, 11.05
duration of covenant
  enforceability of non-competition, 11.13
duty of full and frank disclosure
  non-compete covenants, 11.11
enforceability of covenant
  non-competition, 11.12–11.13
ex parte orders
  non-compete covenants, 11.11
harassment
  application for continuation of interim order, 11.16
inducement to breach of contract
  non-compete covenants, 11.10
interim orders
  non-compete covenants, 11.12
  stalking, 11.16
interlocutory orders
  disciplinary process, 11.02–11.04
  dismissal, 11.05, 11.07
  non-compete covenants, 11.10, 11.13
introduction, 11.01
investigations as to misconduct, against
  unlawful delegation of authority, 11.02–11.04

Injunctions – *contd*
mandatory orders
  dismissal, 11.06
non-compete covenants
  adequacy of damages, 11.12
  balance of convenience, 11.10, 11.12
  duration of covenant, 11.13
  duty of full and frank disclosure, 11.11
  enforceability, 11.12–11.13
  inducement to breach of contract, 11.10
  restraint of trade, 11.13
  scope of covenant, 11.13
  serious issue to be tried, 11.12
  validity, 11.10
picketing
  adequacy of damages, 11.15
  balance of convenience, 11.15
  dispute in jurisdiction not covered by 1990 Act, 11.15
  right to engage in industrial action, 11.14
  serious issue to be tried, 11.15
prohibitory orders
  disciplinary process, 11.02–11.04
restraint of trade
  non-compete covenants, 11.13
right to engage in industrial action
  picketing, 11.14
scope of covenant
  enforceability of non-competition, 11.13
serious issue to be tried
  non-compete covenants, 11.12
  picket injunctions, 11.15
stalking
  application for continuation of interim order, 11.16
traveller and Roma encampments
  basis and safeguards upon grant, 11.09
unknown defendant,
  basis and safeguards upon grant, 11.09
Injurious falsehood
damages for injured feelings, 5.02
economic loss refused, 5.02
Intention of parties
employment status, 4.13
Interference with right to organise
distinction between covered and non-covered public servants, 10.13
favourable treatment given to rival trade union, 10.13
withdrawal from Lansdowne Road Agreement, 10.13

Interim injunctions
  non-compete covenants, 11.12
  stalking, 11.16
Interlocutory injunctions
  disciplinary process, 11.02–11.04
  dismissal, 11.05, 11.07
  non-compete covenants, 11.10, 11.13
International jurisdiction
  material error of law, 4.26
International Labour Organisation
  working hours of share fishermen, 13.24
Intervention by judge
  conduct of hearing, 12.02
Interview process
  sex discrimination, 3.26
Investigations, decisions and fines
  Airbnb
    identity verification, 2.27
  Apple
    retention of data in hashed form, 2.28
  balancing fundamental rights
    freedom of expression and information, 2.29
  behavioural advertising
    consent or pay model, 2.25
  customer verification process
    lawfulness and transparency, 2.24
  data controllers
    guidance on use of CCTV, 2.11–2.21
  data minimisation
    financial reporting, 2.28
    identity verification, 2.27
  Data Protection Commission
    Airbnb, 2.27
    Apple, 2.28
    introduction, 2.23
    Mediahuis, 2.29
    Meta Platforms, 2.25, 2.30
    Microsoft, 2.26
    Ryanair, 2.24
  erasure request
    failure to inform of ability to review refusal, 2.26
    requests for copies of identity, 2.27
    retention of data in hashed form, 2.28
  freedom of expression and information
    balancing fundamental rights, 2.29
  identity verification
    requests for copies of ID, 2.27
  introduction, 2.23
  legitimate interests
    financial reporting, 2.28
  Mediahuis
    freedom of expression and information, 2.29

Investigations, decisions and fines – *contd*
  Meta
    behavioural advertising, 2.25
    visibility of passwords, 2.30
  Microsoft
    erasure request, 2.26
  Ryanair
    customer verification process, 2.24
  visibility of passwords
    employees of social platform, to, 2.30
Investment Strategy (Liquidity Risk) Guidance
  pension trustees, 15.07
Invoicing as self-employed contractor
  employment status, 4.11
IR35
  self-direction as to existence, 17.37
  sports commentator, 17.38
  television presenters, 17.39, 17.41

Job applicants
  protected disclosures, 21.04
  unjustified collection of data, 2.04
Joint Labour Committees
  contract cleaning industry, 13.37
  early years' service, 13.42–13.43
  security industry, 13.45
  statutory review, 13.25
Judicial proceedings immunity
  protected disclosures, 21.06
Judicial review
  conduct of hearing
    apprehension of bias, 12.02
    excessive intervention by judge, 12.02
    fairness of procedure, 12.02
    Traveller community members, 12.02
  discharge from defence forces
    lawfulness of decision-making process, 12.03
    prescribed procedure, 12.03
  employment equality
    age-based retirement, 12.04
    entitlement to contract of indefinite duration, 12.04
    unlawful exclusion from pension scheme, 12.04
  Garda disciplinary proceedings
    cause of action estoppel, 12.05
    finality of decisions, 12.05
    Henderson v Henderson rule, 12.05
    insufficient evidence, 12.05
    res judicata, 12.05
  introduction, 12.01

Judiciary
  contracts of indefinite duration, 7.02
  pensions for part-time workers, 14.03
Justification
  age discrimination, 3.05
  fixed-term contracts, 7.04

***Karshan (Midlands)* test**
  employment status, 4.10
  generally, 17.13–17.14
  impact on couriers, 17.28
Knowledge
  disability discrimination, 3.11, 3.22–3.25

Layoff
  redundancy, 16.04–16.05
Legal advice privilege
  disclosure orders, 4.08
Legislation in 2024
  See also **Statutory instruments**
  automatic enrolment retirement savings system, 13.02
  collective redundancies, 13.03
  employment equality, 13.05
  employment permits, 13.04
  introduction, 13.01
  maternity leave, 13.05
  non-disclosure agreements, 13.05
  pension schemes
    European, 15.06
    Irish, 15.02–15.05
    regulatory, 15.07
  records relating to mother and baby homes, 13.05
  social welfare, 13.05
Legitimate aim
  age discrimination, 3.03, 3.05
  disability discrimination, 3.21
Legitimate interests
  guidance on use of CCTV, 2.21
  financial reporting, 2.28
Less favourable treatment
  age discrimination, 3.08
  fixed-term contracts
    in event of dismissal, 7.05
    length of service, 7.06
    non-discrimination principle, 7.05–7.06
  part-time workers
    causation, 14.02
    intention, 14.02
    judicial pensions, 14.03
    private hire-driver, 14.02
  protected disclosures
    external job applicant, 21.04
  sex discrimination, 3.25

'Like work'
  sex discrimination, 3.29
Litigation
  abuse of process
    multiple claims concerning same issue, 4.02
    re-litigation of decided issue, 4.02
    res judicata, 4.02
  adjournment application
    capacity of witness, 4.05
    error in refusal, 4.04–4.05
    ill-health of claimant, 4.04
  anonymity orders
    dishonest and untruthful evidence, 4.03
  capacity of witness
    adjournment application, 4.05
  costs
    unrepresented unsuccessful party, against, 4.06
  diplomatic immunity
    application of correct test, 4.07
    tort exception for psychiatric injury, 4.07
    waiver, 4.07
  disclosure orders
    iniquity exceptions, 4.08
    privilege, 4.08
    relevance of material disclosed, 4.09
  employment status
    associate partners, 4.13
    contract of service vs contract for services, 4.11
    fixed-term contracts, 4.16
    identification of employer, 4.15–4.16
    intention of parties, 4.13
    invoicing as self-employed contractor, 4.11
    Karshan (Midlands) test, 4.10
    mutuality of obligation test, 4.10
    protected disclosures dismissal, 4.10
    rescue services, 4.12
    separate legal entities, 4.15–4.16
    series of fixed-term contracts, 4.16
    statutory service requirement, 4.10
    vexatious appeals, 4.14
    volunteers, 4.12
    'worker', 4.12–4.13
  frivolous proceedings
    multiple applications to different tribunals, 4.14
  ill-health of claimant
    adjournment application, 4.04
  international jurisdiction
    material error of law, 4.26
  introduction, 4.01

Litigation – *contd*
  legal advice privilege
    disclosure orders, 4.08
  litigation privilege
    disclosure orders, 4.08
  press freedom
    reporting on affidavit not read aloud in open court, 4.17
    transcript of digital audio recording, 4.17
  protected disclosures dismissal
    statutory service requirement, 4.10
  res judicata
    identical referral made out of time, 4.18
    issue previously determined by different tribunal in separate claim, 4.19
  seafarers
    ouster of jurisdiction over discrimination claim, 4.22
  settlement agreements
    action compromised by mediated settlement, 4.20
    binding mediation between parties, 4.21
    consensual variation of a contract, 4.23
    legal advice on transfer to 'disability plan', 4.23
    waiver in respect of future claims, 4.22
  state immunity
    territorial reach of employment protections, 4.25
  striking out
    fair trial possible after five year delay and 'lost' witness, 4.24
    proportionality of decision, 4.24
  substantial disadvantage
    failure to review two-year warning, 4.19
  territorial jurisdiction
    extra-territorial employment protections, 4.25
    material error of law, 4.26
    state immunity, 4.25
  time limits
    alleged misrepresentation by employer, 4.28, 4.32
    cognisable period, 4.38
    delay of three and a half years, 4.29
    determination that misrepresentation did not occur, 4.32
    discretion to extend, 4.41–4.44
    engagement with other agencies, 4.39
    'exceptional circumstances', 4.42, 4.45
    extension of time, 4.31, 4.34–4.41
    ignorance of the law is no excuse, 4.35
    incorrect respondent named, 4.30

Litigation – *contd*
  time limits – *contd*
    internal appeals process delayed, 4.33, 4.37
    missing supporting information or documents, 4.44–4.45
    misunderstanding of emails, 4.43
    misunderstanding of the law, 4.40
    one-day late, 4.37
    personal and professional difficulties, 4.36
    perverse refusal of extension, 4.41
    psychological stress, 4.39
    reasonable cause, 4.35, 4.37, 4.39
    substantial compliance with rules within limit, 4.44–4.45
    vulnerable person, 4.39
    worker becoming aware of pregnancy after dismissal, 4.27
  vexatious proceedings
    multiple applications to different tribunals, 4.14
  without prejudice privilege
    improper behaviour, 4.46
    pre-termination negotiations, 4.46
    protected conversations, 4.46

Litigation privilege
  disclosure orders, 4.08

Loans from remuneration trust
  payment to director/shareholder, 17.40

Locum surgeons
  fixed-term contracts, 7.04

Loss of earnings claims
  refusal to insert term in settlement order, 5.03

Mandatory injunctions
  dismissal, 11.06

Mandatory retirement
  age discrimination, 3.03–3.05

Maternity leave and pay
  issue of P45, 3.34
  legislation, 13.05
  postponement of payment
    cases of serious health conditions, 13.60
  single-parent families, 22.05
  substantial grounds for dismissal, 3.35

Mediahuis
  investigations, decisions and fines
    freedom of expression and information, 2.29

Medical opinion
  disability discrimination, 3.13, 3.17

Index

Meta
  investigations, decisions and fines
    behavioural advertising, 2.25
    visibility of passwords, 2.30
Microsoft
  investigations, decisions and fines
    erasure request, 2.26
Minimum wage
  adequacy, 13.57
  minimum hourly rate, 13.53
Mitigation of risks
  guidance on use of CCTV, 2.21
MMR vaccinations
  payments to GPs, 13.33
Mother and baby home records
  legislation, 13.05
Motor mechanics, electricians and technicians
  employment permits, 13.54
Multiple claims
  abuse of process, 4.02
Mutagens
  protection of workers from exposure risks, 13.34
Mutuality of obligation test
  employment status, 4.10

National insurance contributions
  host employer provisions, 17.42
National minimum wage
  adequacy, 13.57
  deductions from wages
    company's use and benefit, 20.03
    voluntary deductions to save for holidays, 20.03
  minimum hourly rate, 13.53
Newcomer injunctions
  basis and safeguards upon grant, 11.09
Night workers
  failure to comply with obligation to assess health, 22.06
  need to establish specific harm, 22.06
Non-compete covenants
  adequacy of damages, 11.12
  balance of convenience, 11.10, 11.12
  duration of covenant, 11.13
  duty of full and frank disclosure, 11.11
  enforceability, 11.12–11.13
  inducement to breach of contract, 11.10
  restraint of trade, 11.13
  scope of covenant, 11.13
  serious issue to be tried, 11.12
  validity, 11.10
Non-disclosure agreements
  legislation, 13.05

Non-discrimination principle
  fixed-term contracts
    contracts of indefinite duration, 7.02
    less favourable treatment, 7.05–7.06
Northern Ireland
  case law
    equal pay, 23.08
    holiday pay claims, 23.06
    unfair dismissal, 23.07
  compensation
    unfair dismissal awards, 23.05
  domestic abuse
    paid 'safe leave', 23.03
  equal pay, 23.08
  'Good Jobs' Employment Rights Bill, 23.02
  holiday pay claims, 23.06
  introduction, 23.01
  legislative developments, 23.02–23.05
  religious discrimination of teachers, 23.04
  'safe leave' payments
    domestic abuse, 23.03
    school teachers, 23.04
  unfair dismissal
    case law, 23.07
    compensation awards, 23.05
Notice of termination
  goodwill payment in lieu of notice, 19.17

Occupational benefit scheme
  sex discrimination, 3.32
Occupational pension schemes
  de-risking, 15.15
  fees, 15.05
  revaluation, 13.35
Occupational qualification
  age discrimination, 3.02
Office holders and employees
  reimbursement of travel and subsistence, 17.11
Other substantial grounds
  refusal to be vaccinated, 19.18
Outsourced workers
  race discrimination, 3.39
Overhead powerline contractors
  registered employment agreements, 13.41
Overtime pay
  sex discrimination, 3.25

Parent's leave
  extension of periods of leave, 13.44
  refusal of request by employer, 22.07
  single-parent families, 22.05
Partners
  employment status, 4.13

Part-time work
employment status of referees, 17.36
introduction, 14.01
less favourable treatment
causation, 14.02
intention, 14.02
judicial pensions, 14.03
private hire-driver, 14.02
sex discrimination, 3.25
Passwords
visibility to employees of social platform, 2.30
PAYE
assessment guidelines update, 17.05
employee tax credit, 17.18
Employers' Guide, 17.06
reviews where Week 53 applies, 17.10
Penalisation
protected health and safety act
constructive dismissal, 8.03
failure to attend work as directed, 8.03
failure to co-operate with grievance procedure, 8.02
failure to identify 'immediate danger', 8.04
lack of evidenced detriment, 8.06
reduction of variable overtime, 8.05
whistleblowing
external job applicant, 21.04
judicial proceedings immunity, 21.06
less favourable treatment, 21.04
making protected acts and disclosures, 21.05
victimisation, 21.05
Pension contributions
generally, 17.15
Pension schemes
age-based retirement, 12.04
discontinuance, 17.17
Pensions
automatic enrolment retirement savings systems, 15.02
Budget 2025, 15.02
case law
death within pensionable employment, 15.16
de-risking, 15.15
scheme wording, 15.14
trust deed and rules, 15.12–15.13
validity of amendment to scheme, 15.17
choice of claim date for state pension, 15.03
Code of Conduct for PRSA providers
consultation process, 15.10

Pensions – *contd*
death within pensionable employment, 15.16
de-risking defined benefit scheme, 15.15
Digital Operational Resilience (DORA), 15.06
European Insurance and Occupational Pensions Authority
Risk Dashboard, 15.09
Financial Services and Pensions Ombudsman
complaints overview (2023), 15.08
legislative update, 15.04
increase in payments, 15.01
interpretation of trust deed and rules
'interests' of members, 15.14
solvency of scheme, 15.13
'text in context' approach, 15.12
introduction, 15.01
Investment Strategy (Liquidity Risk) Guidance for Trustees, 15.07
legislative update
European, 15.06
Irish, 15.02–15.05
regulatory, 15.07
occupational pension schemes
de-risking, 15.15
fees, 15.05
Pensions Authority
Code of Conduct for PRSA providers, 15.10
Investment Strategy (Liquidity Risk) Guidance, 15.07
PRSA providers
Code of Conduct consultation, 15.10
retirement annuity contracts
end of approvals, 15.11
Revenue update
retirement annuity contracts, 15.11
scheme wording, 15.14
solvency of scheme
interpretation of trust deed and rules, 15.13
Standard Fund Threshold, 15.01
state pension
choice of claim date, 15.03
increase in payments, 15.01
trust deed and rules
construction, 15.14
interpretation, 15.12
statutory interpretation, 15.13
validity of amendment to scheme, 15.17

Index

Pensions Authority
Code of Conduct for PRSA providers, 15.10
Investment Strategy (Liquidity Risk) Guidance, 15.07
Performance improvement plan
capability dismissal, 19.03
constructive dismissal, 19.1
Person with disabilities
age discrimination, 3.02
Personal Injuries Assessment Board Rules
statutory instrument, 13.09
Personal Injuries Resolution Board
statutory instrument, 13.10–13.11
Personal injury
evidence of generic or individual causation, 5.04
material contribution test, 5.04
terms of settlement order, 5.03
Personal service companies
self-direction as to existence, 17.37
sports commentator, 17.38
television presenters, 17.39, 17.41
Picketing injunctions
adequacy of damages, 11.15
balance of convenience, 11.15
dispute in jurisdiction not covered by 1990 Act, 11.15
right to engage in industrial action, 11.14
serious issue to be tried, 11.15
Post-retirement employee benefits
age discrimination, 3.06
Posting of workers
duration of work longer than permit allowed, 6.02
obligation to hold residence permits, 6.02
tax and social security advantages, 6.03
Pregnancy
issue of P45, 3.33
substantial grounds for dismissal, 3.33
Press freedom
reporting on affidavit not read aloud in open court, 4.17
transcript of digital audio recrding, 4.17
Privilege
disclosure orders, 4.08
Prohibitory injunctions
disciplinary process, 11.02–11.04
Proprietary directors
interpretation under TCA 1971, 17.34
Protected disclosures
compensation
contractual cap on damages, 21.02
uplift of award, 21.02

Protected disclosures – *contd*
Criminal Justice Act 2011
failure of suspended Garda officer to make complaint, 20.03
decision-makers inflicting detriment with no knowledge of disclosure, 21.12
detriment
external job applicant, 21.04
judicial proceedings immunity, 21.06
less favourable treatment, 21.04
making protected acts and disclosures, 21.05
penalisation, 21.04–21.06
victimisation, 21.05
disagreeing with way work carried out, 21.12
dismissal
cashflow issues during furlough, 21.09
causative link, 21.08
employment status, 4.10
insufficient qualifying employment, 21.08–21.09
likely breach of legal obligation, 21.09
non-qualifying disclosures, 21.09
employer's knowledge
disclosures not influence decision to dismiss, 21.10
employment status
statutory service requirement, 4.10
external job applicant, 21.04
failure to establish a protected disclosure was made, 21.11
insufficient qualifying employment, 21.08–21.09
introduction, 21.01
judicial proceedings immunity, 21.06
less favourable treatment
external job applicant, 21.04
likely breach of legal obligation, 21.09
non-qualifying disclosures, 21.09
objective belief, 21.13
penalisation
external job applicant, 21.04
judicial proceedings immunity, 21.06
less favourable treatment, 21.04
making protected acts and disclosures, 21.05
victimisation, 21.05
reasonable belief, 21.13

480

Protected disclosures – *contd*
relevant wrongdoing
causal link between detriments and disclosures, 21.07
disagreeing with way work carried out, 21.13
reasonable or objective belief that occurred, 21.13
subjective belief that disclosure in public interest, 21.07
vicarious liability
application to amend claim to add, 21.14
victimisation, 21.05
worker
lack of contractual relationship between parties, 21.15
president-elect of charity, 21.15
Procedural bias
race discrimination, 3.43
Procedural fairness
sex discrimination, 3.30
Provision, criterion or policy
age discrimination, 3.06
disability discrimination, 3.21–3.22, 3.25
race discrimination, 3.39
PRSA providers
Code of Conduct consultation, 15.10
Psychiatric injury
diplomatic immunity, 4.07
Public holiday pay
requirement to be 'on call', 22.08
Public sector workers
fixed-term contracts, 7.03
Public service pay and pensions
MMR vaccination payments to GPs, 13.33

Quarantine
distinction from sick leave, 22.02

Race discrimination
abuse by prisoners to officers, 3.37
accent, 3.43
adverse treatment, 3.42
aggravated damages, 3.41
associative discrimination, 3.44
burden of proof
accent, 3.43
comparators, 3.39
disparate impact, 3.39
general, 3.38, 3.40
harassment, 3.43
procedural bias, 3.43
provision, criterion or policy, 3.39
remuneration of outsourced workers, 3.39

Race discrimination – *contd*
cognisable 6-month period, 3.42
comparators, 3.39
continuing discrimination, 3.42
contradictory findings, 3.37
Covid-19 quarantine, 3.41
disparate impact, 3.39
failure to give reasons, 3.37
harassment
accent, 3.43
Covid-19 quarantine, 3.41
procedural bias, 3.43
substantial disadvantage, 3.41
person not having same protected characteristic but suffers same disadvantage, 3.44
procedural bias, 3.43
provision, criterion or policy, 3.39
rationality of decision, 3.37
remuneration of outsourced workers, 3.39
substantial disadvantage, 3.41
Rationality of decision
race discrimination, 3.37
Reasonable accommodation
See also **Reasonable adjustments**
burden of proof, 3.13
conflicting medical opinion, 3.13
disability at relevant time, 3.13
inference of occurrence of discriminatory act, 3.12
knowledge of the disability, 3.11
medical opinion, 3.13
victimisation, 3.10
Reasonable adjustments
See also **Disability discrimination**
autism spectrum condition, 3.24
factual features of the disability, 3.22
failure to engage with substantive case, 3.19
hypothetical comparator, 3.15
knowledge of the disability, 3.24–3.25
provision, criterion or policy, 3.22, 3.25
redeployment, 3.20
refusal to void previous unsuccessful exam attempts, 3.14
restricted duties, 3.19
substantial disadvantage test, 3.15, 3.22
Recognition of professional qualifications
failure of member State to fulfil obligations, 6.07
Records relating to mother and baby homes
legislation, 13.05
Recruitment process
sex discrimination, 3.26

Index

Redeployment
disability discrimination, 3.20
Redundancy
adequacy of consultation process, 19.19
band of reasonable responses, 19.19
collective redundancy
commencement date of consultation process, 16.03
obligation to inform and consult, 16.02
termination of contracts at retirement, 16.05
information and consultation
collective redundancy, 16.02
date of commencement, 16.03
introduction, 16.01
layoff
notice periods, 16.04–16.05
payments
layoff, 16.04–16.05
notice periods, 16.04–16.05
procedural unfairness, 19.19
retirement
termination of contracts on retirement of owner, 16.05
selection criteria and scoring, 19.19
sex discrimination, 3.34
statutory redundancy
payments, 16.06
unfair dismissal
adequacy of consultation process, 19.19
band of reasonable responses, 19.19
procedural unfairness, 19.19
selection criteria and scoring, 19.19
sex discrimination, 3.34
workforce-level consultation, 19.19
workers' representatives
entitlement to information and consultation, 16.02
workforce-level consultation, 19.19
Redundancy payments
continuation of employment in successor company, 17.32
layoff, 16.04–16.05
Re-engagement
failure to give consideration to practicality, 19.20
headmaster of school, 19.20
Referees
employment status, 17.36
Refusal to be vaccinated
Covid-19 policy, 19.18
justification for interference with rights, 19.18
proportionality of dismissal, 19.18

Refusal to be vaccinated – *contd*
religion and belief discrimination, 19.18
substantive fairness of decision to dismiss, 19.18
Registered employment agreements
overhead powerline contractors, 13.41
Religious discrimination
anti-Muslim views, 3.47
conflict between beliefs and professional duties, 3.45
English nationalism as a protected belief, 3.47
ethos of school known to pupil, 3.46
Grainger criteria, 3.47
legitimate aim, 3.46
professional duties and misconduct, 3.45
prohibition of pupils' prayer rituals on secular school premises, 3.46
teachers' standards, 3.45
Religion and belief discrimination
refusal to be vaccinated, 19.18
Re-litigation
abuse of process, 4.02
Remote working
Code of Practice, 13.32
consideration of request demonstrated by employer, 22.09
employee's individual needs, 22.09
'return to office' policy post-Covid, 22.09
tax relief, 17.20
Remuneration rates
employment permits, 13.20, 13.22
Reportable benefits returns
enhanced requirements, 17.12, 17.16
Reprotoxic substances
protection of workers from exposure risks, 13.34
Res judicata
abuse of process, 4.02
age discrimination, 3.04
Garda disciplinary proceedings, 12.05
identical referral made out of time, 4.18
issue previously determined by different tribunal in separate claim, 4.19
Research and development activities
key employee relief, 17.03
Rescue services
employment status, 4.12
Resignation
conduct of employer, 19.13
constructive dismissal, 19.12–19.13
employer's policy to refuse to allow retraction, 19.16
protection of mental health, 19.12

Rest rooms
  guidance on use of CCTV, 2.20
Restraint of trade
  non-compete covenants, 11.13
Retirement
  constructive dismissal, 19.21
  reasonableness of conduct of employer, 19.21
  termination of contracts on retirement of owner, 16.05
Retirement annuity contracts
  end of approvals, 15.11
Restricted duties
  disability discrimination, 3.19
Retirement age
  firefighters, 13.32
  Garda, 13.52
'Return to office' policies
  request for remote working, 22.09
Revenue
  adverse impact by Covid-19 restrictions
    self-employed individuals, 17.22
  arrears of pay
    employee who has left employment, 17.26
  case law
    Irish High Court, 17.34–17.35
    Irish Tax Appeals Commission, 17.30–17.33
    UK decisions, 17.36–17.42
  Codes of Practice
    determining employment status, 17.29
  couriers
    impact of *Karshan* judgment, 17.28
  director's loan accounts
    amounts drawn down from a credit, 17.31
    conferring a credit, 17.30
  discontinuance of pension schemes, 17.17
  disguised remuneration
    loans from trust to director/shareholder, 17.40
  eBriefs, 17.02–17.29
  emoluments
    amounts drawn down from a credit to director's loan account, 17.31
    conferring a credit to director's loan account, 17.30
  employee relief
    research and development activities, 17.03
  employee tax credit, 17.18
  employer-provided vehicles, 17.04
  employer returns
    reportable benefits, 17.12

Revenue – *contd*
  employment detail summary (EDS), 17.21
  employment status
    amounts drawn down from a company account by sole director, 17.33
    application of *RMC* test, 17.38
    Code of Practice on determination, 17.29
    generally, 17.07
    Karshan judgment, 17.13–17.14
    referees as employees, 17.36
    sports commentator, 17.38
    television presenters, 17.39, 17.41
  Employments Regulations 2024, 17.24
  enhanced reporting obligations
    generally, 17.12, 17.16
    introduction, 17.01
  ex gratia termination payments
    employment-related disputes, 17.35
  examination awards, 17.15
  football referees
    employment status, 17.36
  host employer provisions
    liability for NICs, 17.42
  income tax credits
    individuals over 65 and carers, 17.19
  income tax return (2023)
    ROS Form 11, 17.23
  introduction, 17.01
  IR35
    self-direction as to existence, 17.37
    sports commentator, 17.38
    television presenters, 17.39, 17.41
  national insurance contributions
    host employer provisions, 17.42
  Karshan judgment
    generally, 17.13–17.14
    impact on couriers, 17.28
  loans from remuneration trust
    payment to director/shareholder, 17.40
  office holders and employees
    reimbursement of travel and subsistence, 17.11
  part-time workers
    employment status of referees, 17.36
  PAYE
    assessment guidelines update, 17.05
    employee tax credit, 17.18
    Employers' Guide, 17.06
    reviews where Week 53 applies, 17.10
  pension contributions, 17.15
  pension schemes
    discontinuance, 17.17

Revenue – *contd*
  personal service companies
    self-direction as to existence, 17.37
    sports commentator, 17.38
    television presenters, 17.39, 17.41
  proprietary director
    interpretation under TCA 1971, 17.34
  redundancy payments
    continuation of employment in successor company, 17.32
  referees
    employment status, 17.36
  reimbursement of travel and subsistence
    office holders and employees, 17.11
  remote working relief, 17.20
  reportable benefits returns
    enhanced requirements, 17.12, 17.16
  research and development activities
    key employee relief, 17.03
  retirement annuity contracts, 15.11
  Revenue eBriefs, 17.02–17.29
  Revenue Guidelines on Employment Status
    generally, 17.07
    Karshan judgment, 17.13–17.14
  road haulier drivers
    subsistence rates, 17.27
  salary sacrifice arrangements, 17.25
  Schedule E basis of charge, 17.09
  self-employed individuals
    adversely impacted by Covid-19 restrictions, 17.22
  Special Assignee Relief Programme, 17.08
  sports commentators
    employment status, 17.38
  Tax and Duty Manuals, 17.02
  television presenters
    employment status, 17.39, 17.41
  termination payments
    employment-related disputes, 17.35
  transboundary workers relief
    proprietary directors, 17.34
  travel and subsistence expenses, 17.11
  verification of personal addresses for non-revenue purposes, 17.21
Ridicule
  age discrimination, 3.07
Right to engage in industrial action
  picketing, 11.14
Right to request flexible and remote working
  Code of Practice, 13.32
Right to silence
  privilege against self-incrimination, 1.07
  refusal to comply with instruction to answer questions, 1.07

Road haulier drivers
  subsistence rates, 17.27
Roma encampments
  basis and safeguards upon grant of injunction, 11.09
Ryanair
  investigations, decisions and fines
    customer verification process, 2.24

Safety, health and welfare at work
  carcinogens, mutagens and reprotoxic substances, 13.34
Salary sacrifice arrangements
  generally, 17.25
Schedule E
  basis of charge, 17.09
Sea fishers in Irish fishing fleet
  employment permits, 13.47
Seafarers
  ouster of jurisdiction over discrimination claim, 4.22
Seagoing fishing vessel workers
  working time, 13.23
Sectoral employment orders
  construction industry
    generally, 10.11
    legislation, 13.55
  rates of pay for skilled workers, 10.11
Security industry
  Joint Labour Committee, 13.45
Self-employed contractors
  employment status, 4.11
Selection process
  redundancy, 19.19
  sex discrimination, 3.26
Self-employed individuals
  adversely impacted by Covid-19 restrictions, 17.22
Separate legal entities
  employment status
    fixed-term contracts, 4.16
    generally, 4.15
Series of fixed-term contracts
  employment status, 4.16
  equal treatment, 7.02
  honorary members of judiciary, 7.02
  interim civil servants, 7.03
  justification, 7.04
  locum surgeons, 7.04
  non-discrimination principle, 7.02
  public sector workers, 7.03
Serious issue to be tried
  non-compete covenants, 11.12
  picket injunctions, 11.15

Index

Settlement agreements
action compromised by mediated settlement, 4.20
binding mediation between parties, 4.21
consensual variation of a contract, 4.23
legal advice on transfer to 'disability plan', 4.23
personal injury claims
  refusal to insert no loss of earnings claim, 5.03
waiver in respect of future claims, 4.22

Sex discrimination
additional overtime pay for full-time workers, 3.25
affirmative action, 3.28
ambit of protected characteristic, 3.27
burden of proof, 3.29
comparators, 3.26, 3.29
constructive dismissal, 3.35
detriment, 3.36
equal opportunity measures, 3.28
equal pay, 3.29, 3.34–3.35
evidence linking behaviour to protected characteristic, 3.30
firefighters, 3.35
gender identity, 3.36
gender recognition, 3.31
harassment, 3.27, 3.30
holding protected beliefs, 3.36
inducing a discriminatory act, 3.36
interview process, 3.26
less favourable treatment, 3.25
'like work', 3.29
occupational benefit scheme, 3.32
part-time work, 3.25
pregnancy and maternity leave, 3.33–3.34
procedural fairness, 3.30
recruitment process, 3.26
redundancy, 3.34
selection process, 3.26
unfair dismissal, 3.27, 3.34

Share fishermen
working hours, 13.24

Sick leave
increase of days, 13.21

Social security and welfare
bonus to recipients of payments, 13.13
child maintenance and liable relatives
  means tests, 13.39–13.40
consolidated claims, payments and control
  child maintenance and liable relatives, 13.39
  days not to be treated as days of unemployment, 13.27

Social security and welfare – *contd*
consolidated claims, payments and control – *contd*
  jobseeker's pay-related benefit, 13.58–13.59
  long term carer's qualifying contribution, 13.17
  payments to continue after pensionable age, 13.16
consolidated contributions and insurability
  credited contributions, 13.15
  employment contributions, 13.26
consolidated occupational injuries
  disablement gratuity, 13.56
  increase of benefits and pensions, 13.14
credited contributions, 13.15
days not to be treated as days of unemployment, 13.27
domiciliary care allowance, 13.13
employment contributions, 13.26
EU law
  care leave allowance, 6.08
  equality of treatment, 6.08
  family benefits, 6.08
  migrant workers, 6.08
jobseeker's pay-related benefit
  engaged in casual employment, 13.59
  key features, 13.58
legislation, 13.05
liable relatives
  child maintenance, 13.39–13.40
long term carer's qualifying contribution, 13.17
means tests
  child maintenance, 13.39–13.40
payments to continue after pensionable age, 13.16
qualified child bonus payments, 13.12
temporary provisions, 13.12–13.13

Social work
industrial training, 13.36

Solicitors
apprentices' fees, 13.07

South African nationals
immigration visas, 13.48

Special Assignee Relief Programme (SARP)
generally, 17.08

Sports associations
competition law, 6.05–6.06
'home-grown' player rules, 6.05
player transfer rules, 6.06

Index

Sports commentators
employment status, 17.38
Stalking
application for continuation of interim injunction, 11.16
Stammer
disability discrimination, 3.23
Standard Fund Threshold
pension schemes, 15.01
Standby periods
overall impact of restrictions, 22.10
State immunity
territorial reach of employment protections, 4.25
State pension
See also **Pensions**
choice of claim date, 15.03
increase in payments, 15.01
Status of claimant
agency work, 1.02
Status of employment relationship
amounts drawn down from a company account by sole director, 17.33
associate partners, 4.13
Code of Practice on determination, 13.06, 17.29
contract of service vs contract for services, 4.11
fixed-term contracts, 4.16
identification of employer
    fixed-term contracts, 4.16
    separate legal entities, 4.15–4.16
intention of parties, 4.13
invoicing as self-employed contractor, 4.11
Karshan (Midlands) test, 4.10, 17.13–17.14
mutuality of obligation test, 4.10
protected disclosures dismissal, 4.10
referees, 17.36
rescue services, 4.12
Revenue Guidelines, 17.07
separate legal entities
    fixed-term contracts, 4.16
    generally, 4.15
series of fixed-term contracts, 4.16
sports commentators, 17.38
statutory service requirement, 4.10
taxation
    amounts drawn down from a company account by sole director, 17.33
    application of *RMC* test, 17.38
    Code of Practice on determination, 17.29
    generally, 17.07

Status of employment relationship – *contd*
taxation – *contd*
    Karshan judgment, 17.13–17.14
    referees as employees, 17.36
    Revenue Guidelines, 17.07
    sports commentator, 17.38
    television presenters, 17.39, 17.41
television presenters, 17.39, 17.41
transfer of undertakings
    care home staff, 18.06
vexatious appeals, 4.14
'worker'
    associate partners, 4.13
    volunteers, 4.12
Statutory review
Joint Labour Committees, 13.25
Statutory service requirement
employment status, 4.10
Striking out
fair trial possible after five year delay and 'lost' witness, 4.24
proportionality of decision, 4.24
Substantial disadvantage
disability discrimination, 3.15, 3.22
failure to review two-year warning, 4.19
race discrimination, 3.41
Successive contracts
employment status, 4.16
equal treatment, 7.02
honorary members of judiciary, 7.02
interim civil servants, 7.03
justification, 7.04
locum surgeons, 7.04
non-discrimination principle, 7.02
public sector workers, 7.03
Superannuation
fire brigade employees, 13.51
Surveillance of employees
excessive collection of data, 2.05

Tax and Duty Manuals (TDMs)
generally, 17.02
Taxation
adverse impact by Covid-19 restrictions
    self-employed individuals, 17.22
arrears of pay
    employee who has left employment, 17.26
case law
    Irish High Court, 17.34–17.35
    Irish Tax Appeals Commission, 17.30–17.33
    UK decisions, 17.36–17.42
Codes of Practice
    determining employment status, 17.29

Index

Taxation – *contd*
  couriers
    impact of *Karshan* judgment, 17.28
  director's loan accounts
    amounts drawn down from a credit, 17.31
    conferring a credit, 17.30
  discontinuance of pension schemes, 17.17
  disguised remuneration
    loans from trust to director/shareholder, 17.40
  eBriefs, 17.02–17.29
  emoluments
    amounts drawn down from a credit to director's loan account, 17.31
    conferring a credit to director's loan account, 17.30
  employee relief
    research and development activities, 17.03
  employee tax credit, 17.18
  employer-provided vehicles, 17.04
  employer returns
    reportable benefits, 17.12
  employment detail summary (EDS), 17.21
  employment status
    amounts drawn down from a company account by sole director, 17.33
    application of *RMC* test, 17.38
    Code of Practice on determination, 17.29
    generally, 17.07
    Karshan judgment, 17.13–17.14
    referees as employees, 17.36
    sports commentator, 17.38
    television presenters, 17.39, 17.41
  Employments Regulations 2024, 17.24
  enhanced reporting obligations
    generally, 17.12, 17.16
    introduction, 17.01
  ex gratia termination payments
    employment-related disputes, 17.35
  examination awards, 17.15
  football referees
    employment status, 17.36
  host employer provisions
    liability for NICs, 17.42
  income tax credits
    individuals over 65 and carers, 17.19
  income tax return (2023)
    ROS Form 11, 17.23
  introduction, 17.01
  IR35
    self-direction as to existence, 17.37
    sports commentator, 17.38
    television presenters, 17.39, 17.41

Taxation – *contd*
  national insurance contributions
    host employer provisions, 17.42
  Karshan judgment
    generally, 17.13–17.14
    impact on couriers, 17.28
  loans from remuneration trust
    payment to director/shareholder, 17.40
  office holders and employees
    reimbursement of travel and subsistence, 17.11
  part-time workers
    employment status of referees, 17.36
  PAYE
    assessment guidelines update, 17.05
    employee tax credit, 17.18
    Employers' Guide, 17.06
    reviews where Week 53 applies, 17.10
  pension contributions, 17.15
  pension schemes
    discontinuance, 17.17
  personal service companies
    self-direction as to existence, 17.37
    sports commentator, 17.38
    television presenters, 17.39, 17.41
  proprietary director
    interpretation under TCA 1971, 17.34
  redundancy payments
    continuation of employment in successor company, 17.32
  referees
    employment status, 17.36
  reimbursement of travel and subsistence
    office holders and employees, 17.11
  remote working relief, 17.20
  reportable benefits returns
    enhanced requirements, 17.12, 17.16
  research and development activities
    key employee relief, 17.03
  Revenue eBriefs, 17.02–17.29
  Revenue Guidelines on Employment Status
    generally, 17.07
    Karshan judgment, 17.13–17.14
  road haulier drivers
    subsistence rates, 17.27
  salary sacrifice arrangements, 17.25
  Schedule E basis of charge, 17.09
  self-employed individuals
    adversely impacted by Covid-19 restrictions, 17.22
  Special Assignee Relief Programme, 17.08
  sports commentators
    employment status, 17.38
  Tax and Duty Manuals, 17.02

Index

Taxation – *contd*
  television presenters
    employment status, 17.39, 17.41
  termination payments
    employment-related disputes, 17.35
  transboundary workers relief
    proprietary directors, 17.34
  travel and subsistence expenses, 17.11
  verification of personal addresses for
    non-revenue purposes, 17.21
Television presenters
  employment status, 17.39, 17.41
Temporary work
  joint and several liability of agency and
    user, 19.02
  maternity leave, 19.02
  parental leave, 19.02
  purpose and nature of work, 1.02
  supervisory authority by user, 19.02
  'temporary agency work', 19.02
Termination
  fixed-term contracts, 7.05
Termination payments
  employment-related disputes, 17.35
Terms of employment
  failure to provide written statement,
    1.09–1.10
  pay increases arising from collective
    agreements, 1.08
Territorial jurisdiction
  extra-territorial employment protections,
    4.25
  material error of law, 4.26
  state immunity, 4.25
Third party data processors
  guidance on use of CCTV, 2.15
Time limits
  alleged misrepresentation by employer,
    4.28, 4.32
  belief that claim precluded, 4.40
  cognisable period, 4.38
  delay of three and a half years, 4.29
  determination that misrepresentation did
    not occur, 4.32
  discretion to extend
    'exceptional circumstances', 4.45
    missing supporting information or
      documents, 4.44–4.45
    perverse refusal, 4.41
    substantial compliance with rules within
      limit, 4.44–4.45
  engagement with other agencies, 4.39
  'exceptional circumstances'
    internal appeals process delayed,
      4.37

Time limits – *contd*
  'exceptional circumstances' – *contd*
    misunderstanding of emails,
      4.43
    one-day late, 4.37
    personal and professional difficulties,
      4.36
    reasonable cause, 4.37
    substantial compliance with rules
      within limit, 4.45
    unfitness to attend work, 4.42
  extension of time, 4.31, 4.34–4.41
  ignorance of the law is no excuse,
    4.35
  incorrect respondent named, 4.30
  internal appeals process delayed
    general, 4.33
    one-day late, 4.37
    reasonable cause, 4.37
  missing supporting information or
    documents, 4.44–4.45
  misunderstanding of emails, 4.43
  misunderstanding of the law
    belief that claim precluded, 4.40
  one-day late, 4.37
  personal and professional difficulties,
    4.36
  perverse refusal of extension,
    4.41
  psychological stress, 4.39
  reasonable cause
    engagement with other agencies,
      4.39
    ignorance of the law is no excuse,
      4.35
    one-day late, 4.37
    psychological stress, 4.39
    vulnerable person, 4.39
  substantial compliance with rules within
    limit, 4.44–4.45
  unfitness to attend work, 4.42
  vulnerable person, 4.39
  worker becoming aware of pregnancy
    after dismissal, 4.27
Toilets and rest rooms
  guidance on use of CCTV, 2.20
Torts
  defamation
    damages for injured feelings,
      5.02
    economic loss refused, 5.02
  injurious falsehood
    damages for injured feelings,
      5.02
    economic loss refused, 5.02

Torts – *contd*
  introduction, 5.01
  loss of earnings claims
    refusal to insert term in settlement order, 5.03
  personal injury
    evidence of generic or individual causation, 5.04
    material contribution test, 5.04
    terms of settlement order, 5.03
  settlement orders
    refusal to insert no loss of earnings claim, 5.03
  vicarious liability
    abuse of children by employee caretaker, 5.05
    sufficiently close connection, 5.05

Trade dispute referral
  dismissal of claimant for misconduct, 10.05
  exhaustion of alternative means of resolution, 10.08
  outstanding proceedings between employee and employer, 10.06
  withdrawal of conditional offer of employment, 10.07

Trade union activities
  failure to establish dismissal due to activities, 19.22
  required period of service, 19.22

Trade union recognition
  recommendation to employer, 10.12

Trade unions
  defamation, 10.02
  interference with right to organise, 10.13
  recognition, 10.12

Trans-Atlantic data transfers
  EDPB Information Note
    redress mechanism for EU/EEA individuals, 2.46
  EU-US Data Privacy Framework
    FAQ for European individuals, 2.47
    generally, 2.45

Transboundary workers relief
  proprietary directors, 17.34

Transfer of personal data
  failing to appropriately safeguard, 2.03

Transfer of undertakings
  change to terms post-transfer
    diminution of contractual entitlements, 18.03
  commission of healthcare services
    no economic activity, 18.07

Transfer of undertakings – *contd*
  dismissal
    economic, technical or organisational reason not made out, 18.02
    merger of NHS CCGs after restructure, 18.07
  economic activity
    requirement for supply of goods or services to the market, 18.07
  employment status
    care home staff, 18.06
  information and consultation obligation
    absence of employee representatives, 18.03
    no failure to consult where transfer to buyer, 18.06
  introduction, 18.01
  meaning
    closure of care home and transfer to one of two others, 18.06
    moving outreach team funded by HSE, 18.04
    reorganisation of public health service, 18.07
  public administrative functions
    no economic activity, 18.07
  service provision change
    employment status of care home staff, 18.06
  tortious liability
    transfer from employer to transferee, 18.05
  unlawful variation of terms post-transfer
    diminution of contractual entitlements, 18.03
    measurable change, 18.03

Travel and subsistence expenses
  generally, 17.11

Travellers
  basis and safeguards upon grant of injunction against encampments, 11.09
  conduct of tribunal hearing, 12.02

Unauthorised deductions from wages
  rectification of collective agreements, 10.10

Unfair dismissal
  affirmation of contract
    breach of duty of trust and confidence, 19.14
  agency workers
    joint and several liability of agency and user, 19.02
    maternity leave, 19.02

Index

Unfair dismissal – *contd*
  agency workers – *contd*
    parental leave, 19.02
    supervisory authority by user, 19.02
    'temporary agency work', 19.02
  band of reasonable responses
    conduct, 19.08, 19.10
    redundancy, 19.19
  breach of duty of trust and confidence
    affirmation of contract, 19.14
  capability
    fairness of dismissal, 19.03
    interaction with conduct of employee, 19.03
    performance improvement plan, 19.03
    warning of risk of dismissal, 19.03
  choice of employer
    failure to identify an employer, 19.04
  compensation
    conduct of employee, 19.06
    financial loss, 19.05
    joint and several liability, 19.06
    just and equitable, 19.05
    protected disclosures, 19.07
    quantum, 19.05
    reduction in sum otherwise payable, 19.06–19.07
    social media activity, 19.07
  conduct
    absence of disciplinary procedure, 19.09
    band of reasonable responses, 19.08, 19.10
    deficiencies in disciplinary procedure, 19.10
    fair procedures, 19.08
    freedom of expression, 19.11
    gross misconduct, 19.08–19.10
    interaction with capability of employee, 19.03
    publication of 'commercial secrets', 19.11
    stress-related behaviour, 19.08
    summary dismissal, 19.09–19.10
  constructive dismissal
    affirmation of contract, 19.14
    breach of duty of trust and confidence, 19.14–19.15
    conduct of parties, 19.13
    failure to exhaust internal procedures, 19.12–19.13, 19.15
    performance improvement plan, 19.13
    perverse decision of tribunal, 19.15
    repudiatory breach, 19.13
    resignation due to employer conduct, 19.13
    resignation to protect mental health, 19.12

Unfair dismissal – *contd*
  'dismissal'
    refusal by employer to allow retraction of resignation, 19.16
  freedom of expression
    obligation to protect rights from interference by individuals, 19.11
    publication of 'commercial secrets' in public interest, 19.11
  introduction, 19.01
  notice of termination
    goodwill payment in lieu of notice, 19.17
  other substantial grounds
    refusal to be vaccinated, 19.18
  performance improvement plan
    capability dismissal, 19.03
    constructive dismissal, 19.13
  redundancy
    adequacy of consultation process, 19.19
    band of reasonable responses, 19.19
    procedural unfairness, 19.19
    selection criteria and scoring, 19.19
    sex discrimination, 3.34
    workforce-level consultation, 19.19
  re-engagement
    failure to give consideration to practicality, 19.20
    headmaster of school, 19.20
  refusal to be vaccinated
    Covid-19 policy, 19.18
    justification for interference with rights, 19.18
    proportionality of dismissal, 19.18
    religion and belief discrimination, 19.18
    substantive fairness of decision to dismiss, 19.18
  religion and belief discrimination
    refusal to be vaccinated, 19.18
  resignation
    conduct of employer, 19.13
    constructive dismissal, 19.12–19.13
    employer's policy to refuse to allow retraction, 19.16
    protection of mental health, 19.12
  retirement
    constructive dismissal, 19.21
    reasonableness of conduct of employer, 19.21
  selection criteria
    redundancy, 19.19

Index

Unfair dismissal – *contd*
sex discrimination
ambit of protected characteristic, 3.27
equal pay, 3.34
harassment, 3.27
pregnancy and maternity leave, 3.34
redundancy, 3.34
temporary agency workers
joint and several liability of agency and user, 19.02
maternity leave, 19.02
parental leave, 19.02
supervisory authority by user, 19.02
'temporary agency work', 19.02
trade union activities
failure to establish dismissal due to activities, 19.22
required period of service, 19.22
Unidentifiable persons
basis and safeguards upon grant of injunction, 11.09
Unlawful deduction of wages
Covid-related pay reduction, 20.02
Covid-related special leave, 20.09
custom or practice in appropriate, 20.10
inability to work due to suspension, 20.12
lack of authorisation to reduce pay, 20.13
layoffs, 20.11
oral variation of contract, 20.13
overtime averaging, 20.09
professional footballer under suspension, 20.12
reduced weekly working hours, 20.11
sick pay, 20.08
suspension pay for Garda member after custodial sentence, 20.07
unavoidable impediment periods, 20.12
unpaid bonus, 20.05
unpaid layoff, 20.10

Vaccination refusal
Covid-19 policy, 19.18
justification for interference with rights, 19.18
proportionality of dismissal, 19.18
religion and belief discrimination, 19.18
substantive fairness of decision to dismiss, 19.18
VAT liability
due diligence by employer, 6.09
fake invoices issued by employee, 6.09
Vehicle mechanics, electricians and technicians
employment permits, 13.54

Verification of personal addresses
non-revenue purposes, 17.21
Vexatious proceedings
multiple applications to different tribunals, 4.14
Vicarious liability
abuse of children by employee caretaker, 5.05
disability discrimination, 3.17
protected disclosures
application to amend claim to add, 21.14
sufficiently close connection, 5.05
Victimisation
disability discrimination, 3.10, 3.18
protected disclosures, 21.05
Video surveillance
unlawful distribution, 2.08
Visibility of passwords
employees of social platform, to, 2.30

Wages
Covid-19
reasonableness of pay reduction, 20.02
unlawful deductions during special leave, 20.09
discretionary bonus scheme
employment on pay-out date, 20.05
non-contractual and unquantifiable, 20.06
introduction, 20.01
national minimum wage
company's use and benefit, 20.03
voluntary deductions to save for holidays, 20.03
payment
discretionary bonus scheme, 20.05–20.06
refusal to attend workplace, 20.04
unlawful deductions
Covid-related pay reduction, 20.02
Covid-related special leave, 20.09
custom or practice in appropriate, 20.10
inability to work due to suspension, 20.12
lack of authorisation to reduce pay, 20.13
layoffs, 20.11
oral variation of contract, 20.13
overtime averaging, 20.09
professional footballer under suspension, 20.12
reduced weekly working hours, 20.11
sick pay, 20.08
suspension pay for Garda member after custodial sentence, 20.07
unavoidable impediment periods, 20.12
unpaid bonus, 20.05
unpaid layoff, 20.10

Waiver
  diplomatic immunity, 4.07
Whistleblowing
  compensation
    contractual cap on damages, 21.02
    uplift of award, 21.02
  Criminal Justice Act 2011
    failure of suspended Garda officer to make complaint, 20.03
  decision-makers inflicting detriment with no knowledge of disclosure, 21.12
  detriment
    external job applicant, 21.04
    judicial proceedings immunity, 21.06
    less favourable treatment, 21.04
    making protected acts and disclosures, 21.05
    penalisation, 21.04–21.06
    victimisation, 21.05
  disagreeing with way work carried out, 21.12
  dismissal
    cashflow issues during furlough, 21.09
    causative link, 21.08
    insufficient qualifying employment, 21.08–21.09
    likely breach of legal obligation, 21.09
    non-qualifying disclosures, 21.09
  employer's knowledge
    disclosures not influence decision to dismiss, 21.10
  external job applicant, 21.04
  failure to establish a protected disclosure was made, 21.11
  insufficient qualifying employment, 21.08–21.09
  introduction, 21.01
  judicial proceedings immunity, 21.06
  less favourable treatment
    external job applicant, 21.04
    likely breach of legal obligation, 21.09
    non-qualifying disclosures, 21.09
  objective belief, 21.13
  penalisation
    external job applicant, 21.04
    judicial proceedings immunity, 21.06
    less favourable treatment, 21.04
    making protected acts and disclosures, 21.05
    victimisation, 21.05
  reasonable belief, 21.13

Whistleblowing – *contd*
  relevant wrongdoing
    causal link between detriments and disclosures, 21.07
    disagreeing with way work carried out, 21.13
    reasonable or objective belief that occurred, 21.13
    subjective belief that disclosure in public interest, 21.07
  vicarious liability
    application to amend claim to add, 21.14
  victimisation, 21.05
  worker
    lack of contractual relationship between parties, 21.15
    president-elect of charity, 21.15
Without prejudice privilege
  improper behaviour, 4.46
  pre-termination negotiations, 4.46
  protected conversations, 4.46
Work life balance
  commencement orders, 13.30–13.31
  flexible working, 13.32
  remote working, 13.32
Work returns
  unlawful monitoring, 2.09
'Worker'
  See also **Employment status**
  associate partners, 4.13
  conditional offer of employment, 10.07
  protected disclosures
    lack of contractual relationship between parties, 21.15
    president-elect of charity, 21.15
  volunteers, 4.12
Workers' representatives
  entitlement to redundancy information and consultation, 16.02
Working time
  annual leave
    carrying over period of quarantine, 22.02
    prohibition on allowance in lieu for untaken period prior to resignation of public servant, 22.03
  holiday pay
    cabin crew allowances to be treated as normal pay, 22.04
    requirement to be 'on call', 22.08
  introduction, 22.01
  maternity leave
    single-parent families, 22.05

Working time – *contd*
  night workers
    failure to comply with obligation to assess health, 22.06
    need to establish specific harm, 22.06
  parental leave
    refusal of request by employer, 22.07
    single-parent families, 22.05
  public holiday pay
    requirement to be 'on call', 22.08
  quarantine
    distinction from sick leave, 22.02

Working time – *contd*
  remote working
    consideration of request demonstrated by employer, 22.09
    employee's individual needs, 22.09
    'return to office' policy post-Covid, 22.09
  seagoing fishing vessel workers, 13.23
  share fishermen, 13.24
  standby periods
    overall impact of restrictions, 22.10

Workplace relations
  fixed payment notices, 13.18

Workplace Relations Committee
  Code of Practice on flexible and remote working, 13.32